The Syntax of Portuguese

Portuguese is the second most widely spoken Romance language in the world, and, due to recent interest in comparative syntax, the literature on its syntax has increased exponentially, resulting in exciting discoveries of a range of aspects that have hitherto been overlooked. This book provides a theoretically grounded overview of the major syntactic properties of Portuguese, focusing on the differences between European and Brazilian Portuguese. It shows from a theoretical point of view how different syntactic properties are interconnected by comparing and contrasting the variances between pronominal and agreement systems, null subjects, null complements, and word order. It also highlights how small differences in the specification of syntactic properties may yield quite different dialects. It introduces key theoretical points without technical jargon, making the content accessible to specialists and non-specialists alike. It is essential reading for both academic researchers and students of Portuguese language, comparative syntax, Romance linguistics, and theoretical syntax.

MARY A. KATO is Professor at the Universidade Estadual de Campinas. Recent publications include *The Morphosyntax of Portuguese and Spanish in Latin America* (co-edited with Ordóñez, 2016), and *Português brasileiro: Uma segunda viagem diacrônica* (co-edited with Galves and Roberts, 2019).

ANA MARIA MARTINS is Professor at the Universidade de Lisboa. Recent publications include *Word Order Change* (co-edited with Cardoso, 2018) and *Manual de Linguística Portuguesa* (co-edited with Carrilho, 2016).

JAIRO NUNES is Professor at the Universidade de São Paulo. Recent publications include *Minimalist Essays on Brazilian Portuguese Syntax* (editor, 2009), and *Control as Movement* (with Boeckx and Hornstein, 2010).

CAMBRIDGE SYNTAX GUIDES
General editors:
P. AUSTIN, B. COMRIE, J. BRESNAN, D. LIGHTFOOT, I. ROBERTS, N. V. SMITH

Responding to the increasing interest in comparative syntax, the goal of the Cambridge Syntax Guides is to make available to all linguists major findings, both descriptive and theoretical, which have emerged from the study of particular languages. The series is not committed to working in any particular framework, but rather seeks to make language-specific research available to theoreticians and practitioners of all persuasions.

Written by leading figures in the field, these guides will each include an overview of the grammatical structures of the language concerned. For the descriptivist, the books will provide an accessible introduction to the methods and results of the theoretical literature; for the theoretician, they will show how constructions that have achieved theoretical notoriety fit into the structure of the language as a whole; for everyone, they will promote cross-theoretical and cross-linguistic comparison with respect to a well-defined body of data.

Other books available in this series

O. FISCHER et al.: *The Syntax of Early English*
K. ZAGONA: *The Syntax of Spanish*
K. KISS: *The Syntax of Hungarian*
S. MCHOMBO: *The Syntax of Chichewa*
H. THRÁINSSON: *The Syntax of Icelandic*
P. ROWLETT: *The Syntax of French*
R. D. BORSLEY et al.: *The Syntax of Welsh*
C.-T. J. HUANG et al.: *The Syntax of Chinese*
J. AOUN et al.: *The Syntax of Arabic*
H. HAIDER: *The Syntax of German*
J.-W. ZWART: *The Syntax of Dutch*

The Syntax of Portuguese

MARY A. KATO
Universidade Estadual de Campinas, Brazil

ANA MARIA MARTINS
Universidade de Lisboa, Faculdade de Letras, Centro de Linguística, Portugal

JAIRO NUNES
Universidade de São Paulo, Brazil

Shaftesbury Road, Cambridge CB2 8EA, United Kingdom

One Liberty Plaza, 20th Floor, New York, NY 10006, USA

477 Williamstown Road, Port Melbourne, VIC 3207, Australia

314–321, 3rd Floor, Plot 3, Splendor Forum, Jasola District Centre, New Delhi – 110025, India

103 Penang Road, #05–06/07, Visioncrest Commercial, Singapore 238467

Cambridge University Press is part of Cambridge University Press & Assessment, a department of the University of Cambridge.

We share the University's mission to contribute to society through the pursuit of education, learning and research at the highest international levels of excellence.

www.cambridge.org
Information on this title: www.cambridge.org/9781009321297

DOI: 10.1017/9780511842931

© Mary A. Kato, Ana Maria Martins, and Jairo Nunes 2023

This publication is in copyright. Subject to statutory exception and to the provisions of relevant collective licensing agreements, no reproduction of any part may take place without the written permission of Cambridge University Press & Assessment.

First published 2023
First paperback edition 2025

A catalogue record for this publication is available from the British Library

ISBN 978-0-521-86061-1 Hardback
ISBN 978-1-009-32129-7 Paperback

Cambridge University Press & Assessment has no responsibility for the persistence or accuracy of URLs for external or third-party internet websites referred to in this publication and does not guarantee that any content on such websites is, or will remain, accurate or appropriate.

Contents

List of Tables   *page vii*
Acknowledgments   *x*
List of Abbreviations   *xii*

1 Introduction   *1*

2 The Pronominal System   *5*
   2.1   Introduction   *5*
   2.2   Strong, Weak, and Clitic Personal Pronouns in Portuguese   *6*
   2.3   Feature Composition of Personal Pronouns in Portuguese   *11*
   2.4   Similarities and Differences between European Portuguese and Brazilian Portuguese   *25*
   2.5   Summary   *52*

3 Agreement   *57*
   3.1   Introduction   *57*
   3.2   Agreement within Nominal Domains in Portuguese   *58*
   3.3   Subject–Predicate Agreement in Portuguese   *70*
   3.4   Reanalyzing the Different Agreement Systems in European Portuguese and Brazilian Portuguese   *87*
   3.5   Special Cases of Agreement   *127*
   3.6   Summary   *140*

4 Null Subjects   *142*
   4.1   Introduction   *142*
   4.2   Different Types of Null Subjects   *142*
   4.3   Definite Null Subjects   *147*
   4.4   Indefinite Null Subjects   *215*
   4.5   Expletive Null Subjects   *219*
   4.6   Related Issues   *220*
   4.7   General Summary   *226*

5 Word Order   *230*
   5.1   Introduction   *230*
   5.2   Word Order in Declarative Sentences and Informational Content   *231*
   5.3   Word Order in Interrogative Sentences   *265*
   5.4   Word Order in Exclamative Sentences   *286*
   5.5   Word Order in Nonfinite Domains   *294*
   5.6   Clitic Placement   *299*
   5.7   Summary   *329*

6 Null Objects and Null Possessors   *331*
   6.1   Introduction   *331*
   6.2   Ellipsis of Verbal Projections   *332*
   6.3   Null Direct Objects   *336*
   6.4   Null Oblique Objects   *354*
   6.5   Null Possessors   *359*
   6.6   Summary   *368*

7 Affirmation, Negation, and *yes/no* Questions and Answers   *369*
   7.1   Introduction   *369*
   7.2   Emphatic Affirmation   *369*
   7.3   Syntactic Patterns of Negation   *386*
   7.4   Biased Polar Questions   *416*
   7.5   Minimal Answers to *yes/no* Questions   *423*
   7.6   Summary   *453*

8 Conclusion   *455*

References   *464*
Corpora   *501*
Index   *502*

Tables

2.1	First person pronouns in European Portuguese	*page 26*
2.2	First person pronouns in Brazilian Portuguese	27
2.3	Second person pronouns in European Portuguese	33
2.4	Second person pronouns in Brazilian Portuguese	34
2.5	Third person pronouns in European Portuguese	41
2.6	Third person pronouns in Brazilian Portuguese	42
2.7	Fusion of dative and accusative clitics in European Portuguese	46
2.8	Syncretism of personal pronouns in European Portuguese	54
2.9	Syncretism of personal pronouns in Brazilian Portuguese	55
3.1	Person and number agreement in European Portuguese – finite clauses	77
3.2	Person and number agreement in Brazilian Portuguese – finite clauses	78
3.3	Imperatives in European Portuguese	80
3.4	Imperatives in Brazilian Portuguese	80
3.5	Person and number agreement in European Portuguese – inflected infinitives	83
3.6	Person and number agreement in Brazilian Portuguese – inflected infinitives	83
3.7	Person and number agreement in dialectal European Portuguese – inflected gerunds	86
3.8	Feature composition of personal pronouns in Portuguese – traditional analysis	88
3.9	Feature composition of personal pronouns in Portuguese – eliminating feature mismatch (subject to revision in Table 3.12)	101
3.10	Morphological specifications for personal pronouns and verbal agreement in European Portuguese	103

3.11 Morphological specifications for personal pronouns and verbal agreement in Brazilian Portuguese   *108*
3.12 Pronominal specifications for person and number and verbal agreement in Portuguese (revision of Table 3.9)   *112*
3.13 Ambiguity of finite Infl(ection) in Brazilian Portuguese   *121*
4.1 Frequency of definite null subjects according to person in oral corpora in Portuguese   *148*
4.2 Frequency of definite null subjects in Brazilian theater plays across time   *148*
4.3 First and second person pronouns and verbal agreement morphology in Portuguese finite clauses (fuller paradigm)   *150*
4.4 First and second person pronouns in European Portuguese – syntactic agreement in finite clauses (fuller paradigm)   *156*
4.5 First and second person pronouns in Brazilian Portuguese – syntactic agreement in finite clauses (fuller paradigm)   *161*
4.6 Licensing of first and second person null subjects in finite clauses in European Portuguese (fuller paradigm)   *168*
4.7 Licensing of first and second person null subjects in finite clauses in Brazilian Portuguese (fuller paradigm)   *168*
4.8 First and second person pronouns in European Portuguese – syntactic agreement in finite clauses under impoverishment   *173*
4.9 First and second person pronouns in Brazilian Portuguese – syntactic agreement in finite clauses under impoverishment   *174*
4.10 Third person pronouns and verbal agreement in Portuguese finite clauses   *179*
4.11 Licensing of third person null subjects in Portuguese finite clauses   *185*
4.12 Person and number agreement inflection in finite clauses and null subject licensing in Portuguese   *188*
4.13 First and second person pronouns and verbal agreement morphology in Portuguese inflected infinitives   *189*
4.14 First and second person null subjects and infinitival agreement in European Portuguese   *192*
4.15 First and second person null subjects and infinitival agreement in Brazilian Portuguese   *193*

4.16	Third person pronouns and verbal agreement in Portuguese inflected infinitives	*197*
4.17	Agreement inflection in inflected infinitives and null subject licensing in Portuguese	*199*
4.18	Participial agreement and third person null subjects	*203*
4.19	Agreement inflection in participials and the licensing of first and second person null subjects in European Portuguese	*205*
4.20	Participial agreement and null subject licensing	*209*
4.21	Inflected gerunds in dialectal European Portuguese and null subject licensing	*212*
4.22	Morphological licensing of definite null subjects in European Portuguese – summary	*227*
4.23	Morphological licensing of definite null subjects in Brazilian Portuguese – summary	*228*
5.1	Conjugations of the inflected infinitive and subjunctive future in BP for a regular and an irregular verb	*327*
6.1	Licensing of null objects in European Portuguese and Brazilian Portuguese	*347*
7.1	Short answers with bare verbs and responsive particles in European Portuguese and Brazilian Portuguese	*433*
8.1	Syncretism of personal pronouns with the default form in European Portuguese	*456*
8.2	Syncretism of personal pronouns with the default form in Brazilian Portuguese	*457*
8.3	Pronominal specifications for person and number and verbal agreement in Portuguese	*459*
8.4	Morphological licensing of definite null subjects in European Portuguese	*460*
8.5	Morphological licensing of definite null subjects in Brazilian Portuguese	*461*
8.6	Licensing of null objects in European Portuguese and Brazilian Portuguese	*462*

Acknowledgments

It took us a long time to write this book – much longer than we (and the series editors) expected or wanted. But as the enterprise comes to an end, it is a nice feeling to realize that throughout this time we have been fortunate to receive very valuable feedback on different chapters from students and colleagues that substantially helped us improve the content and presentation of the whole volume. We are deeply thankful to all of them. For their helpful comments and constructive criticism, special thanks to the audiences at the Universidade Estadual de Campinas, Universidade de Lisboa, Universidade de São Paulo, University of Connecticut, Universidad del País Vasco/Euskal Herriko Unibertsitatea, Universiteit Leiden, Universiteit Utrecht, Universidad de Buenos Aires, Rutgers University, Universität Hamburg, New York University, Universidade Federal de Uberlândia, Universidade Federal do Rio de Janeiro, and Universidade Federal de Minas Gerais; the members of the research group "Minimalismo e a Teoria da Gramática" at the Universidade de São Paulo; and the audiences at the following conferences: Romania Nova (2005, 2006, 2010, 2016, 2017), Going Romance (2007, 2013, 2016, 2018), Colloquium on Generative Grammar (2008, 2014), XI Diachronic Generative Syntax (DiGS 2009), XI Congreso de la Sociedad Argentina de Lingüística (2008), Workshop on the Syntax of Answers to Polar Questions (2012), II Congresso Internacional de Linguística Histórica (2012), 12º Congresso Alemão de Lusitanistas (2016), Linguistic Symposium on Romance Languages (2015, 2016, 2017, 2020, 2021), Linguística Formal I (2018), 19th International Conference of the Department of Linguistics of the University of Bucharest (2019), and Abralin ao Vivo (2020). We would also like to thank David Lightfoot for his initial encouragement for us to write this book and Helen Barton for her guidance, support, and patience as she oversaw its progress. Many thanks too to Virginia Catmur, who worked on every single detail of the book to make it clearer and more reader friendly. The writing of the final version has received partial support from CNPq – Conselho Nacional de Desenvolvimento Científico e Tecnológico (first author, grant 304954/2021–7, and third author, grant 303195/2019–3) and FCT – Fundação para a Ciência e a Tecnologia (second author, projects UIDB/00214/2020 and SynAPse – Atlas sintático do português europeu, PTDC/LLT-LIN/32086/2017).

Abbreviations

↓	falling intonation
↑	rising intonation
→	flat intonation
Ø	null constituent
%	indicates that the acceptability of a sentence (or other linguistic expression) is dialectally/idiolectally restricted
?	indicates that a sentence (or other linguistic expression) is marginally acceptable
*	indicates that a sentence (or other linguistic expression) is unacceptable
#	indicates that a sentence is grammatically well formed, but pragmatically odd
φ	person, number, and gender features
1	first person
2	second person
3	third person
3PAC	third person accusative clitic
ACC	accusative case
AFFIRM	affirmative
BP	Brazilian Portuguese
CL	clitic
[±close]	greater or lesser degree of familiarity, intimacy or proximity in social status
COND	conditional
CONFIRM	confirmative
CORDIAL-SIN	Syntax-Oriented Corpus of Portuguese Dialects (see Corpora)
CRPC	Corpus de Referência do Português Contemporâneo (see Corpora)
DAT	dative case
Det	phonetically null determiner

DIM	diminutive
ECM	exceptional case marking
EP	European Portuguese
EXPL	expletive
FEM	feminine
FUT	future
G	gender
GEN	genitive case
GER	gerund
[hum]	human
I	impoverished
IMP	imperative
IMPERF	imperfective
IND	indefinite
INDIC	indicative
INF	infinitive
Infl	inflection
INTERJ	interjection
L1	native language
L2	second language
lit.	literally
MASC	masculine
N	number
n/a	not applicable
NEG	negation
NOM	nominative case
NPI	negative polarity item
NT	neuter
OBL	oblique case
P	person
PAST	past tense
PERF	perfective
PL	plural
PPI	positive polarity item
PPLE	participle
PRES	present tense
PRET	preterite
pro	null pronoun
PRO	null subject of control constructions
pron	pronoun

REFL	reflexive
S	strong
SG	singular
SUBJ	subjunctive
SV	subject–verb order
SVO	subject–verb–object order
T_I	tense subject to impoverishment
TV	thematic vowel
u	unvalued
VP	verb phrase
VS	verb–subject order
VSO	verb–subject–object order
VSVPE	verb stranding VP ellipsis
VXS	verb–arbitrary constituent–subject order
W	weak
wh-	interrogative (constituent)

1

Introduction

Portuguese is a Romance language that branched off from medieval Galician-Portuguese, one of the linguistic communities that emerged from Latin in the Iberian Peninsula. Originating in its northwest area, Portuguese gradually diverged from Galician as it spread to the south in tandem with the expansion of the kingdom of Portugal, which became independent in 1143, giving rise to a political border that ultimately came to be a linguistic border as well. In the fifteenth century Portugal started building a colonial empire and, from then on, Portuguese spread worldwide. Today it is the official language of eight countries (Portugal, Brazil, Angola, Cape Verde, East Timor, Guinea Bissau, Mozambique, and São Tomé and Príncipe) and of an autonomous Chinese territory (Macau), being spoken by about 250 million people. Only in Portugal and Brazil is Portuguese the native language (L1) of the large majority of the population, though. In the other places, the situation differs from country to country, but in general Portuguese is mostly learned at school as a second language (L2) and only a minority of children grows up speaking it.[1]

In part reflecting this difference, the literature on the European and Brazilian varieties of Portuguese (henceforth EP and BP) is much more comprehensive and detailed than the corresponding literature on the other varieties. In fact, the exponential growth in the literature on Portuguese syntax in the past four decades was substantially fueled by studies systematically contrasting EP and BP. Given this asymmetry in the available literature and the comparative perspective we will be taking in this book, our discussion

---

[1] However, it is worth noting that the situation in Angola and Mozambique has considerably changed since their independence in the seventies. With rural populations moving to their capital cities (Luanda and Maputo, respectively), Portuguese has become a *lingua franca* among people with very diverse L1 languages and this in turn has provided the grounds for more children to acquire Portuguese as their native language. In a few decades the percentage of L1 speakers of Portuguese has grown from about 1 percent to about one third of the population in Angola and to 10.7 percent in Mozambique, with a higher proportion of L1 speakers in the province of Maputo and one much higher proportion in the city of Maputo (for figures and discussion, see e.g. I. Castro 2006, Gonçalves 2012, Hagemeijer 2016, and Mutali 2019).

concentrates on major syntactic properties that are common to all or most subvarieties of EP and BP. We will use the long-established term *grammar* to refer to this common syntactic knowledge shared by the majority of native speakers of each variety, generally reflected by their judgments on the well-formedness of linguistic expressions.[2]

The comparative interest in the grammar of Portuguese and in its syntax, in particular, has considerably increased in the past four decades as a reflex of the general interest in comparative syntax prompted by the Principles and Parameters Theory (Chomsky 1981, Chomsky and Lasnik 1993). Building on the literature published in this period, *The Syntax of Portuguese* presents an overview of the major syntactic aspects of Portuguese that may be of relevance to readers interested in Portuguese grammar, theoretical syntax, and comparative linguistics in general.

Before we move on to the presentation of the chapters proper, a few methodological remarks about the scope of the book are in order. The first regards the specific varieties of EP and BP to be considered here. In consonance with the methodological decision made above, we primarily focus our attention on the syntactic knowledge that native speakers of EP and BP have attained which arguably results from the normal process of language acquisition and not from schooling. Accordingly, we discuss differences between spoken and written language only when they provide insights into the nature of the grammars under examination. For instance, third person accusative clitics *o* (MASC.SG), *os* (MASC-PL), *a* (FEM.SG), and *as* (FEM-PL) are acquired through schooling in BP and are mostly employed in written language. Thus, they will not be analyzed as part of the grammar of BP. Interestingly, the syntactic positions these clitics occupy in written BP differ not only from those they occupy in EP but even from those occupied by other clitics in written BP. Therefore, a cursory discussion of written BP in this case may provide independent evidence for excluding third person accusative clitics from the grammar of BP (see Section 5.6.2).

That said, the approach explored here notably diverges from that adopted in traditional reference books in four ways. First, the presentation proceeds under a uniformly theoretically oriented perspective. We have systematized the relevant properties in a way that − we hope − may shed more light on central features of the syntactic architecture of natural languages. The empirical material and theoretical results are discussed using the general framework

---

[2] Ana Maria Martins is a native speaker of EP and Mary A. Kato and Jairo Nunes are native speakers of BP.

of the Principles and Parameters Theory as a point of reference, but technical parlance is kept to a minimum and is made accessible to the non-initiated.

Second, our primary concern is to describe the internal properties of the grammars of EP and BP rather than their use. However, sociolinguistic, diachronic, or acquisition information will also be reported when it highlights the contrasts between EP and BP.

Third, the paradigms we present involve what we believe corresponds to the common features underlying most subvarieties of contemporary EP and BP and may therefore differ from reference books in not including forms that have died out or that are not part of most subvarieties. This does not mean that dialectal properties that are not analyzed as part of the grammar of EP or BP will be simply disregarded. When their discussion leads to a better understanding of these grammars, the relevant data will receive due attention. Take the second person plural nominative pronoun *vós* ('you-PL') and its corresponding second person plural verbal inflection (as in *cantais* 'sing-**2.PL**'), for example. Although traditional textbooks always provide pronominal and verbal paradigms that include *vós* and its corresponding verbal inflection, they are inexistent in BP and are dialectally restricted to Northern varieties in EP. Thus, we will accordingly assume that the grammars of BP and EP (in the sense specified above) do not include *vós* or the corresponding verbal inflection. However, a brief discussion of this loss (see Section 2.4.2) may help us understand why it has a greater impact on the grammar of contemporary BP than on that of contemporary EP (see Section 3.4.2).

Finally, being part of the grammar of the relevant variety is not equivalent to what textbooks elect as "standard." If a given syntactic property is part of the knowledge attained through regular language acquisition and is common to most dialects, it will be included as part of the grammar under discussion even if it is prescriptively considered as substandard. An example of this is the use of the third person pronouns *ele* (MASC.SG), *eles* (MASC-PL), *ela* (FEM.SG), and *elas* (FEM-PL) in object position in BP. Although emphatically condemned by traditional textbooks and sociolinguistically stigmatized, this use can be observed in the (informal) speech of practically all speakers in all dialects of BP. Thus, we will analyze the occurrence of these pronouns in object position as part of the grammar of BP (see Section 2.4.3).

Throughout the book we will adopt the following conventions in the presentation of the data. When the discussion focuses on just one of the varieties of Portuguese analyzed here or the comparison set is relevant only in one variety, and not the other, examples will be identified as "EP" or "BP." When the discussion focuses on their differences, judgments will be provided with respect to each variety. Examples will be left unidentified if they receive the same grammatical judgment in both EP and BP and comparison is not germane to the issue under discussion. A percentage sign preceding "EP" or "BP" ("%EP" or "%BP") indicates that the acceptability of the sentence in question is dialectally/idiolectally restricted.

Following standard practice, we will also add question marks and asterisks preceding an example to signal that, under the indicated reading, the relevant sentences are judged by native speakers as marginal or unacceptable, respectively. Likewise, we will employ "#" introducing an example to indicate that the sentence is grammatically well formed, but pragmatically odd. Finally, if an asterisk, for instance, is placed outside parentheses – *(…) –, this indicates that the absence of the parenthesized material leads to unacceptability; conversely, an asterisk inside parentheses – (* …) – means that the presence of the parenthesized material leads to unacceptability.

Glosses will be detailed only when relevant. Morphological information in the glosses will be preceded by a hyphen if it corresponds to an independent morpheme and by a period if it does not. The parts of the examples or the glosses that are the focus of the discussion will appear in bold.

With these general methodological guidelines in mind, in the following chapters we compare the grammars of EP and BP with respect to all the syntactic properties examined, highlighting the theoretical significance of their contrasts and similarities. Chapter 2 introduces the paradigms of personal pronouns in EP and BP. Chapter 3 presents their agreement systems. Chapter 4 analyzes the properties of null subject constructions of each variety in the face of their differences regarding the pronominal and verbal agreement systems. Chapter 5 is devoted to the word order of major constituents in each variety. Chapter 6 discusses null objects and null possessors in each variety. Chapter 7 describes how EP and BP syntactically encode affirmation, negation, and polar questions and answers. Finally, Chapter 8 briefly summarizes some of the main syntactic differences between EP and BP discussed in the preceding chapters, showing how they are interwoven.

2

The Pronominal System

2.1 Introduction

One distinctive property of natural languages is that they formally identify three types of discourse participants (the speaker, the addressee, and any other third party). Personal pronouns are primary representatives of this tripartite distinction. Despite their lack of descriptive content, their feature [person] allows us to refer to each of these participants. So, we have first person pronouns to identify the speaker, second person pronouns to refer to the addressee, and third person pronouns to refer to any other participant, as respectively exemplified by the Portuguese pronouns *eu* 'I', *você* 'you.SG', and *ele* 'he'.

The specific system of personal pronouns of any given language is generally associated with its core syntactic properties and this is not different in the case of Portuguese. We will see that the differences between the pronominal systems of European Portuguese (EP) and Brazilian Portuguese (BP) are intimately connected to their most flagrant syntactic differences. For instance, their different systems of nominative pronouns correlate with their different agreement systems (see Section 3.4.2), whereas their different systems of genitive pronouns are associated with differences in the interpretation of null possessors (see Section 6.5). Thus, before we discuss these differences in the following chapters, we will first pay close attention to the system of personal pronouns in EP and BP.

The discussion is organized as follows. Section 2.2 presents Cardinaletti and Starke's (1999) tripartite classification of pronouns, exemplified with Portuguese personal pronouns. Section 2.3 briefly describes the feature composition of personal pronouns in Portuguese. Given this general background, in Section 2.4 we proceed to discuss the similarities and differences between EP and BP with respect to each grammatical person. Finally, Section 2.5 presents a summary with the major properties of the pronominal systems of EP and BP.

2.2 Strong, Weak, and Clitic Personal Pronouns in Portuguese

Let us start our discussion with a distinction that will prove very important for the comparison between EP and BP. Traditional textbooks make a distinction between tonic and clitic (CL) pronouns, the latter being unstressed pronouns that have special placement requirements. For instance, in BP the pronouns *você* 'you.SG' and *te* 'you.SG' differ in that the "tonic" pronoun *você* may occupy the canonical postverbal object position, while the clitic *te* must appear preverbally, as illustrated in (2.1).

(2.1)   a. Eu vi **você** ontem. (BP)
            I saw you.SG yesterday
    b. Eu **te** vi ontem. (BP)
            I you.SG$_{[CL]}$ saw yesterday
    'I saw you(SG) yesterday.'

However, this two-way distinction is insufficient to capture the different types of pronouns one finds in natural languages. Based on evidence from several languages, Cardinaletti and Starke (1999) argue that non-clitic ("tonic") pronouns actually involve two distinct classes, which they call *strong* (S) and *weak* (W) pronouns. Among their various syntactic dissimilarities, strong pronouns differ from weak pronouns in being able to appear in isolation and in allowing topicalization, coordination, and modification by focus particles. For instance, take the behavior of the BP pronouns *você* 'you.SG' and *cê* 'you.SG' with respect to each of these properties, as respectively illustrated in (2.2)–(2.5).

(2.2)   *Discourse fragments:*
    a. Quem vai fazer isso? **Você**? (BP)
        who goes do this you.SG
    b. Quem vai fazer isso? *****Cê**? (BP)
        who goes do this you.SG
    'Who is going to do this? You(SG)?'

(2.3)   *Topicalization:*
    a. **Você**, eu convidei. (BP)
        you.SG I invited
    b. *****Cê**, eu convidei. (BP)
        you.SG I invited
    'You(SG), I invited.'

(2.4)   *Coordination:*
    a. O João e **você** foram promovidos. (BP)
        the João and you.SG were promoted
    b. *O João e **cê** foram promovidos. (BP)
        the João and you.SG were promoted
    'João and you(SG) were promoted.'

2.2 Strong, Weak, and Clitic Personal Pronouns   7

(2.5)   *Modification by focus particles:*
    a. Nem **você** comprou o livro. (BP)
       nor you.SG bought the book
    b. *Nem **cê** comprou o livro. (BP)
       nor you.SG bought the book
    'Not even you(SG) bought the book.'

The (a) sentences in (2.2)–(2.5) respectively show that *você* can function as a discourse fragment, can be topicalized and coordinated, and can be modified by the focus particle *nem* 'not even'. By contrast, the (b) sentences show that exactly the opposite holds for *cê*.[1] Thus, according to these tests, *você* in (2.2)–(2.5) is a strong pronoun, whereas *cê* is not.

If BP *cê* is not a strong pronoun, the question now is whether it is a weak pronoun or a clitic.[2] One test that may tease these possibilities apart involves coordinated structures: whereas weak pronouns in subject position can be deleted under coordination, subject clitics cannot. Consider the sentences in (2.6) below, for example. Given that *cê* can receive an arbitrary interpretation, (2.6a) can be a paraphrase of (2.6b), with the indefinite clitic pronoun *se* (see Section 2.4.3). However, the two sentences contrast in that *cê* can be deleted in the second conjunct, but *se* cannot. This shows that *cê* is a weak pronoun and not a clitic.

(2.6)   a. Aqui **cê** não deve chegar atrasado, mas também (**cê**)
       here you.SG not should arrive late but also you.SG
       não deve chegar muito adiantado. (BP)
       not should arrive very early
    b. Aqui não **se** deve chegar atrasado, mas também não
       here not $SE_{[CL]}$ should arrive late but also not
       *(**se**) deve chegar muito adiantado. (BP)
       $SE_{[CL]}$ should arrive very early
    'Here one should not arrive late, but one should not arrive too early either.'

Further confirmation that BP *cê* is not a clitic is provided by its positioning requirements. Although weak pronouns may also have special placement

---

[1] For some BP speakers, *cê* may be allowed in a coordinated structure if it is the first conjunct, as illustrated in (i) below. This asymmetry is arguably due to the fact that the last conjunct receives the stress associated with the whole coordinated structure and weak pronouns are incompatible with prosodic prominence (see (2.10) below). What is relevant for our current discussion is that for all BP speakers, when *cê* is the last conjunct, it systematically contrasts with *você*, as seen in (2.4).

    (i)   Cê e o João foram promovidos. (%BP)
           you.SG and the João were promoted
           'You(SG) and João were promoted.'

[2] For discussion on the status of *cê* in BP, see e.g. Ramos 1996, Vitral 1996, Paredes Silva 1998, Ferreira 2000, 2009, Martins and Nunes 2005, 2009, 2010, Othero 2013, and especially Petersen 2008.

restrictions, they do not occupy the same position as clitics. In (2.6a), for instance, *cê* precedes negation, whereas the clitic *se* in (2.6b) follows it. A similar contrast can be observed when *cê* functions as a verbal complement. Consider the data in (2.7)–(2.9) below, for example. (2.7) shows that, like the clitic *te* in BP, the object pronoun *cê* cannot appear in the postverbal object position, whereas (2.8) and (2.9) show that they differ with respect to the syntactic position where they can surface: *te* must immediately precede the verb (see (2.8a)) and the object pronoun *cê* appears in a specific left periphery position (cf. (2.3b)/(2.8b) vs. (2.9b)). Thus, the positioning requirements of *cê* provide further evidence that it is neither a strong pronoun nor a clitic, but a weak pronoun.

(2.7) a. *O João convidou-**te**? (BP)
the João invited-you.$SG_{[CL]}$
b. *O João convidou **cê**? (BP)
the João invited you.SG
'Did João invite you(SG)?'

(2.8) a. O João **te** convidou? (BP)
the João you.$SG_{[CL]}$ invited
b. *O João **cê** convidou? (BP)
the João you.SG invited
'Did João invite you(SG)?'

(2.9) a. ***Te** que o João convidou? (BP)
you.$SG_{[CL]}$ that the João invited
b. **Cê** que o João convidou? (BP)
you.SG that the João invited
'Was it really you(SG) that João invited?'

The distinction between strong and weak pronouns may be morphologically transparent as in the case of *você* and *cê* in BP, with the weak pronoun being a reduced version of the strong form. However, it is not at all uncommon to find instances of homophony between strong and weak forms across languages. In this case, the identification of each type of pronoun may require a combination of different diagnostics. Take the contrast in (2.10)[3] involving the pronoun *ele* (3.MASC.SG) in BP, for instance.[4]

---

[3] Following standard practice, capital letters as in *ELE* and *ELA* in (2.10b) annotate (contrastive) focus stress.
[4] For discussion see e.g. Britto 1998, 2000, Galves 1997, 2001, Kato 1999, 2002a, Cyrino, Duarte, and Kato 2000, and Barbosa, Duarte, and Kato 2001, 2005.

(2.10) a. **Ele**   é   alto.   (BP)
        pron.3.MASC.SG is   tall
        '**He/it** is tall.'
     b. **ELE**   é   alto (e   não   ELA).   (BP)
        pron.3.MASC.SG is   tall and not   pron.3-FEM.SG
        '**HE/*IT** is tall (and not SHE/*IT).'

One semantic property of strong pronouns is that they are always associated with the feature [+hum]. The fact that in BP *ele* in (2.10a) may refer to a man or any non-human grammatically masculine nominal expression such as *o prédio* 'the building', for instance, indicates that there should be a weak version of *ele* in BP, for only weak pronouns (and clitics) may allow [-hum] readings. Another property of strong pronouns is that they can be prosodically prominent and interpreted as (contrastively) focused. Thus, the acceptability of (2.10b), with prosodic prominence on *ele*, leads us to conclude that there must also be a strong version of *ele* in BP. In other words, *ele* in BP is lexically ambiguous between a weak and a strong pronoun. Notice that this ambiguity does not result in an "everything-goes" situation. In (2.10b), *ele* (and *ela*, as well) can have only a [+hum] reading, for the prosodic prominence signals the use of the strong form. The combination of the feature [±hum] with prosodic prominence therefore allows us to isolate each version of *ele* in BP.

Strong pronouns may "double" clitics or weak pronouns. EP allows clitic doubling only when the clitics are doubled by the corresponding strong pronouns preceded by the preposition *a* 'to', as illustrated in (2.11).[5]

(2.11) a. O   professor repreendeu-**te**   a   **TI**.   (EP)
           the teacher   scolded-pron.2.$SG_{[CL]}$ to pron.2.$SG_{[S]}$
           'The teacher scolded YOU(SG).'
     b. O   professor não **me**   recomendará   a   **mim**
           the teacher   not   pron.1$SG_{[CL]}$ will-recommend to   pron.1$SG_{[S]}$
           nem aos   meus   colegas.   (EP)
           nor to-the my   colleagues.
           'The teacher will not recommend me or my colleagues.'
     c. O   João insultou-**nos**   a   **nós**   os três.   (EP)
           the João insulted-pron.1.$PL_{[CL]}$ to pron.1.$PL_{[S]}$ the three
           'João insulted the three of us.'

That the doubling pronoun in constructions such as (2.11) is strong is indicated by the fact that doubling pronouns in EP are licit only if they bear focus stress, as in (2.11a), or are coordinated or syntactically modified, as in (2.11b) and (2.11c), respectively. Further confirmation that this is so is provided by

---

[5] See e.g. Kato 1999, 2002a for discussion.

the contrast between (2.12a) and (2.12b) below in EP. Whereas the clitic in (2.12a) is ambiguous between [+hum] and [-hum], the clitic in (2.12b) is not, for the strong pronoun enforces the [+hum] reading.

(2.12)   a.   O   João   deixou-**o**   em   casa.   (EP)
             the   João   left-pron.3.MASC.SG$_{[CL]}$ at   home
             'João left **him/it** at home.'
         b.   O   João   deixou-**o**   a   **ELE**   em
             the   João   left-pron.3.MASC.SG$_{[CL]}$ to   pron.MASC.SG$_{[S]}$ at
             casa.   (EP)
             home
             'João left **HIM/*IT** at home.'

BP in turn only allows doubling of weak pronouns,[6] as illustrated in (2.13), with the weak pronouns *cê* and *ele* in subject position resuming the strong pronouns *você* and *ele* in topic position.[7]

(2.13)   a.   **Você**,   **cê**   vai ser promovido com certeza.   (BP)
             you.SG   you.SG$_{[W]}$ go   be   promoted   with certainty
             'You(SG) are surely going to be promoted.'
         b.   **Ele**,   **ele**   é alto.   (BP)
             pron.3.MASC.SG   pron.3.MASC.SG   is tall
             'He/*it is tall.'

Recall that *ele* is ambiguous between a weak and a strong pronoun in BP. Thus, the sentence in (2.13b) without the pronoun in topic position is ambiguous between a [+hum] or [-hum] reading (see (2.10a)). However, given that only strong pronouns can be topicalized (see (2.3)), the topicalized pronoun in (2.13b) must then be a strong form. Furthermore, given that strong personal pronouns must be [+hum], (2.13b) can admit only the [+hum] reading.

In the sections below and the following chapters, we will see that the tripartite distinction *strong/weak/clitic* underlies several of the distinct properties between EP and BP syntax. For purposes of presentation in

---

[6] For discussion see e.g. Britto 1998, 2000, Galves 1997, 2001, Kato 1999, 2002a, Cyrino, Duarte, and Kato 2000, Barbosa, Duarte, and Kato 2001, 2005, and Martins and Nunes 2009.

[7] Some BP speakers may allow clitic doubling as illustrated in (i), although individual speakers may vary with respect to which clitics allow it. For discussion see e.g. Machado-Rocha 2016 and Machado-Rocha and Ramos 2016.

(i)   a.   Ele   **me**   chamou   **eu**.   (%BP)
          he   pron.1.SG$_{[CL]}$ called   pron.1.SG$_{[S]}$
          'He called me.'
      b.   Eu vou **te**   falar   uma   coisa   pra   **você**.   (%BP)
          I   go   pron.2.SG$_{[CL]}$ speak   one   thing   to   pron.2.SG$_{[S]}$
          'I'll tell you something.'

what follows, unambiguous forms will have their specification as strong, weak, and clitic coded by the indices [S], [W], and [CL], respectively. If the relevant form is ambiguous between a strong and a weak pronoun or if the information is irrelevant to the point under discussion, no indices will be added.

2.3 Feature Composition of Personal Pronouns in Portuguese

In terms of their feature composition, Portuguese personal pronouns can be classified with respect to person, number, gender, case, and reflexivity. Person, number, and gender are essentially lexical features in the sense that their values are independent of the syntactic structures where they may occur. By contrast, case and reflexivity are more syntactic in nature, as their values must be licensed in specific syntactic configurations. Let us briefly consider each of these features.

2.3.1 Person

As mentioned in Section 2.1, the feature [person] admits three values: first (1), which refers to the speaker (*eu* 'I') or the speaker and someone else (e.g. *nós* 'we'); second (2), which refers to the addressee(s) (e.g. *tu* 'you.SG') or the addressee(s) and someone else other than the speaker (e.g. *vocês* 'you-PL'); and third (3), which refers to any participant(s) other than the speaker or the addressee(s) (e.g. *ela* 'she'). These values are semantic in nature and must be kept apart from syntactic values (i.e. the kind of syntactic agreement a given pronoun triggers). For instance, in EP *tu* and *você* are both specified as second person (singular) from a semantic point of view, but differ in the kind of syntactic agreement they are associated with: *tu* triggers second person (singular) agreement, whereas *você* triggers third person (singular) agreement (see Section 3.4.1). For purposes of presentation, we will represent the semantic person values on the pronouns and the syntactic person values on the predicates, as illustrated in (2.14).

(2.14) a. **Tu** saíste cedo ontem. (EP)
        pron.2.SG leave-PERF.PAST.2.SG early yesterday
    b. **Você** saiu cedo ontem. (EP)
        pron.2.SG leave-PERF.PAST.3.SG early yesterday
        'You(SG) left early yesterday.'

By formally encoding discourse participants, personal pronouns may also be associated with extralinguistic information about social relations among the participants or their social status.[8] For instance, in EP the second person singular pronoun *tu* (as well as its null counterpart detected by the verbal inflection) conveys more familiarity, intimacy, or proximity in social status with respect to the speaker than the second person singular pronoun *você* (or its null counterpart).[9] Whenever this distinction becomes relevant in what follows, we will use the feature [±close] to represent it; thus, for EP *tu* will be specified as [+close] and *você* as [-close].[10,11]

2.3.2 Number

Regarding number, personal pronouns in Portuguese admit two values: *singular* (SG) and *plural* (PL). Singular and plural pronouns may be distinguished by the nominal plural suffix -*s*, as in *você* 'you.SG' vs. *vocês*

---

[8] This type of extralinguistic information is typically conveyed by address forms. For instance, *o senhor* (lit. *the mister*) and *a senhora* (lit. *the mistress*), which are illustrated in (i) below, convey respect towards the addressee in both EP and BP and are therefore generally used to address elders, superiors, customers, etc. In EP, such address forms may also be combined with titles, as shown in (ii).

(i)   a. **O senhor** está cansado?
          the mister is   tired
          'Are you tired, sir?'
    b. O Pedro viu **a senhora** na livraria.
          the Pedro saw the mistress in-the bookstore
          'Pedro saw you, Ma'am, at the bookstore'.

(ii)   **O Senhor Doutor** dá-me licença? (EP)
           the mister doctor gives-me license
           'May I come in, Doctor?'

[9] For discussion see e.g. Cintra 1972, Faraco 1996, Lopes and Duarte 2007, Lopes 2008, and Bacelar do Nascimento 2020. For some EP speakers, the overt and null versions of *você* contrast in that the overt version is understood as an impolite or disrespectful address form (see e.g. Guilherme and Lara Bermejo 2015, Lara Bermejo and Guilherme 2018, Lara Bermejo 2017, and Bacelar do Nascimento 2020).

[10] This opposition in EP does not hold in some (higher class) social groups, for which *você* may also convey familiarity/intimacy/proximity.

[11] In EP, proper names are also commonly used as address forms (see e.g. Lopes and Duarte 2007 and Bacelar do Nascimento 2020), occupying – like *você* and its null counterpart – the [-close] side of the scale of familiarity/intimacy/proximity. Thus, a sentence such as (i) in EP can be used as a direct question to Maria, as shown by its translation, and indicates that the speaker is in some way [-close] with respect to her.

(i)   A **Maria** quer um café? (EP)
       the Maria wants a coffee
       'Would **you** like some coffee, Maria?'

'you-PL', or via suppletion, as in *eu* (1.SG) vs. *nós* (1.PL). Again, one must distinguish number as a semantic feature on pronouns and number as a syntactic feature, that is, the syntactic agreement associated with the pronoun. The first person plural pronoun *a gente*, for instance, triggers third person singular agreement on verbs, as illustrated in (2.15) (see Section 3.4.1).

(2.15) **A gente** vai viajar amanhã.
pron.*1.PL* go.*3.SG* travel tomorrow
'We are going to travel tomorrow.'

2.3.3 Gender

As for gender, the values are *masculine* (MASC) and *feminine* (FEM). Only a subset of personal pronouns can inflect for gender. These are the pronouns *ele* (3.MASC.SG), *ela* (3-FEM.SG), *o* (3.MASC.SG), *a* (3.FEM.SG) (and their plural counterparts), and the series of possessive pronouns, as exemplified by *nosso* 'our-MASC.SG' and *nossa* 'our-FEM.SG'. If a subject pronoun is not specified for gender, its adjectival or nominal predicate will have its gender specification (partially) determined by the gender of the speaker in the case of a first person pronoun or by that of the addressee in the case of a second person pronoun, as illustrated in (2.16) (see Section 3.4.1).

(2.16) a. **Eu** estou cansado.   [*spoken by a **male***]
       I   am   tired-***MASC**.SG*
       'I am tired.'
     b. **Você** é professora?   [*spoken to a **female***]
       you.*SG* is teacher-***FEM**.SG*
       'Are you a teacher?'

2.3.4 Case

Case is a prototypical syntactic feature as it encodes the syntactic function of a nominal expression in a given sentence. The first person singular pronoun, for instance, is realized with the nominative form *eu* if it is the subject of a finite clause or with the oblique form *mim* if it is the complement of a preposition. In Portuguese, only pronouns are morphologically specified for case and there are five case distinctions: nominative (NOM), accusative (ACC), dative (DAT), oblique (OBL), and genitive (GEN). Below we describe the general syntactic environments where each case is licensed.

2.3.4.1 Nominative

In both EP and BP the nominative case is canonically licensed as the subject of finite clauses (i.e. indicative, subjunctive, and imperative clauses), as shown in (2.17), gerund clauses,[12] as shown in (2.18), and inflected infinitival clauses,[13] as shown in (2.19).

(2.17) a. **Eu** acordei tarde.
  I.NOM woke-up.INDIC.PERF.PAST.1SG late
  'I woke up late.'
 b. O João recomendou que **eu** viajasse
  the João recommended that I.NOM travel.SUBJ.IMPERF.1.SG
  amanhã.
  tomorrow
  'João recommended that I travel tomorrow.'
 c. Dá **tu** a notícia! (EP)
  give.AFFIRM.IMP.2.SG you.NOM.SG the news
  'You(SG) break the news!'

(2.18) Estando **tu** feliz, as crianças também estão. (EP)
 be.GER you.NOM.SG happy the children also are
 'If you(SG) are happy, the children are happy too.'

(2.19) **Tu** chegares cedo foi uma agradável surpresa. (EP)
 you.NOM.SG arrive-INF-2.SG early was a pleasant surprise
 'Your(SG) early arrival was a pleasant surprise.'

Nominative is also the default case in EP and BP.[14] Thus, nominative pronouns can also appear in predicative positions, as in (2.20a), in the left periphery of clauses, as in (2.20b), or in isolation, as in (2.20c).

(2.20) a. O problema é **ele**.
  the problem is he.NOM
  'The problem is him.'
 b. **Eu**, ninguém me viu.
  I.NOM nobody me saw
  'As for myself, nobody saw me.'

---

[12] Central-Southern and Insular EP dialects (see e.g. Cintra 1971 and Segura 2013) allow inflected gerunds, as illustrated in (i) below (see e.g. Mota 1997, Lobo 2001, 2003, 2016a and Ribeiro 2002 for discussion). The subject of these inflected gerunds is also marked with nominative case.

 (i) Em eles **chegandem**, vamos jantar. (%EP)
  in pron.NOM.3.MASC-PL arrive-GER-3.PL go-1.PL dine
  'As soon as they arrive, we will have dinner.'

[13] See e.g. Raposo 1987a, 1987b, 1989, Ambar 1992b, 1998, 2000, Martins 2001, Duarte, Gonçalves, and Miguel 2005, Pires 2006, Modesto 2011, Duarte, Santos, and Gonçalves 2016, and Ambar and Jiménez-Fernández 2017, for discussion.

[14] On default case in Portuguese, see e.g. Kato 1999 and Viotti 2005.

c. A: – Quem   é   que   a   Maria convidou?
       whom   is   that   the Maria invited
       'Who did Maria invite?'
   B: – **Eu**.
       I.NOM
       'Me.'

There is a fair amount of case syncretism in Portuguese. The only pronouns that are unambiguously nominative are *eu* (1.SG) and *tu* (2.SG). All the others can also be associated with another case. *Nós*, for instance, is the nominative as well as the oblique form of the first person plural pronoun (when it is the complement of prepositions other than *com* 'with'), as we will see below.

2.3.4.2 Accusative

Pronouns are realized with accusative case in Portuguese in three general circumstances, all of them involving transitive verbs. The canonical pattern is when the pronoun is the direct object of a transitive verb, as illustrated in (2.21).

(2.21)   A Maria comprou-**o**.   (EP)
         the Maria bought-pron.ACC.3.MASC.SG
         'Maria bought it.'

The second pattern emerges when the pronoun is the logical subject of a gerund or an uninflected infinitival selected by a perception verb (*ver* 'see', *ouvir* 'hear', *escutar* 'listen to', etc.) or a causative verb (*fazer* 'make', *deixar* 'let', etc.), as exemplified in (2.22).[15]

(2.22) a. O João **te**   viu   saindo.   (BP)
           the João you.ACC.SG saw leaving
           'João saw you(SG) leaving.'
        b. Eu ouvi-**os**   cantar.   (EP)
           I   heard-pron.ACC.3.MASC-PL sing
           'I heard them sing.'
        c. O Pedro deixou-**as**   entrar.   (EP)
           the Pedro let-pron.ACC.3.FEM-PL enter
           'Pedro let them in.'

Finally, if the pronoun is the logical subject of a "small clause" (a subject–predicate structure without tense specification) selected by a transitive verb, it

---

[15] See e.g. Raposo 1989, Gonçalves 1999, Martins 2000a, Gonçalves and Duarte 2001, Barbosa and Cochofel 2005, Hornstein, Martins, and Nunes 2006, 2008, and Gonçalves, Carrilho, and Pereira 2016 for discussion.

is also realized as accusative. In (2.23), for example, there is a subject–predicate relation between the pronoun *a* 'her' and the adjective *doente* 'sick' and the small clause structure *[a doente]* is the complement of the transitive verb *encontrar* 'find'.[16]

(2.23) Eu encontrei-**a**   doente.   (EP)
        I found-pron.ACC.3.FEM.SG sick
        'I found her sick.'

Exceptionally, the existential verb *haver* and the copulas *ser* and *estar* can also license accusative case in EP, as illustrated in (2.24) and (2.25).[17]

(2.24) Problemas, havia-**os**   de todos os tipos; mas
        problems   had-pron.ACC.3.MASC-PL of all the types but
        soluções   não   (EP)
        solutions not
        'There were all kinds of problems, but no solutions.'

(2.25) a. Loucas,   elas   não **o**   são, mas agem
           crazy-FEM-PL they   not pron.ACC.3.MASC.SG   are but act
           como se   fossem.   (EP)
           as   if   were
           'They are not crazy, but they act as if they were.'
        b. Vários   projetos   estão   atrasados   e   não
           several projects   are   delayed-MASC-PL   and   not
           o   deveriam   estar.   (EP)
           pron.ACC.3.MASC.SG   should   be
           'Several projects are behind schedule and should not be.'

As in standard circumstances, the accusative clitic *os* in (2.24) agrees in gender and number with the nominal expression it is associated with (*problemas*). In contrast, the accusative clitic in (2.25) surfaces with the default masculine singular form *o* as it is associated with a predicative adjective (*loucas* 'crazy-FEM-PL' in (2.25a) and *atrasados* 'delayed-MASC-PL' in (2.25b)).

O, *os*, *a*, and *as* (and their allomorphs; see Section 2.4.3) are the only unambiguous accusative pronouns in Portuguese. The second person singular clitic *te*, for instance, is ambiguous between accusative (see (2.22a)) and dative.

---

[16] Constructions such as (2.22) and (2.23) are subtypes of what is known in the generative literature as "exceptional case marking" (ECM) constructions, that is, constructions in which a given element assigns case to the subject of its complement.
[17] For discussion see e.g. Eliseu 1984, Matos 1985, and Cyrino 1993, 1997.

2.3.4.3 Dative

In both EP and BP, the "indirect" object of ditransitive verbs is the canonical realization of dative case, as illustrated in (2.26) below.[18] Also in both varieties, only clitics can bear morphological dative case. If the indirect object is not a clitic, it is case-marked by means of a preposition – *a* 'to' in EP and *para/pra* 'to/for' in BP, as shown in (2.27).[19]

(2.26)   a. Eu dei-**lhe** um livro. (EP)
           I gave-CL.DAT.3.SG a book
           'I gave him a book.'
   b. O Pedro ainda não **me** enviou o documento.
           the Pedro still not CL.DAT.1.SG sent the document.
           'Pedro hasn't sent me the document yet.'

(2.27)   a. Eu dei um livro **ao** João. (EP)
           I gave a book to-the João
           'I gave a book to João.'
   b. Eu dei um livro **pro** João. (BP)
           I gave a book to-the João
           'I gave a book to João.'

In the remaining environments, the two varieties substantially differ, as dative licensing in BP is becoming substantially weakened. For instance, a possessor may generally be licensed in EP with dative case, as shown in (2.28) below, whereas in BP this type of construction is allowed only with first and second person clitics.[20]

(2.28)   a. O Pedro consertou o carro **ao** João. (EP: OK; BP: *)
           the Pedro fixed the car to-the João
           'Pedro fixed João's car.'
   b. Puxei o rabo **ao** gato. (EP: OK; BP: *)
           pulled-1.SG the tail to-the cat
           'I pulled the cat's tail.'
   c. Só a Maria **lhe** viu o rosto. (EP: OK; BP: *)
           only the Maria him/her.DAT saw the face
           'Only Maria saw {his/her} face.'
   d. Ninguém **me** apertou a mão. (EP: OK; BP: OK)
           nobody me.DAT pressed the hand
           'Nobody greeted me.'

---

[18] See e.g. Berlinck 1996b, Salles 1997, Torres Morais 2007, Torres Morais and Berlinck 2007, Torres Morais and Salles 2010, and Calindro 2015, 2020 for discussion.
[19] Some dialects of BP also allow the preposition *a* in these contexts. See e.g. Scher 1996 and Cavalcante 2009 for discussion.
[20] For discussion see e.g. Miguel 1992, 1996, 2004, Miguel, Gonçalves and Duarte 2010, Barros 2006, Torres Morais and Salles 2016, Gonçalves and Miguel 2019, and Nunes and Kato forthcoming.

The dative clitic is also replaced in BP by a prepositional phrase in constructions involving adjectival complements, as illustrated in (2.29),[21] and by an accusative pronoun, which is homophonous with the nominative form (see Section 2.4.3), in constructions involving the complement of a psychological ("psych") verb such as *interessar* 'interest' and *agradar* 'please',[22] as illustrated in (2.30). Finally, many constructions such as the ones in (2.31), for example, where the impersonal verb assigns dative case to the clitic, have simply disappeared in BP.[23]

(2.29) a. Aquelas pessoas não **te** eram leais. (EP)
those persons not CL.DAT.2.SG were loyal
'Those people were not loyal to you(SG).'
b. Aquelas pessoas não eram leais a **você**. (BP)
those persons not were loyal to you.SG
'Those people were not loyal to you(SG).'

(2.30) a. Aquilo não **lhe** interessava. (EP)
that not CL.DAT.3.SG interested
'That didn't interest {him/her}.'
b. Aquilo não interessava **ele**. (BP)
that not interested pron.ACC.3.MASC.SG
'That didn't interest him.'
c. Nada **lhes** agradava. (EP)
nothing CL.DAT.3-PL pleased
'Nothing pleased them.'
d. Nada agradava **elas**. (BP)
nothing pleased pron.ACC.3-FEM-PL
'Nothing pleased them(FEM).'

(2.31) a. Não **me** custou nada a escrever o relatório. (EP/*BP)
not CL.DAT.1.SG cost nothing to write the report
'It was not at all hard for me to succeed in writing the report.'
b. Não **me** calhou ir para a tropa. (EP/*BP)
not CL.DAT.1.SG happened go to the army
'I didn't happen to be selected for military service.'

[21] Interestingly, the preposition used in adjectival complements in BP is *a* rather than *para/pra* (cf. (2.29b) vs. (2.27b)). This is also true of psych-verb constructions in formal styles of BP, where the verbal complement may surface with the preposition *a*, as illustrated in (i). See e.g. Costa 2000 and Figueiredo Silva 2007 for discussion.

(i) a. Aqueles resultados não interessavam **ao** João. (%BP)
those results not interested to-the João
'Those results did not interest João.'
b. A proposta agradou **ao** João. (%BP)
the proposal pleased to-the João
'The proposal pleased João.'

[22] For discussion on psych verbs in BP, see e.g. Cançado 1995, 1997.
[23] See e.g. Martins and Nunes 2005, 2017a for discussion.

The third person singular pronoun *lhe* 'him/her' and its plural counterpart *lhes* 'them' are the only forms that are unambiguously dative (but see footnote 41 below). All the other pronouns are ambiguous with respect to other cases. *Me* 'me', for instance, is ambiguous between dative (see (2.26b)) and accusative.

2.3.4.4 Oblique

Pronouns are realized with oblique case in EP and BP when they are the complement of a preposition, as illustrated in (2.32).

(2.32) a. O João não faz nada sem **mim**.
the João not does nothing without pron.***OBL.1.SG***
'João doesn't do anything without me.'
b. A Maria trouxe esses livros para **ti**.   (EP)
the Maria brought these books for pron.***OBL.2.SG.***[+close]
'Maria brought these books for you(SG).'
c. Eu estava a pensar em **si**.   (EP)
I was to think in pron.*2.SG.**OBL*[-close]
'I was thinking about you(SG).'

In BP, a pronoun may also be realized as oblique if it is the subject of an uninflected infinitival that is the complement of the preposition *para/pra* 'to/for', as illustrated in (2.33), a possibility that is dialectally restricted in EP.[24]

(2.33) a. O João trouxe esse artigo pra **mim** ler.   (BP)
the João brought this article for pron.***OBL.1.SG*** read
'João brought this article for me to read.'
b. Pra **mim** ir lá agora vai ser muito difícil.   (BP)
for pron.***OBL.1.SG*** go there now goes be very difficult
'For me to go there now is going to be very hard.'

---

[24] For discussion on this subtype of ECM construction in BP (see footnote 16 above), see e.g. Perini 1974, Lightfoot 1991, Salles 1997, and Hornstein, Martins, and Nunes 2008. In the CORDIAL-SIN corpus, these constructions are attested in some Southern dialects and in the archipelago of Azores, as respectively illustrated in (ia) and (ib).

(i) a. Com isto não é dizer que queria ver os outros mal
with this not is say that wanted to-see the others bad
para **mim** estar bem.   (%EP)
for pron.***OBL.1.SG*** be well
'This is not to say that I wish anyone bad for my own good.'
(CORDIAL-SIN, MLD50)
b. Eu estou inquieta para parar, para apanhar aí
I am restless to stop to gather there
umas primaveras para **mim** levar comigo.   (%EP)
some primroses for pron.***OBL.1.SG*** take with-me
'I am eager to stop to gather some primroses there to take with me.'
(CORDIAL-SIN, MIG47)

In addition to the unambiguous oblique forms *mim* (see (2.32a)), *ti* (see (2.32b)), and *si* (see (2.32c)), Portuguese also has conflated oblique pronouns such as *comigo* 'with me' and *contigo* 'with you(SG)' illustrated in (2.34). These result from morphological fusion involving the preposition *com* 'with', as sketched in (2.35) (see Section 2.4 for details on the specific use of the pronouns in (2.35) in EP and BP).[25]

(2.34)   a. As   crianças   vão   **comigo**.
              the   children   go   with-me
              'The children are coming with me.'
         b. Eu   preciso   conversar   **contigo**.   (EP)
              I   need   talk   with-you.$SG_{[+close]}$
              'I need to talk to you(SG).'

(2.35)   a. com   +   mim   → comigo   'with me'
              with   pron.OBL.1.SG
         b. com   +   ti   → contigo   'with you.SG'
              with   pron.OBL.2.SG $_{[+close]}$
         c. com   +   si   → consigo   'with him/her/them';
              with   pron.OBL.3.SG   'with you.SG' (EP)
         d. com   +   nós   → connosco (EP
              with   pron.OBL.1.PL   orthography) 'with us'
                                           conosco (BP
                                           orthography) 'with us'
         e. com   +   vós   → convosco   'with you-PL'
              with   pron.OBL.2.PL

2.3.4.5 Genitive

Among the cases available in Portuguese, genitive is the only one that is licensed within noun phrases, indicating the possessor (in a broad sense) associated with the head noun.[26] Genitive pronouns agree in gender and number with the possessee, as illustrated in (2.36).

---

[25] These exceptional forms emerged in two diachronic steps. Take *comigo* 'with me', for instance. In Latin, the (ablative) first person singular pronoun *me* and the preposition *cum* 'with' fused, yielding *mecum*, which evolved into the Old Portuguese forms *mego/migo*. Later on, after Latin encliticization of *cum* to personal pronouns was lost, the preposition *com* 'with' was added in initial position to this already fused form, yielding the modern conflated form *comigo*, which in Old Portuguese coexisted with the variant *migo*. For discussion see e.g. Nunes 1919, Williams 1938, Mattos e Silva 1993, 2008, and Houaiss and Villar 2001.

[26] For discussion see e.g. Oliveira e Silva 1984, Perini 1985, Miguel 1992, 1996, 2004, Cerqueira 1993, 1996, Menuzzi 1996, 1999, Müller 1996, Negrão and Müller 1996, Floripi 2003, Rodrigues 2004, 2010, 2020, Avelar 2004, 2006, 2009b, A. Castro 2006, Estrela 2006, Brito 2007, Floripi and Nunes 2009, Lobo 2013a, and Nunes 2018.

(2.36) a. O **meu** carro é
    the.MASC.SG pron.GEN.1.SG.MASC.SG car.MASC.SG is
    vermelho.
    red-MASC.SG
    'My car is red.'
  b. A **minha** casa é
    the.FEM.SG pron.GEN.1.SG-FEM.SG house.FEM.SG is
    pequena.
    small-FEM.SG
    'My house is small.'
  c. Os **nossos** amigos vêm
    the.MASC-PL pron.GEN.1.PL-MASC-PL friend-MASC-PL come
    para o jogo.
    for the game
    'Our friends will come for the game.'

For full noun phrases, the possessor relation is realized by means of the dummy preposition *de* 'of', as shown in (2.37) below, and in this situation the possessor does not agree with the head noun. This possibility is also available for some pronouns, as illustrated in (2.38) (see Section 2.4 for a discussion on the competition between the two possibilities for genitive expression in EP and BP).

(2.37) As páginas **do** livro estão sujas.
    the pages of-the book are dirty
    'The pages of the book are dirty.'

(2.38) a. As páginas **dele** estão sujas. (BP)
    the pages of-pron.3.MASC.SG are dirty
    'Its pages are dirty.'
  b. A filha **de** vocês é muito inteligente. (BP)
    the daughter of pron.2-PL is very intelligent
    'Your(PL) daughter is very smart.'

2.3.5 Reflexivity

Personal pronouns can also be distinguished in terms of reflexivity.[27] The accusative third person singular pronouns *se* and *o*, for instance, contrast in that the denotation of reflexive pronoun *se* must be the same as the

---

[27] Within the Principles and Parameters framework (see e.g. Chomsky 1981, Chomsky and Lasnik 1993), the relevant distinction is formulated in terms of anaphors (corresponding to reflexive and reciprocal expressions), subject to Principle A of the Binding Theory, and pronouns, subject to Principle B. For purposes of presentation, we will stick to the familiar distinction between reflexive and nonreflexive pronouns. Thus, all items below that are simply referred to as *pron(ouns)* or bear the specification [-REFL] correspond to [+pronominal, -anaphoric] elements in Chomsky's (1981) system, whereas the elements that are referred to as *reflexives* or bear the feature [+REFL] correspond to [-pronominal, +anaphoric] elements.

denotation of the (closest) subject, whereas the denotation of the nonreflexive pronoun *o* must be distinct from the (closest) subject, as illustrated in (2.39) below.[28] Although *se* is inherently specified as [+REFL] and *o* as [-REFL], most pronouns in Portuguese are not specified for this feature and therefore are compatible with both reflexive and nonreflexive contexts, as respectively illustrated in (2.40) with the pronoun *me* 'me'.

(2.39) a. Ele$_i$ elogiou-se$_{i/*k}$ na reunião. (EP)
he praised-pron.3.SG.*[+REFL]* in-the meeting
'He praised himself at the meting.'
b. Ele$_i$ elogiou-o$_{k/*i}$ na reunião. (EP)
he praised-pron.3.SG.*[-REFL]* in-the meeting
'He praised him at the meeting.'

(2.40) a. Eu$_i$ não me$_i$ vi no espelho.
I not **pron.1.SG** saw in-the mirror
'I didn't see **myself** in the mirror.'
b. Ele não me viu no cinema.
he not **pron.1.SG** saw in-the cinema
'He didn't see **me** at the movies.'

There are strong correlations in Portuguese between reflexivity, on the one hand, and case, person, and the tripartite distinction *strong/weak/clitic*, on the other. First, there are no nominative reflexives; thus, if a pronoun is marked with nominative, it is necessarily specified as [-REFL]. In addition, genitive pronouns are not specified for reflexivity; the genitive pronoun *nosso* 'our', for example, can occur in both anaphoric and nonanaphoric contexts, as respectively illustrated in (2.41).

(2.41) a. Nós vamos consultar o **nosso** advogado.
we go consult the *pron.GEN.1.PL-MASC.SG* lawyer
'We're going to consult our lawyer.'
b. Eles contrataram o **nosso** advogado.
they hired the *pron.GEN.1.PL-MASC.SG* lawyer
'They hired our lawyer.'

Yet another correlation is that accusative, dative, and oblique case-marked pronouns may have distinct forms associated with [+REFL] and [-REFL] specifications only if their morphological paradigm is associated with third person (syntactic) agreement. Consider the second person singular pronouns *tu* and *você* in EP, for instance. As mentioned in Section 2.3.1 and illustrated in (2.42) below, *você* triggers third person singular agreement, whereas *tu*

---

[28] Following standard practice, coreference is annotated by identical indices and distinct reference by different indices.

2.3 Feature Composition of Personal Pronouns   23

triggers second person singular agreement. Accordingly, one finds the opposition between [+REFL] and [-REFL] in forms corresponding to *você*, for instance, but not in forms corresponding to *tu*, as respectively illustrated in (2.43) and (2.44).

(2.42)   a. **Você**   **sabe**   o que   eu   quero.   (EP)
           pron.2.SG$_{[-close]}$ *know.3.SG*   *what*   *I*   *want*
      b. **Tu**   **sabes**   o que   eu   quero.   (EP)
           pron.2.SG$_{[+close]}$ *know-2.SG*   *what*   *I*   *want*
           'You(SG) know what I want.'

(2.43)   a. **Você**   feriu-**se**?   (EP)
           pron.2.SG$_{[-close]}$ *hurt-2.SG.[+REFL]$_{[-close]}$*
           'Did you hurt yourself?'
      b. *Você$_i$ feriu-o$_i$?   (EP)
           pron.2.SG$_{[-close]}$ *hurt-2.SG.[-REFL]$_{[-close]}$*
           'Did you hurt yourself?'

(2.44)   a. **Tu**   magoas-**te**   com qualquer coisa. (EP)
           pron.2.SG$_{[+close]}$ *hurt-pron.2.SG$_{[+close]}$*   *with any thing*
           'You(SG) get hurt by anything.'
      b. A   Joana   não   **te**   deu   o   recado? (EP)
           the Joana not   ***pron.2.SG$_{[+close]}$***   *gave the message*
           'Didn't Joana give you(SG) the message?'

Finally, there is an interesting correlation between reflexivity and the tripartite distinction *strong/weak/clitic* (see Section 2.2) in BP. If a given verb is not intrinsically reflexive, coreference between the object and the closest subject must be established by a clitic in the unmarked case, as shown in (2.45a) below, or by a strong pronoun if contrast is involved, as shown in (2.45b). Weak pronouns are not compatible with a reflexive reading, as illustrated in (2.45c) with an unstressed pronoun.

(2.45)   a. A Maria **se**   indicaria   pro cargo? (BP)
           the Maria pron.3.SG.[+REFL]$_{[CL]}$ would-nominate for-the position
           'Would Maria nominate herself to the position?'
      b. [A Maria]$_i$ indicaria   **ELA**$_i$ pro cargo? (BP)
           the Maria would-nominate pron.3-FEM.SG$_{[S]}$ for-the position
           'Would Maria nominate HERSELF to the position?'
      c. *[A Maria]$_i$ indicaria   **ela**$_i$ pro cargo? (BP)
           the Maria would-nominate pron.3-FEM.SG$_{[W]}$ for-the position
           'Would Maria nominate herself to the position?'

By contrast, if the verb involves an inherently reflexive predicate such as *chamar-se* 'to be called' or *queixar-se* 'to complain', or a reciprocal predicate such as *encontrar-se* 'to meet' or *abraçar-se* 'to hug', only clitics are allowed, as illustrated in (2.46)–(2.49).²⁹

(2.46) a. Ela **se** chama Maria. (BP)
          she pron.3.SG.[+REFL]$_{[CL]}$ *calls Maria*
     b. *Ela$_i$ chama **ELA**$_i$ Maria. (BP)
          she calls pron.3-FEM.SG$_{[S]}$ *Maria*
     c. *Ela$_i$ chama **ela**$_i$ Maria. (BP)
          she calls pron.3-FEM.SG$_{[W]}$ *Maria*
          'Her name is Maria.'

(2.47) a. O Pedro **se** queixou à polícia. (BP)
          the Pedro pron.3.SG.[+REFL]$_{[CL]}$ *complained to-the police*
     b. *[O Pedro]$_i$ queixou **ELE**$_i$ à polícia. (BP)
          the Pedro complained pron.3.MASC.SG$_{[S]}$ *to-the police*
     c. *[O Pedro]$_i$ queixou **ele**$_i$ à polícia. (BP)
          the Pedro complained pron.3.MASC.SG$_{[W]}$ *to-the police*
          'Pedro complained to the police.'

(2.48) a. Acabou que eles não **se** encontraram. (BP)
          finished that they not pron.3.PL.[+REFL]$_{[CL]}$ *met*
     b. *Acabou que eles$_i$ não encontraram **ELES**$_i$. (BP)
          finished that they not met pron.3.MASC-PL$_{[S]}$
     c. *Acabou que eles$_i$ não encontraram **eles**$_i$. (BP)
          finished that they not met pron.3.MASC-PL$_{[W]}$
          'It turned out that they didn't meet.'

---

²⁹ Reflexive clitics associated with inherently reflexive verbs can be dropped in several dialects of BP, as illustrated in (i) (see e.g. d'Albuquerque 1984, Nunes 1995, Negrão and Viotti 2015, and Carvalho 2016).

(i) a. Ela **(se)** chama Maria. (%BP)
       she pron.3.SG.[+REFL]$_{[CL]}$ *calls Maria*
       'Her name is Maria.'
   b. Eu **(me)** lembrei de você ontem. (%BP)
       I pron.1.SG.[+REFL]$_{[CL]}$ *remembered of you yesterday*
       'I thought of you yesterday.'

In turn, some EP speakers allow (or sometimes require) deletion of a reflexive clitic in a nonfinite clause if it is identical to the subject of its clause or the object of the subordinating clause, as illustrated in (ii) (see e.g. Martins and Nunes 2017a,b for discussion).

(ii) a. O João fez-**nos** encontrar-(***nos**) com o Pedro. (%EP)
       the João made-pron.1.PL$_{[CL]}$ *meet-pron.1.PL.[+REFL]*$_{[CL]}$ *with the Pedro*
       'João made us meet with Pedro.'
   b. O João convenceu-**me** a deitar-(***me**)
       the João convinced-pron.1.SG$_{[CL]}$ *to lie.down-pron.1.SG.[+REFL]*$_{[CL]}$
      mais cedo. (%EP)
      more early
       'João convinced me to go to bed earlier.'

(2.49) a. As crianças **se** abraçaram. (BP)
the children pron.3.PL.[+REFL]$_{[CL]}$ hugged
b. *[As crianças]$_i$ abraçaram **ELAS**$_i$. (BP)
the children hugged pron.3-FEM-PL$_{[S]}$
c. *[As crianças]$_i$ abraçaram **elas**$_i$. (BP)
the children hugged pron.3-FEM-PL$_{[W]}$
'The children hugged each other.'

2.4 Similarities and Differences between European Portuguese and Brazilian Portuguese

Let us now examine the complete system of personal pronouns in EP and BP.

2.4.1 First Person Pronouns

Tables 2.1 and 2.2 below depict the realization of first person pronouns in EP and BP, according to their case specification.[30]

As seen above, EP and BP behave alike in having one series for first person singular pronouns and two series for first person plural pronouns – one represented by *nós* and the other by *a gente*, which is formed by the feminine singular definite article *a* and the common noun *gente* 'folk'. Originally meaning 'the folk' (with the exclusion of the speaker), *a gente* came to be grammaticalized as a personal pronoun referring to a group of people including the speaker.[31] It has lost its specification for gender and, as in the case of the other pronouns that are not specified for gender (see Section 2.3.3), it may trigger masculine or feminine agreement on the predicate, depending on the gender of the members of the group it refers to. Typically, if at least one member of the group is a male or

---

[30] Some dialects of BP admit *eu* and *nós* in accusative positions, as illustrated in (i), in competition with *me* and *a gente*, respectively (see e.g. Kato 1994 for discussion). Some of the dialects that allow *eu* in object position may also allow it to double a clitic (see footnote 7 above).

(i) a. Você pôs **eu** na lista? (%BP)
you.SG put pron.ACC.1.SG in-the list
'Did you put my name on the list'?
b. O João não convidou **nós**. (%BP)
the João not invited pron.ACC.1.PL
'João didn't invite us.'

[31] For discussion on the grammaticalization of *a gente*, see e.g. Menon 1996, Omena and Braga 1996, C. Lopes 1998, 2003, Zilles 2005, and Brocardo and Lopes 2016.

Table 2.1 *First person pronouns in European Portuguese*

	NOM	ACC		DAT		OBL		GEN
	[-REFL]	[-REFL]	[+REFL]	[-REFL]	[+REFL]	[-REFL]	[+REFL]	
1.SG	eu	me[CL]	me[CL]	me[CL]	me[CL]	mim	mim	meu[MASC.SG] meus[MASC-PL] minha[FEM.SG] minhas[FEM-PL]
1.PL	nós	nos[CL]	nos[CL]	nos[CL]	nos[CL]	nós	nós	nosso[MASC.SG] nossos[MASC-PL] nossa[FEM.SG] nossas[FEM-PL]
						comigo	comigo	
						connosco	connosco	
	a gente	a gente	se[CL]	à gente	se[CL]	a gente	a gente	da gente
						com a gente	com a gente	

The first column displays the traditional description of the nominative pronouns in the second column, which will be revised in Section 3.4.2. In the OBL cells, the first entry is the pronominal form used with any preposition other than *com* 'with' and the the second entry (if there is one) indicates whether or not the form associated with *com* is conflated (see Section 2.3.4.4).

Table 2.2 *First person pronouns in Brazilian Portuguese*

	NOM	ACC		DAT		OBL		GEN
	[-REFL]	[-REFL]	[+REFL]	[-REFL]	[+REFL]	[-REFL]	[+REFL]	
1.SG	eu	me[CL]	me[CL]	me[CL]	me[CL]	mim	mim	meu[MASC.SG] / meus[MASC-PL] / minha[FEM.SG] / minhas[FEM-PL]
						comigo	comigo	
1.PL	nós					nós	nós	nosso[MASC.SG] / nossos[MASC-PL] / nossa[FEM.SG] / nossas[FEM-PL]
	a gente	a gente	a gente	pra gente	a gente	a gente	a gente	da gente
			se[CL]		se[CL]	com a gente	com a gente	

The first column displays the traditional description of the nominative pronouns in the second column, which will be revised in Section 3.4.2. In the OBL cells, the first entry is the pronominal form used with any preposition other than *com* 'with' and the second entry (if there is one) indicates whether or not the form associated with *com* is conflated (see Section 2.3.4.4).

2 The Pronominal System

if *a gente* is understood as a generic group that includes the speaker, masculine agreement is triggered, as in (2.50a) and (2.50a′) below; if the relevant group involves only females, feminine agreement is triggered instead, as in (2.50b) and (2.50b′). As seen in (2.50a′) and (2.50b′), variation between singular and plural on the adjectival predicate is allowed in both patterns for EP, but not for BP, which admits only singular (see Section 3.4.1). As for verbal agreement, *a gente* has retained its former syntactic properties, triggering third person singular agreement, as shown by its contrast with *nós* in (2.51).[32]

(2.50)   a. **A gente**   ficou   muito   cansad**o**.   (EP/BP)
            pron.1.PL   *stayed*   *very*   *tired*-**MASC.SG**
   a′. **A gente**   ficou   muito   cansad**os**.   (EP/*BP)
            pron.1.PL   *stayed*   *very*   *tired*-**MASC-PL**

---

[32] We may also find "mixed" patterns, with *a gente* triggering first person plural agreement in some dialects of both BP and EP and *nós* triggering third person agreement in some dialects of BP, as illustrated in (i) below (see e.g. Omena and Braga 1996, Bacelar do Nascimento 1989, Costa, Moura, and Pereira 2001, C. Lopes 1998, 2003, Pereira 2003, Costa and Pereira 2005, 2012, Vianna 2006, and Sória 2013 for discussion).

(i)   a. **A gente**   **vimos**   o   acidente.   (%EP; %BP)
        *pron.**1.PL***   *saw-**1.PL***   *the*   *accident*
        'We saw the accident.'
   b. **Nós**   **viu**   o   acidente.   (%BP)
        *pron.**1.PL***   *saw.**3.SG***   *the*   *accident*
        'We saw the accident.'

Recall that pronouns may have distinct forms associated with [+REFL] and [-REFL] specifications only if they are associated with third person verbal agreement (see Section 2.3.5). Thus, in EP the corresponding reflexive clitic in sentences with the agreement pattern of (ia) is generally *nos* rather than *se*, as shown in (iia) below; accordingly, in BP dialects that allow (ib), the reflexive chosen is *se*, as shown in (iib).

(ii)   a. **A gente**   ferimo-**nos**   no   acidente.   (%EP)
        *pron.**1.PL***   *hurt-pron.ACC.**1.PL**$_{[CL]}$*   *in-the*   *accident*
        'We got hurt in the accident.'
   b. **Nós**   **se**   encontrou   na   festa.   (%BP)
        *pron.**1.PL***   *pron.ACC.**3.SG**.[+REFL]$_{[CL]}$*   *met.**3.SG***   *in-the*   *party*
        'We met at the party.'

However, there are some Insular and Southern EP dialects that use the clitic *se* as the reflexive correlate of *a gente* even in the presence of first person plural agreement and some BP dialects that allow *se* with *nós* and first person plural agreement, as respectively shown in (iiia) and (iiib).

(iii)   a. A   gente   casámos-se   novos.   (%EP)
       pron.1.PL   *married-**1.PL**-pron.**3.SG**.[+REFL]$_{[CL]}$*   *young*
       'We were young when we got married.'
                                                          (CORDIAL-SIN, GRC31)

2.4 Similarities and Differences between EP and BP

	b.	**A gente**	ficou	muito	cans**a**da.	(EP/BP)
		pron.1.PL	*stayed*	*very*	*tired-**FEM.SG***	
	b′.	**A gente**	ficou	muito	cans**a**d**as**.	(EP/*BP)
		pron.1.PL	*stayed*	*very*	*tired-**FEM-PL***	
		'We got very tired.'				

(2.51) a. A gente vai chegar tarde.
        pron.1.PL *go.3.SG* *arrive* *late*
      b. Nós vamos chegar tarde.
        pron.1.PL *go-1.PL* *arrive* *late*
       'We will arrive late.'

At first sight, the two series of first person plural pronouns seem interchangeable in both varieties of Portuguese, as illustrated in (2.52) below.[33] That is not always the case, though. In both EP and BP *a gente* contrasts with

  b. Nós **se** **conhecemo** em 1970. (%BP)
     pron.1.PL *pron.3.SG.[+REFL]₍CL₎* *met-1.PL* *in* *1970*
     'We met each other in 1970.'

Note that the ending for first person plural may independently alternate in BP between -*mos* and -*mo*, as illustrated in (iiib), with the latter being associated with informal registers. See further Chapter 3: footnote 24.

Independent factors seem to be behind the exceptional patterns in (iii), though. The EP dialects that allow (iiia) appear to be in the process of replacing the entire *nós* series by the *a gente* series (see e.g. Martins 2009 for discussion). In turn, *se* in BP seems to be in the process of becoming the unique reflexive for all the persons in some dialects. Sentences with the first person singular pronoun such as (iva) below, for instance, are possible for many speakers and are the preferred (or unique) form in the speech of children as old as eight years. Besides, the heavy sociolinguistic stigmatization ascribed to (iiib) is considerably neutralized in sentences like (ivb), where the first person plural agreement is hosted by an auxiliary and the reflexive is phonologically associated with the main verb.

(iv) a. **Eu** **se** esqueci. (%BP)
        pron.1.SG *pron.3.SG.[+REFL]₍CL₎* *forgot-1.SG*
        'I forgot.'
     b. Onde nós **vamo** **se** encontrar? (%BP)
        where *pron.1.PL* *go-1.PL* *pron.3.SG.[+REFL]₍CL₎* *meet*
        'Where are we going to meet?'

[33] For instance, EP speakers that allow the dative form of *a gente* (see discussion below (2.56) in the text) may allow it to double the clitic *nos* (see Section 2.2), as illustrated in (i) below. For discussion on the co-occurrence of *nós* and *a gente* in BP, see e.g. Menuzzi 2000.

(i) Eles chamam-**nos** à gente sarracenos. (%EP)
    they *call-pron.1.PL₍CL₎* *to-pron.1.PL* *Saracen*
    'They call us Saracen.'
    (CRPC, in Bacelar do Nascimento 1989)

nós in that it cannot be modified by numerals or nominals, as shown in (2.53).³⁴

(2.52) a. **A gente** queria convidar os **nossos** amigos.
pron.NOM.1.PL wanted invite the pron.GEN.1.PL-MASC-PL friends
'We wanted to invite our friends.'

b. **Nós** sabíamos que ele tinha visto **a gente** na
pron.NOM.1.PL knew that he had seen pron.ACC.1.PL in-the
praia.
beach
'We knew that he had seen us on the beach.'

(2.53) a. **Nós três** vamos chegar tarde.
we three go arrive late

b. *__A gente__ **três** {vai/vamos} chegar tarde.
pron.1PL three go.3SG/go-1PL arrive late
'The three of us are going to arrive late.'

c. **Nós brasileiros** adoramos tango.
we Brazilian-PL adore tango

d. *__A gente__ **brasileiros** {adora/adoramos} tango.
pron.1PL Brazilian-PL adore.3SG/adore-1PL tango
'We Brazilians love tango.'

More relevant to our discussion is the fact that *nós* and *a gente* do not enjoy the same status in each variety. In EP, the *nós* series is the unmarked one: it is compatible with both formal and informal registers, it is fully productive with respect to case distinctions, as illustrated in (2.54) below, and its forms can be used in nonreflexive (see (2.54a–f)) and reflexive (see (2.54g)) contexts. On the other hand, the *a gente* series is more restricted. For instance, *a gente* cannot be a reflexive pronoun in EP (see the BP sentence in (2.55g) below) and there are EP speakers (including the second author of this book) for whom its dative and genitive forms (*à gente* and *da gente*) are marginal.³⁵ In addition,

---

³⁴ See e.g. Taylor 2009 for discussion. Interestingly, *a gente* allows similar modification in EP if the modifier is headed by the definite article, as shown in (i) (see e.g. Costa and Pereira 2012).

(i) a. **A gente os dois** fica/ficamos em casa. (EP: OK: BP: *)
pron.1PL the two stay.3SG/stay-1PL in house
'We two are staying at home.'

b. **A gente, os portugueses,** bebe/bebemos bom café. (EP: OK: BP: *)
pron.1PL the Portuguese drink.3SG/drink-1PL good coffee
'We Portuguese drink good coffee.'

³⁵ In the CORDIAL-SIN corpus of EP dialects, *a gente* displays a high frequency of occurrence only in nominative positions. Nonetheless, it is attested across the three main EP dialectal areas (Northern, Central-Southern, and Insular) in all case forms and positions (see e.g. Sória 2013).

some EP speakers take *a gente* to be more marked in that it conveys some form of empathy/solidarity/camaraderie towards the other participants referred to by the pronoun.

(2.54) a. **Nós** não sabíamos o que fazer. (EP)
*pron.**NOM**.1.PL not knew what do*
'We didn't know what to do.'

b. O governo enganou-**nos**. (EP)
*the government deceived-pron.**ACC**.1.PL[CL]*
'The government deceived us.'

c. A loja fez-**nos** um bom desconto. (EP)
*the store made-pron.**DAT**.1.PL[CL] a good discount*
'The store gave us a good discount.'

d. Eles não pensaram em **nós**. (EP)
*they not thought in pron.**OBL**.1.PL*
'They didn't think about us.'

e. A Maria vai **connosco**. (EP)
*the Maria goes with.pron.**OBL**.1.PL*
'Maria is going with us.'

f. A **nossa** hipótese estava errada. (EP)
*the pron.**GEN**.1.PL-FEM.SG hypothesis was wrong*
'Our hypothesis was wrong.'

g. Nós vimo-**nos** na televisão. (EP)
*pron.**NOM**.1.PL saw-pron.1.PL.[+REFL][CL] in-the television*
'We saw ourselves on TV.'

The converse situation holds for BP, where the unmarked series is that represented by *a gente*.[36] Its forms are the most frequently used, uniformly cover all case positions, as illustrated in (2.55) below, and may be used in both reflexive (see (2.55g)) and nonreflexive contexts (see (2.55a–f)).

(2.55) a. **A gente** não sabia o que fazer. (BP)
*pron.**NOM**.1.PL not knew what do*
'We didn't know what to do.'

b. O governo enganou **a gente**. (BP)
*the government deceived pron.**ACC**.1.PL*
'The government deceived us.'

c. A loja deu um bom desconto **pra gente**. (BP)
*the store gave a good discount to-pron.**DAT**.1.PL*
'The store gave us a good discount.'

d. Eles não pensaram **na gente** (BP)
*they not thought in-pron.**OBL**.1.PL*
'They didn't think about us.'

---

[36] See e.g. Omena and Braga 1996, C. Lopes 1998, 2003, Zilles 2005, and references therein for discussion.

32   2 The Pronominal System

    e. A   Maria   vai   com   **a gente**.   (BP)
       the   Maria   goes   with   *pron.OBL.1.PL*
       'Maria is going with us.'
    f. A   hipótese   **da gente**   estava   errada.   (BP)
       the   hypothesis   *of-pron.GEN.1.PL*   was   wrong
       'Our hypothesis was wrong.'
    g. Se   **a gente**   tiver   de   indicar
       if   *pron.NOM.1.PL*   have   of   nominate
       a gente   por   falta
       pron.ACC.1.PL.[+REFL]$_{[S]}$ by   lack
       de   outros   candidatos,   **a gente**   indica.   (BP)
       of   other   candidates   *pron.NOM.1.PL*   nominate
       'If we have to nominate ourselves because there are no other candidates, we'll do so.'

By contrast, the *nós* series suffers from a much more unstable status in the grammar of BP. Its members have been consistently replaced by members of the *a gente* series[37] and one finds considerable variation across speakers' judgments for individual case forms. The oblique conflated form *conosco*, for instance, has been clearly replaced by *com a gente*, whereas the accusative and dative clitic *nos*, although still used, is associated by most speakers (including the two Brazilian authors of this book) with formal style, written language, and schooling (hence its absence from Table 2.2; see Chapter 1). In Section 3.4.2, we will see that the weakness of the *nós* series in BP also has repercussions in its verbal agreement system.

2.4.2 Second Person Pronouns

Tables 2.3 and 2.4 below lay out the paradigms of second person pronouns in EP and BP.

EP has two series of second person singular pronouns: one represented by *tu* and the other represented by *você*, which resulted from the grammaticalization of the archaic address form *Vossa Mercê* (lit. *Your Mercy*). *Você* behaves like the first person plural pronoun *a gente* discussed in Section 2.4.1 in being unspecified for gender, as shown in (2.56), in triggering third person singular agreement, as shown by the contrast with *tu* in (2.57), and in using a specific form for the reflexive, as again shown by the contrast with *tu* in (2.58).

---

[37] As mentioned in footnote 32 above, some EP dialects appear to be undergoing a similar change (see e.g. Martins 2009 and Sória 2013). These innovative EP dialects still diverge from BP in that *a gente* may trigger first person plural agreement on the verb (a marginal agreement pattern in BP).

Table 2.3 *Second person pronouns in European Portuguese*

		NOM	ACC		DAT		OBL		GEN
		[-REFL]	[-REFL]	[+REFL]	[-REFL]	[+REFL]	[-REFL]	[+REFL]	
2.SG	[+close]	*tu*	*te*[CL]	*te*[CL]	*te*[CL]	*te*[CL]	*ti*	*ti*	*teu*[MASC.SG] *teus*[MASC-PL] *tua*[FEM.SG] *tuas*[FEM-PL]
	[-close]	*você*	*o*[CL][MASC] *a*[CL][FEM]	*se*[CL]	*lhe*[CL]	*se*[CL]	*você* *si* *consigo*	*si* *consigo*	*seu*[MASC.SG] *seus*[MASC-PL] *sua*[FEM.SG] *suas*[FEM-PL]
2-PL		*vocês*	*vos*[CL] *os*[CL][MASC] *as*[CL][FEM]	*se*[CL]	*vos*[CL] *lhes*[CL]	*se*[CL]	*vocês* *com vocês* *convosco*	*vocês* *com vocês* *convosco*	*vosso*[MASC.SG] *vossos*[MASC-PL] *vossa*[FEM.SG] *vossas*[FEM-PL]

The first column displays the traditional description of the nominative pronouns in the second column, which will be revised in Section 3.4.2. In the OBL cells, the first entry displays the pronominal forms used with any preposition other than *com* 'with' and the other entries indicate whether or not the forms associated with *com* are conflated (see Section 2.3.4.4).

Table 2.4 *Second person pronouns in Brazilian Portuguese*

	NOM	ACC		DAT		OBL		GEN
	[-REFL]	[-REFL]	[+REFL]	[-REFL]	[+REFL]	[-REFL]	[+REFL]	
2.SG	*você*	*você*	*você*[S]	*pra você*	*pra você*	*você*	*você*	*seu*[MASC.SG] *seus*[MASC.PL] *sua*[FEM.SG] *suas*[FEM.PL]
		te[CL]	*se*[CL]	*te*[CL]	*se*[CL]	*com você*	*com você*	
	cê[W]	*cê*[W]						
2-PL	*vocês*	*vocês*	*vocês*[S]	*pra vocês*	*pra vocês*	*vocês*	*vocês*	*de vocês*
			se[CL]		*se*[CL]	*com vocês*	*com vocês*	
	cês[W]	*cês*[W]						

The first column displays the traditional description of the nominative pronouns in the second column, which will be revised in Section 3.4.2. In the OBL cells, the first entry is the pronominal form used with any preposition other than *com* 'with' and the other entries (if there are any) indicate whether or not the form associated with *com* is conflated (see Section 2.3.4.4).

(2.56) a. **Você**   parece   cansad**o**.   [spoken to a **male**]
       pron.2.SG seems   tired-**MASC.SG**
     b. **Você**   parece   cansad**a**.   [spoken to a **female**]
       pron.2.SG seems   tired-**FEM.SG**
       'You(SG) look tired.'

(2.57) a. **Você**   ontem   **saiu**   cedo.   (EP)
       pron.**2.SG** yesterday left.**3.SG**   early
     b. **Tu**   ontem   **saíste**   cedo.   (EP)
       pron.**2.SG** yesterday left-**2.SG**   early
       'You(SG) left early yesterday.'

(2.58) a. Você   feriu-**se**?   (EP)
       pron.2.SG$_{[-close]}$ hurt-2.SG.**[+REFL]**$_{[-close]}$
       'Did you hurt yourself?'
     b. Você   feriu-**o**?   (EP)
       pron.2.SG$_{[-close]}$ hurt-2.SG.**[-REFL]**$_{[-close]}$
       'Did you hurt him?'
     c. Tu   feriste-**te**?   (EP)
       pron.2.SG$_{[+close]}$ hurt-2.SG$_{[+close]}$
       'Did you hurt **yourself**?'
     d. Ele   feriu-**te**?   (EP)
       he   hurt-2.SG$_{[+close]}$
       'Did he hurt **you(SG)**?'

However, as opposed to the *a gente* series, the *você* series in EP incorporated all the forms corresponding to its former third person specification, as illustrated in (2.59).[38]

(2.59) a. **Você**$_i$ quer   que   eu
       pron.NOM.2.SG$_{[-close]}$ wants   that   I
       a$_i$ ajude?   (EP)
       pron.ACC.2.FEM.SG.**[-REFL]**$_{[-close;\ CL]}$ help
       'Do you(SG) want me to help you(SG)?'
     b. **Você**$_i$ preparou-**se**$_i$
       pron.NOM.2.SG$_{[-close]}$ prepared-pron.ACC.**2.SG.[+REFL]**$_{[-close;\ CL]}$
       bem   para o   exame?   (EP)
       well   for   the   exam
       'Did you prepare yourself well for the exam?'
     c. **Você**$_i$ quer   que   eu
       pron.NOM.2.SG$_{[-close]}$ wants   that   I
       lhe$_i$ conte o que realmente
       pron.DAT.**2.SG.[-REFL]**$_{[-close;\ CL]}$ tell   what really
       aconteceu?   (EP)
       happened
       'Do you(SG) want me to tell you(SG) what really happened?'

---

[38] All the sentences in (2.59) may have an alternative with a null counterpart for nominative *você*, which is the preferred option for EP speakers who dislike overt *você* as an address form (see footnote 9 above).

d. **Você**ᵢ   sabe se o **seu**ᵢ
   pron.NOM.2.SG₍₋ₒₗₒₛₑ₎ knows if the *pron.GEN.2.SG*₍₋ₒₗₒₛₑ₎
   filho já saiu?   (EP)
   son already left
   'Do you(SG) know if your(SG) son has already left?'

e. **Você**ᵢ   precisa ter mais confiança em
   pron.NOM.2.SG₍₋ₒₗₒₛₑ₎ needs have more confidence in
   siᵢ.   (EP)
   pron.OBL.2.SG ₍₋ₒₗₒₛₑ₎
   'You(SG) need to be more self-confident.'

f. **Você**ᵢ   trouxe os documentos
   pron.NOM.2.SG₍₋ₒₗₒₛₑ₎ brought the documents
   consigoᵢ?   (EP)
   with-pron.OBL.2.SG ₍₋ₒₗₒₛₑ₎
   'Did you(SG) bring the documents with you(SG)?'

Interestingly, the oblique forms *si* and *consigo* have been neutralized in terms of the specification [±REFL]. Thus, in addition to reflexive contexts, as in (2.59e,f), they are also allowed in nonreflexive contexts, as exemplified in (2.60), which sounds completely outlandish in BP.

(2.60) a. Eu   preciso falar **consigo**.   (EP)
           I   need   speak *with-pron.OBL.2.SG* ₍₋ₒₗₒₛₑ₎
           'I need to speak with you(SG).'
        b. Eu   só   pensava em   **si**.   (EP)
           I   only   thought in   *pron.OBL.2.SG* ₍₋ₒₗₒₛₑ₎
           'I only thought about you(SG).'

Você and *tu* contrast with respect to the extralinguistic feature [±close] in EP (see Section 2.3.1) and therefore the two series are not interchangeable in this variety. In BP, on the other hand, the [±close] distinction between them was lost[39] and the *você* series replaced the *tu* series in most dialects.[40] This means that although (2.59d), for instance, is acceptable in both EP and BP,

---

[39] It is worth mentioning that *você* in BP still contrasts with address forms like *o senhor* (lit. *the mister*) in that the latter encodes respect towards the addressee (see footnote 8 above).

[40] A good number of dialects in BP still keep some forms of the *tu* series in addition to or in alternation with the *você* series, as illustrated in (i) below. In these dialects, the nominative form may trigger third person singular agreement (see e.g. Menon and Loregian-Penkal 2002, Paredes Silva 2003, and Lopes 2008 for discussion), as illustrated in (ii), and the oblique form can also occur in the subject position of an uninflected infinitival clause selected by the preposition *para/pra* 'to/for' (see Section 2.3.4.4), as illustrated in (iii) (see e.g. Hornstein, Martins, and Nunes 2008 for discussion). Other dialects allow *tu* as the complement of verbs and prepositions, as illustrated in (iv).

there are situations in which it will be appropriate in BP but not in EP, namely, when there is familiarity/intimacy between speaker and addressee. The only remaining form from the *tu* series in the grammar of BP is the accusative/dative clitic *te*, which replaced the corresponding accusative forms *o* and *a* and the dative form *lhe* of the *você* series in EP.[41] As the distinction [±close] is no longer at play in BP, *te* combines with other elements of the *você* series without problems, as illustrated in (2.61) (see also footnote 7 above).

(2.61) a. A **sua** irmã estava **te** procurando. (BP)
 the pron.*GEN.2.SG* sister was pron.*ACC.2.SG* looking-for
 'Your(SG) sister was looking for you(SG).'
 b. **Você** me disse pra **te** telefonar hoje. (BP)
 pron.*NOM.2.SG* me said to pron.*DAT.2.SG* call you
 'You(SG) told me to call you(SG) today.'

As for second person plural pronouns, earlier stages of Portuguese had a specific series involving the nominative form *vós* (which triggered second person plural agreement, as in *cantais* 'sing.INDIC.PRES.**2.PL**'), the accusative/dative clitic *vos* (used in both reflexive and nonreflexive contexts), the non-conflated and conflated oblique forms *vós* and *convosco*, and the genitive form *vosso* (along with its feminine and plural counterparts). As shown in Table 2.4, in

---

(i) Eu encontrei o **teu** pai ontem. (%BP)
 I found the pron.*GEN.2.SG.MASC.SG* father yesterday
 'I met your father yesterday.'

(ii) **Tu** **viaja** hoje? (%BP)
 pron.*NOM.2.SG* travel.*3.SG* today
 'Are you travelling today?'

(iii) O João trouxe esse livro pra **ti** ler. (%BP)
 the João brought this book for pron.*OBL.2.SG* read
 'João brought this book for you to read.'

(iv) a. Eu vi **tu** no cinema ontem. (%BP)
 I saw pron.*2.SG*. in-the cinema yesterday
 'I saw you at the movies yesterday.'
 b. Ela gosta tanto de **tu**! (%BP)
 she likes much of pron.*2.SG*
 'She likes you so much!'

[41] Some Northeastern dialects of BP have instead generalized the use of *lhe*, employing it as an accusative pronoun for the *você* series, as illustrated in (i) (see e.g. Neves 2000 for discussion).

(i) Eu **lhe** vejo amanhã. (%BP)
 I pron.*2.SG[CL]* see tomorrow
 'I'll see you tomorrow.'

BP this series was completely replaced by the series represented by *vocês*, the plural form of the second person singular *você*. By contrast, in EP the *vós* and the *vocês* series blended, yielding the irregular paradigm shown in Table 2.3 and illustrated in (2.62a) below.[42] As with what we saw in (2.59), the new paradigm also allows the third person plural clitics *os/as* (in accusative contexts) and *lhes* (in dative contexts) to be used as nonreflexive second person plural pronouns, in alternation with *vos*, as respectively exemplified in (2.62b) and (2.62c).[43]

(2.62) a. Eu   asseguro-**vos**   que   **vocês**   não
            I   assure-pron.*DAT.2.PL*   that   pron.*NOM.2-PL*   not
            imaginam o que   o   **vosso**   professor
            imagine what   the   pron.GEN.2.PL-MASC   teacher
            disse   de   **vocês**.   (EP)
            said   of   pron.OBL.2-PL
            'I assure you(PL) that you(PL) can't imagine what your(PL) teacher said about you(PL).'

---

[42] Some Northern dialects of continental EP still preserve the primitive regular *vós* series. (i) and (ii) respectively exemplify the nominative and oblique form *vós* of dialectal EP (see e.g. Segura 2013 and Lara Bermejo 2017).

  (i) **Vós**   tínheis   um, não tínheis?   (%EP)
       pron.NOM.2-PL   had.*PAST.2.PL*   one not had.*PAST.2.PL*
       'You(PL) had got one of those, hadn't you?'
                                                             (CORDIAL-SIN, LAR20)
  (ii) O   carvão   que   der   é metade para **vós**   e   metade
       the charcoal   that   will.give is half   for pron.OBL.2.PL and half
       para nós.   (%EP)
       for pron.OBL.1.PL
       'Any charcoal that we obtain is half for you(PL) and half for us.'
                                                             (CORDIAL-SIN, GRJ67)

[43] Both types of variants (the conservative form *vos* and the forms based on third person plural clitics) are considered part of standard EP (see e.g. Raposo 2013 and Lara Bermejo 2017). In formal registers of (written) BP, the third person clitics *o(s)*, *a(s)*, and *lhe(s)* can also be used as second person pronouns, as illustrated in (i), but not the clitic *vos* (cf. (ib) and (id) vs. (2.62) in EP).

  (i) a. Esta carta   é   para avisá-**la**   de que
          this letter   is   to   warn-pron.ACC.2.FEM.SG[CL] of that
          seu seguro   expirou.   (%BP)
          your insurance expired
          'This letter is to warn you that your insurance has expired.'
       b. Eu gostaria de convidá-**los**   para a   cerimônia. (%BP)
          I would.like of invite-pron.ACC.2.MASC-PL[CL]   to   the ceremony
          'I would like to invite you to the ceremony.'
       c. Esta mensagem é   para   **lhe**   dar
          this message is   to   pron.DAT.2.SG[CL]   give
          os   parabéns   pelo   seu   novo   livro.   (%BP)
          the congratulations for-the your new   book
          'This message is to congratulate you on your new book.'
       d. Eu gostaria   de   **lhes**   dar as boas vindas
          I would.like of   pron.DAT.2-PL[CL]   give the welcome
          e   desejar que   vocês   tenham   um excelente congresso. (%BP)
          and wish   that   you-PL   have   an excellent conference
          'I would like to welcome you and wish you an excellent conference.'

b. Vocês_i   querem   que   eu
    pron.NOM.2-PL want   that   I
    {**vos/os**_i}   ajude? (EP)
    pron.ACC.2.PL.[-REFL]/pron.ACC.2.MASC-PL.[-REFL] help
    'Do you(PL) want me to help you(PL)?'
c. Vocês_i   querem   que   eu
    pron.NOM.2-PL want   that   I
    {**vos/lhes**_i}   conte o que
    pron.DAT.2.PL.[-REFL]/pron.DAT.2-PL.[-REFL] tell   what
    realmente   aconteceu?   (EP)
    really   happened
    'Do you(PL) want me to tell you(PL) what really happened?'

In both EP and BP, the nominative form *vocês* triggers third person plural agreement, as shown in (2.63a) and, accordingly (see Section 2.3.5), is associated with the distinct reflexive form *se*, as illustrated in (2.63b).

(2.63) a. **Vocês**   **poderiam**   ajudar   o   Pedro?
          pron.NOM.2-PL *could.3-PL*   help   the Pedro
          'Could you(PL) help Pedro?'
       b. **Vocês**   nunca   **se**   entendem.
          pron.NOM.2-PL never   *2.PL.[+REFL]_[CL]* understand
          'You(PL) never understand each other.'

A final development took place in BP, with the emergence of two weak pronouns *cê* and *cês*, based on *você* and *vocês*.[44] As weak pronouns, *cê* and *cês* have special placement requirements different from clitics, as discussed in Section 2.2. More specifically, nominative *cê/cês* can appear only in subject position or preceding the complementizer-like element in the left periphery of

---

[44] Some dialects of BP have the forms *ocê* and *ocês* instead of *você* and *vocês* in all possible case forms, as illustrated in (i). See e.g. Ramos 1996, Vitral 1996, Paredes Silva 1998, and Petersen 2008 for discussion.

(i) a. **Ocê**   nem vai acreditar!   (%BP)
       pron.NOM.2.SG nor go believe
       'You(SG) won't believe it!'
    b. O   professor vai   reprovar **ocês**.   (%BP)
       the teacher goes fail   pron.ACC.2-PL
       'The teacher is going to fail you(PL).'
    c. Eu trouxe   um presente pr'**ocês**.   (%BP)
       I   brought a   gift   for-pron.DAT.2-PL
       'I brought you(SG) a gift.'
    d. O   João vai viajar sem   **ocê**.   (%BP)
       the João goes travel without pron.OBL.2.SG
       'João is going to travel without you(SG).'
    e. Eu preciso falar com o   pai   d'**ocês**.   (%BP)
       I   need   talk   with the father of-pron.GEN.2-PL
       'I need to talk to your(PL) father.'

the clause, as illustrated in (2.64) below. In turn, accusative *cê/cês* can occupy only this left periphery position, as exemplified in (2.65). For all remaining cases and syntactic positions, the *você* and *vocês* series fill in for the gaps in the *cê* and *cês* series, as illustrated in (2.66) with the accusative second person singular clitic *te* and the genitive second person plural form *de vocês*.[45]

(2.64) a. **Cê**   quer   casar   comigo?   (BP)
          pron.NOM.2.SG*[W]* wants marry   with-me
          'Do you(SG) want to marry me?'
       b. **Cês**   que   sabem!   (BP)
          pron.NOM.2-PL*[W]* that   know
          'It's up to you(PL)!'

(2.65) a. **Cê**   que o   João contratou recentemente? (BP)
          pron.ACC.2.SG*[W]* that the João hired   recently
          'Is it in fact you(SG) that João hired recently?'
       b. **Cês**   que   a   Maria   convidou   pro
          pron.ACC.2-PL*[W]* that   the   Maria   invited   for-the
          espetáculo?   (BP)
          show
          'Are you(PL) the people that Maria invited to the show?'

(2.66) a. **Cê**   não   mencionou que o   Pedro tinha
          pron.NOM.2.SG*[W]* not   mentioned that the Pedro had
          te
          visto.   (BP)
          pron.ACC.2.SG*[CL]* seen
          'You(SG) didn't mention that Pedro had seen you(SG)'
       b. **Cês**   precisam conversar com o professor **de**
          pron.NOM.2-PL*[W]* need   talk   with the teacher of
          vocês.   (BP)
          pron.2-PL
          'You(PL) need to talk to your(PL) teacher'

2.4.3 Third Person Pronouns

Let us now consider the paradigms of third person pronouns in EP and BP, presented in Tables 2.5 and 2.6.

---

[45] Some BP dialects also admit conflated dative and oblique forms of *cê(s)*, as illustrated in (i) (see e.g. Petersen 2008 for discussion).

(i) a. Eu trouxe isso **p'cê**   ontem.   (%BP)
        I brought this to-pron.2.SG*[W]* yesterday
        'I brought this for you(SG) yesterday.'
     b. Eu queria falar **c'cês**.   (%BP)
        I wanted speak with-pron.2-PL*[W]*
        'I would like to speak with you(PL).'

Table 2.5 *Third person pronouns in European Portuguese*

	NOM	ACC		DAT		OBL		GEN
	[-REFL]	[-REFL]	[+REFL]	[-REFL]	[+REFL]	[-REFL]	[+REFL]	
3.MASC.SG	*ele*[S]	*o*[CL]	*se*[CL]	*lhe*[CL]	*se*[CL]	*ele* / *com ele*	*ele* / *si* / *com ele* / *consigo*	*dele* / *seu*[MASC.SG] / *sua*[FEM.SG] / *seus*[MASC-PL] / *suas*[FEM-PL]
3.FEM.SG	*ela*[S]	*a*[CL]	*se*[CL]	*lhe*[CL]	*se*[CL]	*ela* / *com ela*	*ela* / *si* / *com ela* / *consigo*	*dela* / *seu*[MASC.SG] / *sua*[FEM.SG] / *seus*[MASC-PL] / *suas*[FEM-PL]
3.MASC-PL	*eles*[S]	*os*[CL]	*se*[CL]	*lhes*[CL]	*se*[CL]	*eles* / *com eles*	*eles* / *si* / *com eles* / *consigo*	*deles* / *seu*[MASC.SG] / *sua*[FEM.SG] / *seus*[MASC-PL] / *suas*[FEM-PL]
3.FEM-PL	*elas*[S]	*as*[CL]	*se*[CL]	*lhes*[CL]	*se*[CL]	*elas* / *com elas*	*elas* / *si* / *com elas* / *consigo*	*delas* / *seu*[MASC.SG] / *sua*[FEM.SG] / *seus*[MASC-PL] / *suas*[FEM-PL]
indefinite	*se*[CL]						*si* / *consigo*	

The first column displays the traditional description of the nominative pronouns in the second column, which will be revised in Section 3.4.2. In the OBL cells, the first entry displays the pronominal forms used with any preposition other than *com* 'with' and the other entries indicate whether or not the form associated with *com* is conflated (see Section 2.3.4.4).

Table 2.6 *Third person pronouns in Brazilian Portuguese*

	NOM	ACC		DAT		OBL		GEN
	[-REFL]	[-REFL]	[+REFL]	[-REFL]	[+REFL]	[-REFL]	[+REFL]	
3.MASC.SG	*ele*	*ele*	*ele*[S]	*pra ele*	*pra ele*	*ele*	*ele*	*dele*
			se[CL]		*se*[CL]	*com ele*	*com ele*	
3.FEM.SG	*ela*	*ela*	*ela*[S]	*pra ela*	*pra ela*	*ela*	*ela*	*dela*
			se[CL]		*se*[CL]	*com ela*	*com ela*	
3.MASC-PL	*eles*	*eles*	*eles*[S]	*pra eles*	*pra eles*	*eles*	*eles*	*deles*
			se[CL]		*se*[CL]	*com eles*	*com eles*	
3.FEM-PL	*elas*	*elas*	*ela*[S]	*pra elas*	*pra elas*	*elas*	*elas*	*delas*
			se[CL]		*se*[CL]	*com elas*	*com elas*	
indefinite	*se*[CL]						*si*	

The first column displays the traditional description of the nominative pronouns in the second column, which will be revised in Section 3.4.2. In the OBL cells, the first entry is the pronominal form used with any preposition other than *com* 'with' and the other entry (if there is one) indicates whether or not the form associated with *com* is conflated (see Section 2.3.4.4).

Each of the case subsystems in Tables 2.5 and 2.6 displays considerable differences between EP and BP. Take the nominative pronouns illustrated in (2.67) below, for example. All the sentences are acceptable in both EP and BP, but with different meanings. In BP, the pronouns of (2.67) are ambiguous between a [+hum] and a [-hum] interpretation. By contrast, in EP the [-hum] interpretation is somewhat marginal and subject to variation among speakers. This difference can be accounted for by the nominative forms *ele*, *eles*, *ela*, and *elas* being typically strong in EP, whereas in BP they may be strong or weak (see Section 2.2).[46] As we will see in Section 4.6.3, this difference has implications for the interpretation of null subjects in EP and BP.[47]

(2.67) a. **Ele** é alto.
 pron.3.MASC.SG is tall
 'He is tall.' (EP/BP: OK)
 'It is tall.' (**EP: %; BP: OK**)
 b. **Eles** são altos.
 pron.3.MASC-PL are tall
 'They are tall.' (*eles = os meninos* 'the boys' → EP/BP: OK)
 (*eles = os edifícios* 'the buildings'→ **EP: %; BP: OK**)
 c. **Ela** é bonita.
 pron.3-FEM.SG is beautiful
 'She is beautiful.' (EP/BP: OK)
 'It is beautiful.' (**EP: %; BP: OK**)
 d. **Elas** são bonitas.
 pron.3-FEM-PL are beautiful
 'They are beautiful.' (*elas = as meninas* 'the girls' → EP/BP: OK)
 (*elas = as casas* 'the houses'→ **EP: %; BP: OK**)

---

[46] See e.g. Britto 1998, 2000, Kato 1999, 2002a, Cyrino, Duarte, and Kato 2000, Barbosa, Duarte, and Kato 2001, 2005, Raposo 2013, and Weingart 2020 for discussion.

[47] The nominative pronoun *ele* can also be used as an expletive in some dialects of EP, as illustrated in (i) below (adapted from Mateus *et al.* 2003). This expletive differs from traditional expletives such as English *it* or *there* in that it conveys some sort of expressive emphasis. For discussion see e.g. Uriagereka 1995a, 2004, Raposo and Uriagereka 1996, Silva-Villar 1998, Carrilho 2003, 2005, 2008, 2009, Betoni 2013, and Section 4.6.1.

(i) a. **Ele** choveu toda a noite. (%EP)
 EXPL rained all the night
 'It rained all night long.'
 b. **Ele** há cada uma! (%EP)
 EXPL has such one
 'There are such things!'
 c. Tudo está mais caro: **ele** é o leite, **ele** é
 everything is more expensive EXPL is the milk EXPL is
 a fruta, **ele** é o peixe. (%EP)
 the fruit EXPL is the fish
 'Everything is getting more expensive: milk, fruit, fish.'

Let us now examine the accusative paradigms. The clitics *o, a, os,* and *as,* illustrated in (2.68) below, are the only forms that are unambiguously accusative. Each of them has two allomorphs, depending on the phonological properties of the verb immediately preceding it. If the verb ends with /r/ or /s/, this last phoneme is dropped and the clitic is realized with [l] preceding it, as illustrated in (2.69); on the other hand, if the verb ends in a nasal diphthong, [n] is added to the clitic, as shown in (2.70).

(2.68) a. As crianças não **o** viram. (EP)
the children not pron.*ACC.3.MASC.SG_[CL]* saw
'The children didn't see him/it.'
b. Quem **os** contratou? (EP)
who pron.*ACC.3.MASC-PL_[CL]* hired
'Who hired them?'
c. O João leu-**a** cuidadosamente. (EP)
the João read-pron.*ACC.3.FEM.SG_[CL]* carefully
'João read it carefully.'
d. Eu não **as** quero. (EP)
I not pron.*ACC.3.FEM-PL_[CL]* want
'I don't want them.'

(2.69) a. O João vai comprá-**las**. [*comprar + as*] (EP)
the João goes buy-pron.*ACC.3.FEM-PL_[CL]*
'João is going to buy them.'
b. Tu sabe-**lo** bem. [*sabes + o*] (EP)
you.*SG_[+close]* know-pron.*ACC.3.MASC.SG_[CL]* well
'You(SG) know it well.'
c. Nós convidámo-**la** ontem. [*convidamos + a*] (EP)
we invited-pron.*ACC.3.FEM.SG_[CL]* yesterday
'We invited her yesterday.'

(2.70) Eles sabem-**no** bem. [*sabem* (['sabẽj̃]) *+ o*] (EP)
they know-pron.*ACC.3.MASC.SG_[CL]* well
'They know it well.'

As we can see in Table 2.6, these clitics are not part of the grammar of BP in the sense defined in Chapter 1. Their residual preservation in BP is actually due to schooling. Hence, they do not occur in the speech of pre-school children or illiterate adults and are generally associated with formal registers, written language, and a high level of formal education.[48] Table 2.6 shows that

---

[48] For discussion see e.g. Omena 1978, Tarallo 1983, Duarte 1986, 1989, Corrêa 1991, Kato 1993b, 2017, Nunes 1993, 2011, 2015a, 2019a, Galves 2001, Kato, Cyrino, and Corrêa 2009 and Section 5.6.2.

2.4 Similarities and Differences between EP and BP 45

they have been replaced by pronouns homophonous with the nominative form (*ele*, *ela*, *eles*, and *elas*), as illustrated in (2.71).

(2.71) a. Quando você comprou **ele**? (BP)
when you.SG bought pron.3.MASC.SG
'When did you(SG) buy it?'

b. Eu procurei a Maria, mas não encontrei **ela**
I looked-for the Maria but not found pron.3-FEM.SG
em lugar nenhum. (BP)
in place none
'I looked for Maria, but couldn´t find her anywhere.'

c. Você convidou **eles** pra festa? (BP)
you.SG invited pron.3.MASC.SG to-the party
'Did you(SG) invite them to the party?'

d. Você precisa carregar **elas** com bastante cuidado. (BP)
you.SG need carry pron.3-FEM-PL with much care
'You(SG) must carry them carefully.'

The loss of morphologically unambiguous accusative clitics prompted a complete reorganization in the grammar of BP. First, this loss also affected the clitics *o* and *a* when they are specified as second person singular (see Table 2.3 and footnote 43 above); as seen in Table 2.4, they were replaced by *você* and *te* in BP. Second, the new series of accusative pronouns (*ele*, *ela*, *eles*, and *elas*) cannot relate to constituents other than noun phrases; hence, constructions where an accusative clitic stands for a predicate, as illustrated in (2.72) (see Section 2.3.4.2), simply died out in BP.[49]

(2.72) Tímida, ela não **o** é. (EP)
shy-FEM.SG she not pron.ACC.3.MASC.SG is
'Shy, she is not.'

The third reflex of the reorganization of the system has to do with fused clitics. In EP, when the accusative clitics *o(s)*, *a(s)* are combined with dative clitics, they must be fused, as sketched in Table 2.7 and illustrated in (2.73) below. The dative clitic *se* is exceptional in this regard, for it does not have a form for the fused version and does not allow the nonfused version either, as

---

[49] For discussion see e.g. Cyrino 1993, 1997, Kato, Cyrino, and Corrêa 2009, Raposo 1998b, and Kato 2017.

Table 2.7 *Fusion of dative and accusative clitics in European Portuguese*

Dative clitics	Accusative clitics			
	o (3.MASC.SG)	*os* (3.MASC-PL)	*a* (3.FEM.SG)	*as* (3.FEM-PL)
me (1.SG)	*mo*	*mos*	*ma*	*mas*
te (2.SG)	*to*	*tos*	*ta*	*tas*
lhe (3.SG)	*lho*	*lhos*	*lha*	*lhas*
se (3.SG.REFL)				
nos (1.PL)	*no-lo*	*no-los*	*no-la*	*no-las*
vos (2.PL)	*vo-lo*	*vo-los*	*vo-la*	*vo-las*
lhes (3-PL)	*lho*	*lhos*	*lha*	*lhas*
se (3.PL.REFL)				

shown in (2.74).[50] Once BP had lost the accusative clitics *o(s)* and *a(s)* (as well as the dative clitics *vos*, *lhe*, and *lhes*; see Tables 2.4 and 2.6), the fused forms of Table 2.7 were also lost.

---

[50] In EP, nominative *se* – like dative *se* – cannot be followed by an accusative pronoun, as illustrated in (i) below, unless a dative clitic intervenes between *se* and the accusative clitic, as illustrated in (ii) (see e.g. Naro 1976, Nunes 1990, 1991, Martins 2003, 2013b, and Martins and Nunes 2016 for discussion).

(i)   a.   *Alugou-**se-as**.   (EP)
            rented-pron.$NOM.3_{[CL]}$-pron.$ACC.3.FEM\text{-}PL_{[CL]}$
            'One rented them.'
    b.   *Penteia-**se-te**.   (EP)
            combs-pron.$NOM.3_{[CL]}$-pron.$ACC.2.SG_{[CL]}$
            'One combs you.'

(ii)   Comprou-**se-lhos**.(EP)
         bought-pron.$NOM.3_{[CL]}$-pron.$DAT.3.ACC.3.MASC\text{-}PL_{[CL]}$
         'Someone bought them to/from him/her/them.'

However, some Southern and Insular EP dialects permit the co-occurrence of nominative *se* with a third person singular accusative clitic, as shown in (iii).

(iii)   a.   Deixa-**se-a**   crescer.   (%EP)
            lets-pron.$NOM.3_{[CL]}$-pron.$ACC.3.FEM.SG$ grow
            'We/people let it grow.'
                                              (CORDIAL-SIN, PST01)

(2.73) a. O João deu-**mo**. (EP)
      *the João gave-**pron.DAT.1.SG₍CL₎-pron.ACC.3.MASC.SG₍CL₎***
      'João gave it to me.'
  b. Eu dei-**to**. (EP)
      I gave-pron.DAT.2.SG₍+close; CL₎-pron.ACC.3.MASC.SG₍CL₎
      'I gave it to you(SG).'
  c. O João enviou-**lha**. (EP)
      *the João sent-**pron.DAT.3₍CL₎-pron.ACC.3.FEM.SG₍CL₎***
      'João sent it to him/her/them.'
  d. A Maria recomendou-**no-las**. (EP)
      *the Maria recommended-**pron.DAT.1.PL₍CL₎-pron.ACC.3.FEM-PL₍CL₎***
      'Maria recommended them to us.'
  e. Eu não **vo-lo** direi. (EP)
      *I not **pron.DAT.2.PL₍CL₎-pron.ACC.3.MASC.SG₍CL₎** will-say*
      'I won't tell you(PL).'

(2.74) *O João deu-se-o. (EP)
      *the João gave-**pron.DAT.3.[+REFL]₍CL₎-pron.ACC.3.MASC.SG₍CL₎***
      'João gave it to himself.'

Lastly, the diachronic change affecting third person accusative clitics in BP was not restricted to a mere replacement of some forms by others in the same environments, but actually had far-reaching interpretive consequences. Consider the pairs in (2.75) from EP and (2.76) from BP, for instance.[51]

(2.75) a. [A Maria]ᵢ incluiu todos na lista, mas
      the Maria included all in-the list but
      esqueceu-se de
      forgot-pron.ACC.3.SG.[+REFL₍CL₎] of
      incluir-**se**ᵢ. (EP)
      include-pron.ACC.3.SG.[+REFL]₍CL₎

    b. Pode-**se-a** guardar na "freeze." (%EP)
        can-pron.NOM.3₍CL₎-pron.ACC.3.FEM.SG₍CL₎ keep in-the refrigerator
        'We/one can keep it in the fridge.'
        (CORDIAL-SIN, STE36)

    c. Abre-**se-o** de um metro de
        opens-pron.NOM.3₍CL₎-pron.ACC.3.MASC.SG₍CL₎ of one meter of
        fundura. (%EP)
        depth
        'We/people dig it to a depth of one meter.'
        (CORDIAL-SIN, ALC15)

---

[51] See e.g. Moreira da Silva 1983 and Galves 1986a, 2001 for data and discussion.

b. *[A   Maria]ᵢ   incluiu   todos   na   lista, mas
   the   Maria   included   all   in-the list   but
   esqueceu-se   de
   forgot-pron.ACC.3.SG.[+REFL]₍CL₎   of
   incluí-laᵢ.   (EP)
   include-pron.ACC.3.FEM.SG.[-REFL]₍CL₎
   'Maria included everybody in the list, but forgot to include herself.'

(2.76) a. [A   Maria]ᵢ   incluiu   todos   na   lista, mas esqueceu de
          the   Maria   included   all   in-the list   but forgot   of
          seᵢ   incluir.   (BP)
          pron.ACC.3.SG.[+REFL]₍CL₎ include
       b. [A   Maria]ᵢ   incluiu   todos   na   lista, mas esqueceu de
          the   Maria   included   all   in-the list   but forgot   of
          incluir ELAᵢ.   (BP)
          include pron.ACC.3-FEM.SG₍S₎
          'Maria included everybody in the list, but forgot to include herself.'

(2.75) illustrates the fact that the accusative clitic *se* is [+REFL], whereas the accusative clitic *a* is [-REFL]; hence, coreference is possible between *se* and *a Maria* in (2.75a), but not between *a* and *a Maria* in (2.75b). Now, recall that BP *ele(s)* and *ela(s)* are ambiguous between weak and strong pronouns and, furthermore, that a strong pronoun can be used as a reflexive in contrastive contexts (see Section 2.3.5). Thus, we expect to find sentences involving reflexivity where *ele(s)/ela(s)* are legitimate, but *o(s)/a(s)* are not. The contrast between (2.75b) in EP and (2.76b) in BP, which allows the reflexive reading, shows that this prediction is indeed borne out.

It is also worth noting that the reorganization caused by the loss of the clitics *o(s)* and *a(s)* went beyond the nuclear grammar of BP, also affecting its peripheral usage associated with schooling, written language, and formal registers.[52] For instance, the placement of the clitics *o(s)* and *a(s)* and the other clitics in these registers is not the same, as illustrated in (2.77) and (2.78) below.[53] We return to a more detailed discussion of this point in Section 5.6.2.

(2.77) a. O   João   o   tinha   visto.   (written BP)
          the   João   pron.ACC.3.MASC.SG₍CL₎   had   seen
          'João had seen him/it.'
       b. *O   João   me   tinha   visto.   (BP)
          the   João   pron.ACC.1.SG₍CL₎   had   seen
          'João had seen me.'

---

[52] See e.g. Kato 2005, Kato, Cyrino, and Corrêa 2009, and Nunes 2011, 2015a, 2019a for discussion.
[53] See e.g. Figueiredo Silva 1990, Cyrino 1993, Nunes 1993, 2011, 2015a, 2019a, Pagotto 1993, and Galves, Ribeiro, and Torres Morais 2005.

(2.78) a. *O João tinha **o** visto. (written BP)
the João had pron.*ACC.3.MASC.SG*[CL] seen
'João had seen him/it.'
b. O João tinha **me** visto. (BP)
the João had pron.*ACC.1.SG*[CL] seen
'João had seen me.'

Regarding dative, oblique, and genitive pronouns, we find more simplifications in the grammar of BP. As seen in Table 2.6, BP has lost the unambiguous dative forms *lhe* and *lhes* and uses periphrastic forms such as those in (2.79) instead.

(2.79) a. Eu dei um livro **pra ele**. (BP)
I gave a book to pron.*3.MASC.SG*
'I gave him a book.'
b. O João enviou os documentos **pra elas**. (BP)
the João sent the documents to pron.*3-FEM-PL*
'João sent them the documents.'

In addition, the oblique reflexive forms *si* and *consigo* have become obsolete. Thus, although both options in (2.80) and (2.81) are allowed in EP (with a preference for (2.81) possibly due to the ambiguity of *si* and *consigo* between third and second person), BP admits only the version in (2.81).[54]

(2.80) a. [A Maria]ᵢ só pensa em **si**ᵢ. (EP: OK; BP: *)
the Maria only thinks in pron.*OBL.3.[+REFL]*
'Maria only thinks about herself.'

---

[54] On the incompatibility between *a gente* and *si*, see e.g. Menuzzi 2000. On the competition between the forms *ele(s)/ela(s)* and *si/consigo* in EP, see e.g. Estrela 2006, Lobo 2013a, and Weingart 2020. Although the pronouns *ele(s)/ela(s)* and the reflexive *si* can alternate in cases like (2.80a) and (2.81a) or (i) in EP, the distribution of *si* is more restricted because it requires its antecedent to be a subject, as shown in (ii) (see e.g. Lobo 2013a).

(i) a. [O Pedro]ᵢ viu uma cobra atrás de **si**ᵢ. (EP)
the Pedro saw a snake behind of pron.*OBL.3. [+REFL]*
b. [O Pedro]ᵢ viu uma cobra atrás **dele**ᵢ. (EP)
the Pedro saw a snake behind of-pron.*3.MASC.SG*
'Pedro saw a snake behind himself.'

(ii) a. [O **Pedro**]ᵢ soube diretamente d[o **João**]ₖ que alguém
the Pedro knew directly from-the João that someone
tinha falado mal de **si**ᵢ/*ₖ. (EP)
had spoken badly of pron.*OBL.3.[+REFL]*
'Pedroᵢ heard directly from Joãoₖ that someone had spoken badly of **him**ᵢ/*ₖ.'
b. [O **Pedro**]ᵢ soube diretamente d[o **João**]ₖ que alguém
the Pedro knew directly from-the João that someone
tinha falado mal **dele**ᵢ/ₖ. (EP)
had spoken badly of-pron.*OBL.3.MASC.SG*
'Pedroᵢ heard directly from Joãoₖ that someone had spoken badly of **him**ᵢ/ₖ.'

b. [O João]ᵢ trouxe os documentos **consigo**ᵢ. (EP: OK; BP: *)
the João brought the documents with-pron.OBL.3.[+REFL]
'João brought the documents with him.'

(2.81) a. [A Maria]ᵢ só pensa **nela**ᵢ. (EP/BP)
the Maria only thinks in-pron.OBL.3.-FEM.SG
'Maria only thinks about herself.'
b. [O João]ᵢ trouxe os documentos com **ele**ᵢ. (EP/BP)
the João brought the documents with pron.OBL.3.MASC.SG
'João brought the documents with him.'

Finally, the genitive forms *seu(s)* and *sua(s)*, which in EP can be associated with third person or ([-close]) second person singular, became restricted to the second person singular in BP. Thus, the sentence (2.82) below has only the reading 'your car' in BP, whereas in EP this is the preferred but not exclusive reading. For the reading 'his car', for instance, BP must resort to the periphrastic form *dele*, as illustrated in (2.83), which is also a possibility available in EP.[55]

---

[55] On the replacement of *seu(s)* and *sua(s)* by *dele(s)* and *dela(s)* in BP, see e.g. Oliveira e Silva 1984 and Cerqueira 1993, 1996. There is a residual use of *seu(s)* and *sua(s)* as third person in BP when they are bound by quantified expressions (especially those introduced by the quantifier *cada* 'each'), as illustrated in (ia) below (see e.g. Menuzzi 1996, Negrão and Müller 1996, Negrão 1997, and Menuzzi and Lobo 2016 for discussion). However, the acceptability of (ib) (for some speakers) suggests that the prepositional version is also replacing the *seu* series in these contexts.

(i) a. [Cada paciente]ᵢ ligou pro **seu**ᵢ médico. (BP)
each patient called to-the **pron.GEN.3.SG** doctor
b. [Cada paciente]ᵢ ligou pro médico **dele**ᵢ. (%BP)
each patient called to-the doctor **of-pron.3.SG**.
'[Each patient]ᵢ called hisᵢ doctor.'

Some BP dialects (in particular, some dialects of Minas Gerais) make a distinction between the genitive pronouns *seu* and *seus* (and their corresponding feminine forms) when they appear postverbally: *seu* is interpreted as second person singular and *seus* as second person plural (see e.g. Pereira 2016). Thus, in these dialects the sentences in (ii), for example, do not involve lack of number agreement between the noun and the genitive pronoun as may appear at first sight; rather, the number specification of the genitive pronouns is independent from the number specification of the noun.

(ii) a. Ana, preciso de **fotos** **sua**. (%BP)
Ana need-1.SG of picture-**PL** pron.GEN.2-FEM.SG
'Ana, I need some of your(SG) pictures.'
(recorded in Lavras (Minas Gerais), 2016: Pereira 2016)
b. O **projeto** **seus** prevê
the project.**SG** pron.GEN.2.MASC-**PL** predicts
aplicação no ensino? (%BP)
application in-the teaching
'Do you(PL) expect your(PL) project to have any teaching applications?'
(recorded in Diamantina (Minas Gerais), 2013: Pereira 2016)

(2.82) O João viu o **seu**   carro   no
        the João saw the pron.GEN.3/2.SG car   in-the
        estacionamento.   (**seu** = 'your' → EP: OK; BP: OK
        parking-lot   **seu** = 'his' → EP: OK; BP: *)
        'João saw your/his car in the parking lot.'

(2.83) O João viu o carro **dele**   no
        the João saw the car of-pron.3.MASC.SG in-the
        estacionamento.   (EP/BP)
        parking-lot
        'João saw his car in the parking lot.'

The last line in Tables 2.5 and 2.6 contains the so-called indefinite (IND) or impersonal *se*, illustrated in (2.84) below. In both EP and BP nominative *se* is interpreted as an indefinite of sorts and may license an oblique reflexive (only *si* in BP and *si* and *consigo* in EP), as shown in (2.85).

(2.84) Não **se**   deve   fumar   aqui   dentro.
        not pron.NOM.3.IND$_{[CL]}$ should smoke   here   inside
        'One should not smoke in here.'

(2.85) a. Quando só **se**   pensa em
           when   only pron.NOM.3.IND$_{[CL]}$ thinks in
           si,   tudo   pode dar errado.   (EP/BP)
           pron.OBL.3[+REFL] everything can give wrong
           'When one only thinks about oneself, everything can go wrong.'
        b. Não **se**   deve   ter
           not pron.NOM.3.IND$_{[CL]}$ should have
           consigo   muito dinheiro.   (EP/*BP)
           with.pron.OBL.3[+REFL] much   money
           'One should not have a lot of money on oneself.'

The lack of accusative and dative reflexives for the indefinite *se* series is generally attributed to a co-occurrence restriction on two instances of *se*, as illustrated in (2.86).[56]

(2.86) *Levanta-**se**-**se**   cedo
        gets.up-pron.ACC.3.[+REFL]$_{[CL]}$-pron.NOM.3.IND$_{[CL]}$ early
        neste   país.   (EP)
        in-this   country
        'People get up early in this country.'

Interestingly, EP and BP differ even with respect to the nature of this co-occurrence restriction.[57] In EP, it is sensitive to syntactic information and not

---

[56] See e.g. Naro 1976, Nunes 1990, and Martins and Nunes 2016, 2017b for discussion.
[57] See e.g. Martins and Nunes 2016, 2017b for discussion.

linear proximity. Consider the contrast in (2.87) below, for instance. At first sight, the contrast is the opposite of what one would expect, given that in the acceptable sentence in (2.87a) there is just a single verb separating the two clitics, but in the unacceptable sentence in (2.87b) there are two. Upon closer inspection, one can see that the subject of the embedded clause in (2.87a) is *ele* 'he', whereas the null subject of the lower clauses of (2.87b) is interpreted as being the indefinite clitic *se*. In other words, in EP the computation of the co-occurrence restriction seen in (2.86) takes into consideration the properties of the local subject.

(2.87) a. Soube-**se**   ter-**se**   ele
 knew-pron.NOM.3.IND$_{[CL]}$ have-pron.ACC.3.[+REFL]$_{[CL]}$ he
 suicidado.   (EP)
 committed-suicide
 'It was heard that he committed suicide.'
 b. *Conseguiu-**se**   evitar sentar-**se**
 managed-pron.NOM.3.IND$_{[CL]}$ avoid sit-pron.ACC.3.[+REFL]$_{[CL]}$
 na   última   fila.   (EP)
 in-the   last   row
 'One managed to avoid sitting in the last row.'

In (BP), on the other hand, the co-occurrence restriction takes into account only linear adjacency. As illustrated in (2.88), if there is phonological material intervening between the two clitics, the restriction does not apply:

(2.88) a. Não   **se**   deve
 not   pron.NOM.3.IND$_{[CL]}$ should
 se   levantar   tarde.   (BP)
 pron.ACC.3.[+REFL]$_{[CL]}$ raise   late
 'One shouldn't get up late.'
 b. Pode-**se**,   salvo engano, **se**
 can-pron.NOM.3.IND$_{[CL]}$ saving mistake pron.ACC.3.[+REFL]$_{[CL]}$
 sentar   em   qualquer   lugar.   (BP)
 sit   in   any   place
 'One can, if I'm not mistaken, sit in any seat.'

We return to indefinite *se* in Sections 3.5.3 and 5.6.2, when we compare the types of agreement it triggers in EP and BP, as well its behavior with respect to clitic placement.

2.5 Summary

Leaving indefinite *se* aside for the moment (see Section 3.5.3 for discussion), Tables 2.8 and 2.9 below reorganize the system of personal pronouns in EP and BP, based on the discussion of the previous sections. Before we examine the tables proper, let us make a couple of points regarding their presentation. First, we take the nominative form to be representative of each series of pronouns, as

2.5 Summary

nominative is the default case in Portuguese (see Section 2.3.4.1); hence, it is the only case in both tables that has each of its cells filled. Second, the presentation capitalizes on the different kinds of syncretism that occur in EP and BP. Accordingly, the nominative column is in the middle of the tables, pronouns that are ambiguous between strong and weak forms are combined, and prepositional genitives are distinguished from synthetic ones. Thus, the lack of cell divisions to the left and right of the nominative forms *ele* and *ela* in Table 2.8, for instance, indicates that the corresponding oblique and prepositional genitive forms are the same. Finally, putting aside conflated oblique forms, the specific prepositions associated with a given case are ignored. For instance, the lack of cell divisions between the nominative *a gente* in Table 2.8 and the [-REFL].OBL and prepositional GEN columns indicates that it may combine with the prepositions *com* (*com a gente*) and *de* (*da gente*).

The darker shaded areas in Tables 2.8 and 2.9 outline some of the major differences between the pronominal systems in EP and BP after the incorporation of the series represented by *você*, *vocês*, and *a gente* in each grammar. The geometrical figures formed by the darker shaded areas extend along the vertical dimension in EP, but along the horizontal dimension in BP. This means that the incorporation of these series of pronouns in the grammar of EP resulted in some syncretism with respect to person (for instance, *o(s)/a(s)/lhe(s)* and *consigo* can be second or third person), but the case system was basically kept intact. By contrast, the incorporation of these forms into the grammar of BP was accompanied by a drastic simplification of its case distinctions. This difference becomes very clear when we compare the *vocês* series in the two varieties. As illustrated in (2.89)–(2.93), EP may use up to six different forms depending on the case the pronoun has, whereas BP uses a single form for all cases.

(2.89) **Vocês** querem pedir mais alguma coisa? (EP/BP)
pron.*NOM*.2-*PL* want order more some thing
'Would you(PL) like to order anything else?'

(2.90) a. A vovó adora-{**vos/os**}. (EP)
the grandma adores-pron.*ACC*.2.*PL*/pron.*ACC*.2.*MASC-PL*
b. A vovó adora **vocês**. (BP)
the grandma adores pron.*ACC*.2-*PL*
'Grandma loves you(PL).'

(2.91) a. O João não {**vos/lhes**} trouxe nada. (EP)
the João not pron.*DAT*.2.*PL*/pron.*DAT*.2-*PL* brought nothing
b. O João não trouxe nada pra **vocês**. (BP)
the João not brought nothing for pron.*DAT*.2-*PL*
'João didn't bring you(PL) anything.'

Table 2.8 *Syncretism of personal pronouns in European Portuguese*

	[+REFL]	[-REFL]	[-REFL]	[+REFL]	[-REFL]	prepositional	synthetic
	ACC / DAT	ACC	DAT	OBL	NOM	GEN	GEN
1.SG	me[CL]	me[CL]	me[CL]	mim / comigo	eu		meu[MASC.SG] / meus[MASC-PL] / minha[FEM.SG] / minhas[FEM-PL]
2.SG[+close]	te[CL]	te[CL]	te[CL]	ti / contigo	tu		teu[MASC.SG] / teus[MASC-PL] / tua[FEM.SG] / tuas[FEM-PL]
2.SG[-close]	se[CL]	o[MASC.CL] / a[FEM.CL]	lhe[CL]	si / consigo	você		seu[MASC.SG] / seus[MASC-PL] / sua[FEM.SG] / suas[FEM-PL]
3.SG	se[CL]	o[MASC.CL] / a[FEM.CL]	lhe[CL]	si / consigo	ele[MASC] / ela[FEM]		seu[MASC.SG] / seus[MASC-PL] / sua[FEM.SG] / suas[FEM-PL]
3-PL	se[CL]	os[MASC.CL] / as[FEM.CL]	lhes[CL]	si / consigo	eles[MASC] / elas[FEM]		seu[MASC.SG] / seus[MASC-PL] / sua[FEM.SG] / suas[FEM-PL]
2-PL	vos[CL]	vos[CL]	vos[CL]	convosco	vocês		vosso[MASC.SG] / vossos[MASC-PL] / vossa[FEM.SG] / vossas[FEM-PL]
1.PL	nos[CL]	nos[CL]	nos[CL]	connosco	a gente / nós		nosso[MASC.SG] / nossos[MASC-PL] / nossa[FEM.SG] / nossas[FEM-PL]

The first column displays the traditional description of the nominative pronouns in boldface, which will be revised in Section 3.4.2.

Table 2.9 *Syncretism of personal pronouns in Brazilian Portuguese*

	[+REFL]	[-REFL]		[+REFL]	[-REFL]	[-REFL]	prepositional	synthetic
	ACC / DAT	ACC	DAT	OBL	OBL	NOM	GEN	GEN
1.SG	*me*[CL]			*mim* / *comigo*		*eu*		*meu*[MASC.SG] *meus*[MASC-PL] *minha*[FEM.SG] *minhas*[FEM-PL]
2.SG	*se*[CL]	*te*[CL]				*você*		*seu*[MASC.SG] *seus*[MASC-PL] *sua*[FEM.SG] *suas*[FEM-PL]
		cê[W]				*cê*[W]		
2-PL	*se*[CL]	*cês*[W]				*vocês*		
						cês[W]		
3.SG/3-PL	*se*[CL]					*ele*[MASC.SG] *ela*[FEM.SG] *eles*[MASC-PL] *elas*[FEM-PL]		
1.PL	*se*[CL]					*a gente*		
						nós		*nosso*[MASC.SG] *nossos*[MASC-PL] *nossa*[FEM.SG] *nossas*[FEM-PL]

The first column displays the traditional description of the nominative pronouns in boldface, which will be revised in Section 3.4.2.

(2.92) a. Eu   vou   **convosco**.   (EP)
              I   go   with.pron.**OBL**.2.PL
       b. Eu   vou   com   **vocês**.   (EP/BP)
              I   go   with   pron.**OBL**.2-PL
       'I'm going with you(PL).'

(2.93) a. Os   **vossos**   documentos ainda não
              the   pron.**GEN**.2.PL-MASC-PL documents   still   not
              estão prontos.   (EP)
              are   ready
       b. Os   documentos   de   **vocês**   ainda não
              the   documents   of   pron.**GEN**.2-PL still   not
              estão prontos.   (BP)
              are   ready
       'Your(PL) documents are not ready yet.'

It is a well documented fact that when languages lose case distinctions, they change towards a more rigid word order. This is one of the implications of the differences encoded in Tables 2.8 and 2.9 that we will explore in the chapters that follow. We will see that the difference between EP and BP with respect to the possible word orders they admit (see Chapter 5), their different agreement systems (see Section 3.4.2), and their differences in licensing null arguments (see Chapters 4 and 6), for instance, are all related to the differences in their pronominal systems.

3

Agreement

3.1 Introduction

Natural languages may redundantly encode some grammatical features. In the sentence in (3.1) below, for instance, all lexical items are specified as plural and all elements but the verb are specified as feminine. The systematic covariation in morphological features among lexical items or phrases is referred to as *syntactic agreement* – the topic of this chapter.

(3.1)   **As**   alun**as**   estrangeir**as**   chega**ram**
        *the.**FEM-PL***   *student-**FEM-PL***   *foreign-**FEM-PL***   *arrived-3.**PL***
        adiantad**as**.
        *early-**FEM-PL***
        'The foreign female students arrived early.'

Syntactic agreement may involve either elements in a specification or modification relation within a single phrase or elements in a subject–predicate relation within a sentence. In (3.1), for example, we have agreement in gender and number internal to the noun phrase[1] *as alunas estrangeiras*, agreement in number between this noun phrase and the verbal predicate *chegaram*, and agreement in gender and number between the noun phrase and the adjectival predicate *adiantadas*. In this chapter we discuss how each of these types of agreement is instantiated in the grammars of European Portuguese (EP) and Brazilian Portuguese (BP).

The chapter is organized as follows. Section 3.2 discusses agreement within nominal domains. Section 3.3 is reserved for subject–predicate agreement. In Section 3.4, we propose a reinterpretation of the traditional analysis of agreement with personal pronouns in Portuguese. In Section 3.5, we discuss

---

[1] In the wake of Abney's (1987) work, most linguists have standardly reanalyzed noun phrases (NPs) as determiner phrases (DPs). Given that this distinction will not be specifically relevant in the following discussion, we will stick to the traditional terminology and, accordingly, take determiners to be specifiers of nouns.

special cases of agreement and, finally, Section 3.6 briefly summarizes the major architectural differences between EP and BP that are associated with their different agreement systems.

3.2 Agreement within Nominal Domains in Portuguese

Agreement within nominal domains, also referred to as "concord," is restricted to gender and number features in Portuguese. The parts of speech that can be specified for these features and appear within noun phrases are the following: nouns (e.g. *primo* 'cousin-**MASC.SG**', *primas* 'cousin-**FEM-PL**'), adjectives (e.g. *bonitos* 'beautiful-**MASC-PL**', *cara* 'expensive-**FEM.SG**'), articles (e.g. *o* 'the.**MASC.SG**', *umas* 'a-**FEM-PL**'), demonstratives (e.g. *aqueles* 'that.**MASC-PL**', *essa* 'this-**FEM.SG**'), possessive pronouns (e.g. *meus* 'my.**MASC-PL**', *minha* 'my-**FEM.SG**'), quantifiers (e.g. *muitos* 'many-**MASC-PL**', *alguma* 'some-**FEM.SG**'), interrogative pronouns (e.g. *quais* 'which-**PL**'), and relative pronouns (e.g. *o qual* 'lit.: the.**MASC.SG** which.**SG**', *cujas* 'whose-**FEM-PL**').

Below we describe how agreement in gender and number within noun phrases is realized in Portuguese.

3.2.1 Gender Agreement

In Portuguese, gender admits two values: masculine and feminine.[2] With nouns referring to humans and other animals, these values generally correspond to biological gender (male and female), as exemplified by the pairs *esposo* 'spouse-**MASC.SG**'/*esposa* 'spouse-**FEM.SG**' and *gato* 'cat-**MASC.SG**'/*gata* 'cat-**FEM.SG**'. However, a specific value may be lexically specified with no correspondence to biological gender. This is the case of *criança* 'child' and *cobra* 'snake', for instance, which are always feminine, and *tatu* 'armadillo' and *jacaré* 'alligator', which are always masculine, regardless of whether they refer to males or females. Additionally, some nouns are not specified for gender, thus being compatible with both masculine and feminine specifiers/modifiers (depending on whether they refer to males or females), as illustrated by *o estudante/especialista alto* 'lit.: the.**MASC.SG** student.SG/specialist.SG

---

[2] A small group of pronouns (the demonstrative *isto* 'this' and the indefinite *algo* 'something', for instance) are at times analyzed as having their gender feature specified as neuter. We will not make this fine-grained distinction here, as the gender agreement triggered by these pronouns can always be analyzed as default masculine.

tall-**MASC**.SG' and *a estudante/especialista alta* 'lit.: the.**FEM**.SG student.SG/specialist.SG tall-**FEM**.SG'.

From a morphological point of view, gender may be encoded via suppletion, as in the case of the pairs *pai/mãe* 'father/mother' and *boi/vaca* 'ox/cow', or via the thematic vowels *-o* and *-a*, with *-o* encoding masculine and *-a* feminine, as in *amigo/amiga* 'friend-**MASC**.SG/friend-**FEM**.SG'.[3] Feminine marking may also be encoded by vowel lowering as in the pair *avô/avó* (*av*[o]/*av*[ɔ]) 'grandfather'/'grandmother' or (redundantly) *novo/nova* (*n*[o]*vo*/*n*[ɔ]*va*) 'new-**MASC**.SG'/'new-**FEM**.SG'. When biological gender is not at stake, there is a strong tendency for nouns ending with the thematic vowel *-a* to be feminine (e.g. *casa* 'house.**FEM**.SG') and with the thematic vowel *-o* to be masculine (e.g. *prédio* 'building.**MASC**.SG'). However, there do exist cases where this correlation does not hold, as exemplified by *problema* 'problem.**MASC**.SG', which ends in *-a* but is masculine, and *tribo* 'tribe.**FEM**.SG', which ends in *-o* but is feminine.

In both EP and BP, gender agreement must hold between the head of the noun phrase (see footnote 1 above) and all of its specifiers and modifiers, unless the modifier is a prepositional phrase, as illustrated in (3.2).

(3.2) a. o   meu   querido   amigo
         the.*MASC.SG* my.*MASC.SG* dear-*MASC.SG* friend-*MASC.SG*
         engraçado   da   Argentina
         funny-*MASC.SG* of-the.*FEM.SG* Argentina.*FEM.SG*
         'my dear funny (male) friend from Argentina'
    b. a   minha   querida   amiga
         the.*FEM.SG* my-*FEM.SG* dear-*FEM.SG* friend-*FEM.SG*
         engraçada   do   Rio
         funny-*FEM.SG* of-the.*MASC.SG* Rio.*MASC.SG*
         'my dear funny (female) friend from Rio'

As happens in other languages, an exception to the lack of agreement when prepositional phrases are involved concerns relative pronouns within prepositional phrases. As shown in (3.3), the definite article that is part of the complex relative pronoun *o qual/a qual* inflects for gender and agrees with its antecedent:[4]

(3.3) a. o   homem com o   qual   eu falei
         the.*MASC.SG* man   with the.*MASC.SG* which.SG I spoke
         'the man with whom I spoke'
    b. a   mulher com a   qual   eu falei
         the.*FEM.SG* woman with the.*FEM.SG* which.SG I spoke
         'the woman with whom I spoke'

---

[3] For discussion see e.g. Câmara Jr. 1970, Villalva 2000, 2003, Lucchesi 2009, Armelin 2015, Mota 2016, 2020a,b, Carvalho 2018, and Rio-Torto 2020.

[4] This exceptional behavior is arguably related to the fact that there is a predication relation between the antecedent of the relative pronoun and the relative clause.

As opposed to the relative pronoun *o qual*, whose gender and number are determined by its antecedent, as seen in (3.3), the relative pronoun *cujo* 'whose' agrees with the noun it modifies, as shown in (3.4) below.

(3.4) a. a   mulher   cujo   filho   viajou   (EP)
           the.*FEM.SG* woman   whose-*MASC.SG*   child-*MASC.SG*   traveled
           'the woman whose son traveled'
       b. o   homem   cuja   filha   viajou   (EP)
           the.*MASC.SG* man   whose-*FEM.SG*   child-*FEM.SG*   traveled
           'the man whose daughter traveled'

The usage of *cujo* constitutes the only major difference between the grammars of EP and BP with respect to gender agreement within nominal domains, as this relative pronoun has got lost in BP. In all the remaining constructions, the two varieties behave essentially in the same fashion.[5]

3.2.2 Number Agreement

The feature [number] in Portuguese admits two values: singular and plural. Singular is the unmarked form, while plural is canonically marked with the suffix -*s*, as in the pair *casa/casas* 'house.FEM.SG/house.FEM-PL',

---

[5] For some speakers of BP, the quantifier *menos* 'less/few' and the adverb *meio* 'a little' allows for gender agreement, as illustrated in (i).

(i)   a. Tinha   menas   pessoas.   (%BP)
          had.*3.SG* minus(*FEM*)   person.*FEM-PL*
          'There were fewer people.'
      b. Eu fiquei   meia   confusa.   (%BP)
          I stayed   half-*FEM* confused-*FEM.SG*
          'I got a bit confused.'

Some speakers of BP also allow the neuter quantifier *tudo* 'everything' (see footnote 2 above) to alternate with inflecting versions of *todo* 'every' when in postnominal or "floating" positions (see e.g. Cançado 2006, Vicente 2006, and Lacerda 2011, 2016):

(ii) a. {Todos/*tudo}   os   alunos   vão
          all-*MASC-PL*/everything.*NT.SG*   the.*MASC-PL*   student-*MASC-PL*   go
          viajar.
          travel
      b. Os   alunos   {todos/**tudo**}   vão
          the.*MASC-PL*   student-*MASC-PL*   all-*MASC-PL*/everything.*NT.SG*   go
          viajar.   (%BP)
          travel
      c. Os   alunos   vão {todos/**tudo**}
          the.*MASC-PL*   student-*MASC-PL*   go all-*MASC-PL*/everything.*NT.SG*
          viajar.   (%BP)
          travel
          'All the students are going to travel.'

and its variants, as illustrated by the pairs *mês/meses* 'month.MASC.SG/ month.MASC-PL', *papel/papéis* 'paper.MASC.SG/paper.MASC-PL', and *portão/portões* 'gate.MASC.SG/gate.MASC-PL'.[6] As with the realization of feminine (see Section 3.2.1), plural can also be (redundantly) marked by vowel lowering, as in *porco/porcos* (*p*[o]*rco/p*[ɔ]*rcos*) 'pig-MASC.SG'/ 'pig-MASC-PL' or *corajoso/corajosos* (*coraj*[o]*so/coraj*[ɔ]*sos*) 'courageous-MASC.SG/courageous-MASC-PL'.

Some specifiers/modifiers are intrinsically singular, intrinsically plural, or simply not specified with respect to number. For instance, the quantifier *cada* 'each' is invariably singular and the quantifier *vários* 'several' is always plural.[7] Hence, the former can combine only with singular nouns and the latter only with plural ones, as illustrated in (3.5a–b) below. In turn, the interrogative pronoun *que* 'what' is not specified for number and is thus compatible with both singular and plural nouns (see (3.5c)).[8]

(3.5)   a. cada livro   /*cada livros
        each book.MASC.SG each   book.MASC-PL
        'each book'
       b. vários   livros   /*vário   livro
        various-MASC-PL book.MASC-PL various-MASC.SG book.MASC.SG
        'several books'
       c. que livro   /que livros
        what book.MASC.SG what book.MASC-PL
        'which book/which books'

As with gender, number agreement may affect all modifiers of the noun, except for prepositional phrases, as illustrated in (3.6) below. Also as with gender, the relative pronoun *o qual* 'which' and its feminine counterpart agree in number with their antecedent even when they are inside a prepositional

---

[6] For discussion see e.g. Mota 2016.
[7] The quantifier *bastante* 'many/much' has become morphologically specified as singular in BP, despite its plural meaning. Thus, it behaves like *cada* 'each' (see (3.5a)) in being incompatible with a plural noun, as illustrated in (i).

(i)   a. O   João   precisava   de   **bastantes**   livros.   (EP/*BP)
         the   João   needed   of   many-PL   book-PL
      b. O   João   precisava   de   **bastante**   livros.   (*EP/*BP)
         the   João   needed   of   many.SG   book-PL
      c. O   João   precisava   de   **bastante**   livro.   (*EP/BP)
         the   João   needed   of   many.SG   book
      'João needed many books.'

[8] In some dialects of BP (the dialect of Minas Gerais, for instance), the interrogative pronoun *que* can inflect for plural, as illustrated in (i) (see e.g. Nunes 2007):

(i)   **Ques**   livro   você   comprou?   (%BP)
      *what-**PL**   book   you   bought*
      'Which books did you buy?'

phrase (see (3.7)) and the EP relative pronoun *cujo* 'whose' and its feminine counterpart agree in number with the head they modify (see (3.8)).

(3.6) a. aquele   outro   professor
       that.*MASC.SG*   other-*MASC.SG* teacher.*MASC.SG*
       estrangeiro   das   crianças
       foreign-*MASC.SG* of-the.*FEM-PL* child.*FEM-PL*
       'that other foreign teacher of the children's'
    b. as   novas   pontes   largas
       the.*FEM-PL*   new-*FEM-PL*   bridge.*FEM-PL* wide-*FEM-PL*
       daquele   rio
       of-that.*MASC.SG* river.*MASC.SG*
       'the new wide bridges over that river'

(3.7) a. o   homem com o   qual   eu falei
       the.*MASC.SG* man.*SG* with the.*MASC.SG* which.*SG* I spoke
       'the man with whom I spoke'
    b. os   homens com os   quais   eu falei
       the.*MASC-PL* man-*PL* with the.*MASC-PL* which-*PL* I spoke
       'the men with whom I spoke'

(3.8) a. o   autor   cujos   livros
       the.*MASC.SG* author.*MASC.SG* whose-*MASC-PL*   book.*MASC-PL*
       vendem   bem   (EP)
       sell   well
       'the author whose books sell well'
    b. os   alunos   cujo
       the.*MASC-PL* student-*MASC-PL*   whose-*MASC.SG*
       projeto   me   impressionou   (EP)
       project.*MASC.SG* me   impressed
       'the students whose project impressed me'

Whereas EP and BP essentially pattern alike with respect to gender agreement within noun phrases, they differ considerably with respect to number agreement. Full agreement within the noun phrase as in (3.9) below is mandatory across EP dialects. BP, on the other hand, displays a much wider and more intricate range of possibilities across dialects/idiolects,[9] which can be grouped into three basic patterns: full agreement, as in (3.9), nonagreement as in (3.10), and partial agreement, as in (3.11).[10]

---

[9] For discussion see e.g. Scherre 1988, 1994, Menuzzi 1994, Scherre and Naro 1998b, Naro and Scherre 2007, and Baxter 2009.
[10] The distinct behavior of number in the two varieties when compared to gender suggests that number in Portuguese is not an intrinsic property of nouns, but rather a property of determiners or a bound lexical item encoding number and heading a projection of its own (NumP). For discussion see e.g. Magalhães 2004, Munn and Schmitt 2005, Augusto, Ferrari Neto, and Corrêa 2006, and Costa and Figueiredo Silva 2006a.

(3.9)   aqueles   carros   brasileiros
        that.*MASC-PL* car.*MASC-PL* Brazilian-*MASC-PL*
        pequenos   (EP/BP)
        small-*MASC-PL*
        'those small Brazilian cars'

(3.10) a. aqueles   carro   brasileiro   pequeno   (%BP)
           that.*MASC-PL* car.*MASC*   Brazilian-*MASC*   small-*MASC*
           'those small Brazilian cars'
        b. umas   amiga   minha   argentina   (%BP)
           a-*FEM-PL*   friend-*FEM*   my-*FEM*   Argentine-*FEM*
           'some female Argentine friends of mine'
        c. os   mesmo   político   corrupto   (%BP)
           the.*MASC-PL* same-*MASC*   politician-*MASC* corrupt-*MASC*
           'the same corrupt politicians'
        d. essas   minha   camisa   velha   (%BP)
           this-*FEM-PL* my-*FEM*   shirt.*FEM*   old-*FEM*
           'these old shirts of mine'

(3.11) a. ?aqueles   carros   brasileiros   pequeno   (%BP)
           that.*MASC-PL* car.*MASC-PL* Brazilian-*MASC-PL* small-*MASC*
        b. ?aqueles   carros   brasileiro   pequeno   (%BP)
           that.*MASC-PL* car.*MASC-PL* Brazilian-*MASC* small-*MASC*
           'those small Brazilian cars'

As opposed to what may seem to be the case at first sight, the patterns in (3.9)–(3.11) do not mean that realization of plural agreement morphology inside noun phrases is simply optional in BP. There are in fact several restrictions that constrain such realization or lack thereof. Let us consider some of them in more detail.

3.2.2.1 Nonagreement

The three general patterns in (3.9)–(3.11) do not enjoy the same sociolinguistic status in BP: (3.9) is the prescriptive option and (3.10) and (3.11) represent nonstandard possibilities. Despite its lack of sociolinguistic prestige, the pattern in (3.10) is very frequent in informal speech across all dialects. In turn, (3.11) seems to involve a mixed pattern and its acceptability is less uniform across speakers. There seems to be a directional implication, though: speakers who accept (3.11) also accept (3.10), but speakers who admit (3.10) do not necessarily allow (3.11). In a sense, the pattern in (3.10) is the "canonical" option among the nonstandard possibilities and this has very interesting consequences for the grammar of BP, as we will see shortly (see Section 3.2.2.3).

Although the nonagreement pattern in (3.10) shows that BP allows plural morphology to be realized only once within the noun phrase, it is simply not the case that any element within the noun phrase can bear the plural morpheme. The sentences in (3.10) contrast sharply with (3.12a) below, for instance, where the plural morpheme is realized only on the noun. Interestingly, (3.12b) seems to be parallel to (3.12a) and is acceptable, nonetheless.

(3.12)   a. *aquele carros   (BP)
           that   *car-MASC-PL*
           'those cars'
       b. que livros   (BP)
           which book-MASC-PL
           'which books'

The generalization that emerges from comparing (3.10) with (3.12) is that, in the nonagreement pattern, the plural morpheme is realized on the determiner if the determiner is compatible with plural; otherwise, it will be realized by the head noun. Thus, given that *aquele* 'that' can bear a plural morpheme, it must be the host for the plural specification; hence, the contrast between (3.10a) and (3.12a).[11] On the other hand, given that the interrogative determiner *que* 'which' is not specified for number (see (3.5c)), the realization of plural morphology on the noun in (3.12b) becomes obligatory (the absence of *-s* on *livros* in (3.12b) necessarily leads to a singular interpretation).[12]

Another factor that has great influence on the acceptability of the lack of realization of plural morphology has to do with the degree of markedness associated with specific morphophonological realizations.[13] Take the sentences in (3.13) below, for instance. Their different degrees of acceptability are arguably related to the different morphophonological adjustments

---

[11] An exception to this general pattern arises in some dialects of BP when the definite article is followed by a possessive pronoun. In this case the possessive rather than the determiner may bear the plural morpheme, as illustrated in (i) (see Costa and Figueiredo Silva 2006a).

     (i)   o   meus   livro   (%BP)
         the.MASC my.MASC.PL book.MASC
         'my books'

[12] As should be expected, in BP dialects that allow plural inflection on *que* (see footnote 8 above), the pattern of full agreement is as in (ia) below and nonagreement as in (ib). The nonagreement version in (3.12b) is plainly ungrammatical in these dialects.

     (i)   a. ques   livros   (%BP)
            what-PL book.MASC-PL
         b. ques   livro   (%BP)
            what-PL book.MASC
            'which books'

[13] For discussion see e.g. Scherre 1988, 1994 and Scherre and Naro 1998a.

triggered by the affixation of the plural morpheme {-s}. The noun *livro* 'book' in (3.13a), for instance, requires no additional adjustments when affixed with the plural morpheme (*livro/livros*). By contrast, the plural forms of the nouns in (3.13b–d) require different morphophonological adjustments: vowel lowering in the preceding nonadjacent syllable in the case of *jogo/jogos* (*j*[o]*go/j*[ɔ]*gos*) 'game/games'), changes in the adjacent diphthong in the case of *limão/limões* (*lim*[ẽw̃]/*lim*[õj̃]*s*) 'lemon/lemons', and introduction of an epenthetic vowel followed by resyllabification in the case of *flor/flores* (*flo-res*) 'flower/flowers'. As (3.13) shows, the more marked the surface realization of the plural marking, the higher the degree of unacceptability of its absence.

(3.13) a. os   livro   (%BP)
            the.*MASC-PL* book.*MASC*
            'the books'
        b. ?os   j[o]go   (%BP)
            the.*MASC-PL* game.*MASC*
            'the games'
        c. ??os   limão   (%BP)
            the.*MASC-PL* lemon.*MASC*
            'the lemons'
        d. ??as   flor   (%BP)
            the.*FEM-PL* flower.*FEM*
            'the flowers'

An interesting contrast regarding the realization of gender and number can be observed with respect to vowel lowering. We have seen that vowel lowering may redundantly mark feminine as in *gostoso/gostosa* (*gost*[o]*so/ gost*[ɔ]*sa*) 'tasty-**MASC.SG**/tasty-**FEM**.SG' or plural as in *gostoso/ gostosos* (*gost*[o]*so/gost*[ɔ]*sos*) 'tasty-**MASC.SG**'/'tasty-**MASC-PL**'. We have also seen that in BP gender agreement is obligatory within noun phrases, but not number agreement. Accordingly, we find that the redundant marking of feminine via vowel lowering is obligatory, but the redundant marking of plural is blocked if the plural morpheme is missing, as illustrated in (3.14).[14]

(3.14) a. aquelas   comida   gostosa   (gost[ɔ]sa/*gost[o]sa) (%BP)
            that-*FEM-PL* food.*FEM* tasty-*FEM*
            'those tasty foods'
        b. aqueles   prato   gostoso   (gost[o]so/*gost[ɔ]so) (%BP)
            that.*MASC-PL* dish.*MASC* tasty-*MASC*
            'those tasty dishes'

---

[14] See Nunes 2007 for discussion.

3.2.2.2 Partial Agreement

Let us now consider the contrasts in (3.15) and (3.16), which involve cases of partial agreement within the noun phrase.

(3.15) a. ?essas minhas camisas velha (%BP)
      this-FEM-PL my-FEM-PL shirt.FEM-PL old-FEM
   b. *essas minha camisas velhas
      this-FEM-PL my-FEM shirt.FEM-PL old-FEM-PL
      'these old shirts of mine'

(3.16) a. ?aqueles carros pequeno (%BP)
      that.MASC-PL car.MASC-PL small-MASC
   b. *aqueles carro pequenos
      that.MASC-PL car.MASC small-MASC-PL
      'those small cars'

As with the nonagreement pattern (see (3.10) vs. (3.12a)), it is not the case that the optionality of plural realization in the partial agreement pattern affects each lexical item independently of the others. As a general rule, the noun delimits a boundary for number agreement in that prenominal modifiers are more likely to display plural agreement than postnominal ones (see (3.15a) vs. (3.15b)).[15] In addition, if the noun does not bear plural, realization of plural on a modifier to its right leads to various degrees of unacceptability (see (3.16a) vs. (3.16b)).

3.2.2.3 Bare Singulars with Count Nouns

The difference between EP and BP with respect to the realization of number within noun phrases has far-reaching consequences. To see this, let us first consider the French sentence in (3.17), which contains a plural indefinite in object position, and compare it with the EP sentences in (3.18).

(3.17) Jean a acheté **des** livres. (French)
      *Jean has purchased **IND.PL** book.MASC-PL*
      'Jean bought some books.'

(3.18) a. O João nunca compra livros usados. (EP)
         the João never buys book.MASC-PL used-MASC-PL
         'João never buys second-hand books.'
   b. A Maria gosta de goiabas vermelhas. (EP)
      the Maria likes of guava.FEM-PL red-FEM-PL
      'Maria likes red guavas.'

In the French sentence in (3.17), the plural determiner *des* encodes indefiniteness. Given the similarity in interpretation between the plural noun phrase in

---

[15] For discussion see e.g. Scherre 1988, 1994 and Menuzzi 1994.

(3.17) and those in (3.18) (and their English translations), it is reasonable to analyze (3.18) along the lines of (3.19) below, where a null determiner parallel to French *des* encodes indefiniteness.[16] Furthermore, given that EP only allows the full agreement pattern (see (3.9)), the number feature of such null determiner must be specified as plural, in consonance with the specification of the other elements.

(3.19) a. O   João   nunca   compra   **Det**_[N:PL]   livros   usados.   (EP)
            the João never buys   book.*MASC-**PL*** used-*MASC-**PL***
        b. A   Maria gosta   de   **Det**_[N:PL]   goiabas   vermelhas.   (EP)
            the Maria likes   of   guava.*FEM-**PL*** red-*FEM-**PL***

As for BP, it also admits plural indefinites such as those in (3.18). However, they are judged as somewhat marked and are associated with formal registers. The most natural rendition of (3.18) in BP is as in (3.20), with an apparent bare singular count noun in object position – a possibility that is completely unavailable in EP.[17]

(3.20) a. O   João   nunca   compra   **livro**   **usado.**   (BP)
            the João never buys   book.*MASC* used-*MASC*
            'João never buys second-hand books.'
        b. A   Maria gosta   de   **goiaba**   **vermelha**.   (BP)
            the Maria likes   of   guava.*FEM* red-*FEM*
            'Maria likes red guavas.'

As the translations indicate, the direct objects in (3.20) are interpreted in a way parallel to the plural indefinites in (3.17) and (3.18) despite the lack of an overt marking for plural. At first sight, this apparent syntax–semantics mismatch is just a by-product of the availability of the nonagreement pattern in the grammar of BP. Given that (dialects/idiolects of) BP may allow plural within the noun phrase to be realized just on the determiner (see (3.10)) and that indefinites may be associated with a null determiner (see (3.18)), sentences like (3.20) could involve a null determiner specified for plural, as in (3.19). In other words, sentences like (3.20) would not involve a bare singular, but a plural indefinite under the nonagreement possibility for plural encoding in BP. Although reasonable, this approach fails to account for the fact that bare singulars are not always interpreted as plural. In nongeneric sentences

---

[16] See e.g. Raposo 1998a for discussion.
[17] For discussion on bare singulars in BP, see e.g. Saraiva 1996, 1997, Schmitt and Munn 1999, 2002, Müller 2002, Müller and Oliveira 2004, Lopes 2005, Munn and Schmitt 2005, Dobrovie-Sorin and Pires de Oliveira 2008, Dobrovie-Sorin 2010, Ferreira 2010, Pires de Oliveira and Rothstein 2011, Cyrino and Espinal 2015, Menuzzi, Figueiredo Silva, and Doetjes 2015, and Wall 2017.

such as (3.21a) and (3.21b) below, for example, the bare singular allows both plural and singular interpretation, as indicated by the pronouns in the second clause (see footnote 17 above). This indicates that the number feature of the null determiner may be unvalued (**Det$_{[N]}$**), thus being compatible with singular or plural contexts. From this perspective, the bare singulars of (3.21) should be represented as in (3.22).

(3.21) BP:
    a. O   João   comprou **livro**   **usado**   ontem, mas
       the   João   bought   book.MASC used-MASC yesterday but
       ele   não   era   barato.
       pron.3.MASC.SG not   was   cheap-MASC.SG
       'João bought a second-hand book yesterday, but it was not cheap.'
    a'. O   João   comprou **livro**   **usado**   ontem, mas
       the   João   bought   book.MASC used-MASC yesterday but
       eles   não   eram   baratos.
       pron.3.MASC.PL not   were   cheap-MASC-PL
       'João bought some second-hand books yesterday, but they were not cheap.'
    b. Tinha   **professor**   na   festa, mas **ele**
       had-3.SG teacher.MASC in-the party but   pron.3.MASC.SG
       parecia   bem   entediado.
       seemed   well   bored-MASC.SG
       'There was a teacher at the party, but he seemed very bored.'
    b'. Tinha   **professor**   na   festa, mas **eles**
       had-3.SG teacher.MASC in-the party but   pron.3.MASC.PL
       pareciam bem   entediados.
       seemed   well   bored-MASC-PL
       'There were teachers at the party, but they seemed very bored.'

(3.22) BP:
    a. O João comprou [**Det$_{[N]}$** livro usado] ontem ...
    b. Tinha [**Det$_{[N]}$** professor] na festa ...

The availability of a null determiner underspecified for number in BP makes room for additional contrasts with EP. For instance, BP may allow count nouns with uninflected/singular quantifiers that are usually associated with mass nouns, as illustrated in (3.23) below. It is worth observing that although the relevant noun phrases in (3.23a) and (3.23b) have a plural counterpart, (3.23c) does not, as shown in (3.24).

(3.23) a. Eu tenho   **muito**   **amigo**   pra visitar.   (BP)
       I   have.1.SG much-MASC friend-MASC for visit
       'I have many friends to visit.'

b. **Quanta** coisa que aquele alpinista já deve
   how.much-FEM thing.FEM that that.MASC alpinist already must
   ter visto! (BP)
   have seen
   'How many things must that mountaineer have seen!'
c. O João comprou **um** **tanto** **de**
   the João bought.3.SG a.MASC.SG bunch.MASC.SG of
   livro! (BP)
   book.MASC
   'João bought so many books!'

(3.24) a. Eu tenho muitos amigos pra visitar. (BP)
       I have.1.SG much-MASC-PL friend-MASC-PL for visit
       'I have many friends to visit.'
    b. Quantas coisas que aquele alpinista já
       how.much-FEM-PL thing.FEM-PL that that.MASC alpinist already
       deve ter visto! (BP)
       must have seen
       'How many things must that mountaineer have seen!'
    c. *O João comprou um tanto /uns
       the João bought.3.SG a.MASC.SG bunch.MASC.SG /a.MASC-PL
       tantos de livros! (BP)
       bunch.MASC-PL of book.MASC-PL
       'João bought so many books!'

Further indication that bare singulars in BP may involve a null determiner underspecified for number is provided by data such as (3.25) below. As observed in Section 3.2.2.1, the nonagreement pattern, despite being very common in informal speech, is sociolinguistically stigmatized. This is even more so if the relevant unrealized plural involves marked morphophonological processes such as vowel lowering, changes in the preceding diphthong, or resyllabification (see (3.13b–d)). Interestingly, no sociolinguistic stigmatization is attached to the analogous constructions with bare singulars in (3.25), whose nouns would undergo the processes mentioned above if the noun phrase were plural.

(3.25) a. Eu perdi uma porção de **j[o]go** na última copa. (BP)
       I missed a portion of game in-the last cup
       'I missed a lot of games in the last world cup.'
    b. O João esqueceu de comprar **limão**. (BP)
       the João forgot of buy lemon
       'João forgot to buy lemons.'
    c. A Maria vende **flor** na feira. (BP)
       the Maria sells flower in-the fair
       'Maria sells flowers at the fair.'

The contrast between (3.18) in EP and (3.20) in BP is also reflected in the format of their compounds. As shown in (3.26), the basis for nominalized verb phrases involves bare plurals in EP, but bare singulars in BP.[18]

(3.26) a. EP: *quebra-cabeças* 'jigsaw puzzle', *abre-latas* 'can opener',
            (lit. *breaks-head-**PL***)   (lit. *opens-can-**PL***)
            saca-rolhas 'corkscrew'
            (lit. *take.out-cork-**PL***)
      b. BP: *quebra-**cabeça*** 'jigsaw puzzle', *abridor de **lata*** 'can opener',
            (lit. *breaks-**head***)   (lit. *opener of **can***)
            *saca-**rolha*** 'corkscrew'
            (lit. *take.out-**cork***)

In sum, the contrast between EP and BP with respect to number agreement within noun phrases goes much beyond noun phrases *per se* and has interesting semantic and morphological consequences. In particular, the fact that the grammar of BP allows for overt number marking to be encoded only on the determiner has paved the way for the emergence of a null determiner underspecified for number, which has in turn led to the availability of two other distinctive properties of the grammar of BP: bare singulars with count nouns and compounds with bare singulars.

3.3 Subject–Predicate Agreement in Portuguese

3.3.1 *Agreement with Nominal and Adjectival Predicates*

In Portuguese, a nominal or adjectival predicate may agree with its subject in gender and number, as illustrated in (3.27) below. Agreement proceeds regardless of whether or not the subject of the relevant predication is also the syntactic subject of the sentence. In (3.27), for instance, the bracketed subject of the underlined nominal and adjectival predicates is the syntactic subject in (3.27a–b), but the syntactic object in (3.27c–d).

(3.27) a. [Es**sas** médic**as**] também são professor**as**.
         this-**FEM-PL** doctor-**FEM-PL** also   are teacher-**FEM-PL**
         'These female doctors are also teachers.'
     b. [**Os** caval**os**] ficaram calm**os**.
         the.**MASC-PL** horse.**MASC-PL** stayed calm-**MASC-PL**
         'The horses became calm.'
     c. Só o João considera [esses candidat**os**]
         only the João considers this.**MASC-PL** candidate-**MASC-PL**
         polític**os** de confiança.
         politician-**MASC-PL** of trust
         'Only João considers these candidates to be trustworthy politicians.'

---

[18] See e.g. Nunes 2007, Cyrino and Espinal 2015, and Villalva 2020 for discussion.

d. A Maria achou [**as** alunas] <u>bem</u>
   *the Maria thought the.**FEM-PL** student-**FEM-PL** well*
   <u>prepara**das**</u>.
   *prepared-**FEM-PL***
   'Maria considered the female students to be well prepared.'

The similarities and contrasts between EP and BP with respect to agreement within noun phrases (see Sections 3.2.1 and 3.2.2) are by and large replicated in the domain of agreement involving nominal and adjectival predicates. That is, gender agreement is obligatory in both EP and BP (see (3.27)), but number agreement need not be enforced in dialects of BP, as illustrated in (3.28).

(3.28) a. [Ess**as** médic**as**] também são **professora**. (%BP)
   *this-**FEM-PL** doctor-**FEM-PL** also are teacher-**FEM***
   'These female doctors are also teachers.'
   b. [**Os** caval**os**] ficaram **calmo**. (%BP)
   *the.**MASC-PL** horse.**MASC-PL** stayed calm-**MASC***
   'The horses became calm.'
   c. Só o João considera [ess**es** candidat**os**]
   *only the João considers this.**MASC-PL** candidate-**MASC-PL***
   político de confiança. (%BP)
   *politician-**MASC** of trust*
   'Only João considers these candidates to be trustworthy politicians.'
   d. A Maria achou [**as** alun**as**]
   *the Maria thought the.**FEM-PL** student-**FEM-PL***
   bem **preparada**. (%BP)
   *well prepared-**FEM***
   'Maria considered the female students to be well prepared.'

Likewise, the lack of realization of plural in nominal and adjectival predicates is sociolinguistically stigmatized and its acceptability is subject to factors such as morphophonological markedness (see footnote 13 above). There is also a tendency for symmetry between the two types of agreement in that the specific pattern of agreement internal to the subject in general correlates with the parallel pattern of agreement exhibited by the nominal or adjectival predicate. Thus, if all inflecting elements within the subject realize plural, the corresponding predicate is likely to realize plural, as well (see (3.27)); conversely, if only the determiner realizes plural within the subject, the corresponding predicate is more likely to lack plural specification, as in (3.29).[19]

---

[19] See e.g. Scherre 1988, 1994, Scherre and Naro 1998b, and Costa and Figueiredo Silva 2006a.

(3.29) a. [Ess**as** **médica**] também são **professora**. (%BP)
 *this-**FEM-PL** doctor-**FEM** also are teacher-**FEM***
 'These female doctors are also teachers.'
 b. [**Os** **cavalo**] ficaram **calmo**. (%BP)
 *the.**MASC-PL** horse.**MASC** stayed calm-**MASC***
 'The horses became calm.'
 c. Só o João acha considera [esses
 *only the João thinks considers **MASC-PL** this.*
 candidato] **político** de confiança. (%BP)
 *candidate-**MASC** politician-**MASC** of trust*
 'Only João considers these candidates to be trustworthy politicians.'
 d. A Maria achou [**as** **aluna**] bem **preparada**. (%BP)
 *the Maria thought the.**FEM-PL** student-**FEM** well prepared-**FEM***
 'Maria considered the female students to be well prepared.'

This tendency to symmetry reaches its limit when bare singulars are involved. As discussed in Section 3.2.2.3, bare singulars with count nouns in BP can be analyzed as involving a null determiner underspecified for number. Once the null determiner is not morphologically specified for number, it should fail to trigger number agreement. Thus, if a nominal or adjectival predicate takes an (apparent) bare singular for its subject, it should inflect for gender but not for number. (3.30) below shows that this is indeed the case. The nominal or adjectival predicates in (3.30) seem to display singular agreement because the nominal morpheme associated with singular does not have phonetic expression (see Section 3.2.2).

(3.30) a. [Médic**o**] sempre chega atrasado(*s). (BP)
 *doctor-**MASC** always arrives late.**MASC**-(*PL)*
 'Doctors always arrive late.'
 b. [Mul**a**] é mais teimos**a**(*s) que cavalo. (BP)
 *mule.**FEM** is more stubborn-**FEM**-(*PL) than horse*
 'Mules are more stubborn than horses.'
 c. Esse produtor transforma [dançar**in**a] em atriz(*es) (BP)
 *this producer transforms dancer-**FEM** in actress-(*PL)*
 'This producer transforms dancers into actresses.'
 d. Esse candidato só falta chamar [eleitor] de
 *this candidate only lacks call voter.**MASC** of*
 palhaço(*s) (BP)
 *clown-**MASC**-(*PL)*
 'The only thing that is missing is for this candidate to call voters clowns.'

Finally, if the (apparent) bare singular is embedded in indefinite partitive expressions such as *um punhado de* 'a bunch of' or *uma porção de* 'a portion of', gender agreement is determined by the bare singular and not by the head of the partitive, as shown in (3.31).[20]

---

[20] For related discussion, see Rodrigues 2006 and Scherre and Naro 1998a.

(3.31) a. [Um   punhado   de aluna]   ficou
          a.MASC.SG   *handful.MASC.SG* *of* *student-FEM* *stayed*
          indigna**da**.   (BP)
          outraged-FEM
          'A lot of female students were outraged.'
     b. [Um   montão   de professora]   ficou
          a.MASC.SG   *pile.MASC.SG*   *of* *teacher-FEM* *stayed*
          surpres**a**.   (BP)
          surprised-FEM
          'A lot of female teachers were surprised.'
     c. [Uma   porção   de aluno]   ficou
          a-FEM.SG   *portion.FEM.SG* *of* *student-MASC* *stayed*
          indigna**do**.   (BP)
          outraged-MASC
          'A lot of students were outraged.'
     d. [Uma   cacetada   de aluno]   ficou
          a-FEM.SG   *drubbing.FEM.SG* *of* *student-MASC* *stayed*
          surpres**o**.   (BP)
          surprised-MASC
          'A lot of students were surprised.'

3.3.2 Agreement with Verbal Predicates

Verbal predicates may involve agreement in gender and number or person and number. Below we discuss each of these in turn.

3.3.2.1 Gender and Number Agreement in Participials

Verbal participials may display agreement in gender and number if they are passive, as in (3.32) below, or if they head "absolutive" constructions, as in (3.33). Absolutive participial constructions are reduced temporal clauses with no complementizers or finite verbs. They may involve transitive verbs, as in (3.33a–b), as well as unaccusative verbs – traditional intransitive verbs whose only argument displays object behavior (see Section 3.5.1.1) – as in (3.33c–d).[21]

(3.32) a. [**Os**   projetos]   foram arquiva**dos**.
          the.MASC-PL   *project.MASC-PL* *were* *filed-MASC-PL*
          'The projects were filed.'
     b. [**As**   propostas]   foram aprova**das**.
          the.FEM-PL   *proposal.FEM-PL* *were* *approved-FEM-PL*
          'The proposals were approved.'

---

[21] For discussion on unaccusative verbs in Portuguese, see e.g. Eliseu 1984, Whitaker-Franchi 1989, Ciríaco and Cançado 2006, and Cançado, Godoy, and Amaral 2013.

(3.33) a. Compra**dos** [**os** equipamen**tos**], o trabalho
bought-***MASC-PL*** the.***MASC-PL*** equipment.***MASC-PL*** the work
recomeçou.
restarted
'Once the equipment was bought, the work restarted.'
b. Fei**tas** [**as** con**tas**], nós tivemos de
made-***FEM-PL*** the.***FEM-PL*** calculation.***FEM-PL*** we had of
cancelar o pedido.
cancel the order
'Once we'd done the sums, we had to cancel the order.'
c. Saí**dos** [**os** resulta**dos** da eleição], todos
left-***MASC-PL*** the.***MASC-PL*** result.***MASC-PL*** of-the election all
foram comemorar.
went celebrate
'Once the results of the election were in, everyone went out to celebrate.'
d. Chega**das** [**as** ferramen**tas**], o Pedro conseguiu
arrived-***FEM-PL*** the.***FEM-PL*** tool.***FEM-PL*** the Pedro managed
resolver o problema.
solve the problem
'Once the tools arrived, Pedro managed to solve the problem.'

The similarities and dissimilarities between EP and BP as far as participial agreement is concerned do not differ from what was described with respect to agreement involving nominal and adjectival predicates (see Section 3.3.1). The only confounding issue is that absolute participial constructions generally have postposed subjects – a possibility also available for passives – and this is a factor that independently inhibits agreement, as will be discussed in Section 3.5.1. Thus, BP differs from EP in that it may allow lack of number agreement in passive constructions with preverbal subjects, as shown in (3.34), and lack of both gender and number agreement in passives with postverbal subjects and participial absolute clauses, as shown in (3.35).[22]

(3.34) a. [**Os** proje**to**] foram arquiva**do**. (%BP)
the.***MASC-PL*** project.***MASC*** were filed-***MASC***
'The projects were filed.'
b. [**As** propos**ta**] foram aprova**da**. (%BP)
the.***FEM-PL*** proposal.***FEM*** were approved-***FEM***
'The proposals were approved.'

(3.35) a. Ainda não foi envia**do** **as** encomen**da**. (%BP)
still not was sent-***MASC*** the.***FEM-PL*** package.***FEM***
'The packages have not been sent yet.'

---

[22] See Simioni 2010, 2011 for a fuller discussion and analysis of these agreement paradigms.

b. Foi cobrad**o** todas as tarifa. (%BP)
   *was charged-**MASC** all-**FEM-PL** the.**FEM-PL** fee.**FEM***
   'All the fees were charged.'
c. Feit**o** [as conta], nós tivemos de cancelar
   *made-**MASC** the.**FEM-PL** calculation.**FEM** we had of cancel*
   o pedido. (%BP)
   the order
   'Once we'd done the sums, we had to cancel the order.'
d. Chegad**o** [as ferramenta], o Pedro conseguiu
   *arrived-**MASC** the.**FEM-PL** tool.**FEM** the Pedro managed*
   resolver o problema. (%BP)
   solve the problem
   'Once the tools arrived, Pedro managed to solve the problem.'

3.3.2.2 Person and Number Agreement

A finite verb or inflected infinitival in both EP and BP as well as inflected gerunds in some Southern and Insular dialects of EP agree in person and number with the syntactic subject of their clause, regardless of whether it is overt or null. Given that syntactic subjects in Portuguese are canonically marked with nominative case and only pronouns can be morphologically distinguished in terms of case (see Section 2.3.4), the differences between EP and BP with respect to person and number agreement should be related to some extent to their specific set of nominative pronouns (see Section 2.5). This is what we will see in the sections that follow.

3.3.2.2.1 Person and Number Agreement in Finite Clauses

Finite clauses constitute the typical configuration where subject–verb agreement surfaces. In Portuguese, finite clauses can be in the indicative, subjunctive, or imperative mood and in all three the verb agrees with its subject in person and number, as respectively illustrated in (3.36).

(3.36) a. Eu não jogo futebol.
   *pron.**1.SG** not play-INDIC.PRES.**1.SG** soccer*
   'I don't play soccer.'
b. Talvez nós poss**amos** viajar amanhã.
   *maybe pron.**1.PL** can-SUBJ.PRES.**1.PL** travel tomorrow*
   'Maybe we can travel tomorrow.'
c. S**ê** breve! (EP)
   *be.IMP.AFIRM.**2.SG** brief*
   'Be brief!'

Putting aside a more detailed discussion of individual tenses for the moment, let us take the indicative present to be representative of the agreement patterns one may find in EP and BP finite clauses. Tables 3.1 and 3.2 below present the different agreement inflections available in each dialect, illustrated with the verb *dançar* 'dance'.

Tables 3.1 and 3.2 show that EP and BP have both lost the nominative second person plural pronoun *vós* (see Section 2.4.2) in tandem with second person plural agreement (e.g., *dançais* 'dance-2.PL').[23] This gap aside, EP displays five possibilities for inflection for person in the indicative present, whereas BP has four.[24] This difference is due to the loss of the

---

[23] As mentioned in Section 2.4.2 (see Chapter 2: footnote 42), some Northern EP dialects have preserved *vós* and the corresponding second person plural agreement, as illustrated in (i).

(i) Alugastes   **vós**   os   quartos.   (%EP)
     rented-2.PL *pron.NOM.2.PL* *the* *rooms*
     'You(PL) rented the rooms. / It was you(PL) who rented the rooms.'
     (CORDIAL-SIN, VPA20)

The CORDIAL-SIN corpus shows that the Central-Southern (see e.g. Cintra 1971 and Segura 2013) and Insular EP dialects have lost *vós* and the second person plural verbal inflection. Northern dialects (see e.g. Cintra 1971 and Segura 2013), on the other hand, display the *vós* series in parallel with the *vocês* series. Within the same group of dialects, we may also find replacement of *vós* by *vocês* associated with second person plural verbal inflection, as illustrated in (ii), as well as variation in the agreement pattern, as exemplified by (iii) (see e.g. Lara Bermejo 2015, 2017 and Selph 2021).

(ii) **Vocês**   andais   a   gastar   dinheiro. (%EP)
      pron.2.NOM-PL   *walk.2.PL* *to* *spend* *money*
      'You(PL) are going around spending your money.'
      (CORDIAL-SIN, COV01)

(iii) **Vocês**   escolhei,   'lei'   as   folhas   como
      you.2.NOM-PL   *choose.2.PL*   *read.2.PL*   *the* *pages*   *as*
      vocês   quiserem,   diante   do   advogado, e
      you.2.NOM-PL   *want-3.PL*   *before*   *of-the* *lawyer* *and*
      vocês   escolhei.
      you.2.NOM-PL   *choose.2.PL*
      'You(PL) decide, "read" the documents as you wish, in the presence of the lawyer, and decide.'
      (CORDIAL-SIN, COV10)

[24] In EP, the first person plural agreement suffix *-mos* must be reduced to *-mo* when it precedes the first person plural clitic *nos* or the third person accusative clitics *o(s)/a(s)*, as shown in (i).

(i) a. Encontrámo-nos   no   cinema.   (EP)
         met-1.PL-pron.1.PL[CL]   *in-the* *cinema*
         'We met at the movies.'
     b. Encontrámo-los   no   cinema.   (EP)
         met-1.PL-pron.3.ACC-PL[CL] *in-the* *cinema*
         'We met them at the movies.'

3.3 Subject–Predicate Agreement

Table 3.1 *Person and number agreement in European Portuguese – finite clauses*

Nominative pronouns	Person and number agreement triggered	Surface forms: *dançar* 'dance' (indicative present)
eu 'I'	1.SG	*danço*
tu 'you(SG)$_{[+close]}$'	2.SG	*danças*
você 'you(SG)$_{[-close]}$'		
ele 'he/it(MASC)' *ela* 'she/it(FEM)'	3.SG	*dança*
a gente 'we'		
nós 'we'	1.PL	*dançamos*
vocês 'you(PL)'		
eles 'they(MASC)' *elas* 'they(FEM)'	3.PL	*dançam*

The second column displays the traditional description of verbal agreement morphology in Portuguese, which will be revised in Section 3.4.2.

Given that BP enforces proclisis on finite verbs (see Section 5.6.2), the rule illustrated in (i) is inapplicable in this variety. However, the ending for first person plural may independently alternate in BP between *-mos* and *-mo*, as illustrated in (ii), with the latter being associated with informal registers.

(ii) a. Nós   saí**mos**   correndo   do   prédio.   (BP)
        pron.1.PL left.1.PL   running   of-the building
    b. Nós   saí**mo**   correndo   do   prédio.   (%BP)
        pron.1.PL left.1.PL   running   of-the building
       'We ran out of the building.'

Although this alternation seems to be tied to the overall underspecification of BP's pronominal system, as will be discussed in Section 3.4.2, the variant *-mo* has a more limited distribution than *-mos*: it is incompatible with some specific tenses, as illustrated in (iii) with the contrast between the indicative perfective past and the subjunctive future (see Nunes 2015b), and more generally, it cannot be associated with tenses whose first person plural form has stress on the antepenultimate syllable, as illustrated in (iv) with the subjunctive imperfective past and the indicative imperfective past.

(iii) a. Quando nós   chega**mos**/chega**mo**,   a   reunião começou.   (%BP)
         when   pron.1.PL arrive.IND.PERF.PAST-1.PL the meeting began
         'When we arrived, the meeting began.'
     b. Quando nós   chegar**mos**/*chegar**mo**, a   festa vai começar. (%BP)
         when   pron.1.PL arrived-SUBJ FUT-1.PL the party goes begin
         'When we arrive, the party will begin.'

78   3 Agreement

Table 3.2 *Person and number agreement in Brazilian Portuguese – finite clauses*

Nominative pronouns	Person and number agreement triggered	Surface forms: *dançar* 'dance' (indicative present)
eu 'I'	1.SG	*danço*
você 'you(SG)' *cê* 'you(SG)_[w]' *ele* 'he/it(MASC)' *ela* 'she/it(FEM)' *a gente* 'we'	3.SG	*dança*
nós 'we'	1.PL	*dançamos*
vocês 'you(PL)' *cês* 'you(PL)_[w]' *eles* 'they(MASC)' *elas* 'they(FEM)'	3.PL	*dançam*

The second column displays the traditional description of verbal agreement morphology in Portuguese, which will be revised in Section 3.4.2.

nominative pronoun *tu* in the grammar of BP (see Section 2.4.2) and its corresponding second person singular agreement (see *danças* in Table 3.1).[25]

At first sight, Tables 3.1 and 3.2 suggest that EP and BP are very similar with respect to person and number agreement. However, a closer look at the

(iv) a. Se   nós   resolvêssemos/*resolvêssemo   o problema,   o
        if   pron.1.PL solve.**SUBF.IMPERF.PAST-1.PL** the problem   the
        professor ia   ficar   surpreso.   (%BP)
        teacher   went   become   surprise
        'If we solved the problem, the teacher would be surprised.'
    b. Nós sempre jantávamos/*jantávamo   naquele restaurante.   (%BP)
        we   always   dine.**IND.IMPERF.PAST-1.PL**   in-that restaurant
        'We always used to have dinner at that restaurant.'

[25] As already mentioned in Section 2.4.2 (see Chapter 2: footnote 40), some BP dialects (dialects of Bahia, Maranhão, Pará, Rio Grande do Sul, and Santa Catarina, for instance) have kept the nominative form *tu*. However, in these dialects *tu* triggers "third person singular agreement," as illustrated in (i), either categorically or in variation with the second person singular agreement.

(i)   O que que tu   **quer**?   (%BP)
       what that pron.2.SG want.**3.SG**
       'What do you want?'

agreement possibilities that are frequently found in nonstandard BP but are rare or simply nonexistent in dialects of EP indicates that the erosion of the ending for first person plural in BP (see footnote 24 above) is only the tip of the iceberg. Recall that although EP and BP both have two series of first person plural pronouns – represented by *nós* and *a gente* – they differ with respect to the status each series enjoys: the *nós* series is the unmarked one in EP, but the marked one in BP (see Section 2.4.1). Some forms of the *nós* series (the accusative and dative clitic *nos* 'us' and the conflated oblique form *conosco* 'with us') have already been replaced by members of the *a gente* series in the grammar of BP (see Table 2.2) and its nominative form seems to be facing a similar fate. And as *a gente* in BP is being used more frequently than *nós* in nominative positions, so is the corresponding "third person singular agreement" it triggers (see Section 3.4.2 for further discussion). In fact, it is not uncommon in nonstandard BP for *nós* to be associated with "third person singular agreement," as illustrated in (3.37) below, in a clear contrast with what one finds in dialectal EP.[26]

(3.37) No final **nós** sempre **acaba** concordando. (%BP)
in-the end pron.1.PL always finish.3.SG agreeing
'In the end we always end up agreeing.'

Also worth mentioning is the fact that the pressure towards third person singular agreement morphology in BP does not exclusively affect *nós*. In nonstandard BP, second person plural and third person plural pronouns may also be associated with third person singular morphology, as illustrated in (3.38), again in clear contrast with EP.[27]

(3.38) a. Vocês não **sabe** o que aconteceu! (%BP)
pron.2-PL not know.3.SG what happened
'You(PL) don't know what happened.'
b. Eles nunca **pensa** em ninguém. (%BP)
pron.3.MASC-PL never know.3.SG in nobody
'They never think about anybody else.'

---

[26] In the CORDIAL-SIN corpus, only a handful of cases resembling (3.37) are attested (see Sória 2013). It is worth noting that in BP the pattern illustrated in (3.37), although very common, is considerably more stigmatized than its alternative with an eroded first person plural agreement as in (i) (see footnote 24 above).

(i) No final nós sempre **acabamo** concordando. (%BP)
in-the end pron.1.PL always finish.1.PL agreeing
'In the end we always end up agreeing.'

[27] For discussion see e.g. Lemle and Naro 1977, Guy 1981, Galves 1993, and Scherre and Duarte 2016.

Table 3.3 *Imperatives in European Portuguese*

Pronoun	Indicative present	Affirmative imperative	Subjunctive present	Negative imperative
tu 'you(SG)$_{[+close]}$'	*danças* →	*dança*	*dances* →	*não dances*
você 'you(SG)$_{[-close]}$'	*dança*	*dance*	← *dance* →	*não dance*
nós 'we'	*dançamos*	*dancemos*	← *dancemos* →	*não dancemos*
vocês 'you(PL)'	*dançam*	*dancem*	← *dancem* →	*não dancem*

Table 3.4 *Imperatives in Brazilian Portuguese*

Pronoun	Indicative present	Affirmative imperative	Subjunctive present	Negative imperative
você 'you(SG)$_{[-close]}$'	*dança* →	*dança/dance*	← *dance* →	*não dance*
nós 'we'	*dançamos*	*dancemos*	← *dancemos* →	*não dancemos*
vocês 'you(PL)'	*dançam*	*dancem*	← *dancem* →	*não dancem*

The loss of the specific verbal agreement inflection associated with *tu* (see footnote 25 above) and *vós* in BP had consequences beyond its agreement system, affecting its imperative mood, as well. To see this, let us first consider the imperative mood in EP. As illustrated with the verb *dançar* 'dance' in Table 3.3 above, the verbal form associated with *tu* in the imperative affirmative is obtained by deleting the /s/ of the corresponding form in the indicative present; all the other forms follow the subjunctive present form.

The main motivation for analyzing the affirmative imperative form *dança* in EP as being derived from the indicative second person singular form *danças* and not from the indicative third person form *dança* is that in the older stages of Portuguese that had the second person plural pronoun *vós* and in the EP dialects that still maintain *vós* or the second person plural agreement inflection (see footnote 23 above), the rule for the derivation of the affirmative imperative form is the same: deletion of /s/ of the second person plural indicative form (e.g. *dançais* 'sing.INDIC.PRES.2.PL' → *dançai* 'sing.AFFIRM.IMP.2.PL').

In BP, on the other hand, there was no underlying form with /s/ to begin with, as the agreement forms associated with *tu* and *vós* had been lost. Informally speaking, what BP did in this situation was to move the arrow in the indicative present column of Table 3.3 one cell down, as shown in Table 3.4. That is, the affirmative imperative form for *você* in BP came to have the possibility of being derived from either the indicative or the subjunctive form, with very interesting idiolectal and geographical variations.[28]

In sum, a simple count of the number of person and number distinctions that EP and BP allow can be very misleading. In EP the five distinctions displayed in Table 3.1 are stable, whereas BP seems to be undergoing a wholesale weakening of its verbal agreement morphology. Thus, in addition to the system with four distinctions for the indicative present listed in Table 3.2, one finds dialects/idiolects with three distinctions (1.SG, 3.SG and 3.PL, with the exclusion of 1.PL) or just two (1.SG and 3.SG). This contrast between EP and BP is at the heart of their differences with respect to subject-to-subject movement and the licensing of null subjects, as we will see in Section 3.4.3 and Chapter 4.

3.3.2.2.2 Person and Number Agreement in Inflected Infinitivals

In addition to ordinary uninflected infinitivals, Portuguese also has inflected infinitivals, which manifest agreement in person and number with the syntactic subject of the clause.[29] Such infinitivals may occur in argument or adjunct positions. When in argument position, they are sensitive to the selectional properties of the matrix predicate. Thus, one may find verbs such as *querer* 'want', which selects only for uninflected infinitives (see (3.39)), and verbs such as *convencer* 'convince', which is compatible with both types (see (3.40)).[30]

(3.39) Os professores querem {**viajar**/*viajarem}.
        the teachers   want-3.PL travel-INF/travel-INF-3.PL
        'The teachers want to travel.'

(3.40) O João convenceu os alunos a {**viajar**/**viajarem**}.
        the João convinced the students to travel-INF/travel-INF-3.PL
        'João convinced the students to travel.'

---

[28] For discussion see e.g. Faraco 1982, 1986, Menon 1984, Scherre 2004, 2007, Cardoso 2006, and Scherre, Cardoso, Lunguinho, and Salles 2007.

[29] On inflected infinitives in Portuguese, see e.g. Maurer Jr. 1968, Raposo 1987a, 1987b, 1989, Ambar 1998, 2000, Mensching 2000, Martins 2001, 2006a, Pires 2006, Modesto 2011, 2016, Barbosa and Raposo 2013, Gonçalves, Santos and Duarte 2014, Duarte, Santos and Gonçalves 2016, Ambar and Fernández-Jiménez 2017, and Barbosa, Flores and Pereira 2018.

[30] The subject of the infinitivals in (3.39) and (3.40) is null and must be interpreted as being coreferential with the subject of the subordinating clause in the case of (3.39) and the object in the case of (3.40) (see Chapter 4: footnote 3). These are known in the generative literature as subject and object control constructions, respectively (see e.g. Chomsky 1981, Chomsky and Lasnik 1993, Hornstein 1999, and Boeckx, Hornstein, and Nunes 2010). There appear to be no cases of subject or object control constructions where the subordinating verb selects only for inflected infinitivals.

As for adjunct clauses, infinitivals are obligatorily inflected if their subject is overt, as in (3.41), and optionally inflected if their subject is null and interpreted as being the same as the subject of the subordinating clause (i.e. if it is a subject control construction; see footnote 30 above), as in (3.42):[31]

(3.41) O professor telefonou antes de [vocês {saírem/*sair}].
the teacher called before of you-PL leave-INF-3.PL/leave-INF
'The teacher called before you(PL) left.'

(3.42) [Os alunos]ᵢ saíram sem [Øᵢ {cumprimentarem/cumprimentar}
the students left-3.PL without greet-INF-3.PL/greet-INF
o João].
the João
'The students left without greeting João.'

Putting aside lexical selection, let us consider the differences between EP and BP with respect to their agreement paradigms for inflected infinitivals (Tables 3.5 and 3.6).

As illustrated in Tables 3.5 and 3.6 below, EP displays four morphological distinctions in inflected infinitivals and BP, three. Again, this difference reflects the loss of the second person singular pronoun *tu* and its corresponding agreement morphology in the grammar of BP (see Section 2.4.2). Besides, EP and BP each have one fewer morphological distinction in inflected infinitivals than in the paradigm for the indicative present (see Section 3.3.2.2.1), for the agreement form triggered by the first person singular pronoun *eu* is never morphologically distinct from the 3.SG form (see *dançar* in Tables 3.5 and 3.6); in fact, they are homophonous with the uninflected form (see Section 4.3.1.2 below for further discussion).

In common with finite clauses (see Section 3.3.2.2.1), a simple comparison between the number of morphological distinctions existing in EP and BP may be deceptive. As the first person plural form *a gente* has replaced *nós* in BP, first plural person agreement also has lost ground to "third person singular agreement," making room for a simple two-way distinction (e.g. 3.SG *dançar* vs. 3.PL *dançarem*).[32] Moreover, as mentioned in Section 3.3.2.2.1, there are

---

[31] See Nunes and Raposo 1997, 1998 and Martins and Nunes 2017c for a discussion of different factors that may favor or require inflected infinitivals in environments of optionality.

[32] Interestingly, the infinitive is one of the verbal forms that prevents deletion of -*s* in the ending corresponding to first person plural (see footnote 24 above), as illustrated in (i) (see Nunes 2015b).

(i) Eles tiveram de insistir para nós {dançarmos/*dançarmo} na festa. (BP)
they had of insist for we dance-INF-1.PL in-the party
'They had to insist in order for us to dance at the party.'

Table 3.5 *Person and number agreement in European Portuguese – inflected infinitives*

Nominative pronouns	Person and number agreement triggered	Surface forms: *dançar* 'dance' (inflected infinitive)
nós 'we'	1.PL	*dançarmos*
tu 'you(SG)$_{[+close]}$'	2.SG	*dançares*
eu 'I'	1.SG	
você 'you(SG)$_{[-close]}$'	3.SG	*dançar*
ele 'he/it(MASC)' *ela* 'she/it(FEM)'		
a gente 'we'		
vocês 'you(PL)'	3.PL	*dançarem*
eles 'they(MASC)' *elas* 'they(FEM)'		

The second column displays the traditional description of verbal agreement morphology in Portuguese, which will be revised in Section 3.4.2.

Table 3.6 *Person and number agreement in Brazilian Portuguese – inflected infinitives*

Nominative pronouns	Person and number agreement triggered	Surface forms: *dançar* 'dance' (inflected infinitive)
nós 'we'	1.PL	*dançarmos*
eu 'I'	1.SG	
você 'you(SG)' *cê* 'you(SG)$_{[w]}$'	3.SG	*dançar*
ele 'he/it(MASC)' *ela* 'she/it(FEM)'		
a gente 'we'		
vocês 'you(PL)' *cês* 'you(PL)$_{[w]}$'	3.PL	*dançarem*
eles 'they(MASC)' *elas* 'they(FEM)'		

The second column displays the traditional description of verbal agreement morphology in Portuguese, which will be revised in Section 3.4.2.

BP dialects where the only distinction made in finite clauses is between 1.SG and 3.SG, that is, all noun phrases but the first person singular pronoun trigger "third person singular agreement" (see (3.37) and (3.38)). Given that 1.SG and 3.SG are not morphologically distinct in infinitivals (not even in EP), these dialects end up allowing a single form to be associated with any person and number combinations, as illustrated in (3.43).[33]

(3.43) Não vai ser fácil [{eu/você/ele/ela/a gente/nós/vocês/eles/elas} **falar**
not goes be easy I/you.SG/he/she/we.3.SG/we.1.PL/you-PL/ speak-INF
they.MASC/they.FEM
disso]. (%BP)
of-this
'It's not going to be easy for {me/you(SG)/him/her/us/you(PL)/them} to talk about this.'

Interestingly, sentences such as (3.44) below are not allowed even in dialects that allow (3.43). Notice that one cannot attribute the ill-formedness of (3.44) in these dialects to the fact that the embedded subject is not associated with plural morphology on the infinitive; otherwise, (3.43) should also be excluded when the pronouns *nós* 'we', *vocês* 'you-PL', and *eles/elas* 'they' are involved.

(3.44) *O João quer [os alunos **viajar**]
the João wants the students travel-INF
'João wants the students to travel.'

Recall that the verb *querer* 'want' in Portuguese selects only for uninflected infinitives (see (3.39)). Assuming that this is also true in dialects that allow (3.43), we are led to the conclusion that the crucial difference between an "uninflected" and an "inflected" infinitive in these dialects is not the realization of verbal agreement morphology, but the ability to license an overt subject. Thus, in these dialects (3.43) counts as inflected and (3.44) as uninflected. Put differently, all dialects of BP behave alike in making a distinction between inflected and uninflected infinitivals, but individual dialects may differ with respect to how many morphological distinctions there are if the infinitive is inflected, varying from three (see Table 3.6) to zero (see (3.43)). Importantly, there is no EP dialect that allows only "inflected infinitivals without inflection," as in (3.43).

The availability of (3.43) in dialects of BP is most certainly related to another salient difference between EP and BP infinitivals (see Section 2.3.4.4), namely, the fact that the latter generally allow instances of exceptional case marking (see Chapter 2: footnote 16) where the subject of an infinitive is assigned oblique case by the preposition *para/pra* 'to/for', as illustrated in (3.45)

---

[33] For discussion and consequences, see e.g. Pires 2006 and Nunes 2015b.

below, whereas in EP this possibility is dialectally restricted (see Chapter 2: footnote 24).³⁴ In other words, in the absence of overt agreement morphology, an infinitival clause in BP may be interpreted as uninflected and its subject can then be case-marked by a preposition selecting the infinitival.

(3.45)   a. O   João trouxe o   documento pra **mim**   assinar. (BP)
             *the   João brought the document   for pron.**OBL.1.SG** sign*
             'João brought the document for me to sign.'
         b. Pra **mim**   acordar cedo, eu preciso dormir bem cedo. (BP)
             *for pron.**OBL.1.SG** wake.up early I   need   sleep   well early*
             'In order for me to wake up early, I need to go to sleep very early.'

In sum, when all subvarieties of EP and BP are taken into consideration, one realizes that their differences go much beyond what is pictured in Tables 3.5 and 3.6. In EP, agreement in inflected infinitivals is as stable as in finite clauses, whereas in BP it is subject to variation across dialects and there are dialects that simply make no overt morphological distinction between inflected and uninflected infinitivals. This overall weakness of agreement within infinitivals in BP has cleared the way for the emergence of exceptional case marking structures (see (3.45)), as well as constructions involving subject-to-subject movement originating in an inflected infinitival, as will be discussed in Section 3.4.3.

3.3.2.2.3 Person and Number Agreement in Inflected Gerunds in Dialectal European Portuguese

Central-Southern and Insular dialects of EP may also display person and number agreement in gerund clauses, as illustrated in (3.46) below, although individual dialects may differ with respect to which combinations of person and number are permitted.³⁵ Table 3.7 below illustrates the paradigm when all forms are realized.

(3.46)   a. Em tu   **querendos!**   (%EP)
             *in   pron.2.SG want-**GER-2.SG***
             'Whenever you(SG) want it!'
                                                                             (CORDIAL-SIN, CBV41)

---

³⁴ For discussion see e.g. Perini 1974, Lightfoot 1991, and Salles 1997. As mentioned in Section 2.4.2 (see Chapter 2: footnote 40), BP dialects that have preserved *tu* (you.SG) may also allow sentences such as (i), with the oblique form *ti* as the subject of the infinitive (see e.g. Hornstein, Martins, and Nunes 2008).

(i)   Eu fiquei quieto pra **ti**   dormir. (%BP)
         *I   stayed quiet   for pron.**OBL.2.SG** sleep*
         'I kept quiet so that you could sleep.'

³⁵ See e.g. Dias Martins 1954, Mota 1997, Lobo 2001, 2003, 2016a, and Ribeiro 2002 for discussion. We will follow the orthographical convention adopted by CORDIAL-SIN to transcribe inflected first person plural gerunds; hence the lack of an accent on the antepenultimate (stressed) syllable in *separandomos* in (3.46b) and similar examples.

Table 3.7 *Person and number agreement in dialectal European Portuguese – inflected gerunds*

Nominative pronouns	Person and number agreement triggered	Surface forms: *dançar* 'dance' (inflected gerund)
eu 'I'	1.SG	
você 'you(SG)*[-close]*'		
ele 'he/it(MASC)' *ela* 'she/it(FEM)'	3.SG	*dançando*
a gente 'we'		
tu 'you(SG)*[+close]*'	2.SG	*dançandos*
nós 'we'	1.PL	*dançandomos*
vocês 'you(PL)'		
eles 'they(MASC)' *elas* 'they(FEM)'	3.PL	*dançandem*

The second column displays the traditional description of verbal agreement morphology in Portuguese, which will be revised in Section 3.4.2.

    b. Mas em se   **separandomos**,   o   senhor pensa numa coisa
        but in REFL$_{CL}$ get-apart-**GER-1.PL** the mister thinks in-a thing
        e   eu penso   noutra.   (%EP)
        and I   think   in-other
        'But when we are apart, you(SG) think one way and I think another.'
                                                                  (CORDIAL-SIN, CPT27)
    c. Em o   **querendem**   levar,   podem-no   levar. (%EP)
        in   it   want-**GER-3.PL** take   can-3.PL-it take
        'You(PL) can take it whenever you(PL) want.'
                                                                 (CORDIAL-SIN, CBV39)

We will leave a discussion of the differences between inflected and uninflected gerunds in these dialects to Section 4.3.4.1. What is relevant for our current purposes is to observe that there is no dialect of BP that displays inflection on gerunds. Thus, although we cannot make a direct comparison between EP and BP with respect to inflected gerunds, their mere existence in dialects of EP but not BP is already very telling. Inflected gerunds in dialects of EP may be seen as the reverse image of BP dialects that allow "inflected infinitivals without inflection" as in (3.43). Put in more general terms, inflected infinitivals without inflection in BP dialects and inflected gerunds in EP dialects are the most transparent illustrations of their opposite tendencies: dialect variation in BP leans towards fewer agreement distinctions, whereas dialect variation in EP in general tends to explore additional combinatory possibilities for the agreement distinctions it has available. The question is, of course, what lies behind these opposite trends.

This is the topic of our next section.

3.4 Reanalyzing the Different Agreement Systems in European Portuguese and Brazilian Portuguese

The grammars of EP and BP appear superficially to be very similar as far as person and number agreement is concerned. At first sight, the only difference is that BP has one fewer morphological distinction than EP: four vs. five distinctions in the indicative present (see Tables 3.1 and 3.2) and three vs. four distinctions in inflected infinitival clauses (see Tables 3.5 and 3.6). However, we have also seen that this simple count of the number of morphological distinctions has been insufficient to account for the fact that there is a lot of dialectal variation in BP, which in general leans towards a great simplification of the agreement paradigm. Thus, the issue is what formal properties exert such pressure towards simplification in BP that do not operate in EP.

There are two salient differences between the grammars of EP and BP that are suggestive in this regard. First, the pronoun *tu* and the corresponding second person singular agreement have been lost in the grammar of BP (see Section 2.4.2). Second, the *a gente* series has acquired unmarked status in BP and its nominative form triggers "third person singular agreement" (see Section 2.4.1). The question is how exactly these facts have interacted so that the agreement system of BP has become substantially unstable, making room for the attested dialectal variation.

Below we propose an account of the agreement differences between EP and BP that is based on two factors: (i) what the feature specification for nominative pronouns is in each variety; and (ii) how the inflection on the verb is to be optimally matched with the features present on nominative pronouns in each variety.

3.4.1 *The Feature Composition of Personal Pronouns and Apparent Agreement Mismatches*

In Chapter 2, when we introduced the pronominal systems of EP and BP, pronouns were glossed according to their semantic features and their morphological specifications (the type of agreement they trigger) were actually represented on the relevant predicate. In doing this, we were following the

Table 3.8 *Feature composition of personal pronouns in Portuguese – traditional analysis*

Nominative pronouns	Person, number, and gender	
	Semantic specification	Morphological specification
eu 'I'	[P:1; N:SG]	[P.N:1.SG]
tu 'you(SG)' (EP)	[P:2; N:SG]	[P.N:2.SG]
você 'you(SG)'	[P:**2**; N:SG]	[P.N:**3**.SG]
ele 'he/it(MASC)'	[P:3; N:SG; (G:MASC)]	[P.N:3.SG; G:MASC]
ela 'she/it(FEM)'	[P:3; N:SG; (G:FEM)]	[P.N:3.SG; G:FEM]
nós 'we'	[P:1; N:PL]	[P.N:1.PL]
a gente 'we'	[P:**1**; N:**PL**]	[P.N:**3.SG**]
vocês 'you(PL)'	[P:**2**; N:PL]	[P.N:**3**.PL]
eles 'they(MASC)'	[P:3; N:PL; (G:MASC)]	[P.N:3.PL; G:MASC]
elas 'they(FEM)'	[P:3; N:PL; (G:FEM)]	[P.N:3.PL; G:FEM]

traditional view on subject–predicate agreement in Portuguese, which encompasses two assumptions: (i) it is (mainly) the morphological specifications of pronouns that determine syntactic agreement on a given predicate; and (ii) the morphological specifications of pronouns need not match their semantic specifications. Under this traditional view, the feature composition of personal pronouns in Portuguese is as depicted in Table 3.8 above (the nominative form is taken to be representative of all case forms).[36]

The first point worth mentioning regarding Table 3.8 is that it subscribes to the standard view that a featural analysis of a given property involves a relation between an attribute (say, person) and a value (say, 1). Here, we will not dwell on the organization of person, number, and gender specifications on the semantics side and simply assume that, for semantic purposes, there exists a list of these specifications associated with the corresponding pronouns. Our attention will instead focus on the morphological organization of these specifications, as they are crucial for syntactic agreement. The third column of Table 3.8 depicts the traditional view according to which the pronouns of the first column have their person and number attributes morphologically fused, as the verbal agreement inflection they are associated with typically has a single

[36] For discussion, see Galves 1993 and Lopes and Rumeu 2007.

3.4 The Different Agreement Systems in EP and BP   89

morpheme to convey the values for both person and number.[37] That said, let us examine in more detail the traditional assumption that the semantic and morphological features of pronouns need not match.

One instance of the lack of correspondence between these types of features depicted in Table 3.8 is somewhat trivial: the presence of morphological gender features on *ele(s)* and *ela(s)* is not necessarily associated with the presence of their semantic counterparts. Recall that morphological gender in Portuguese correlates with biological gender (male vs. female) only when referring to animals (see Section 3.2.1). The fact that *país* 'country' is masculine and *raiz* 'root' is feminine, for instance, is an arbitrary lexical property that is morphologically relevant but devoid of semantic import. Assuming that third person pronouns "inherit" the relevant properties of the noun phrases they are associated with, a third person pronoun will be specified as masculine for both semantic and morphological computations if related to a noun phrase headed by *homem* 'man', for example, but only for morphological computations if related to a noun phrase headed by *país* 'country'. Crucially, the latter possibility does not constitute a real instance of mismatch. It is not the case that the value of one piece of morphological specification (feminine in the case of *raiz*) is different from the value of the corresponding semantic specification, for *raiz* does not have specification for semantic gender to begin with. As far as gender is concerned, the morphological specification of *raiz* is simply richer than its semantic specification.

Once we have made the distinction between presence vs. absence of a given specification, on the one hand, and different values for the same features, on the other, the pronouns *você*, *a gente*, and *vocês* stand out in Table 3.8 as the only ones where semantic and morphological features mismatch: *você* and *vocês* involve a mismatch in person values and *a gente* a mismatch in both person and number values. It is no coincidence that these are the pronouns that seem to display exceptional behavior. Recall that they all originate from former nouns phrases (*Vossa(s) Mercê(s)* 'Your Mercy/Mercies' and *a gente* 'the folk') and entered the language much later than the other pronouns (see Sections 2.4.1 and 2.4.2). Therefore, it is reasonable to think that the exceptional behavior depicted in Table 3.8 is somehow related to the grammaticalization process that reanalyzed *você*, *vocês*, and *a gente* as pronouns. Given that standard nonpronominal noun phrases in Portuguese have values for number but not for person, we may tentatively conjecture that the

---

[37] The story is slightly more complex for third person pronouns, which trigger person and number agreement with finite verbs, inflected infinitivals, and inflected gerunds (see Section 3.3.2.2), but gender and number agreement with participials (see Section 3.3.2.1). For the purposes of this exposition, we will leave this complication aside, as it will be resolved in the ensuing discussion.

grammaticalization of these pronouns involved the assignment of the relevant value to the unvalued person attribute of the original expressions. The question that then arises is why these pronouns, once grammaticalized into the language, ended up triggering "third person agreement."

Appearances can be misleading, though, for the verbal agreement inflections that are traditionally analyzed as encoding third person singular and third person plural are not themselves transparent. Take the verbal forms in (3.47a) and (3.47b) below, for instance. The form *dança* in (3.47a) clearly involves a stem (*danç-*) and a thematic vowel (*-a*) specifying that the verb belongs to the first conjugation, but there is no overt morpheme encoding person or number. Thus, the verbal form in (3.47a) is compatible with two different morphological analyses: as involving a single null fused morpheme (represented by Ø) corresponding to both (third) person and (singular) number, as in (3.47a′), or involving two independent null morphemes, one corresponding to third person and the other to singular number, as in (3.47a″). Accordingly, the morpheme *-m* of *dançam* in (3.47b) may be analyzed as simultaneously encoding (third) person and (plural) number, as (3.47b′), or as encoding just (plural) number in association with a null morpheme encoding (third) person, as in (3.47b″).

(3.47) a. {Ele/ela}   **dança**   bem.
        pron.3.MASC.SG/pron.3-FEM.SG dance-TV-? well
        '{He/she} dances well.'
    a′. danç-a-**Ø**
        dance-TV-[P.N:3.SG]
    a″. danç-a-**Ø-Ø**
        dance-TV-[P:3]-[N:SG]
    b. {Eles/elas}   **dançam**   bem.
        pron.3.MASC-PL/pron.3-FEM-PL dance-TV-? well
        '{They(MASC)/they(FEM)} dance well.'
    b′. danç-a-**m**
        dance-TV-[P.N:3.PL]
    b″. danç-a-**Ø-m**
        dance-TV-[P:3]-[N:PL]

Which is the correct analysis: (3.47a′)/(3.47b′) or (3.47a″)/(3.47b″)? This question is analogous to the zebra problem faced by biologists: are zebras white with black stripes or black with white stripes? In both circumstances, the options under consideration are able to correctly describe the phenomena at an observational level. However, both biologists and linguists are actually looking for the inner forces that interact to yield what we obtain at the observational level; this is by no means a trivial task.

In the linguistic case at hand, the traditional analysis is the one associated with (3.47a′) and (3.47b′), presumably by analogy with the other verbal agreement morphemes, which simultaneously encode person and number; the verbal suffixes -*o*, -*s*, and -*mos* in Table 3.1, for instance, simultaneously encode 1.SG, 2.SG, and 1.PL, respectively. However, the properties of first and second person agreement morphemes by themselves do not provide compelling grounds for subsuming third person agreement under the morphological template of the former. After all, these are associated with unequivocal first and second person pronouns that are themselves monomorphemic. In other words, the person and number features of the pronouns *eu*, *tu*, and *nós* are independently taken to be fused, for they cannot be identified in isolation. By contrast, in the case of third person pronouns *eles* and *elas*, plural is conveyed by an independent morpheme (-*s*), dissociated from person; this morpheme is also independent from gender, as seen in the feminine form *elas*, which clearly has three independent morphemes: the root *el-* encoding third person, the nominal thematic vowel -*a* bearing feminine gender specification, and the suffix -*s* encoding plural number. This invites us to generalize this morphological template to also include the other third person pronouns of Table 3.8 along the following lines: *ele*: [P:3 – G:MASC – N:SG]; *eles*: [P:3 – G:MASC – N:PL]; and *ela*: [P:3 – G:FEM – N:SG]. Now, if the morphological organization of verbal agreement morphemes should in principle mirror the morphological organization of the elements they agree with, as seen above with respect to first and second persons, third person agreement inflection should be independent of number, as in (3.47a″) and (3.47b″), and not fused with it, as in (3.47a′) and (3.47b′).

Interesting evidence for taking the suffix -*m* in (3.47b) as encoding only plural and not third person plural as standardly assumed is provided by the EP data in (3.48)–(3.50).[38]

(3.48) a. O João ouviu **tu** chegares. (EP)
the João heard pron.*NOM.2.SG* arrive-INF-*2.SG*
b. O João ouviu-**te** chegar. (EP)
the João heard-pron.*ACC.2.SG* arrive-INF
c. *O João ouviu-**te** chegares. (EP)
the João heard-pron.*ACC.2.SG* arrive-INF-*2.SG*
'João heard you(SG) arrive.'

(3.49) a. O João ouviu **nós** chegarmos.
the João heard pron.*NOM.1.PL* arrive-INF-*1.PL*
b. O João ouviu-**nos** chegar. (EP)
the João heard-pron.*ACC.1.PL* arrive-INF
c. *O João ouviu-**nos** chegarmos. (EP)
the João heard-pron.*ACC.1.PL* arrive-INF-*1.PL*
'João heard us arrive.'

---

[38] See Hornstein, Martins, and Nunes 2006, 2008 for discussion.

(3.50) a. O   João ouviu   **eles**   **chegarem**
           *the João heard   pron.**NOM.3.MASC-PL**   arrive-INF-3-PL*
        b. O   João ouviu-**os**   chegar   (EP)
           *the João heard-pron.**ACC.3.MASC-PL**   arrive-INF*
        c. O   João ouviu-**os**   chegarem   (%EP)
           *the João heard-pron.**ACC.3.MASC-PL**   arrive-INF-3-PL*
           'João heard them arrive.'

Perception and causative verbs in Portuguese can select for inflected or uninflected infinitives. When an inflected infinitive is selected, its subject is accordingly marked with nominative case, as illustrated in (3.48a), (3.49a), and (3.50a). In turn, when an uninflected infinitive is selected, the embedded subject is assigned accusative case by the matrix verb, as exemplified by (3.48b), (3.49b), and (3.50b) (see Section 2.3.4.2), because an uninflected infinitive is unable to assign case to its subject. Given this background, the contrast between (3.48c) and (3.49c), on the one hand, and (3.50c), on the other, is rather unexpected. If the infinitive is inflected, its subject should be marked as nominative and accusative case assignment by the matrix verb should be blocked. This accounts for the ungrammaticality of (3.48c) and (3.49c) for all speakers and of (3.50c) for some speakers. The question is why some EP speakers allow (3.50c) or, to restate the problem more clearly, why the inflected infinitive in (3.50c) does not automatically license nominative case in the grammar of these speakers.

In this regard, two points are worth noting. First, person is arguably the agreement feature of inflected infinitivals that is responsible for nominative case assignment.[39] As we have seen, finite verbs in both EP and BP and inflected gerunds in some dialects of EP (see Section 3.3.2.2.3) inflect for person, and nominative is licensed within their clauses (see Section 2.3.4.1); conversely, participial verbs in passives inflect for gender and number but not person (see Section 3.3.2.1) and their inflection does not independently license nominative. Second, the infinitive has been traditionally analyzed as a "nominal form" of the verb, for infinitival clauses generally have the distribution of noun phrases. Thus, it would not be surprising if some infinitivals lacked the feature [person], for noun phrases do not display values for the feature person (see Section 4.3.2 for related discussion). With these two observations in mind, we can now understand what is going on in sentences like (3.50c). Its infinitive can be analyzed either as a standard inflected infinitive bearing the features [person] and [number], as represented in (3.51a) below, or as a defective personless inflected infinitive, bearing only number,

---

[39] In Chomsky's (2000, 2001) Agree-based system, for example, this amounts to saying that person is the feature that allows the φ-set of a Tense head to count as complete and value a case feature as nominative.

3.4 The Different Agreement Systems in EP and BP 93

as represented in (3.51b) (see footnote 39 above). For speakers who analyze *chegarem* as involving only a standard inflected infinitive (see (3.51a)), the embedded subject must be assigned nominative case; hence, an accusative clitic as the subject of an inflected infinitival will be uniformly ruled out in the grammar of these speakers, regardless of which clitic is involved. In contrast, for speakers who allow *chegarem* to be analyzed as involving just plural, as in (3.51b), the infinitive will be unable to assign case to the embedded subject if so specified. The embedded subject must then be licensed with accusative case by the matrix verb; hence the grammaticality of (3.50c) for these speakers. Crucially, this potential ambiguity arises for *chegarem* in (3.50c) but not for *chegares* (see (3.48c)) or *chegarmos* (see (3.49c)), whose person and number features are fused and associated with a single morpheme.

(3.51) a. *O João ouviu-os   chegare-Ø-m   (EP)
           the João heard-pron.ACC.3.MASC-PL arrive-INF-3-PL
        b. O João ouviu-os   chegare-m   (%EP)
           the João heard-pron.ACC.3.MASC-PL arrive-INF-PL
           'João heard them arrive.'

Note that this account of the contrast between (3.48c) and (3.49c), on the one hand, and (3.50c), on the other, holds only if person and number verbal inflection are each associated with a different morpheme when third person is at stake, mirroring what we have seen with the third person pronouns *ele/eles/ela/elas*. This implies that the most adequate analysis of (3.47a) and (3.47b) is indeed the one in terms of (3.47a″) and (3.47b″), as represented in (3.52).

(3.52) a. {Ele/ela}   danç-a-Ø-Ø   bem
           pron.3-MASC-SG/pron.3-FEM-SG   dance-TV-3-SG well
           '{He/she} dances well.'
        b. {Eles/elas}   danç-a-Ø-m   bem
           pron.3-MASC-PL/pron.3-FEM-PL   dance-TV-3-PL well
           '{They(MASC)/they(FEM)} dance well.'

Let us now return to the original question that initiated this whole discussion of the morphological organization of person and number in the verbal agreement inflection when third person is involved: why do the pronouns *você*, *vocês*, and *a gente* trigger third person agreement on verbs? Consider *você* and *vocês*, first. Here we have a morphologically transparent case of singular/plural alternation by means of addition of the plural morpheme *-s*. If *-s* clearly marks number, it must be the case that *você-* encodes person. The traditional analysis is that, for morphological purposes, the value of this person attribute should be 3 rather than 2. There are two tacit reasons for why this has been the canonical way to describe verbal agreement with *você/vocês* in Portuguese. The first, already mentioned, is that the surface forms of verbs agreeing with *você/vocês* are the same as those associated with the indisputable third person pronouns *ele/eles* in both EP and BP. The second reason is that, in EP, the combination of 2 plus SG in the case of *você* should be associated with the second person singular agreeing morpheme *-s* (see Table 3.1) and this does not happen. There is no dialect in EP that admits (3.53) below, for instance.

(3.53) *Você cantas muito bem.
you.SG$_{[-close]}$ sing-TV-2.SG very well
'You(SG) sing very well.'

Although reasonable, neither of these motivations is compelling. First of all, the paradigm of the *vocês* series in EP has retained elements of the old second person plural *vós* series (see Section 2.4.2), as illustrated in (3.54) below. This indicates that at least the combination of 2 and PL is independently found in EP. In fact, in some of the EP dialects that preserved the old second person plural morpheme *-is* (see Section 2.4.2), it may be associated with *vocês*, as illustrated in (3.55) (see footnote 23 above).

(3.54) a. Eu asseguro-**vos** que eles não convenceram o
       I   assure-pron.DAT.2.PL that they not convinced the
       vosso   chefe.   (EP)
       pron.GEN.2.PL boss
       'I assure you(PL) that they didn't convince your(PL) boss.'
    b. A Maria vai **convosco**.   (EP)
       the Maria goes with.pron.2.PL
       'Maria will go with you(PL).'

(3.55) **Vocês** andais a gastar dinheiro.   (%EP)
       you-PL walk.**2.PL** to spend money
       'You(PL) are going around spending your money.'
                                          (CORDIAL-SIN, COV01)

As for the ungrammaticality of (3.53) in EP, recall that /s/ is the phonological realization of a morpheme with the specifications for person and number fused ([P.N:2.SG]), reflecting the fusion of these features on the pronoun *tu*. On the other hand, the regular alternation *você/vocês* clearly shows that in this case number is independent from person. Hence, one is not forced to assume that the autonomous specifications 2 and SG on *você* ([P:2 – N:SG]) should necessarily be associated with a fused agreement morpheme. Observe that the specification [N:SG], which is not phonetically realized, is independently motivated by the alternation *ela/elas*, for instance (see (3.52)). Thus, everything should work perfectly well if the independent specification [P:2] patterns like [P:3] in not being assigned an overt phonological exponent. To put it differently, these specifications should fall under the Elsewhere Condition for the phonetic realization of verbal agreement inflection.[40] In the case of the indicative present tense, for example, one could have the correspondence rules in (3.56) below for EP and the Elsewhere Condition in (3.56b) would assign no phonological realization to specifications different from the ones listed in (3.56a). That being so, BP would differ from EP only in not having the rule *[P.N:2.SG] ↔ {-s}*.[41]

(3.56)   Correspondence rules for the morphological realization of verbal agreement inflection in the indicative present in EP:
  a. [P.N:1.SG]   ↔   {-o}
     [P.N:2.SG]   ↔   {-s}
     [P.N:1.PL]   ↔   {-mos}
     [N:PL]   ↔   {-m}
  b. Ø elsewhere

According to (3.56), the sentences in (3.57) below should be completely parallel to those of (3.52), with 2 in place of 3. The specification [N:PL] of the verbal inflection (3.57b) is associated with the morpheme {-m} (see (3.56a)) and all the remaining person and number specifications of the agreement inflection of (3.57a) and (3.57b) are assigned no phonological content, in accordance with the Elsewhere Condition in (3.56b). If this is so, it is not the case that the morphological specification of *você/vocês* mismatches their semantic value for person. Both their semantic and morphological person specifications are valued as 2. The fact that the verbal agreement inflection associated with *você* and *vocês* is the same as that associated with third person pronouns is interpreted as a superficial by-product of the Elsewhere Condition in (3.56b).

(3.57)   a. Você   danç-a-Ø-Ø   bem
            pron.[P:2]-[N:SG] dance-TV-[P:2]-[N:SG] well
            'You(SG) dance well.'
         b. Vocês   danç-a-Ø-m   bem.
            pron.[P:2]-[N:PL] dance-TV-[P:2]-[N:PL] well
            'You(PL) dance well.'

Let us now examine the case of *a gente*, starting by its number specification. Following the standard analysis, *a gente* in Table 3.8 is analyzed as being semantically plural, but morphologically singular. Again, appearances may be misleading. It is true that *a gente* does not have a plural morphological counterpart. It is also true that the verbal agreement inflection associated with

---

[40] See e.g. Kiparsky 1973.
[41] We are using the term *correspondence rule* in the sense of Distributed Morphology (see e.g. Halle and Marantz 1993), according to which the pieces of morphological information provided by the syntactic component are assigned phonetic outputs (the phonetic "exponents") in the morphological component.

a gente is superficially the same as that associated with *ele/ela* and *você*, which are analyzed as being specified as singular. There is however an alternative analysis of the number specification of *a gente* that captures the verbal agreement forms it is associated with without inducing a mismatch between its semantic and morphological specifications for number. Given that *a gente* does not have a morphological counterpart to participate in the singular–plural alternation as in *eu/nós, você/vocês, ele/eles*, suppose that *a gente* is morphologically neutral with respect to this distinction. More specifically, suppose that *a gente* has a number attribute without a value ([N]). That being so, consider the representation of the number specifications of a sentence such as (3.58) (leaving aside the representation of person for the moment).

(3.58) A gente   danç-a-Ø   bem
         pron.*[N]* dance-TV-*[N:u]* well
         'We dance well.'

In (3.58), the number feature of the agreement inflection should have its value determined by the value of the number feature of the subject. However, given that the number attribute of *a gente* does not have a value, the number specification of the agreement inflection remains unvalued (represented by *u*). Notice now that the specification [N:u] falls under the Elsewhere Condition in (3.56b) and is assigned no phonetic content. As far as number is concerned, the verb then surfaces with the same form as that associated with *ele/ela* and *você* (see (3.52a) and (3.57a)). If this proposal is on the right track, it is not really the case the morphological specification for number of *a gente* ([N]) mismatches its semantic specification ([N:PL]). It is simply the case that the semantic specification of number for *a gente* is richer than its morphological specification.

There is in fact independent evidence from EP that shows that the morphological number specification of *a gente* does not have a value. Recall that the fact that *a gente* is not specified for gender allows it to be compatible with both masculine and feminine agreement on the predicate, depending on the gender of the members of the group it refers to (see Section 2.4.1), as illustrated in (3.59).

(3.59) a. A gente   chegou   esfomead**o**.   (EP/BP)
            pron.*[N]* arrived starving-***MASC***-*N:u*
         b. A gente   chegou   esfomead**a**.   (EP/BP)
            pron.*[N]* arrived starving-***FEM***-*N:u*
            'We arrived starving.'

Interestingly, *a gente* is also compatible with plural on the embedded predicate in EP, as illustrated in (3.60).

3.4 The Different Agreement Systems in EP and BP

(3.60)   a. A gente chegou esfomeados.   (EP/*BP)
pron.[N] arrived starving-MASC-PL
b. A gente chegou esfomeadas.   (EP/*BP)
pron.[N] arrived starving-FEM-PL
'We arrived starving.'

If the morphological specification of number for *a gente* does not have a value, as conjectured above, it is not surprising that it can be compatible with plural. Notice that in (3.59) and (3.60), EP and BP display a similar behavior with respect to gender but not with respect to number. However, this is not something new. Recall that EP and BP diverge with respect to agreement within nouns phrases along the same lines: gender agreement is mandatory for both EP and BP, but the realization of plural is not always enforced in BP (see Section 3.2). In the case at hand, there is no morphological triggering force for plural specification on the adjectival predicate, for the morphological number specification of *a gente* does not have a value; hence, plural is simply blocked in BP. As for EP, the number feature on the adjectival predicate may be valued by the semantic number specification of *a gente*, namely, [N:PL].

Let us now examine the morphological specification of person for *a gente*. The traditional view, summarized in Table 3.8, is that the person feature of *a gente* is semantically valued as 1, but morphologically valued as 3. Again, the reason for this position is that the surface form of verbs agreeing with *a gente* does not differ from the surface form of verbs agreeing with *ele/ela*. We have seen above that this is a very weak reason for supporting such a mismatch. Notice that in the case of *você/vocês*, we can make the case that there is morphological evidence that these pronouns are morphologically specified as 2. In EP, the forms *você* 'you.SG', *vos* 'you.ACC/DAT.PL', *vosso* 'you.GEN.PL-MASC.SG', and *convosco* 'with you-PL' (see (3.54)) are all morphologically related and all refer to the addressee. This strongly suggests that they have maintained the second person specification of the old form *vós*. In BP, the last three forms have been lost (see Section 2.4.2), but the fact that *você* has replaced *tu* suggests that it could also be specified as 2 (but see Section 3.4.2). In the case of *a gente*, on the other hand, there is no comparable morphological clue that could identify it as morphologically bearing [P:1] to match its meaning or [P:3] to match the surface agreement it is associated with. Moreover, the surface agreement morphology for person associated with *a gente* is not a reliable diagnostic either, as it may result from an Elsewhere Condition computation (see (3.56b)). Let us then assume that, as in the case of number, the morphological person specification of *a gente* does not have a value either ([P]). Finally, the fact that *a gente* cannot be associated with the plural morpheme *-s* indicates that its person and number features are fused. That being so, *a gente* should bear the specification [P.N].

Independent evidence supporting this conclusion is found in different dialects of EP, where *a gente* can double the first person plural pronoun *nós* (see Chapter 2: footnote 33) or form a double subject construction with the indefinite clitic *se*, as illustrated in (3.61) below.[42] Under the assumption that in both constructions there must be some form of agreement/compatibility between the elements in boldface, it is arguably the absence of value for person and number in the morphological specification of *a gente* that makes it morphologically compatible with different pronouns.

(3.61)   a. Eles chamam-**nos**   **à gente**   sarracenos. (%EP)
           they call-pron.1.PL_[CL]   *to-pron.[P.N]*   *Saracen*
           'They call us Saracen.'
                                         (CRPC, cited in Bacelar do Nascimento 1989)
   b. Chama-**se**-lhe   **a gente**   espigas.   (%EP)
           *call-3-SG-**SE**-it.DAT*   *pron.[P.N]*   *spikes*
           'We call them spikes.'
                                                    (CORDIAL-SIN, AAL03)

If *a gente* is specified as [P.N], we must now determine whether the corresponding verbal agreement morphology also has its person and features fused ([P.N:u]), whether these features are independent ([P:u-N:u]), or whether these two possibilities may be resorted to, but have their origins in different reasons. This particular issue is related to the more general question of when agreement features should undergo fusion. We have already seen that the morphological organization of agreement features generally mirrors the morphological organization of the expressions they agree with. For instance, person and number agreement features are fused in Portuguese when they agree with the pronoun *nós*, which has the corresponding features fused (see (3.49a)), but not when they agree with *elas* (see (3.52b)), whose person and number features are morphologically independent from one another. This should in principle lead us to expect the agreement inflection associated with *a gente* to have its person and number features fused, mimicking the morphological organization of these features on the pronoun. There is a difference between *nós* and *a gente*, though. Descriptively speaking, the person and number features of the agreement inflection associated with *nós* are pressed into undergoing fusion in order to comply with the correspondence rule *{-mos}* ↔ *[P.N:1.PL]* in (3.56a); in other words, a single phonetic realization encompasses more than one piece of morphological information. By contrast, no such pressure is at work with *a gente*, for its agreement inflection falls under the Elsewhere Condition in (3.56b) and it is not assigned a phonetic exponent; in other words, whether or

---

[42] See Martins 2009 and footnote 75 below for discussion.

3.4 The Different Agreement Systems in EP and BP

not fusion takes place ([P.N:u] or [P:u-N:u]), the agreement inflection associated with *a gente* is not phonetically realized.

There is in fact evidence suggesting that fusion may be seen as a last resort operation that applies only when it is independently required. The evidence involves two patterns of semantic agreement found in different dialects. The first is mainly found in Azorean dialects of EP and involves *a gente* associated with ("third person") plural verbal agreement, as illustrated in (3.62) below.[43] From the perspective taken here, (3.62) should be seen as a case of agreement between the number feature of the agreement inflection and the semantic number specification of *a gente* ([N:PL]). Crucially, it must be the case that this pattern of agreement involves independent person and number features on the agreement inflection, as annotated by the gloss of (3.62) for, otherwise, semantic agreement affecting the person feature of the agreement inflection should value it as 1.

(3.62) Que **a gente** tosquia**vam** as ovelhas duas vezes no
 that pron.*[P.N]* shear-*[P:u]*-*[N:PL]* the sheep two time in-the
 ano. (%EP)
 year
 'Because we used to shear the sheep twice a year.'
 (CORDIAL-SIN, MIG58)

The other pattern, registered in dialects of both EP and BP, displays full agreement in person and number with the semantic specification of *a gente*. Unsurprisingly, the verb surfaces with first person plural morphology (see Chapter 2: footnote 32), as illustrated in (3.63), with person and number fused in order to comply with the correspondence rule *[P.N:1.PL]* ↔ *{-mos}* in (3.56a).[44]

---

[43] See Pereira 2003, Carrilho and Pereira 2009, and Costa and Pereira 2012, 2013 for discussion.

[44] In EP, first person plural agreement with *a gente* can be found with the finite forms of the verb, with inflected infinitivals, and with inflected gerunds in Central-Southern dialects (see Section 3.3.2.2.3), as respectively illustrated in (i)–(iii).

(i) Agora estes rapazes novos não sabem aquilo que **a gente** pass**ámos**. (%EP)
 now these boys new not know that that pron.*[P.N]* passed-*1.PL*
 'These youngsters have no idea of all we've been through.'
 (CORDIAL-SIN, CLC15)

(ii) E então, é muito natural **a gente** a conviver**mos** com os outros aqui.
 and then is very natural pron.*[P.N]* to live.together-INF-*1.PL* with the others here
 no campo, pois a gente não sabe muitas das vezes quase nada. (%EP)
 in-the field for pron.*[P.N]* not know many of-the times almost nothing
 'So, it's very natural for us to live together with the others here in the countryside, for most of the times we know almost nothing.'
 (CORDIAL-SIN, PAL20)

(iii) estando**mos** **a gente** a falar (%EP)
 be-GER-*1.PL* pron.*[P.N]* to talk
 'this is just us talking' [parenthetical]
 (CORDIAL-SIN, CBV41)

(3.63)   A gente   dançamos   bem.   (%EP; %BP)
         pron.[P.N] dance-TV-[P.N:1.PL] well
         'We dance well.'

We will thus proceed under the assumption that the person and number features of agreement inflection will undergo fusion only if independently triggered by the correspondence rules for the realization of morphological inflection. The representation of (3.58) should thus be updated as in (3.64).

(3.64)   A gente   danç-a-Ø-Ø   bem
         pron.[P.N] dance-TV-[P:u]-[N:u] well
         'We dance well.'

In (3.64), the person feature of the agreement inflection cannot receive a specific value from the subject, because the morphological person specification for *a gente* does not have a value. The person specification of the agreement inflection then remains unvalued ([P:u]). As such, it falls under the Elsewhere Condition in (3.56b) and receives no phonological exponent, giving the impression that *a gente* is triggering third person agreement.[45] Again, this is not a case of morphology–semantics mismatch; the semantic specification for person of *a gente* is simply richer than its morphological counterpart in that it has a value associated with it.

Table 3.9 below summarizes the revised morphological specifications for Portuguese pronouns proposed above.

Regardless of whether this pattern of agreement is obligatory or optional for individual EP speakers, when it is employed an associated adjectival predicate must also be plural, as shown in (iii) below (see e.g. Costa and Pereira 2012, 2013 for discussion). In contrast, BP speakers that allow *a gente* with first person plural verbal inflection (see Chapter 2: footnote 32) accept both possibilities in (iii). The additional possibility in (iiib) in these dialects of BP is arguably related to the fact that in BP the realization of plural need not be enforced on adjectival predicates (see Section 3.3.1).

(iii)   a. A gente   estamos   cansados.   (%EP: OK; %BP: OK)
           pron[P.N] be.PRES-1.PL tired-MASC-PL
        b. A gente   estamos   cansado.   (%EP: *; %BP: OK)
           pron[P.N] be.PRES-1.PL tired-MASC-N:u
           'We are tired.'

[45] If nominative case assignment is a by-product of an Agree relation between the subject and the verbal inflection, as proposed by Chomsky (2000, 2001), there arises the question of how *a gente* in (3.64), for instance, is licensed with nominative case despite the fact that it does not have values for its person and number specifications. We assume here that the matching between the person and number attributes of *a gente* and the corresponding attributes of the inflection suffices to license case valuation. Thanks to Andrés Saab (p.c.) for bringing this issue to our attention.

Table 3.9 *Feature composition of personal pronouns in Portuguese – eliminating feature mismatch (subject to revision in Table 3.12)*

Nominative pronouns	Person, number, and gender	
	Semantic specification	Morphological specification
eu 'I'	[P:1; N:SG]	[P.N:1.SG]
tu 'you(SG)' (EP)	[P:2; N:SG]	[P.N:2.SG]
você 'you(SG)'	[P:2; N:SG]	[**P:2**-N:SG]
ele 'he/it(MASC)'	[P:3; (G:MASC); N:SG]	[P:3-G:MASC-N:SG]
ela 'she/it(FEM)'	[P:3; (G:FEM); N:SG]	[P:3-G:FEM-N:SG]
nós 'we'	[P:1; N:PL]	[P.N:1.PL]
a gente 'we'	[P:1; N:PL]	[**P.N**]
vocês 'you(PL)'	[P:2; N:PL]	[**P:2**-N:PL]
eles 'they(MASC)'	[P:3; (G:MASC); N:PL]	[P:3-G:MASC-N:PL]
elas 'they(FEM)'	[P:3; (G:FEM); N:PL]	[P:3-G:FEM-N:PL]

According to Table 3.9, *a gente* involves a case where the pronoun is more specified semantically than morphologically (with respect to both person and number), whereas *ele(s)* and *ela(s)* illustrate the case where the pronouns may be more specified morphologically than semantically (with respect to gender). But there are no cases in Table 3.9 where the morphological information mismatches the semantic information. In particular, if the morphological specification of the pronouns *você*, *vocês*, and *a gente* is as in Table 3.9 and not as in Table 3.8, the traditional description – according to which *você* and *a gente* trigger third person singular agreement and *vocês* third person plural agreement – is simply incorrect. It just happens that the verbal agreement specifications [P:3], [P:2], [P:u], [N:SG], and [N:u] associated with these pronouns all fall under the Elsewhere Condition in (3.56b) and receive no phonetic content. Thus, the agreement mismatch ascribed to these pronouns is just an illusion conjured up by the opacity of surface verbal forms traditionally described as involving third person agreement.

That being so, we can considerably simplify the traditional account of subject–predicate agreement in Portuguese by retaining only the assumption that subject–predicate agreement involving personal pronouns in Portuguese is (mainly) determined by their morphological properties and dropping the assumption that the morphological specifications of pronouns may mismatch their semantic specifications.

102   3 Agreement

Now that the apparent mismatch problems have been dealt with, in the next section we discuss specific differences between EP and BP regarding the feature specification of their pronouns that arguably underlie some of their key syntactic differences.

3.4.2 The Feature Composition of Personal Pronouns and Syntactic Agreement

Let us take stock, bearing in mind the feature composition of Portuguese personal pronouns discussed in Section 3.4.1 (see Table 3.9).

The loss of the second person plural pronoun *vós* and the grammaticalization of *você(s)* and *a gente* as personal pronouns has not had a great impact in EP (see Section 2.5). As far as the morphological specifications for person and number are concerned, the feature [person] continues to have three possible values (1, 2, or 3), which can then combine with the two values for the feature [number] (SG or PL) and yield a paradigm with up to five verbal distinctions in finite domains and four in inflected infinitivals, as illustrated in Table 3.10 below, with the relevant correspondence rules given in (3.65).

(3.65) *Correspondence rules for the morphological realization of verbal agreement inflection in EP:*
   a. [P.N:1.PL] ↔ {-mos}
      [N:PL]   ↔ {-m}
   b. [P.N:1.SG] → {-o} / INDIC.PRES __
                  → {-i} elsewhere
   c. [P.N:2.SG] → {-ste} / INDIC.PERF.PAST __
                  → {-s} elsewhere
   d. Ø elsewhere

The first three finite tenses in Table 3.10 are the only ones that have a specific verbal agreement inflection for first person singular in EP. The other tenses, represented in Table 3.10 by the indicative imperfective past, behave like inflected infinitivals in that the pronoun *eu* is apparently associated with third person singular agreement, as exemplified in (3.66), with the indicative imperfective past and the subjunctive present, respectively.

(3.66) a. {**Eu**/você/ele/a gente}   **dançava**   bastante
           *I/you.SG/he/pron.[P.N] dance-**INDIC.IMPERF.PAST** a.lot*
           naquela   época.
           in-that   time
           '{I/you(SG)/he/we} used to dance a lot at that time.'

Table 3.10 *Morphological specifications for personal pronouns and verbal agreement in European Portuguese*

Personal pronouns		Verbal inflection				
		Surface forms: *dançar* 'dance'				
Nominative form	Morphological specification	Indicative present	Indicative perfective past	Indicative future	Indicative imperfective past	Inflected infinitive
eu 'I'	[P.N:1.SG]	*danço*	*dancei*	*dançarei*	*dançava*	*dançar*
você 'you(SG)'	[P:2-N:SG]	*dança*	*dançou*	*dançará*	*dançava*	*dançar*
ele 'he/it(MASC)'	[P:3-G:MASC-N:SG]	*dança*	*dançou*	*dançará*	*dançava*	*dançar*
ela 'she/it(FEM)'	[P:3-G:FEM-N:SG]	*dança*	*dançou*	*dançará*	*dançava*	*dançar*
a gente 'we'	[P.N]	*dança*	*dançou*	*dançará*	*dançava*	*dançar*
tu 'you(SG)'	[P.N:2.SG]	*danças*	*dançaste*	*dançarás*	*dançavas*	*dançares*
nós 'we'	[P.N:1.PL]	*dançamos*	*dançamos*	*dançaremos*	*dançávamos*	*dançarmos*
vocês 'you(PL)'	[P:2-N:PL]	*dançam*	*dançaram*	*dançarão*	*dançavam*	*dançarem*
eles 'they(MASC)'	[P:3-G:MASC-N:PL]	*dançam*	*dançaram*	*dançarão*	*dançavam*	*dançarem*
elas 'they(FEM)'	[P:3-G:FEM-N:PL]	*dançam*	*dançaram*	*dançarão*	*dançavam*	*dançarem*

b. A   Maria quer que {**eu**/você/ele/a gente}   **dance**
   *the   Maria wants that I/you.SG/he/pron.[P.N] dance-**SUBJ.PRES***
   bastante.
   a.lot
   'Maria wants {me/you(SG)/him/us} to dance a lot.'

As will be discussed in more detail in Section 4.3.1.1, these defective tenses involve morphological impoverishment, that is, a case of feature deletion triggered by a given morphological context.[46] In the case at hand, the tenses represented by the indicative imperfective past in Table 3.10 trigger deletion of either the person or the number specification of the agreement inflection associated with *eu* (before these features undergo fusion). Leaving the discussion of which feature is actually deleted to Section 4.3.1.1, notice that the result of deleting either [P:1] or [N:SG] of the agreement inflection associated with *eu* falls under the Elsewhere Condition in (3.65d) and is assigned no phonetic content. This is what gives the impression that, in these tenses, *eu* triggers third person singular agreement. Given that the tenses that undergo impoverishment are not relevant for the correspondence rule in (3.65b), its formulation amounts to saying that {-o} is the morpheme that corresponds to the agreement specification [P.N:1.SG] in the present tense and {-i} in the other tenses that have this agreement specification, namely, the indicative perfective past and the indicative future.

In BP, the finite tenses that have a specific morpheme for first person singular have become restricted to the indicative present and the indicative perfective past. The indicative future seen in Table 3.10 in EP has been replaced in BP by the periphrastic future (a form that also exists in EP), which is formed by the present tense of the auxiliary *ir* 'go' and an uninflected infinitival (e.g. *vou dançar* 'go.1SG dance-INF'). In addition to the changes in the pronominal system mentioned above and the loss of the indicative future, BP has undergone two additional changes that have contributed to reducing the number of verbal agreement distinctions even further: the pronoun *tu* and the corresponding second person singular agreement have been lost (see Section 2.4.2), and *a gente* has become the canonical form for encoding a semantically first person plural pronoun (see Section 2.4.1). Finally, dialectal variation in BP also generally leans towards additional simplification of the paradigm, as illustrated in (3.37), (3.38), and (3.43), repeated below in (3.67) (see also footnote 25 above).

(3.67)   a. No   final **nós**   sempre **acaba**   concordando.   (%BP)
   *in-the end pron.**1.PL** always finish-**3.SG** agreeing*
   'In the end we always end up agreeing.'

---

[46] On the notion of morphological impoverishment, see e.g. Bonet 1991.

b. Vocês   não **sabe**   o que aconteceu!   (%BP)
    pron.2-PL not know.3.SG what happened
c. Eles   nunca **pensa**   em ninguém.   (%BP)
    pron.3.MASC-PL never know.3.SG in nobody
d. Não   vai ser fácil [{eu/você/ele/ela/a gente/nós/vocês/eles/elas}
    *not   goes be easy I/you.SG/he/she/we.[P.N]/we.1.PL/you-PL/
                                                they.MASC/they.FEM*
    fazer isso]   (%BP)
    do-INF this
    'It's not going to be easy for {me/you(SG)/him/her/us/you(PL)/them}
    to do this.'

The combination of all these factors has certainly had a drastic effect on the agreement system of BP. However, when we compare EP and BP with respect to the number of morphological distinctions for their verbal agreement inflection, we find that BP has only one agreement distinction fewer than EP (the agreement associated with *tu*) and this does not seem to provide sufficient grounds for deriving their general agreement differences or their different behavior with respect to null subject licensing (see Chapter 4). We believe that the lack of a truly explanatory account of these substantial differences between the two varieties stems from the tacit assumption that the morphological specifications of BP pronouns essentially correspond to those of their EP counterparts (see Table 3.9). If BP pronouns had the same attributes and values as their EP counterparts, they should behave in the same way in determining the values of the features of verbal agreement inflection and their general agreement systems should be completely parallel. Given that this is not the case, let us then consider a different approach.

Suppose that the weaker nature of the verbal agreement system in BP is actually a reflex of a wholesale feature underspecification in its pronominal system.[47] Take, for instance, the EP pronouns with fused person and number features in Table 3.10 (*eu*, *tu*, and *nós*). The values for person and number are both necessary to properly identify the agreement morphology associated with each of these pronouns: the person value distinguishes *eu* ([P.N:1.SG]) from *tu* ([P.N:2.SG]) and the number value distinguishes *eu* from *nós* ([P.N:1.PL]). With the loss of *tu* in BP, on the other hand, the person value for *eu* has become redundant. Let us then assume that it can be dispensed with, yielding the specification ([P.N:SG]).

If *eu* in BP is specified simply as ([P.N:SG]), *nós* need not be doubly specified either, for there is no other pronoun with fused person and number features that has the values 1 or PL. Interestingly, some of the variation

---

[47] See e.g. Nunes 2019b, 2020a and Martins and Nunes 2021 for discussion.

106   3 Agreement

involving *nós* in BP seems to be related precisely to the issue of whether it is redundantly specified for person and number ([P.N:1.PL]) or specified for person only ([P.N:1]). Recall that the verbal agreement associated with *nós* in BP is subject to idiolectal/dialectal variation and may alternate between -*mos* and -*mo* (see footnotes 24 and 32 above). Bearing this in mind, let us consider the paradigm in (3.68) in BP.

(3.68)   a. Nós   fica**mos**   tranquilos   durante a   entrevista. (BP)
            pron.1.PL stayed-1.PL calm-MASC-PL during   the interview
         b. Nós   fica**mo**   tranquilo   durante a   entrevista.   (%BP)
            pron.1   stayed-1   calm-MASC   during   the interview
         c. Nós   fica**mos**   tranquilo   durante a   entrevista.   (%BP)
            pron.1   stayed-1   calm-MASC   during   the interview
         d. *Nós   fica**mo**   tranquilos   durante a   entrevista.   (%BP)
            pron.1   stayed-1   calm-MASC-PL during   the interview
            'We remained calm during the interview.'

In (3.68a) the plural morphology on the adjective shows that the subject must be specified for plural and the agreeing morphology on the verb shows that it must be specified for person; hence, *nós* for these speakers is specified as [P.N:1.PL]. In turn, the lack of plural morphology in the adjective in (3.68b) and (3.68c) may indicate that, for some speakers, *nós* is not morphologically specified for number; the reduced agreement form -*mo* is then allowed in addition to or in alternation with the form -*mos* (see footnotes 24 and 32 above). In other words, for speakers who allow (3.68b) and (3.68c), *nós* may be specified simply as [P.N:1]. Crucially, (3.68d) does not seem to be allowed even by speakers that admit (3.68b). The reason is that the plural morpheme on the adjective shows that *nós* must be specified as plural and therefore it should trigger full person and number agreement on the verb, as in (3.68a), blocking the unambiguous simplex [P.N:1] morpheme -*mo*. BP speakers may in fact allow both (3.68a) and (3.68b), distinguishing them in terms of register, the former signaling formal register and the latter colloquial register. Let us then assume that, in the colloquial register – the one to be analyzed here – *nós* is specified as [P.N:1].

If *eu* is morphologically specified as [P.N:SG] and *nós* as [P.N:1], there is no need to attribute values to the person features of the other pronouns: the putative values are not associated with an overt morpheme and these pronouns can be properly singled out even if their person feature does not have a value. Put differently, the putative values for the person feature of the pronouns *você(s)*, *ele(s)*, and *ela(s)* in Table 3.9 make no contribution to morphological distinctions in the verbal agreement system of BP. Let us then assume that these pronouns are also underspecified in that their morphological specification for person does not have a value.

What about the number specification of the pronouns *você(s)*, *cê(s)*, *ele(s)* and *ela(s)* in BP? Clearly, *vocês/cês*, *eles*, and *elas* must have their number feature valued as PL thanks to the independent morpheme *-s*, which encodes plurality. So, the question to be answered really concerns the pronouns *você/cê*, *ele*, and *ela*. There are two logical possibilities to entertain: their number feature can be valued as SG or not valued at all; in either case, the number specification of a verbal form agreeing with these pronouns should be assigned no phonetic content (see Section 3.4.1). In other words, we are again facing a zebra problem, for the phenotype of the verbal agreement associated with these pronouns is consistent with two genotypes. We may find a hint for a get-out from this conundrum, though, by reexamining the way number is computed within noun phrases in BP. As illustrated by the non-agreement pattern in (3.69) below, for instance, BP is very fond of unencumbered morphological forms (see Section 3.2.2). Crucially, one should not take the absence of the plural morpheme *-s* on *carro*, *amarelo*, and *amassado* in (3.69) as indicating that these lexical items are specified as SG, for this would create a conflict with the transparent specification for plural on the demonstrative.

(3.69) aqueles   carro   amarelo   amassado   (%BP)
        that.MASC-PL car.MASC yellow-MASC dented-MASC
        'those dented yellow cars'

A more plausible approach is to assume that, in BP, nouns and nominal modifiers may have a value for number only when they encode plurality. This being so, there would be no mismatch in number values among the lexical items of (3.69). Suppose that this conclusion is not restricted to standard noun phrases but also extends to BP pronouns. The morphological specification for number of the pronouns *você/cê*, *ele*, and *ela* in BP should then be unvalued.

Table 3.11 below, coupled with the correspondence rules given in (3.70), summarizes the results of the discussion above.[48]

---

[48] For discussion see e.g. Nunes 2008a, 2015b, 2019b, 2020a and Martins and Nunes 2021. BP dialects that have preserved *tu* with its distinctive agreement inflection (see footnote 25 above) can be accommodated in the picture outlined in Table 3.11 if *tu* in these dialects is morphologically specified as [P.N:2] and the phonetic realization for its agreement inflection is determined by the correspondence rule in (i). The prediction is that in these dialects, *tu* should pattern with *nós* due to its person specification; hence, it should be banned from hyper-raising constructions (see Section 3.4.3) and its null counterpart should be morphologically licensed (see

Table 3.11 *Morphological specifications for personal pronouns and verbal agreement in Brazilian Portuguese*

Personal pronouns		Verbal inflection			
Nominative form	Morphological specification	Indicative present	Indicative perfective past	Indicative imperfective past	Inflected infinitive
eu 'I'	[P.N:SG]	*-o*	*-i*		
você/cê 'you (SG)'	[P-N]				
ele 'he/it(MASC)'	[P-G:MASC-N]				
ela 'she/it(FEM)'	[P-G:FEM-N]				
a gente 'we'	[P.N]				
nós 'we'	[P.N:1]		*-mo(s)*		
vocês/cês 'you(PL)'	[P-N:PL]				
eles 'they(MASC)'	[P-G:MASC-N:PL]		*-m*		
elas 'they(FEM)'	[P-G:FEM-N:PL]				

(3.70) *Correspondence rules for the morphological realization of verbal agreement inflection in BP:*
    a. [P.N:1] ↔ {-mo(s)}
        [N:PL] ↔ {-m}
    b. [P.N:SG] → {-o} / INDIC.PRES __
                  → {-i} / INDIC.PERF.PAST __
    c. Ø elsewhere

Besides having different semantic features, each of the pronouns in Table 3.11 can be individually singled out on a morphological basis. Take the pronouns with fused person and number features, for example. *A gente* sets itself apart from *eu* and *nós* in that its person and number amalgam does not have a value; in turn, *eu* and *nós* differ from each other with respect to the value

Section 4.3.1). We leave for another occasion a more detailed discussion of the impact of the distinctive agreement inflection associated with *tu* in these dialects.

(i) *Correspondence rule for the agreement inflection with* tu *in BP dialects that have preserved a distinct form for this inflection:*
    [P.N:2] → {-ste} / INDIC.PERF.PAST __
           → {-s} elsewhere

3.4 The Different Agreement Systems in EP and BP 109

associated with the fused features (SG for *eu* and 1 for *nós*). With respect to the pronouns that have independent person and number features, the value for number or lack thereof distinguishes two groups: the pronouns *vocês/cês*, *eles*, and *elas*, specified as PL, and *você/cê*, *ele*, and *ela*, with no number value. Gender makes an additional tripartite distinction, with *ele(s)* having the value MASC, *ela(s)* having the value FEM, and *você(s)/cê(s)* not being specified for gender (see Sections 2.4.2 and 2.4.3). Finally, the feature [weak] (see Section 2.2) sets *cê* and *cês* apart from *você* and *vocês*. So, the individuation and interpretation of each pronoun are adequately captured in Table 3.11 and, in this regard, it is no different from Table 3.9. What makes Table 3.11 distinctive is that it captures the intuition that BP verbal agreement system is weak by looking not at the surface verbal agreeing forms themselves, but at the underlying feature (under)specification of the pronouns that determine such forms. Another distinctive trait of Table 3.11 is that, as far as verbal agreement in person and number is concerned, it has no redundancy in feature specifications; it actually portrays the smallest set of attribute values for nominative pronouns in BP that suffices to account for its verbal agreement patterns.

Similar considerations apply to the pronouns *vocês/cês* and *eles/elas*. If the morphological person specification of these pronouns is not associated with a value in BP, as postulated in Table 3.11, the agreeing forms associated with them should have their number specification valued as plural, but their person specification should remain unvalued and receive no phonetic content. In other words, it is the plural morpheme -*s* of these pronouns that values the number feature of the agreement inflection, which is then realized by the morpheme orthographically represented as -*m* (see (3.70a)).

As for the pronoun *eu* in Table 3.11, it behaves like its EP counterpart in having its person and number attributes fused, capturing the fact that it is not derivationally related to either of its (semantically) plural counterparts (*nós* or *a gente*). However, in the face of the massive underspecification of person in BP displayed in Table 3.11, the pronoun *eu* follows suit and its person attribute is not assigned a value either. Recall that Table 3.11 is meant to list the minimal set of morphological specifications to account for verbal agreement in BP. Thus, from this perspective it is not necessary that the lexical entry of *eu* have its morphological specification for person valued, in order for the agreement morphemes -*o* and -*i* to be properly associated with *eu*. According to Table 3.11, *eu* is the only pronoun in BP specified as SG and the correspondence rule in (3.70b) makes crucial reference to this value; thus, the agreement morphemes -*o* and -*i* cannot be associated with *você/cê*, *a gente*,

110   3 Agreement

or *ele/ela*, for instance, because these pronouns are not morphologically valued for number: the agreement inflection associated with them is accordingly not specified as SG, but remains unvalued and is assigned no phonetic content, in consonance with (3.70c).

The only context in BP that seems to require that the morphological person specification of *eu* be valued as 1 involves coordinated subjects. In BP, like in EP, a coordinated subject involving *eu* triggers first person plural agreement, as illustrated in (3.71) below (see Section 3.5.1.2). This seems to indicate that the specification of *eu* as 1 must be computed for purposes of agreement resolution involving coordinated subjects.

(3.71)   A Maria e   eu vamos   viajar amanhã. (BP)
         the Maria and I   go.1.PL   travel tomorrow
         'Maria and I are going to travel tomorrow.'

Appearances here are misleading, though. (3.71) does not necessarily show that the morphological specification of *eu* must be valued as 1. Recall that *a gente* in neither EP nor BP has its morphological specification for person valued (see Section 3.4.1). Interestingly, a coordinated subject involving *a gente* in BP also triggers first person plural agreement, as illustrated in (3.72) below. Given that *a gente* is not morphologically specified as 1, the conclusion is that agreement resolution in (3.72) resorts to semantic agreement. In other words, it is the semantic specification of *a gente* as 1 that is computed in the agreement resolution for the coordinated subject in (3.72). However, once semantic agreement is independently required for coordination involving *a gente*, it should also be available for coordination involving *eu*. In other words, the first person plural agreement in (3.71) does not commit us to assuming value 1 in the morphological specifications of *eu*, for the agreement in (3.71) may also be resolved via computation of the semantic specifications for *eu*. That being so, we will proceed assuming the minimal morphological specification for *eu* to be [P.N:SG], as in Table 3.11.[49]

(3.72)   a. **A gente**   e   três   outros   membros   da
            pron.[P.N]   *and*   *three*   *other*   *members* *of-the*
            comissão   estamos encarregados do   relatório.   (BP)
            committee   *be-1.PL* *charged*   *of-the* *report*
            'We and three other members of the of the committee are in charge of the report.'

---

[49] See Section 4.3.3.2 for a discussion of the marginal role of semantic agreement in the licensing of null subjects in BP.

b. O   professor e   **a gente**   resolve**mos**
   the   *teacher*   *and pron.[P.N]* *resolved-1.PL*
   falar   com   o   diretor.   (BP)
   speak *with*   *the*   *director*
   'We and the teacher decided to speak to the director.'

As for the pronoun *nós*, Table 3.11 suggests reasons for why it is losing terrain to *a gente* in BP. *A gente* has no value for number or person. Accordingly, the verbal agreement inflection associated with it remains unvalued, resulting in superficially bare forms, much in consonance with BP's liking. *Nós*, on the other hand, is an oddball in the system in that it is the only pronoun whose lexical entry has a valued person feature. As we will see later in Chapter 4, this exceptional specification also has direct consequences for the licensing of its corresponding null subject.

Table 3.11 also paves the way for a better understanding of other agreement differences among BP dialects.[50] For instance, dialects where all pronouns but *eu* apparently trigger third person singular, as illustrated in (3.67) (see also footnote 25 above), have simply eliminated (3.70a) from the correspondence rules for verbal agreement inflection in BP. With these rules eliminated, the person and number specifications of verbal forms associated with the pronouns *nós*, *vocês/cês*, and *eles/elas* fall under the Elsewhere Condition in (3.70c) and receive no phonetic content in the morphological component (see (3.70c)), giving the impression that these pronouns trigger third person singular agreement. Again, there is no feature mismatch between the semantic and morphological specifications of these pronouns in the dialects that allow (3.67); it is simply the case that their semantic specification is richer than their morphological specification in that it includes values for their person and number attributes (see Section 3.4.1).

Table 3.12 below revises Table 3.9 in the face of this discussion and lays out a comparison with EP.

Table 3.12 shows that although each nominative pronoun may have different morphological specifications for person and number in EP and BP, the corresponding agreeing verbs may have the same surface form, thanks to the correspondence rules in each variety (see (3.65) and (3.70)). In particular, the Elsewhere Conditions in (3.65d) in EP and (3.70c) in BP assign Ø to a motley set of agreement specifications ([P:2], [P:3], [P:u], [N:SG], and [N:u], in EP and [P:u] and [N:u] in BP), giving the impression that the pronouns *você*

---

[50] For discussion, see Nunes 2015b, 2019b.

Table 3.12 *Pronominal specifications for person and number and verbal agreement in Portuguese (revision of Table 3.9)*

Nominative pronouns	Morphological specification for person and number				Surface forms: *dançar* 'dance' (indicative present)
	EP		BP		
	Pronoun specification	Agreement inflection	Pronoun specification	Agreement inflection	
tu 'you(SG)'	[P.N:2.SG]	[P.N:2.SG]			*danças*
eu 'I'	[P.N:1.SG]	[P.N:1.SG]	[P.N:SG]	[P.N:SG]	*danço*
nós 'we'	[P.N:1.PL]	[P.N:1.PL]	[P.N:1]	[P.N:1]	*dançamos*
você 'you(SG)'	[P:2-N:SG]	[P:2-N:SG]			
ele 'he/it(MASC)' *ela* 'she/it(FEM)'	[P:3-N:SG]	[P:3-N:SG]	[P-N]	[P:u-N:u]	*dança*
a gente 'we'	[P.N]	[P:u-N:u]	[P.N]		
vocês 'you(PL)'	[P:2-N:PL]	[P:2-N:PL]			
eles 'they(MASC)' *elas* 'they(FEM)'	[P:3-N:PL]	[P:3-N:PL]	[P-N:PL]	[P:u-N:PL]	*dançam*

and *a gente* are morphologically specified as third person singular and *vocês* as third person plural (see Section 3.4.1).

For the sake of completeness, let us now consider verbal agreement with nonpronominal noun phrases, as illustrated in (3.73).

(3.73) a. O menino dança bem.
  the boy dance well
  'The boy dances well.'
 b. Os meninos dançam bem.
  the-PL boy-PL dance-PL well
  'The boys dance well.'

We have seen that the feature [person] is relevant for the licensing of nominative case (see footnote 39 above); thus, the nonpronominal noun phrases in (3.73) should in principle have a person feature. Furthermore, only pronouns seem to be able to bear an intrinsic value for their person feature. This leads us to conclude that the person feature of nonpronominal noun phrases (or, more precisely, the person feature of the determiner of these phrases; see footnote 1 above) does not have a value. That being so, the person feature of the verbal agreement inflection associated with *o menino* 'the boy' in (3.73a) and *os meninos* 'the boys' in (3.73b) remains unvalued ([P:u]) and, as such, it is not assigned phonetic content, in accordance with the Elsewhere Conditions in (3.65d) in EP and (3.70c) in BP.

Let us now consider the number feature of the nonpronominal noun phrases in (3.73). In (3.73b) the value for the number feature of the subject is PL; hence the verbal inflection will be specified as [P:u-N:PL] and only the number feature is assigned a phonetic exponent, in consonance with the correspondence rules in (3.65a) in EP and (3.70a) in BP. As for (3.73a), the number of the subject is valued as SG in EP and the corresponding verbal inflection ([P:u-N:SG]) is assigned no phonetic exponent, in accordance with the Elsewhere Condition in (3.65d). Given the overall pattern of agreement in BP, on the other hand, (3.73a) may receive two different analyses: the number feature of the subject is valued as SG as in EP or it has no value. In either circumstance, the Elsewhere Condition in (3.70c) assigns no phonetic exponent to the corresponding verbal inflection ([P:u-N:SG] or [P:u-N:u], respectively). Crucially, [N:SG] is not realized as -*o*, for instance, for this phonetic exponent is to be associated with a fused person and number and not just number (see (3.70b)). Here we will not attempt to choose between these possible analyses; given that BP allows more than one pattern of number agreement within the noun phrase (see Section 3.2.2), it is not unlikely that the two possibilities are indeed available in BP. For our purposes, what is relevant is that the surface form of the verb in (3.73a) may be identical in EP and BP even if their underlying feature specifications turn out to be different, thanks to the Elsewhere Conditions for the realization of person and number in (3.65d) and (3.70c).

We can now understand why dialectal variation in EP and BP goes in opposite directions, despite the fact that they superficially diverge with respect to just one inflection. Given the robust feature specification of its pronominal system, dialectal variation in EP leans towards additional forms of agreement, as seen, for example, in (3.46a), (3.62), (i) in footnote 44 above, and (3.55), repeated below in (3.74a–d). Thus, there are dialects that allow for inflected gerunds (see (3.74a)), dialects that resort to semantic agreement when the pronoun does not have a value for its morphological attributes, as is the case of *a gente* (see (3.74b,c)) and dialects that add a correspondence rule for the realization of agreement when the valued person feature of the inflection should otherwise fall under the Elsewhere Condition, as is the case with *vocês* (see (3.74d)).

(3.74) a. Em tu querendos! (%EP)
in pron.2.SG want-GER-2.SG
'Whenever you(SG) want it!'
(CORDIAL-SIN, CBV41)

b. Que a gente tosquiavam as ovelhas duas vezes no ano. (%EP)
that pron.[P.N] shear-[N:PL] the sheep two time in-the year
'Because we used to shear the sheep twice a year.'
(CORDIAL-SIN, MIG58)

c. Agora estes rapazes novos não sabem aquilo que a gente
now these boys new not know that that pron.[P.N]
passámos. (%EP)
passed-1.PL
'These youngsters have no idea of all we've been through.'
(CORDIAL-SIN, CLC15)

d. Vocês andais a gastar dinheiro. (%EP)
you-PL walk.2.PL to spend money
'You(PL) are going around spending your money.'
(CORDIAL-SIN, COV01)

By contrast, the pronominal system of BP has become substantially underspecified and still seems to be under pressure towards further underspecification. The most radical dialects have eliminated the correspondence rules in (3.70a), yielding sentences with plural subjects and verbs in their bare form, as illustrated in (3.75a). Additionally, the dialects that have preserved *tu* (see Section 2.4.2 and footnote 25 above) have also reanalyzed its morphological matrix as [P-N], allowing sentences such as (3.75b), where *tu* is also associated with bare agreement forms.

(3.75)   a. No final **nós/vocês/eles**   sempre **acaba**
             in-the end we/you-PL/they.MASC always finish-[P:u]-[N:u]
             concordando.   (%BP)
             agreeing
             'In the end we/you(PL)/they always end up agreeing.'
   b. Tu   não **sabe**   o que aconteceu!   (%BP)
       you.SG not know-[P:u]-[N:u] what happened
       'You(SG) don't know what happened.'

Notice that, according to Table 3.12, EP and BP assign the same feature specification only to *a gente* ([P.N]). Interestingly, this is the only pronoun that displays a comparable behavior in both EP and BP with respect to ellipsis underlying null subjects, as we will see in Chapter 4. Another property that stands out in Table 3.12 is that, except for the agreement inflection associated with *nós*, the feature [person] of the agreement inflection in BP seems to be relevant only to license nominative case (see footnotes 39 and 45 above). As far as agreement is concerned, it is basically inert as it induces no changes in the final shape of the verb. One then wonders what would happen if the person feature went missing in the agreement inflection of BP. This is the topic of the next section.

3.4.3 *Defective Agreement Specification and Hyper-Raising in Brazilian Portuguese*

Let us consider the sentences in (3.76) and (3.77), where the overt verbal morphology is glossed according to the specifications for agreement inflection in BP (see Table 3.12).[51]

(3.76)   a. Parece que esses professores **elogiam**   bastante os alunos.
             seem   that these teachers   praise-PL a.lot   the students
             'It seems that these teachers praise the students a lot.'
   b. É difícil   esses professores **reclamarem**   dos   alunos.
       is difficult these teachers   complain-INF-PL of-the students
       'These teachers rarely complain about the students.'

(3.77)   a. *Parece esses professores **elogiar**   bastante os alunos.
             seem   these teachers   praise-INF a.lot   the students

---

[51] With the exception of hyper-raising constructions, the sentences in this section are judged in the same way in both EP and BP, although their verbal agreement inflection is associated with different feature specifications, as seen in Table 3.12. Given that the focus of this section is hyper-raising constructions in BP we will, for purposes of exposition, present glosses only according to BP specifications.

b. Esses professores **parecem** elogiar bastante os alunos.
   these teachers seem-*PL* praise-*INF* a.lot the students
   'It seems that these teachers praise the students a lot.'

In (3.76), the embedded subject is arguably licensed with nominative case by the inflection on the embedded verb – a finite verb in (3.76a) and an inflected infinitival in (3.76b) (see Section 2.3.4.1). By contrast, the embedded subject of (3.77a) cannot have its case licensed, for the verb *parecer* 'seem' has selected an uninflected infinitival. However, the ungrammaticality of (3.77a) can be repaired if the embedded subject moves to the matrix subject position, as seen in the "raising" construction in (3.77b), for the finite inflection on the matrix verb can license nominative case.

Given the paradigm in (3.76)–(3.77), the BP data in (3.78) are very surprising.[52]

(3.78) a. Esses professores **parecem** que **elogiam** bastante os alunos. (BP)
        these teachers seem-*PL* that praise-*PL* a.lot the students
        'It seems that these teachers praise the students a lot.'
      b. Esses professores **são** difíceis de **reclamarem** dos alunos. (BP)
        these teachers be-*3.PL* difficult of complain-*INF-PL* of-the students
        'These teachers rarely complain about the students.'

Once the embedded verb is inflected, the subject should be licensed in the embedded clause and further movement to the matrix subject position, triggering agreement with the matrix verb, should be blocked. In fact, these "hyper-raising" constructions are disallowed in EP.[53] One then

---

[52] For discussion see e.g. Ferreira 2000, 2009, Duarte 2004, 2007, Martins and Nunes 2005, 2009, 2010, and Nunes 2008a, 2010a,b, 2011, 2015b, 2016, 2017, 2019b, 2020b.

[53] A superficially similar construction may be derived in both EP and BP if the embedded subject is topicalized to the matrix clause, as illustrated in (i) below, but in this case there is no subject-to-subject movement and agreement with the matrix verb does not take place.

(i) Os meninos **parece** que vão viajar.
    the boys seem that go.*PL* travel
    'It seems that the boys are going to travel.'

The hyper-raising constructions in (3.78) are also different from another similar construction in EP, dubbed by Rooryck and Costa (2000) a *pseudo-raising construction* (see (iia) below), which they argue does not involve subject-to-subject movement. They observe that these constructions in EP allow any type of pronominal subject, but not indefinites, as shown by the contrast between (iia) and (iib);

3.4 The Different Agreement Systems in EP and BP

wonders why inflectional agreement in BP does not necessarily license nominative case.

A closer look at hyper-raising constructions in BP shows that they are actually sensitive to specific combinations of person and number agreement

---

furthermore, the verb of the embedded clause must be predicative, as shown by the contrast between (iia) and (iic). Exactly the opposite holds of hyper-raising in BP (see e.g. Nunes 2019b, 2020b): it is sensitive to the type of pronoun involved (in particular, *nós* is not allowed in subject hyper-raising), as shown in (iiia); it allows indefinites, as shown in (iiib); and it is compatible with eventive predicates in the embedded clause, as shown in (iiic). Moreover, hyper-raising constructions in BP allow idiom chunks, but seemingly analogous constructions in EP do not, as shown in (iv) and (v). For discussion see e.g. Martins and Nunes 2005, 2009, 2010 and Nunes 2008a, 2016, 2019b, 2020b.

(ii) EP (adapted from Rooryck and Costa 2000)
    a. **Nós** parecemos que estamos felizes.
       we seem-1.PL that are-1.PL happy
       'We seem to be happy.'
    b. *[**Umas meninas**] parecem que estão doentes.
       some girls seem-3-PL that are sick
       'A few girls seem to be sick.'
    c. *Tu pareces que **comes** o bolo.
       pron.2.SG seem-2.SG that eat-2.SG the cake
       'You seem to be eating the cake.'

(iii) *BP*:
    a. ***Nós** parecemos que tomamos a decisão certa.
       we seem-1 that took-1 the decision right
       'We seem to have made the right decision.'
    b. [**Umas meninas**] parecem que foram reprovadas na prova de química.
       some girls seem-PL that were failed in-the exam of chemistry
       'Some girls seem to have failed the chemistry exam.'
    c. Eles pareciam que iam **bater** um no outro.
       they seemed-PL that went-PL hit one in-the other
       'It seemed that they were going to hit each other.'

(iv) *BP*:
    a. A vaca foi pro brejo.
       the cow went to-the swamp
       Idiomatic reading: 'Things went bad.'
    b. [**A vaca**] parece que foi pro brejo.
       the cow seems that went to-the swamp
       Idiomatic reading: 'It seems that things went bad.'

(v) EP:
    a. A formiga já tem catarro.
       the ant already has phlegm
       Idiomatic reading: 'The child thinks he/she is already an adult.'
    b. *[**A formiga**] parece que já tem catarro.
       the ant seems that already has phlegm
       Idiomatic reading: 'It seems that the child thinks {he/she} is already an adult.'

values.[54] Assuming the correspondence rules for agreement inflection in BP as given in (3.70), consider the impersonal constructions in (3.79) and their hyper-raising counterparts in (3.80), for example.

(3.79)   a. Parece que eu **elogio** bastante os alunos.
         seem that I praise-**SG** a.lot the students
         'It seems that I praise the students a lot.'
      b. Parece que {você/ele/ela/a gente} **elogia** bastante os alunos.
         seem that you.SG/he/she/pron.[P.N] praise a.lot the students
         'It seems that {you(SG)/he/she/we} praise the students a lot.'
      c. Parece que nós **elogiamos** bastante os alunos.
         seem that we praise-**1** a.lot the students
         'It seems that we praise the students a lot.'
      d. Parece que {vocês/eles/elas} **elogiam** bastante os
         seem that you-PL/they.MASC/they.FEM praise-**PL** a.lot the
         alunos.
         students
         'It seems that {you(PL)/they} praise the students a lot.'

(3.80)   a. %Eu **pareço** que **elogio** bastante os alunos.   (BP)
            I seem-**SG** that praise-**SG** a.lot the students
            'It seems that I praise the students a lot.'
         b. {Você/ele/ela/a gente} **parece** que **elogia** bastante os alunos. (BP)
            you.SG/he/she/pron.[P.N] seem that praise a.lot the students
            'It seems that {you(SG)/he/she/we} praise the students a lot.'
         c. *Nós **parecemos** que **elogiamos** bastante os alunos.   (BP)
            we seem-**1** that praise-**1** a.lot the students
            'It seems that we praise the students a lot.'
         d. {Vocês/eles/elas} **parecem** que **elogiam** bastante
            you-PL/they.MASC/they.FEM seem-**PL** that praise-**PL** a.lot
            os alunos.   (BP)
            the students
            'It seems that {you(PL)/they} praise the students a lot.'

In (3.79), the embedded subject is licensed in the embedded clause and all pronouns are allowed. In (3.80), on the other hand, the embedded subject undergoes subject-to-subject movement, but only the constructions employing traditional "third person" agreement (singular or plural) are acceptable in the grammar of BP (see (3.80b) and (3.80d)). Constructions involving traditional "first person plural" agreement are uniformly excluded (see (3.80c)) and constructions involving traditional "first person singular" agreement are subject to idiolectal variation (see (3.80a)). A similar pattern appears in hyper-raising out of inflected infinitivals (see the impersonal constructions in (3.81)

---

[54] See e.g. Nunes 2008a, 2015b, 2019b, and 2020b for discussion.

and their hyper-raising counterparts in (3.82) below), the only difference being that hyper-raising of *eu* is now uniformly accepted across speakers.[55]

(3.81) a. É difícil {eu/você/ele/ela/a gente} **reclamar** de alguém.
is difficult I/you.SG/he/she/ pron.[P.N] complain-INF of somebody
'{I/you(SG)/he/she/we} rarely complain(s) about people.'
b. É difícil nós **reclamarmos** de alguém.
is difficult we complain-INF-1 of somebody
'We rarely complain about people.'
c. É difícil {vocês/eles/elas} **reclamarem** de
is difficult you-PL/they.MASC/they.FEM complain-INF-**PL** of
alguém.
somebody
'{You(PL)/they} rarely complain about people.'

(3.82) a. Eu **sou** difícil de **reclamar** de alguém. (BP)
I be-**1.SG** difficult of complain-INF of somebody
'I rarely complain about people.'
b. {Você/ele/ela/a gente} **é** difícil de **reclamar** de
you.SG/he/she/pron.[P.N] be.**3.SG** difficult of complain-INF of
alguém. (BP)
somebody
'{You(SG)/he/she/we} rarely complain(s) about people.'
c. *Nós **somos** difíceis de **reclamarmos** de alguém. (BP)
we be-**1** difficult of complain-INF-**1** of somebody
'We rarely complain about people.'
d. {Vocês/eles/elas} **são** difíceis de **reclamarem**
you-PL/they.MASC/they.FEM be-**3.PL** difficult of complain-INF-**PL**
de alguém. (BP)
of somebody
'{You(PL)/they} rarely complain about people.'

The reader might have noticed that the specific pattern of person and number combinations in the embedded clause that allows or forbids hyper-raising of the embedded subject is reminiscent of BP's agreement paradigm

---

[55] For discussion see e.g. Galves 1987, Ferreira 2000, Nunes 2008a, and Oliveira 2009. In BP, the (postverbal) infinitival clause of impersonal constructions may be optionally introduced by a dummy preposition, as illustrated in (ia) below. However, in the case of hyper-raising constructions, the presence of a dummy preposition is obligatory (see (ib)). See e.g. Nunes 2008a, 2009, 2010b, 2020b for an account of the role of dummy prepositions in licensing hyper-raising.

(i) a. É difícil **(d)**esses professores elogiarem os alunos. (BP)
is difficult **of**-these teachers praise.INF-PL the students
b. Esses professores são difíceis ***(de)*** elogiarem os alunos. (BP)
these teachers are difficult **of** praise-INF-PL the students
'These teachers rarely praise the students.'

seen in Table 3.11. In other words, hyper-raising is possible if the verbal form in the embedded clause does not involve an overt morpheme for person or number (see *elogia* in (3.80b) and *reclamar* in (3.82a,b)) and blocked if it involves an overt morpheme for person (see *elogiamos* in (3.80c) and *reclamarmos* in (3.82c)); in turn, when the embedded verbal form involves specification only for number, hyper-raising is possible if the number morpheme is valued as plural (see *elogiam* in (3.78a)/(3.80d)) and *reclamarem* in (3.78b)/(3.82d)), but shows idiolectal variation when the number morpheme is valued as singular (see *elogio* in (3.80a)). Thus, the question before us is how to use these fine-grained distinctions to account for the correlation between availability of hyper-raising and combinations of person and number values in BP, as well as the difference between BP and EP in allowing hyper-raising in the first place (see footnote 53 above).

Recall that the feature [person] is the one that is involved in nominative case licensing in Portuguese (see Section 3.4.1). Given that the embedded subjects of (3.76), (3.79), and (3.81) are licensed in the embedded clauses, we are led to the conclusion that the embedded verbal inflection (Infl) of these sentences is associated with both number and person so that the embedded subject can have its nominative case licensed in the embedded clause. In this regard, BP is no different from EP. By contrast, the acceptable hyper-raising constructions of (3.78), (3.80), and (3.82) indicate that the embedded Infl need not always be associated with the feature [person] in BP; otherwise, subject-to-subject movement would be blocked, as in EP. In other words, in order for the data in (3.76)–(3.82) to be accounted for, it must be the case that, in the grammar of EP, the Infl of finite clauses and inflected infinitivals is obligatorily associated with person and number (thus, uniformly excluding hyper-raising), whereas, in the grammar of BP, Infl may optionally bear both person and number (thus allowing for impersonal constructions such as (3.76), (3.79), and (3.81)) or just number (thus permitting hyper-raising constructions as well).[56] The obvious question then is whether it makes sense to postulate such an option for BP Infl.[57]

Interestingly, Table 3.11 has shown that the morphological underspecification of personal pronouns in BP has led to such a massive underspecification

---

[56] Recall from Section 3.4.1 that, in some dialects of EP, inflected infinitivals that are the complement of perception and causative verbs may also be optionally associated with Infl bearing person and number or just number (see (3.51)).

[57] For the proposal that Infl in BP may be ambiguous in that it can carry either a complete or an incomplete set of Φ-features, see Ferreira 2000, 2009. For the formulation of this ambiguity in terms of the optional presence of the feature [person], see Nunes 2008a, 2015b, 2019b.

Table 3.13 *Ambiguity of finite Infl(ection) in Brazilian Portuguese*

Nominative pronouns	Person and number			
	Morphological specification	Surface forms: *dançar* 'dance' (indicative present)	Infl [P:u-N:u]	Infl [N:u]
eu 'I'	[P.N:SG]	*danço*	[P.N:SG]	%[N:SG]
você/cê 'you(SG)'	[P-N]	*dança*	[P:u-N:u]	[N:u]
ele 'he/it(MASC)'				
ela 'she/it(FEM)'				
a gente 'we'	[P.N]			
nós 'we'	[P.N:1]	*dançamo(s)*	[P.N:1]	
vocês/cês 'you-PL'	[P-N:PL]	*dançam*	[P:u-N:PL]	[N:PL]
eles 'they(MASC)'				
elas 'they (FEM)'				

in its agreement system that it is fair to say that, for the most part, the person feature on the agreement inflection is of no morphological significance in BP. Only one agreement inflection (-*mo(s)*) requires making reference to a person value (1); all the other agreement inflections can be properly distinguished based just on the value specification for number (SG, PL, or u), as shown by the correspondence rules for the realization of verbal agreement in BP stated in (3.70) and repeated below in (3.83). Let us suppose then that Infl in BP is in fact ambiguous in that it may bear both person and number or just number, as depicted in Table 3.13 below.[58]

(3.83) Correspondence rules for the morphological realization of verbal agreement inflection in BP:
   a. [P.N:1]   ↔   {-mo(s)}
      [N:PL]   ↔   {-m}

---

[58] In Table 3.13 we represent only the more complex pattern with finite clauses, where there is a split among speakers with respect to hyper-raising of *eu* 'I' (see (3.80a)). As mentioned above, in the case of infinitivals, hyper-raising of *eu* is possible for all BP speakers (see (3.82a)). This is undoubtedly related to the fact that the surface form of an infinitival with *eu* as its subject is the bare form (even in EP), as depicted in Tables 3.10 and 3.11. We will return to this case in Section 4.3.2.2. See Nunes 2015b for discussion.

b. [P.N:SG] → {-o} / INDIC.PRES ___
          → {-i} / INDIC.PERF.PAST ___
c. Ø elsewhere

Given the correspondence rules in (3.83), Table 3.13 shows that, in BP, a verbal form with no agreement morphemes (e.g. *dança*) or a form marked only with plural (e.g. *dançam*) can be obtained either with Infl bearing person and number or with Infl bearing number only. In the case of the pronouns *você/cê*, *ele/ela*, *vocês/cês*, and *eles/elas*, their person and number features are morphologically autonomous and therefore the number feature of a full Infl or an underspecified Infl enters into a direct agreement relation with the morphological number feature of the pronoun, being valued as PL and realized as {-m} (see (3.83a)) when agreeing with *vocês/cês* and *eles/elas*, and remaining unvalued and receiving no phonetic realization (see (3.83c)) when agreeing with the valueless number feature of *você/cê* and *ele/ela*. In the case of *a gente*, its person and number features are fused, but neither of them has a value; given that this feature amalgam does not have a value ([P.N]), *a gente* does not trigger fusion of the corresponding features of a fully specified Infl, because each of the features of Infl ([P:u] and [N:u]) falls under the elsewhere case in (3.83c) and receives no phonetic exponent (see Section 3.4.1). From this it follows that, regardless of whether the agreement inflection associated with *a gente* has person and number ([P:u-N:u]) or just number ([N:u]), the verbal form is realized without overt agreement morphology. This is what gives the illusion that *a gente* triggers third person singular agreement, as discussed in Section 3.4.1. As for the agreement form associated with *nós* (e.g. *dançamos*), it can be obtained only if Infl has both person and number, because the fused feature complex of *nós* is valued as 1, and this is not a possible value for number. Finally, given that the pronoun *eu* has its person and number feature fused and valued as SG, it triggers the corresponding fusion and valuation with respect to the feature of a fully specified Infl and is realized as {-o} (as in *danço* in Table 3.13), in compliance with (3.83b). In turn, the percentage sign in the last column of Table 3.13 is meant to indicate that whether or not an underspecified Infl can agree with *eu* is subject to individual variation. Descriptively speaking, some speakers do not allow a single feature to agree with a valued amalgam of features; for these speakers, the agreement form *danço* in Table 3.13 cannot be obtained in this scenario. Other speakers seem to be tuned not to the fact that number is not dissociated from person in the feature matrix of *eu*, but to the value of the feature amalgam (SG). Since SG is a possible value for number, these speakers allow the form *danço* in Table 3.13 to be derived through agreement between *eu* and an Infl bearing number only. Put differently, for these speakers the correspondence rule in (3.83b) actually reads as (3.84), showing once again that the feature [person] is not morphologically salient in BP.

(3.84)   [(P.)N:SG]   →   {-o} / INDIC.PRES ___   (%BP)
                     →   {-i} / INDIC.PERF.PAST ___

From this perspective, hyper-raising constructions such as (3.85a) and (3.85b) below, for instance, can be obtained along the lines of (3.85a′) and (3.85b′), where the surface forms of the agreeing verbs are not transparent with respect to their feature composition. The embedded Infl in (3.85a′) and (3.85b′) has only number and is therefore incapable of assigning nominative to its subject, as opposed to the matrix Infl, which has both number and person.

(3.85)   a. Elas   **parecem**   que **elogiam**   bastante os alunos.   (BP)
            they(FEM)   seem-**PL**   that praise-**PL** a.lot   the students
            'It seems that they(FEM) praise the students a lot.'
         a′. [elas$_{[P\text{-}G:FEM\text{-}N:PL]}$ parece-**Infl**$_{[P:u\text{-}N:PL]}$ [que __ elogia-**Infl**$_{[N:PL]}$ bastante os alunos]]

         b. Vocês   **parecem**   que **elogiam**   bastante os alunos.   (BP)
            you(PL)   seem-**PL**   that praise-**PL** a.lot   the students
            'It seems that you(PL) praise the students a lot.'
         b′. [vocês$_{[P\text{-}N:PL]}$ parece-**Infl**$_{[P:u\text{-}N:PL]}$ [que __ elogia-**Infl**$_{[N:PL]}$ bastante os alunos]]

Notice that one need not stipulate that, in hyper-raising constructions, the embedded Infl is defective and that of the matrix clause is complete.[59] If the matrix Infl in (3.85a′) or (3.85b′) were defective, the moved subject would not have its case licensed. Alternatively, if the embedded Infl in (3.85a), for instance, were complete, the embedded subject would be licensed in the embedded clause, preventing subject-to-subject movement and yielding the impersonal construction in (3.86a).

(3.86)   a. Parece que elas   elogiam   bastante os alunos.
            seem   that they.FEM praise-PL a.lot   the students
            'It seems that they(FEM) praise the students a lot.'
         b. [Parece [que elas$_{[P\text{-}G:FEM\text{-}N:PL]}$ elogia-**Infl**$_{[P:u\text{-}N:PL]}$ bastante os alunos]]

Similar considerations apply to hyper-raising involving the pronouns *ela*, *você*, and *a gente*, for instance, as shown in (3.87) below. The only difference is that the number feature of both the matrix and the embedded Infl remains unvalued because these pronouns do not have a value for number in their morphological specification:

---

[59] See Ferreira 2000, 2009 for discussion.

124   3 Agreement

(3.87) a. Ela parece que elogia bastante os alunos.   (BP)
        she seem that praise a.lot   the students
        'It seems that she praises the students a lot.'
        a'. [ela_{[P-G:FEM-N]} parece-Infl_{[P:u-N:u]} [que __ elogia-Infl_{[N:u]} bastante os alunos]

        b. Você   parece que elogia bastante os alunos.   (BP)
        you(SG) seem that praise a.lot   the students
        'It seems that you praise the students a lot.'
        b'. [você_{[P-N]} parece-Infl_{[P:u-N:u]} [que __ elogia-Infl_{[N:u]} bastante os alunos]

        c. A gente parece que elogia bastante os alunos.   (BP)
        we   seem   that praise a.lot   the students
        'It seems that we praise the students a lot.'
        c'. [a gente_{[P.N]} parece-Infl_{[P:u-N:u]} [que __ elogia-Infl_{[N:u]} bastante os alunos]

Let us now examine the impossibility of hyper-raising involving *nós* (see (3.80c) and (3.82c)). Consider, for instance, the abstract representation of the embedded clause of (3.80c), repeated below in (3.88a), just before the pronoun moves to the matrix clause:

(3.88) a. *Nós parecemos que elogiamos bastante os alunos.   (BP)
            we   seem-1   that praise-1   a.lot   the students
            'It seems that we praise the students a lot.'
        b. [que nós_{[P.N:1]} elogia-Infl_{[N:1]} ...]

If the embedded Infl of (3.88a) had both person and number, the person feature would be valued by *nós*, which would then be licensed with nominative in the embedded clause and would be prevented from moving to the matrix subject position, along the lines we saw in (3.79c). As we mentioned above, in order for a hyper-raising construction to be derived, the embedded Infl must involve just a number feature. This is what we find in the representations in (3.85) and (3.87), on the one hand, and (3.88b), on the other. However, there is a crucial difference between them. In (3.85) and (3.87), the number feature of the pronoun that triggers agreement with Infl (*eles* and *vocês*) is realized by an autonomous morpheme ({-s}). By contrast, in (3.88b) the number feature of the subject pronoun is fused with the person feature; worse than that, the value for the amalgam [P.N] is a person value (1) rather than a number value. We may thus take the agreement failure at the stage represented in (3.88b) to be responsible for the ungrammaticality of (3.88a). In effect, given the rules for the phonetic realization of verbal agreement inflection in (3.83), there is no way for the form *elogiamos* in (3.88a) to be obtained if the embedded Infl bears only number.

Let us finally consider the hyper-raising construction involving *eu* in (3.80a), repeated below in (3.89a).

(3.89) a. %Eu pareço que elogio bastante os alunos.   (BP)
           I seem-SG that praise-SG a.lot   the students
           'It seems that I praise the students a lot.'
      b. [parece-**Infl**$_{[P.N:SG]}$ [que eu$_{[P.N:SG]}$ elogia-**Infl**$_{[N:SG]}$ ...]]

As discussed in Section 3.4.2, *eu* in BP is morphologically specified as [P.N: SG], that is, it has an unvalued person attribute fused with a number attribute valued as singular. When *eu* agrees with a complete Infl, it triggers fusion of the person and number features of Infl, which are then valued as SG and realized as {-o}, in consonance with the correspondence rule in (3.83b). This is what is expected to happen in the matrix clause of (3.89b) after *eu* moves to the matrix subject position, for the matrix Infl is complete. The question is what happens in the embedded clause. In order for *eu* to be able to move, the embedded Infl must bear only number, as discussed above. However, if this is the case, the single number feature of Infl should not be able to agree with the number feature fused with person in the feature matrix of *eu*. This accounts for why some speakers treat *nós* and *eu* alike as far as hyper-raising is concerned. For these speakers, the problem is not the movement of *eu* itself, but the agreement failure between the subject and the embedded Infl, which in the case of (3.89a) cannot give rise to verbal form *elogio*.

What about the speakers who allow hyper-raising with *eu*, but not with *nós*? As discussed with regard to Table 3.13, although person and number are fused in both *nós* and *eu* in BP, the amalgam [P.N] has a person value in the case of *nós* (1), but a number value in the case of *eu* (SG). This suggests that speakers that allow (3.89a) disregard the fact that person and number are fused and instead compute the value of the amalgam (perhaps reanalyzing the relevant correspondence rule as (3.84)); hence, they allow agreement between an Infl bearing only number with an amalgam with a number value (*eu*: [P.N:SG]) but not with an amalgam with a person value (*nós*: [P.N:1]).[60] Thus, this low-level

---

[60] Recall that we suggested that, in formal registers of BP, *nós* is specified as [P.N:1.PL] (see Section 3.4.2). The fact that the agreement failure in the embedded clause of (3.88a) similarly results in ungrammaticality in these registers also falls under the rule that a single number feature cannot enter into an agreement relation with a fused conglomerate involving (valued) person and number features.

variation among speakers lends additional support to the morphological specifications for BP pronouns depicted in Table 3.11.

To put it in general terms, if the embedded finite clause contains Infl$_{[N]}$ and *nós* (for all speakers) or *eu* (for some speakers) as its subject (see footnote 58 above), the resulting structure (with hyper-raising) will not be legitimate, because Infl will fail to agree with the subject. Thus, if *nós* (or *eu* for some speakers) is the subject of an embedded finite clause, the resulting structure will be licit only if the embedded Infl is complete, with both person and number features. However, if this is so, the embedded subject will have its case licensed in the embedded clause (see (3.79c) and (3.81b)) and will be prevented from undergoing subject-to-subject movement (see (3.80c) and (3.82c)). Thus, hyper-raising constructions involving *nós* (and *eu* for some speakers) as the moved subject are doomed to be ungrammatical in BP regardless of whether or not the embedded Infl is complete or defective (see footnote 60 above). Divergence in judgments among speakers with respect to *eu* depends on whether or not the grammars of individual speakers can disregard an unvalued fused person feature for purposes of agreement when Infl has only a number feature. If they can, Infl is valued as SG and hyper-raising constructions with *eu* are allowed; if they cannot, these hyper-raising constructions are ruled out.[61]

In conclusion, simplification of the morphological specifications of BP pronouns has yielded a system that highly favors bare verbal forms. Bare forms may be associated with *você/cê*, *ele/ela*, and *a gente* in all tenses and with

---

[61] In addition to subject hyper-raising constructions, BP also allows constructions such as (i) below, where both the matrix and the embedded subject positions are filled (see e.g. Duarte 2004, 2007). Martins and Nunes (2010) and Nunes (2016) argue that sentences such as (ia) and (ib) involve hyper-raising of an embedded topic, which may also surface in the embedded clause, as respectively shown in (iia) and (iib). Speakers who do not allow hyper-raising of *eu* as a subject may allow hyper-raising of *eu* as a topic, as illustrated in (ib). This is possible because, in cases of topic hyper-raising, the embedded Infl must have both person and number in order to license the case of the embedded subject.

(i)   a.   **Os alunos** parecem que **eles** vão viajar amanhã.   (BP)
            the students seem-PL that they go.3.PL travel tomorrow
            'It seems that the students are going to travel tomorrow.'
     b.   **Eu** pareço que **eu** vou ser despedido.   (BP)
            I seem-1.SG that I go.1.SG be fired
            'It seems that I'm going to be fired.'
(ii)   a.   Parece que **os alunos**, **eles** vão viajar amanhã.   (BP)
            seem that the students they go.3.PL travel tomorrow
            'It seems that the students are going to travel tomorrow.'
     b.   Parece que **eu**, **eu** vou ser despedido.   (BP)
            seem that I I go.1.SG be fired
            'It seems that I'm going to be fired.'

eu in all tenses but the indicative present and indicative perfective past (see Table 3.11; recall that BP has lost the synthetic forms of the indicative future tense – see Section 3.4.2). Moreover, there is only one verbal agreement morpheme that is associated with person (*-mo(s)*). This massive underspecification in BP has given rise to hyper-raising constructions, where the Infl of a finite clause or inflected infinitival is associated only with number, forcing its subject to undergo subject-to-subject movement to get its case licensed. In a sense, the weakening of BP's agreement paradigm has ended up broadening the possibilities for subject-to-subject movement to take place. Importantly, the fact that hyper-raising is sensitive to specific person and number combinations associated with the embedded Infl provides compelling evidence for the drastic underspecification of both the pronominal and verbal paradigms of BP discussed in Section 3.4.2.

3.5 Special Cases of Agreement

In this section we discuss some general cases where subject–predicate agreement does not seem to hold and show that appearances may be misleading.

3.5.1 Agreement Asymmetries and Word Order

As happens in many languages, subject–predicate agreement in Portuguese may be affected by the position of the subject with respect to the verb. More specifically, postverbal subjects appear to differ from preverbal subjects in being able to escape subject–verb agreement. Here we discuss two such cases: agreement with unaccusative verbs and agreement with coordinated subjects.

3.5.1.1 Agreement with Unaccusative Verbs

Consider the contrast between (3.90) and (3.91) below, where only overt agreement morphemes are glossed. Sentences like (3.91b), where the verb does not seem to agree with its subject, are pervasively found in BP and are well attested in EP dialects (especially Southern and Insular dialects). However, we will see in this section that lack of verbal agreement in sentences such as (3.91b) is only apparent.[62]

---

[62] For discussion see e.g. Berlinck 2000, Kato 2000, 2002b, Coelho 2000, Costa 2001, Carrilho 2003, Kato and Tarallo 2003, Cardoso, Carrilho, and Pereira 2011, and Lobo and Martins 2017.

128   3 Agreement

(3.90)   a. Três barcos chegaram ontem.
         *three boats   arrived-**PL** yesterday*
      b. *Três barcos **chegou** ontem.
         three boats   arrived yesterday
         'Three boats arrived yesterday.'

(3.91)   a. **Chegaram** três barcos ontem.
         *arrived-**PL** three boats yesterday*
      b. **Chegou** três barcos ontem.   (BP/%EP)
         arrived three boats yesterday
         'There arrived three boats yesterday.'

Before we start discussing the agreement asymmetry illustrated by the contrast between (3.90) and (3.91), the first thing to note is that it is not the case that any subject can appear in postverbal position in both EP and BP or that any postverbal subject can fail to trigger agreement. Take monoargumental verbs, for example. Although they are traditionally analyzed as intransitive, they actually involve two distinct classes: the "unaccusative" and the "unergative" verbs. The unaccusative class encompasses verbs whose single argument displays semantic and syntactic properties of canonical objects (i.e. it is an internal argument), whereas the unergative class involves verbs whose only argument has semantic and syntactic properties of canonical subjects (i.e. it is an external argument). The argument of the unaccusative verb *chegar* 'arrive', for instance, behaves like the direct object of a transitive verb like *demolir* 'demolish' in being able to participate in absolutive participial constructions (see Section 3.3.2.1), as opposed to the argument of the unergative verb *dançar* 'dance', as shown in (3.92).[63]

(3.92)   a. Demolid**as**   **as**   casas,   a   nova
         *demolish-**PPLE-FEM-PL** the.**FEM-PL** house.**FEM-PL** the new*
         construção   começou.
         construction   began
         'Once the houses had been demolished, the new construction began.'
      b. Chegad**os**   todos   **os**
         *arrive-**PPLE-MASC-PL** all-**MASC-PL** the.**MASC-PL***
         convidados,   a   reunião podia   começar.
         *guest-**MASC-PL** the meeting could   start*
         'After all the guests had arrived, the meeting could start.'

---

[63] For additional tests for the distinction between unaccusatives and unergatives in Portuguese and further discussion, see e.g. Eliseu 1984, Whitaker-Franchi 1989, Ciríaco and Cançado 2006, and Cançado, Godoy, and Amaral 2013.

c. *Dançad**os**   todos   **os**   convidados,
    dance-PPLE-MASC-PL all-MASC-PL the.MASC-PL guest-MASC-PL
    a   festa   acabou.
    the   party   ended
    'Once all the guests had danced, the party ended.'

This distinction between internal and external arguments is very relevant for the agreement asymmetries seen in (3.90) and (3.91). First, BP differs from EP in generally disallowing postverbal subjects that are external arguments, as illustrated in (3.93) (see Chapter 5). So, the agreement asymmetry seen in (3.91) can be witnessed in BP only with unaccusative verbs, for postverbal subjects with unergative verbs are generally not permitted in the first place.

(3.93) a. Chegaram uns   amigos   meus   ontem.   (EP/BP)
          arrived-PL some-PL friend-PL my-PL yesterday
          'There arrived some friends of mine yesterday.'
       b. Dançam uns   amigos   meus   nessa companhia. (EP/*BP)
          dance-PL some-PL friend-PL my-PL in-this company
          'Some friends of mine dance in this company.'

EP, on the other hand, allows postverbal subjects with both kinds of verbs, as seen in (3.93). Interestingly, only unaccusative verbs may allow lack of agreement with a postverbal subject in dialectal EP, as illustrated by the contrast between the unaccusative verb *nascer* 'be born' and the unergative *cantar* 'sing' (see (3.94) and (3.95)):

(3.94) a. Já   nasceram   os filhotes. (BP/EP)
          *already be.born.PAST-**PL** the puppies*
       b. Já   **nasceu**   os filhotes. (BP/%EP)
          *already be.born.PAST-3-**SG** the puppie*s
          'The puppies have already been born.'

(3.95) a. Cantam uns   amigos   meus   nesse coro. (EP)
          *sing-**PL** some-PL friend-PL my-PL in-this choir*
       b. **Canta** uns   amigos   meus   nesse coro. (EP)
          sing   some-PL friend-PL my-PL in-this choir
          'Some friends of mine sing in that choir.'

These distinctions between unaccusative and unergative verbs follow from the different nature of their argument. Given that the argument of an unaccusative verb has the semantic and syntactic properties of an object, it may appear in postverbal position, for this is the neutral position objects occupy in Portuguese. Likewise, unaccusative verbs may fail to trigger verbal agreement, for objects never trigger person and number agreement in Portuguese.

Hence, the internal arguments in (3.91b) and (3.94b) are just displaying their object nature as far as positioning and agreement properties are concerned. The agreement asymmetry between (3.90) and (3.91) is therefore parallel to what one finds in French constructions like (3.96), where the internal argument triggers agreement when occupying the subject position but not when occupying the object position.

(3.96)   *French*:
      a. Trois enfants **sont** **arrivés**.
         three children be.3.*PL* arrive-*PPLE.MASC-PL*
         'Three children arrived.'
      b. Il **est** **arrivé** trois enfants.
         it be.3.*SG* arrive-*PPLE.MASC.SG* three children
         'There arrived three children.'

The lack of agreement with the internal argument in (3.91b) and (3.94b) can now be accounted for if the subject position of these sentences is occupied by a null expletive akin to French *il* in (3.96b). In other words, lack of subject–verb agreement in sentences like (3.91b) and (3.94b) is only apparent, because the subject in the relevant configurations is actually a preverbal null expletive pronoun, which triggers (default) third person singular agreement (see Section 4.5). Furthermore, the contrast between EP and BP with respect to the acceptability of sentences like (3.91b) and (3.94b) (fully productive in BP but dialectally restricted in EP) reflects the general preference for bare agreeing forms in BP, as discussed in the previous sections.

There remain differences between EP and BP with respect to agreement in unaccusative constructions. Consider the data in (3.97) below, for instance.[64] In (3.97a), the agreement with the internal argument qualifies it as a proper subject and, as such, it should be able to control the reference of the null subject in the adjunct infinitival clause. In the "non-agreeing" construction in (3.97b), on the other hand, the subject position is occupied by a null expletive and the internal argument should fail to control the reference of the embedded subject. In fact, the predicted contrast holds in EP, but not in BP, which allows control by the internal argument in both cases. The fact that subject agreement is not a requirement in BP for a given element to qualify as a proper controller seems to be another consequence of BP's preference for bare forms whenever possible. Recall that there are actually BP dialects where the first person singular pronoun *eu* is the only subject that triggers overt agreement morphology on the verb and only in two tenses (see Section 3.4.2).

---

[64] See e.g. Carrilho 2003 for discussion.

(3.97) a. Chegaram muitas gaivotas sem   fazer   qualquer ruído. (BP/EP)
           arrived-**PL** many seagulls without make-INF any   noise
       b. **Chegou** muitas gaivotas sem   fazer   qualquer ruído. (**BP/*EP**)
           arrived many seagulls without make-INF any   noise
          'Many seagulls arrived silently.'

Another prediction arises with respect to case. If the null expletive in subject position is assigned nominative in "non-agreeing" constructions, the internal argument cannot bear nominative case. In EP, this is indeed the case, as illustrated in (3.98) and (3.99), which show the contrast between the grammatical "agreeing" sentences in (3.98a)/(3.99a) and the ungrammatical "non-agreeing" ones in (3.98b)/(3.99b).[65]

(3.98) a. Já   chegaram eles   todos à   praia. (EP)
          already arrived-**PL** pron.**NOM**.3-MASC-**PL** all   to.the beach
       b. *Já   **chegou** eles   todos à   praia. (EP)
          already arrived pron.**NOM**.3-MASC-**PL** all   to.the beach
          'They have all arrived at the beach already.'

(3.99) a. Cheguei   **eu**   e   vocês   partiram. (EP)
          arrived-**1.SG** I.**NOM** and you-PL left-PL
       b. ***Chegou** eu   e   vocês   partiram. (EP)
          arrived   I.**NOM** and you-PL left-PL
          'I arrived and you(PL) left.'

In BP, on the other hand, sentences such as (3.100), which are analogous to (3.98b) and (3.99b), are acceptable for many speakers.

(3.100) E   aí   **chega**   eu/vocês/nós/eles   lá   e
        and   then   arrive   I/you-PL/we/they   there   and
        não   tem   ninguém   na   casa!   (%BP)
        not   have   nobody   in-the   house
        'And then I/you(PL)/we/they arrive there and there's nobody home!'

In addition to constituting another instance of BP's preference for bare forms, the acceptability of sentences such as (3.100) for some speakers appears to be related to the fact that there is a massive case syncretism in BP (see Table 2.9), with the nominative form being the default. If so, whichever case the internal argument is associated with in "non-agreeing" constructions, it surfaces with default nominative in BP.[66]

3.5.1.2 Agreement with Coordinated Subjects

In Section 3.5.1.1, we saw that although "non-agreeing" constructions with unaccusative verbs are allowed by some EP speakers (see (3.91b)/(3.94b)), this does not happen with unergative verbs (see (3.95b)). In the face

---
[65] See e.g. Costa 2001 for discussion.
[66] See e.g. Viotti 2005, 2007 for discussion.

132   3 Agreement

of this contrast, the fact that EP speakers uniformly admit both agreement patterns with the postverbal subject of (3.101), which involves the unergative verb *mentir* 'lie', becomes very surprising.

(3.101) a. A   Maria e   o   João mentiram.
             the   Maria and the João lied-**PL**
         b. *A   Maria e   o   João **mentiu**.
             the   Maria and the João lied
         c. Mentiram a   Maria e   o   João.   (EP)
             lied-**PL** the Maria and the João
         d. **Mentiu** a   Maria e   o   João. (EP)
             lied   the Maria and the João
             'Maria and João lied.'

The examples in (3.102) below further show that, when there is no plural agreement in postverbal constructions, the verb necessarily agrees with the first member of the coordinated sequence (so-called *first conjunct agreement*). This in turn suggests that, in sentences like (3.101d), we also have first conjunct agreement rather than lack of agreement.

(3.102) a. Tu   e   a   Maria cantam/*cantas/***canta** nesse coro. (EP)
             pron.2.SG and the Maria sing.***PL***/sing-***2.SG***/sing in-this choir
             'You(SG) and Maria sing in this choir.'
         b. Nesse coro, cantam   tu   e   a   Maria.   (EP)
             in-this choir sing-***PL*** pron.2.SG and the Maria
         c. Nesse coro, cantas   tu   e   a   Maria.   (EP)
             in-this choir sing-***2.SG*** pron.2.SG and the Maria
         d. *Nesse coro, **canta** tu   e   a   Maria.   (EP)
             in-this choir sing   pron.2.SG and the Maria
         e. Nesse coro, **canta** a   Maria e   tu.   (EP)
             in-this choir sing   the Maria and pron.2.SG
         f. *Nesse coro, cantas   a   Maria e   tu.   (EP)
             in-this choir sing-***2.SG*** the Maria and pron.2.SG
             'In this choir, you(SG) and Maria sing.'

The data above can be accounted for if the constructions in (3.101d), (3.102c), and (3.102e) actually involve a biclausal structure associated with deletion of the verb of the second clause, rather than coordination of noun phrases.[67] That is, these sentences should be associated with the structures in (3.103).

---

[67] For further arguments, see Colaço 2005, where this analysis was proposed for EP. On gender and number agreement under coordination within noun phrases, see e.g. Colaço 2016.

(3.103) a. [**Mentiu** a Maria] e [~~mentiu~~ o João]   (EP)
         lied   the Maria and lied   the João
    b. Nesse coro, [**cantas** tu]   e [~~canta~~ a Maria] (EP)
         in-this choir sing-**2.SG** pron.2.SG and sing the Maria
    c. Nesse coro, [**canta** a Maria] e [~~cantas~~ tu]   (EP)
         in-this choir sing the Maria and sing-**2.SG** pron.2.SG

Crucially, the deletion process seen in (3.103), also known as *gapping*, cannot apply to the first member of a coordinated structure. Thus, sentences such as (3.101b) with *mentir* and (3.102a) with *cantar* cannot be generated through gapping and their ungrammaticality follows from lack of agreement with the coordinated subject, which must trigger plural agreement (see (3.101a)/(3.102a)).

As for BP, recall that it productively allows postverbal subjects only with unaccusative verbs. That said, let us examine the paradigm in (3.104) in BP, with the unaccusative verb *sair* 'leave'.[68]

(3.104) a. Eu e   a Maria **saímos**/*saí/*saiu   (BP/EP)
         I   and the Maria left-**1.PL**/left-**1.SG**/left
    b. **Saímos** eu e a Maria.   (BP/EP)
         left-**1.PL** I and the Maria
    c. **Saí** eu e a Maria.   (BP/EP)
         left-**1.SG** I and the Maria
       'Maria and I left.'

BP patterns similarly to EP with respect to (3.104) and the sentences in (3.104a–c) may be subject to the same analysis as that applied to EP in (3.101) and (3.102). In other words, (3.104a) must involve agreement between the coordinated subject and the verb, which then surfaces with first person plural morphology (see Section 3.4.2), for it cannot be derived through gapping. When the verb precedes all the arguments, a potential structural ambiguity arises. (3.104b) is parallel to (3.102b) in that the two noun phrases are conjoined and the coordinate subject is the constituent that triggers (first person plural) agreement. In turn, (3.104c) illustrates the possibility of a biclausal structure with gapping along the lines of (3.105) (see (3.103)).

(3.105) [**Saí** eu] e [~~saiu~~ a Maria]
         left-**1.SG** I and left the Maria

---

[68] For purposes of presentation, the agreement glosses in (3.104) and (3.105) follow EP specifications. Note that, in *saiu*, -*u* is a tense marker; there is no overt morpheme encoding agreement.

Finally, given that BP independently has the option (unavailable in EP) of having an internal argument with default nominative and the unaccusative verb with the bare form, as seen in (3.100), the pattern in (3.106) is also allowed.

(3.106) **Saiu** eu e a Maria. (BP/*EP)
left I and the Maria
'Maria and I left.'

3.5.2 Agreement with Impersonal Predicates

Impersonal constructions in Portuguese frequently display alternating agreement patterns, with the verb carrying what is traditionally analyzed as third person singular or third person plural morphology, as illustrated in (3.107)–(3.109).

(3.107) a. **Faltam** vinte minutos para o avião sair.
lack-**PL** twenty minutes for the plane leave
b. **Falta** vinte minutos para o avião sair.
lack twenty minutes for the plane leave
'The plane will leave in twenty minutes.'

(3.108) a. **Choveram** toneladas de água esta noite.
rained-**PL** tons of water this night
b. **Choveu** toneladas de água esta noite.
rained tons of water this night
'It has rained a lot tonight.'

(3.109) a. Agora **são** três horas em Paris. (BP/EP)
now be.3.**PL** three hours in Paris
b. Agora **é** três horas em Paris. (BP/%EP)
now be.3.**SG** three hours in Paris
'Now it's three o'clock in Paris.'

Idiosyncratic lexical differences aside (see (3.109) in EP), the two patterns of agreement are allowed in both EP and BP. As should be expected by now, EP and BP differ with respect to the preferred pattern, though. The unmarked pattern in EP is the one with plural morphology on the verb, whereas BP favors the pattern with bare forms. In other words, we have the same scenario as that depicted for unaccusatives (see Section 3.5.1.1).

Given the analysis of unaccusative constructions discussed in Section 3.5.1.1, the "non-agreeing" impersonal constructions in (3.107)–(3.109) can also be analyzed in terms of a null expletive occupying the subject position and triggering third person singular agreement, whereas the agreeing versions can be analyzed in terms of agreement with the internal argument. Interestingly, however, the agreeing impersonal constructions differ from the agreeing unaccusative constructions in that the internal argument cannot appear in preverbal position, as illustrated in (3.110) (with flat intonation).[69]

(3.110) a. *Vinte minutos faltam para o avião sair.
twenty minutes lack-**PL** for the plane leave
'The plane will leave in twenty minutes.'
b. *Toneladas de água choveram esta noite.
tons of water rained-**PL** this night
'It has rained a lot tonight.'
c. *Agora três horas **são** em Paris.
now three hours be.3.**PL** in Paris
'Now it's three o'clock in Paris.'

Some speakers of EP and BP extend the alternating pattern of agreement seen above to existential constructions that canonically trigger third person singular agreement, as illustrated in (3.111) and (3.112).[70,71]

(3.111) a. **Havia** muitos gatos nesse jardim. (EP)
had many cats in-this garden
b. Havi**am** muitos gatos nesse jardim. (%EP)
had-**PL** many cats in-this garden
'There were many cats in this garden.'

(3.112) a. **Tinha** muitos gatos nesse jardim. (BP)
had many cats in-this garden
b. Tinh**am** muitos gatos nesse jardim. (%BP)
had-**PL** many cats in-this garden
'There were many cats in this garden.'

In consonance with what we have seen regarding the agreement preferences of EP and BP, nonstandard agreeing constructions such as (3.111b) are

---

[69] This freezing effect may be accounted for if the internal argument of impersonal constructions receives inherent case in the sense of Chomsky 1986. For discussion of the correlation between inherent case and movement to subject position, see e.g. Nunes 2008a, 2010b, 2017. The word order in (3.110) is allowed in EP only if the subject constituent has undergone (contrastive/mirative) focus-movement, which correlates with a specific intonation contour.

[70] EP uses the verb *haver* for existential constructions, whereas BP employs the verb *ter*. For discussion see e.g. Ribeiro 1993, Franchi, Negrão, and Viotti 1998, Viotti 1998, 1999, Avelar 2004, 2009b, Avelar and Callou 2007, Kato 2006, Duarte and Kato 2008, and Carrilho and Pereira 2009.

[71] Some speakers of EP and BP also extend the agreement pattern to the prepositional object of the verb *tratar-se de* 'to be about', as illustrated in (i).

(i) a. **Trata**-se de trabalhos muito importantes.
treat-REFL$_{[CL]}$ of works very important-PL
b. **Tratam**-se de trabalhos muito importantes. (%EP/%BP)
treat-**PL**-REFL$_{[CL]}$ of works very important-PL
'These are very important works.'

quite common in spoken EP and appear to be a feature of urban dialects, whereas BP counterparts such as (3.112b) are associated with speakers with more formal education. Again, speakers who accept the agreement versions do not allow movement of the internal argument, as illustrated in (3.113).

(3.113) a. *Muitos gatos haviam nesse jardim. (EP)
many cats had-**PL** in-this garden
b. *Muitos gatos tinham nesse jardim. (BP)
many cats had-**PL** in-this garden
'There were many cats in this garden.'

3.5.3 Agreement in se Constructions

Like other Romance languages, Portuguese also allows constructions with the so-called indefinite (or impersonal) clitic *se*.[72] Basically any type of verb can participate in indefinite *se* constructions in EP, as illustrated in (3.114), whereas BP does not admit indefinite *se* with raising verbs (see (3.114f)).[73]

(3.114) a. *Transitive verbs with prepositional complements:*
Precisa-se de cozinheiros.
need-SE of cooks
'Cooks wanted.'
b. *Unergative verbs:*
Vive-se bem nesta cidade.
live-SE well in-this city
'One lives well in this city.'
c. *Unaccusative verbs:*
Chegava-se cedo ao trabalho.
arrived-SE early at-the work
'One used to arrive early at work.'
d. *Passive verbs:*
Quando se é **promovido**, as coisas ficam mais fáceis.
when SE be.3.SG promoted the things stay more easy
'When one is promoted, things become easier.'

---

[72] For discussion see e.g. Naro 1976, Galves 1986b, 1987, Cinque 1988, Nunes 1990, 1991, Raposo and Uriagereka 1996, Cavalcante 2006, Martins 2009, Duarte 2013a, Negrão and Viotti 2015, and Martins and Nunes 2016.
[73] See e.g. Quicoli 1982, Cinque 1988, and Nunes 1990, 1991 for discussion.

e. *Copular verbs:*
Não se **ficou** contente com a nova situação.
not SE stayed happy with the new situation
'People were not happy with the new situation.'

f. *Raising verbs:*
Parecia-se estar apreensivo. (EP/*BP)
seemed-SE be apprehensive
'One seemed apprehensive.'

In all the cases above, the clitic *se* is associated with default (third person singular) agreement in EP and in BP (see Section 3.4.2) and is arguably assigned nominative case. As for gender agreement, *se* behaves as if it were not specified for gender, thus being sensitive to the gender of the speaker. A generic sentence such as (3.115a), for instance, with default masculine agreement, may be uttered by a male or a female, whereas (3.115b), with a feminine participle, indicates that the speaker is female.[74]

(3.115) a. É revoltante quando se é demitido sem um
*is upsetting when SE be.3.SG fired-**MASC** without a*
motivo justo.
motive fair
'It is upsetting when one is fired unfairly.'

b. Quando se é **recomendada** para um
*when SE be.3.SG recommended-**FEM** for a*
cargo, a responsabilidade aumenta.
job the responsibility increases
[spoken by a **female**]
'When one is recommended for a job, one's responsibility increases.'

---

[74] The sentences in (3.116) also show that *se* triggers default number agreement on the participle. As illustrated in (i), there are dialects of EP that admit plural agreement, though. For a possible correlation of this pattern with dialectal subject doubling with the indefinite clitic *se* (see footnote 75 below), see Martins 2009.

(i) a. Não se andava **calçados**. (%EP)
not SE walked with.shoe.on-MASC-PL
'We didn't go around wearing shoes.'
(CORDIAL-SIN, CDR25)

b. Na idade é que é; uma pessoa quando se é **novos**, poder (%EP)
in-the age is that is a person when SE is young-MASC-PL can-INF
'There is a right time for everything; when one is young, one must be strong willed.'
(CORDIAL-SIN, ALV36)

When *se*-constructions involve transitive verbs with prepositionless "third person" plural complements, the verb may agree with the internal argument, as illustrated in (3.116):[75]

(3.116) a. **Ouviu**-se as três explosões na cidade toda. (EP/BP)
           heard.*SE the three explosions in-the city all*
        b. Ouviram-se as três explosões na cidade toda. (EP/*BP)
           heard-***PL**-SE the three explosions in-the city all*
           'The three explosions were heard throughout the city.'

In (3.116a), as in (3.114), the indefinite clitic *se* is the controller of subject–verb agreement and bears nominative case. In (3.116b), on the other hand, it is the internal argument that controls agreement and has nominative case. For this reason, constructions such as (3.116b) are generally called *impersonal passives* and, accordingly, the clitic *se* in these constructions is analyzed as a passive marker.

Evidence for the different nature of the constructions in (3.116) (in EP) is provided by the contrasts between (3.117) and (3.118).[76]

(3.117) a. **Cria**-se facilmente avestruzes. (EP)
           raise-SE easily ostriches
           'One raises ostriches easily.'

---

[75] The indefinite clitic *se* can be associated with different nominative pronouns in a double subject construction found in some EP dialects, as illustrated in (i) below, with the doubling pronoun setting an inclusive or exclusive reading for *se* (see Martins 2009). Verbal agreement in this case is determined by the doubling pronoun: hence, default ("third person singular") agreement in (ia), first person plural agreement in (ib), and third person plural agreement in (ic).

(i) a. **A gente**   não   **se**   **come**,   mas   os   de   Lisboa
       ***pron.[P.N]** not   **SE**$_{IND}$ eat*   *but   the   of   Lisbon*
       diz   que   comem   daquele   peixe.   (%EP)
       says   that   eat   of-that   fish
       'Here we don't eat that fish but we heard that in Lisbon people eat it.'
                                                                         (CORDIAL-SIN, CLC25)
    b. Há   várias   qualidades   de   peixe   que   até   ainda
       has   several   qualities   of   fish   that   even   already
       nós   não   **se**   conhecemos.   (%EP)
       ***we**   not   **SE**   know-1.PL*
       'There are so many fish species that even we (fishermen) do not know them all yet.'
                                                                         (CORDIAL-SIN, ALV29)
    c. Sei   é   de   real   certeza   que   isto   era
       know.1.SG   is   of   real   certainty that   this   was
       com   o que   **se**   **eles** batiam   o   centeio.   (%EP)
       *with   what   **SE**   **they** beat-3-PL the   rye*
       'What I know for sure is that this was the thing that people used to husk the rye.'
                                                                         (CORDIAL-SIN, SRP15)

[76] For discussion see e.g. Martins and Nunes 2016.

b. **Cria**-se avestruzes **despreocupado**. (EP)
raise-SE ostriches unpreoccupied
'One raises ostriches without any worries.'
c. Cria-se-**as** facilmente. (%EP)
raise-SE-*pron.ACC.3.FEM-PL$_{[CL]}$* easily
'One raises them easily.'
d. Pode-se criá-**las** facilmente. (EP)
can-SE raise-INF-*pron.ACC.3.FEM-PL$_{[CL]}$* easily
'One can raise them easily.'

(3.118) a. **Criam**-se facilmente avestruzes. (EP)
raise-**PL**-SE easily ostriches
'One raises ostriches easily.'
b. *****Criam**-se avestruzes **despreocupado**. (EP)
raise-**PL**-SE ostriches unpreoccupied
'One raises ostriches without any worries.'
c. *****Criam**-se-**as** facilmente. (EP)
raise-**PL**-SE-*pron.ACC.3.FEM-PL$_{[CL]}$* easily
d. *****Podem**-se criá-**las** facilmente. (EP)
can-**PL**-SE raise-INF-*pron.ACC.3.FEM-PL$_{[CL]}$* easily
'One can raise them easily.'

In (3.117), *se* is an indefinite subject and bears nominative. Hence, it may control a subject-oriented secondary predicate like the one in (3.117b) and the internal argument is free to receive accusative case (see (3.117c–d)). Sentences like (3.117c) belong to Southern EP dialects and are judged grammatical by the second author. In other EP dialects the sequence *se* + accusative clitic is always excluded.[77] However, (3.117d), where the clitic sequence is broken, is acceptable in all dialects, which shows that the internal argument of indefinite *se* constructions receives accusative even in the dialects that do not allow (3.117c). In turn, *se* in (3.118) is a passive marker and the internal argument receives nominative case. Hence, *se* cannot license subject-oriented secondary predicates (see (3.118b)) and the internal argument cannot surface as an accusative clitic in any dialect even if it is not adjacent to *se* (see (3.118c–d)).

EP and BP behave differently with respect to *se* constructions involving transitive verbs with prepositionless complements. While both indefinite *se* and passive *se* are allowed in EP, only indefinite *se* is admitted in BP.[78] BP also departs from EP in apparently being able to drop indefinite *se* in generic tenses, yielding an indefinite reading for a null third person singular subject,

---

[77] See e.g. Naro 1976, Nunes 1990, 1991, and Martins and Nunes 2016 for discussion.
[78] The passive *se* in BP is acquired through schooling and is confined to formal or literary language. For discussion see e.g. Galves 1986b, 1987, Nunes 1990, 1991, and Cavalcante 2006.

as illustrated in (3.119) below (see Section 4.4.2).[79] Both of these differences again conform with the generalization that BP favors lack of overt verbal agreement morphology and the use of bare forms whenever possible.

(3.119) a. Não **usa** mais esse estilo de redação. (BP)
　　　　　not　use　more　this　style　of　writing
　　　　　'One doesn't use this writing style anymore.'
　　　b. **Casava**　　　　muito cedo no　　século passado. (BP)
　　　　　marry-IMPERF very　early in-the century passed
　　　　　'People used to get married very young in the last century.'
　　　c. No　futuro　**vai** descobrir remédio para tudo　　quanto
　　　　　in-the future　go discover　medicine for　everything which
　　　　　é　　doença. (BP)
　　　　　is　sickness
　　　　　'In the future medicines will be discovered for every sickness.'

3.6 Summary

In Chapter 2, we saw that case morphology in BP is weaker than in EP in that fewer case distinctions are overtly marked (see Table 2.9). In the current chapter we observed a similar scenario with respect to agreement morphology. Generally speaking, BP favors bare forms whenever possible. The morphological realization of plural agreement, for instance, is not always enforced in BP within noun phrases or in nominal, adjectival, or participial predicates (see Sections 3.2.2, 3.3.1, and 3.3.2.1). Specifically in the case of noun phrases, the possibility of recording number only on the determiner has made it possible for bare singulars with count nouns to become acceptable in BP (see Section 3.2.2.3), in sharp contrast with EP.

As for verbal agreement morphology, the differences are almost insignificant at first sight: EP has up to five agreement distinctions in finite clauses and four in inflected infinitivals (see Tables 3.1 and 3.5), whereas BP displays one fewer distinction in each case (see Tables 3.2 and 3.6). However, a mere count of the number of inflectional distinctions does not account for other sharp syntactic differences between EP and BP, such as the dialectal variation in BP that always leans towards bare forms (see Sections 3.3.2.2.1 and 3.3.2.2.2) or their differences regarding null subject licensing (see Chapter 4). The hypothesis entertained in Table 3.11 above is that the weakening of person and

---

[79] For discussion see e.g. Galves 1986b, 1987, Nunes 1990, 1991, Lunguinho and Medeiros Jr. 2009, and Carvalho 2018, 2019.

3.6 Summary

number morphology in BP grammar is not restricted to inflectional morphemes, but affects the personal pronouns, as well. More specifically, all the verbal agreement distinctions can be captured in an optimal way, with no mismatches between morphological and semantic specifications, if personal pronouns in BP are drastically underspecified from a morphological point of view, with *eu* being specified as SG, the morpheme *-s* of the pronouns *vocês/cês* and *eles/elas* as PL, *nós* as 1, and no additional value for the other person and number attributes. Under this view, the agreement systems of EP and BP are similar only superficially, for the forms that have the same phonetic shape in the two dialects may be derived from different underlying specifications. In particular, verbal forms that have been traditionally analyzed as carrying third person singular inflection in EP are analyzed in BP as always involving forms with unvalued person and number features. This is due to the fact that the values 3 for person and SG for number are not assigned a phonetic exponent in EP; hence, verbal forms with these values in EP are indistinguishable from corresponding verbal forms in BP with no value for such features.

From this perspective, all verbal agreement morphemes in BP apart from the (traditional) first person plural form *-mos* can be analyzed as being derived from an underlying form involving unvalued specification for person and number or an underlying form involving valued specification just for number (see Table 3.13 above). This overall morphological opacity in BP has paved the way for the emergence of hyper-raising constructions, where an embedded inflected domain (finite or infinitival) is specified only for number, allowing its subject to undergo subject-to-subject movement to a higher domain (see Section 3.4.3). In this sense, the wholesale simplification of the agreement paradigms in BP when compared to EP have ended up broadening the types of raising constructions allowed in the language.

In the next chapter, we will see that the underlying differences between the agreement systems of EP and BP also correlate with their differences in the licensing of null subjects.

4

Null Subjects

4.1 Introduction

One remarkable property of natural languages is that they may allow predicate arguments to be left phonetically unexpressed. Interestingly, languages vary with respect to the kinds of arguments they allow to be phonetically null and the syntactic environments where such argument drop is licensed. European Portuguese (EP) and Brazilian Portuguese (BP) provide a concrete example of how fascinating this issue of null arguments can be: although they both allow null subjects and null complements, they differ considerably with respect to the specific arguments that can be left unexpressed. In this chapter, we examine null subjects in each variety, leaving a discussion of null complements to Chapter 6.

The chapter is organized as follows. In Section 4.2, we introduce the three types of null subjects we will discuss here: definite, indefinite, and expletive null subjects. In Sections 4.3, 4.4, and 4.5 we examine the properties of each type in both varieties. In Section 4.6 we discuss some issues related to the differences between EP and BP regarding null subjects. Finally, Section 4.7 summarizes the major properties discussed in the chapter.

4.2 Different Types of Null Subjects

There are several types of null subjects and languages vary with respect to the types they license. The first distinction one may make hinges on whether the environment where the null subject is found can independently host an overt subject. Take the contrast between Portuguese and English illustrated in (4.1) and (4.2), for example.[1]

(4.1)   a. **Eu** vou viajar amanhã.
            I   *go.1.SG*   *travel*   *tomorrow*
            'I'm going to travel tomorrow.'
      b. [Ø vou viajar amanhã]
            go.1.SG   *travel*   *tomorrow*

(4.2)   a. **I** am going to travel tomorrow.
      b. *[Ø am going to travel tomorrow]

The overt subject may alternate with a null counterpart in (4.1) in Portuguese, but not in (4.2) in English. However, this does not entail that English never allows null subjects. As shown in (4.3) and (4.4), a null subject may in fact be the only option for certain configurations in English.

(4.3)   a. *Mary began [**herself** to understand the problem]
      b. Mary began [Ø   to understand the problem]

(4.4)   a. *It is forbidden [**people** to park here]
      b. It is forbidden [Ø   to park here]

Similarly, the fact that the null subject of (4.1b) in Portuguese can alternate with its overt counterpart does not mean that this alternation is always available in Portuguese. As illustrated in (4.5), there are environments in Portuguese that replicate the pattern seen in (4.3) and (4.4) in English, where a null subject is allowed, but an overt one is not.

(4.5)   a. *O João queria [**ele** vir aqui]
            the João wanted he come here
      b. O João queria [Ø vir aqui]
            the João wanted   come here
            'João wanted to come here.'

The lack of alternation in (4.3)–(4.5) is arguably due to their case properties. In Section 2.3.4 we saw that different syntactic positions may be associated with different cases and that in Portuguese only

---

[1] We saw in Section 3.4.2 that verbal agreement morphology is superficially the same in EP and BP but has different underlying specifications in the two varieties (see Table 3.12). Given that the pronoun *eu* 'I' is morphologically specified as 1.SG in EP but just as SG in BP, the corresponding verbal inflection on the verb of (4.1), for instance, should accordingly be glossed as 1.SG in EP and SG in BP. To simplify the presentation, we will however gloss agreement morphemes in terms of their traditional description and resort to fine-grained specifications only when this is the issue under discussion.

pronouns exhibit morphological distinctions for case. The same holds true of English. However, this does not entail that noun phrases other than pronouns in Portuguese or English are not sensitive to case. We can see the relevance of "abstract" case for noun phrases in general with the contrast between the Portuguese verbs *amar* 'love' and *gostar* 'like' illustrated in (4.6) below. Although *amar* and *gostar* are very similar in meaning, the noun phrase *o João* can be the syntactic complement of *amar* in (4.6a), but not of *gostar* in (4.6b). In order for *gostar* to license a noun phrase as its complement, the meaningless preposition *de* 'of' must be inserted before the noun phrase, as seen in (4.6c). Furthermore, note that it is not simply the case that *gostar* must select a prepositional phrase; as shown in (4.6d), when the complement is a clause and not a noun phrase, the dummy preposition is not required.

(4.6) a. A Maria ama o João.
the Maria loves the João
'Maria loves João.'
b. *A Maria gosta o João.
the Maria likes the João
'Maria likes João.'
c. A Maria gosta do João.
the Maria likes of-the João
'Maria likes João.'
d. A Maria gostaria que o João viesse.
the Maria like-PRET.FUT that the João come-SUBJ.PAST
'Maria would like João to come.'

Once the case properties of *amar* and *gostar* are taken into consideration, the puzzle in (4.6) dissolves. As shown by the data in (4.7) below, *amar* licenses accusative case, but *gostar* does not. That being so, the unacceptability of (4.6b) in contrast to (4.6d) can be accounted for if nominal phrases in general, but not clauses, require being licensed with case even if they do not overtly display case distinctions.[2] The acceptability of (4.6c) can now be accounted for if the dummy preposition can license *o João* with oblique case, which is confirmed by the morphological shape of the pronoun in (4.7c). Accordingly, the contrasts in (4.3), (4.4), and (4.5) can be accounted for if their infinitival clauses do not have case available for their subjects.

(4.7) a. A Maria ama-o. (EP)
the Maria loves-pron.ACC.3.MASC.SG$_{[CL]}$
'Maria loves him.'

---

[2] This requirement has become known as the Case Filter (see e.g. Chomsky 1981 and Vergnaud 2008).

b. *A Maria gosta-o. (EP)
the Maria likes-pron.ACC.3.MASC.SG$_{[CL]}$
'Maria likes him.'
c. A Maria gosta de mim.
the Maria likes of me$_{OBL}$
'Maria likes me.'

In this chapter we will set aside null subjects found in obligatorily caseless positions such as those in (4.3b), (4.4b), and (4.5b)[3] and focus on null subjects like that in (4.1b), whose lack of phonetic realization is not due to unavailability of case. We will also put aside null subjects of imperatives and coordinated structures as in (4.8), which are generally allowed crosslinguistically even in languages that disallow null subjects like the one in (4.1b).

(4.8) a. [Ø abra a porta, por favor]
open the door by favor
'Open the door, please.'
b. O João abriu a porta e [Ø entrou]
the João opened the door and entered
'João opened the door and came in.'

In the generative literature, languages that consistently allow null subjects in case-marked positions are referred to as *pro-drop* languages and languages that require case-marked subject positions to be filled with an overt expression as *non-pro-drop* languages. The intuition behind this terminology is that null subjects in pro-drop languages behave like pronouns in that they may refer, but do not have the type of descriptive content that we find in standard noun phrases such as *the beautiful house*. Metaphorically speaking, it is as if subject pronouns could be dropped in pro-drop languages. This does not mean that overt and null pronominal subjects can freely alternate in pro-drop languages, though. In general, the overt version behaves as a strong pronoun and the null version as a weak pronoun, in the sense of Cardinaletti and Starke 1999 (see Section 2.2). Thus, an overt subject pronoun in pro-drop languages may convey a shift in the topic of discussion, single out the relevant denotation when more than one interpretation is potentially accessible, or be interpreted as being focused or emphatic; by contrast, the null subject is found in more neutral contexts.[4] EP is a prototypical pro-drop language, whereas

---

[3] The null subject of (4.3b), (4.4b), and (4.5b) (see Chapter 3: footnote 30) corresponds to PRO in the Principles and Parameters Theory (see e.g. Chomsky 1981, Chomsky and Lasnik 1993).

[4] The apparent preference for a null subject over its overt counterpart in neutral contexts found in pro-drop languages is commonly referred to as the *Avoid Pronoun Principle* (see e.g. Chomsky 1981).

English is a prototypical non-pro-drop language. As for BP, it does allow phonetically empty subjects, but they are generally much more restricted than their EP cousins, as we shall see.[5]

In this chapter we will discuss three general classes of null subjects. The first encompasses what we will refer to as *definite* null subjects. These involve null subjects whose denotation is determined by the corresponding verbal agreement morphology, as in (4.9a), the utterance context, as in (4.9b), another element in the sentence, as in (4.9c), or another element in the discourse, as in (4.9d).

(4.9)   a.   Ø   termine**i**   o   trabalho.
             finished-1.SG   *the*   *work*
             'I finished the work.'
       b.   Ø   aceita   um   cafezinho?
             accept   *a*   *coffee-DIM*
             'Would you(SG) like some coffee?'
       c.   [O João]$_i$ disse que [Ø$_i$ já   almoçou].
             the João   *said*   *that*   *already had.lunch*
             'João said that he had already had lunch.'
       d.   A: –   [O João]$_i$ estava   muito   feliz   ontem.
                    the João   *was*   *very*   *happy*   *yesterday*
                    'João was very happy yesterday.'
             B: –   A médica   confirmou que [Ø$_i$ está   curado].   (EP)
                    the doctor-FEM confirmed that   *is*   *cured-MASC*
                    'The doctor has confirmed that he has been cured.'

The second class that we will discuss involves null subjects that receive a fixed indefinite interpretation when associated with specific verbal inflections. The sentence in (4.10) below, for instance, can appear out of the blue, with the third person plural inflection on the verb indicating that the agent (the null subject) excludes the speaker, but is otherwise left unspecified. We will refer to such null subjects as *indefinite*.

(4.10)   Ø$_{IND}$ demitiram o   João.
               fired-3PL   *the João*
               'João was fired.'

---

[5] For discussion on the availability and interpretation of null subjects in Portuguese, as well as their alternation with overt pronouns, see e.g. Chao 1983, Moreira da Silva 1983, Tarallo 1983, Negrão 1986, Galves 1987, 1993, 1997, 1998, 2001, Brito 1991b, Duarte 1993, 1995, 2000, Barbosa 1995, 1996, 2019, Lobo 1995, 2013b, Figueiredo Silva 1996, Britto 1998, 2000, Kato 1999, 2000, 2002a, Ferreira 2000, 2009, Kato and Negrão 2000, Modesto 2000, Barbosa, Duarte, and Kato 2001, 2005, Rodrigues 2002, 2004, Martins and Nunes 2005, 2009, 2010, 2021, Nunes 2008a, 2009, 2010a,b, 2011, 2016, 2017, 2020a, Holmberg, Nayudu, and Sheehan 2009, Petersen 2011, Camacho 2013, 2016, Lobo and Martins 2017, Saab 2016, Coelho, Nunes, and Santos 2018, and Kato and Duarte 2021.

Finally, the third class involves *expletive* null subjects. These are taken to involve null pronominal elements that occupy the subject position but are not assigned a denotation. Their postulation is somewhat theory-internal as it is based on the existence of overt counterparts in non-pro-drop languages. In English, for instance, the subject position of the sentences in (4.11) below cannot be left empty and must be filled by the dummy pronominal elements *it* or *there*, despite the fact that they are assigned no denotation. If every clause must have a syntactic subject regardless of its interpretation, then sentences analogous to (4.11) in Portuguese should also involve a null pronominal expletive in the subject position, as represented in (4.12).[6]

(4.11) a. *(**It**) rained yesterday.
        b. *(**There**) was a clown at the party.

(4.12) a. Ø$_{EXPL}$ choveu ontem.
           rained yesterday
           'It rained yesterday.'
        b. Ø$_{EXPL}$ havia um palhaço na   festa. (EP)
           had   a   clown   in-the party
           'There was a clown at the party.'

In the following sections we discuss the similarities and differences between EP and BP with respect to each type of null subject mentioned above.

4.3 Definite Null Subjects

Although EP and BP both allow definite null subjects, they exhibit considerable quantitative and qualitative differences regarding these null arguments.[7] Table 4.1 below, for instance, depicts the rate of usage of null subjects in two comparable samples of oral corpora in EP and BP, reported in Duarte 2000. It shows that, for each person, it is always the case that definite null subjects are employed in a much more robust way in EP than in BP.[8]

---

[6] The requirement that every clause have a syntactic subject is referred to as the *Extended Projection Principle* (EPP) in the Principles and Parameters Theory (see e.g. Chomsky 1981 and Chomsky and Lasnik 1993).
[7] For discussion, see references in footnote 5 above.
[8] See Duarte 2000 for details and discussion.

Table 4.1 *Frequency of definite null subjects according to person in oral corpora in Portuguese*

	EP	BP
1st person	65%	26%
2nd person	76%	10%
3rd person	79%	42%

Adapted from Duarte 2000.

Table 4.2 *Frequency of definite null subjects in Brazilian theater plays across time*

Year of play						
1845	1882	1918	1937	1955	1975	1992
80%	77%	75%	54%	50%	33%	26%

Adapted from Duarte 1993.

Diachronic studies have also documented a substantive decrease over time in the frequency of definite null subjects in BP.[9] Table 4.2, for instance, presents the results of Duarte's (1993) study on the overall frequency of definite null subjects in seven theater plays written by Brazilian authors between 1845 and 1992.[10] We can see that, in less than two centuries, the frequency drops from 80 percent to 26 percent.[11]

Notice that Table 4.1 also hints at some qualitative differences between the two varieties in that the frequency of null subjects is much more sensitive to the type of person in BP than in EP. This is undoubtedly related to the differences in their pronominal and verbal agreement systems discussed in Chapters 2 and 3. With this in mind, in the following sections we will describe the null subjects available in each variety, paying close attention to their morphological specifications, as well as the verbal agreement morphology they are associated with. We will discuss first and second person null subjects separately from third person null subjects because of their intrinsic different

---

[9] For discussion see e.g. Tarallo 1983, Duarte 1993, 1995, 2000, Martins and Nunes 2009, and Nunes 2011.
[10] See Duarte 1993 for details and discussion.
[11] EP and BP also show different profiles as far as the acquisition of null subjects is concerned, with BP being somewhat influenced by schooling in this regard. See e.g. Simões 1997, 1999, R. Lopes 2003, Magalhães 2003, 2006, 2007, Gonçalves 2004, Magalhães and Santos 2006, and Lobo 2016b for discussion.

interpretive properties. Overt first and second person pronouns can generally be used in out-of-the-blue contexts, because their feature specifications suffice to identify them as the utterance's speaker or the addressee. Accordingly, their null counterparts can be interpreted in the same manner (if they are morphologically licensed, as we shall see shortly). By contrast, the interpretation of a third person pronoun must piggyback on the interpretation of another nominal phrase in the discourse even when it is overt.[12] A sentence such as (4.13) below, for instance, is pragmatically odd in an out-of-the-blue context, regardless of whether the third person pronoun is overt or null. For this reason, definite third person null subjects will be examined in contexts where there could be an appropriate nominal expression in the sentence or in the discourse that could in principle ground their denotation. This will help us to properly identify the role verbal inflectional morphology plays in identifying third person null subjects.

(4.13) **Ela/Ø** fala francês bem.
 she speaks French well
 'She speaks French well.'

4.3.1 *Definite Null Subjects in Finite Clauses*

4.3.1.1 **First and Second Person Null Subjects in Finite Clauses**

Let us re-examine the inventory of first and second person nominative pronouns in EP and BP (see Sections 2.4.1 and 2.4.2) and the verbal agreement inflections they are associated with (see Section 3.4.2), starting with the paradigm that displays the larger number of distinctions. As observed in Section 3.4.2, the indicative present, the indicative perfective past, and the indicative future are the only tenses in Portuguese that have a specific agreement morpheme for *eu* 'I'.[13] This is illustrated in Table 4.3 below, with the indicative present tense.

As we can see in Table 4.3, first and second person pronouns can be divided in two groups, depending on whether or not they are associated with unambiguous verbal inflection in finite clauses. The first group involves *eu* 'I', *nós* 'we', and *tu* 'you.SG', each of which may be associated with a distinctive verbal agreement inflection. In turn, the second group encompasses *a gente* 'we', *você/cê* 'you.SG', and *vocês/cês* 'you-PL', which are associated with the

---

[12] Here we put aside situations where an overt third person pronoun can be deictically identified through extralinguistic means such as pointing.
[13] As mentioned in Section 3.4.2, the indicative future has been replaced by the periphrastic future in BP, which ends up reducing to two the number of tenses that have a regular distinctive agreement inflection for *eu* in BP.

Table 4.3 *First and second person pronouns and verbal agreement morphology in Portuguese finite clauses (fuller paradigm)*

Nominative pronouns	Verbal inflection: *dançar* 'dance' (indicative present)
eu 'I'	*danço*
tu 'you(SG)' (EP)	*danças*
nós 'we'	*dançamos*
você 'you(SG)'	*dança*
cê 'you(SG)$_{[W]}$' (BP)	
a gente 'we'	
vocês 'you(PL)'	*dançam*
cês 'you(PL)$_{[W]}$' (BP)	

agreement inflection that is homophonous to the one triggered by third person pronouns (see Sections 3.4.1 and 4.3.1.2 below).

Taken at face value, this distinction could play a significant role in the licensing of subject dropping. After all, verbal agreement morphology by itself suffices to identify the subject of the clause if it corresponds to pronouns of the first group. So, if null subject licensing were tied to unambiguous agreement inflection, the expectation would be that null subjects corresponding to pronouns of the first group should be morphologically licensed by the related agreement inflection, as opposed to null subjects corresponding to pronouns of the second group. Surprisingly, the lack of ambiguity in the verbal agreement inflection does not seem to play a major role with respect to null subject licensing, as we shall see shortly. In fact, at first sight this seems to be a totally obvious fact. Data such as (4.14) and (4.15), for instance, appear to show that null subjects corresponding to each of the pronouns in Table 4.3 can be licensed regardless of whether or not they can be unambiguously identified by the verbal inflection.[14]

---

[14] The acceptability judgments relative to the examples in (4.14) and similar empirical paradigms correspond to the readings indicated in parentheses. For presentation purposes, agreement morphemes are glossed in terms of their traditional description unless fine-grained specifications become relevant (see footnote 1 above). Also for reasons of presentation, we will not represent the null counterparts of the pronouns *cê*/*cês* in BP, as they arguably have the same distribution as the null counterparts of the longer forms *você*/*vocês*.

(4.14) a. A: – Você terminou as tarefas?
you.SG finished the tasks
'Have you(SG) finished the tasks?'
B: – [Ø terminei] (Ø = eu)
finished-1.SG
'Yes, I have.'
b. A: – Eu devo reclamar?
I should-1.SG complain
'Should I complain?'
B: – [Ø deves] (EP: Ø = tu)
should-2.SG
'Yes, you(SG) should.'
c. A: – Eu estou enganado?
I am mistaken
'Am I mistaken?'
B: – [Ø está] (Ø = você)
be.PRES.3.SG
'Yes, you(SG) are.'
d. A: – Vocês abriram os envelopes?
you-PL opened-3.PL the envelopes
'Did you(PL) open the envelopes?'
B: – [Ø abrimos] (Ø = nós)
opened-1.PL
'Yes, we did.'
e. A: – A gente não vai ter que esperar muito, ou vai?
we not go.3.SG have that wait much or go.3.SG
'We won't have to wait long, will we?'
B: – [Ø vai, sim] (Ø = a gente)
go.3.SG yes
'Yes, we will.'
f. A: – Você acha que nós convencemos o diretor?
you.SG think that we convince-1.PL the director
'Do you(SG) think we convinced the director?'
B: – [Ø convenceram, sim] (Ø = vocês)
convinced-3PL yes
'Yes, you(PL) certainly did.'

(4.15) a. [Ø vou pensar no seu caso] (Ø = eu)
go.1.SG think in-the your case
'I'll think about your case.'
b. [Ø fizeste uma excelente proposta] (EP: Ø = tu)
made-2.SG a excellent proposal
'You(SG) made an excellent proposal.'
c. [Ø quer entrar]? (Ø = você)
want.3.SG enter
'Would you(SG) like to come in?'

d. [Ø devemos sair agora] (Ø = *nós*)
   should-1.PL leave now
   'We should leave now.'
e. A gente não tinha escolha. [Ø só podia sair quando
   we   not had   choice   only could.3.SG leave when
   a   aula   terminava]   (Ø = *a gente*)
   the class ended
   'We had no choice. We could only leave after the class was over.'
f. [Ø fizeram boa viagem]?   (Ø = *vocês*)
   made-3.PL good trip
   'Did you(PL) have a nice trip?'

The only differences between EP and BP in (4.14) and (4.15) are irrelevant to our present discussion. Recall that *tu* and the agreement inflection it is associated with are not part of the grammar of BP and the weak pronouns *cê* and *cês* are not part of the grammar of EP (see Sections 2.4.2 and 3.3.2.2 and Table 4.3). Hence, (4.14b) and (4.15b) are independently excluded in BP and the null subjects of (4.14c,f) and (4.15c,f) can also correspond to *cê* or *cês* in BP, but not in EP (see footnote 14 above). However, upon closer inspection this unexpected similarity between EP and BP turns out to be illusory. Starting with the answers in (4.14), notice that the subject is not the only constituent that is left unexpressed. In Section 6.2, we will show that this type of answer to *yes/no* questions in Portuguese is actually the result of ellipsis applying to a constituent that includes all the arguments of the verb. Thus, the answers in (4.14) do not really involve the type of null subject we are interested in.

As for (4.15), the nature of the empty subjects may be different in EP and BP or even within the same variety. Let us consider why, by first examining the apparently unrelated data in (4.16) and (4.17) in EP.

(4.16)   EP:
a. O João   comprou o   novo livro do   Saylor onde?
   the João   bought   the new book of-the   Saylor where
   'Where did João buy Saylor's new book?'
b. Onde comprou o   João o   novo livro do   Saylor?
   where bought the João the new book of-the   Saylor
   'Where did João buy Saylor's new book?'
c. O   novo livro do   Saylor, o   João comprou onde?
   the new book of-the   Saylor the João bought where
   'Regarding Saylor's new book, where did João buy it?'
d. *Onde o   novo livro do   Saylor, comprou o   João?
    where the new book of-the   Saylor bought the João
   'Regarding Saylor's new book, where did João buy it?'

(4.17) EP:
- a. E o novo livro do Saylor? O João comprou-o onde?
  and the new book of-the Saylor the João bought-it where
- a'. E o novo livro do Saylor? O João comprou onde?
  and the new book of-the Saylor the João bought where
- b. E o novo livro do Saylor? Onde o comprou o João?
  and the new book of-the Saylor where it bought the João
- b'. E o novo livro do Saylor? *Onde comprou o João?
  and the new book of-the Saylor where bought the João

'What about Saylor's new book? Where did João buy it?'

(4.16a) and (4.16b) show that interrogative elements can optionally move to the beginning of the clause in EP (see Section 5.3.2) and the contrast between (4.16c) and (4.16d) shows that such movement cannot proceed across a topicalized object. In turn, (4.17) shows that whereas an object clitic is compatible with an *in-situ* or a moved interrogative constituent (see (4.17a) and (4.17b)), a null object with the same interpretation can co-occur with an *in-situ*, but not a moved interrogative element (see (4.17a') and (4.17b')). Thus, the null object in (4.17b') patterns in the same way as the topicalized object in (4.16d). In other words, the contrasts between (4.16c) and (4.16d), on the one hand, and (4.17a') and (4.17b'), on the other, can receive a uniform account if (4.17b') involves a null topicalized object.[15]

Returning to the sentences in (4.15), one must determine whether their subjects are null pronominals or null topics, that is, a case of pro-drop or, rather, a case of "topic drop."[16] Based on what we saw in (4.17b'), we may find the answer by determining whether the empty constituent in sentences like those in (4.15) is compatible with a moved interrogative constituent. If it is, we have a null pronominal subject; if it is not, we have a null topic.

---

[15] See Raposo 1986 for the original proposal and Chapter 6 for additional references and further discussion. As we will see in Section 5.3.2, movement of interrogative elements does not trigger subject–verb inversion in BP; hence the sentences corresponding to (4.16b), (4.16d), and (4.17b) in BP all have subject–verb order. (4.17b') contrasts with its BP counterpart in (i) below in that the latter is acceptable with a null object. This indicates that null objects in sentences like (i) in BP are not the result of topicalization. We return to this issue in Section 6.3.

- (i) E o novo livro do Saylor? Onde o João comprou?   (BP)
  and the new book of-the Saylor where the João bought
  'What about Saylor's new book? Where did João buy it?'

[16] See e.g. Ross 1982 and Huang 1984 for discussion.

154   4 Null Subjects

Interestingly, EP and BP give different answers in this regard, as we can see in (4.18).[17]

(4.18) a. [Em que   candidato Ø voto   desta
           in   which candidate   vote-1.SG of-this
           vez]?   (Ø = eu → EP: OK; BP: ??)
           time
           'Which candidate do I vote for this time?'
        b. [O que Ø viste]?   (Ø = tu → EP: OK)
           what   saw.2.SG
           'What did you(SG) see?'
        c. [O que Ø quer   fazer]?   (Ø = você → EP: OK; BP: *)
           what   want.3.SG do
           'What do you(SG) want to do?'
        d. [Quem Ø devíamos   contratar]? (Ø = nós → EP: OK; BP: OK)
           whom   should-1.PL hire
           'Who should we hire?'
        e. [Quando Ø deve   viajar]?   (Ø = a gente → EP: *; BP: *)
           when   should-3.SG   travel
           'When should we travel?'
        f. [Quando Ø viajaram]?   (Ø = vocês → EP: OK; BP: ??)
           when   traveled-3.PL
           'When did you(PL) travel?'

Let us examine EP first. With the exception of the null counterpart of *a gente*, all other null subjects are compatible with the moved interrogative constituent in EP. This indicates that we have a null pronominal in these cases and not a null topic, which is in consonance with the description of EP as a prototypical pro-drop language. As for (4.18e), with the null counterpart of *a gente*, we cannot simply say that it is unacceptable due to some pragmatic oddity, for the alternative version of (4.18e) with the null subject corresponding to *nós* (and 1.PL verbal agreement), uttered in the same context, is acceptable. In addition, we cannot simply attribute the contrast between (4.15e) and (4.18e) to the fact the null counterpart of *a gente* finds its overt counterpart in the previous discourse in the former but not in the latter. If (4.18e) is inserted in a discourse sequence parallel to (4.15e), as shown in (4.19), it still remains unacceptable.

---

[17] As we will see in Section 5.3.2, the order between the subject and the verb in interrogative clauses may be different in EP and BP. Assuming that things are kept constant when null subjects are involved, the empty subjects in sentences like (4.18), for instance, should occupy different positions in each variety. For purposes of exposition, we will however put this issue aside and represent the null subject as always preceding the relevant verb or auxiliary.

(4.19) [A gente]ᵢ tem   uma dúvida. *[Quando Øᵢ deve
        we   have.3.SG a   doubt   when   should.3.SG
        viajar]?   (Ø = a gente → EP: *; BP: *)
        travel
        'We have a question. When should we travel?'

The conclusion to be drawn from these observations is that the null subject corresponding to *a gente* in sentences such as (4.15e), (4.18e), and (4.19) must be analyzed as an instance of topic drop; hence, it is acceptable in (4.15e), where it can be anchored in the previous discourse, but not in (4.18e) and (4.19), where the moved interrogative constituent blocks such discourse licensing (see (4.17b′)). To put it in different terms, the null counterpart of *a gente* in EP cannot be morphologically licensed by the agreement inflection it is associated with.[18]

One wonders why this should be so, though. Clearly, it cannot be due to the fact that *a gente* belongs to the second group of pronouns in Table 4.3 and is not associated with unambiguous verbal agreement morphology. After all, *você* and *vocês* also belong to this group, but their null counterparts can be morphologically licensed in EP (see (4.18c) and (4.18f)). Furthermore, *a gente* and *você* are superficially associated with the same agreement morphology. The answer must thus reside in the more abstract feature specification of the agreeing forms associated with these pronouns, as we shall now see.

Our discussion of the pronominal and verbal agreement systems in Section 3.4.1 led us to the conclusion that the pronouns *você* and *vocês* in EP have values for both person and number, but *a gente* does not. This means that a given verbal inflection will have its person and number features valued if it syntactically agrees with *você*, for instance, but will remain unvalued if it agrees with *a gente* (see Chapter 3: footnote 44), as illustrated in the third column of Table 4.4 (see also Table 3.12).

Neither the agreement specification associated with *você* ([P:2; N:SG]) nor the agreement specification associated with *a gente* ([P:u; N:u]) are assigned an overt morpheme in EP, as shown in the fourth column of Table 4.4, for their morphological realization falls under the Elsewhere Condition in (4.20d) below (reproduced from (3.65d)). In other words, the fact that the person and number agreement inflections associated with *você* and *a gente* in EP have the same phonetic realization (namely, none) does not entail that they have the same underlying values. So it is conceivable that different patterns of null subject licensing are tied to different feature value specifications.

---

[18] For discussion see e.g. Pereira 2003, Costa and Pereira 2005, 2013, and Sória 2013.

Table 4.4 *First and second person pronouns in European Portuguese – syntactic agreement in finite clauses (fuller paradigm)*

Nominative pronouns	Morphological specification	Person and number		Surface forms: *dançar* 'dance' (indicative present)
		Syntactic agreement [P:u-N:u]	Correspondence rules	
eu 'I'	[P:N:1.SG]	dança-[P:N:1.SG]	dança-*o*	danço
tu 'you(SG)'	[P:N:2.SG]	dança-[P:N:2.SG]	dança-*s*	danças
você 'you(SG)'	[P:2-N:SG]	dança-[P:2-N:SG]	dança-*Ø-Ø*	dança
nós 'we'	[P:N:1.PL]	dança-[P:N:1.PL]	dança-*mos*	dançamos
a gente 'we'	[P.N]	dança-[P:u-N:u]	dança-*Ø-Ø*	dança
vocês 'you(PL)'	[P:2-N:PL]	dança-[P:2-N:PL]	dança-*Ø-m*	dançam

(4.20) *Correspondence rules for the morphological realization of verbal agreement inflection in EP:*
a. [P.N:1.PL] ↔ {-mos}
   [N:PL] ↔ {-m}
b. [P.N:1.SG] → {-o} / INDIC.PRES ___
   → {-i} elsewhere
c. [P.N:2.SG] → {-ste} / INDIC.PERF.PAST ___
   → {-s} elsewhere
d. Ø elsewhere

Let us then suppose that valuation of verbal inflection features plays a role in the licensing of definite null subjects (perhaps as a way to ensure the recoverability of unexpressed subjects). Table 4.4 suggests that the exceptional behavior of the null counterpart of *a gente* seen in (4.18e) is no accident, for the agreement inflection associated with *a gente* is the only one that has none of its features valued. Of the two features associated with the agreement inflection in Table 4.4, person seems to be more prominent than number in that it may be connected with nominative case assignment (see Sections 3.4.1 and 3.4.3). Let us then assume that a given verbal inflection is able to license a definite null subject in Portuguese only if its most prominent feature is valued, along the lines of (4.21).[19]

(4.21) *Prominent Feature Valuation Condition*
A given verbal inflection Infl can morphologically license the ellipsis of a definite pronominal subject in Portuguese only if the most prominent feature of Infl is valued, where feature prominence has the following scale: *person* > *number* > *gender* > *case*.

According to (4.21), the agreement inflection associated with the indicative present tense, the indicative perfective past, and the indicative future in EP (see Table 3.10) can license any null first or second person subject, with the exception of the null counterpart of *a gente*. Only in the latter case is the person feature not valued. Assuming that this proposal is on the right track, there is actually no such thing as null subject licensing via unambiguous agreement inflection. The cases covered by unambiguous agreement are just subcases of the more general condition in (4.21). That is, the unambiguous agreeing forms associated with *eu*, *tu*, and *nós* in Table 4.3 all contain a valued person feature (see Table 4.4), in consonance with (4.21).

This proposal also predicts that if the morphological specifications of the nominative pronouns in Table 4.4 were different, this could indirectly affect null subject licensing, for the corresponding agreement inflections would also

---

[19] For different analyses of null subjects in terms of deletion, see e.g. Perlmutter 1971, Duguine 2013, Roberts 2010, Saab 2016, and Sheehan 2016. For the specific proposal in terms of the Prominent Feature Valuation Condition, see Martins and Nunes 2021 and Nunes 2020a.

have different specifications. With this in mind, let us now examine the judgments BP speakers ascribe to the sentences in (4.18), repeated here in (4.22) for convenience.

(4.22)   a. [Em que candidato Ø voto desta vez]?
in which candidate vote-1.SG of-this time
(Ø = *eu* → EP: OK; BP: ??)
'Which candidate do I vote for this time?'
  b. [O que Ø viste]?
what saw.2.SG
(Ø = *tu* → EP: OK)
'What did you(SG) see?'
  c. [O que Ø quer fazer]?
what want.3.SG do
(Ø = *você* → EP: OK; BP: *)
'What do you(SG) want to do?'
  d. [Quem Ø devíamos contratar]?
whom should-1.PL hire
(Ø = *nós* → EP: OK; BP: OK)
'Who should we hire?'
  e. [Quando Ø deve viajar]?
when should-3.SG travel
(Ø = *a gente* → EP: *; BP: *)
'When should we travel?'
  f. [Quando Ø viajaram]?
when traveled-3.PL
(Ø = *vocês* → EP: OK; BP: ??)
'When did you(PL) travel?'

First of all, it is worth observing for the sake of clarity that the markings "??" and "*" in (4.22) are taken to annotate increasing degrees of unacceptability. Second, it should be pointed out that it is not the case that the sentences in (4.22) annotated with "??" are unintelligible to BP speakers. These markings are meant to indicate that the relevant sentences sound marked and are associated with written language and formal style (see Chapter 1). Crucially, BP speakers always prefer the alternatives with an overt subject (even in the case of *nós*), as in (4.23), and in this regard BP sets itself apart from prototypical pro-drop languages like EP.

(4.23)   BP:
    a. Em que candidato **eu** voto desta vez?
in which candidate I vote-1.SG of-this time
'Which candidate do I vote for this time?'
    b. O que {**você/cê**} quer fazer?
what you.SG/you.SG₍W₎ want.3.SG do
'What do you(SG) want to do?'
    c. Quem **nós** devíamos contratar?
whom we should-1.PL hire
'Who should we hire?'
    d. Quando **a gente** deve viajar?
when we should-3.SG travel
'When are we supposed to travel?'

e. Quando {**vocês/cês**} viajaram?
   when you-PL/you-PL_[W] traveled-3.PL
   'When did you(PL) travel?'

The general pattern of unacceptability in BP of constructions that block topic drop such as (4.22) and its preference for the overt counterparts in (4.23) indicate that, in BP, the empty subjects in (4.15), repeated here in (4.24), involve not null pronominals, but rather null topics.[20]

(4.24) a. [Ø vou pensar no seu caso] (Ø = *eu*)
         go.1.SG think in-the your case
         'I'll think about your case.'
      b. [Ø quer entrar]? (Ø = *você*)
         want.3.SG enter
         'Would you(SG) like to come in?'
      c. [Ø devemos sair agora] (Ø = *nós*)
         should-1.PL leave now
         'We should leave now.'
      d. A gente não tinha escolha. [Ø só podia
         we not had choice only could.3.SG
         sair quando a aula terminava] (Ø = *a gente*)
         leave when the class ended
         'We had no choice. We could only leave after the class was over.'
      e. [Ø fizeram boa viagem]? (Ø = *vocês*)
         made-3.PL good trip
         'Did you(PL) have a nice trip?'

Supporting evidence for this conclusion is provided by empty subjects in embedded clauses. Topic drop generally targets matrix rather than embedded subjects. Even in a non-pro-drop language like English, for instance, one may find instances of topic drop affecting subjects in "diary contexts," as illustrated in (4.25a); crucially, such a phenomenon is restricted to matrix subjects, as shown by the ungrammaticality of (4.25b) in a diary context.[21]

(4.25) a. Must call Mom tonight.
      b. *John said (that) must call Mom tonight.

Bearing this in mind, consider the data in (4.26), for example.

(4.26) a. O professor disse que [Ø escrevo bem] (Ø = *eu* → EP: OK; BP: ??)
         the teacher said that write.1.SG well
         'The teacher said that I write well.'
      b. Ninguém duvidava que [Ø ias encontrar uma
         nobody doubted that went.2.SG find a
         solução] (Ø = *tu* → EP: OK)
         solution
         'Nobody doubted that you(SG) were going to find a solution.'

---

[20] For discussion see e.g. Modesto 2000, Ferreira 2000, and Rodrigues 2004.
[21] See e.g. Haegeman 1990, 2013 for discussion.

160   4 Null Subjects

    c. Eu acho que [Ø está   com fome]   (Ø = *você* → EP: OK; BP: *)
       I   think that   be.3.SG with hunger
       'I think that you(SG) are hungry.'
    d. A   Maria   acha   que   [Ø   fizemos   a
       the   Maria   thinks that   made-1.PL   the
       escolha certa]   (Ø = *nós* → EP: OK; BP: OK)
       choice right
       'Maria thinks that we made the right choice.'
    e. Eles   pensam   que   [Ø   não   vai
       they   think   that   not   go.3.SG
       reclamar]   (Ø = *a gente* → EP: *; BP: *)
       complain
       'They think that we are not going to complain.'
    f. Eu percebo que [Ø estão   cansados]   (Ø = *vocês* → EP: OK; BP: ??)
       I   perceive that   be-3.PL tired
       'I see that you(PL) are tired.'

If topic drop generally does not apply to embedded subjects, it is not surprising that (4.26) in BP replicates the corresponding patterns of acceptability of (4.22): both involve contexts that disfavor topic drop. Notice that with the exception of the null counterpart of *a gente* (see (4.26e)), all the remaining empty subjects are grammatical in EP and this is not unexpected either, for null pronominals are generally not sensitive to such asymmetries between matrix and embedded clauses.

Let us now examine each of the null subjects in BP presented in (4.22) and (4.26), starting with the null counterparts of *nós* and *eu*. (4.23c), with the overt form *nós*, sounds more natural in BP than (4.22d), with its null counterpart. Still, the null counterpart of *nós* in (4.22d) is much more acceptable in BP than the other null subjects of (4.22), including the null counterpart of *eu* in (4.22a). Notice that the overt counterparts of these pronouns are the only ones in BP that are associated with unambiguous verbal agreement morphology (see Table 4.3). Thus, if lack of morphological ambiguity in the verbal agreement morphology were to play a role in the licensing of null subjects in BP, the null counterparts of *eu* and *nós* should pattern alike. Curiously, the degree of acceptability of the null counterpart of *eu* is much closer to that of the null counterpart of *vocês/cês* (see (4.22f)/(4.26f)) than that of the null counterpart of *nós*. This clearly indicates that the phonological distinctions of their corresponding agreement morphemes are not by themselves what is relevant for the licensing of null subjects in BP. If we consider instead the interaction between the morphological specifications of the agreement inflection associated with these pronouns, as sketched in Table 4.5 below (which reinterprets Table 3.11), on the one hand, and the correspondence rules in (4.27) (= (3.70)), on the other, the picture becomes quite revealing.

Table 4.5 *First and second person pronouns in Brazilian Portuguese – syntactic agreement in finite clauses (fuller paradigm)*

Nominative pronouns	Person and number			Surface forms: *dançar* 'dance' (indicative present)
	Morphological specification	Syntactic agreement [P:u-N:u]	Correspondence rules	
eu 'I'	[P.N:SG]	*dança*-[**P.N:SG**]	*danç-o*	*danço*
você/cê 'you(SG)'	[P-N]	*dança*-[**P:u-N:u**]	*dança-Ø-Ø*	*dança*
nós 'we'	[P.N:1]	*dança*-[**P.N:1**]	*dança-mo(s)*	*dançamo(s)*
a gente 'we'	[P.N]	*dança*-[**P:u-N:u**]	*dança-Ø-Ø*	*dança*
vocês/cês 'you(PL)'	[P-N:PL]	*dança*-[**P:u-N:PL**]	*dança-Ø-m*	*dançam*

(4.27) *Correspondence rules for the morphological realization of verbal agreement inflection in BP:*
a. [P.N:1] ↔ {-mo(s)}
   [N:PL] ↔ {-m}
b. [P.N:SG] → {-o} / INDIC.PRES __
   → {-i} / INDIC.PERF.PAST __
c. Ø elsewhere

In Table 4.5, *nós* is the only pronoun that is valued for person and so is its corresponding agreement inflection. Hence, it is not surprising that the null counterpart of *nós* is the most acceptable null subject in BP (see (4.22d) and (4.26d)), for it complies with the Prominent Feature Valuation Condition in (4.21). The reader might have noted that it is not a coincidence that the null counterpart of *nós* displays exceptional behavior in BP and the null counterpart of *a gente* exceptional behavior in EP (see (4.22e) and (4.26e)). Recall that although the overt forms of these pronouns exist in both dialects, the *nós* series is the one that is marked in BP, whereas the *a gente* series is the one that is marked in EP (see Section 2.4.1). Thus, the general association of the null counterpart of *nós* with formal style and written language in BP may be seen as a side effect of the on-going wholesale replacement of the *nós* series by the *a gente* series in this variety.

Let us now consider the fact that the unambiguous inflection associated with *eu* patterns in the same way as the ambiguous inflection associated with *vocês/cês* in marginally licensing their corresponding null subjects in BP (see (4.22a)/(4.26a) and (4.22f)/(4.26f)). Notice that *eu* and *vocês* are the only pronouns in Table 4.5 that specify a value for the number feature in the agreement inflections associated with them. Recall that according to the Prominent Feature Valuation Condition in (4.21), number is the second most prominent feature in the scale of prominence. Let us then suppose that number valuation may marginally license ellipsis of the corresponding overt pronouns in finite clauses in BP, perhaps as a reflex of the meager morphological role played by person valuation in BP (see Section 3.4.3). That being so, *eu* and *vocês/cês* can undergo ellipsis in (4.22) and (4.26) (see (4.22a)/(4.26a) and (4.22f)/(4.26f)), but *você/cê* or *a gente* cannot (see (4.22c)/(4.26c) and (4.22e)/(4.26e)). Crucially, neither the person feature nor the number feature of the verbal agreement inflection associated with *você/cê* and *a gente* is valued in BP (see Table 4.5); hence, the null counterparts of these pronouns cannot be elided (even marginally).

This proposal provides a straightforward account for an interesting contrast between *você* in EP and *você/cê* in BP. In EP, the person feature of *você* is valued (see Table 4.4); thus, it should pattern like *vocês*, which also has a valued person feature, and unlike *a gente*, whose person and number features are unvalued. This indeed holds true. As seen in (4.22c)/(4.26c) and (4.22f)/(4.26f), the null counterparts of *você* and *vocês* can be licensed by the corresponding inflection agreement in EP in consonance with the Prominent Feature Valuation Condition in (4.21), but the null counterpart of *a gente* cannot (see (4.22e)/(4.26e)). In contrast, in BP *você/cê* and *vocês/cês* do not have a valued person feature in their morphological specification, but number valuation in the agreement inflection related to the latter marginally licenses ellipsis. Thus, *você/cê* in BP should pattern like *a gente* rather than *vocês/cês* in that their null counterparts cannot be licensed by the corresponding agreement inflection. This prediction is also met (see (4.22c,e)/(4.26c,e) vs. (4.22f)/(4.26f)).

The data in (4.28) point to the same conclusion.

(4.28)   a. [Ø parece   estar de mau humor]   (Ø = *a gente* → EP: *; BP: *)
           seem.3.SG be   of bad mood
         'We seem to be in a bad mood.'
     b. [Ø parece   estar de mau humor]   (Ø = *você* → EP: OK; BP: *)
           seem.3.SG be   of bad mood
         'You(SG) seem to be in a bad mood.'
     c. [Ø parecem estar de mau humor]   (Ø = *vocês* → EP: OK; BP: ??)
           seem.3.PL be   of bad mood
         'You(PL) seem to be in a bad mood.'

(4.28) involves declarative clauses with a raising verb (see Section 3.4.3) and replicates the pattern seen in (4.26), with the null subject in the embedded clause, and (4.22), with the null subject in a matrix clause with a moved interrogative constituent. In the three sets of sentences, the null counterpart of *a gente* is not licensed in either variety and the null counterparts of *você* and *vocês* can be licensed in EP, as the agreement inflection associated with them has a valued person feature. In BP, on the other hand, the null counterparts of *você/cê* pattern like *a gente* in not being licensed, whereas the null counterpart of *vocês/cês* is marginally acceptable thanks to the valued number feature associated with their verbal agreement inflection.

The paradigm in (4.28) suggests that the licensing of the null counterparts of *você/cê* and *vocês/cês* in BP seen earlier in (4.15c,f), repeated below in (4.29), is not actually carried out by the agreement inflection. Recall (see Section 4.1) that imperatives may license a second person null subject (see (4.8a)) even in languages that do not generally allow null subjects. In other words, illocutionary force may also play a role in licensing (some) null subjects. The null subjects corresponding to *você/cê* and *vocês/cês* in (4.29) seem to illustrate another instance of null subject licensing contingent on the illocutionary force of the sentence. More specifically, a direct *yes/no* question seems to be able to license a null subject corresponding to these pronouns, as it explicitly engages the addressee in the discourse interaction.

(4.29) a. [Ø quer entrar]?   (Ø = *você* → EP: OK; BP: OK)
           want.3.SG enter
           'Would you(SG) like to come in?'
      b. [Ø fizeram boa viagem]?   (Ø = *vocês* → EP: OK; BP: OK)
           did-3.PL good trip
           'Did you(PL) have a nice trip?'

Evidence that null subject licensing in (4.29) is grounded by the illocutionary force of the sentence rather than the verbal agreement morphology is provided by the fact that gerundive rhetorical interrogatives like (4.30) in BP do not involve agreement inflection, but are able to license the null counterparts of *você/cê* and *vocês/cês*. In fact, these are the only elements that can be licensed in this construction: not only must the null subject of (4.30) be interpreted as *você/cê* or *vocês/cês*, but any overt subject is excluded. This strongly indicates that a sentence with a direct *yes/no* question as its illocutionary force is independently capable of licensing null subjects corresponding to the addressee in BP.

(4.30) [Ø estacionando em lugar proibido,
         parking   *in*   *place* *prohibited*
         hem?!]   (Ø = *você/cê/vocês/cês* → BP: OK)
         INTERJ
         'Parking in a forbidden spot, aren't you?'

Let us now examine another point in which *você/cê* patterns in the same way as *a gente* and unlike *vocês/cês* in BP. Consider the data in (4.31), for instance.

(4.31) a. [A gente]$_i$ acha que [Ø$_i$ deve participar
           we   think.3.SG that   should.3.SG *participate*
          mais]
          more   (Ø = *a gente* → EP: OK; BP: OK)
          'We think that we should be more involved.'
      b. [A gente]$_i$ vai rever os testes que [Ø$_i$
         we   go.3.SG review the tests that
         fez]
         did.3.SG   (Ø = *a gente* → EP: OK; BP: *)
         'We are going to review the tests that we did.'

We have seen that the null counterpart of *a gente* cannot be morphologically licensed by the corresponding agreement inflection (see (4.19), (4.22e), (4.26e), and (4.28a)). This problem could in principle be circumvented in the

4.3 Definite Null Subjects

sentences in (4.31), for they provide an environment where the null counterpart of *a gente* could be anaphorically licensed by its overt counterpart in the matrix clause. At first sight, the grammaticality of (4.31a) in both dialects suggests that such anaphoric licensing operates in the same manner. (4.31b), on the other hand, shows that the answer cannot be this trivial, for anaphoric licensing is successful in EP, but not in BP. Interestingly, the pattern seen in (4.31) is replicated in both varieties with the null counterpart of a third person pronoun such as *ele* 'he', as illustrated in (4.32).

(4.32) a. Ele$_i$ acha que [Ø$_i$ deve participar
 he think.3.SG that should.3.SG participate
 mais] (Ø = *ele* → EP: OK; BP: OK)
 more
 'He$_i$ thinks that he$_i$ should be more involved.'
 b. Ele$_i$ vai rever os testes que
 he go.3.SG review the tests that
 [Ø$_i$ fez]$_i$ (Ø = *ele* → EP: OK; BP: *)
 did.3.SG
 'He$_i$ is going to review the tests that he$_i$ did.'

The fact that the null counterpart of *a gente* is behaving like the null counterpart of a third person pronoun is not surprising. Given that it cannot rely on morphological licensing, it could in principle resort to anaphoric licensing, which generally assigns interpretation to third person pronouns by anchoring their denotation onto that of an antecedent in the sentence or in the discourse. What is unexpected is the distinction that BP makes, allowing anaphoric licensing into a complement clause (see (4.31a) and (4.32a)), but not into a relative clause (see (4.31b) and (4.32b)). We will discuss this issue in detail in Section 4.3.1.2 below. For our current purposes, suffice it to observe that the two types of embedded clauses differ independently with respect to allowing syntactic movement from within their domains, with complement clauses being generally transparent and adjunct clauses opaque (see Section 4.3.1.2 below). Thus, the provisional generalization that emerges from the data above is that the null counterpart of *a gente* is not licensed within an opaque embedded clause in BP even if the appropriate antecedent is available (see (4.31b)).

As we should by now expect, the null counterparts of *você* in BP again patterns in the same way as the null counterpart of *a gente* in this regard, and not as the null counterpart of *vocês* (the same applies to *cê/cês*). In other words, the null counterpart of *você* in BP can be licensed anaphorically if it sits within a transparent domain (see (4.33a)), but not within an opaque domain (see (4.33b)), whereas the null counterpart of *vocês* in BP is fully acceptable in transparent domains (see (4.34a)) and marginal in opaque domains (see (4.34b)).

166   4 Null Subjects

(4.33) a. Você$_i$ prometeu   que   [Ø$_i$ vai   participar
          you.SG   promised.3.SG that   go.3.SG   participate
          mais]   (Ø = você → EP: OK; BP: OK)
          more
          'You(SG) promised to be more involved.'
       b. Você$_i$ precisa   rever   os   testes   que [Ø$_i$ fez]
          you.SG   need.3.SG   review   the tests   that   did.3.SG
                                                         (Ø = você → EP: OK; BP: *)
          'You(SG) need to review the tests that you(SG) did.'

(4.34) a. Vocês$_i$ prometeram   que   [Ø   vão$_i$ participar
          you-PL   promised.3.PL that   go-3.PL   participate
          mais]   (Ø = vocês →EP: OK; BP: OK)
          more
          'You(PL) promised to be more involved.'
       b. Vocês$_i$ precisam   rever   os   testes   que [Ø$_i$
          you-PL   need-3.PL   review   the tests   that
          fizeram]   (Ø = vocês → EP: OK; BP: ??)
          did-3.PL
          'You(PL) need to review the tests that you(PL) did.'

For the sake of completeness, let us finally examine the behavior of the null counterparts of *nós* and *eu* in transparent and opaque embedded domains when they are anteceded by their overt counterparts within the same sentence. With respect to the null counterpart of *nós*, the presence of an overt antecedent and the type of embedded clause in which it appears do not have any effect on their general pattern of acceptability in EP or BP, as illustrated in (4.35) below. That is, the null counterpart of *nós* is (morphologically) licensed in both EP and BP, although the overt counterpart remains the preferred option in BP, as illustrated in (4.36).[22]

(4.35) a. Nós$_i$ descobrimos   que   [Ø$_i$ estávamos
          we   discovered-1.PL   that   be-PAST-1.PL
          errados]   (Ø = nós → EP: OK; BP: OK)
          wrong
          'We found out that we were wrong.'
       b. Nós$_i$ não   recomendamos   o   curso   que   [Ø
          we   not   recommend-1.PL   the   course   that
          fizemos]$_i$ (Ø = nós → EP: OK; BP: OK)
          did-1.PL
          'We don't recommend the course that we took.'

---

[22] Recall that the preference for null over overt subjects in pro-drop languages applies to neutral contexts (see Section 4.2). Thus, the sentences in (4.36), (4.37b), and (4.38b) are perfectly acceptable in EP if the embedded overt subject pronoun bears emphatic/contrastive stress.

4.3 Definite Null Subjects   167

(4.36) a. Nós   descobrimos   que   [nós   estávamos
           we   discovered-1.PL that   we   be-PAST-1.PL
           errados]   (EP: ??; BP: OK)
           wrong
           'We found out that we were wrong.'
        b. Nós   não   recomendamos   o   curso   que   [nós
           we   not   recommend-1.PL   the   course that we
           fizemos]   (EP: ??; BP: OK)
           did-1.PL
           'We don't recommend the course that we took.'

As for the null counterpart of *eu*, the picture is more complex. In opaque embedded domains, the pattern is the same as we saw earlier: full acceptability in EP and marginality in BP, which displays the usual preference for the overt counterpart, as illustrated in (4.37).

(4.37) a. Eu$_i$ não   gostei   dos   últimos   artigos   que   [Ø$_i$
           I   not   liked-1.SG of-the   last   articles that
           li]   (Ø = eu → EP: OK; PB: ??)
           read-1.SG
        b. Eu   não   gostei   dos   últimos   artigos   que
           I   not   liked-1.SG of-the   last   articles that
           [eu li]   (EP: ??; PB: OK)
           I   read-1.SG
           'I didn't like the latest articles that I read.'

On the other hand, if the embedded clause is a transparent domain, BP speakers are split with respect to their judgments. For some speakers, there is no contrast between transparent and opaque domains. That is, for these speakers, the null subject of the transparent embedded clause in (4.38a) below is only marginally accepted, patterning like the null subject of (4.37a). For other speakers, the null subject of sentences such as (4.38a), with an antecedent, is acceptable, contrasting with sentences like (4.39), with no antecedent. Importantly, the version with the overt counterpart in (4.38b) is well formed for both these groups of BP speakers. We will return to these fine-grained distinctions in Section 4.3.1.2 below, after discussing general properties of intrasentential anaphoric licensing in both varieties.

(4.38) a. Eu$_i$ acho   que   [Ø$_i$ fiz   um bom
           I   think-1.SG that   did-1.SG   a good
           trabalho]   (Ø = eu → EP: OK; %BP: ??; %BP: OK)
           job
        b. Eu   acho   que   eu   fiz   um bom
           I   think-1.SG that   I   did-1.SG   a good
           trabalho.   (EP: ??; BP: OK)
           job
           'I think that I did a good job.'

Table 4.6 *Licensing of first and second person null subjects in finite clauses in European Portuguese (fuller paradigm)*

		Morphological licensing	Intrasentential anaphoric licensing	
			In opaque domains	In transparent domains
Null counterpart of	eu 'I'	✓	✓	✓
	tu 'you(SG)'	✓	✓	✓
	você 'you(SG)'	✓	✓	✓
	nós 'we'	✓	✓	✓
	vocês 'you(PL)'	✓	✓	✓
	a gente 'we'	*	✓	✓

Table 4.7 *Licensing of first and second person null subjects in finite clauses in Brazilian Portuguese (fuller paradigm)*

		Morphological licensing	Intrasentential anaphoric licensing	
			In opaque domains	In transparent domains
Null counterpart of	nós 'we'	✓	✓	✓
	eu 'I'	??	??	%?? / %✓
	vocês/cês 'you(PL)'	??	??	✓
	a gente 'we'	*	*	✓
	você/cê 'you(SG)'	*	*	✓

(4.39) O Pedro acha que [Ø fiz um bom
 the Pedro thinks that did-1.SG a good
 trabalho]   (Ø = eu → EP: OK; BP: ??)
 job
 'Pedro thinks that I did a good job.'

Putting aside instances of topic drop and licensing by certain types of illocutionary force, Tables 4.6 and 4.7 below summarize the factors that may license first and second person null subjects in EP and BP discussed thus far.

Tables 4.6 and 4.7 clearly illustrate the sharp differences between EP and BP as far as first and second person null subjects are concerned. EP displays a very uniform behavior across different domains. The only exception is the null counterpart of *a gente*. Given that it does not value the person feature of the agreement inflection associated with it, its null counterpart cannot be morphologically licensed and requires being anteceded by the overt form. However, it may be located in a transparent or opaque domain with respect to its antecedent.

By contrast, BP presents a much more complex picture, as judgments do not show a simple opposition acceptable/unacceptable, but rather a wider scale of unacceptability. The null counterpart of *nós* is the only pronoun that displays constant behavior across different syntactic environments, which is accounted for if *nós* is the only pronoun in BP that triggers valuation of the person feature of the agreement inflection associated with it (see Section 3.4.2 and Table 4.5); hence, ellipsis of *nós* can be morphologically licensed in consonance with the Prominent Feature Valuation Condition in (4.21). In turn, the null counterparts of *você/cê* and *a gente* display a completely parallel behavior in BP: they cannot be morphologically licensed by the verbal agreement inflections associated with them and must sit in a transparent domain with respect to their antecedents in order to be anaphorically licensed. Finally, the null counterparts of *eu* and *vocês/cês* display parallel behavior except for contexts in which they sit in a transparent domain with respect to their antecedents. Their marginal acceptability in the other environments is attributed to the fact that they value the number feature of the agreement inflection associated with them (see Section 3.4.2 and Table 4.5) and number valuation in finite clauses marginally licenses ellipsis of their overt counterparts.

Let us now examine finite tenses with one fewer agreement distinction, that is, tenses where the agreement inflection for *eu* is not different from traditional third person singular agreement (see Section 3.4.2). These involve the indicative imperfective past, the indicative conditional, and all the subjunctive tenses, as illustrated in (4.40).[23]

---

[23] These are all simple tenses. Compound tenses are formed by an auxiliary with inflection for a simple tense, followed by a nonfinite form of the main verb. The subjunctive perfective past, for instance, is formed with the auxiliary *ter* 'have' in the subjunctive present followed by the participle of the main verb (e.g. *tenhamos saído* 'have.SUBJ.PRES-1.PL leave-PPLE'); hence, the possibilities for null subject licensing in complex tenses replicate the possibilities for the simple tenses associated with the auxiliary. For expository purposes, we will discuss only simple tenses here.

(4.40) a. {Eu/você/a gente} trabalha**va** bastante naquela
 I/you.SG/we work-INDIC.IMPERF much in-that
 época.
 time
 '{I/you(SG)/we} worked a lot at that time.'
 b. {Eu/você/a gente} não **teria** outra
 I/you.SG/we not have-INDIC.COND other
 oportunidade.
 opportunity
 '{I/you(SG)/we} would not have another chance.'
 c. O diretor quer [que {eu/você/a gente} avalie
 the director wants that I/you.SG/we evaluate-SUBJ.PRES
 o projeto].
 the project
 'The director wants {me/you(SG)/us} to evaluate the project.'
 d. Eles esperavam [que {eu/você/a gente} resolvesse
 they expected that I/you.SG/we resolve-SUBJ.IMPERF
 o problema].
 the problem
 'They hoped that {I/you(SG)/we} would solve the problem.'
 e. Os resultados vão ser divulgados [quando
 the results go be released when
 {eu/você/a gente} concluir a pesquisa].
 I/you.SG/we conclude-SUBJ.FUT the research
 'The results will be released when {I/you(SG)/we} finish the research.'

The apparent agreement mismatch between the feature specification of the pronoun *eu* and the pattern of agreement it is associated with in the tenses above can be accounted for if it results from morphological impoverishment (feature deletion triggered by a given morphological context).[24] In the case at hand, the agreement inflection related to *eu* should have some morphological specification deleted when it co-occurs with the tense morphemes of (4.40) so that the surface form of the agreeing verb is not different from the form associated with third person singular. The question is then which feature is deleted.

For BP, the answer is straightforward. Recall that *eu* in BP is specified only as SG and consequently, a verb agreeing with *eu* also becomes specified just for SG (see Section 3.4.2 and Table 4.5) Hence, morphological impoverishment in the case of BP simply entails deletion of SG. In other words, if a given agreement inflection in BP specified as [P:u-N:SG] has the number specification deleted, the remaining unvalued person feature will be assigned no phonetic content, in compliance with the Elsewhere Condition in (4.27c),

---

[24] On the notion of morphological impoverishment, see e.g. Bonet 1991.

4.3 Definite Null Subjects   171

repeated below in (4.41c) for convenience. The final surface form will then not display any overt morpheme for number or person, which gives the illusion that the verb exhibits third person singular agreement.

(4.41) *Correspondence rules for the morphological realization of verbal agreement inflection in BP:*
    a. [P.N:1]   ↔   {-mo(s)}
       [N:PL]   ↔   {-m}
    b. [P.N:SG] →   {-o} / INDIC.PRES ___
                    →   {-i} / INDIC.PERF.PAST ___
    c. Ø elsewhere

In the case of EP, on the other hand, the situation is less trivial. As *eu* in EP is specified as 1.SG, so should any finite verb agreeing with it. The question then is whether impoverishment in EP for the tenses illustrated in (4.40) means deletion of 1 or deletion of SG. Again, we cannot make a decision based on surface agreement, for both possibilities arguably result in the same surface form, according to the Elsewhere Condition in (4.20d), repeated below in (4.42d). That is, if impoverishment deletes 1, the verb will not surface with overt agreeing morphology, for SG alone is assigned no phonetic exponent; likewise, if impoverishment deletes SG, the verb will not surface with overt agreeing morphology either, for 1 alone is assigned no phonetic exponent.

(4.42) *Correspondence rules for the morphological realization of verbal agreement inflection in EP:*
    a. [P.N:1.PL] ↔   {-mos}
       [N:PL]   ↔   {-m}
    b. [P.N:1.SG] →   {-o} / INDIC.PRES ___
                      →   {-i} elsewhere
    c. [P.N:2.SG] →   {-ste} / INDIC.PERF.PAST ___
                      →   {-s}elsewhere
    d. Ø elsewhere

The choice between these options can however be determined if we take into account the Prominent Feature Valuation Condition in (4.21). In other words, licensing of the null counterpart of *eu* should be possible in EP if morphological impoverishment deletes SG, but not if it deletes 1. With these two possibilities in mind, let us consider the sentences in (4.43), under the interpretation where the null subject corresponds to *eu*.

(4.43) a. Todos   achavam [que Ø trabalhava
          everyone thought   that   work-INDIC.IMPERF
          na   fábrica]   (Ø = *eu* → EP: OK; BP: *)
          in-the   factory
          'Everyone thought I worked at the factory.'

b. Eles não   imaginam   [o que Ø
   they not   imagine   what
   gostaria   de fazer]   (Ø = *eu* → EP: OK; BP: *)
   like-INDIC.COND   of do
   'They can't imagine what I would like to do.'
c. A   diretora   quer   [que Ø contrate
   the   director   wants   that   hire-SUBJ.PRES
   outra   secretária]   (Ø = *eu* → EP: OK; BP: *)
   other secretary
   'The director wants me to hire another secretary.'
d. O   professor   esperava   [que Ø
   the   teacher   expected   that
   estudasse   mais]   (Ø = *eu* → EP: OK; BP: *)
   study-SUBJ.PRES   more
   'The teacher hoped that I would study more.'
e. [Se Ø   não   ultrapassar   os
   if   not   exceed -SUBJ.FUT the
   120 km/h], a   gasolina vai dar.   (Ø = *eu* → EP: OK; BP: *)
   120 km/h   the gasoline go give
   'If I don't go over 120 km/h, there will be enough gas.'

(4.43) shows that EP systematically allows the interpretation of the null subjects of clauses involving the tenses in (4.40) as being *eu*, but BP does not. This can be analyzed as showing that in both varieties impoverishment deletes SG. In the case of EP, the null counterpart of *eu* can be morphologically licensed by the surviving valued person feature of the corresponding agreement inflection, in consonance with the Prominent Feature Valuation Condition (see (4.21)). By contrast, impoverishment resulting in deletion of SG in the agreement inflection associated with *eu* in BP blocks ellipsis of the pronoun and the interpretation of the null subject of the sentences in (4.40), as *eu* is precluded. Thus, the same impoverishment rule applying to EP and BP has different consequences for the licensing of a null subject corresponding to *eu*, in virtue of the different specifications each variety assigns to the overt version of this pronoun (see Section 3.4.2).

The inner workings of impoverishment in the two varieties are illustrated with the subjunctive present in Tables 4.8 and 4.9 below, where T_I stands for a tense subject to impoverishment.[25]

---

[25] It is arguably the case that the features [person] and [number] of the verbal agreement inflection are fused after agreeing with pronouns that have these features fused. This is the case for the pronoun *eu* and the agreement associated with it in both EP and BP. This suggests that impoverishment applies before fusion takes place. Since nothing that follows hinges on this refinement, we will put it aside for expository purposes. For an alternative analysis of impoverishment in the indicative imperfective past, with deletion of person, see Bassani and Lunguinho 2011.

Table 4.8 *First and second person pronouns in European Portuguese – syntactic agreement in finite clauses under impoverishment*

Nominative pronouns	Morphological specification	Person and number			
		Syntactic agreement [P:u-N:u]	Impoverishment: If V-T_r-[P:1-N:SG] → V-T_r-[P:1]	Correspondence rules	Surface forms: *dançar* 'dance' (subjunctive present)
eu 'I'	[P.N:1.SG]	dance-[P.N:1.SG]	dance-[P:1]	dance-Ø	dance
tu 'you(SG)'	[P.N:2.SG]	dance-[P.N:2.SG]	n/a	dance-s	dances
você 'you(SG)'	[P:2-N:SG]	dance-[P:2-N:SG]	n/a	dance-Ø-Ø	dance
nós 'we'	[P.N:1.PL]	dance-[P.N:1.PL]	n/a	dance-*mos*	dance*mos*
a gente 'we'	[P.N]	dance-[P:u-N:u]	n/a	dance-Ø-Ø	dance
vocês 'you(PL)'	[P:2-N:PL]	dance-[P:2-N:PL]	n/a	dance-Ø-*m*	dance*m*

Table 4.9 *First and second person pronouns in Brazilian Portuguese – syntactic agreement in finite clauses under impoverishment*

Nominative pronouns	Person and number				Surface forms: *dançar* 'dance' (subjunctive present)
	Morphological specification	Syntactic agreement [P:u-N:u]	Impoverishment: If V-T₁-[P:u-N:SG] → V-T₁-[P:u]	Correspondence rules	
eu 'I'	[P.N:SG]	dance-[P.N:SG]	dance-[P:u]	dance-Ø	dance
você 'you(SG)'	[P-N]	dance-[P:u-N:u]	n/a	dance-Ø-Ø	dance
nós 'we'	[P.N:1]	dance-[P:1-N:u]	n/a	dance-*mo(s)*	dance*mo(s)*
a gente 'we'	[P.N]	dance-[P:u-N:u]	n/a	dance-Ø-Ø	dance
vocês 'you(PL)'	[P-N:PL]	dance-[P:u-N:PL]	n/a	dance-Ø-*m*	dance*m*

4.3 Definite Null Subjects   175

According to Tables 4.8 and 4.9, a subjunctive present verb agreeing with *eu* has the same surface form in both EP and BP, but differs in its powers to license the null subject corresponding to *eu* after the application of impoverishment. This once again shows that surface agreement morphology is in fact irrelevant for null subject licensing. What really matters is the underlying feature specification of the agreeing verb in each variety. In the case of EP, the agreeing form involves a surviving valued person feature ([P:1]) and hence can license the null counterpart of *eu*, in consonance with the Prominent Feature Valuation Condition (see (4.21)). By contrast, the surviving specification of the analogous surface form in BP ([P:u]) cannot license the ellipsis of the overt pronoun *eu*.

The same conclusion is reached when we examine the sentences in (4.43) under the interpretation of the null subjects as *você* and *a gente*, as shown in (4.44).

(4.44) a. Todos   achavam [que Ø trabalhava
           everyone thought   that   work-INDIC.IMPERF
           na   fábrica]   (Ø = *você* → EP: OK; BP: *)
           in-the   factory   (Ø = *a gente* → EP: *; BP: *)
           'Everyone thought {you(SG)/we} worked at the factory.'
        b. Eles   não   imaginam [o que Ø gostaria
           they   not   imagine   what   like-INDIC.COND
           de   fazer]   (Ø = *você* → EP: OK; BP: *)
           of   do   (Ø = *a gente* → EP: *; BP: *)
           'They can't imagine what {you(SG)/we} would like to do.'
        c. O   diretor   quer [que Ø contrate   outra
           the   director wants that   hire-SUBJ.PRES   other
           secretária]   (Ø = *você* → EP: OK; BP: *)
           secretary   (Ø = *a gente* → EP: *; BP: *)
           'The director wants {you(SG)/us} to hire another secretary.'
        d. O   professor esperava [que Ø estudasse
           the   teacher   expected   that   study-SUBJ.PRES
           mais]   (Ø = *você* → EP: OK; BP: *)
           more   (Ø = *a gente* → EP: *; BP: *)
           'The teacher hope that {you(SG)/we} would study more.'
        e. [Se Ø   não   ultrapassar   os   120 km/h],   a
           if   not   exceed-SUBJ.FUT   the   120 km/h   the
           gasolina vai dar.   (Ø = *você* → EP: OK; BP: *)
           gasoline go give   (Ø = *a gente* → EP: *; BP: *)
           'If {you(SG)/we} don't go over 120 km/h, there will be enough gas.'

Again, the surface form of the agreeing verb is the same regardless of whether the null subject is *você* or *a gente*. However, only when the null subject is interpreted as *você* in EP can the agreement license the corresponding subject; this is not possible for the null counterpart of *você* in BP nor for the null counterpart of *a gente* in either variety. As we can see in Tables 4.8 and 4.9, only the surface form associated with *você* in EP has an underlying form with a valued person feature. Hence, the Prominent Feature Valuation Condition in (4.21) provides the correct interpretation regarding null subject licensing by the same surface form associated with different underlying feature specifications.

The impoverishment rule proposed above also provides independent evidence for the role of number valuation in marginally licensing null subjects in finite clauses in BP. Recall that, in the absence of an intrasentential antecedent, the null counterparts of *eu* and *vocês* behave alike in BP finite tenses with a fuller agreement paradigm (see Table 4.7) in that they can be marginally licensed. Given that impoverishment deletes only the SG specification of the agreement inflection associated with *eu* (see Table 4.9), the prediction is that, in impoverished tenses in BP, the null counterparts of *eu* and *vocês/cês* should not pattern alike, for only the latter could still be marginally licensed. The contrast between the sentences in (4.43) and that in (4.45) below show that this prediction is correct.

(4.45) Eu   quero que   Ø   entreguem   o   trabalho
        I   want   that   deliver-SUBJ.PRES-3.PL   the work
        no   prazo.   (Ø = *vocês* → EP: OK; BP:??)
        in-the time
        'I want you(PL) to deliver the work on time.'

Additional evidence for the impoverishment rule in Table 4.7 is provided by hyper-raising constructions in BP involving *eu*. Consider the contrast between (4.46) and (4.47), for instance.

(4.46) a. Eles   parecem que nadam   bem.   (BP)
           they(MASC)   seem-**PL** that swim-**PL** well
           'They(MASC) seem to swim well.'
        b. [eles$_{\text{[P-G:MASC-N:PL]}}$ parece-**Infl**$_{\text{[P:u-N:PL]}}$ [que __ nada-**Infl**$_{\text{[N:PL]}}$ bem]]

(4.47) a. %Eu pareço   que nado   bem.   (BP)
           I   seem-**SG** that swim-**SG** well
           'I seem to swim well.'
        b. [eu$_{\text{[P.N:SG]}}$ parece-**Infl**$_{\text{[P.N:SG]}}$ [que __ nada-**Infl**$_{\text{[N:SG]}}$ bem]]

Recall that Infl in BP may bear person and number or just number (see Table 3.13). When Infl is specified only for number, the subject of its clause is not assigned nominative and must undergo raising to the higher clause in search of case licensing (see Section 3.4.3). This is what we see in (4.46b). By contrast, when the raised element is the pronoun *eu* as in (4.47b), speakers' judgments split. In Section 3.4.3, this variation in judgment was taken to depend on whether or not the grammar of individual speakers allows Infl with just number to enter into an agreement relation with a pronoun with fused number and person. This proposal predicts that in contexts where no such potential problem arises, hyper-raising of *eu* should yield uniform results across speakers. With that in mind, let us now consider the sentence in (4.48a).

(4.48) a. Eu parecia que nadava bem. (BP)
I *seem-INDIC.IMPERF that swim-INDIC.IMPERF well*
'I seemed to swim well.'
b. [eu[P.N:SG] parece-T₁-Infl[P:u] [que __ nada-T₁-Infl bem]]

(4.48a) also involves hyper-raising of *eu*, as sketched in (4.48b). Interestingly, however, (4.48a) is judged as acceptable even by speakers who do not admit (4.47a). The relevant difference here is that the tense of the embedded clause of (4.48a) (indicative imperfective past) is one of the tenses that triggers impoverishment in Portuguese. As seen in Table 4.7, this means that the specification SG is independently deleted in both Infls of (4.48b). Once this specification is gone, no potential failure of agreement arises and the source of disagreement among speakers disappears.[26]

4.3.1.2 Third Person Null Subjects in Finite Clauses

Let us now examine third person null subjects in finite clauses in EP and BP. The first thing to check is whether they involve pro-drop or topic drop. Recall that one test to distinguish these two possibilities involves null subjects in clauses with moved interrogative constituents (see Section 4.3.1.1). Bearing this in mind, consider the data in (4.49) and (4.50) (see footnote 17 above).

(4.49) a. A: – Onde está a Maria?
where is the Maria
'Where's Maria?'
B: – [Ø acabou de sair] (Ø = *ela* → EP: OK; BP: OK)
finished-3.SG of leave
'She's just left.'
b. A: – Onde estão os meninos?
where are the boys
'Where are the boys?'
B: – [Ø acabaram de sair] (Ø = *eles* → EP: OK; BP: OK)
finished-3.PL of leave
'They've just left.'

---

[26] See Nunes 2015b and 2020a for discussion.

(4.50) a. A: – Onde está a Maria?
  where is the Maria
  'Where's Maria?'
 B: – O que Ø fez desta vez? (Ø = ela → EP: OK; **BP: ***)
  what did-3.SG of-this time
  'What did she do this time?'

 b. A: – Os alunos pareciam preocupados.
  the students seemed worried
  'The students seemed worried.'
 B: – Que prova Ø fizeram hoje? (Ø = eles → EP: OK; **BP: ??**)
  which exam did-3.PL today
  'Which exam did they do today?'

In both (4.49) and (4.50), the null subjects could potentially be identified by the nominal expression present in the question in the previous discourse. EP and BP behave alike with respect to (4.49), but not with respect to (4.50). Note that topic drop can be licensed in (4.49), but not in (4.50) due to the presence of the fronted interrogative constituent (see Section 4.3.1.1). This indicates that third person null subjects in (4.49) and (4.50) should be analyzed as instances of topic drop in BP (hence their contrast in BP), but can be analyzed as instances of pro-drop in EP (hence the lack of contrast between (4.49) and (4.50) in EP).

This distinction in turn follows from the feature specification of third person pronouns discussed in Section 3.4.2. Despite being associated with the same verbal agreement forms in EP and BP, these pronouns have different underlying person and number specifications in the two varieties, as seen in Table 3.12 and repeated below in Table 4.10.

According to Table 4.10, all third person pronouns in EP and their corresponding verbal agreement inflection have their person and number specifications valued; by contrast, in BP only number is valued and only when the pronoun is plural. These distinctions are not detected at first sight, for the verbal agreement specifications [P:3] and [N:SG] in EP and [P:u] and [N:u] in BP fall under the Elsewhere Condition of their morphological realization rules in (4.51d) and (4.52c) (= (4.20d) and (4.27c)) and are assigned no phonetic content.

(4.51) *Correspondence rules for the morphological realization of verbal agreement inflection in EP:*
 a. [P.N:1.PL] ↔ {-mos}
  [N:PL] ↔ {-m}
 b. [P.N:1.SG] → {-o} / INDIC.PRES ___
  → {-i} elsewhere
 c. [P.N:2.SG] → {-ste} / INDIC.PERF.PAST ___
  → {-s} elsewhere
 d. Ø elsewhere

4.3 Definite Null Subjects   179

Table 4.10 *Third person pronouns and verbal agreement in Portuguese finite clauses*

Nominative pronouns	Person and number				Surface forms: *dançar* 'dance' (indicative present)
	EP		BP		
	Morphological specification	Agreement inflection	Morphological specification	Agreement inflection	
ele 'he'	[P:3-N:SG]	[P:3-N:SG]	[P-N]	[P:u-N:u]	*dança*
ela 'she'					
eles 'they(MASC)'	[P:3-N:PL]	[P:3-N:PL]	[P-N:PL]	[P:u-N:PL]	*dançam*
elas 'they(FEM)'					

(4.52) *Correspondence rules for the morphological realization of verbal agreement inflection in BP:*
 a. [P.N:1]   ↔   {-mo(s)}
    [N:PL]   ↔   {-m}
 b. [P.N:SG] →   {-o} / INDIC.PRES ___
              →   {-i} / INDIC.PERF.PAST ___
 c. Ø elsewhere

However, when pronominal null subject licensing is taken into account, the effects of the different specifications in Table 4.10 immediately arise. Given that the person inflection associated with third person pronouns is valued in EP, it can license their null counterparts in compliance with the Prominent Feature Valuation Condition (see (4.21)). Hence, the null counterparts of third person pronouns can be licensed in EP even in environments such as (4.50). In BP, on the other hand, the person feature is not valued; thus, third person null subjects in matrix clauses are fully legitimate only when they result from topic drop, as in (4.49). The contrast between third person singular and third person plural in (4.50) is also expected. Recall from Section 4.3.1.1 that in BP a valued number feature can marginally allow ellipsis of an overt pronoun (see (4.22a,f) and (4.26a,f), for example). This being so, number valuation in (4.50b) marginally allows ellipsis, leading to an amelioration effect when compared to (4.50a), which cannot resort to ellipsis as its number feature is not valued.

Let us now examine third person null subjects in embedded clauses.

(4.53) a. [a Maria]$_i$ acha   [que Ø   vai   viajar amanhã] (EP: Ø$_{i/k}$; **BP:** Ø$_{i/*k}$)
            the Maria   thinks that   go-3.SG travel tomorrow
            'Maria$_i$ thinks that she$_{i/k}$/he is going to travel tomorrow.'

180   4 Null Subjects

    b. [os alunos]$_i$ disseram [que Ø conversaram com a
       the students said that talked with the
       diretora]   (EP: Ø$_{i/k}$; **BP:** Ø$_{i/??k}$)
       dirctor]
       '[The students]$_i$ said that they$_{i/k}$ talked with the director.'

(4.53) shows that third person null subjects are allowed in embedded clauses in both EP and BP, but with different interpretations. In the case of EP, the embedded null subject can be interpreted as referring to the matrix subject or some other compatible nominal expression that was salient in the previous discourse (indicated by the index k); for instance, the null subjects of (4.53) may respectively refer to João or the teachers if these were the topics of conversation in the previous discourses. In BP, on the other hand, the matrix reading is allowed, but the extrasentential reading is admitted (and marginally so) only with the third person plural.

The fact that the extrasentential interpretation of the null subjects of (4.53) is disallowed in BP in the case of the third person singular and marginally allowed in the case of the third person plural is not surprising in the face of the contrast between (4.49) and (4.50), which showed that third person null subjects in matrix clauses are cases of topic drop and not pro-drop. Recall that topic drop is typically a matrix clause phenomenon (see (4.26)). What is however unexpected is the lack of contrast between the third person singular and the third person plural null subjects in (4.53) under the intrasentential reading, as opposed to what we saw in (4.50).

The data in (4.54) and (4.55) further show that linking the embedded null subject to a nominal expression within its sentence is not a sufficient condition to license it in BP.

(4.54)   a. O pai d[a Maria]$_i$ acha [que Ø$_i$ está
        the father of-the Maria thinks that be.PRES-3.SG
        grávida]   (EP: OK; **BP:** *)
        pregnant
        'Maria$_i$'s father thinks that she$_i$ is pregnant.'
   b. A professora d[os meus filhos$_i$] disse [que Ø$_i$ passaram
        the teacher of-the my-PL son-PL said that passed
        de ano]   (EP: OK; **BP:** ??)
        of year
        '[My children]$_i$'s teacher said that they$_i$ passed their year-end exams.'

(4.55)   a. [O João]$_i$ disse que a gerente confirmou [que Ø$_i$
        the João said that the.FEM manager confirmed that
        vai ser promovido]   (EP: OK; **BP:** *)
        go-3.SG be promoted-MASC
        'Maria$_i$ said that the manager confirmed that she$_i$'s going to be promoted,'

4.3 Definite Null Subjects   181

b. [Os   estagiários]ᵢ   ouviram que a   diretora disse
    the.MASC-PL trainee-MASC-PL   heard   that the director said
    [que   Øᵢ chegaram   atrasados
    that   arrived-3.PL   delayed-MASC-PL
    para a   reunião]   (EP: OK; **BP: ??**)
    to   the meeting
    '[The trainees]ᵢ heard that the director said that theyᵢ arrived late for the meeting.'

All the null subjects of (4.54) and (4.55) are acceptable with the intended interpretation in EP, which again confirms that these are ordinary cases of pro-drop in this variety. In BP, on the other hand, the sentences with a third person singular null subject are excluded (see (4.54a) and (4.55a)) and those with a third person plural null subject are marginally acceptable (see (4.54b) and (4.55b)), replicating the pattern we saw earlier in (4.50). It is worth noting that the sentences in (4.54) and (4.55) are morphologically and pragmatically biased towards establishing the intended coreference, but this is to no avail in BP. The most natural rendition of the meaning indicated by the translations of (4.54) and (4.55) in BP has an overt pronoun in the embedded subject position.

Another interesting contrast between EP and BP regards the interpretation of the null subjects of certain subjunctive clauses, as illustrated in (4.56).[27]

(4.56) [O João]ᵢ quer   [que Ø viaje   na   próxima
        the João wants that   travel-SUBJ.PRES-3.SG in.the   next
        semana]   (Øᵢ → EP/BP: *;
        week   Øₖ → EP: OK; BP: *)
        'João wants him to travel next week.'

As with what we find in other Romance languages, the subjunctive clause that is complement of verbs like *querer* 'want' imposes an obviative interpretation on its subject with respect to the subordinating subject (i.e. the two subjects must have disjoint reference). Thus, in neither EP or BP can the embedded subject of (4.56) be interpreted as being João. This possibility of interpretation being excluded, the null subject of (4.56) can be interpreted in EP as referring to some other salient person being spoken about in the previous discourse. By contrast, there is no such possibility in BP: (4.56) is simply unacceptable, regardless of the interpretation of the null subject. This suggests that the obviation applies to pronouns, and (4.56) is not a configuration where a null pronoun can be licensed in BP.

In sum, the contrast between EP and BP regarding the interpretation of the null subjects of (4.50) and (4.53)–(4.56) leads to the conclusion that embedded

---

[27] For discussion see e.g. Raposo 1985, Negrão 1986, and Petersen 2011.

null subjects in BP do not involve pro-drop (otherwise, they should behave like their EP counterparts). This in turn leads us to expect that whatever is responsible for the full acceptability of the interpretation of the embedded null subjects of (4.53) as coreferential with the matrix subject in BP, it should not be based on null pronouns. There is in fact interesting independent evidence that the null subjects of (4.53) are not null pronominals. Consider the data in (4.57) and (4.58), for instance.[28]

(4.57) [O   João]$_i$ tinha dito [que $Ø_i$ ia
the João had said that go-INDIC-IMPERF
reclamar da decisão] e a Maria também tinha.
complain of-the decision and the Maria also had
'João$_i$ had said that he$_i$ was going to complain about the decision and Maria$_k$ had also (said that **she$_k$** was going to complain about the decision).' (EP: OK; BP: OK)
'João$_i$ had said that he$_i$ was going to complain about the decision and Maria had also (said that **he$_i$** was going to complain about the decision).' (EP: OK; **BP: ***)

(4.58) Só [a Maria]$_i$ acha [que $Ø_i$ vai ganhar a eleição]
only the Maria thinks that go-3.SG win the election
'Only Maria$_i$ thinks that she$_i$ will win the election (no one else is **self** confident).' (EP: OK; BP: OK)
'Only Maria$_i$ thinks that she$_i$ will win the election (no one else believes that **she$_i$** will win).' (EP: OK; **BP: ***)

As indicated above, the sentences in (4.57) and (4.58) have two interpretations in EP, but only one in BP. Crucially, the two interpretations are available in analogous sentences in BP when an overt pronoun occupies the embedded subject position, as show in (4.59) and (4.60) below. The fact that the ambiguity associated with unequivocal pronouns in (4.59) and (4.60) is found in (4.57) and (4.58) in EP but not in BP strongly indicates that the last pairs of sentences involve a null pronominal in EP, but not in BP.

(4.59) [O   João]$_i$ tinha dito [que **ele**$_i$ ia
the João had said that he go-INDIC-IMPERF
reclamar da decisão] e a Maria também tinha.
complain of-the decision and the Maria also had
'João$_i$ had said that he$_i$ was going to complain about the decision and Maria had also (said that **she** was going to complain about the decision).' (EP: OK; BP: OK)
'João$_i$ had said that he$_i$ was going to complain about the decision and Maria had also (said that **he$_i$** was going to complain about the decision).' (EP: OK; **BP: OK**)

---

[28] For discussion see e.g. Negrão 1986, Ferreira 2000, 2009, and Rodrigues 2004.

(4.60) Só [a Maria]ᵢ acha [que **elaᵢ** vai ganhar a eleição]
only the Maria thinks that she go-3.SG win the election
'Only Mariaᵢ thinks that sheᵢ will win the election (no one
else is **self** confident).' (EP: OK; BP: OK)
'Only Mariaᵢ thinks that sheᵢ will win the election (no one
else believes that **sheᵢ** will win).' (EP: OK; **BP: OK**)

We are thus left with the issue of the nature of the null subject of (4.53) in BP if it is neither a case of topic drop nor a case of pronominal ellipsis. The contrasts between BP and EP in (4.54) and (4.55) show that the licensing of embedded third person null subjects in BP is subject to much stricter conditions than those that apply to anaphoric licensing of null third person pronouns in EP. In particular, an embedded null subject in BP requires an antecedent (see (4.53)) that must sit in the next subordinating clause (see (4.55)) and not be immediately dominated by another noun phrase (see (4.54)). Interestingly, this cluster of properties actually describes subject-to-subject movement. Recall that verbal agreement inflection in BP may be ambiguous in involving both person and number or just number (see Section 3.4.3). In the latter situation, the embedded subject does not receive Case within its clause and moves to the next higher subject position, as illustrated in (4.61).

(4.61) a. Eles **parecem** que **gostam** de nadar. (BP)
they(MASC) seem-PL that like-PL of swim
'They seem to like to swim.'
b. [eles₍ₚ₋G:MASC-N:PL₎ parece-**Infl**₍P:u-N:PL₎ [que __ gosta-**Infl**₍N:PL₎ de nadar]]

Once this hyper-raising possibility is available in BP, it could in principle be resorted to in the derivation of sentences such as (4.53) as well, as sketched in (4.62).²⁹ In other words, if the null subjects of sentences such as (4.53) in BP are syntactic gaps that result from subject-to-subject movement,³⁰ we can account for the tighter restrictions we find on the licensing of embedded null subjects in BP (see (4.54)/(4.55)).

---

[29] We are glossing over some technical details here. It is arguably the case that on their way to the matrix subject position, the subjects in (4.62) first move to a position where they can establish a thematic relation with the matrix predicates. For further details and arguments for a movement analysis of definite null subjects in BP, see e.g. Ferreira 2000, 2009, Rodrigues 2002, 2004, Nunes 2008a, 2009, 2010a, 2017, and Petersen 2011.
[30] *Traces* in generative terminology (see e.g. Chomsky 1973).

184   4 Null Subjects

(4.62) BP:
    a. [a Maria]$_i$ acha [que Ø$_i$ vai   viajar amanhã]
       the Maria thinks that go-3.SG travel tomorrow
       'Maria$_i$ thinks that she$_i$/he is going to travel tomorrow.'
    a'. [[a Maria] acha-Infl$_{[P:u-N:u]}$ [que __ ir.PRES-Infl$_{[N:u]}$ viajar amanhã]]

    b. [os alunos]$_i$ disseram [que Ø$_i$ conversaram com a diretora]
       the students said   that   talked   with the director
       '[The students]$_i$ said that they$_{i/k}$ talked with the director.'
    b'. [[os alunos] dissera-Infl$_{[P:u-N:PL]}$ [que __ conversara-Infl$_{[N:PL]}$ com a diretora]]

Evidence for a movement approach to third person null subjects in BP along the lines of (4.62) is provided by island effects.[31] The subjects in (4.62) move out of a complement clause and complement clauses are generally transparent to movement, as illustrated in (4.63a) below with the movement of the interrogative phrase. By contrast, relative clauses are syntactic islands, as they do not allow movement from within them, as illustrated in (4.63b).

(4.63) BP:
    a. Que livro a Maria disse que o João comprou?
       what book the Maria said that the João bought
       'Which book did Maria say that João bought?'
    a'. [que livro] a Maria disse [que o João comprou __]

    b. *Que livro a Maria conversou com o estudante que comprou?
       which book the Maria talked   with the student that bought
    b'. *[que livro] a Maria conversou com o estudante [que comprou __]

As mentioned in Section 4.3.1.1, a third person singular null subject is allowed in BP as the subject of a complement clause, but not as the subject of a relative clause, as shown in (4.64) (= (4.32)). If the null subjects in (4.53) are the result of movement, the contrast in (4.64) is exactly what we should expect, for they replicate the pattern seen in (4.63).

(4.64)   a. Ele$_i$ acha   que [Ø$_i$ deve   participar
         he   think.3.SG that   should.3.SG participate
         mais]   (Ø = ele → EP: OK; BP: OK)
         more
       'He$_i$ thinks that he$_i$ should be more involved.'
    b. Ele$_i$ vai   rever os testes que [Ø fez]$_i$ (Ø = ele → EP: OK; BP: *)
       he go.3.SG review the tests that   did.3.SG
       'He$_i$ is going to review the tests that he$_i$ did.'

Also predicted is the contrast in BP between (4.65a) and (4.65b) below and that between (4.64b) and (4.65b).

---

[31] In the sense of Ross 1967.

(4.65) a. Eles$_i$ acham [que Ø$_i$ devem participar mais] (EP: OK; BP: OK)
 they think that should-3.PL participate more
 'They$_i$ think that they$_i$ should be more involved.'
 b. Eles$_i$ vão rever os testes [que Ø$_i$ fizeram] (EP: OK; BP: ??)
 they go review the tests that did-3.PL
 'They$_i$ are going to review the tests they$_i$ did.'

In (4.65a) movement from within the complement clause is possible; hence, the third person plural null subject is fully acceptable. In (4.65b), on the other hand, the relative clause does not allow movement from within it. However, the agreement inflection on its verb has its number feature valued, which may marginally allow pronominal ellipsis in BP; hence, the marginal acceptability of the null subject of (4.65b) in BP. This possibility is not available in (4.64b), for the number feature of the agreement inflection remains unvalued (see Table 4.10). The fully acceptable versions of (4.64b) and (4.65b) in BP actually involve overt pronouns in the embedded clauses, as shown in (4.66).

(4.66) a. Ele$_i$ vai rever os testes [que **ele**$_i$ fez] (EP: ?: BP: OK)
 he goes review the tests that he did-3.SG
 'He$_i$ is going to review the tests he$_i$ did.'
 b. Eles$_i$ vão rever os testes [que **eles**$_i$ fizeram] (EP: ?; BP: OK)
 they go review the tests that they did-3.PL
 'They$_i$ are going to review the tests they$_i$ did.'

Also expected is the fact that in EP all four sentences in (4.64) and (4.65) are fully acceptable, but the ones in (4.66) are slightly marginal (unless the embedded subject is contrastive or emphasized in some way). The agreement inflection associated with third person pronouns is valued in EP (see Table 4.10) and is, therefore, able to license the instances of null pronominals in (4.65). As for the marginality of (4.66) in EP, it is an effect of the preference for null subjects in neutral contexts in canonical pro-drop languages (see footnote 4 above).

The behavior of third person null subjects in EP and BP finite clauses is summarized in Table 4.11.

Table 4.11 *Licensing of third person null subjects in Portuguese finite clauses*

		Morphological licensing	Intrasentential anaphoric licensing	
			In opaque domains	In transparent domains
Null counterpart of	*ele* 'he' *ela* 'she'	EP: OK; BP: *	EP: OK; BP: *	EP: OK; BP: OK
	eles 'they(MASC)' *elas* 'they(FEM)'	EP: OK; BP: ??	EP: OK; BP: ??	EP: OK; BP: OK

186   4 Null Subjects

The movement analysis of embedded third person null subjects in BP also provides an account of the intriguing contrasts involving first and second person null subjects depending on whether or not they are within a syntactic island, as observed in Section 4.3.3.1. Consider the BP data in (4.67)–(4.69), for example (the corresponding sentences are all acceptable in EP).

(4.67) a. {Você/a gente}$_i$ prometeu   [que Ø$_i$ vai   participar
            you.SG/we   promised-3.SG that   go-3.SG participate
            mais]   (BP: OK)
            more
            '{You(SG)/we} promised to be more involved.'
        b. {Você/a gente}$_i$ vai   rever os testes [que Ø$_i$ fez] (BP: *)
            you.SG/we   go-3.SG review the tests   that   did-3.SG
            '{You(SG)/we} are going to review the tests that {you(SG)/we} did.'

(4.68) a. Vocês$_i$ prometeram [que Ø$_i$ vão   participar mais] (BP: OK)
            you-PL promised-3.PL that   go-3.PL participate more
            'You(PL) promised to be more involved.'
        b. Vocês$_i$ precisam rever os testes [que Ø$_i$ fizeram]   (BP: ??)
            you-PL need-3.PL review the tests   that   did-3.PL
            'You(PL) need to review the tests that you(PL) did.'

(4.69) a. Eu$_i$ acho   [que Ø$_i$ estudei   o
            I   think-1.SG that   studied-1.SG the
            suficiente]   (%BP: OK; %BP: ??)
            sufficient
            'I think I studied enough.'
        b. Eu$_i$ não   gostei   dos   últimos artigos [que Ø$_i$
            I   not   liked-1.SG of-the last   articles that
            li]   (BP: ??)
            read-1.SG
            'I didn't like the last articles I read.'

Subject-to-subject movement constitutes a viable approach in the case of the (a) sentences of (4.67)–(4.69), but not in the case of the (b) sentences, as the latter involve an island configuration (a relative clause). Accordingly, (4.67a) and (4.68a) are fully acceptable and (4.67b) is unacceptable. As for (4.68b) and (4.69b), the number valuation in the agreement inflection associated with *vocês* and *eu* marginally allows ellipsis of these pronouns; thus, although these sentences cannot be derived via movement, they are marginally acceptable thanks to the marginal role that number valuation plays in the licensing of null subjects in BP. Finally, speakers' judgments split with respect to (4.69a). The problem is not the movement of the embedded subject, for the embedded clause is a transparent domain (see (4.67a) and (4.68a)), but the agreement in the embedded clause. As discussed in Section 3.4.3, in order for subject-to-subject movement out of the embedded clause to be possible in BP, the embedded Infl must bear only number. Some speakers do not allow a number feature to enter into an agreement relation with the fused person and number specification of *eu*; these speakers then analyze the embedded clauses of sentences like (4.69a) as involving an Infl with both person and number, which yields a marginal result like that in (4.69b) thanks to the marginal availability of ellipsis. For speakers who allow an underspecified Infl to agree with *eu*, the movement alternative is viable and (4.69a) patterns in the same way as (4.67a) and (4.68a).

4.3.1.3 Summary

Table 4.12 below summarizes the discussion so far.

As the pronouns in each variety have different underlying morphological specifications, they trigger different patterns of valuation for the agreement inflection associated with them. The Prominent Feature Valuation Condition (see (4.21)) then determines which agreement specifications are able to license the ellipsis of a pronominal subject. In EP, all inflections but the one associated with *a gente* have their person feature valued; hence, all null pronouns but the null counterpart of *a gente* can be morphologically licensed. In BP, by contrast, *nós* is the only pronoun that values the person feature of the agreement inflection associated with it; hence, the null counterpart of *nós* is the only one that is fully acceptable in BP. The pronouns *eu*, *vocês/cês*, and *eles/elas* in BP actually value the number feature of the agreement inflection associated with them. Given that number is the second most prominent feature in the scale of prominence (see (4.21)), their null counterparts can be marginally licensed by the corresponding agreement inflection. Finally, the null counterparts of *você/cê*, *ele/ela*, and *a gente* in BP cannot be morphologically licensed because the agreement inflection associated with them has neither person nor number valued. Accordingly, if impoverishment deletes the value of the number inflection associated with *eu* in BP (see Table 4.9), its null counterpart will also fail to be morphologically licensed (even marginally).

Null subjects may however arise in BP as the output of subject-to-subject movement (see (4.62)). In this scenario, the restrictions associated with the null subjects in BP (they must occur in a transparent domain and be interpreted as the subject of the next subordinating clause containing them; see (4.54)–(4.55), (4.64)–(4.65), and (4.67)–(4.69)) follow from conditions that independently apply to subject-to-subject movement.

4.3.2 Definite Null Subjects in Inflected Infinitivals

4.3.2.1 First and Second Person Null Subjects in Inflected Infinitivals

As discussed in Section 3.3.2.2.2, inflected infinitivals in Portuguese have one fewer agreement distinction than the fuller paradigm of agreement in finite clauses, with EP displaying two cases of unambiguous agreement

Table 4.12 *Person and number agreement inflection in finite clauses and null subject licensing in Portuguese*

Nominative pronouns	Morphological specification for person and number					
	EP			BP		
	Pronoun specification	Agreement inflection	Null subject licensing	Pronoun specification	Agreement inflection	Null subject licensing
tu 'you(SG)'	[P.N:2.SG]	[P.N:2.SG]	OK			
nós 'we'	[P.N:1.PL]	[P.N:1.PL]	OK	[P.N:1]	[P.N:1]	OK
eu 'I'	[P.N:1.SG]	[P.N:1.SG]	OK	[P.N:SG]	[P.N:SG]	
vocês 'you(PL)'	[P:2-N:PL]	[P:2-N:PL]	OK	[P-N:PL]	[P:u-N:PL]	??
eles 'they(MASC)' *elas* 'they(FEM)'	[P:3-N:PL]	[P:3-N:PL]	OK			
você 'you(SG)'	[P:2-N:SG]	[P:2-N:SG]	OK	[P-N]	[P:u-N:u]	*
ele 'he' *ela* 'she'	[P:3-N:SG]	[P:3-N:SG]	OK			
a gente 'we'	[P.N]	[P:u-N:u]	*	[P.N]		

4.3 Definite Null Subjects

Table 4.13 *First and second person pronouns and verbal agreement morphology in Portuguese inflected infinitives*

Nominative pronouns	Surface forms: *dançar* 'dance': (inflected infinitive)
eu 'I'	*dançar*
você 'you(SG)'	
cê 'you(SG)[W]' (BP)	
a gente 'we'	
tu 'you(SG)' (EP)	*dançares*
nós 'we'	*dançarmos*
vocês 'you(PL)'	*dançarem*
cês 'you(PL)[W]' (BP)	

inflection (those associated with *tu* and *nós*) and BP only one (that associated with *nós*). In particular, the agreement inflection associated with the pronoun *eu* is also subject to a process of impoverishment, which gives rise to a surface form that is identical to the uninflected infinitive, as shown in Table 4.13 above.

We have seen in Section 4.3.1.1 that, in the case of finite clauses, morphological uniqueness plays no role in the licensing of null subjects. Rather, what was relevant for the licensing of pronominal null subjects via inflectional agreement was the Prominent Feature Valuation Condition stated in (4.21) and repeated here in (4.70), for convenience.

(4.70) *Prominent Feature Valuation Condition*
A given verbal inflection Infl can morphologically license the ellipsis of a definite pronominal subject in Portuguese only if the most prominent feature of Infl is valued, where feature prominence has the following scale: *person* > *number* > *gender* > *case*.

So, the question we have to determine is whether inflected infinitivals behave differently in licensing their null subjects via unambiguous agreement morphology or whether the Prominent Feature Valuation Condition is able to provide a uniform account of null subjects in both finite and nonfinite domains.

We may start by asking which feature of the agreement inflection associated with *eu* is deleted by the impoverishment process in inflected infinitivals. Again, the answer involving BP is not hard to establish. If *eu* in BP is specified only as SG (see Section 3.4.2), it is this feature specification in the corresponding agreement inflection that must undergo impoverishment. Such deletion should

190   4 Null Subjects

then block ellipsis of the overt counterpart of *eu*, which is marginally allowed with tenses with the fuller agreement paradigm (see Section 4.3.1.1). As for EP, *eu* is specified for both person and number and the corresponding agreement inflection is also specified for these features. We may then determine whether it is the person feature or the number feature that is deleted under impoverishment, by examining if EP allows the null subject corresponding to *eu* to be morphologically licensed in inflected infinitivals.

Bearing this in mind, let us consider the data in (4.71) (see footnote 1 above).

(4.71) a. Eles   ouviram-**me**$_i$ atentamente e   lamentaram [Ø$_i$ estar
            they   *heard-me*   *attentively*   *and*   *regretted*   *be*
            sem   tempo   para   os   ajudar]   (Ø = *eu* → EP: OK)
            without *time* *to*   *them*   *help*

        a'. *Eles   **me**$_i$ ouviram atentamente e   lamentaram [Ø$_i$ estar
            they   *me*   *heard*   *attentively*   *and*   *regretted*   *be*
            sem   tempo   para   ajudar   eles]   (Ø = *eu* → BP: *)
            without *time* *to*   *help*   *them*

            'They listened to me carefully and regretted that I didn't have time to help them.'

        b. O   professor lamentou   [Ø   estares   sem
            the   *teacher*   *regretted*   *be-2.SG*   *without*
            trabalho]   (Ø = *tu* → EP: OK)
            work

            'The teacher regretted that you(SG) are jobless.'

        c. O professor   lamentou [Ø$_i$ estar   sem   trabalho], mas
            the teacher   *regretted*   *be*   *without work*   *but*
            infelizmente   não   pode   atribuir-**lhe**$_i$
            unfortunately *not*   *can*   *assign-you.SG*
            a   bolsa.   (Ø = *você* → EP: OK)
            the   *fellowship*

        c'. *O   professor   lamentou [Ø$_i$ estar   sem   trabalho], mas
            the   *teacher*   *regretted*   *be*   *without work*   *but*
            infelizmente   não   pode   **te**$_i$ atribuir
            unfortunately *not* *can*   *you.SG*   *assign*
            a   bolsa.   (Ø = *você* → BP: *)
            the   *fellowship*

            'The teacher regretted that you(SG) are jobless, but unfortunately he cannot assign you(SG) the fellowship.'

        d. O   professor lamentou [Ø   estarmos   sem
            the   *teacher* *regretted*   *be-1.PL*   *without*
            trabalho]   (Ø = *nós* → EP: OK; PB: OK)
            work

            'The teacher regretted that we are jobless.'

        e. *Eles ouviram **a gente**$_i$ atentamente   e   lamentaram [Ø$_i$ estar sem
            they *heard*   *us*   *attentively* *and regretted*   *be*   *without*
            tempo para   os   ajudar]   (Ø = *a gente* → EP: *)
            time to   *them* *help*

e'. *Eles ouviram **a gente**ᵢ atentamente e lamentaram [Øᵢ estar sem
    they heard   us   attentively   and regretted   be   without
    tempo para ajudar eles]   (Ø = *a gente* → BP: *)
    time to   help   them
    'They listened to us carefully and regretted that we didn't have time to help them.'
f. Seria   bom [Ø arrumarem as malas] (Ø = *vocês* → EP: OK; PB: ??)
    would.be good   arrange   the bags
    'You(PL)'d better pack your luggage.'

Putting aside the null counterpart of *eu* in (4.71a) and (4.71a′) for the moment, the paradigm in (4.71) replicates what we saw in the case of null subjects in embedded finite clauses (see (4.26)). In EP, the null counterparts of *tu, você, nós*, and *vocês* can be morphologically licensed, but not the null counterpart of *a gente*. In BP, on the other hand, only the null counterpart of *nós* is fully acceptable; the null counterpart of *vocês* is marginal and the null counterparts of *você* and *a gente* are completely excluded. The explanation for this pattern is the same as the one we had before: *a gente* in EP and BP and *você* in BP are not morphologically valued for person or number; therefore, the Prominent Feature Valuation Condition prevents the agreement inflections associated with them from morphologically licensing their null counterparts. The different behavior of the null counterpart of *você* in the two varieties, despite being associated with the same surface agreeing form, in itself leads to the conclusion that null subject licensing in inflected infinitivals is not based on unambiguous agreement forms.

That being so, let us return to the null counterpart of *eu* in (4.71a) and (4.71a′). The infinitival form is the same in EP and BP. However, only in EP can the null subject be appropriately interpreted as the speaker. This mirrors what we saw with respect to the finite tenses that undergo impoverishment (see (4.40)) and the explanation can be the same: in both varieties, impoverishment deletes the number specification of the inflectional agreement associated with *eu*, as sketched in Tables 4.14 and 4.15. Such deletion does not prevent the null counterpart of *eu* from being licensed in EP, because the remaining person feature of the agreement inflection is valued, thus being in consonance with the Prominent Feature Valuation Condition. In BP, on the other hand, the surviving person feature is not valued and therefore the null counterpart of *eu* cannot be licensed (even marginally).

The data in (4.71) and their analysis in Tables 4.14 and 4.15 below show that, despite appearances, the null counterpart of *eu* forms a natural class with the null counterpart of *você* in EP infinitivals, but with the null counterparts of *a gente* and *você* in BP infinitivals. In EP, the infinitival agreement inflections associated with *eu* and *você* have a valued person feature and are therefore able to morphologically license the corresponding null subjects in

Table 4.14 *First and second person null subjects and infinitival agreement in European Portuguese*

Nominative pronouns	Morphological specification	Person and number		Surface forms: *dançar* 'dance': (inflected infinitive)
		Syntactic agreement [P:u-N:u]	Impoverishment: If V-INF-[P:1-N:SG] → V-INF-[P:1]	Correspondence rules	
eu 'I'	[P.N:.SG]	*dançar*-[P.N:1.SG]	*dançar*-[P:1]	*dançar*-∅	*dançar*
você 'you(SG)'	[P:2-N:SG]	*dançar*-[P:2-N:SG]	n/a	*dançar*-∅-∅	
a gente 'we'	[P.N]	*dançar*-[P:u-N:u]	n/a	*dançar*-∅-∅	
tu 'you(SG)'	[P.N:2.SG]	*dançar*-[P.N:2.SG]	n/a	*dançar*-*s*	*dançares*
nós 'we'	[P.N:1.PL]	*dançar*-[P.N:1.PL]	n/a	*dançar*-*mos*	*dançarmos*
vocês 'you(PL)'	[P:2-N:PL]	*dançar*-[P:2-N:PL]	n/a	*dançar*-∅-*m*	*dançarem*

Table 4.15 *First and second person null subjects and infinitival agreement in Brazilian Portuguese*

Nominative pronouns	Morphological specification	Person and number			Surface forms: *dançar* 'dance'; (inflected infinitive)
		Syntactic agreement [P:u-N:u]	Impoverishment: If V-INF-[P:u-N:SG] → V-INF-[P:u]	Correspondence rules	
eu 'I'	[P:N:SG]	*dançar*-[P.N:SG]	*dançar*-[P:u]	*dançar*-Ø	*dançar*
você 'you(SG)'	[P:N]	*dançar*-[P:u-N:u]	n/a	*dançar*-Ø-Ø	
a gente 'we'	[P.N]	*dançar*-[P:u-N:u]	n/a	*dançar*-Ø-Ø	
nós 'we'	[P.N:1]	*dançar*-[P.N:1]	n/a	*dançar*-*mos*	*dançarmos*
vocês 'you(PL)'	[P-N:PL]	*dançar*-[P:u-N:PL]	n/a	*dançar*-Ø-*m*	*dançarem*

consonance with (4.70). In BP, on the other hand, the infinitival agreement inflections associated with *eu*, *você*, and *a gente* cannot license their null counterparts because they are devoid of a valued person feature.

Notice that the intriguing contrasts between EP and BP in (4.71) are completely obliterated in infinitival constructions such as (4.72) below, where all the sentences are grammatical in both varieties.

(4.72) a. Eu$_i$ escrevi este artigo para Ø$_i$ discutir com
   I wrote this article to discuss with
   a professora. (Ø = *eu* → EP: OK; BP: OK)
   the teacher
   'I wrote this article to discuss with the teacher.'
 b. Você$_i$ deve organizar os dados para Ø$_i$ discutir com
   you.SG should organize the data to discuss with
   o professor. (Ø = *você* → EP: OK; BP: OK)
   the teacher
   'You(SG) should organize the data to discuss with the teacher.'
 c. [A gente]$_i$ preparou um projeto para Ø$_i$ discutir com
   we prepared a project to discuss with
   o professor. (Ø = *a gente* → EP: OK; BP: OK)
   the teacher
   'We prepared a project to discuss with the teacher.'

Crucially, the antecedents of the null subjects of the adjunct clauses in (4.72) sit in the subject position of the subordinating clause and this constitutes an environment that admits both inflected and uninflected infinitivals (see Section 3.3.2.2.2), as illustrated in (4.73) below. Thus, the grammatical versions of (4.72) that correspond to ungrammatical versions in (4.71) can be independently licensed thanks to the uninflected infinitival possibility, which involves not a null pronominal subject, but a null caseless subject (see Section 4.2 and footnote 3 above).

(4.73) Deves organizar os resultados antes de [Ø {**conversar/conversares**}
   should-2.SG organize the results before of talk/talk-2.SG
   com o professor] (Ø = *tu* → EP: OK)
   with the teacher
   'You(SG) must organize the results before talking with the teacher.'

Let us examine one final consequence of the impoverishment rule in Table 4.15 for BP. As mentioned in Section 4.3.1.1, even BP speakers who do not allow hyper-raising constructions such as (4.74a) (= (4.47a)), which involves hyper-raising of *eu* out of an embedded clause in the present tense, admit similar constructions like (4.75a) (= (4.48a)), whose embedded clause is in the indicative imperfective past tense.

(4.74) a. Eu   pareço   que   nado   bem.   (%BP)
        I   seem-**SG**   that swim-**SG** well
        'I seem to swim well.'
    b. [eu_{[P:N:SG]} parece-Infl_{[P:u-N:SG]} [que __ nada-**Infl**_{[N:SG]} bem]]

(4.75) a. Eu   parecia   que nadava   bem.   (BP)
        I   seem-*INDIC.IMPERF* that swim-*INDIC.IMPERF* well
        'I seemed to swim well.'
    b. [eu_{[P:N:SG]} parece-T_I-Infl_{[P:u]} [que __ nada-T_I-**Infl** bem]]

Recall from Section 3.4.3 that, in order for hyper-raising to take place, the embedded Infl must be specified only for number. This is in principle possible in both (4.74b) and (4.75b). So, hyper-raising *per se* is licit in both constructions. The distinction is in fact morphological in nature. In order for the structure in (4.74b) to surface as in (4.74a), the number feature of the embedded Infl must agree with a pronoun with fused person and number features. Although this is generally precluded (thus preventing hyper-raising of *nós*; see (3.88a)), some speakers seem to capitalize on the value of the fused amalgam (SG – a number value), allowing hyper-raising in this case; hence the variation in judgments we find for sentences such as (4.74a). In (4.75b), on the other hand, no problem arises, for the indicative imperfective past (like the subjunctive present) is one of the tenses that deletes the number feature of Infl under impoverishment; hence, the embedded verb surfaces with no agreement inflection (see Table 4.9) and BP speakers uniformly judge (4.75a) as an acceptable sentence.

If inflected infinitivals in BP undergo impoverishment along the lines of the description in Table 4.15, the prediction is that hyper-raising of *eu* out of inflected infinitivals should pattern in a similar way to (4.75a) and not to (4.74a). The prediction is correct. As mentioned in Section 3.4.3, a sentence such as (4.76a) below, which involves hyper-raising out of an inflected infinitival, is acceptable even for speakers who dislike (4.74a). As in (4.75b), impoverishment independently deletes the number specification of (4.76b) and the verb surfaces with a form identical to the uninflected infinitival.

(4.76) a. Eu sou   difícil   de   **nadar**   bem em competição.   (BP)
        I am   difficult of   swim-*INF* well in competition
        'I rarely swim well in competitions.'
    b. [eu_{[P:N:SG]} sou difícil de [__ nada-**INF**_I bem em competição]]

196   4 Null Subjects

4.3.2.2 Third Person Null Subjects in Inflected Infinitivals

Inflected infinitivals do not essentially differ from finite clauses (see Table 4.11) in regard to third person null subjects. As depicted in Table 4.16, the verbal agreement inflection associated with inflected infinitivals is valued for both person and number in EP, but only for number specification in BP and only when the pronoun is plural.

We should thus expect parallel behavior between finite clauses and inflected infinitivals as far as the licensing of third person null subjects is concerned. That this prediction is correct is illustrated by the sentences in (4.77).

(4.77) a. [O João]ᵢ discutiu com o chefe hoje. É muito improvável
         the João discussed with the boss today is very improbable
         [Øᵢ ser   promovido no   fim do   ano]   (EP: OK; BP: *)
         be-INF promoted in-the end of-the year
         'Joãoᵢ argued with the boss today. It's very unlikely that he'll be promoted at the end of the year.'
     b. A Maria já   ligou para [os convidados]ᵢ. Vai ser impossível
        the Maria already called to the guests   go be impossible
        [Øᵢ chegarem antes das   nove horas]   (EP: OK; BP: ??)
        arrive-PL before of-the nine hours
        'Maria has already called the guests. It is going to be impossible for them to arrive before nine o'clock.'

The syntactic context in (4.77a–b) is one that licenses inflected infinitivals in both EP and BP. In EP, the null subject of the inflected infinitival can pick up its antecedent in the previous sentence. In BP, on the other hand, this connection is only marginally established in the case of the third plural null subject. This contrast can be accounted for if the infinitival agreement inflections associated with third person pronouns are able to morphologically license their null counterparts in EP thanks to their valued person feature, but not in BP (see Table 4.16 below). The amelioration effect noticed in (4.77b) in BP is due to the marginal availability of ellipsis when the agreement inflection has its number feature valued.

Let us finally examine the data in (4.78) and (4.79).

(4.78) a. Eu nunca imaginei   que fosse   tão fácil [alguém
         I   never imagined that be-SUBJ.IMPERF so easy somebody
         convencer   as pessoas dessa maneira]   (EP: OK; BP: OK)
         convince-3.SG the people of-this manner
         'I never thought that it would be so easy for someone to convince people this way.'

Table 4.16 *Third person pronouns and verbal agreement in Portuguese inflected infinitives*

Nominative pronouns	Person and number				Surface forms: *dançar* 'dance' (inflected infinitive)
	EP		BP		
	Morphological specification	Agreement inflection	Morphological specification	Agreement inflection	
ele 'he'	[P:3-N:SG]	[P:3-N:SG]	[P-N]	[P:u-N:u]	*dançar*
ela 'she'					
eles 'they(MASC)'	[P:3-N:PL]	[P:3-N:PL]	[P-N:PL]	[P:u-N:PL]	***dançarem***
elas 'they(FEM)'					

b. É fácil [[algumas pessoas] perderem a paciência nesta
   is easy some people lose-INF-3.PL the patience in-this
   situação]   (EP: OK; BP: OK)
   situation
   'It is easy for people to lose patience in this situation.'

(4.79) a. Eu nunca imaginei que **alguém**ᵢ fosse tão fácil
   I never imagined that somebody be-SUBJ.IMPERF so easy
   de [Øᵢ convencer as pessoas dessa
   of   convince-3.SG the people of-this
   maneira]   (EP: *; BP: OK)
   manner
   'I never thought that it would be so easy for someone to convince people this way.'

b. [**Algumas pessoas**]ᵢ são fáceis de [Øᵢ perderem a paciência
   some people are easy of   lose-INF-3.PL the patience
   nesta situação]   (EP: *; BP: OK)
   in-this situation
   'It is easy for people to lose patience in this situation.'

In both (4.78) and (4.79) the infinitival clause is the argument of the adjective *fácil* 'easy'. As this is an environment that allows inflected infinitives, the noun phrases *alguém* 'someone' in (4.78a) and *algumas pessoas* 'some people' in (4.78b) can be appropriately licensed with nominative case inside the infinitival clause. Hence, both sentences are allowed in EP and BP. (4.79), in turn, displays instances of hyper-raising out of the inflected infinitival, something that is not permitted in EP, but is allowed in BP thanks to the ambiguity of its infinitival Infl, which may bear person and number or just number (see Section 3.4.3). The sentences in (4.79) in BP are derived along the lines of (4.80), with the infinitival subject moving to the next subject position in order to be licensed with case. In other words, this is another instance of embedded null subjects in BP that are the result of subject-to-subject movement.

(4.80) a. **alguém** fosse-Infl₍P:u-N:u₎ tão fácil de [__ convencer-**Infl**₍N:u₎ as pessoas ...]

b. [**Algumas pessoas**] se-Infl₍P:u-N:PL₎ fáceis de [__ perder-**Infl**₍N:PL₎ a paciência]

4.3.2.3 Summary

Table 4.17 below summarizes our discussion of null subject licensing in inflected infinitivals.

Table 4.17 *Agreement inflection in inflected infinitives and null subject licensing in Portuguese*

Nominative pronouns	Morphological specification for person and number					
	EP			BP		
	Pronoun specification	Agreement inflection	Null subject licensing	Pronoun specification	Agreement inflection	Null subject licensing
tu 'you(SG)'	[P.N:2.SG]	[P.N:2.SG]	OK			
nós 'we'	[P.N:1.PL]	[P.N:1.PL]	OK	[P.N:1]	[P.N:1]	OK
vocês 'you(PL)'	[P:2-N:PL]	[P:**2**; N:PL]	OK			
eles 'they(MASC)' *elas* 'they(FEM)'	[P:3-N:PL]	[P:3-N:PL]	OK	[P-N:PL]	[P:u; N:**PL**]	??
eu 'I'	[P.N:1.SG]	[P:**1**]	OK	[P.N:SG]	[P:u]	
você 'you(SG)'	[P:2-N:SG]	[P:**2**-N:SG]	OK	[P-N]	[P:u-N:u]	*
ele 'he' *ela* 'she'	[P:3-N:SG]	[P:3-N:SG]	OK	[P-N]	[P:u-N:u]	
a gente 'we'	[P.N]	[P:u-N:u]	*	[P.N]	[P:u-N:u]	

200   4 Null Subjects

Table 4.17 shows that, as far as null subject licensing is concerned, inflected infinitivals in each variety pattern in the same way as its finite clauses with impoverished tenses (see Tables 4.8 and 4.9). That is, in both varieties impoverishment deletes the specification [N:SG] of infinitival agreement inflection associated with *eu*. This does not have any impact on the licensing of the null counterpart of *eu* in EP, for the remaining person feature is valued; by contrast, in the case of BP, it excludes the possibility of marginal acceptability of the null counterpart of *eu*, for the only valued feature is deleted. Thus, we see again that, in EP, all subject pronouns but *a gente* can be perfectly elided and, in BP, only the null counterpart of *nós* yields fully acceptable results.

4.3.3   *Definite Null Subjects in Participial Clauses*

A series of interacting factors comes into play when we examine the licensing of null subjects in participial clauses in the face of Prominent Feature Valuation Condition, repeated here in (4.81).

(4.81)   *Prominent Feature Valuation Condition*

A given verbal inflection Infl can morphologically license the ellipsis of a definite pronominal subject in Portuguese only if the most prominent feature of Infl is valued, where feature prominence has the following scale: *person* > *number* > *gender* > *case*.

First of all, participial verb forms are specified for gender and number, but not for person, as illustrated in (4.82) (see Section 3.3.2.1).

(4.82)   Uma   vez   apresentad**as**   [as   propostas],
         one   time   present-*PPLE-**FEM-PL***   the.*FEM-PL*   proposal.*FEM-PL*
         o   Pedro encerrou   a   reunião.
         the Pedro closed-off the meeting
         'Once the proposals were presented, Pedro ended the meeting.'

Thus, we should in principle expect the second most prominent feature in the scale of prominence in (4.81), namely, number, to be the feature involved in null subject licensing in participial clauses. As we will see below, EP conforms to this prediction. However, BP does not seem to assign the same degree of morphological prominence to number where participial clauses are concerned. Recall that participial agreement in BP may involve only gender but cannot involve only number, as illustrated in (4.83) and (4.84) below (see Section 3.3.2.1). Notice that the problem with (4.84b), in particular, is not simply an incompatibility with the default masculine form. Verb–subject orders may induce default agreement in BP (see Sections 3.5.1 and 3.3.2.1), as shown in (4.85).³² The problem with (4.84b) (and (4.83b)) is that the realization of number is more marked than that of gender.

(4.83) a. As   proposta   foram analisada.   (%BP)
           *the.FEM-PL proposal.FEM were analyze-PPLE-**FEM***
      b. *As   proposta   foram analisad**os**.
           *the.FEM-PL proposal.FEM were analyzed-**MASC-PL***
           'The proposals were analyzed.'

(4.84) a. Uma vez   analisad**a**   as   propostas,
          *one time   analyze-PPLE-**FEM** the.FEM-PL proposal.FEM-PL*
          a   reunião foi   encerrada.   (%BP)
          the meeting was   closed
      b. *Uma vez   analisad**os**   as   propostas,
          *one   time analyze-PPLE-**MASC-PL** the.FEM-PL proposal.FEM-PL*
          a   reunião foi   encerrada.
          the meeting was   closed
          'Once the proposals had been analyzed, the meeting was ended.'

(4.85) Uma vez   analisad**o**   as   propostas,
          *one time   analyze-PPLE-**MASC** the.FEM-PL proposal.FEM-PL*
          a   reunião foi   encerrada.   (%BP)
          the meeting was   closed
          'Once the proposals had been analyzed, the meeting was ended.'

Data such as (4.83)–(4.85) lead us to conjecture that, as far as participial agreement is concerned, the most prominent feature is number in EP, but gender in BP. Let us then test this hypothesis by examining the licensing of null subjects in participial clauses in each variety, starting with third person pronouns.

4.3.3.1 Third Person Null Subjects in Participial Clauses
Take the data in (4.86), for example.

(4.86) a. Ninguém esperava muito d[o   João]$_i$. Mas [depois de Ø$_i$
          nobody   expected much of-the João   but after of
          nomead**o**   para o cargo], a
          *appoint-PPLE-**MASC.SG** to   the position the*
          empresa melhorou   consideravelmente.   (EP: OK; BP: OK)
          company improved   considerably
          'Nobody expected much of João. But after his appointment to the position, the company considerably improved.'
      b. Os trabalhadores não gostaram muito d[a   nova lei]$_i$. Mas [uma
          the workers   not liked   much of-the new law but one
          vez Ø$_i$ votad**a**],   a   greve acabou. (EP: OK; BP: OK)
          *time   vote-PPLE-**FEM.SG** the strike ended*
          'The workers didn't like the new law very much. But once it was passed, the strike ended.'

---
³² For discussion, see Simioni 2010, 2011.

c. Todos só falavam d[os novos funcionários]ᵢ. [Depois de
   all   only spoke of-the new   employees   after   of
  Øᵢ contratad**os**],   a   produção dobrou.   (EP: OK; BP: OK)
    hire-*PPLE-**MASC-PL** the production doubled*
'Everybody only talked about the new employees. After they were hired, production doubled.'

d. Todos esperavam pel[as novas vagas de trabalho]ᵢ.
   all   waited   for-the new   vacancies   of   work
[Mas depois de Øᵢ anunciad**as**],
*but   after   of   announce-PPLE-**FEM-PL***
a diretora cancelou o concurso.   (EP: OK; BP: OK)
the director canceled the tender
'Everyone was waiting for the new job vacancies. But after they were announced, the director canceled the tender.'

The null subjects of the participial clauses of (4.86) are all licensed in both EP and BP, regardless of their gender or number specifications. This is the first set of data discussed here where EP and BP pattern alike with respect to null subject licensing. At first sight, this is rather surprising, for third person pronouns have different morphological specifications in the two varieties (see Section 3.4.2) and this was in fact what determined the different behavior of their null counterparts seen in finite clauses and inflected infinitivals (see Tables 4.12 and 4.17). The puzzle disappears, though, if the most prominent feature in participial inflection is number in EP and gender in BP, as conjectured above. As we can see in Table 4.18 below, the participial agreement inflection associated with third person pronouns is always valued for number in EP and always valued for gender in BP: hence, the licensing of third person null subjects in participial clauses in both varieties is in full compliance with the Prominent Feature Valuation Condition (see (4.81)).

4.3.3.2 First and Second Person Null Subjects in Participial Clauses

Let us now consider the licensing of first and second person null subjects in the participial clauses of (4.87).

(4.87)   a. [Depois de Ø {contratado/contratada}], os meus problemas
           after   of   hire-PPLE-MASC/FEM the my problems
        acabaram.   (Ø = *eu* → EP: OK; BP: ?)
        finished
'After I was hired, my problems were over.'

Table 4.18 *Participial agreement and third person null subjects*

Nominative pronouns	EP			BP		
	Morphological specification for gender and number	Participial inflection	Null subject licensing	Morphological specification for gender and number	Participial inflection	Null subject licensing
ele 'he'	[G:MASC-N:SG]	[G:MASC-N:**SG**]	OK	[G:MASC-N]	[G:**MASC**-N:u]	OK
ela 'she'	[G:FEM-N:SG]	[G:FEM-N:**SG**]	OK	[G:FEM-N]	[G:**FEM**-N:u]	OK
eles 'they(MASC)'	[G:MASC-N:PL]	[G:MASC-N:**PL**]	OK	[G:MASC-N:PL]	[G:**MASC**-N:PL]	OK
elas 'they(FEM)'	[G:FEM-N:PL]	[G:FEM-N:**PL**]	OK	[G:FEM-N:PL]	[G:**FEM**-N:PL]	OK

204   4 Null Subjects

b. Tínhamos grande   apreço   por ti.   Mas   [depois de Ø
   had-1PL   big   consideration by   you.SG but   after   of
   {eleito/eleita}],   as   coisas mudaram
   elect-PPLE-MASC/FEM the things changed
   muito.   (Ø = tu → EP: OK)
   much
   'We thought very highly of you(SG). But after you(SG) were
   elected, things changed a lot.'

c. Não   se   preocupe.   [Uma vez   Ø   chamada
   not   yourself worry   one   time   call-PPLE-FEM.SG
   para   a   entrevista], as   chances de você   ser
   for   the   interview   the   chances of you.SG   be
   contratada são boas.   (Ø = você → EP: OK; BP: ?)
   hired   are good
   'Don't worry. Once you(SG) have been called for the interview, your
   chances of being hired are good.'

d. [A gente] estava   muito confiante. [Uma vez Ø
   we   was   very   confident one time
   {eleito/eleita}],   a   crise   ainda   poderia   ser
   elect-PPLE-MASC.SG/FEM.SG   the crisis   still   could   be
   revertida.   (Ø = a gente → EP: *; BP: *)
   reversed
   'We were very confident. Once we were elected, the crisis could still be
   reversed.'

e. Nós   estávamos   muito confiantes. [Uma vez   Ø
   we   were   very   confident   one   time
   {eleitos/eleitas}],   a   crise
   elect-PPLE-MASC-PL/FEM-PL   the   crisis
   ainda   poderia   ser   revertida.   (Ø = nós → EP: OK; BP: ?)
   still   could   be   reversed
   'We were very confident. Once we were elected, the crisis could still
   be reversed.'

f. Vocês   não   perceberam   o   óbvio.   [Depois de Ø
   you-PL   not   perceived   the   obvious   after   of
   {demitidos/demitidas}],   tudo   ia   ficar mais
   fire-PPLE-MASC-PL/FEM-PL   everything went stay more
   difícil.   (Ø = vocês → EP: OK; BP: ?)
   difficult
   'You(PL) didn't see the obvious. After you(PL) were fired, everything
   was going to become much harder.'

EP displays a familiar picture: it licenses the null counterpart of all pronouns, but not the null counterpart of *a gente* (see (4.87d)). This follows from our hypothesis that, in EP, number is the relevant feature to be computed for purposes of the Prominent Feature Valuation Condition (see (4.81)). As we

4.3 Definite Null Subjects

Table 4.19 *Agreement inflection in participials and the licensing of first and second person null subjects in European Portuguese*

Nominative pronouns	Morphological specification	Syntactic agreement	Null subject licensing
eu 'I'	[P.N:1.SG]	[G:u-N:**SG**]	OK
tu 'you(SG)'	[P.N:2.SG]	[G:u-N:**SG**]	OK
você 'you(SG)'	[P:2-N:SG]	[G:u-N:**SG**]	OK
a gente 'we'	[P.N]	[G:u-N:u]	*
nós 'we'	[P.N:1.PL]	[G:u-N:**PL**]	OK
vocês 'you(PL)'	[P:2-N:PL]	[G:u-N:**PL**]	OK

can see in Table 4.19 above, all pronouns but *a gente* value the number specification of the participial inflection; hence, only *a gente* cannot have its null counterpart morphologically licensed.

On the other hand, if in BP gender is the relevant feature to be computed by the Prominent Feature Valuation Condition (see (4.81)) in participials, as conjectured above, the judgments for BP in (4.87) are unexpected. After all, first and second person pronouns are not morphologically specified for gender (see Section 2.3.3); thus, all null pronouns in (4.87) in BP should pattern like the null counterpart of *a gente*, contrary to fact. Nonetheless, we also see that first and second person pronouns trigger semantic agreement, as illustrated in (4.88).

(4.88) a. **Eu** estou cansado.   [*spoken by a **male***]
              I   am   tired-***MASC***
              'I am tired.'
         b. **Você** parece cansada.   [*spoken to a **female***]
              you.SG seem   tired-***FEM***
              'You(SG) seem tired.'

Suppose then that the marginal licensing of first and second person null subjects in (4.87) in BP is actually due to semantic agreement. If so, we need only account for why semantic agreement in gender does not suffice to license the null counterpart of *a gente* in BP.

One possibility is that the semantic agreement seen in (4.87) for BP is actually full agreement, that is, semantic agreement for purposes of null subject licensing in participials must involve both gender and number. This does not make a difference in the agreement paradigm for the pronouns *eu*, você, nós, and vocês, but it does in the case of *a gente*, which is semantically plural. Consider the sentence in (4.89), for instance.

(4.89) [A gente]$_i$ estava muito confiante. [Uma vez Ø$_i$
we was very confident one time
{eleitos/eleitas}], a crise ainda poderia
elect-PPLE-MASC-PL/FEM-PL the crisis still could
ser revertida. (EP: OK; BP: ?)
be reversed
'We were very confident. Once we were elected, the crisis could still be reversed.'

(4.89) differs minimally from (4.87d) in that plural is added to the participial agreement. The result is that (4.89) becomes fully acceptable in EP and marginally so in BP. This difference results from structural ambiguity. Recall that members of the *a gente* and the *nós* series very often alternate (see Section 2.4.1); thus, the null subject of (4.89) could also be the null counterpart of *nós*. In EP, this would lead to a fully acceptable result, for the valued number specification of the participial agreement associated with *nós* licenses its null counterpart (see (4.87e)). In BP, by contrast, gender is the most prominent feature in participial agreement and given that neither *nós* nor *a gente* is morphologically specified for gender, full semantic agreement must be resorted to; hence, regardless of whether Ø in (4.89) is the null counterpart of *nós* or *a gente*, it falls under the general pattern of marginal acceptability of first and second person null subjects in BP seen in (4.87).

Let us finally consider the data in (4.90).

(4.90) a. [Uma vez Ø$_i$ {nomeado/nomeada}],
one time appoint-PPLE-MASC.SG/FEM.SG
eu$_i$ procurei resolver os problemas
I searched solve the problems
pessoalmente. (EP: OK; BP: OK)
personally
'Once I was appointed, I personally tried to solve the problems.'
b. [Depois de Ø$_i$ {eleito/eleita}], tu$_i$
after of elect-PPLE-MASC.SG/FEM.SG you.SG
ficaste mais confiante. (EP: OK)
stayed more confident
'After being elected, you(SG) became more confident.'
c. [Depois de Ø$_i$ {promovido/promovida}],
after of promote-PPLE-MASC.SG/FEM.SG
você$_i$ ficou com pouco tempo de lazer. (EP: OK; BP: OK)
you.SG stayed with few time of leisure
'After being promoted, you(SG) had little leisure time.'
d. [A gente]$_i$ só viu o tamanho do problema
we only saw the size of-the problem
[depois de Ø$_i$ {contratado/contratada}] (EP: OK; BP: OK)
after of hire-PPLE-MASC.SG/FEM.SG
'We only realized how big the problem was after being hired.'

e. [Mesmo depois de Ø$_i$ {inscritos/inscritas}
   even   after   of   register-PPLE-MASC.PL/FEM.PL
   formalmente], vocês$_i$ ainda podiam desistir. (EP: OK; BP: OK)
   formally   you-PL still   could   give.up
   'Even after being formally registered, you(PL) could still withdraw.'

(4.90) differs from (4.87) in that the null subjects of the participial clauses are coreferential with the subjects of the subordinating clauses. Interestingly, all the null subjects of (4.90) are fully acceptable in both EP and BP, including the null counterpart of *a gente* (see (4.90d)). The exceptional pattern of this configuration is not something new, though. Recall that the null counterparts of *eu* and *você* in BP and the null counterpart of *a gente* in both EP and BP, which cannot be morphologically licensed in inflected infinitivals (see Section 4.3.2.1), can be licensed if they sit in the subject position of an uninflected adjunct infinitival and are coreferential with the subject of the subordinating clause, as seen in (4.72), repeated below in (4.91). This indicates that the phonetic emptiness of the embedded subjects of (4.90) and (4.91) does not result from ellipsis of pronominal subjects, as in (4.87), but is related to the phonetic emptiness of caseless positions in general (see Section 4.2 and footnote 3 above).³³

(4.91) a. Eu$_i$ escrevi este artigo para Ø$_i$ discutir com
           I   wrote   this article to   discuss with
           a professora.   (Ø = *eu* → EP: OK; BP: OK)
           the teacher
           'I wrote this article to discuss with the teacher.'

---

³³ Under a movement analysis of adjunct control (see e.g. Hornstein 1999 and Boeckx, Hornstein, and Nunes 2010), for instance, the sentences in (4.90) can be analyzed as involving two or three instances of movement, depending on whether or not the participial clause is fronted. As sketched in (i) below, the pronoun first undergoes sideward movement (in the sense of Nunes 2001, 2004) from the participial clause to some thematic position within the matrix verb phrase (see (ia)). After the participial clause adjoins to the matrix verb phrase, the pronoun then moves to the matrix subject position (see (ib)). This is the derivation of (4.90d), for instance; for the remaining sentences of (4.90), the participial clause moves further to the beginning of the sentence (see (ic)).

(i)   a. [verb phrase ... **pron**$_i$ ...]   [participial clause ... ─$_i$ ...]

      b. [matrix clause **pron**$_i$ ... [[verb phrase ... ─$_i$ ...] [participial clause ... ─$_i$ ...]]]

      c. [[**participial clause** ... ─$_i$ ...]$_k$ ... [matrix clause pron$_i$ ... [[verb phrase ... ─$_i$ ...] ─$_k$]]]

b. Você$_i$ deve   organizar os dados para Ø$_i$ discutir com
   you.SG   should   organize   the   data   to   discuss with
   o   professor.   (Ø = você → EP: OK; BP: OK)
   the   teacher
   'You(SG) should organize the data to discuss with the teacher.'
c. [A gente]$_i$ preparou um   projeto para Ø$_i$ discutir com
   we   prepared   a   project to   discuss with
   o   professor.   (Ø = a gente → EP: OK; BP: OK)
   the   teacher
   'We prepared a project to discuss with the teacher.'

4.3.3.3 Summary

Table 4.20 below summarizes the discussion of this section. As number is the most prominent feature in EP participials, it can license pronominal ellipsis when syntactically valued: hence, all pronouns but *a gente* can be elided in EP participials. In BP, on the other hand, the most prominent feature is gender; hence, syntactic agreement can license the null counterparts only of third person pronouns. The null counterparts of first and second person pronouns (including *a gente*) can however be marginally licensed in BP if they trigger (full) semantic agreement with the participial inflection (see (4.87) and (4.89)).

4.3.4   Definite Null Subjects in Gerunds

One can identify (at least) three types of gerund clauses in Portuguese, despite their superficial similarities: (i) obligatorily controlled gerunds; (ii) inflected gerunds; and (iii) agreementless case-marking gerunds. The first type involves the same configuration as that seen above with participials (see (4.90)) and uninflected infinitivals (see (4.91)): the gerund is an adjunct clause whose null subject must be interpreted as being coreferential with the subject of the subordinating clause. As with what we have seen with uninflected infinitives and participials, EP and BP pattern alike in placing no restriction on the pronoun that licenses the null subject, as illustrated in (4.92).

(4.92) a. [Ø$_i$ saindo do   escritório], eu$_i$ encontrei a   Maria.
            leaving of-the office   I   met   the Maria
           'Leaving the office, I met Maria.'
        b. **Tu**$_i$ puseste   o   nosso trabalho em risco, [Ø$_i$
            you.SG   put-INDIC.PERF   the our   work   in   risk
            atrasando o   relatório].
            delaying the   report
           'By delaying the report, you(SG) put our work at risk.'

Table 4.20 *Participial agreement and null subject licensing*

Nominative pronouns	EP			BP		
	Syntactic agreement	Null subject licensing	Syntactic agreement	Null subject licensing	Semantic agreement	Null subject licensing
tu 'you(SG)'	[G:u-N:**SG**]	OK				
ele 'he'	[G:**MASC**-N:**SG**]	OK	[G:**MASC**-N:u]	OK		
ela 'she'	[G:**FEM**-N:**SG**]	OK	[G:**FEM**-N:u]	OK		
eles 'they(MASC)'	[G:**MASC**-N:**PL**]	OK	[G:**MASC**-N:**PL**]	OK		
elas 'they(FEM)'	[G:**FEM**-N:**PL**]	OK	[G:**FEM**-N:**PL**]	OK		
eu 'I'	[G:u-N:**SG**]	OK	[G:u-N:u]	*	[G:**MASC**-N:**SG**]	?
					[G:**FEM**-N:**SG**]	
nós 'we'	[G:u-N:**PL**]	OK	[G:u-N:u]	*	[G:**MASC**-N:**PL**]	?
					[G:**FEM**-N:**PL**]	
você 'you(SG)'	[G:u-N:**SG**]	OK	[G:u-N:u]	*	[G:**MASC**-N:**SG**]	?
					[G:**FEM**-N:**SG**]	
vocês 'you(PL)'	[G:u-N:**PL**]	OK	[G:u-N:**PL**]	*	[G:**MASC**-N:**PL**]	?
					[G:**FEM**-N:**PL**]	
a gente 'we'	[G:u-N:u]	*	[G:u-N:u]	*	[G:**MASC**-N:**PL**]	?
					[G:**FEM**-N:**PL**]	

210   4 Null Subjects

c. **Você**ᵢ fez uma boa escolha, [Øᵢ contratando o João].
   you.SG made a good choice hiring the João
   'You(SG) made a good choice by hiring João.'
d. **Ele**ᵢ entrou na sala [Øᵢ correndo].
   he entered in-the living.room running
   'He ran into the living room.'
e. **Ela**ᵢ saiu [Øᵢ cantarolando uma canção desconhecida].
   she left singing a song unknown
   'She left singing an unknown song.'
f. [Øᵢ saindo daqui], **[a gente]**ᵢ telefona para o Pedro.
   leaving of-here we call to the Pedro
   'After we get out of here, we'll call Pedro.'
g. **Nós**ᵢ vamos encontrar o problema [Øᵢ relendo os relatórios].
   we go find the problem rereading the reports
   'We're going to find the problem by rereading the reports.'
h. **Vocês**ᵢ causaram uma boa impressão [Øᵢ fazendo perguntas
   you-PL caused a good impression making questions
   difíceis].
   difficult
   'You(PL) made a good impression by asking tough questions.'
i. [Øᵢ fazendo pouco barulho], **eles**ᵢ entraram na sala
   making few noise they.MASC entered in-the room
   sem chamar a atenção.
   without calling the attention
   'Making little noise, they entered the room without calling attention to themselves.'
j. **Elas**ᵢ convenceram o chefe, [Øᵢ argumentando
   they(FEM) convinced the boss arguing
   que os problemas foram resolvidos rapidamente].
   that the problems were resolved rapidly
   'They(FEM) convinced the boss by arguing that the problems had been solved quickly.'

As in (4.90) and (4.91), the phonetic nullness of the subject of controlled gerunds is arguably related to properties of this adjunct configuration and not to ellipsis of subject pronouns proper (see footnotes 3 and 33 above). So we will put aside controlled gerund adjuncts like those in (4.92) and focus on the other two kinds of gerunds.

4.3.4.1 Definite Null Subjects in Inflected Gerunds in Dialectal European Portuguese

As mentioned in Section 3.3.2.2.3, Central-Southern and Insular dialects of EP allow for inflected gerunds, although individual dialects may differ with respect to the specific combinations of person and number they allow. We will put aside a detailed discussion of these individual dialects and focus on some of their common properties, instead. First of all, inflected gerunds also undergo an impoverishment process affecting the agreement associated with *eu*, which gives the impression that *eu* triggers third person singular agreement; this yields a form that is identical to the uninflected one, as can be seen in last column of Table 4.21 below.[34]

Interestingly, this impoverishment process does not prevent the null counterpart of *eu* from being morphologically licensed. In a sentence such as (4.93) below, for instance, the null subject of the gerund clause can be interpreted as *eu* (as well as *você*, *ele*, and *ela*). This indicates that, as with inflected infinitivals, impoverishment deletes the number specification of the gerund inflection associated with *eu*, leaving its person feature intact ([P:1]). Once this feature is valued, the null counterpart of *eu* can be licensed in compliance with the Prominent Feature Valuation Condition (see (4.81)).

(4.93) %EP:
[Em   Ø   chegando   a   casa],   o   cão   tem   de   ir
in   arrive-**GER**   to   home   the   dog   has   of   go
à   rua.   (Ø = *eu*/*você*/*ele*/*ela* → OK; Ø = *a gente* → *)
to-the   street
'When {I/you(SG)/*we/he/she/it$_i$} {arrive/arrives} home, [the dog]$_i$ needs to go out.'

As should by now be expected, the null subject of (4.93) cannot be interpreted as *a gente*, despite the fact that it is associated with a gerund form that is not distinct from that associated with *eu*, *você*, *ele*, and *ela*. Given that *a gente* is unable to value the person feature of the gerund agreement inflection, the Prominent Feature Valuation Condition blocks its ellipsis.

---

[34] It is possible to disambiguate ambiguous gerund forms in some environments. For instance, inflected and uninflected gerunds contrast in that the former can occur with adverbial complementizers that are typical of finite clauses, as illustrated by (ia) below with *quando* 'when'. Notice that, taken in isolation, the gerund form *estando* 'being' in (ib) is ambiguous, for it may correspond to the uninflected version or the inflected version associated with *eu*, *você*, *ele*, and *ela* (see Table 4.21). Interestingly, sentences like (ib), whose third person singular specification is not phonetically realized, are ungrammatical in all EP dialects that do not have inflected gerunds. This shows that the agreement specification on inflected gerunds is syntactically computed even when it has no overt manifestation. See Lobo 2001, 2003, 2016a for discussion.

(i) a. Que elas **quando começandem**   a   aparecer ...   (%EP)
        that they **when**   start-**GER-3.PL** to   *appear*
        'Because when the time comes that they [a kind of insect] are born ... '
                                                                  (CORDIAL-SIN, LVR33)
    b. O pão, **quando estando** lêvedo, (...)   a   massa é   mais leve. (%EP)
        the bread **when** **be-GER** *fermented*   the dough is more light
        'When the bread is fermented, the (bread) dough is lighter.'
                                                                  (CORDIAL-SIN, PAL30)

212   4 Null Subjects

Table 4.21 *Inflected gerunds in dialectal European Portuguese and null subject licensing*

Nominative pronouns	Gerund agreement inflection	Null subject licensing	Surface forms: *dançar* 'dance' (inflected gerund)
eu 'I'	[P:1]	OK	*dançando*
você 'you(SG)'	[P:2-N:SG]	OK	
ele 'he' *ela* 'she'	[P:3-N:SG]	OK	
a gente 'we'	[P.N]	*	
tu 'you(SG)'	[P.N:2.SG]	OK	*dançandos*
nós 'we'	[P.N:1.PL]	OK	*dançando**mos**
vocês 'you(PL)'	[P:2-N:PL]	OK	*dançandem*
eles 'they(MASC)' *elas* 'they(FEM)'	[P:3-N:PL]	OK	

(4.94) below presents a paradigm with null subjects corresponding to each of the pronouns in Table 4.21. As the reader can verify there, all of these except for the null counterpart of *a gente* are associated with an inflection with a valued person feature.

(4.94) %EP:
    a. Em **querendo**!   (Ø = *eu*/*ele*/*ela*/*você*/*a gente)
       in   want-**GER**
       'Whenever {I/you(SG)/he/she/it} {want/wants}!'
    b. Em **querendos**!   (Ø = *tu*)
       in   want-**GER-2.SG**
       'Whenever you(SG) want!'
    c. Em **querendomos**!   (Ø = *nós*)
       in   want-**GER-1.PL**
       'Whenever we want!'
    d. Em **querendem**!   (Ø = *eles*/*elas*/*vocês*)
       in   want-**GER-3.PL**
       'Whenever {you(PL)/they} want!'

4.3.4.2 Definite Null Subjects in Agreementless Case-Marking Gerunds

Let us now consider the data in (4.95), leaving aside word order differences for the moment (see Section 5.5).

(4.95) a. **Comendo eu** esta comida toda, vou ficar doente. (EP)
 eating I this food all go.1.SG stay sick
 a'. **Eu comendo** esta comida toda, vou ficar doente. (BP)
 I eating this food all go.1.SG stay sick
 'If I eat all of this food, I'll get sick.'
 b. **Escrevendo nós** a carta, as nossas chances aumentam. (EP)
 writing we the letter the our chances increase
 b'. **Nós escrevendo** a carta, as nossas chances aumentam. (BP)
 we writing the letter the our chances increase
 'If we write the letter, we have a better chance.'
 c. **Fazendo eles** o que foi pedido, os problemas vão
 making they.MASC what was asked the problems go
 terminar. (EP)
 finish
 c'. **Eles fazendo** o que foi pedido, os problemas vão
 they.MASC making what was asked the problems go
 terminar. (EP)
 finish
 'If they do what was asked, the problems will end.'

The gerund clauses in (4.95) contain an overt nominative pronoun, but no agreement that could in principle license it. Suppose that the gerund inflection of this class of gerunds has a case feature valued as nominative and this is what licenses the pronouns in (4.95). If something along these lines is correct, it may have consequences for null subject licensing. Recall that case may also be computed with respect to the Prominent Feature Valuation Condition, repeated here in (4.96) for convenience.

(4.96) *Prominent Feature Valuation Condition*
A given verbal inflection Infl can morphologically license the ellipsis of a definite pronominal subject in Portuguese only if the most prominent feature of Infl is valued, where feature prominence has the following scale: *person* > *number* > *gender* > *case*.

Given that the type of gerunds illustrated in (4.95) have no inflection for person, number, or gender, one may conclude that here case counts as the most prominent feature with respect to (4.96). Thus, if these agreementless case-marking gerunds independently license ellipsis, (4.96) leads us to predict that any pronominal subject bearing case should be able to undergo ellipsis. Or, to put it in different words, all pronouns should have their null counterparts morphologically licensed in agreementless case-marking gerunds. (4.97) below shows that this prediction is correct.

(4.97) a. [Ø   entrando   no   mar], o meu relógio
          entering   in-the   sea   the my watch
       parou.   (Ø = *eu* → EP: OK; BP: OK)
       stopped
       'When I went into the sea, my watch stopped.'
    b. [Ø comendo a   sopa toda], a   mãe   deixa-te   comer a
          eating   the soup all   the mother let-pron.2.SG eat   the
       mousse de   chocolate.   (Ø = *tu* → EP: OK)
       mousse   of   chocolate
       'If you(SG) eat up all your soup, Mom will let you(SG) have the chocolate mousse.'
    c. [Ø agindo honestamente], todos vão votar em
          acting   honestly   all   go vote in
       você.   (Ø = *você* → EP: OK; BP: OK)
       you.SG
       'If you(SG) act with integrity, everyone will vote for you(SG).'
    d. [Ø$_i$ trabalhando bem], a   diretora
          working   well   the director
       contrata-{o$_i$/a$_i$/os$_i$/as$_i$}   no   mês
       hire-{him/her/you.SG/them.MASC/them.FEM/you.PL} in-the month
       que vem.   (Ø = *ele/ela/eles/elas/você/vocês* → EP: OK)
       that comes
       'If {he/she/you(SG)/they/you(PL)} {works/work} well, the director will hire {him/her/you(SG)/them/you(PL)} next month.'
    d'. [Ø$_i$ trabalhando bem], a diretora
           working   well   the director
        contrata-{ele$_i$/ela$_i$/eles$_i$/elas$_i$/você$_i$/vocês$_i$}
        hire-{him/her/them.MASC/them.FEM/you.SG/you.PL}
        no   mês   que vem.   (Ø = *ele/ela/eles/elas/você/vocês* → BP: OK)
        in-the month that comes
        'If {he/she/they/you(SG)/you(PL)} {works/work} well, the director will hire {him/her/them/you(SG)/you(PL)} next month.'
    e. [Ø trabalhando bem], a   diretora vai aumentar o   nosso salário
          working   well   the director goes raise   the our   salary
       este mês.   (Ø = *nós* → EP: OK; BP: OK)
       this   month
       'If we work well, the director is going to raise our salary this month.'
    f. Eles disseram   para a gente ter   cuidado,   pois,
       they   said   to   us   have care   for
       [Ø entrando   no   mar], a   comunicação
          entering   in-the   sea   the   communication
       seria   interrompida.   (Ø = *a gente* → EP: OK; BP: OK)
       would be interrupted
       'They told us to be careful, for if we went into the sea, contact would be lost.'

g. Não   entrem   no   avião!   [Ø entrando no   avião],
   not   enter   in-the   plane   *entering in-the   plane*
   perdemos   a   comunicação
   lose   the   communication
   com vocês.   (Ø = *vocês* → EP: OK; BP: OK)
   with-you-PL
   'Don't go into the plane! If you(PL) do, we'll lose contact with you(PL).'

Notice that the null counterpart of *a gente* is no longer exceptional, as it can be licensed in both varieties (see (4.97f)). It may look surprising that absence of agreement may end up licensing the null counterpart of *a gente*. However, this may look strange only under the assumption that null subjects are licensed by unambiguous morphology. We have seen again and again that this assumption is incorrect, though. Rather than overt morphological distinctions, what is relevant for null subject licensing is the underlying feature specification of the verbal inflection. Thus far, the null counterpart of *a gente* had not been morphologically licensed because the inflection associated with it did not have person, number, or gender valued. These features are however irrelevant in the case of agreementless case-marking gerunds, which have case as the feature able to morphologically license null subjects. Given that *a gente*, like the other pronouns, does have case specifications, it patterns like the other pronouns in having its null counterpart licensed in agreementless case-marking gerunds.

4.4 Indefinite Null Subjects

Thus far, we have analyzed definite null subjects in Portuguese in terms of ellipsis of overt personal nominative pronouns under the restrictions dictated by the Prominent Feature Valuation Condition (see (4.96)). Portuguese indefinite null subjects, on the other hand, seem to require a different analysis as they do not obviously have overt counterparts. Although it is conceivable that their feature specifications allow them to be described in terms of obligatory ellipsis, for presentational purposes we will put this possibility aside and proceed under the assumption that null indefinite pronouns are inherently phonetically null.[35]

---

[35] The same considerations apply to null expletives, to be discussed in Section 4.5 below.

4.4.1 Third Person Plural Indefinite Null Subjects

Like other null subject languages, both EP and BP have an indefinite third person plural null subject. It is interpreted as excluding the speaker and is restricted to external arguments. That is, it may be employed with transitive and unergative verbs (i.e. traditional intransitive verbs whose sole argument behaves like the subject of transitive verbs; see Section 3.5.1.1), as shown in (4.98), but not with passive or unaccusative verbs (i.e. traditional intransitive verbs whose sole argument patterns in the same way as the object of transitive verbs; see Section 3.3.2.1), as illustrated by the sentences in (4.99) (which are acceptable with a definite interpretation for their null subjects in EP, and further restricted in BP to topic-drop contexts).

(4.98)   a. Ø$_{IND}$ roubaram   o   meu carro.
                   stole-*3.PL* *the* *my* *car*
               'My car was stolen.'
    b. Ø$_{IND}$ falaram   muito bem de você   na   reunião.
               spoke-3.PL *very* *well* *of* *you.SG* *in-the* *meeting*
       'People spoke fondly of you(SG) at the meeting.'
    c. Ø$_{IND}$ gritaram   naquela sala.
              scream-3.PL *in-that* *room*
       'Someone screamed in that room.'

(4.99)   a. *Ø$_{IND}$ foram   roubados.
               be.PAST-3.PL *robbed*
       '{Someone/people} {was/were} robbed.'
    b. *Ø$_{IND}$ morreram durante a   guerra.
             died-3.PL *during* *the* *war*
       '{Someone/people} died during the war.'
    c. *Ø$_{IND}$ nasceram   durante os   feriados.
             be.born.PAST-3.PL *during* *the* *holidays*
       '{Someone/people} {was/were} born during the holidays.'

4.4.2 Third Person Singular Indefinite Null Subjects

There are two types of third person singular indefinite null subjects in Portuguese. The first, illustrated in (4.100) below, is interpreted existentially and is available only in BP. It is likely that such constructions came into existence in BP as a by-product of the on-going loss of the indefinite clitic *se* in the language (see Section 3.5.3).[36]

---

[36] For discussion see e.g. Galves 1987, Nunes 1990, 1991, Lunguinho and Medeiros Jr. 2009, Martins and Nunes 2021, and especially Carvalho 2018, 2019.

(4.100) a. Ø_IND vende   cerveja nessa   praia.   (EP: *; BP: OK)
             sell-*3.SG* *beer*   *in-this* *beach*
             '{People sell beer on this beach/Beer is sold on this beach}.'
         b. Ø_IND não   fabrica   mais   esse   tipo   de
             not *manufacture-3.SG* *more* *this* *type* *of*
             carro.   (EP: *; BP: OK)
             car
             '{People don't manufacture this type of car anymore./This type of car is no longer manufactured.}'

The second type, illustrated in (4.101), is interpreted generically and is found in both BP and EP.[37]

(4.101) a. Meu querido, isto aqui é assim: [Ø_IND deitou, Ø_IND
             my dear   this here is so   lain.down-3.SG
             pagou].   (EP/BP)
             paid-3.SG
             'My dear, here (in the physiotherapy clinic) it works like this: once one lies down, one must pay for the session.'
         b. Antigamente era assim: [Ø_IND falava
             in.the.old.days was thus   spoke-INDIC.IMPERF-3.SG
             mais de uma língua,   Ø_IND 'tava
             more of one language   be-INDIC.IMPERF-3.SG
             empregado]   (EP/BP)
             employed
             'In the old days, it was like this: anyone who spoke more than one language would have a job.'

The existential indefinite null subject is considerably more restricted than the generic one.[38] As illustrated in (4.102) below, for instance, the existential indefinite cannot be an internal argument (see (4.102a)) and is not compatible with episodic tense interpretations (see (4.102b)) or individual level predicates (i.e. verbs that describe permanent properties; see (4.102c)). By contrast, generic indefinite null subjects exhibit no such restrictions, as can be seen in (4.103).

(4.102) a. *Ø_IND é   sempre elogiado no   ensaio.   (BP)
              be.PRES.3.SG   *always praised in-the rehearsal*
             '{Someone/one} is always praised during rehearsals.'
         b. *Ø_IND dançou   muito no   carnaval. (BP)
              dance-INDIC.PERF-3.SG *much in-the carnival*
             '{Someone/people} danced a lot during carnival.'
         c. *Ø_IND nessa   escola **sabe**   matemática de   verdade. (BP)
              *in-this school **know**-3.SG mathematics of truth*
             'In this school people truly know mathematics.'

---
[37] See Nunes 1991, Carvalho 2018, 2019, and Martins and Nunes 2021.
[38] See Carvalho 2018, 2019 for the properties of each type and further discussion.

(4.103) a. Em geral é assim: [Ø_{IND} é
in general is thus be.PRES.3.SG
elogiado no ensaio, Ø_{IND} faz uma
praised in-the rehearsal make-3.SG a
apresentação ruim] (EP/BP)
presentation bad
'In general it's like this: if one is praised during the rehearsal, one gives a bad performance.'

b. É o que acontece sempre: [Ø_{IND} dançou
is what happens always dance-INDIC.PERF-3.SG
muito no carnaval, Ø_{IND} dorme até tarde
much in the carnival sleep 3.SG until late
na quarta-feira de cinzas]. (EP/BP)
in-the Wednesday of ashes
'There are no exceptions: If one dances a lot during carnival, one sleeps until late on Ash Wednesday.'

c. Nessa escola é assim: [Ø_{IND} sabe matemática,
in this school is thus know-3.SG mathematics,
Ø_{IND} passa de ano; Ø_{IND} não sabe, Ø_{IND}
pass-3.SG of year not know-3.SG
não passa]. (EP/BP)
not pass-3.SG
'In this school, it's like this: one only passes the year-end exams if one knows mathematics.'

A sentence such as (4.104a) below is ambiguous in BP.[39] The null subject can be interpreted as an existential indefinite or as coreferential with the matrix subject. If some constituent is fronted in the embedded clause, as illustrated in (4.104b), only the indefinite reading is maintained, though.

(4.104) a. [O João]_k disse que [Ø_{k/IND} vende cerveja nessa praia]. (BP)
the João said that sell-3.SG beer in-this beach
'João_k said that {he_k/people} {sells/sell} beer on this beach.'

b. [O João]_k disse que [nessa praia Ø_{*k/IND} vende cerveja]. (BP)
the João said that in-this beach sell-3.SG beer
'João said that people sell beer on this beach.'

Recall that definite embedded third person null subjects in BP are gaps resulting from subject-to-subject movement (see Section 4.3.2.2). The ungrammaticality of the definite reading in (4.104b) can then be accounted for if the fronted constituent blocks movement of the embedded subject.[40]

---

[39] See Alexiadou and Carvalho 2017 and Carvalho 2018, 2019 for discussion.
[40] For discussion, see Ferreira 2000, 2009, Rodrigues 2004, Nunes 2010a, 2020b, and Carvalho 2018, 2019.

4.5 Expletive Null Subjects

In non-pro-drop languages such as English, the subject position is filled with an "expletive" pronoun when the subject does not receive a thematic role, as illustrated in (4.105).

(4.105) a. It rains a lot in this part of the country.
b. There were three toys in the yard.

The pronouns *it* and *there* in (4.105) have no denotation and their major function is just to fill the subject position. They differ in their agreement properties, though. In clauses with *it*, the expletive triggers third person agreement on the verb it is associated with (see (4.105a)), whereas in constructions with the expletive *there*, the verb agrees with the (indefinite) argument that would occupy the subject position if *there* were not present (in (4.105b), for example, the verb agrees with *three toys*).

In pro-drop languages, analogous constructions leave their subject position empty, as illustrated in (4.106) below. Under the assumption that all clauses must have a subject regardless of its phonetic realization (see footnote 6 above), constructions like that in (4.106) are generally analyzed as involving null expletives.[41]

(4.106) a. Ø$_{EXPL}$ chove   muito em São Paulo.
                  rain-3.SG much in São Paulo
   'It rains a lot in São Paulo.'
b. Ø$_{EXPL}$ havia   vários restaurantes na   minha rua. (EP)
                had-3.SG several restaurants in-the my   street
b'. Ø$_{EXPL}$ tinha   vários restaurantes na   minha rua. (BP)
                 had-3.SG several restaurants in-the my   street
   'There were several restaurants on my street.'

As the translation of the sentences in (4.106) and (4.107) below show, null expletives in EP and BP are used in basically the same contexts in which one finds overt expletives in non-pro-drop languages: with weather verbs (see (4.106a)), existential verbs (see (4.106b)), unaccusative verbs (see (4.107a)), passivized verbs (see (4.107b)), and a variety of impersonal predicates that select for nominal or clausal arguments (see (4.107c–f)).

(4.107) a. Ø$_{EXPL}$ chegaram   uns turistas da   China.
                   arrived-3.PL some tourists from-the China
   'There arrived some tourists from China.'
b. Ø$_{EXPL}$ ainda não foram   enviadas algumas das   cartas.
                 still not be.PAST-3.PL sent   some   of-the letters
   'Some of the letters have not been sent yet.'

---

[41] But see Viotti 2007 for arguments against this view.

c. Ø_EXPL eram   três   horas quando o João
         be.INDIC.IMPERF-3.PL three hours when   the João
   chegou.
   arrived
   'It was three o'clock when João arrived.'
d. Ø_EXPL parece   que os estudantes terminaram o trabalho.
         seem-3.SG that the students finished   the work
   'It seems that the students finished their work.'
e. Ø_EXPL é verdade que o João foi contratado.
         is truth   that the João was hired
   'It's true that João was hired.'
f. Ø_EXPL foi difícil nós chegarmos   aqui.
         was difficult we arrive-INF-1.PL here
   'It was hard for us to get here.'

EP and BP essentially exhibit the same behavior as far as null expletive constructions are concerned. The only relevant contrast is associated with their independent differences with respect to agreement with postverbal nominal expressions. As discussed in Sections 3.3.2.1, 3.5.1.1, and 3.5.2, lack of agreement with postverbal unaccusative subjects is generally allowed in BP and is dialectally restricted in EP. Thus, we may also find the patterns in (4.108) in addition to those in (4.107a–c) in BP.[42]

(4.108) a. Ø_EXPL chegou   uns turistas da   China.   (BP)
             arrived-3.SG some tourists from-the China
       'There arrived some tourists from China.'
   b. Ø_EXPL ainda não foi   enviado
             still not be.PAST-3.SG sent-MASC.SG
      algumas   das   cartas.   (BP)
      some-FEM-PL of-the.FEM-PL letter.FEM-PL
      'Some of the letters have not been sent yet.'
   c. Ø_EXPL era   três horas quando o João
             be.INDIC.IMPERF-3.SG three hours when   the João
      chegou.   (BP)
      arrived
      'It was three o'clock when João arrived.'

4.6 Related Issues

4.6.1 Overt Expletives in Dialectal European Portuguese

By and large, overt expletives are not found in pro-drop languages. However, some dialects of EP admit constructions such as (4.109) below, with

---

[42] See Kato 2002b for discussion.

an overt expletive (*ele*).[43] Interestingly, the version with the overt expletive may occur side by side with the version with the null expletive, as illustrated in (4.109a) and (4.109b).

(4.109)   %EP (adapted from Carrilho 2005):
   a. Ah,   se   Ø_{EXPL} chover   era melhor, mas
      INTERJ if   rain-FUT.SUBJ.3SG was better   but
      ele   não   chove   amanhã.
      EXPL   *not   rain.PRES.3.SG   tomorrow*
      'Oh, it would be better if it rains, but it won't rain tomorrow.'
                                                         (CORDIAL-SIN, MST11)
   b. É   a   estrela-da-manhã (...) e   Ø_{EXPL} há   a   estrela...
      is   the   star of-the morning   and   has the star
      Bom,   **ele**   há   várias   estrelas, não   é?
      *good   **EXPL*** *has   several   stars   not   is*
      'That's the morning star (...) and there is the star ... Well, there are several stars, aren't there?'
                                                         (CORDIAL-SIN, AAL92)
   c. **Ele**   tem-me   acontecido   aqui   cada   uma!
      EXPL *has-me   happened   here   such   one*
      'I have suffered such things here!'
                                                         (CORDIAL-SIN, COV23)

Despite appearances, there are several reasons to think that the expletive *ele* in dialectal EP is not like the expletive *it* or *there* in English.[44] For instance, constructions involving the expletive *ele* are interpreted as somewhat more emphatic or more expressive than analogous counterparts with the null expletive. In addition, *ele* does not control verbal agreement, as shown in (4.110) below, and may even co-occur with an overt subject occupying the preverbal subject position, as shown in (4.111). In fact, *ele* may precede different types of left peripheral phrases such as initial adverbs, hanging topics, topicalized objects, *wh*-phrases, and focus-moved phrases, as respectively illustrated in (4.112).

(4.110)   %EP (adapted from Carrilho 2005):
   a. **Ele**   subiram   os   impostos.
      EXPL(SG)   *raised-3.PL   the   taxes*
      'The taxes were raised.'
   b. **Ele**   boto-lhe   assim   a   água   ao   meu.
      EXPL(not-1)   *put-1.SG-it_{DAT}*   *thus   the water   to-the   mine*
      'I put water in mine like this.'
                                                         (CORDIAL-SIN, MST35)

---

[43] For discussion see e.g. Uriagereka 1995a, 2004, Raposo and Uriagereka 1996, Silva-Villar 1998, Carrilho 2003, 2005, 2008, 2009, and Betoni 2013.
[44] See references in footnote 43 above and especially Carrilho 2005.

(4.111) %EP (adapted from Carrilho 2005):
a. Tinham   que estar (...) que **ele**   **os porcos** não os
   had-3.PL that be-INF   that **EXPL** **the pigs** not them
   vissem.
   see-IMPERF.SUBJ-3.PL
   'They had to be in such a way that the pigs would not see them.'
                                            (CORDIAL-SIN, PFT13)
b. Que **ele**   eu gosto de socorrer (...) as   pessoas, homem!
   that **EXPL** I   like of help-INF   the people man
   'I like to help people, man!'
                                            (CORDIAL-SIN, COV23)

(4.112) %EP (adapted from Carrilho 2008):
a. **Ele**   agora já   ninguém costuma cozer.
   EXPL now already nobody uses   bake.bread
   'Now nobody is in the habit of baking bread anymore.'
                                            (CORDIAL-SIN, OUT32)
b. E **ele**   eu, o homem leu aquilo diante de mim!
   and **EXPL** I   the man read that before of me
   'And, as for me... the man read that before me!'
                                            (CORDIAL-SIN, COV18)
c. **Ele**   a fome   não havia!
   EXPL the hunger not had
   'Hunger didn't exist!'
                                            (CORDIAL-SIN, VPA06)
d. Não sendo no   Natal,   **ele**   quem é que os   come?!
   not being in-the Christmas **EXPL** who is that them eat
   Ninguém!
   nobody
   'If they are not eaten by Christmas, who will eat them?! Nobody!'
                                            (CORDIAL-SIN, OUT50)
e. Que **ele**   até com um pau se   malha.
   that **EXPL** even with a stick REFL threshes
   'Actually, we thresh even with a stick.'
                                            (CORDIAL-SIN, MST37)

The data in (4.109)–(4.112) indicate that the expletive *ele* in dialectal EP occupies not the subject position, but rather a position in the left periphery of the clause encoding expressiveness and/or evidentiality, which accords well with the fact that EP is a prototypical pro-drop language. This in turn implies that overt expletive constructions such as (4.109a), for example, are actually associated with two expletives: an overt one in the left periphery and a null one in the subject position, as represented in (4.113).

(4.113) ...mas **ele** Ø_{EXPL} não chove amanhã (%EP)
but **EXPL** not rain.PRES.3.SG tomorrow

4.6.2 Filling Out Null Expletive Positions in Brazilian Portuguese

We have seen in Section 4.3 that definite null subjects are highly restricted in BP and this has led to a significant decrease in the overall use of definite null subjects in the language (see Tables 4.1 and 4.2). This pressure towards filling out subject positions with overt expressions has affected null expletive positions, as well.

Two types of constructions clearly illustrate this trend in BP.[45] The first involves the fronting of a prepositionless locative expression to the subject position, triggering verbal agreement, as illustrated in (4.114a′) and (4.114b′).

(4.114) BP:
    a. Chove muito nessas cidades.
       rain.PRES.3.SG much in-these cities
    a′. Essas cidades chov**em** muito.
       these cities rain.PRES-**3.PL** much
       'It rains a lot in these cities.'
    b. Cabe muita coisa nessas gavetas.
       fit.PRES.3SG many thing in-these drawers
    b′. Essas gavetas cab**em** muita coisa.
       these drawers fit-**3.PL** many thing
       'Many things can fit in these drawers.'

The second construction involves part-whole structures where a prepositionless possessor moves to the subject position, also triggering verbal agreement, as shown in (4.115a′) and (4.115b′).

(4.115) BP:
    a. Quebrou o ponteiro dos relógios.
       broke.3.SG the pointer of-the watches
    a′. Os relógios quebrar**am** o ponteiro.
       the watches broke-**3.PL** the pointer
       'The hands of the watches broke.'

---

[45] For discussion see e.g. Pontes 1987, Kato 1989, Figueiredo Silva 1996, Britto 1998, Galves 1998, 2001, Negrão 1999, Lobato 2006, Lunguinho 2006, Negrão and Viotti 2008, Avelar and Cyrino 2008, Avelar 2009a, Avelar and Galves 2011, Bastos-Gee 2011, Munhoz 2011, Munhoz and Naves 2012, Andrade and Galves 2014, Costa, Augusto, and Rodrigues 2014, Nunes 2016, 2017, Gonçalves and Miguel 2019, Kato and Ordóñez 2019, Meireles and Cançado 2020, Rodrigues 2020, Kato and Duarte 2021, and Nunes and Kato forthcoming.

b. Acabou a bateria dos celulares.
   *finished.**3.SG*** the battery of-the cell.phones
   'The battery of the cell phones is dead.'
b'. Os celulares acabaram a bateria.
   the cell.phones finished-***3.PL*** the battery
   'The cell phones ran out of battery.'

Interestingly, the possessor can be very deeply embedded, as shown in (4.116a') below, and one may also find mixed constructions where the possessor moves from within the locative expression, as illustrated in (4.116b').[46]

(4.116) BP:
   a. Diminuiu o tamanho da hélice do motor desses
      *diminished-**3.SG*** the size of-the propellor of-the engine of-these
      barcos.
      boats
      'The size of the propellor of the engine of these boats got reduced.'
   a'. Esses barcos diminuíram o tamanho da hélice do
      these boats *diminished-**3.PL*** the size of-the propellor of-the
      motor.
      engine
      'These boats had the size of the propellors of their engine reduced.'
   b. Cabe muita coisa na parte interna da lateral desses
      *fit-**3.SG*** many thing in-the part internal of-the side of-these
      porta-malas.
      car-trunks
   b'. Esses porta-malas cabem muita coisa na parte interna da
      these car-trunks *fit-**3.PL*** many thing in-the part internal of-the
      lateral.
      side
      'You can fit a lot inside the side compartments of these car trunks.'

4.6.3 *Null Subjects and the Distinction between Strong and Weak Pronouns*

We have seen in Section 4.3 that, as far as definite pronominal subjects are concerned, EP behaves like a prototypical pro-drop language in the sense that null pronouns constitute the default choice for unmarked contexts, whereas overt pronouns mark shift in the topic of discussion, focus, or emphasis, for example. In BP, on the other hand, an overt pronoun is not associated with marked contexts and this follows from the fact that the

---

[46] See e.g. Nunes 2017 and Nunes and Kato forthcoming for discussion.

licensing of definite null subjects in BP has become very severely restricted. This difference between EP and BP can be recast in terms of the distinction between strong and weak pronouns (see Section 2.2). More specifically, in EP overt nominative pronouns can be generally analyzed as strong forms and their null counterparts as weak forms, whereas in BP overt nominative pronouns may be ambiguous between weak and strong forms.[47]

The idea is that once BP lost the option of encoding unmarked contexts via a definite null subject, the system was restructured in such a way that other forms came to play the role previously played by null pronominals. This becomes clear with the emergence of two unambiguously weak pronouns – the pronouns *cê* and *cês* (see Section 2.2).[48] From this perspective, the remaining overt nominative pronouns in BP have become ambiguous regarding the strong/weak distinction. With respect to first and second person pronouns, this is suggested by their sheer frequency when compared to their EP counterparts. As we can infer from Section 4.3 (Table 4.1), oral corpora in BP display 74 percent of overt first person pronouns and 90 percent of overt second person pronouns, whereas comparable oral corpora in EP show 35 and 24 percent, respectively. As for third person pronouns, recall that strong forms are interpreted as [+hum], whereas weak forms are compatible with [+hum] or [-hum] (see Section 2.2). Thus, nominative third person pronouns in BP are compatible with [+hum] or [-hum] interpretation, whereas their EP counterparts are generally interpreted as [+hum], as illustrated in (4.117) below.[49] In (4.117a), *ele* may refer to, say, *o João* ('the. MASC.SG João') or *o carro* ('the.MASC.SG car') in BP, but generally only to *o João* in EP; likewise, *ela* in (4.117b) may refer to *a Maria* ('the.FEM.SG Maria') or *a vassoura* ('the.FEM.SG broom') in BP, but generally only to *a Maria* in EP.

(4.117) a. Ele   está   na   garagem.
        pron.MASC.SG is   in-the garage
        'He is in the garage.'   (EP: OK; BP: OK)
        'It is in the garage.'   (EP: %; BP:OK)

---

[47] For discussion, see Barbosa 1995, 1996, Galves 1997, Duarte 1998, Kato 1999, 2002a, Britto 1998, 2000, Costa 2003, and Barbosa, Duarte, and Kato 2005.
[48] See Petersen 2008 for discussion.
[49] For discussion see e.g. Britto 1998, 2000 and Barbosa, Duarte, and Kato 2005. It is worth noting that, as far as EP is concerned, this correlation seems to be better described as a strong tendency rather than a categorical statement, for examples with nominative *ele* and *ela* interpreted as [-hum] can be attested in EP corpora.

b. Ela   está na   sala.
   pron-FEM.SG is in-the living.room
   'She is in the living room.'   (EP: OK; BP: OK)
   'It is in the living room.'   (EP: %; BP:OK)

4.7 General Summary

We have seen that although both EP and BP admit definite null subjects, they have more differences than similarities with respect to the nature and distribution of the null subjects allowed, as Tables 4.22 and 4.23 below highlight. EP behaves like a prototypical pro-drop language. With the exception of the null counterpart of the pronoun *a gente*, those of the other pronouns are productively employed as the unmarked choice for pronominal usage. By contrast, in BP the overt pronouns constitute the unmarked option and the acceptability of their null counterparts varies depending on the pronoun and the syntactic environment.

As discussed in detail in Section 4.3.1, BP has just one fewer morphological distinction in its verbal agreement inflection than EP. However, this difference in itself is insufficient as an explanation for their very different syntactic properties in respect of agreement and null subject licensing. This led us to consider the hypothesis that the crucial difference was in fact the morphological specification of personal pronouns in the two dialects (see Section 3.4.2). From this perspective, identical verbal forms in both dialects may have different underlying specifications, for the pronouns they agree with are phonologically the same in both dialects, but have different morphological specifications. In other words, we have a typical "zebra scenario" (see Section 3.4.1): different underlying specifications associated with the same superficial form.

This zebra scenario can be unveiled by taking into account the relevant agreement feature involved in null subject licensing, as specified by the Prominent Feature Valuation Condition:[50]

(4.118)   *Prominent Feature Valuation Condition*
          A given verbal inflection Infl can morphologically license the ellipsis of a definite pronominal subject in Portuguese only if the most prominent feature of Infl is valued, where feature prominence has the following scale: *person > number > gender > case*.

---

[50] See Martins and Nunes 2021 for discussion.

Table 4.22 *Morphological licensing of definite null subjects in European Portuguese – summary*

		Finite clauses			Inflected infinitivals	Participials	Agreementless case-marking gerunds
		Fuller paradigm	Impoverished paradigm				
Null counterpart of	*eu* 'I'	✓	✓		✓	✓	✓
	tu 'you(SG)'	✓	✓		✓	✓	✓
	você 'you(SG)'	✓	✓		✓	✓	✓
	ele 'he' *ela* 'she'	✓	✓		✓	✓	
	nós 'we'	✓	✓		✓	✓	✓
	vocês 'you(PL)'	✓	✓		✓	✓	✓
	eles 'they(MASC)' *elas* 'they(FEM)'	✓	✓		✓	✓	✓
	a gente 'we'	*	*		*	*	✓

Table 4.23 *Morphological licensing of definite null subjects in Brazilian Portuguese – summary*

		Finite clauses		Inflected infinitivals	Participials	Agreementless case-marking gerunds
		Fuller paradigm	Impoverished paradigm			
Null counterpart of	*nós* 'we'	✓	✓	✓	*	✓
	vocês 'you(PL)'	??	??	??	*	✓
	eles 'they(MASC)' *elas* 'they(FEM)'	??	??	??	✓	✓
	eu 'I'	??	*	*	*	✓
	você 'you(SG)'	*	*	*	✓	✓
	ele 'he' *ela* 'she'	*	*	*	*	✓
	a gente 'we'	*	*	*	*	✓

Given the different morphological specifications for the personal pronouns of EP and BP (see Section 3.4.2), the Prominent Feature Valuation Condition provides a straightforward account of their differences regarding null subject licensing, as well as the intricate pattern internal to BP, with different null subjects clustering together or being set apart depending on the tense of the clause (see Tables 4.22 and 4.23 above)[51].

As for indefinite null subjects, BP is richer than EP in that it has an additional type of indefinite singular null subject (see Section 4.4.2). This innovation accords well with BP's general preference for unmarked/default agreement forms (see Chapter 3). Finally, EP and BP generally pattern alike with respect to null expletive constructions, but BP shows a tendency to have dislocated elements to fill the position that would be reserved for a null expletive (see Section 4.6.2) and some EP dialects have an apparent overt expletive (*ele*), which is actually linked to interpretations associated with the sentence left periphery.

---

[51] The lightest shading in the cells marked with "*" in the participials columns of Tables 4.22 and 4.23 is meant to indicate that, although the relevant null pronoun cannot be morphologically licensed in this environment, it may be licensed via semantic agreement.

5

Word Order

5.1 Introduction

Changes in the basic word order of a given language are generally associated with different discourse settings or imposed by morphophonological restrictions. In the case of European Portuguese (EP) and Brazilian Portuguese (BP), the unmarked constituent order of a simple declarative sentence is SVO, that is, the subject followed by the verb, followed by the object(s), as illustrated in (5.1) below. However, we may also find the orders in (5.2), for instance, with one of the objects preceding the subject, under certain discourse situations to be discussed below.[1] (5.3a) in turn shows that the SVO order is not licit if the object is a clitic and the main verb has participial morphology; in such a case, the clitic surfaces phonologically attached to the right of the auxiliary verb in EP, as shown in (5.3b), and to the left of the main verb in BP, as shown in (5.3c).

(5.1)   a.   O   João   recomendou   este   livro   à   Maria   (EP)
                the João recommended this book to-the Maria
         b.   O   João   recomendou   este   livro   para   a   Maria.   (BP)
                the João recommended this book to   the Maria
            'João recommended this book to Maria.'

(5.2)   a.   **Este livro**, o   João   recomendou   à   Maria.   (EP)
                this book the João recommended to-the Maria
       a′.   **Este livro**, o   João   recomendou   para   a   Maria. (BP)
                this book the João recommended to   the Maria
            'This book, João recommended to Maria.'
         b.   **À**   **Maria**, o   João   recomendou   este   livro.   (EP)
                to-the Maria the João recommended this book
       b′.   **Para a   Maria**, o   João   recomendou   este   livro.   (BP)
                to   the Maria the João recommended this book
            'To Maria, João recommended this book.'

---

[1] Recall that nonpronominal datives are introduced by the preposition *a* 'to' in EP and the preposition *para/pra* 'to/for' in BP (Section 2.3.4.3).

(5.3)   a. *O João tinha **visto-me**.
         the João had seen-me*[CL]*
      b. O João **tinha-me** visto. (EP: OK; BP: *)
         the João had-me*[CL]* seen
      c. O João tinha [**me** visto]. (EP: *; BP: OK)
         the João had me*[CL]* seen
      'João had seen me.'

In this chapter we will discuss possible orders other than SVO in EP and BP and the discourse and morphophonological factors that trigger them.[2] In Section 5.2 we discuss the relation between constituent order and informational content in declarative sentences.

In Sections 5.3 and 5.4 we discuss word order in interrogative and exclamative sentences. Section 5.5 is devoted to a brief discussion of word order in nonfinite domains. Section 5.6 discusses clitic placement. Finally, Section 5.7 presents a summary of the main differences between EP and BP in respect of word order.

5.2 Word Order in Declarative Sentences and Informational Content

In this section we examine the relation between the order of major constituents in declarative sentences and informational content.[3]

5.2.1 Thetic and Categorical Judgments

An interesting fact about natural languages is that they often syntactically distinguish the presentation of a situation from the assignment of a property to a given entity (a *thetic judgment* from a *categorical judgment* in the sense of Kuroda 1972). A categorical judgment expresses an aboutness relation between an entity and a predicate, whereas a sentence expressing a thetic judgment describes a situation in which no single entity is assigned a topic status, that is, the sentence is not about a specific entity but the whole

---

[2] For discussion on word order see e.g. Duarte 1987, 1997, Raposo 1987a, 1994, 1995, 2000, Ambar 1992a, 1999, Martins 1994a,b, 2013b, 2020b, Barbosa 1997, 2001, 2006, Costa 1998, 2001, 2004, Martins and Costa 2016, and Martins and Lobo 2020 for EP; and Nascimento 1984, Kato 1989, 2000, Berlinck 1996a, 2000, Kato and Raposo 1996, Galves 2001, Kato and Tarallo 2003, Pilati 2006, Viotti 2007, Coelho and Martins 2012, Tescari Neto 2012, Silva 2013, Kato and Martins 2016, Berlinck and Coelho 2018, and Lacerda 2020 for BP.

[3] For purposes of presentation, we will use traditional glosses for agreement morphemes, setting aside the more refined proposal laid out in Section 3.4.2.

situation. An appropriate answer to the question *What is happening?*, for instance, presents a thetic judgment, whereas an adequate answer to the question *What happened to João?* presents a categorical judgment.

In this section we examine how EP and BP use word order to encode this distinction.[4]

5.2.1.1 The Position of the Subject and the Thetic–Categorical Distinction

As a general rule, subject–verb inversion yielding VS(O) order expresses thetic judgments, whereas the SV(O) order is compatible with both categorical and thetic judgments. Thus, in both EP and BP the SV sentence in (5.4a) below can be interpreted as an appropriate answer to the question of how the previous month fared with respect to unemployment (a categorical judgment) or an answer to the question of how the economy in general is going (a thetic judgment). The VS sentence in (5.4b), on the other hand, is compatible only with the latter scenario.

(5.4) a. A   taxa de desemprego   do   mês   passado caiu.
          the rate of unemployment of-the month passed fell
       b. Caiu a   taxa de desemprego   do   mês   passado.
          fell the rate of unemployment of-the month passed
          'Last month's unemployment rate fell.'

The expression of a thetic judgment by means of VS order is highly sensitive to the class of verbs involved, though. "Intransitive" verbs, for instance, may display a different behavior depending on their subtypes. As discussed in Section 3.5.1.1, this group actually involves two different classes: unaccusative verbs, whose subject may display the syntactic behavior of objects, and unergative verbs, whose subject behaves like the subject of standard transitive verbs. By and large, VS order is more pervasively allowed with unaccusative than with unergative verbs in EP, whereas in BP it is essentially restricted to unaccusatives.[5] Thus, while EP permits SV and VS orders with the unaccusative verbs in (5.5) and the unergative verbs in (5.6) below, for example, BP is less permissive. In particular, the VS order

---

[4] On the importance of the distinction between categorical and thetic judgments for word order in Portuguese, see e.g. Duarte 1987, 1996, 2013b, Martins 1994a, Raposo and Uriagereka 1995, Martins and Costa 2016, and Lobo and Martins 2017 for EP, and Kato 1989, 2007, Britto 1998, 2000, and Kato and Duarte 2018 for BP.

[5] For discussion see e.g. Nascimento 1984, Ambar 1992a, Berlinck 1996a, 2000, Duarte 1997, Costa 1998, 2004, Barbosa, Duarte, and Kato 2005, Barbosa 2006, 2009, Costa and Figueiredo Silva 2006b, Kato and Martins 2016, and Martins and Costa 2016.

with unergatives in BP is (marginally) allowed only with a few verbs (see (5.6a′)/(5.6b′) vs. (5.6c′)/(5.6d′)) and, even within the set of unaccusative verbs, BP does not license VS order with copular verbs, as illustrated in (5.5d′), with the copula *estar* 'be'.

(5.5)   a. Um soldado morreu.
            a   soldier died
        a′. Morreu um soldado
            died   a   soldier
            'A soldier died.'
        b. A primavera já chegou.
            the spring   already arrived
        b′. Já   chegou a   primavera.
            already arrived the spring
            'Spring has already arrived.'
        c. Alguns problemas surgiram quando menos se esperava.
            some   problems   arose   when   less SE_{IND} expected
        c′. Surgiram alguns problemas quando menos se esperava.
            arose   some   problems   when   less SE_{IND} expected
            'There arose problems when we least expected them.'
        d. Para minha grande surpresa, o gato estava no jardim.
            to   my   big   surprise   the cat   was   in-the garden.
        d′. Para minha grande surpresa, estava o gato no jardim.   (EP: OK; BP: *)
            to   my   big   surprise   was   the cat   in-the garden
            'To my great surprise, the cat was in the garden.'

(5.6)   a. Um desconhecido telefonou ontem.
            a   stranger   called   yesterday
        a′. Telefonou um desconhecido ontem.   (EP: OK; BP: ?)
            called   a   stranger   yesterday
            'A stranger called yesterday.'
        b. Um aluno meu trabalhava nesta fábrica.
            a   student my   worked   in-this factory
        b′. Trabalhava um aluno meu nesta fábrica.   (EP: OK; BP: ?)
            worked   a   student my   in-this factory
            'A student of mine worked at this factory.'
        c. Os candidatos e o entrevistador gritaram o tempo todo durante o debate.
            the   candidates   and   the   interviewer   shouted   the   time all   during   the   debate
        c′. Gritaram os candidatos e o entrevistador o tempo todo durante o debate.   (EP: OK; BP: *)
            shouted   the   candidates   and   the   interviewer   the time   all   during   the   debate
            'The candidates and the interviewer shouted throughout during the debate.'

d. Uma criança espirrou, mas não sei qual.
   a child sneezed but not know.1.SG which
d'. Espirrou uma criança, mas não sei qual. (EP: OK; BP: *)
    sneezed a child but not know.1.SG which
    'A child sneezed, but I don't know which one.'

There is also an intricate interaction in BP between the (in)definite nature of postverbal subjects and the presence of locatives. With unaccusative verbs and VS order, indefinite subjects can co-occur with a locative expression, but definite subjects cannot, as illustrated in (5.7) below. (5.8), in turn, shows that no such contrast arises with preverbal subjects.

(5.7) BP:
   a. Caíram **muitas** flores (no chão).
      fell many flowers in-the ground
      'Many flowers fell down (on the ground).'
   a'. Caíram **as** flores (*no chão).
       fell the flowers in-the ground
       'The flowers fell down (on the ground).'
   b. Apareceram **uns** personagens (no canto do palco).
      appeared some characters in-the corner of-the stage
      'Some characters appeared (at the corner of the stage).'
   b'. Apareceram **os** personagens (*no canto do palco).
       appeared the characters in-the corner of-the stage
       'The characters appeared (*at the corner of the stage).'

(5.8) BP:
   a. Muitas flores caíram (no chão).
      many flowers arrived in-the ground
      'Many flowers fell down (on the ground).'
   a'. As flores caíram (no chão).
       the flowers fell in-the ground
       'The flowers fell down (on the ground).'
   b. Uns personagens apareceram (no canto do palco).
      some characters appeared in-the corner of-the stage
      'Some characters appeared (at the corner of the stage).'
   b'. Os personagens apareceram (no canto do palco).
       the characters appeared in-the corner of-the stage
       'The characters appeared (at the corner of the stage).'

As for unergative verbs, their (marginal) acceptability with VS order in BP is generally restricted to indefinite subjects, as shown by the contrast between (5.6b') and (5.9a) below. However, if a locative associated with an unergative verb is preposed, a definite subject is (marginally) allowed with VS order, as illustrated by the contrasts in (5.9).[6]

(5.9) BP:
    a. *Trabalhava o meu filho nesta fábrica.
       worked   the my son in-this factory
    a'. ?Nesta fábrica trabalhava o meu filho.
       in-this factory worked   the my son
       'My son worked in this factory.'
    b. *Canta a Maria nesse coro.
       sings the Maria in-this choir
    b'. ?Nesse coro canta a Maria.
       in-this choir sings the Maria
       'Maria sings in this choir.'

Interestingly, transitive verbs that select a locative complement in BP behave like unergatives in this regard. The verb *morar* 'live', for instance, disallows VS order with definite subjects (see (5.10a) vs. (5.10b)) unless the locative is preposed (see (5.10b) vs. (5.10c)).

(5.10) BP:
    a. Morava um escritor famoso nesse prédio.
       lived a writer famous in-this building
       'A famous writer lived in this building.'
    b. *Morava o Jobim nesse prédio.
       lived the Jobim in-this building
    c. ?Nesse prédio morava o Jobim.
       in-this building lived the Jobim
       'Jobim lived in this building.'

All the VS sentences in (5.7)–(5.10) are acceptable in EP under a thetic interpretation, regardless of the definiteness of the subjects. VS order in EP is, in fact, more sensitive to (sensorial) evidentiality.[7] Roughly speaking, in EP SV order can report both perceptually grasped and unobserved situations/events, whereas sentences with VS order appear to depend upon the actual perceptual intake of a situation. In (5.11) below, with unaccusative verb *chegar* 'arrive', for instance, VS order is blocked if the place of arrival is outside the visual, auditory or sensorial reach of the speaker. Similarly, the VS order in (5.12), with the unergative verb *telefonar* 'call', is blocked if the speaker is not a participant in the reported event/situation.

---

[6] For discussion see e.g. Kato 2002b, Pilati 2006, Avelar and Cyrino 2008, and Buthers and Duarte 2012.
[7] For discussion see e.g. Martins and Costa 2016 and Martins 2020b.

(5.11) EP:
a. O   teu   pai   já   chegou.
   the   your   father already arrived
   'Your father has already arrived {here / at ours / for dinner}.'
   'Your father has already arrived {back at his home / in Paris by now}.'
b. Já   chegou   o   teu   pai.
   already   arrived   the   your   father
   'Your father has already arrived {here / at ours / for dinner}.'
   *'Your father has already arrived {back at his home / in Paris by now}.'

(5.12) EP:
a. A   Maria   telefonou.
   the Maria   called
   'Maria called {here / this afternoon}.'
   'Maria called {that office where she is applying for a job}.'
b. Telefonou   a   Maria.
   called   the Maria
   'Maria called {here / this afternoon}.'
   *'Maria called {that office where she is applying for a job}.'

Since VS sentences in EP generally describe apprehended/perceived situations, we expect VS order to be blocked in negative sentences, for one arguably does not perceive what does not occur. This expectation is indeed fulfilled. To see this, consider the following scenario. The president is very sick and rumored to be already dead. Someone looks through the window, sees the crowd cheering, and asks what is happening. An opponent of the president may (sarcastically) answer with the affirmative sentences in (5.13a) or (5.13a′), but a supporter can give a negative answer only using SV order, as in (5.13b); the VS order in (5.13b′) does not result in an appropriate answer in this context.[8]

(5.13) EP:
[*Context*: Someone asks what happened.]
a. O   presidente   morreu.
   the president   died
a′. Morreu   o   presidente.
    died   the   president
    'The president has died.'
b. O   presidente   não   morreu.
   the president   not   died

---

[8] In EP, (5.13b′) may be appropriate in other circumstances, such as, for instance, an answer to a question about who did not die in the explosion (a context for information focus; see Section 5.2.2.1). Thus, the annotation "*" in (5.13b′) and the remaining sentences of this chapter is to be understood as signaling an unacceptable sentence given the context under consideration.

b'. *Não morreu o presidente.
  not died the president
  'The president hasn't died.'

Let us finally consider sentences with transitive verbs. In both EP and BP, transitive verbs generally disallow VS order as a way to convey a thetic judgment. An SVO sentence such as (5.14) below, for instance, may be interpreted in both EP and BP as a statement about Maria, explaining why she is sad (a categorical judgment), or the presentation of a state of affairs in the face of a question such as *Why is everyone scouring the room?* (a thetic judgment). By contrast, a VSO sentence such as (5.15) cannot be interpreted as a thetic judgment in EP[9] and is ruled out in BP regardless of the context.

(5.14)   A Maria perdeu a carteira.
         the Maria lost the wallet
         'Maria lost her wallet.'

(5.15)   [*Context*: Someone asks what happened.]
         *Perdeu a Maria a carteira.
         lost the Maria the wallet
         'Maria lost her wallet.'

Similarly, a VS sentence with ditransitive verbs like (5.16b) is ruled out in BP regardless of the context and a sentence like (5.17b) cannot be used to convey a thetic judgment in EP even in a context of sensorial evidentiality.[10]

(5.16)   BP:
         a. O João me deu um presente.
            the João me gave a present
         b. *Me deu o João um presente.
            me gave the João a present
            'João gave me a present.'

(5.17)   EP:
         [*Context*: Someone sees a chocolate cake on the table.]
         a. A mãe comprou-nos bolo de chocolate.
            the mother bought-us cake of chocolate
         b. *Comprou-nos a mãe bolo de chocolate.
            bought-us the mother cake of chocolate
            'Mom bought us chocolate cake.'

---

[9] (5.15) may however be appropriate in EP if the subject is contrastively focused, for instance (see Section 5.2.2.2).
[10] (5.17b) may be appropriate in EP if the subject is contrastively focused, for example (see Section 5.2.2.2).

Some apparently exceptional environments allowing VS order with transitive verbs are indeed expected. Take passive constructions, for example. If a transitive verb is passivized, it should behave like an unaccusative verb, for its subject corresponds to the object of the associated active transitive verb. Unsurprisingly, passive verbs allow VS order in both EP and BP, as illustrated in (5.18).

(5.18) Foram   descobertas novas ruínas romanas em Portugal.
        were   discovered   new   ruins   Roman   in Portugal
        'New Roman ruins were discovered in Portugal.'

Another apparently exceptional environment involves noncanonical complements. In a sentence such as (5.19a) below, for instance, *a maratona* 'the marathon' does not behave like a regular direct object as it cannot be pronominalized (see (5.19b,b′)) and is interpreted more like the measure of the race. In other words, the verb *correr* 'run' seems to keep its unergative properties even in this transitive frame. Also unsurprisingly, EP allows the VS order in (5.20) under a thetic interpretation, but BP does not.

(5.19) a.   Cem   atletas   correram   a   maratona.
             100   athletes   ran   the   marathon
             'There were 100 athletes running the marathon.'
        b.   EP: *Cem atletas   correram-**na**.
             100   athletes ran-it$_{[CL]}$
        b′. BP: *Cem atletas   correram   **ela**.
             100   athletes ran   it$_{[W]}$

(5.20) Correram cem atletas   a   maratona. (EP: OK; BP:*)
        ran   100 athletes   the marathon
        'There were 100 athletes running the marathon.'

The restriction on VS order with transitive verbs in a thetic setting can however be voided in some specific contexts in EP, but not in BP. An auxiliary, for instance, may make the VS order with transitive verbs available in EP, as illustrated by the sentences in (5.21), uttered in a thetic context.

(5.21) [*Context*: Someone looks out of the window.]
        a.   Um cão   está a   atacar   o   gato.   (EP)
             a   dog   is   to   attack   the cat
        a′. Um cachorro está atacando   o   gato.   (BP)
             a   dog   is   attacking   the cat
        b.   Está um cão a   atacar   o   gato.   (EP)
             is   a   dog to   attack   the cat
        b′. *Está um cachorro atacando   o   gato. (BP)
             is   a   dog   attacking   the cat
        'A dog is attacking the cat.'

Another construction that exceptionally allows VS order with transitive verbs in EP involves a matrix clause with the verb in the indicative imperfective past tense, articulated with an adverbial clause that locates the situation described by the matrix clause in the speaker's perceptual field, as illustrated in (5.22) below. Occurrences of this type of VS indicate that the situation described is somehow unexpected.

(5.22)   EP:
   a. Ontem   quando cheguei   a   casa,   **comia**
      yesterday when   arrived-1.SG at   house eat-INDIC.IMPERF
      o   **João**   a   sopa   sem   fazer   fita.
      the João   the   soup   without making   fuss
      'Yesterday when I arrived home, João was eating his soup without making a fuss.'
   b. Ontem   quando cheguei   a   casa,   **via**
      yesterday when   arrived-1.SG at   house see-INDIC.IMPERF
      o   **João**   um   **filme**   na   televisão.
      the João   a   movie   in-the television
      'Yesterday when I arrived home, João was watching a movie on TV.'

This construction may also employ unergative verbs (even unergative verbs that may resist subject inversion), as shown in (5.23).

(5.23)   EP:
   a. Quando   cheguei   à   casa   do   meu   pai,
      when   arrived   at-the   house   of-the my   father
      trabalhava   ele   no   jardim.
      work-INDIC.IMPERF   he   in-the   garden
      'When I arrived at my father's house, he was working in the garden.'
   b. Ontem   quando   cheguei   a   casa,
      yesterday when   arrived-1.SG at   house
      dormia   o   bebé   tranquilamente.
      sleep-INDIC.IMPERF   the   baby   peacefully
      'Yesterday when I arrived home, the baby was sleeping peacefully.'

An interesting case, also restricted to EP, involves verbs that allow an alternation between an accusative and a dative complement, as illustrated in (5.24) below. The dative frame allows VS order, whereas the accusative frame permits it only if the object is pronominalized, as shown in (5.25) and (5.26).

(5.24)   EP:
   a. Um cão mordeu o   Pedro.
      a   dog bit   the Pedro
      'A dog bit Pedro.'
   a'. Um cão mordeu-o.
       a   dog bit-him.ACC_{[Cl]}
       'A dog bit him.'

b. Um cão mordeu ao   Pedro.
   a   dog bit   to-the Pedro
   'A dog bit Pedro.'
b'. Um cão mordeu-lhe.
   a   dog bit-him.DAT$_{[Cl]}$
   'A dog bit him.'

(5.25) EP:
[*Context*: Someone looks out of the window.]
a. *Mordeu um cão o   Pedro.
   bit   a dog the Pedro
b. ?Mordeu um cão ao   Pedro.
   bit   a dog to-the Pedro
   'A dog bit Pedro.'

(5.26) EP:
[*Context*: Someone asks why João is screaming.]
a. Mordeu-o   um cão.
   bit-him.ACC$_{[Cl]}$ a dog
   'A dog bit him.'
b. Mordeu-lhe   um cão.
   bit-him.DAT$_{[Cl]}$ a dog
   'A dog bit him.'

Let us finally consider a specific correlation between word order and the categorical–thetic distinction in BP. As subject–verb inversion and null subjects have become substantially restricted in BP (see Chapter 4), subject doubling has come to be employed to express this distinction.[11] If the doubling noun phrase precedes the subject pronoun, as in (5.27), we have a categorical judgment; if it follows the pronoun (in fact, the whole predicate), as in (5.28), we have a thetic judgment.

(5.27) BP (categorical judgment):
a. A **Clarinha, ela** cozinha que é   uma maravilha.
   the Clarinha she cooks   that is a   wonder
   'Clarinha cooks wonderfully.'
b. **O meu carro, ele** só   me   dá   dor   de cabeça.
   the my car   it only me   gives ache of head
   'My car only gives me headaches.'
c. É   claro que **um bom emprego, ele** começa pelo   respeito
   is   clear that a   good job   it starts by-the respect
   aos   funcionários.
   to-the employees
   'It's clear that a good job begins with respect for the employees.'

---

[11] See e.g. Pontes 1987, Kato 1989, 1999, Britto 1998, 2000, and Galves 1998 for discussion.

d. Eu acho que **qualquer professor, ele** deve sempre
 I think that any teacher he should always
 falar francamente com os alunos.
 speak frankly with the students
 'I think that every teacher must speak frankly with his students.'

(5.28) BP (thetic judgment):
 a. **Ele** só come arroz e feijão, **o João**.
  he only eats rice and beans the João
  'João only eats rice and beans.'
 b. **Ela** não trabalha no fim de semana, **a Maria**.
  she not works in-the end of week the Maria
  'Maria does not work on weekends.'
 c. **Ele** tá pronto, **o vestido azul**.
  it is ready the dress blue
  'The blue dress is ready.'
 d. **Ele** foi traduzido em vinte línguas, **esse livro**.
  it was translated in twenty languages this book
  'This book was translated into twenty languages.'

Although we may also find constructions with doubling of an overt subject pronoun in EP, they are felt as marked. In BP, on the other hand, they are much more frequent and much more diversified. In the case of doubling to the left, in particular, it may occur in matrix (see (5.27a,b)) and embedded clauses (see (5.27c,d)) and the subject may be animate (see (5.27a,d)), inanimate (see (5.27b,c)), definite (see (5.27a,b)), indefinite (see (5.27c)), or quantificational (see (5.27d)). This diversity in contrast with EP is arguably related to the fact that the nominative forms *ele(s)/ela(s)* may be weak or strong pronouns in BP but are typically strong pronouns in EP (see Section 4.6.3); hence, sentences like (5.27b–d) and (5.28c,d), for instance, are to be ruled out (or are marginal) in EP, for the relevant doubled expressions are incompatible with a strong pronoun.

The two varieties also differ with respect to the structure assigned to constructions with doubling to the right. In EP, the doubled expression behaves as if it is a sentence-external constituent. Thus, it more naturally follows a question tag (see Section 7.4.2), as illustrated in (5.29a); if the doubled expression precedes the question tag, as in (5.29b), it requires a marked pause preceding it, which again indicates that it occupies a clause-external position.[12] In BP, on the other hand, the doubled expression cannot follow the question tag and does not trigger insertion of a pause in (5.29b), indicating that it sits in a clause-internal position.

---

[12] See e.g. Costa 2004 and Duarte 2013b for discussion.

(5.29) a. Ele terminou o relatório, **não terminou**, o Paulo? (EP: OK; BP: *)
       he finished the report not finished the Paulo
    b. Ele terminou o relatório o **Paulo, não terminou**? (EP: *; BP: OK)
       he finished the report the Paulo not finished
       'Paulo finished the report, didn't he?'

5.2.1.2 Topicalization of Non-Subjects

In Section 5.2.1.1, we have seen that SV order may generally convey a categorical interpretation, in which case the subject is interpreted as the topic about which something is said. This is generally referred to as an instance of unmarked topics. If a categorical judgment is made about an element other than the subject of the sentence, that is, if such an element is interpreted as the topic of the sentence (an instance of a marked topic construction), SV order can be maintained and the topic appears before the subject, as illustrated in (5.30).[13]

(5.30) a. Esse filme, eu vi na semana passada.
       this movie I saw in-the week passed
       'I saw this movie last week.'
    b. A esses jogadores, o treinador ofereceu excelentes
       to these players the coach offered excellent
       condições de trabalho. (EP)
       conditions of work
    b'. Pra esses jogadores, o treinador ofereceu excelentes
       to these players the coach offered excellent
       condições de trabalho. (BP)
       conditions of work
       'The coach offered excellent working conditions to these players.'
    c. Nesses países o João nunca teve dificuldade em trabalhar.
       in-these countries the João never had difficulty in work
       'João never found it difficult to work in these countries.'

In (5.30a), the topic is the direct object, in (5.30b) and (5.30b′) the indirect object (see footnote 1 above), and in (5.30c) a locative adjunct. The topics in (5.30a), (5.30b), and (5.30b′) can also be doubled by a pronominal element: a clitic in EP and a weak pronoun in BP, as respectively shown in (5.31) and (5.32) below.[14] Notice that doubling of the indirect object may keep *a* in EP (cf. (5.30b) vs. (5.31b)), but not *pra* in BP (cf. (5.30b′) vs. (5.32b)). This

---

[13] For discussion see e.g. Pontes 1987, Duarte 1987, 2003a, 2013b, Kato 1989, Galves 1998, Bastos 2001, Costa 2004, Kato and Raposo 1996, 2007, Bastos-Gee 2009, 2011, Santos 2018, and Lacerda 2020.

[14] If on the right of the pronoun, the doubled expression occupies a clause-external position, as illustrated in (i) for EP (see e.g. Costa 2004 and Duarte 2013b) and (ii) for BP.

suggests that *a* in (5.30b)/(5.31b) is a morphological realization of dative case, whereas *pra* in (5.30b′)/(5.32b) is a standard preposition.[15]

(5.31) EP:
    a. **Esse filme**, vi-**o** na semana passada.
       this movie saw-1.SG-it₍CL₎ in-the week passed
       'I saw this movie last week.'
    b. **(A) esses jogadores**, o treinador ofereceu-**lhes** excelentes condições de trabalho.
       to these players the coach offered-them.DAT₍CL₎ excellent conditions of work
       'The coach offered excellent working conditions to these players.'

(5.32) BP:
    a. **Esse filme**, eu vi **ele** na semana passada.
       this movie I saw it in-the week passed
       'I saw this movie last week.'
    b. **(*Pra) esses jogadores**, o treinador ofereceu excelentes condições de trabalho pra **eles**.
       to these players the coach offered excellent conditions of work to them
       'The coach offered excellent working conditions to these players.'

A sentence may have more than one fronted topic, as illustrated in (5.33) below. The topic status of the fronted elements in (5.33) can be clearly seen in (5.34), where the objects are doubled.

(5.33) a. À minha sobrinha, este jogo, só vou comprar (EP) quando ela tiver 12 anos.
       to-the my niece this game only go.1.SG buy when she have.SUBJ.FUT 12 years
    b. Pra minha sobrinha, este jogo, eu só vou comprar quando ela tiver 12 anos. (BP)
       to-the my niece this game I only go.1.SG buy when she have.SUBJ.FUT 12 years
       'I'll only buy this game for my niece when she turns 12.'

(i)   EP:
    a. Eu comprei-**o** ontem, **esse livro**.
       I bought-it yesterday this book
    b. *Eu comprei-**o esse livro** ontem.
       I bought-it this book yesterday
       'I bought this book yesterday.'

(ii)   *BP*:
    a. Eu comprei **ele** ontem, **esse livro**.
       I bought it yesterday this book
    b. *Eu comprei **ele esse livro** ontem.
       I bought it this book yesterday
       'I bought this book yesterday.'

[15] For discussion see e.g. Berlinck 1996b, Salles 1997, Torres Morais 2007, Torres Morais and Berlinck 2007, Torres Morais and Salles 2010, and Calindro 2015, 2020.

(5.34) a. À   minha   sobrinha, este   jogo,   só
          to-the my   niece   this   game   only
          lho   vou   comprar quando ela
          DAT[CL].3.SG-it[CL]   *go.1.SG buy   when   she*
          tiver   12 anos   (EP)
          have.SUBJ.FUT   years
     b. A   minha   sobrinha, este jogo, eu só   vou
         the my   niece   this game I only go.1.SG
         comprar **ele** pra **ela** quando ela tiver   12 anos.   (BP)
         buy   it   to her   when   she have.SUBJ.FUT 12 years
         'I'll only buy this game for my niece when she turns 12.'

Topicalization does not interfere with clitic placement.[16] The clitics in the topicalization structures in (5.35) below, for example, follow the typical pattern of enclisis in EP and proclisis in BP (see Section 5.6 for detailed discussion).

(5.35) a. Esse   documento, o   João **enviou-te**   na   semana
           this document   the João sent-you.SG[CL]   in-the week
           passada.   (EP)
           passed
       a'. Esse   documento, o   João **te**   **enviou** na   semana
           this document   the João you.SG[CL]   sent   in-the week
           passada.   (BP)
           passed
           'This document, João sent you(SG) last week.'
       b. Com   essas palavras doces, a   Maria **convenceu-me**.   (EP)
           with these words   sweet   the Maria convinced-me[CL]
       b'. Com   essas palavras doces, a   Maria **me**   **convenceu**. (BP)
           with these words   sweet   the Maria me[CL]   convinced
           'With these sweet words, Maria convinced me.'

Finally, marked topic constructions provide a licensing environment for VS order in EP, but not in BP. In particular, VS transitive sentences with marked topics such as (5.36) are perfectly acceptable in EP,[17] but close to unintelligible in BP.

(5.36) a. O   mapa do   tesouro, esconderam os   piratas na   própria
           the map   of-the   treasure hid-3PL   the pirates in-the own
           ilha.   (EP: OK; BP: *)
           island
           'The pirates hid the treasure map on the island itself.'

---

[16] For discussion see e.g. Raposo 1994, 1995, 2000, Martins 1994a, 2013b, Costa and Martins 2011, and Martins and Costa 2016.
[17] See e.g. Duarte 1987 for discussion.

b. O queijo, levou o rato enquanto o gato
   the cheese took the mouse while the cat
   dormia. (EP: OK; BP: *)
   slept
   'The mouse took the cheese away while the cat slept.'

Some properties of topicalization structures become clearer when constituents other than the subject are topicalized, due to the difference in word order they impose. One of these properties is the referential content of the topicalized element. As a general rule, topics must be salient elements in the context. Hence, one frequently finds demonstratives within topicalized expressions, as they explicitly connect the sentence with the previous discourse or the utterance context (see (5.30)–(5.35)). By the same token, negative expressions and bare quantifiers are not prone to topicalization,[18] as shown in (5.37) below, with the comma indicating the same prosodic contour as in (5.30)–(5.36). Quantifiers may however be topicalized if they are modified in a way to make them salient in the discourse, as exemplified in (5.38), with a relative clause.

(5.37) a. *Nenhum livro, o João leu.
          no book the João read
          'João read no books.'
       b. *Tudo, o João comprou.
          everything the João bought
          'João bought everything.'

(5.38) Tudo o que a Maria recomendou, o João comprou.
       everything the that the Maria recommended the João bought
       'João bought everything Maria recommended.'

5.2.2 Focus Structures

The term *focus* identifies a sentential constituent that is taken by the speaker to convey new information to the hearer or information that the speaker assumes to contradict the hearer's beliefs or expectations. The former is referred to as *information focus* and the latter as *contrastive focus*. In this section we discuss how these two kinds of foci interact with word order.[19]

---

[18] For discussion see e.g. Duarte 1987, 1997, A. M. Martins 1997, 2013b, and Barbosa 2006.

[19] For discussion see e.g. Costa and Martins 2011, Martins and Costa 2016, and Martins and Lobo 2020.

5.2.2.1 Information Focus and Word Order

Wh-questions typically establish discourse contexts that license information focus, as the constituent that answers the question is exactly the expression that provides the requested unknown information. The underlined constituents in (5.39), for instance, can be appropriately interpreted as information focus in the contexts given. Observe that the information focus may involve not only parts of the sentence (narrow information focus), as in (5.39a) and (5.39b), but also the whole sentence (broad information focus), as in (5.39c).[20]

(5.39)   a. [*Context*: Someone asks what Maria ate.]
         A   Maria   comeu   <u>bacalhau</u>.
         the Maria   ate   cod
         'Maria ate cod.'
    b. [*Context*: Someone asks what Maria did.]
         A   Maria   <u>viajou</u>   <u>com</u>   <u>os</u>   <u>amigos</u>.
         the Maria   traveled with the friends
         'Maria traveled with her friends.'
    c. [*Context*: Someone asks what happened.]
         <u>A</u>   <u>Maria</u>   <u>ganhou</u>   <u>a</u>   <u>eleição</u>.
         the Maria   won   the election
         'Maria won the election.'

Notice that the sentences in (5.39) display the unmarked SVO order in both EP and BP. In both varieties, information focus must be prosodically prominent and sentential stress in unmarked sentences falls on the rightmost constituent; if that constituent is (part of) the information focus, no rearrangements take place.[21] This is the case in (5.39). Given that the rightmost constituent of each of the sentences of (5.39) is (part of) the information focus, the unmarked SVO order with unmarked stress on the last constituent is kept unaltered in both varieties.

This similarity is not the general rule, though. If the information focus does not correspond to the rightmost constituent of an unmarked order, the two varieties differ in how they deal with this mismatch.[22] Take the

---

[20] An appropriate answer in the context of (5.39a), for instance, may also be *comeu o bacalhau* 'ate the cod' or just *o bacalhau* 'the cod'. Here and in the discussion that follows, we put such short answers aside, for we will be concerned only with the issue of which word orders within a sentence can provide a full answer compatible with the question in the context.
[21] See e.g. Costa 1998, 2004 for discussion.
[22] For discussion see e.g. Costa 1998, 2004, Costa and Figueiredo Silva 2006b, Kato and Martins 2016, and Martins and Lobo 2020.

answers in (5.40) and (5.41), for instance, where boldface annotates marked stress.[23]

(5.40)   [*Context*: Somebody asks who ate the fish.]
    a. Comeu o peixe o **João**. (EP: OK; BP: *)
       ate   the fish   the João
       'João ate the fish.'
    b. Comeu o **João**. (EP: OK; BP: *)
       ate   the João
       'João did.'
    c. **O João** comeu o peixe. (EP: *; BP: OK)
       the João ate   the fish
       'João ate the fish.'
    d. **O João** comeu. (EP: *; BP: OK)
       the João ate
       'João did.'

(5.41)   [*Context*: Someone asks who saw Maria at the movies.]
    a. Viu a Maria no cinema o **João**. (EP: OK; BP: *)
       saw the Maria in-the cinema the João
       'João saw Maria at the movies.'
    b. Viu o **João**. (EP: OK; BP: *)
       saw the João
       'João did.'
    c. **O João** viu a Maria no cinema. (EP: *; BP: OK)
       the João saw the Maria in-the cinema
       'João saw Maria at the movies.'
    d. **O João** viu. (EP: *; BP: OK)
       the João saw
       'João did.'

The contexts in (5.40) and (5.41) involve a transitive verb and request an answer with information focus on the subject. This yields a situation in which *o João* is the information focus in the answers, but *o peixe* 'the fish' in (5.40) and *no cinema* 'at the movies' in (5.41) should in principle be assigned unmarked stress for being the rightmost constituent of the sentence. To solve this conflict, EP places the subject in the final position, allowing it to receive unmarked stress (see (5.40a,b)

---

[23] (5.40c,d) and (5.41c,d) – with marked stress on the subject and conveying an exhaustive answer – are taken to be ungrammatical in EP. The SV order in these sentences is admitted in both BP and EP under a different specific intonational pattern which conveys the meaning that the answer is not exhaustive. Under this intonation, (5.40c,d), for example, may mean that the speaker is committed only to her/his statement about João, implying that people other than João may have done so too. In the discussion that follows, we will put this special intonation aside (see e.g. Lacerda 2020 for discussion) and examine all the relevant sentences with marked stress under the exhaustive interpretation.

and (5.41a,b)). BP, on the other hand, generally resists subject inversion, as we have seen in Section 5.2.1; its solution is to assign a marked stress to the preverbal subject, rendering it prosodically prominent (see (5.40c,d) and (5.41c,d)).[24]

The same contrast is found with intransitive verbs, regardless of whether they are unergative, as shown in (5.42) and (5.43), or unaccusative, as shown in (5.44) and (5.45).

(5.42) [*Context*: Someone asks who cried.]
    a. Chorou o João.   (EP: OK; BP: *)
       cried the João
    b. **O João** chorou.   (EP: *; BP: OK)
       the João cried
       'João did.'

(5.43) [*Context*: Someone asks who worked on Sunday.]
    a. Trabalhou no domingo a Maria.   (EP: OK; BP: *)
       worked in-the Sunday the Maria
    b. **A Maria** trabalhou no domingo.   (EP: *; BP: OK)
       the Maria worked in-the Sunday
       'Maria worked on Sunday.'

(5.44) [*Context*: Someone asks who always arrives late.]
    a. Chega sempre atrasado o Pedro.   (EP: OK; BP: *)
       arrives always late the Pedro
    b. **O Pedro** chega sempre atrasado.   (EP: *; BP: OK)
       the Pedro arrives always late
       'Pedro always arrives late.'

(5.45) [*Context*: Someone asks who was born in Lisbon.]
    a. Nasceram em Lisboa os netos da Rita. (EP: OK; BP:*)
       were.born in Lisbon the grandchildren of-the Rita
    b. **Os netos** da **Rita** nasceram em Lisboa. (EP: *; BP: OK)
       the grandchildren of-the Rita were.born in Lisbon
       'Rita's grandchildren were born in Lisbon.'

The ungrammaticality of (5.44a) and (5.45a) in BP is particularly interesting, given that BP allows VSX order with unaccusatives as a way to encode a thetic

---

[24] Although focus-induced V(X)S order has no place in BP nowadays, residual instances with focus operators like *só* 'only', for instance, are (marginally) allowed. Thus, (ia) can be an appropriate answer in BP to the context question, although the SV version in (ib) is still the preferred option.

(i)   BP:
    [*Context*: Someone asks who did not enjoy the trip.]
    a. Só não gostaram da viagem os meninos pequenos.
       only not liked of-the trip the kids small
    b. Só os meninos pequenos não gostaram da viagem.
       only the kids small not liked of-the trip
       'Only the younger kids didn't enjoy the trip.'

5.2 Word Order in Declarative Sentences 249

judgment, as seen in Section 5.2.1.1. Notice that an answer in the context of (5.44) and (5.45) with a marked stress on the subject under VSX order is equally unacceptable in BP:

(5.46) a. [*Context*: Someone asks who always arrives late.]
        *Chega   o   **Pedro** sempre atrasado.   (EP/BP)
        arrives   the   Pedro   always   late
        'Pedro always arrives late.'
    b. [*Context*: Someone asks who was born in Lisbon.]
        *Nasceram **os netos** da **Rita** em Lisboa. (EP/BP)
        were.born   the grandchildren of-the Rita in Lisbon
        'Rita's grandchildren were born in Lisbon.'

One case in which BP exceptionally patterns with EP in allowing VXS with focal prominence of the subject is found in certain registers where the speaker is narrating an event that s/he is witnessing (in sports broadcasting, for example) or the speaker is organizing the event itself, as illustrated in (5.47) below.[25] This particular pattern of VXS is generally restricted to sentences with indicative present tense and its predicates normally includes predictable events such as a referee raising his arm to end a soccer game in (5.47a) or someone being authorized to speak in a formal meeting in (5.47b). These predicates also often involve grammaticalized phrasal complexes like *ter a palavra* 'have the turn to speak' (lit. *have the word*) in (5.47b).

(5.47) a. Ergue o braço o juiz.   (EP/BP)
        raises the arm the referee
        'The referee raises his arm.'
    b. Tem a palavra agora o secretário do Conselho (EP/BP)
        has the word now the secretary of-the council.
        'Now, the Council's secretary will speak.'

As seen above in (5.40)–(5.45), information focus on the subject gives rise to VXS order in EP. VSX is in fact generally excluded in this scenario, as illustrated by the contrast in (5.48).[26]

---

[25] See e.g. Pilati 2006 and Lobo and Martins 2017 for discussion.
[26] The inadequacy of (5.48b) in the relevant context can be voided in EP if the object is not expressed (see Section 6.3), as in (ia) below, or if a pause is inserted between the subject and the object, as in (ib) (with "#" annotating the pause). In these cases, the subject counts as the rightmost constituent for purposes of assignment of sentential stress, thus becoming compatible with a focus interpretation. No such repair is available in BP.

(i)   [*Context*: Someone asks who made dinner.]
       a. Fez o Pedro.   (EP: OK; BP: *)
           made the Pedro
       b. Fez o Pedro, # o jantar. (EP: OK; BP: *)
           made the Pedro   the dinner
           'Pedro made the dinner.'

(5.48) [*Context*: Someone asks who made dinner.]
    a. Fez o jantar o Pedro.   (EP: OK; BP: *)
       made the dinner the Pedro
    b. *Fez o Pedro o jantar.   (EP: *; BP: *)
       made the Pedro the dinner
       'Pedro cooked dinner.'

Interestingly, VSX order in EP may be licensed in a multiple question context such as that in (5.49) below, where the subject and the object are interpreted as information focus.[27] As one would by now expect, BP allows only SV order in (5.49b), a possibility that is also available in EP.

(5.49) [*Context*:
    A: – O jantar na mesa?! Quem fez o quê?
          the dinner on-the table who did what
       'Dinner is served?! Who did what?']
    a. B: – Fez o João os bifes   (EP: OK; BP: *)
            made the João the steaks
            e o Pedro as batatas.
            and the Pedro the potatoes
    b. B: – O João fez os bifes   (EP: OK; BP: OK)
            the João made the steaks
            e o Pedro as batatas.
            and the Pedro the potatoes
       'João cooked the steaks and Pedro, the potatoes.'

An exception to this general pattern shows up if the expected VXS is independently prevented. Under the relevant interpretation prompted by the context in (5.50) below, for instance, the possessive pronoun *seu* 'his' is to be interpreted as being linked to the quantified expression *cada orientador* 'each advisor'. Independently, such connection may succeed if the quantifier precedes the pronoun, but not if the quantifier follows it. Thus, in EP the VOS order in (5.50a) is precluded in favor of VSO order in (5.50b).[28] BP also marginally accepts the VSO order in this context, but still prefers the SVO order in (5.50c), which is also acceptable in EP in this context.

(5.50) [*Context*: Someone asks who called the students.]
    a. *Telefonou para os seus$_i$ orientandos
       called   to   the his   advisees
       [cada orientador]$_i$.   (EP: *; BP: *)
       each advisor
    b. Telefonou [cada orientador]$_i$ para os seus$_i$
       called   each advisor   to   the his
       orientandos.   (EP: OK; BP: ?)
       advisees

---

[27] See e.g. Costa 2004 for discussion.
[28] See e.g. Costa and Figueiredo Silva 2006b for discussion.

c. [Cada orientador]ᵢ telefonou para os seusᵢ
    each advisor   called   to the his
    orientandos.   (EP: OK; BP: OK)
    advisees
    'Each advisor called his advisees.'

Another context where BP shows its tendency to avoid VS order involves environments of quotative inversion in a narrative style, where the content of what is said precedes the saying verb, as illustrated in (5.51) below.²⁹ VS order in such contexts is obligatory in EP, whereas in BP both SV and VS orders are possible (the VS order in BP is associated with written language, though).

(5.51) a. "Estas   meninas não   gostam de
            these   girls   not   like   of
            bonecas," disse   a   mãe.   (EP: OK; BP: OK)
            dolls   said   the   mother
        a'. "Estas   meninas não   gostam de
            these   girls   not   like   of
            bonecas," a   mãe   disse.   (EP: *; BP: OK)
            dolls   the   mother said
            '"These girls don't like dolls," their mother said.'
        b. "O que   aconteceu?," perguntou
            what   happened   asked
            o   leão à   girafa.   (EP: OK)
            the   lion to-the giraffe
        b'. "O que   aconteceu?," o   leão
            what   happened   the   lion
            perguntou à   girafa.   (EP: *)
            asked   to-the giraffe
        b". "O que   aconteceu?," perguntou o   leão
            what   happened   asked   the   lion
            para a   girafa.   (BP: OK)
            to   the giraffe
        b.''' "O que   aconteceu?," o   leão perguntou
            what   happened   the lion asked
            para a   girafa.   (BP: OK)
            to   the giraffe
            '"What happened?," the lion asked the giraffe.'

Let us finally consider the order between complements in ditransitive structures. In both EP and BP, direct objects precede indirect and oblique objects in unmarked orders. Thus, if the indirect/oblique object is the information focus of the sentence, the unmarked order is maintained in both

---

[29] For discussion see e.g. Matos 2013b, Lobo and Martins 2017, and Martins and Lobo 2020.

varieties, for the indirect or oblique object can receive default sentential stress by being the rightmost constituent. This is illustrated in (5.52) and (5.53).

(5.52) [*Context*: Someone asks who João gave a book to.]
    a. O   João deu   um livro à   Maria. (EP)
       the João gave a   book to-the Maria
    b. O   João deu   um livro pra   Maria. (BP)
       the João gave a   book to-the Maria
    'João gave a book to Maria.'

(5.53) [*Context*: Someone asks where Pedro put the packages.]
    O   Pedro pôs os   pacotes na   cozinha.
    the Pedro put the   packages in-the kitchen
    'Pedro put the packages in the kitchen.'

If the direct object is the information focus instead, the two varieties differ. In EP, the direct object is placed after the indirect or oblique object, as shown in (5.54a) and (5.55a) below. Although this order is acceptable in BP, as shown in (5.54a′) and (5.55a), the preferred option is to keep the unmarked order and assign a marked stress on the direct object (deaccenting the indirect or oblique object), as shown in (5.54b′) and (5.55b) – a possibility that is not available in EP (see (5.54b) and (5.55b)).[30]

(5.54) [*Context*: Someone asks what João gave to Maria.]
    a.   O   João deu à   Maria um livro. (EP)
        the João gave to-the Maria a   book
    a′. O   João deu pra   Maria um livro. (BP)
        the João gave to-the Maria a   book
    b.   *O   João deu **um livro** à   Maria. (EP)
        the João gave a   book   to-the Maria
    b′. O   João deu **um livro** pra   Maria. (BP)
        the João gave a   book   to-the Maria
    'João gave Maria a book.'

(5.55) [*Context*: Someone asks what Pedro put on the table.]
    a. O   Pedro pôs na   mesa uma garrafa de vinho. (EP: OK; BP: OK)
       the Pedro put in-the table a   bottle of wine
    b. O   Pedro pôs **uma garrafa de vinho** na   mesa. (EP: *; BP: OK)
       the Pedro put a   bottle of wine in-the table
    'Pedro put a bottle of wine on the table.'

5.2.2.2 Contrastive Focus and Word Order

Contrastive focus singles out a constituent that is taken by the speaker to express information that in some way or other contradicts what

---

[30] In EP, a marked stress on the direct object in sentences like (5.54b) and (5.55b) leads to a contrastive focus interpretation (see Section 5.2.2.2).

s/he assumes to be the hearer's beliefs or expectations in a given discourse context.[31] The most transparent illustration of this type of focus involves cases with a pair of consecutive statements by different speakers, where the second statement corrects the first one, as illustrated in (5.56).

(5.56) [*Context*:
        A: – O João colocou os livros na estante.
        the João put the books in-the bookshelf
        'João put the books on the bookshelf.]
  a. B: – Não, O PEDRO colocou os livros na estante.
        no the Pedro put the books in-the bookshelf
        'No, Pedro put the books on the bookshelf.'
  b. B: – Não, o João ESPALHOU os livros na estante.
        no the João spread the books in-the bookshelf
        'No, João spread the books on the bookshelf.'
  c. B: – Não, o João colocou OS DISCOS na estante.
        no the João put the disks in-the bookshelf
        'No, João put the records on the bookshelf.'
  d. B: – Não, o João colocou os livros NA ESCRIVANINHA.
        no the João put the books in-the desk
        'No, João put the books on the desk.'
  e. B: – Não, o João ESPALHOU OS DISCOS NA ESCRIVANINHA.
        no the João spread the disks in-the desk
        'No, João spread the records on the desk.'

In each of B's sentences in (5.56), capital letters annotate heavy stress and convey the information that the capitalized expression is to be understood as replacing the analogous constituent in the sentence uttered by A. (5.56a), for instance, is to be understood as stating that it was Pedro and not João who put the books on the bookshelf.

Both EP and BP allow contrastive focus to be encoded by means of heavy stress, as in (5.56), with no change in the unmarked order. They differ though, when the contrastive focus is fronted (heavy stress is optional in this case). In EP, such fronting triggers VS order regardless of the verb involved, as exemplified by the contrasts between the (a) and (b) sentences of (5.57)–(5.62) below. In BP, on the other hand, SV is allowed for all types of sentences (see the (b) sentences of (5.57)–(5.62)), whereas VS is sensitive to the type of verbs involved, being generally banned with transitive verbs (see (5.57a) and (5.58a)), but (marginally) allowed with unaccusative and unergative verbs, as shown by the (a) sentences of (5.59)–(5.62).[32]

---

[31] For discussion see e.g. Costa and Martins 2011, Kato and Martins 2016, and Martins and Lobo 2020.
[32] For discussion see e.g. Raposo 1995, 2000, Ambar 1999, Costa and Martins 2011, Martins and Costa 2016, and Martins and Lobo 2020.

(5.57) [*Context*:
A: – O João trabalha muito, mas ganha bem.
the João works   much   but   earns   well
'João works a lot but is well paid.']
a. B: – 1000 euros   recebe   ele   por mês.   Isto é um
1000 euros   receives he per month this is a
bom salário?!   (EP: OK; BP: *)
good salary
b. B: – 1000 euros   ele recebe   por mês.   Isto é um
1000 euros   he receives per month this is a
bom salário?!   (EP: *; BP: OK)
good salary
'He earns 1000 euros a month. Is this a good salary?!'

(5.58) a. Outros dois estagiários despediu o   chefe ontem.   (EP: OK; BP: *)
other   two trainees   fired   the boss yesterday
b. Outros dois estagiários o   chefe despediu ontem.   (EP: *; BP: OK)
other   two trainees   the boss fired
'The boss fired two other trainees yesterday.'

(5.59)   [*Context*:
A: – A gente   nem   sabia   que   esta árvore
we   not.even   knew   that   this tree
ia   florir. As   flores   apareceram   em   agosto.
went bloom the   flowers   appeared   in   August
'We didn't even know that this tree would bloom. The flowers appeared in August.']
a. B: – Não, em setembro   apareceram as   flores.   (EP: OK; BP: OK)
no   in September appeared   the flowers
b. B: – Não, em setembro   as flores   apareceram. (EP: *; BP: OK)
no   in September the flowers appeared
'No, the flowers appeared in September.'

(5.60) a. Dentro de um táxi nasceu   o   João!   (EP: OK; BP: ?)
inside of a   cab was.born the João
b. Dentro de um táxi o   João nasceu!   (EP: *; BP: OK)
inside of a   cab the João was.born
'João was born in a cab!'

(5.61) [*Context*: Someone wants to doublecheck in which pool the champion swam.]
a. Na   piscina da   direita nadou o   campeão.   (EP: OK; BP: ?)
in-the pool   of-the right   swam the champion
b. Na   piscina da   direita o   campeão nadou.   (EP: *; BP: OK)
in-the pool   of-the right   the champion swam
'The champion swam in the pool on the right.'

(5.62) a. Em   condições   deploráveis   trabalhavam   os
in   conditions   deplorable   worked   the
empregados!   (EP: OK; BP: OK)
employees

b. Em   condições deploráveis os empregados
   in   conditions deplorable the employees
   trabalhavam!   (EP: *; BP: OK)
   worked
   'The employees worked in deplorable conditions!'

Deviation from this general pattern in EP is found when the fronted focus involves focus particles such as *só* 'only', *até* 'even', or *nem* 'not even' and quantifiers like *pouco(s)/pouca(s)* 'few-{MASC/FEM}(-PL)', *nenhum/nenhuma* 'no-{MASC/FEM}', or *ninguém* 'no one'. As illustrated in (5.63) below, VS in EP becomes exceptionally optional in these circumstances.³³ BP in turn displays the by now familiar ban on VS with transitive verbs and (marginal) acceptability with unaccusative and unergative verbs.

(5.63) a. Só   na   Maria confia o   João.   (EP: OK; BP: *)
           only in-the Maria trusts the João
      a'. Só   na   Maria o   João confia.   (EP: OK; BP: OK)
           only in-the Maria the João trusts
           'João only trusts Maria.'
      b. Até   a   salada comeu o   João.   (EP: OK; BP: *)
           even the salad   ate   the João
      b'. Até   a   salada o   João comeu.   (EP: OK; BP: OK)
           even the salad   the João ate
           'João even ate the salad.'
      c. Nem   com a   forte   tempestade caíram as
           not.even with the strong   storm   fell   the
           folhas.   (EP: OK; BP: ?)
           leaves
      c'. Nem   com a   forte   tempestade as   folhas
           not.even with the strong   storm   the leaves
           caíram.   (EP: OK; BP: OK)
           fell
           'Not even with the strong storm did the leaves fall.'
      d. Nem sempre vence o   favorito   (EP: OK; BP: ?)
           not always wins   the favorite
      d'. Nem sempre o   favorito vence.   (EP: OK; BP: OK)
           not always the favorite wins
           'The favorite doesn't always win.'
      e. Poucos pacientes examinou o   médico ontem. (EP: OK; BP: *)
           few   patients   examined the doctor yesterday
      e'. Poucos pacientes o   médico examinou ontem. (EP: OK; BP: OK)
           few   patients   the doctor examined yesterday
           'The doctor only examined a few patients yesterday.'
      f. Em ninguém confiava o   João.   (EP: OK; BP: *)
           in nobody   trusted   the João

---

[33] For discussion see e.g. Costa and Martins 2011 and Martins and Lobo 2020.

f′. Em ninguém o João confiava.   (EP: OK; BP: OK)
    in   nobody   the João trusted
    'João trusted no one.'
g. De nenhum deles   suspeitava eu. (EP: OK; BP: *)
   of   none   of-them suspected   I
g′. De nenhum deles   eu suspeitava. (EP: OK; BP: OK)
    of   none   of-them I suspected
    'I suspected none of them.'

VS may also be employed in EP when the subject is contrastively focused, as shown in (5.64).[34] As expected, this order is not allowed in BP.

(5.64) a. Agora perdeu A MARIA a carteira! Já   (EP: OK; BP: *)
          now lost   the Maria the wallet already
          não bastava o João ter perdido o casaco?!
          not sufficed the João have lost the jacket
          'Now, Maria has lost her wallet! As if it wasn't enough that João had lost his jacket?!'
       b. [*Context*:
          A: – O jantar que vocês prepararam estava delicioso.
              the dinner that you-PL prepared was delicious
              'The dinner you(PL) prepared was delicious.']
          B: – Fiz EU tudo. Ele não fez nada.   (EP: OK; BP: *)
              did I everything he not did nothing
              'I did everything. He didn't do anything.'
       c. Oxalá   alugue   O JOÃO o apartamento, não a
          hopefully rent-SUBJ the João the apartment   not the
          Maria.
          Maria   (EP: OK; BP: *)
          'I hope that João will rent the apartment, not Maria.'
       d. Talvez tenha   O LADRÃO dito a verdade. (EP: OK; BP: *)
          maybe have-SUBJ the thief told the truth
          'Maybe it was the thief who told the truth.'

VS order is also found in EP in coordinate structures like those in (5.65), where each conjunct has the same verb and the complement in the second conjunct (when the verbs are transitive) is null.[35] The subjects of (5.65) contrast in that they are presented as being mutually exclusive, as in (5.65a), or the first subject is taken to not exhaust the predicate, as in (5.65b–d).

(5.65) EP:
       a. Contas   tu.   (a   história) ou conto eu. Não os
          tell   you.SG the   story   or tell   I   not the
          dois   ao   mesmo tempo!
          two   at-the same time
          'Either you(SG) tell the story or I do. Not both of us at the same time!'

---

[34] For discussion see e.g. Barbosa 2009, Martins and Costa 2016, Martins and Lobo 2020, and Martins 2020b.
[35] For discussion see e.g. Martins 2020b.

5.2 Word Order in Declarative Sentences   257

b. [*Context*:
   A: – O   João   quer   um   dos   meus   gatinhos.
         the   João   wants   one   of-the   my   kittens
         'João wants one of my kittens.']
   B: – <u>Quer</u>   <u>o</u>   <u>João</u>   (um   gatinho)   e   <u>quero</u>   <u>eu.</u>
         wants   the   João   a   kitten   and   want   I
         Não   te   esqueças   de   mim.
         not   you.REFL_[CL]   forget   of   me
         'João does want (one of your kittens) and so do I. Don't forget about me!'

c. [*Context*:
   A: – O   João   adora   chocolate.
         the   João   adores   chocolate
         'João loves chocolate.']
   B: – <u>Adora</u>   <u>o</u>   <u>João</u>   chocolate   e   <u>adora</u>   <u>a</u>   <u>Maria.</u>
         adores   the   João   chocolate   and   adores   the   Maria
         Não   o   dês   todo   a   ele.
         not   it   give-IMP-2.SG   all   to   him
         'João loves chocolate and so does Maria. Don't give it all to him.'

d. [*Context*:
   A: – A   Justiça   vai   mal.
         the   justice   goes   badly
         'The judicial system is not working.']
   B: – <u>Vai</u>   <u>a</u>   <u>Justiça</u>   e   <u>vai</u>   <u>o</u>   <u>País.</u>
         goes   the   justice   and   goes   the   country
         'As goes the judicial system, so goes the nation.'

Focus and topic constructions may yield the same word order when fronting is involved. They may however be teased apart by reference to different syntactic diagnostics. As seen in Section 5.2.1.2, a topic may be doubled by a clitic in EP and by a weak pronoun in BP and topicalization does not interfere with clitic placement. The opposite situation is found with focalization: foci trigger proclisis and cannot be doubled. Consider the contrast between the topicalization structures in (5.66) and the focalization structures in (5.67), for example.

(5.66) a. **Este artigo**, a   Maria   leu-o   ontem.   (EP)
            this article   the   Maria   read-it_[CL]   yesterday
        b. **Este artigo**, a   Maria   leu   ele   ontem.   (BP)
            this article   the   Maria   read   it   yesterday
            'Maria read this article yesterday.'

(5.67) a. *****Só este artigo** a   Maria   leu-o   ontem.   (EP)
            only this article   the   Maria   read-it_[CL]   yesterday
        a'. *****Só este artigo** a   Maria   o   leu   ontem.   (EP)
            only this article   the   Maria   it_[CL]   read   yesterday

b. *Só este artigo a   Maria leu ele ontem.   (BP)
   only this article the Maria read it yesterday
   'Maria read only this article yesterday.'

(5.66) replicates the pattern of topicalization seen in Section 5.2.1.2: the topic is doubled by a pronominal element and, in the case of (5.66a), we find the typical enclitic pattern that we would find in EP if the topic were not present. As for (5.67), we have added the focus particle *só* 'only' to make sure that the sentence-initial material receives a focus interpretation. However, this creates a problem in the case of (5.67a), as focus particles independently trigger proclisis (see Section 5.6.1). So, the ungrammaticality of (5.67a) could be attributed to an unrelated problem of clitic placement. This problem is however circumvented in (5.67a′) and the result is still unacceptable, indicating that its problem is that its focus was doubled. In other words, (5.67a′) in EP patterns like BP in (5.67b), where there is no issue of clitic placement.

Let us now examine the sentences in (5.68) in EP.

(5.68)   EP:

a. *Topicalization*:
   Este filme, a   Maria **recomendou-me**   ontem.
   this movie   the Maria recommended-me$_{[CL]}$ yesterday
   'This movie Maria recommended to me yesterday.'

b. *Focalization*:
   Este filme   **me**   **recomendou** a   Maria ontem.
   this movie me$_{[CL]}$ recommended   the Maria yesterday
   'It was this movie that Maria recommended to me yesterday.'

The pattern of clitic placement displayed by both sentences indicates that we have a topicalization structure in (5.68a), but a focalization structure in (5.68b). This in turn predicts that the sentence-initial material can be doubled by a clitic in (5.68a), but not in (5.68b). That this prediction is correct is shown in (5.69).

(5.69)   EP:

a. *Topicalization*:
   Este filme, a   Maria recomendou-mo   ontem.
   this movie   the Maria recommended-me$_{[CL]}$.it$_{[CL]}$ yesterday
   'This movie Maria recommended to me yesterday.'

b. *Focalization*:
   *** Este filme**   mo   recomendou a   Maria ontem.
   this movie   me$_{[CL]}$.it$_{[CL]}$ recommended the Maria yesterday
   'It was this movie that Maria recommended to me yesterday.'

Focus constructions also contrast with topic constructions in allowing extraposition of relative clauses,[36] as illustrated in (5.70), and in disallowing the stranding of the quantifier *todos/todas* 'all-MASC-PL/FEM-PL',[37] as shown in (5.71).

(5.70) EP:
    a. *Topicalization:*
       *Crianças, também conheço <u>que não gostam de chocolate</u>.
       children also know-1.SG that not like of chocolate
       'I also know children that don't like chocolate.'
    b. *Focalization*:
       Poucas crianças conheço <u>que não gostam de chocolate</u>.
       few children know-1.SG that not like of chocolate.
       'I know few children that don't like chocolate.'

(5.71) EP:
    a. *Topicalization*:
       Estes livros, ofereceu-me a Maria <u>todos</u>.
       these books offered-me the Maria all
       'Maria gave me all these books.'
    b. *Focalization*:
       *Estes livros me ofereceu a Maria <u>todos</u>.
       these books me offered the Maria all
       'Maria gave me all these books.'

Finally, it is worth observing that although topics and foci may be fronted in both EP and BP, the order between them is fixed: topics must precede foci, as illustrated in (5.72) below.[38] Thus, a fronted constituent with a question word cannot precede a topic, as shown in (5.73), for question words are intrinsically associated with focus.

(5.72) a. **Os livros, nem das estantes** o João tirou.
       the books not.even from-the bookshelves the João took
    b. ***Nem das estantes, os livros**, o João tirou.
       not.even from-the bookshelves the books the João took
       'João didn't even take the books from the bookshelves.'

(5.73) a. **Esses relatórios, quando** é que os alunos devem entregar?
       these reports when is that the students should deliver
    b. ***Quando** é que, **esses relatórios**, os alunos devem entregar?
       when is that these reports the students should deliver
       'When are the students supposed to hand in their reports?'

---

[36] See e.g. Cardoso 2010, 2016 for discussion.
[37] See e.g. Duarte 1997 for discussion.
[38] Recall that focus fronting with particles like *nem* 'not even' as in (5.72) is exceptional in EP in that VS order is optional (see (5.63)).

5.2.2.3 Clefting

As with many other languages, EP and BP may also employ the syntactic process referred to as *clefting* to encode information and contrastive focus.[39] Clefting reorganizes the constituents of a given sentence around the copula *ser* 'be' and the complementizer-like element *que* 'that' in a way that highlights the focalized constituents. Let us examine some of the diversity of clefting patterns that are available in EP and BP.

The first pattern worth noting involves the copula in the third person singular form of the indicative present (*é*) and the focalized element preceding or following the copula, as sketched in (5.74) and illustrated in (5.75) below.[40] The possibility in (5.74a) is available in both EP and BP, whereas that in (5.74b) is allowed only in BP.

(5.74)   a. X$_{[focus]}$ **é que** [$_{clause}$ ...]
        b. É X$_{[focus]}$ **que** [$_{clause}$ ...]

(5.75) a. Eu **é que** trabalho mais de 10 horas por dia
          I is that work-1.SG more of 10 hours by day
          nesta empresa. (EP: OK; BP: OK)
          in-this company
      a'. É eu **que** trabalho mais de 10
          is I that work-1.SG more of 10
          horas por dia e empresa. (EP: *; BP: OK)
          hours by day in-this company
          'It is me who works more than 10 hours a day in this company.'
      b. Desse equipamento **é que** o João precisava. (EP: OK; BP: OK)
          of-this equipment is that the João needed
      b'. É desse equipamento **que** o João precisava. (EP: *; BP: OK)
          is of-this equipment that the João needed
          'It was this equipment that João needed.'

---

[39] For discussion see e.g. Lopes-Rossi 1993, Costa and Duarte 2001, Modesto 2001, Ambar, Kato, Mioto, and Veloso 2003, Ambar 2005, Alexandre 2006, Kato and Ribeiro 2006, 2009, Lobo 2006, Mioto and Negrão 2007, Costa and Lobo 2009, Kato 2009, Guesser 2011, Kato and Mioto 2011, 2015, 2016, Menuzzi 2012, Mioto 2012, Barbosa 2013, Cardoso and Alexandre 2013, Resenes 2014, Mioto and Lobo 2016, and Martins and Lobo 2020.

[40] Although we will not flag the distinction between information and contrastive focus in the paradigms in (5.75)–(5.92) below, it should be pointed out that clefted constituents may allow for both interpretations. See e.g. Martins and Lobo 2020 for discussion.

Another pattern, sketched in (5.76) below, is arguably related to the possibility in (5.74b), for it is found only in BP.[41] The copula is not present and the focalized constituent precedes *que*:

(5.76)   X[focus] **que** [clause ...]

(5.77)   a. A   Maria   **que**   foi   promovida.   (EP: *; BP: OK)
            the Maria that was promoted
            'It was Maria who was promoted.'
         b. Esse   autor   **que**   o   professor   recomendou,   não   aquele
            this author that the teacher recommended not that
            outro.   (EP: *; BP: OK)
            other
            'It was this author that the teacher recommended, not the other one.'

An additional pattern, allowed in both EP and BP, has the copula agreeing in person and number with the focalized constituent (if it is a noun phrase) and in tense with the embedded verb, as sketched in (5.78) and exemplified in (5.79).

(5.78)

(5.79)   a. **Fui**   eu   **que**   identifiquei   o
            be.INDIC.PRET-1.SG   I   that   identify-INDIC.PRET-1.SG   the
            problema.   (EP: OK; BP: OK)
            problem
            'It was me who identified the problem.'
         b. **Foram**   essas   vacinas   **que**   o   governo
            be.INDIC.PRET-1.PL these   vaccines that   the government
            testou.   (EP: OK; BP: OK)
            tested
            'It was these vaccines that the government tested.'

Given the pattern in (5.78) as the baseline, the focus may also be fronted and precede the copula, as sketched in (5.80) below. Sentences with these formats, as in (5.81), are generally allowed in BP, but dialectally restricted in EP.[42]

(5.80)   X[focus] **SER que** [clause ... V ...]
         person and number agreement / tense agreement

---

[41] For discussion see e.g. Mioto and Figueiredo Silva 1995, Kato 2014, and Mioto and Lobo 2016.
[42] See e.g. Vercauteren 2010, 2015 for discussion.

262   5 Word Order

(5.81) a. O   governo   **foi**   que   não
          the   government   be.INDIC.PRET-3.SG   that   not
          soube   lidar   com a   greve.   (EP: %; BP: OK)
          know.INDIC.PRET-3.SG deal with the   strike
          'It was the government that didn't know how to handle the strike.'
       b. Os   impostos   **eram**   que
          the   taxes   be.INDIC.IMPERF-3.PL   that
          estavam   muito altos.   (EP: %; BP: OK)
          be.INDIC.IMPERF-3.PL very   high
          'It was the taxes that were very high.'

Yet another pattern looks like (5.78), but, instead of *que*, we find the pronouns *quem* 'who' or *o que* 'what' taking the focus as their antecedent, as sketched in (5.82) and illustrated in (5.83).

(5.82)
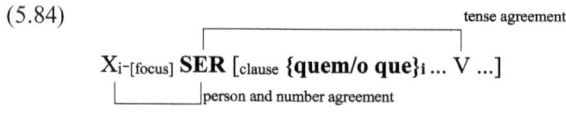

(5.83) a. **Eram**   [essas ideias]ᵢ [o que]ᵢ
          be.INDIC.IMPERF-3.PL these   ideas   what
          ele   criticava.   (EP: OK; BP: OK)
          he   criticized-INDIC.IMPERF-3.SG
          'It was these ideas that he criticized.'
       b. **Foi**   [o   João]ᵢ **quem**ᵢ falou,
          be.INDIC.PRET-3.SG   the João   who   speak-INDIC.PRET-3.SG
          não   o   Pedro.   (EP: OK; BP: OK)
          not   the Pedro
          'It was João who spoke, not Pedro.'

A variant of this pattern places the focus before the copula, as sketched in (5.84) and illustrated in (5.85).

(5.84)   ┌──────── tense agreement ────────┐
                  │   │
         Xᵢ-[focus] **SER** [clause {**quem/o que**}ᵢ ... V ...]
                │_____│person and number agreement

(5.85) a. [Essas   ideias]ᵢ **eram**   [o que]ᵢ   ele
          these   ideas   be.INDIC.IMPERF-3.PL   what   he
          criticava.   (EP: OK; BP: OK)
          criticized-INDIC.IMPERF-3.SG
          'It was these ideas that he criticized.'
       b. [O   João]ᵢ **foi**   **quem**ᵢ falou,
          the   João   be.INDIC.PRET-3.SG   who   speak-INDIC.PRET-3.SG
          não   o   Pedro.   (EP: OK; BP: OK)
          not   the   Pedro
          'It was João who spoke, not Pedro.'

Another pattern based on that in (5.82) fronts the post-focus material, as sketched in (5.86) and exemplified in (5.87).

(5.86) [clause {**quem/o que**}ᵢ ... V ...] **SER** Xᵢ₋[focus]
        with tense agreement between clause and SER, and person and number agreement between SER and Xᵢ

(5.87) a. **[O que]ᵢ** ele criticava   **eram**
          what   he criticized-INDIC.IMPERF-3.SG be.INDIC.IMPERF-3.PL
          [essas   ideias]ᵢ.   (EP: OK; BP: OK)
          these   ideas
          'What he criticized was these ideas.'
       b. **Quem**ᵢ falou   **foi**   [o
          who   speak-INDIC.PRET-3.SG be.INDIC.PRET-3.SG   the
          João]ᵢ, não o   Pedro.   (EP: OK; BP: OK)
          João   not the   Pedro
          'The one who spoke was João, not Pedro.'

Given that default third person singular agreement with VS order is generally allowed in BP (see Section 3.5.1), all the sentences in (5.79), (5.83a) and (5.87a), for instance, may surface with default agreement in BP, as shown in (5.88) below (notice though that tense agreement between the copula and the main verb is enforced). In EP, on the other hand, default agreement in this environment is possible only if the focus is a plural third person pronoun or noun phrase and is not the subject of the main predicate; hence, default agreement is ruled out in (5.88a) (cf. (5.79a)), but possible in (5.88b–d).[43]

(5.88) a. **Foi**   eu   que identifiquei
          be.INDIC.PRET-3.SG I   that identify-INDIC.PRET-1.SG
          o   problema.   (EP: *; BP: OK)
          the   problem
          'It was me who identified the problem.'
       b. **Foi**   essas   vacinas que o   governo
          be.INDIC.PRET-3.SG these   vaccines that the   government
          testou.   (EP: OK; BP: OK)
          tested
          'It was these vaccines that the government tested.'
       c. **Era**   [essas   ideias]ᵢ   [o que]ᵢ
          be.INDIC.IMPERF-3.SG   these   ideas   what
          ele criticava.   (EP: OK; BP: OK)
          he   criticized-INDIC.IMPERF-3.SG
          'It was these ideas that he criticized.'

---

[43] See e.g. Martins and Lobo 2020 for discussion.

d. [O que]ᵢ ele criticava **era**
   what   he criticized-INDIC.IMPERF-3.SG be.INDIC.IMPERF-3.SG
   [essas   ideias]ᵢ.   (EP: OK; BP: OK)
   these   ideas
   'What he criticized was these ideas.'

Finally, EP and BP also allow a pattern like that in (5.89) and exemplified in (5.90), where neither *que* nor the pronoun *quem* or *o que* is present and the focus appears in sentence-final position preceded by the copula, which surfaces in the third person singular form agreeing in tense with the preceding verb.[44]

(5.89) $\overbrace{\phantom{\text{XXXXXX}}}^{\text{tense agreement}}$
         [clause ... V ...] **SER**[3.SG] X[focus]

(5.90) a. Ele   criticava   **era**
          he   criticized-INDIC.IMPERF-3.SG be.INDIC.IMPERF-3.SG
          essas ideias.   (EP: OK; BP: OK)
          these ideas
          'What he criticized was these ideas.'
       b. O   gerente   contratou   **foi**
          the manager   hired-INDIC.PERF.3.SG be.INDIC.PERF.3.SG
          os   candidatos experientes.   (EP: OK; BP: OK)
          the candidates experienced
          'The ones who the manager hired were the experienced candidates.'
       c. Eu quero   **é**
          I want-INDIC.PRES.1.SG   be.INDIC.PRES.3.SG
          café.   (EP: OK; BP: OK)
          coffee
          'What I want is coffee.'

In both EP and BP, cleft constructions such as those in (5.90) may also be preceded by *mas* 'but', which usually corresponds to the adversative coordinating conjunction but here encodes some sort of emphasis, as illustrated in (5.91a–c) below. In EP (subject to variation among speakers) but not in BP, *mas* accompanied by the copula may also appear in sentence-final position, as shown in (5.91d). In this case, the copula does not agree in tense with the main verb, as exemplified by the contrast between (5.91e) and (5.91f).[45]

---

[44] For discussion see e.g. Casteleiro 1979, Wheeler 1982, Costa and Duarte 2001, Vercauteren 2010, 2015, Barbosa 2013, Kato and Mioto 2015, 2016, and Martins and Lobo 2020.

[45] See e.g. Bolrinha 2017 and Martins and Lobo 2020 for discussion.

(5.91) a. Ele   criticava   **mas era**
          he   criticized-INDIC.IMPERF-3.SG but be.INDIC.IMPERF-3.SG
          [essas ideias].   (EP: OK; BP: OK)
          these ideas
          'What he criticized was indeed these ideas.'
     b. O   gerente   contratou **mas foi**   os
        the   manager   hired   but was   the
        candidatos experientes.   (EP: OK; BP: OK)
        candidates experienced
        'The ones who the manager actually hired were the experienced candidates.'
     c. Eu quero **mas é** café.   (EP: OK; BP: OK)
        I   want   but is   coffee
     d. Eu quero café, **mas é**!   (EP: %; BP: *)
        I   want   coffee but is
        'What I really want is coffee.'
     e. O   João comeu um chocolate, **mas é**!   (EP: %; BP: *)
        the João ate   a   chocolate   but is
     f. *O João comeu um chocolate, **mas foi**!   (EP: *; BP: *)
        the João ate   a   chocolate   but was
        'What João really ate was a chocolate bar.'

Some of the patterns discussed are not mutually exclusive and double clefting may be allowed, as exemplified in (5.92a) in EP and BP (with patterns (5.74a) and (5.84)) and (5.92b) in BP (with patterns (5.76) and (5.84)).[46]

(5.92) a. Esse equipamento de segurança **é que foi   o que**
          this equipment   of safety   is that was   what
          salvou o   Pedro.   (EP: OK; BP: OK
          saved the Pedro
          'It was this safety equipment that saved Pedro's life.'
       b. A Maria **que foi com quem** o   João dançou. (EP: *; BP: OK)
          the Maria that was with whom the João danced
          'It was with Maria that João danced.'

5.3 Word Order in Interrogative Sentences

It is often the case in natural languages that interrogative sentences display a word order pattern different from that of declaratives. In this section we examine the order of constituents in interrogative sentences in EP and BP,

---

[46] For discussion see e.g. Mioto and Figueiredo Silva 1995, Vercauteren 2015, and Martins and Lobo 2020.

focusing on the two main types of interrogatives: *yes/no* questions and *wh*-questions.⁴⁷

Yes/no questions typically inquire about the truth of a whole proposition, as illustrated in (5.93) below, and may be satisfied by an affirmative or negative answer, saying that the proposition is true or false.⁴⁸ The speaker who utters (5.93), for instance, asks her/his addressee if the proposition *a Maria comeu o bolo.* 'Maria ate the cake.' is true or false.

(5.93)   A   Maria   comeu   o   bolo?
            the   Maria   ate   the cake
            'Did Maria eat the cake?'

In turn, a *wh*-question typically requests information about a syntactic constituent so that the truth of the relevant proposition can be inspected. In uttering the sentence in (5.94) below, for instance, the speaker asks her/his addressee who is the person (or persons) P such that the proposition *P comeu o bolo.* 'P ate the cake.' is true.

(5.94)   Quem   comeu   o   bolo?
            who   ate   the cake.
            'Who ate the cake?'

In *wh*-questions, the constituent under question must contain an interrogative pronoun (*quem* 'who' or *que/o que* 'what'), an interrogative adverb (*quando* 'when', *onde* 'where', *como* 'how', *porque* (EP) / *por que* (BP) 'why',⁴⁹ or *quanto* 'how much'), an interrogative determiner (*que* 'what', *qual/quais* 'which.SG/which.PL', or *quantos/quantas* 'how.many-MASC-PL/how.many-FEM-PL'), or (in EP) the interrogative degree adverb *quão* 'how'.

Let us then consider different word orders conditioned by these two types of interrogatives.⁵⁰

---

⁴⁷ For discussion see e.g. Ambar 1992a, 2013, Duarte 1992, Lopes-Rossi 1993, Kato and Raposo 1996, Barbosa 2001, Duarte and Kato 2002, Kato and Mioto 2005, Mioto and Lobo 2016, and Dimitrova 2020.
⁴⁸ A detailed description of answers to *yes/no* questions is provided in Section 7.5.
⁴⁹ The difference between the interrogative adverbs *porque* in EP and *por que* in BP is only an orthographic convention.
⁵⁰ *Yes/no* questions and *wh*-questions may also carry an illocutionary force different from those described above and be employed in other contexts. For instance, the *yes/no* question in (i) below functions as an imperative and the *wh*-questions in (ii) respectively express an invitation and a positive response. Here we will set aside cases of questions with a different illocutionary force, unless they are associated with a special word order.

(i)   Você   pode   calar   a   boca?   (BP)
        you.SG   *can*   *shut*   *the mouth*
        'Can you(SG) shut up?

5.3.1 Word Order in yes/no Questions

EP and BP may distinguish interrogative *yes/no* questions from the corresponding unmarked declarative SVO sentences, exclusively through intonation. The two sentences in (5.95), for example, are identical but are interpreted differently, depending on their intonation: if the sentence is assigned a falling intonation (↓), it is interpreted as declarative (see (5.95a)); if assigned a rising intonation (↑), it is typically interpreted as a *yes/no* question (see (5.95b)).

(5.95) a. O   Paulo fala   inglês.↓
           the Paulo speaks English
           'Paulo speaks English.'
       b. O   Paulo fala   inglês?↑
           the Paulo speaks English
           'Does Paulo speak English?'

These two intonational patterns are combined in so-called tag questions, as illustrated in (5.96) below.[51] A tag question is comprised of a statement with falling intonation and an elliptical interrogative clause with rising intonation, which asks the addressee to confirm the veracity of the statement.

(5.96) a. Vocês   **pediram** bacalhau,↓ não **pediram**?↑
           you-PL   asked   cod   not asked
           'You(PL) have asked for cod, haven't you(PL)?'
       b. O   Pedro **tem** estudado bastante,↓ não **tem**?↑
           the Pedro has   studied   a.lot   not has
           'Pedro has studied a lot, hasn't he?"

The tag part involves the finite main or auxiliary verb of the previous statement (see (5.96a) and (5.96b), respectively), inverting its polarity. So, the tag part in the sentences in (5.96) is negative because the previous statement is an affirmative declarative sentence. When the declarative sentence is negative, the two varieties diverge. BP may simply drop the negation associated with the declarative verb in the tag part, as illustrated in (5.97a) below, whereas EP resorts to specific tag expressions, as illustrated in (5.97b–c), a possibility that is also available in BP for some of the forms. We will return to a detailed discussion of tag questions and their answers in Sections 7.4.2 and 7.5.

(ii)   A: – Por que você   não janta com a gente?   (BP)
             why   you.SG not dine with we
             'Why don't you(SG) have dinner with us?'
       B: – Por que não?   (BP)
             why   not
             'Why not?'

[51] For more detailed information on the prosodic distinction between declarative and *yes/no* interrogative sentences, see for e.g. Frota and Moraes 2016; for tag questions, see e.g. Martins 2016a and Section 7.4.2.

268 5 Word Order

(5.97) a. O Paulo não **fala** inglês, **fala**? (EP: *; BP: OK)
 the Paulo not speaks English speaks
 b. O Paulo não fala inglês, **não é**? (EP: OK; BP: OK)
 the Paulo not speaks English not is
 c. O Paulo não fala inglês, **pois** não? (EP: OK; BP: *)
 the Paulo not speaks English CONFIRM not
 'Paulo doesn't speak English, does he?'

    EP may resort to VS order (in addition to the unmarked SV order) in one special type of *yes/no* question, exemplified in (5.98) below, where the speaker is just wondering and does not expect the addressee to have the relevant information that would allow her/him to answer the question. These sentences obligatorily have the verb in the indicative future or conditional.[52]

(5.98) EP:

    a. **Terá** o avião chegado mais cedo?
 have-*INDIC.FUT* the airplane arrived more early
 'I wonder if the plane has arrived early.'
    b. **Faria** o presidente uma coisa dessas?
 do-*INDIC.COND* the president one thing of-these
 'Would the president do such a thing?'

    In this type of context, BP resorts to the frozen expression *será que* (lit. be-*INDIC.FUT that*), also available in EP, which enforces SV order, as shown in (5.99).

(5.99) Será que o presidente faria uma coisa
 be-*INDIC.FUT* that the president do-*INDIC.COND* one thing
 dessas? (EP/BP)
 of-these
 'Would the president do such a thing?'

    EP and BP may also optionally display postverbal subjects (with VXS order) in positively biased negative interrogatives that express evaluative comments, as illustrated in (5.100). In fact, VS imposes a stronger positive bias than SV. In other words, the VS sentences in (5.100a) and (5.100b) are interpreted as evaluative statements and the speaker does not necessarily expect a reply; in the SV sentences in (5.100a′) and (5.100b′), on the other hand, there is some expectation for a response, which may even be in a direction contrary to the bias.

(5.100) EP/BP:

    a. Não está um gigante o meu filho?
 not is a giant the my son

---

[52] See Ambar 1992a for discussion.

a'. O meu filho não está um gigante?
    the my son not is a giant
    'Hasn't my son grown into a giant?'
b. Não está horrível esta sopa?
    not is horrible this soup
b'. Esta sopa não está horrível?
    this soup not is horrible
    'Isn't this soup horrible?'

As in declaratives (see Sections 5.2.1.1 and 5.2.2.2), interrogatives may display VS order with unaccusative and some unergative verbs in both EP and BP, as respectively illustrated in (5.101a–b) below. In turn, VSO interrogatives with transitive verbs are interpreted with contrastive focus on the subject in EP, but are simply not allowed in BP, as exemplified in (5.101c).

(5.101) a. Já chegaram os convidados? (EP: OK; BP: OK)
           already arrived-3.PL the guests
           'Have the guests arrived yet?'
       b. Telefonou alguém? (EP: OK; BP: OK)
           called someone
           'Has anybody called?'
       c. Compra o João as bebidas para o piquenique? (EP: OK; BP: *)
           buys the João the drinks to the picnic
           'Is it João who will buy the drinks for the picnic?'

5.3.2 Word Order in Single Wh-Questions

EP and BP allow for their *wh*-phrases to remain *in situ* (i.e. in their unmarked surface positions)[53] or to move to a designated clause-initial position,[54] as respectively illustrated in (5.102) below.

---

[53] For discussion, see Ambar and Veloso 2001, Ambar 2003, Kato and Mioto 2005, Pires and Taylor 2007, Nunes and Santos 2009, Kato 2013, 2019, 2020a,b, Nunes 2013, 2014, 2018, 2021b, and Figueiredo Silva and Grolla 2016. There is no consensus in the literature about the actual position of surface *in-situ wh*-phrases. Kato (2013), for instance, proposes that echo questions (with rising intonation) are the only true *in-situ wh*-questions in BP; other putative *in-situ wh*-questions (with falling intonation) are taken to undergo short movement to a sentence-internal focus position. Ambar and Veloso (2001) and Ambar (2003), on the other hand, propose that putative *in-situ wh*-questions in EP actually undergo movement to a position in the high left periphery, followed by movement of the rest of the sentence across it. For arguments and details of these proposals, see Kato 2013, 2019, 2020a,b Ambar and Veloso 2001 and Ambar 2003.

[54] For different views on this designated clause-initial position and discussion, see e.g. Ambar 1992a, 2003, Mioto 1994, 2011, Kato and Raposo 1996, Lopes-Rossi 1993, Ambar and Veloso 2001, and Barbosa 2001.

(5.102) a. O João estudou **em que** escola?
the João studied in which school
b. **Em que** escola o João estudou? (BP)
in which school the João studied
b'. **Em que** escola estudou o João? (EP)
in which school studied the João
'In which school did João study?'

In many languages (English, for instance), the *in-situ* option in single *wh*-questions is generally limited to echo questions, that is, metalinguistic questions where the speaker does not hear part of what her/his interlocutor has said and asks for clarification. EP and BP are not restricted in this way, though. In addition to allowing an echo reading, a sentence such as (5.102a), for instance, can convey the same request for information as (5.102b)/ (5.102b'). Also unlike other languages (e.g. French), *in-situ wh*-phrases in EP and BP are not restricted to matrix clauses, either. Sentences such as (5.103a) and (5.103b), which have an *in-situ wh*-phrase in the embedded clause, are well formed in both varieties.

(5.103) a. A Maria acha que o João comprou **o quê**?
the Maria thinks that the João bought what
a'. **O que** é que a Maria acha que o João comprou?
what is that the Maria thinks that the João bought
'What does Maria think João bought?'
b. O Pedro disse que a Ana foi **onde** ?
the Pedro said that the Ana went where
b'. **Onde** é que o Pedro disse que a Ana foi?
where is that the Pedro said that the Ana went
'Where did Pedro say Ana went?'

The fact that both the *in-situ* and the movement possibilities are generally available does not mean that they are identical in meaning. Although the meaning differences may be rather subtle in most of the cases, by and large *in-situ wh*-questions indicate that speaker and hearer (strongly) share common ground, whereas movement *wh*-questions are somewhat neutral in this regard. Thus, in a context such as that in (5.104) below, Maria and her teacher do not share the same background knowledge regarding the poem, as it is being presented to the teacher as Maria asks the question. The movement *wh*-question in (5.104b) is compatible with this scenario, but not the *in-situ wh*-question in (5.104a) (The "*" in (5.104a) encodes its unacceptability given the context under consideration; see footnote 8 above). The most natural interpretation of (5.104a) is that the teacher is in a position to judge the poem at that moment, after having read it earlier, for instance.

(5.104) [*Context*: Maria has just finished writing a poem and hands it to her language teacher, to seek his opinion.]
    a.   *O senhor acha **o quê** deste poema?
        the mister thinks what of-this poem
    b.   **O que** é que o senhor acha deste poema?
        what is that the mister thinks of-this poem
        'What do you think about this poem, Sir?'

A clearer case illustrating the same point involves *wh*-expressions such as *que diabo* 'what the hell', which lexically encodes the information that the constituent inquired after is not part of a common ground. In both EP and BP, the movement option is obligatory with such expressions, as exemplified in (5.105).[55]

(5.105) a. *O João bebeu **que diabo**?
           the João drank which devil
      b. **Que diabo** é que o João bebeu?
           which devil is that the João drank
           'What the hell did João drink?'

Syntactic conditions may also license only one of the options. Embedded questions, for instance, require movement, as illustrated in (5.106) below. However, if the embedded question is headed by the interrogative complementizer *se* 'if', movement is precluded, as shown in (5.107b), and the *in-situ* option is only marginally allowed in BP, as shown in (5.107a), with the interpretation of the sentence being that of a matrix *wh*-question.[56]

(5.106) a. *A Maria não sabe o João comprou **que livro**.
           the Maria not knows the João bought which book
      b. A Maria não sabe **que livro** o João comprou.
           the Maria not knows which book the João bought
           'Maria doesn't know which book João bought.'

(5.107) a. ?A Maria não sabe se o João comprou **que livro**? (BP)
           the Maria not knows if the João bought which book
           'Which book doesn't Maria know if João bought (it)?'
      b. *A Maria não sabe **que livro** se o João comprou.
           the Maria not knows which book if the João bought
           'Maria doesn't know which book João bought.'

---

[55] Some Northeastern dialects of BP allow expressions such as *que diabo* 'what the hell' to remain *in situ* under a special intonation.
[56] For discussion see e.g. Mioto and Lobo 2016.

In turn, "syntactic islands" such as relative clauses in (5.108a,a′) or coordinate clauses in (5.108b,b′) block the movement option, leaving *in-situ wh*-phrases as the only possibility.

(5.108) a. O   João   entrevistou o   autor   que escreveu **que**   **livro**?
the João interviewed the author that wrote which book
a′. ***Que livro** é que o João entrevistou o autor que escreveu?
which book is that the João interviewed the author that wrote
'Which book is it that João interviewed the author who wrote it?'
b. A Maria vai despedir o João e contratar **quem**?
the Maria goes fire the João and hire whom
b′. ***Quem** é que a Maria vai despedir o João e contratar?
whom is that the Maria goes fire the João and hire
'Who is Maria going to hire after firing João?'

So far, we have examined cases where EP and BP behave similarly. It should nevertheless be pointed out that, even in the case of similarities, they display considerable quantitative differences. In particular, *in-situ wh*-questions are much more frequent in BP than EP.[57]

Let us now examine some differences between BP and EP regarding movement *wh*-questions (We return to movement *wh*-questions with clefting in Section 5.3.4). One of these differences has already been noted in Chapter 4. In EP, all pronouns but *a gente* 'we' can be null in the presence of a moved *wh*-constituent, whereas in BP there is a finer range of acceptability, depending on the particular null pronoun, as shown in (5.109).[58]

(5.109) a. [Quando Ø devemos viajar]? (Ø = *nós* 'we'→ EP: OK; BP: OK)
when should-1.PL travel
'When are we supposed to travel?'
b. [O que Ø viste]? (Ø = *tu* 'you(SG)$_{[+close]}$' → EP: OK)
what saw.2.SG
'What did you see?'
c. [Em que candidato Ø voto desta
in which candidate vote-1.SG of-his
vez]? (Ø = *eu* 'I' → EP: OK; BP: ??)
time
'Which candidate do I vote for this time?'
d. [Quando Ø viajaram]? (Ø = *vocês* 'you-PL' → EP: OK; BP: ??)
when traveled-3.PL
'When did you(PL) travel?'

---

[57] In a comparison of EP and BP corpora, Kato and Mioto (2005) report that the proportion of *in-situ wh*-questions is 1:8 (EP to BP).

[58] As in Chapter 4, the pattern of (un)acceptability of null subjects presented here is judged relative to the pattern of their overt counterparts.

e. [Que prova Ø fizeram hoje]? (Ø = *eles/elas* 'they' → EP: OK; BP: ??)
   which exam did-3.PL today
   'Which exam did they do today?'
f. [O que Ø quer fazer]? (Ø = *você* 'you(SG)'→ EP: OK; BP: *)
   what want.3.SG do
   'What do you(SG) want to do?'
g. [O que Ø fez desta vez]? (Ø = *ele* 'he' → EP: OK; BP: *)
   what did-3.SG of-this time
   'What did he do this time?'
h. [Quando Ø deve viajar]? (Ø = *a gente* 'we' → EP: *; BP: *)
   when should-3.SG travel
   'When are we supposed to travel?'

As discussed in Chapter 4, a null subject in Portuguese can result from pronominal ellipsis or topic drop. As topic drop is incompatible with a moved *wh*-question, the null subjects in (5.109) must result from pronominal ellipsis, which is regulated by the Prominent Feature Valuation Condition (see (4.21)). The different degrees of acceptability in (5.109) thus follow from whether or not the relevant pronouns are able to value the most prominent feature of the verbal agreement inflection Infl (see Chapter 4 for discussion and details). In particular, the diversified pattern of acceptability seen in (5.109) for BP is due not to the movement of the *wh*-constituent *per se*, but to the morphological feature specification of the elided pronoun (see Section 4.3.3.3). For instance, as *você* in BP does not have its person and number features morphologically valued, it cannot value the features of Infl and its ellipsis is precluded. Thus, a null instance of *você* co-occurring with a moved *wh*-phrase has become restricted to frozen expressions, as illustrated in (5.110), and is no longer productively used in BP (cf. (5.109f)).

(5.110) Como Ø tem passado? (Ø = *você* 'you(SG)' → EP: OK; BP: OK)
    how have passed
    'How have you(SG) been?'

The other salient difference between EP and BP with respect to movement *wh*-questions has to do with BP's independent restrictions on VS order. When the subject is an overt pronoun, for instance, VS is obligatory in EP, but generally banned in BP, as illustrated in (5.111).[59]

(5.111) a. O que eu devo fazer? (EP: *; BP: OK)
       what I should do

---

[59] For discussion see e.g. Ambar 1992a, Torres Morais 1993, Ribeiro 1995a,b, and Kato and Mioto 2005.

a'. O que devo eu fazer? (EP: OK; BP: *)
   what should I do
   'What should I do?'
b. Para onde você enviou os documentos? (EP: *; BP: OK)
   to where you.SG sent the documents
b'. Para onde enviou você os documentos? (EP: OK; BP: *)
   to where sent you.SG the documents
   'Where did you(SG) send the documents to?'
c. Que artigos ela leu? (EP: *; BP: OK)
   which articles she read
c'. Que artigos leu ela? (EP: OK; BP: *)
   which articles read she
   'Which articles did she read?'
d. Como nós encontramos a Ana? (EP: *; BP: OK)
   how we find the Ana
d'. Como encontramos nós a Ana? (EP: OK; BP: *)
   how find we the Ana
   'How do we find Ana?'
e. O que vocês querem? (EP: *; BP: OK)
   what you-PL want
e'. O que querem vocês? (EP: OK; BP: *)
   what want you-PL
   'What do you(PL) want?'

Interestingly, the VS order in this context is generally excluded in BP even with unaccusative and unergative verbs, as respectively exemplified in (5.112). In fact, only the copula verbs *ser* 'be' and *estar* 'be' allow VS order (in addition to SV) in BP, as shown in (5.113). The only exception involves the verb *ir* 'go' in the formulaic expression in (5.114).

(5.112) a. Quando eles chegam? (EP: *; BP: OK)
   when they arrive
a'. Quando chegam eles? (EP: OK; BP: *)
   when arrive they
   'When do they arrive?'
b. Onde ela dorme? (EP: *; BP: OK)
   where she sleeps
b'. Onde dorme ela? (EP: OK; BP: *)
   where sleeps she
   'Where does she sleep?'

(5.113) a. Onde ele está? (EP: *; BP: OK)
   where he is
a'. Onde está ele? (EP: OK; BP: ?)
   where is he
   'Where is he?'

          b. Quem você   é?   (EP: *; BP: ?)
             who   you.SG is
          b'. Quem é você?   (EP: OK; BP: OK)
              who is you.SG
              'Who are you(SG)?'

(5.114)   a. *Como você   vai?   (EP: *; BP: *)
              how   you.SG go
          b. Como vai você?   (EP: OK; BP: OK)
             how   go   you.SG
             'How are you(SG) doing?'

When the *wh*-element in a matrix *wh*-question is a bare interrogative pronoun or interrogative adverb (as opposed to a *wh*-determiner coupled with a noun), EP also enforces VS, as illustrated in (5.115) and (5.116) below. Again, in BP VS is (marginally) allowed only with unaccusative (see (5.116a')) and unergative verbs (see (5.116b')).

(5.115)   a. Quem as crianças convidaram para a festa?   (EP: *; BP: OK)
             whom the children invited   to the party
          a'. Quem convidaram as crianças para a festa?   (EP: OK; BP: *)
              whom invited   the children to the party
              'Who did the children invite to the party?'
          b. Onde o Pedro tinha deixado o pacote?   (EP: *; BP: OK)
             where the Pedro had   left   the package
          b'. Onde tinha o Pedro deixado o pacote?   (EP: OK; BP: *)
              where had the Pedro left   the package
              'Where had Pedro left the package?'
          c. Quando a Maria enviou a carta para a escola? (EP: *; BP: OK)
             when   the Maria sent   the letter to the school
          c'. Quando enviou a Maria a carta para a escola? (EP: OK; BP: *)
              when   sent   the Maria the letter to the school
              'When did Maria send the letter to the school?'

(5.116)   a. Como essa paixão nasceu?   (EP: *; BP: OK)
             how this passion was.born
          a'. Como nasceu   essa paixão?   (EP: OK; BP: OK)
              how was.born this passion
              'How was this passion born?'
          b. Como os dinossauros espirravam?   (EP: *; BP: OK)
             how the dinosaurs sneezed
          b'. Como espirravam os dinossauros?   (EP: OK; BP: ?)
              how sneezed   the dinosaurs
              'How did dinosaurs sneeze?'

EP may exceptionally allow SV order in the context above if some material intervenes between the bare interrogative pronoun or adverb and the subject, provided that the bare *wh*-element is not the interrogative pronoun *que* 'what', as shown in (5.117).[60]

(5.117) EP:
    a. Quem na tua opinião o João encontrou?
       whom in-the your opinion the João met
       'Who, in your opinion, has João met?'
    b. Onde na tua opinião o João poderá ter ido?
       where in-the your opinion the João may have gone
       'Where, in your opinion, might João have gone?'
    c. *Que na tua opinião o João encontrou?
       what in-the your opinion the João found
       'What, in your opinion, has João found?'

Two environments allow for both SV and VS orders in EP (although in each case the VS order sounds more neutral).[61] The first is illustrated in (5.118) below; the *wh*-constituent involves a *wh*-determiner and a noun and the subject is not pronominal. The second environment involves an embedded question, as illustrated in (5.119).

(5.119) a. Que amigos o João encontrou no cinema? (EP: OK; BP: OK)
       which friends the João met in-the cinema
    b. Que amigos encontrou o João no cinema? (EP: OK; BP: *)
       which friends met the João in-the cinema
       'Which friends did João meet at the movies?'

(5.119) a. Não sei quem os meninos viram na
       not know-1.SG whom the boys saw in-the
       praia. (EP: OK; BP: OK)
       beach
    b. Não sei quem viram os meninos na
       not know-1.SG whom saw the boys in-the
       praia. (EP: OK; BP: *)
       beach
       'I don't know who the boys saw on the beach.'

In both cases, SV is the only possibility available in BP, unless the relevant verbs are unaccusative or unergative, as respectively shown in (5.120) and (5.121).

(5.120) a. A que horas o avião chega? (EP: OK; BP: OK)
       at which hours the airplane arrives
    a'. A que horas chega o avião? (EP: OK; BP: OK)
       at which hours arrives the airplane
       'At what time does the airplane arrive?'

---

[60] For discussion, see Ambar 1992a and Ambar and Veloso 2001.
[61] For discussion, see Ambar 1992a, Lopes-Rossi 1993, Ambar, Kato, Mioto, and Veloso 2003, and Kato and Mioto 2005.

       b. Em que   fábrica o   João trabalhava? (EP: OK; BP: OK)
          in which factory the João worked
       b'. Em que fábrica trabalhava o   João? (EP: OK; BP: ?)
          in which factory worked   the João
          'In which factory did João use to work?'
(5.121) a. A   Maria perguntou onde o   Pedro nasceu. (EP: OK; BP: OK)
          the Maria asked   where the Pedro was.born
       a'. A   Maria perguntou onde nasceu   o   Pedro. (EP: OK; BP: OK)
          the Maria asked   where was.born the Pedro
          'Maria asked where Pedro was born.'
       b. O   professor não sabia onde os alunos
          the teacher   not knew where the students
          trabalhavam.   (EP: OK; BP: OK)
          worked
       b'. O   professor não sabia onde trabalhavam os
           the teacher   not knew where worked   the
           alunos.   (EP: OK; BP: ?)
           students
           'The teacher didn't know where the students worked.'

EP also (marginally) allows movement *wh*-questions with VXS order if the subject is not a pronoun, as illustrated in (5.122) and (5.123).[62] Unsurprisingly, BP allows this order only with unaccusatives, as seen in (5.123).[63]

(5.122) a. Onde pendurou os   quadros   o   João? (EP: ?; BP: *)
          where hung   the paintings the João
          'Where did João hang the paintings?'
       b. Quando comprou o   carro o   Pedro? (EP: ?; BP: *)
          when   bought the car   the Pedro
          'When did Pedro buy the car?'
(5.123) a. Quando   vai chegar ao   mercado essa nova
          when   goes arrive to- the market this new
          tecnologia?   (EP: OK; BP: OK)
          technology
          'When is this new technology going to reach the market?'
       b. Onde   está hoje o   império soviético? (EP: OK; BP: OK)
          where is   today the empire Soviet
          'Where is the Soviet empire today?'

Let us finally examine the contrast between the interrogative pronouns *que* 'what' and *o que* 'what' in both EP and BP.[64] As seen in (5.117c), repeated

---

[62] For discussion, see Ambar 1992a, Kato 1992, 2005, and Kato and Mioto 2005.
[63] For discussion see e.g. Kato 2000 and Kato and Mioto 2005.
[64] For discussion see e.g. Ambar 1992a and Menuzzi 2004.

below in (5.124a), *que* does not allow intervening material separating it from the verb, as opposed to *o que*, as shown in (5.124b). A similar contrast also shows up in embedded questions, where VS order is obligatory with *que* but optional with *o que*, as shown in (5.125).

(5.124) EP:
    a. ***Que** na tua opinião o João encontrou?
        what in-the your opinion the João found
    b. **O que** na tua opinião o João encontrou?
        what in-the your opinion the João found
        'What, in your opinion, has João found?'

(5.125) EP:
    a. Não sei {**o que** /*que} o João comprou.
        not know-1.SG what what the João bought
    b. Não sei {**o que** /**que**} comprou o João.
        not know-1.SG what what bought the João
        'I don't know what João bought.'

In BP, *que* also has a more limited distribution than *o que*. In particular, it cannot surface *in situ* in subject or object positions, but can appear as the complement of a preposition, as shown in (5.126a–c) below.[65] Moreover, it cannot occupy the designated clause-initial position unless it is the complement of a preposition, as shown by the contrast between (5.126d) and (5.126e).

(5.126) BP:
    a. {**O que** /*que} aconteceu?
        what what happened
        'What happened?'
    b. O João comeu {**o quê** /*quê}?
        the João ate what what
        'What did João eat?'
    c. Você precisa {**do quê** /**de quê**}?
        you need of-what of what
        'What do you(SG) need?'
    d. {**O que** /*que} o João comeu?
        what what the João ate
        'What did João eat?'
    e. {**Do que** /**de que**} você precisa?
        of-what of what you need
        'What do you(SG) need?'

Interestingly, the ungrammatical versions with *que* in (5.126a,b,d) may be rescued if *que* moves to the focus position of the reduced clefted construction with just the homophonous complementizer *que* (see (5.76)), as shown in

---

[65] An orthographic convention dictates that *que* and *o que* must be written with a circumflex accent (*quê* and *o quê*) when sitting in a stressed position.

(5.127) below (see Section 5.3.4 for further discussion). This restricted distribution of the interrogative pronoun *que* in both EP and BP suggests that it may be a weak form (see Section 2.2).⁶⁶

(5.127) BP:
    a. **Que** que aconteceu?
        what that happened
        'What happened?'
    b. **Que** que o João comeu?
        what that the João ate
        'What did João eat?'

5.3.3 Word Order in Multiple Wh-Questions

EP and BP allow for multiple *wh*-questions, that is, *wh*-questions involving more than one *wh*-constituent, as illustrated in (5.128a) below.⁶⁷ The answer to such multiple *wh*-questions typically involves a list of pairs such that each member of the pair corresponds to one *wh*-constituent in the question, as can be seen in (5.128b).

(5.128) a. A: – **Quem** comprou **o quê**?
           who bought what
           'Who bought what?'
    b. B: – **A Maria** comprou **um livro**, **o João** (comprou) **um caderno**
           the Maria bought a book the João bought a notebook
        e o **Pedro** (comprou) **uma caneta**.
        and the Pedro bought a pen.
        'Maria bought a book, João a notebook, and Pedro a pen.'

The availability of both *in-situ* and movement *wh*-questions seen in Section 5.3.2 extends to multiple *wh*-questions, as well. Thus, we find cases where all *wh*-phrases remain *in situ*, as in (5.129), and cases where one (and

---

⁶⁶ Recall that the weak pronouns *cê* 'you.SG' and *cês* 'you-PL' in BP, like the interrogative pronoun *que* in (5.126b)/(5.127b), cannot surface in object position, but may appear preceding the clefting complementizer *que*, as illustrated in (i) (see (2.9)).

(i)   BP:
     a. *O João convidou cê?
        the João invited you.SG
        'Did João invite you(SG)?'
     b. Cê que o João convidou?
        you.SG that the João invited
        'Was it really you(SG) that João invited?'

⁶⁷ See e.g. Nunes 2021a for discussion.

only one) of the *wh*-phrases moves to the designated clause-initial position, as in (5.130).

(5.129) a. A   Maria pôs **o quê onde?**
            the Maria put what where
            'Where did Maria put what?'
     b. O   mecânico consertou **o quê quando?**
            the mechanic fixed   what when
            'When did the mechanic fix what?'

(5.130) a. **Onde** a   Maria pôs **o quê?**   (BP)
            where the Maria put what
     a′. **Onde** pôs a   Maria **o quê?**   (EP)
            where put the Maria what
            'Where did Maria put what?'
     b. **Quando** o   mecânico consertou **o quê?** (BP)
            when   the mechanic fixed   what
     b′. **Quando** consertou o   mecânico **o quê?** (EP)
            when   fixed   the mechanic   what
            'When did the mechanic fix what?'

The movement version inherits all the restrictions seen in Section 5.2.2 with respect to single *wh*-questions. (5.130), for instance, displays SV order in BP, but VS order in EP. Likewise, if one of the *wh*-phrases in a multiple question is the subject, the answer may have VS order in EP, but not in BP, as illustrated in (5.131).[68]

(5.131) A: – **Quem** comprou **o quê?**
              who   bought   what
              'Who bought what?'
     B: – O   João   comprou o   peixe e   a
              the João   bought the fish and the
              Maria comprou o   arroz.   (EP: OK; BP: OK)
              Maria bought the rice
     B′: – Comprou o   João o   peixe e   comprou a   Maria
              bought the João the fish and bought the Maria
              o   arroz.   (EP: OK; BP: *)
              the rice
              'João bought the fish and Maria bought the rice.'

There are also some additional restrictions having to do with the relation between the *wh*-phrases involved. First, a multiple question may involve at most three *wh*-constituents, as illustrated in (5.132).

---

[68] For discussion, see Lobo and Martins 2017.

(5.132) a. **Quem** enviou **o quê a quem**? (EP)
who sent what to whom
'Who sent what to who?'
b. ***Quem** enviou **o quê a quem quando**? (EP)
who sent what to whom when
'*Who sent what to who when?'
c. **Quem** enviou **o quê para quem**? (BP)
who sent what to whom
'Who sent what to who?'
d. ***Quem** enviou **o quê para quem quando**? (BP)
who sent what to whom when
'*Who sent what to who when?'

Second, there can be at most one *wh*-adjunct per multiple question, as illustrated by the contrast between (5.133a), with an argument and an adjunct *wh*-phrase, and (5.133b), with two adjunct *wh*-phrases.

(5.133) a. O João comprou **o quê onde**?
the João bought what where
'Where did João buy what?'
b. *O João comprou o livro **onde quando**?
the João bought the book where when
'*Where did João buy the book when?'

Third, there is a hierarchy regarding the unique *wh*-phrase that can be fronted in a multiple *wh*-question. In the main, the subject has precedence over an adjunct or an object (see (5.134)); an adjunct has precedence over an object (see (5.135)); and there is no precedence of an object over another object (see (5.136)).[69]

(5.134) a. **Quem** viaja **quando**?
who travels when
a'. ***Quando quem** viaja? (BP)
when who travels
a''. ***Quando** viaja **quem**? (EP)
when travels who
'Who travels when?'
b. **Quem** estudou **o quê**?
who studied what
b'. ***O que quem** estudou? (BP)
what who studied
b''. ***O que** estudou **quem**? (EP)
what studied who
'Who studied what?'

---

[69] Within the Principles and Parameters Theory (see e.g. Chomksy 1981, Chomsky and Lasnik 1993), restrictions such as those illustrated in (5.132)–(5.135) are generally analyzed in terms of the Empty Category Principle (see e.g. Lasnik and Saito 1984).

(5.135) a. **Como** o João consertou **o quê**? (BP)
how the João fixed what
a′. ***O que** o João consertou **como**? (BP)
what the João fixed how
b. **Como** consertou o João **o quê**? (EP)
how fixed the João what
b′. ***O que** consertou o João **como**? (EP)
what fixed the João how
'How did João fix what?'

(5.136) a. **O que** o João enviou **para quem**? (BP)
what the João sent to whom
'What did João send to whom?'
a′. **Para quem** o João enviou **o quê**? (BP)
to whom the João sent what
'To whom did João send what?'
b. **O que** enviou o João **a quem**? (EP)
what sent the João to whom
'What did João send to whom?'
b′. **A quem** enviou o João **o quê**? (EP)
to whom sent the João what
'To whom did João send what?'

5.3.4 Word Order in Clefted Wh-Questions

Given that there is a close connection between *wh*-questions and focus (see Section 5.2.2.1) and that clefting syntactically encodes focus (see Section 5.2.2.3), the fact that *wh*-questions may be combined with clefting comes as no surprise. Let us then consider the major types of clefted *wh*-questions available in EP and BP.[70]

The patterns in (5.137) and (5.139) are both allowed in EP and BP, as respectively exemplified in (5.138) and (5.140).

(5.137) *wh*- **é que** [clause ...]

(5.138) a. Quem **é que** terminou a tarefa?
who is that finished the homework
'Who has finished their homework?'
b. Quando **é que** o João viaja?
when is that the João travels
'When will João travel?'

---

[70] For discussion, see Kato and Ribeiro 2006, 2009, Mioto and Lobo 2016, and Kato 2018, 2020a,b.

(5.139)   wh- **SER que** [clause ... V ...]
                         ⌜‾‾‾‾‾‾‾‾‾‾‾‾‾tense agreement‾‾‾‾‾‾‾‾‾‾‾‾‾⌝

(5.140) a. O que **foi** **que** o João disse?
           what was that the João said
           'What did João say?'
        b. Onde **era** mesmo **que** a Maria morava?
           where was really that the Maria lived
           'Where exactly did Maria live?'

In general, these structures inherit the order possibilities available in simple interrogative *wh*-questions. Thus, null subjects may be generally admitted in EP but not in BP, as illustrated in (5.141) below, and SV and VS orders are both generally available in EP (although the SV order is the normal option and the VS order may yield marginal results), whereas BP basically restricts VS to unaccusatives, as illustrated in (5.142) and (5.143).[71] Likewise, the VXS possibility is acceptable in EP, in variation with the VSX order, but banned in BP, as shown in (5.144).

(5.141) a. Onde **é** **que** Ø viu esta notícia?
           where is that saw this news
           (Ø = *você* 'you(SG)' → EP: OK; BP: *)
           'Where did you(SG) see this news?'
        b. Que pacotes **é** **que** Ø pôs na garagem?
           which packages is that put in-the garage
           (Ø = *ela* 'she' → EP: OK; BP: *)
           'Which packages did she put in the garage?
        c. Quando **é** **que** Ø voltaram das férias?
           when is that returned from-the vacations
           (Ø = *eles* 'they' → EP: OK; BP: ??)
           'When did they come back from their vacations?'

---

[71] For discussion see e.g. Duarte 1992, Lopes-Rossi 1993, Duarte and Kato 2002, Kato and Mioto 2005, 2016, Kato and Ribeiro 2009, and Kato 2019. See Kato 2019 for a discussion of an innovative cleft type of *wh*-questions in BP, with the copula in sentence initial position, as illustrated in (i).

(i) *BP child language* (Lessa de Oliveira 2003):
     É quem que tá tocano violão?
     is who that is playing guitar
     'Who is playing the guitar?'

d. O que é **que** Ø fizemos de
what is that did of
errado? (Ø = *nós* 'we' → EP: OK; BP: OK)
wrong
'What did we do wrong?'

(5.142) a. O que é **que** o Pedro comprou para o jantar? (EP: OK; BP: OK)
what is that the Pedro bought for the dinner
a′. O que é **que** comprou o Pedro para o jantar (EP: OK; BP: *)
what is that bought the Pedro for the dinner
'What did Pedro buy for dinner?'
b. Onde é **que** esse seu amigo encontrou um
where is that this your friend found a
carro roxo? (EP: OK; BP: OK)
car purple
b′. Onde é **que** encontrou esse seu amigo um
where is that found this your friend a
carro roxo? (EP: OK; BP: *)
car purple
'Where did this friend of yours find a purple car?'

(5.143) a. Como é **que** esse seu interesse por literatura
how is that this your interest for literature
surgiu? (EP: OK; BP: OK)
arose
a′. Como é **que** surgiu esse seu interesse por
how is that arose this your interest for
literatura? (EP: OK; BP: OK)
literature
'How did your interest in literature come about'?
b. Quando é **que** o seu filho mais novo
when is that the your son more new
nasceu? (EP: OK; BP: OK)
was.born
b′. Quando é **que** nasceu o seu filho mais
when is that was.born the your son more
novo? (EP: OK; BP: OK)
new
'When was your youngest child born?'

(5.144) a. O que é **que** propôs de novo esse autor? (EP: OK; BP: *)
what is that proposed of new this author
a′. O que é **que** propôs esse autor de novo? (EP: OK; BP: *)
what is that proposed this author of new
'What novelty has this author proposed?'
b. Onde é **que** expôs os quadros o João? (EP: OK; BP: *)
where is that exhibited the paintings the João

5.3 Word Order in Interrogative Sentences

b'. Onde **é que** expôs o João os quadros? (EP: OK; BP: *)
where is that exhibited the João the paintings
'Where did João exhibit the paintings?'

In BP, the most frequent type of clefted *wh*-questions (in spoken language) is that sketched in (5.145), with only the complementizer-like element *que*, as illustrated in (5.146).[72] This type of clefted question, which is inexistent in EP, is compatible with all *wh*-phrases and may occur both in matrix (see (5.146a–c)) and embedded clauses (see (5.146d,e)). It is blocked only in infinitival *wh*-questions, as shown in (5.147).

(5.145) *wh*- **que** [clause . . .]

(5.146) BP:
a. Quem **que** chegou atrasado?
   who that arrived late
   'Who arrived late?'
b. Por que **que** você fez isso?
   why that you.SG did this
   'Why did you(SG) do this?'
c. Que **que** você quer?
   what that you.SG want
   'What do you(SG) want?'
d. Ele perguntou quando **que** você vai viajar.
   he asked when that you.SG go travel
   'He asked when you(SG) are going to travel.'
e. A Maria não sabe quanto **que** isso custa.
   the Maria not knows how.much that this costs
   'Maria doesn't know how much this costs.'

(5.147) BP:
a. O que (***que***) fazer numa situação dessas?
   what that do-INF in-a situation of-these
   'What should one do in a situation like this?'
b. Eu queria saber onde (***que***) deixar as caixas.
   I wanted know where that leave the boxes
   'I wanted to know where I should leave the boxes.'

Multiple *wh*-questions with movement (see Section 5.3.3) may also be combined with clefting, as illustrated in (5.148).

---

[72] For discussion see e.g. Mioto and Figueiredo Silva 1995, Kato 2014, 2020a,b, and Figueiredo Siva and Grolla 2016.

(5.148) a. Quem é que fez o quê?   (EP: OK; BP: OK)
            who   is that did what
            'Who did what?'
         b. Quem foi que consertou o quê? (EP: OK; BP: OK)
            who   was that fixed   what
            'Who fixed what?'
         c. Quem que montou   o quê?   (EP: *; BP: OK)
            who   that assembled what
            'Who assembled what?'

Finally, we have seen in Section 5.2.2.3 that different patterns of clefting are not always mutually exclusive and the same holds for clefted *wh*-questions, as shown in (5.149a) in EP and BP and (5.149b) in BP.

(5.149) a. Quem é que foi que o João contratou? (EP: OK; BP: OK)
            whom is that was that the João hired
            'Who was it that João hired?'
         b. Que que é que foi que a Maria descobriu? (EP: *; BP: OK)
            what that is that was that the Maria discovered
            'What was it that Maria discovered?'

5.4 Word Order in Exclamative Sentences

In addition to their characteristic intonational contour, different types of exclamative sentences resort to specific word orders to convey their illocutionary force.[73] Take the exclamatives in (5.150) below, for example, which involve a root subjunctive clause licensed by negation.[74] This type of exclamative, which is available only in EP, requires VSX order regardless of verb type, thus being compatible with transitive (see (5.150a)), unergative (see (5.150b)), and unaccusative (see (5.150c)) verbs.

(5.150) EP:
         a. Vai   lá   depressa, não me **compre**   ele o livro errado!
            go.2.SG there quickly   not me buy-SUBJ he the book wrong
            'Catch him; I don't want him buying the wrong book!'
         b. O   chão está molhado! Vê lá   não **escorregue o João**
            the floor is   wet   see there not slip-SUBJ the João
            com os   pacotes escada abaixo!
            with the packages stair down
            'The floor is wet! João should take care not to slide down the stairs with the packages!'

---

[73] For discussion see e.g. Raposo 1995, 2000, Ambar 1999, 2002, 2016, Martins 2013c, Barbosa, Santos, and Veloso 2020, and Dimitrova 2020.
[74] For discussion see e.g. Ambar 1992a.

c. Cuidado, não me **caia**　　o　miúdo daí!
   watch-out not me fall-SUBJ the kid from-there
   'Be careful, I don't want the kid falling down!'

Another case of VS exclamatives exclusive to EP is illustrated in (5.151) below.[75] It involves a "concessive" construction built from two indicative clauses coordinated by *e* 'and', with VS order in the first conjunct. This type of exclamative conveys the speaker's disapproval of (or disappointment with) an unpredicted event or situation described in the second conjunct with respect to the situation described by the first conjunct. The VS order in the first conjunct introduces a counter-expectation, anticipating a contrast between the two conjuncts. If there were SV order in the first conjunct of the sentences in (5.151), the implicit evaluative/emotive layer would disappear and we would have the mere description of a state of affairs.[76] Like the subjunctive exclamatives exemplified in (5.150), coordinate nondegree exclamatives employ VSX order in the first conjunct, regardless of verb type. Thus, we may find coordinate exclamatives with transitive (see (5.151a–c)), unergative (see (5.151d)), and unaccusative (see (5.151e)) verbs.

(5.151) EP:
   a. **Convidei eu** a　Maria para jantar e　ela não apareceu.
      invited I the Maria for dinner and she not appeared
      'I invited Maria for dinner but she didn't come.'
   b. **Ama o João** a　Maria tanto　e　ela nem　olha para ele.
      loves the João the Maria so.much and she not.even looks to him
      'João loves Maria so much but she won't even look at him.'
   c. **Ouvia　eu** as　notícias　tão　sossegada　e　tu
      listened I the news so quiet and you.SG
      foste　ligar　o　aspirador!
      went turn.on the vacuum.cleaner
      'I was listening quietly to the news and you(SG) went and turned on the vacuum cleaner!'
   d. **Tossiu　o　bebé** toda　a　noite　e
      coughed the baby all the night and
      não　podemos　levá-lo　ao　médico.
      not can-1.PL take-him to-the doctor
      'The baby coughed all night, but we can't take him to the doctor.'

---

[75] For further details and discussion, see e.g. Martins 2013c.
[76] With SV order in the first conjunct, the coordinating link would accordingly be more naturally expressed by the adversative conjunction *mas* 'but', instead of the additive conjunction *e* 'and'.

e. **Cheguei**   eu   na   hora   combinada e   já
   arrived-1.SG I   in-the hour   agreed   and   already
   tinham todos saído.
   had   all   left.
   'I arrived at the time at the agreed time, but everybody had already left.'

Let us now consider quantifying exclamatives. This type of exclamatives expresses the speaker's emotional state (surprise, amazement, disapproval, etc.) regarding some quantity or the degree to which a given property holds in relation to some implicit expected scale. When they involve *wh*-pronouns, quantifying exclamative sentences require fronting of the *wh*-phrase in both EP and BP, as illustrated in (5.152).

(5.152) EP/BP:
    a. **Quantos presentes** a Maria ganhou!
       how.many gifts   the Maria got
    a'. *A Maria ganhou **quantos presentes**!
       the Maria got   how.many gifts
       'Maria received so many gifts!'
    b. **Com que rapidez** as crianças saíram da sala de aula!
       with what speed the children left of-the room of class
    b'. *As crianças saíram da sala de aula **com que rapidez**!
       with what speed the children left of-the room of class
       'How quick the kids were in getting out of the classroom!'
    c. **Como** os meninos estudaram para a prova!
       how the boys   studied   for the exam
    c'. *Os meninos estudaram para a prova **como**!
       the boys   studied   for a exam how
       'How hard the boys studied for the exam!'

The unmarked order for this this type of exclamative with transitive verbs is SV in both EP and BP, as shown in (5.153) below. Quantifying exclamatives with *wh*-pronouns thus noticeably differ from *wh*-questions in EP (see Section 5.3.2) in not displaying obligatory subject–verb inversion.

(5.153) EP/BP:
    a. Quantos livros o João leu!
       how.many books the João read
    a'. ?*Quantos livros leu o João!
       how.many books read the João
       'João read so many books!'
    b. O que um pai faz pelo filho!
       what a father does by-the son
    b'. ?*O que faz um pai pelo filho!
       what does a father by-the son
       'A parent does so much for his/her child!'

5.4 Word Order in Exclamative Sentences

As for unergative and unaccusative verbs, both SV and VS orders are allowed in EP, whereas BP displays the usual marginal acceptability with VS order:

(5.154) a. Que alto as crianças gritaram!   (EP: OK; BP: OK)
           what high the children screamed
      a'. Que alto gritaram as crianças!   (EP: OK; BP: ?)
           what high screamed the children
           'How loudly the children screamed!'
       b. Que cedo a Maria chegou hoje!   (EP: OK; BP: OK)
           what early the Maria arrived today
      b'. Que cedo chegou a Maria hoje!   (EP: OK; BP: ?)
           what early arrived the Maria today
           'How early Maria arrived today!'

A fact about quantifying exclamatives with *wh*-pronouns worth noting is that they allow expletive negation in both EP and BP, as illustrated in (5.155) below. Expletive negation is so called because it does not negate the assertion of its clause, as the translations of the sentences of (5.155) show, but rather adds emphasis to what is being expressed (see Section 7.3.4 for discussion).[77] Interestingly, expletive negation may interact with word order and license the otherwise illicit VS order with transitive verbs in both EP and BP (compare (5.156) with (5.153)).

(5.155) EP/BP:
      a. Quantos livros o João **não** leu!
         how.many books the João not read
         'João read so many books!'
      b. O que um pai **não** faz pelo filho!
         what a father not does by-the son
         'A parent does so much for his/her child!'

(5.156) EP/BP:
      a. Quantos livros **não** leu o João!
         how.many books not read the João
         'João read so many books!'
      b. O que **não** faz um pai pelo filho!
         what not does a father by-the son
         'A parent does so much for his/her child!'

---

[77] For discussion see e.g. Matos 2003. Quantifying exclamatives are also compatible with true negation. Thus sentence (5.155a), for example, is ambiguous between a positive and a negative interpretation: 'João read so many books!' or 'João read so few books!' See e.g. González Rodríguez 2008 for discussion.

In this type of exclamative, the *wh*-phrase may also be followed by the complementizer-like element *que* in both EP and BP, as illustrated in (5.157) below, unless we have a bare *wh*-element, as shown in (5.158).[78] In this case, EP uniformly excludes *que*, whereas BP displays this restriction only with *como* 'how', as shown in (5.158d).[79]

(5.157)   EP/BP:
    a. Quantos   presentes **que**   a   Maria ganhou!
       how.many gifts   that the Maria got
       'Maria received so many gifts!'
    b. Com que   rapidez **que**   as   crianças saíram da   sala de aula!
       with what   speed   that the children left   of-the room of class
       'How quick the kids were in getting out of the classroom!'
    c. Que problema **que**   ele arranjou!
       what problem   that he got
       'What a problem he got!'
    d. Que medo **que** me deu!
       what scare that me gave
       'What a scare I got!'

(5.158)   a. O que **que** um pai   faz   pelo   filho!   (EP: *; BP: OK)
       what   that a   father does by-the son
       'A parent does so much for his/her child!'
    b. Quanto **que** eu me   diverti naquele verão! (EP: *; BP: OK)
       how.much that I myself had.fun in-that   summer
       'How much fun I had in that summer!'
    c. Onde **que** eu fui   me   meter!   (EP: *; BP: OK)
       where that I   went myself put
       'I ended up putting myself in a very bad situation.'

---

[78] See e.g. Barbosa, Santos, and Veloso 2020 for discussion.

[79] (5.158a) sounds more natural in BP if it is associated with expletive negation, as in (ia) below. BP allows an exclamative idiomatic expression with *onde* 'where' and the idiomatic reading is maintained in the presence of *que*, as shown in (ib). If assigned a rising intonation, the sentence in (5.158d) may be interpreted in BP as a regular manner question (see Section 5.3.4) or as expressing doubt regarding the veracity of the statement that the boys studied for the exam.

(i)   BP:
    a. O que **que** um pai   **não** faz   pelo   filho!
       what   that a   father not does by-the son
       'A parent does so much for his/her child!'
    b. Onde **(que)** eu fui   amarrar o   meu   burro!
       where that I   went tie   the my   donkey
       'What a bad situation I put myself in!'

d. *Como **que** os meninos estudaram para a prova! (EP: *; BP: *)
   how that the boys studied for the exam
   'How hard the boys studied for the exam!'

Quantifying exclamatives may also involve a fronted bare quantifier or a quantifier phrase, as illustrated in (5.159) and (5.160) below.[80] EP permits both types, and SV and VS orders are allowed regardless of the presence of expletive negation. By contrast, BP does not allow the bare quantifier possibility and the quantifier phrase alternative does not allow expletive negation and is restricted to SV order.[81]

(5.159) a. Muito ele lê!   (EP: OK; BP: *)
             much he reads
         a'. Muito lê ele!   (EP: OK; BP: *)
             much reads he
         b. Muito ele **não** lê!   (EP: OK; BP: *)
             much he not   reads
         b'. Muito **não** lê ele! (EP: OK; BP: *)
             much not   reads he
             'He reads such a lot!'

(5.160) EP:
         a. Muita cerveja o   João bebeu ontem!   (EP: OK; BP: OK)
             much beer   the João drank yesterday
         a'. Muita cerveja bebeu o   João ontem!   (EP: OK; BP: *)
             much beer   drank the João yesterday
         b. Muita cerveja o   João não bebeu ontem!   (EP: OK; BP: *)
             much beer   the João not drank yesterday
         b'. Muita cerveja não bebeu o   João ontem!   (EP: OK; BP: *)
             much beer   not drank the João yesterday
             'João drank so much beer yesterday!'

Another type of exclamative has its evaluative overtone anchored on a fronted evaluative adjective, as illustrated in (5.161) below with the adjective

---

[80] For discussion see e.g. Raposo 1995, 2000, Ambar 1999, and Costa and Martins 2011.
[81] "*" in (5.159a,a'b) and (5.160b,b') for BP is meant to annotate inadequacy as a quantifying exclamative (see footnote 8 above). These sentences can be assigned a sound interpretation in BP if the fronted phrases are interpreted as corrective contrastive focus, for instance.

grande 'big'.⁸² These qualifying exclamatives allow both SV and VS orders with transitive verbs in EP, but only SV in BP.⁸³

(5.161) a. Grande sarilho tu me arranjaste! (EP)
           big   trouble you me brought-2.SG
      a'. Grande sarilho me arranjaste tu! (EP)
           big   trouble me brought-2.SG you.SG
           'You(SG) got me into such a lot of trouble!'
      b. Uma grande encrenca o senhor me arrumou! (BP)
           a   big   problem the mister me got
      b'. *Uma grande encrenca me arrumou o senhor! (BP)
           a   big   problem me got   the mister
           'You(SG) brought me a real big problem!'

Qualifying exclamatives differ from quantifying exclamatives (see footnote 77 above) in that they are not compatible with true negation and typically exclude expletive negation, although in EP sentences like (5.162a) below are marginally acceptable. In BP, on the other hand, expletive negation is uniformly ruled out in qualifying exclamatives. The BP sentence with negation in (5.162b), for example, can be assigned the contrastive focus interpretation indicated in the translation

---

⁸² See e.g. Ambar 1999 for discussion.
⁸³ At first sight, exclamative constructions like those in (i) below, which allow both SV and VS orders (see Naro and Votre 1986, 1999, and Tarallo and Kato 1989), constitute counterexamples to the general pattern found in exclamatives with transitive verbs in BP (see (5.153a'), (5.153b'), and (5.161b')). However, notice that the direct object of *faturar* 'earn' and *custar* 'cost' in (i) expresses a quantity, behaving more like the measure of the event encoded by the verb. Furthermore, these verbs do not license passives, as shown in (ii). Thus, the conclusion is that these verbs are actually unaccusative and the SV/VS alternation in (i) just reflects the general pattern of unaccusatives in BP (see Section 5.2.1.1)

(i)   BP:
      a. Uma ninharia a nossa loja faturou ontem!
         a   pittance the our store earned yesterday
      a'. Uma ninharia faturou a nossa loja ontem!
         a   pittance earned the our store yesterday
         'Our store earned a pittance yesterday!'
      b. 100 mil esse carro custava!
         100 thousand this car cost
      b'. 100 mil custava esse carro!
         100 thousand cost this car
         'This car used to cost 100 grand!'

(ii)   a. *Uma ninharia foi faturada pela nossa loja ontem.
         a   pittance was earned by-the our store yesterday
         'Our store earned a pittance yesterday!'
      b. *100 mil foram custados por esse carro.
         100 thousand were cost by this car
         'This car cost 100 grand.'

(see footnote 8 above), but cannot be interpreted as a qualifying exclamative (be it affirmative or negative).

(5.162) a. ?Grande sarilho **não** me arranjaste tu! (EP)
    big trouble not me brought-2.SG you.SG
    'You(SG) got me into such a lot of trouble!'
  b. *Uma grande encrenca o senhor **não** me arrumou! (BP)
    a big problem the mister not me got
    'You(SG) did not bring me a real big problem (as you(SG) were supposed to).'

Given this difference between quantifying and qualifying exclamatives with respect to negation, a curious additional contrast arises with respect to exclamatives of the type illustrated in (5.163) below, which are anchored on a relative clause and display SV order. In EP, (5.163) is ambiguous: it can be interpreted as a quantifying exclamative expressing amazement at the number of books João read or as a qualifying exclamative expressing amazement at the kinds of books João read. In BP, on the other hand, only the qualifying reading is available.[84] If *não* is added to (5.163), as in (5.164), the sentence can have only, or strongly favors, the quantifying meaning in EP and can no longer be interpreted as a qualifying exclamative in BP. In other words, (5.164) can be used in BP as an answer to the question of which books Maria is organizing, for instance, but not to express disapproval about the content of the books João is reading.

(5.163) Os livros que o João leu!
    the books that the João read
    EP: 'João has read so many books!' or 'The type of books that João has read!'
    BP: 'The type of books that João has read!'

(5.164) Os livros que o João **não** leu!
    the books that the João not read
    EP: 'João has/hasn't read so many books!'
    BP: 'The books that João didn't read!'

---

[84] Although the qualifying interpretation in (5.163) is available with the definite determiner in BP, the most natural way to express this reading in BP is with the quantifier *cada* 'each':

(i) Cada livro que o João leu! (BP)
    each book that the João read
    'The type of books that João has read!'

5.5 Word Order in Nonfinite Domains

The general direction of the contrast between EP and BP seen with respect to declarative, interrogative, and exclamative sentences (see Sections 5.2, 5.3, and 5.4), with BP being less prone to admitting orders other than the unmarked, is also detected within nonfinite domains. Let us briefly examine some examples, starting with inflected infinitives.[85]

When the inflected infinitive is the complement of epistemic or declarative predicates, VS order is obligatory in EP, as shown in (5.165) below, unless the subject is focalized, as shown in (5.166). As with declaratives (see Section 5.2.2.1), VOS is also possible in EP if the subject is the information focus, as shown in (5.167). BP, on the other hand, also (marginally) permits SV in (5.165) in addition to the VS alternative and disallows VOS in (5.167).

(5.165) a. O   professor acredita os   alunos   **terem**   feito
            *the teacher   believes the students have-**INF-3.PL** done*
            um bom   trabalho.   (EP: *; BP: ?)
            a   good   job
        a′. O   professor acredita **terem**   os   alunos feito
            *the teacher   believes have-**INF-3.PL** the students done*
            um bom   trabalho.   (EP: OK; BP: OK)
            a   good   job
            'The teacher believes the students to have done a good job.'
        b. O   governo   declarou as   propostas **estarem**   mal
            *the government declared the proposals be-**INF-3.PL** badly*
            elaboradas.   (EP: *; BP: ?)
            elaborated
        b′. O   governo   declarou **estarem**   as propostas mal
            *the government declared be-**INF-3.PL** the proposals badly*
            elaboradas.   (EP: OK; BP: OK)
            elaborated
            'The government stated that the proposals were poorly formulated.'

(5.166) O diretor afirmou só   esses três   projetos **serem**
        *the director affirmed only these three project be-**INF-3.PL***
        viáveis.   (EP: OK; BP: OK)
        viable
        'The director said that only these three projects were viable.'

---

[85] For discussion see e.g. Raposo 1987a, 1994, Ambar 1992a, 1994, 1998, 2000, Barbosa 2002, Duarte, Gonçalves, and Miguel 2005, Ambar, Negrão, Veloso, and Graça 2007, Barbosa and Raposo 2013, and Duarte, Santos, and Gonçalves 2016.

(5.167) O   João   acredita **terem**   feito   um   mau   negócio
         the João   believes have-**INF-3.PL**   done   a   bad   business
         os   vizinhos.   (EP: OK; BP: *)
         the neighbors
         'João thinks that the neighbors made a bad deal.'

In turn, when the inflected infinitival is the complement of a factive predicate, EP and BP pattern alike, allowing both SV and VS orders, as shown in (5.168).

(5.168) a. Os   alunos   lamentaram as   notas   **terem**
           the   students   regretted   the   grades have-**INF-3.PL**
           sido baixas.   (EP: OK; BP: OK)
           been low
        b. Os   alunos   lamentaram **terem**   as   notas
           the   students   regretted   have-**INF-3.PL** the   grades
           sido baixas.   (EP: OK; BP: OK)
           been low
        'The students regretted that their grades were low.'

In agreementless case-marking gerunds (see Section 4.3.4.2), VS is obligatory in EP, as shown in (5.169)–(5.171), unless the gerund clause is introduced by the preposition *em* 'in', as shown in (5.172a,a′). Even in this case, VS may be possible with unaccusatives, as shown in (5.172b,b′). In BP, on the other hand, the construction with *em* is no longer available, but the SV order is pervasive. The VS order is only (marginally) allowed in cases involving unaccusatives (see (5.170)) or auxiliaries (see (5.171)).[86]

(5.169) a. Eu **comendo** esta comida toda, vou   ficar doente. (EP: *; BP: OK)
            I   eating   this food   all   go.1.SG stay   sick
        a′. **Comendo** eu esta comida toda, vou   ficar
            eating   I   this food   all   go.1.SG stay
            doente.   (EP: OK; BP: *)
            sick
        'If I eat all of this food, I'll get sick.'
        b. Eles   **fazendo** o que foi   pedido, os
            they.MASC   doing   what   was   asked   the
            problemas   vão   terminar.   (EP: *; BP: OK)
            problems   go   finish
        b′. **Fazendo** eles   o que foi   pedido, os
            doing   they.MASC   what   was   asked   the
            problemas   vão   terminar.   (EP: OK; BP: *)
            problems   go   finish
        'If they do what was asked, their problems will end.'

---

[86] For discussion see e.g. Britto 1994, Lobo 2003, and Fiéis and Lobo 2010.

(5.170) a. Eu **chegando** durante o dia, a reunião continua
　　　　 I   arriving during the day the meeting continues
　　　　 marcada.　　　　　　　　　　　　　　　　(EP: *; BP: OK)
　　　　 marked
　　 a'. **Chegando** eu durante o dia, a reunião continua
　　　　 arriving   I during the day the meeting continues
　　　　 marcada.　　　　　　　　　　　　　　　　(EP: OK; BP: ?)
　　　　 marked
　　　　 'If I arrive during the day, the meeting will remain on schedule.'
　　 b. Os juros **caindo,** a economia vai sair da
　　　　 the interests falling the economy goes leave of-the
　　　　 recessão.　　　　　　　　　　　　　　　(EP: *; BP: OK)
　　　　 recession
　　 b'. **Caindo** os juros, a economia vai sair da
　　　　 falling the interests, the economy goes leave of-the
　　　　 recessão.　　　　　　　　　　　　　　　(EP: OK; BP: OK)
　　　　 recession
　　　　 'If the interest rate falls, the economy will move away out of recession.'

(5.171) a. O João **tendo** saído da reunião, nós não
　　　　 the João having left from-the meeting we not
　　　　 conseguimos chegar a uma conclusão.　(EP: *; BP: OK)
　　　　 managed-1.PL arrive to a conclusion
　　 a'. **Tendo** o João saído da reunião, nós não
　　　　 having the João left from-the meeting we not
　　　　 conseguimos chegar a uma conclusão.　(EP: OK; BP: OK)
　　　　 managed-1.PL arrive to a conclusion
　　　　 'As João had left the meeting, we didn't manage to reach
　　　　 a conclusion.'
　　 b. A reunião **tendo** acabado, a decisão foi divulgada
　　　　 the meeting having finished the decision was made.public
　　　　 imediatamente.　　　　　　　　　　　　(EP: *; BP: OK)
　　　　 immediately
　　 b'. **Tendo** a reunião acabado, a decisão foi divulgada
　　　　 having the meeting finished the decision was made.public
　　　　 imediatamente.　　　　　　　　　　　　(EP: OK; BP: OK)
　　　　 immediately
　　　　 'As the meeting had finished, the decision was published immediately.'

(5.172) EP:
　　 a. Em eu **terminando** o que estou a fazer, vamos sair.
　　　　 in I finishing what am to do go-1.PL leave
　　 a'. *Em **terminando** eu o que estou a fazer, vamos sair.
　　　　 in finishing I what am to do go-1.PL leave
　　　　 'When I finish what I'm doing, we'll go out.'
　　 b. Em a primavera **chegando**, começo a preparar uma viagem.
　　　　 in the spring arriving start-1.SG to prepare a trip

b'. Em **chegando** a primavera, começo a preparar uma viagem.
    in arriving the spring start-1.SG to prepare a trip
    'When spring comes, I'll start preparing for a trip.'

With inflected gerunds in dialectal EP (see Sections 3.3.2.2.3 and 4.3.4.1), SV and VS are both allowed, as illustrated in (5.173).[87]

(5.173) %EP:
  a. Eles **tendem**   as coisas em casa, fazem a toda a hora.
     they having-GER-3.PL the things at home do-3.PL at every the hour
     'When they have everything they need at home, they can do it anytime they want.'
                                                                  (CORDIAL-SIN, AAL36)
  b. **Vindem**   as águas novas, aparecem uns carochinhos.
     come-GER-3.PL the waters new   appear   some little.beetles
     'When it starts raining, those little beetles appear.'
                                                                  (CORDIAL-SIN, LVR33)

Finally, as far as participial clauses are concerned, EP and BP surprisingly display the same behavior.[88] VS order is enforced if the participial clause is bare, as shown in (5.174) below. If the participial clause is introduced by some connective, the three possible patterns obtain, depending on the connective. For instance, we may have obligatory SV order with *com* 'with', as shown in (5.175a,a'), obligatory VS order with *quando* 'when', as in (5.175b,b'), or both orders with *antes de* 'before', as in (5.175c,c').

(5.174) a. *As tarefas   **concluídas**,   saímos   para
            the tasks   conclude-PPLE-FEM-PL left-1PL to
            comemorar.   (EP: *; BP: *)
            celebrate
         b. **Concluídas**   as tarefas, saímos   para
            conclude-PPLE-FEM-PL the tasks   left-1PL to
            comemorar.   (EP: OK; BP: OK)
            celebrate
            'After the tasks were done, we went out to celebrate.'

(5.175) a. Com as   tarefas   **concluídas**,   saímos
            with the   tasks   conclude-PPLE-FEM-PL left-1PL
            para comemorar.   (EP: OK; BP: OK)
            to celebrate

---

[87] For discussion see e.g. Lobo 2001, 2003 and Ribeiro 2002.
[88] For discussion see e.g. Ambar 1992a, 2000 and Santos 1999.

a'. *Com **concluídas** as tarefas,
with conclude-PPLE-FEM-PL the tasks
saímos para comemorar. (EP: *; BP: *)
left-1PL to celebrate
'After the tasks were done, we went out to celebrate.'

b. *Quando as tarefas **concluídas**,
when the tasks conclude-PPLE-FEM-PL
vamos sair para comemorar. (EP: *; BP: *)
go-1PL leave to celebrate

b'. Quando **concluídas** as tarefas, vamos
when conclude-PPLE-FEM-PL the tasks go-1PL
sair para comemorar. (EP: OK; BP: OK)
leave to celebrate
'When the tasks are done, we'll go out to celebrate.'

c. Antes das tarefas **concluídas**,
before of-the tasks conclude-PPLE-FEM-PL
não vamos sair. (EP: OK; BP: OK)
not go-1PL leave

c'. Antes de **concluídas** as tarefas,
before of conclude-PPLE-FEM-PL the tasks
não vamos sair. (EP: OK; BP: OK)
not go-1PL leave
'We won't leave before the tasks are done.'

Interestingly, if the participial clause is introduced by a prepositional periphrasis ending with *de* 'of', contraction between *de* and the adjacent determiner of the subject is obligatory, as seen in (5.175c). In this regard, participial clauses differ from inflected infinitivals, where contraction is optional, as illustrated by the contrast between (5.176) and (5.177).[89] In EP the contraction option, though common, is considered nonstandard.

(5.176) a. *Depois **de as** tarefas
after of the tasks
terminadas, fomos almoçar. (EP: *; BP: *)
finish-PPLE-FEM-PL went-1PL have.lunch

b. Depois **das** tarefas terminadas,
after of-the tasks finish-PPLE-FEM-PL
fomos almoçar. (EP: OK; BP: OK)
went-1PL have.lunch
'After the tasks were finished, we went for lunch.'

---

[89] For an analysis of this contrast in terms of the structural size of the clause being introduced by the prepositional periphrasis, see Ximenes 2002, Ximenes and Nunes 2004, and Nunes and Ximenes 2009.

(5.177) a. Depois **de** o João ter terminado
 after *of* *the João have finish-PPLE*
 as tarefas, fomos almoçar. (EP: OK; BP: OK)
 the tasks went-1PL have.lunch
 b. Depois **do** João ter terminado as
 after *of-the João have finish-PPLE the*
 tarefas, fomos almoçar. (EP: %; BP: OK)
 tasks went-1PL have.lunch
 'After João finished his tasks, we went for lunch.'

5.6 Clitic Placement

We saw in Section 2.2 that clitics are unstressed pronominal elements that have special positioning requirements. Following traditional terminology, we say that we have *proclisis* when the clitic precedes its verbal host and *enclisis* when the clitic follows it. In this section, we examine clitic placement in EP and BP, discussing some of the intriguing properties of each variety.[90] Before we move to the discussion proper, a couple of remarks are in order.

EP has distinct proclisis and enclisis configurations, whereas BP essentially has a uniform proclitic system. Enclisis in BP is more associated with written language and schooling and, as such, it is to be generally found in formal texts such as newspaper editorials and academic articles or in literary texts.[91] Following the methodology presented in Chapter 1, we put such prescriptivist cases aside and focus on cases that reflect native speakers' intuitions that are arguably the reflex of a regular process of language acquisition and do not result from schooling. An exception will be made with respect to third person accusative clitics *o(s)/a(s)*, though. As mentioned in Section 2.4.3, in BP these clitics are acquired through schooling and are viewed as sociolinguistic markers of a high degree of education.[92] Interestingly, the conditions

---

[90] For discussion see e.g. Cyrino 1993, Pagotto 1993, Martins 1994a,b, 2000a, 2011, 2013b, 2021a, Uriagereka 1995b, Ribeiro 1995a,b, Abaurre and Galves 1996, Barbosa 2000, Duarte and Matos 2000, Raposo 1994, 1995, 2000, Galves 2001, Duarte 2003b, Galves, Ribeiro, and Torres Morais 2005, Magro 2007, and Luís and Kaiser 2016.
[91] For discussion see e.g. Pagotto 1993, Abaurre and Galves 1996, Galves 2001, Carneiro 2005, Galves, Ribeiro, and Torres Morais 2005, Kato 2005, 2017, and Carneiro and Galves 2010.
[92] For discussion see e.g. Omena 1978, Tarallo 1983, Duarte 1986, 1989, Corrêa 1991, Kato 1993b, Nunes 1993, 2015a, 2019a, Cyrino 1997, Galves 2001 and Kato, Cyrino, and Corrêa 2009.

regulating the placement of these clitics differ from the conditions governing the placement of other clitics in BP or of clitics in general in EP. It will thus be illustrative to discuss the placement of these clitics, as well.

For presentation purposes, we will discuss EP and BP separately, contrasting proclisis and enclisis possibilities in EP and the two groups of clitics in BP.

5.6.1 Clitic Placement in European Portuguese

EP displays a very intricate pattern of clitic placement.[93] By and large, enclisis is the default possibility, whereas proclisis is triggered by a very diversified set of factors. Let us look at some of them.

The sentences in (5.178) below illustrate the fact that preverbal negative elements trigger proclisis in EP. Notice that (5.178a–c) involve finite clauses and (5.178d–e) nonfinite clauses – an inflected infinitival in (5.178d) and a gerund clause in (5.178e). This shows that the distinction [±finite], which is a key factor in determining clitic placement in other Romance languages such as Spanish, Catalan, and Italian, is not operative in EP clitic placement.

(5.178) EP:
    a. Ele <u>não</u> {**me** agradeceu /*agradeceu-**me**}.
        he   not   me   thanked   thanked-me
        'He didn't thank me.'
    b. <u>Ninguém</u> {**me** telefonou /*telefonou-**me**}.
        nobody   me   called   called-me
        'Nobody called me.'
    c. <u>Nem</u> eu {o   vi   /*vi-**o**}, <u>nem</u> ele {**me** viu /*viu-**me**}.
        nor   I   him saw saw-him nor   he   me   saw saw-me
        'I didn't see him nor did he see me.'
    d. É melhor <u>não</u> {**lhe** contares   /*contares-**lhe**} nada.
        is better   not him tell-INF-2.SG tell-INF-2.SG-him nothing
        'It would be better if you(SG) didn't tell him anything.'
    e. Ele saiu <u>não</u> {**me** agradecendo /*agradecendo-**me**}.
        he left not me thanking   thanking-me
        'He left without thanking me.'

At first sight, the pattern in (5.179) below is unexpected, as enclisis to an uninflected infinitive is allowed (for some speakers)[94] despite the presence of negation. However, upon close inspection, we see that the difference resides in

---

[93] For discussion see e.g. A. M. Martins 1994a,b, 1997, 2000a, 2011, 2013b, 2021a, Raposo 1994, 1995, 2000, Duarte and Matos 2000, Costa and Martins 2003, Duarte 2003b, Magro 2005, 2007, and Rodygina 2009.
[94] Some EP speakers (including the second author) generally dislike enclisis in negative infinitival clauses, as in all other types of negative clauses.

the status of *não* 'not', which in EP may be ambiguous between the standard marker of predicate negation or a marker of constituent negation (see Section 7.3). Under the latter interpretation, *não* forms a complex predicate with the verb (*não fazer* 'not do') and, in this regard, it patterns like the "negative" prefix *des-* 'un-' in not triggering proclisis, as shown in (5.180). Thus, in environments where predicate negation is independently required, proclisis is the only alternative available, as illustrated by the sentences in (5.181).[95] The negative polarity item *ninguém* 'anybody' in (5.181a) and the contrastive focus in (5.181b) must be licensed by predicate negation (see Section 7.31), which then triggers proclisis.

(5.179) Eu decidi não {**o** fazer /%fazê-**lo**}. (EP)
I decided not it do-INF do-INF-it
'I decided not to do it.'

(5.180) Eu decidi {***o** desfazer /desfazê-**lo**}. (EP)
I decided it un-do-INF un-do-INF-it
'I decided to undo it.'

(5.181) EP:
    a. Eu decidi não {**o** dar /*dá-**lo**} a ninguém.
        I decided not it give-INF give-INF-it to nobody
       'I decided not to give it to anybody.'
    b. Eu decidi não {**o** dar /*dá-**lo**} à Maria, mas sim ao Pedro.
        I decided not it give-INF give-INF-it to-the Maria but yes to-the Pedro.
       'I decided to give it not to Maria, but to Pedro.'

A preverbal focalized element also triggers proclisis, as shown in (5.182) below. Given the intrinsic association between *wh*-phrases and focus (see Section 5.3.2), preverbal *wh*-phrases trigger proclisis as well, as shown in (5.182c).

(5.182) EP:
    a. [*Context:*
        A: – Esqueceste-te do aniversário da Maria, não foi?
            forgot-2.SG-yourself_{[CL]} of-the birthday of-the Maria not was
           'You(SG) forgot Maria's birthday, didn't you(SG)?']
        B: – Ora vê! O novo livro do Saylor {**lhe** comprei /*comprei-**lhe**} eu.
            now see the new book of-the Saylor her bought-1.SG bought-1.SG-her I
           'Wrong! I bought her Saylor's new book.'

---

[95] For discussion see e.g. Duarte 2003a and Costa and Martins 2003.

b. [*Context:*
A: – O João enviou o relatório na semana passada.
   the João sent the report in-the week passed
   'João sent the report last week.']
B: – ONTEM {o enviou /*enviou-o} o mentiroso!
   yesterday it sent sent-it the liar
   'Only yesterday did the liar send it!'
c. Quem {te contou /*contou-te}?
   who you.SG told told-you.SG
   'Who told you(SG)?'

Pairs of sentences like that in (5.183) below may give the false impression that variation between proclisis and enclisis is permitted with some adverbs. The different positioning of the clitic in (5.183) is in fact a reflex of the fact that different preverbal adverbs may be either foci or topics; as we can see in the translations of the sentences of (5.183), the locative *ali* 'there' receives a focus interpretation in (5.183a), but a topic interpretation in (5.183b). Actually, the same type of effect may also arise with non-adverbial constituents. The response in (5.182a), for instance, would exhibit the opposite pattern of clitic placement in a context inducing the interpretation of the fronted object as a topic, as illustrated in (5.184). In other words, rather than showing that the adverb *ali* is lexically specified as being compatible with both proclisis and enclisis, what (5.183) actually shows is that the lexical content of *ali* is such that it allows it to be either topicalized or focalized.

(5.183) EP:
a. Ali se construiu o mosteiro.
   there SE_{IND} built the monastery
   'It was there that the monastery was built.'
b. Ali constrói-se de forma selvagem.
   there builds-SE_{IND} of way wild
   'In that place, people are building unrestrainedly.'

(5.184) [*Context:*
A: – Quando compraste o novo livro do Saylor?
   when bought-2SF the new book of-the Saylor
   'When did you(SG) buy Saylor's new book?']
B: – O novo livro do Saylor, {*o comprei /comprei-o}
   the new book of-the Saylor it bought-1.SG bought-1.SG-it
   ontem. (EP)
   yesterday
   'I bought Saylor's new book yesterday.'

As should be expected, preverbal focalizing particles or adverbs function as proclisis triggers. These include particles that denote exclusion (*só* 'only', *somente* 'only', *apenas* 'only', *logo* 'unexpectedly among all possibilities', *antes* 'instead', etc.) and inclusion (*também* 'also', *até* 'even', *mesmo* 'even', etc.) and adverbs encoding aspect (*já* 'already', *ainda* 'still', *quase* 'almost', *mal* 'almost not', etc.) and modality (*talvez* 'maybe', *acaso* 'by any chance', etc.), as illustrated in (5.185).

(5.185) EP:
    a. Só   tu   {**me** fazes /*fazes-**me**} rir.
       only you.SG me make make-me   laugh
       'Only you(SG) make me laugh.'
    b. Até o gato {**me** mordeu /*mordeu-**me**}
       even the cat me bit   bit-me
       'Even the cat bit me.'
    c. O carro quase {**a** atropelou /*atropelou-**a**}.
       the car   almost her hit   hit-her
       'The car almost hit her.'
    d. Talvez a Maria {**o** contrate   /*contrate-**o**}.
       maybe the Maria him hire.SUBJ.PRES hire.SUBJ.PRES-him
       'Maybe Maria will hire him.'

Preverbal emphatic expressions also trigger proclisis, as shown in (5.186) below.[96] The interesting thing about the sentences in (5.186) is that the underlined expressions lose their original adverbial interpretation (manner in (5.186a), place in (5.186b), and time in (5.186c)) when they appear in a preverbal position; if that happens, they are interpreted as conveying emphasis and enforce proclisis.

(5.186) EP:
    a. Bem {**nos** custou   /*custou-**nos**} vender a   casa.
       well us   cost.3.SG cost.3.SG-us sell   the house
       'It was really painful for us to sell the house.'
    b. Lá   {**se** perdeu /*perdeu-**se**} uma grande oportunidade!
       there SE_{IND} lost   lost-SE_{IND} a   big   opportunity
       'We missed a great opportunity!'
    c. Ontem sempre {**nos**   rimos   /*rimo-**nos**}   um
       yesterday always ourselves laughed.1PL laughed.1PL-ourselves a
       bocado e   ficámos mais   animados.
       bit   and stayed   more   animated
       'Yesterday we ended up laughing a lot and felt more cheerful.'

---

[96] For discussion see e.g. Martins 1994a,b, 2013b,c, 2016a, Raposo 1994, and Magro 2007.

A slightly more complex pattern is found with preverbal quantifiers.[97] Take the determiner *muito(s)/muita(s)* 'many-MASC/FEM', for instance. At first sight, it is compatible with either proclisis or enclisis, as illustrated in (5.187) below. However, the position of the clitic is associated with a different interpretation in each case, as indicated by the translations.

(5.187) EP:
    a. Muitas pessoas **se** vacinam todos os anos.
       many-FEM-PL people themselves vaccinate all the years
       'Every year there is a large number of people who get vaccinated.'
    b. Muitas pessoas vacinam-**se** todos os anos.
       many-FEM-PL people vaccinate-themselves all the years
       'Many people are such that they get themselves vaccinated every year.'

Like many quantifiers in EP, *muitos* is ambiguous between receiving a quantificational/nonspecific interpretation and a "referential"/specific interpretation. Thus, whereas (5.187a) says that the cardinality (i.e. the number of the members) of the set of people who are vaccinated every year in relation to the set of people is large (a quantificational/nonspecific interpretation), (5.187b) says that there is a specific group of people who get vaccinated every year (whose members could in principle be identified) and this is a numerous group (a referential/specific interpretation). Although often subtle, this difference becomes crystal-clear in cases such as (5.188) below, for the referential/specific reading is pragmatically anomalous, as the event of committing suicide is not iterative.

(5.188) EP:
    a. Muitas pessoas **se** suicidam todos os anos.
       many-FEM-PL people themselves commit.suicide all the years
       'Every year there is a large number of people who commit suicide.'
    b. #Muitas pessoas suicidam-**se** todos os anos.
       many-FEM-PL people commit.suicide-themselves all the years
       #'Many people are such that they commit suicide every year.'

The different patterns of clitic placement associated with different quantifiers by and large follow their quantificational/nonspecific or referential/specific interpretation, for only the former triggers proclisis, as illustrated in (5.187) and (5.188). The two uses can be independently distinguished through the apposition of a name or names identifying the member(s) of the set, which is compatible with the referential/specific interpretation, but not with the quantificational/nonspecific reading. The masculine singular determiner

---

[97] For discussion see e.g. A. M. Martins 1994a,b, 1997, Raposo 1994, and Costa and Martins 2003.

algum 'some', for instance, does not allow such an apposition, whereas its plural feminine counterpart *algumas* does, as shown in (5.189) below. Accordingly, *algum* triggers proclisis, but *algumas* does not, as illustrated in (5.190).[98]

(5.189) EP:
    a. *Algum aluno meu, o João, saiu da sala.
        some.MASC.SG student my the João left from-the room
        'Some student of mine, namely, João, left the room.'
    b. Algumas alunas minhas, a Maria e a Susana, saíram da sala.
        some-FEM-PL students my the Maria and the Susana left from-the room
        'Some students of mine, namely, Maria and Susana, left the room.'

(5.190) EP:
    a. Algum aluno {**me** telefonou /*telefonou-**me**}.
        some.MASC.SG student me called called-me
        'Some student called me.'
    b. Algumas alunas {***me** viram /viram-**me**} cair.
        some students me saw saw-me fall
        'Some students saw me fall down.'

---

[98] Notice that most – if not all – proclitic sentences like those in (5.182)–(5.190) seem to carry some sort of implicit "negative" meaning, as illustrated in (i) below. If this proves to be correct, the superficial diversity of types of proclisis seen in (5.182)–(5.190) may perhaps be reducible to the general case of negation illustrated in (5.178).

(i) EP:
    a. <u>Poucas</u> pessoas **se** salvaram.
        few people themselves saved
        'Few people escaped.' → Many people did not.
    b. De <u>pouco</u> **te** serviu seres honesto.
        of few yourself served be-INF-2SG honest
        'Being honest was of little use for you.' → Being honest hasn't done you(SG) much good.
    c. <u>Ali</u> **se** construiu o mosteiro.
        there SE_{IND} built the monastery
        'It was there that the monastery was built.' → The monastery wasn't built anywhere but there.
    d. <u>Só</u> tu **me** fazes rir.
        only you.SG me make laugh
        'Only you(SG) make me laugh.' → Nobody else does.
    e. O carro <u>quase</u> **a** atropelou.
        the car almost her hit
        'The car almost hit her.' → The car didn't hit her after all.
    f. <u>Bem</u> **te** avisei.
        well you.SG advised-1SG
        "I told you(SG) so!" → You(SG) didn't listen to me (and suffered the consequences).

Connective elements introducing an embedded clause trigger proclisis in the embedded clause. This property is clearer in the case of finite clauses, which are generally preceded by a connector, as illustrated in (5.191) below. Thus, the complementizers *que* and *se* in (5.191a) and (5.191b), the conjunctions *quando* 'when' and *porque* 'because' in (5.191c) and (5.191d), and the relative pronoun *que* in (5.191e) all trigger proclisis within the clause they introduce.[99]

(5.191)   EP:

    a. Espero   que ele {**me** conte   /*conte-**me**}
        hope-1.SG that he me tell-SUBJ.PRES tell-SUBJ.PRES-me
        tudo.
        everything
        'I hope he will tell me everything.'
    b. A Maria perguntou se o   Pedro {se   desculpou /*desculpou-se}.
        the Maria asked   if the Pedro himself excused   excused-himself
        'Maria asked if Pedro had apologized.'
    c. Faço   isso quando ele {**me** telefonar   /*telefonar-**me**}.
        do-1.SG that when   he me call-.SUBJ.FUT call-.SUBJ.FUT-me
        'I'll do that when he calls me.'
    d. Eu disse isso porque ela {**me** pediu /*pediu-**me**}.
        I said this because she me asked asked-me
        'I said that because she asked me.'
    e. Vou   jantar com o meu amigo que {**me** telefonou /*telefonou-**me**}.
        go.1SG dine with the my friend that me called   called-me
        'I'm having dinner with that friend of mine that called.'

If the embedded clause is not introduced by a connector and does not have a proclisis trigger within it, enclisis is enforced as the default option; hence, the contrast in clitic placement in the pairs of sentences in (5.192)–(5.194) below, with proclisis in the finite embedded clause in (5.192a), (5.193a), and (5.194a) triggered by the complementizers and enclisis in the infinitival clause in (5.192b) and (5.193b) and the subjunctive clause of (5.194b), in the absence of proclisis triggers. The contrast in (5.194) is of particular interest as it shows that subjunctive mood is not a proclisis trigger; rather, subjunctive clauses generally display proclisis because they are normally introduced by a connector. It is also worth pointing out that the lack of a connector in (5.194b) obligatorily activates VS order, placing proclitic *me* in a clause-initial position – a possibility that is independently excluded in EP.[100]

---

[99] Some finite complement clauses with indicative mood marginally allow enclisis, but proclisis is without exception the unmarked pattern of clitic placement in this context (see e.g. Martins 1994a, 2013b and Ribeiro 1995a). Speakers' judgments greatly vary with respect to the acceptability of the marginal enclitic option.

[100] Exceptional instances of clause-initial proclisis in EP such as those illustrated in (i) involve an emphatic interpretation on the verb and should thus be viewed as cases

(5.192) EP:
   a. Ele julgou que {**me** enganava /*enganava-**me**}.
      he judged that me deceived   deceived-me
   b. Ele julgou {***me** enganar   /enganar-**me**}.
      he judged me   deceive-INF deceive-INF-me
      'He thought he was deceiving me.'

(5.193) EP:
   a. Toda a   gente viu <u>que</u> {**lhe** trouxeram   /*trouxeram-**lhe**}
      all   the   people saw that him brought-3.PL brought-3.PL-him
      um   papagaio.
      a   parrot
   b. Toda a   gente viu {***lhe** trazerem   /trazerem-**lhe**}
      all   the   people saw him   bring-INF-3.PL bring-INF-3.PL-him
      um   papagaio.
      a   parrot
      'Everybody saw that a parrot was brought to him.'

(5.194) EP:
   a. Se ele {**me** desse   /*desse-**me**}   ouvidos,
      if he me give-SUBJ.IMPERF give-SUBJ.IMPERF-me ears
      isso não aconteceria.
      this not   happen-INDIC.COND
   b. {***Me** desse   /desse-**me**}   ele ouvidos
      me   give-SUBJ.IMPERF give-SUBJ.IMPERF-me he ears
      e   isso não aconteceria.
      and this not happen-INDIC.COND
      'If he listened to me, this wouldn't happen.'

Let us now consider the sentences in (5.195) below, which are challenging in that the infinitival clause is preceded by what looks like a *bona fide* connector (the preposition *de* 'of'), but enclisis is allowed in addition to proclisis. Again, appearances are misleading and we may be facing another instance of ambiguity. In this particular case, the question is whether *de* in (5.195) counts as a clause-introducing complementizer or a preposition.

---

of proclisis triggered by emphasis (see (5.186)). However, these cases are very marked, subject to lexical restrictions, and their acceptability is not uniform across speakers. For discussion, see Magro 2007 and Martins 2013b.

(i)   %EP:
   a. **Te**   garanto   que   é   verdade!
      you.SG warrant-1.SG that is   true
      'It is surely true.' → 'You(SG) have my word that it is undoubtedly true.'
   b. **Te**   arrenego,   desgraçado!
      you.SG disown-1.SG damned
      'I disown you(SG), you bastard!'

(5.195) Deixei de {te ouvir /ouvir-te}. (EP)
 stopped-1.SG of you.SG hear-INF hear-INF-you.SG
 'I can't hear you(SG) anymore.'

The data suggest that we in fact have three possibilities in EP regarding particles preceding nonfinite clauses: (a) particles that behave like complementizers in obligatorily triggering proclisis: for instance, the particle *em* 'in' introducing gerund clauses (see (5.196a)) and prepositional particles introducing inflected infinitives[101] (see (5.196b–d)):

(5.196) EP:
 a. Em uma comida {lhe agradando /*agradando-lhe}, não
    in   a   food   him   pleasing   pleasing-him   not
    quer   comer   outra coisa.
    want.3.SG eat-INF other thing
    'Whenever he likes some food, he doesn't want to have anything else.'
 b. Vive   com medo de {o   roubarem   /*roubarem-no}.
    live.3.SG with fear of him rob-INF-3.PL rob-INF-3.PL-him
    'He lives in fear of being robbed.'
 c. Para {me   agradarem   /*agradarem-me},   convidaram também
    to   me   please-INF-3.PL please-INF-3.PL-me invited-3.PL also
    o   João.
    the João
    'To please me, they also invited João.'
 d. Ele saiu sem   {lhe darmos   /*darmos-lhe}   autorização.
    he left without him give-INF-1.PL give-INF-1.PL-him authorization
    'He left without us giving him permission.'

(b) particles that behave like prepositions and do not trigger proclisis: for instance, the particles *a* 'to' (though some dialectal variation can be found) and *com* 'with' when introducing infinitival clauses (see (5.197a,b)) and, interestingly, the particle *se* of infinitival embedded questions (see (5.197c)):

(5.197) EP:
 a. Ele imaginou os   caranguejos a   {*lhe morderem
    he imagined the crabs   to him   bite-INF-3PL
    /morderem-lhe}   os pés.
    bite-INF-3PL-him the feet
    'He imagined crabs biting his feet.'

---

[101] This statement excludes *a* 'to' and *com* 'with', which correlate with enclisis (see (5.197a,b)), and *em* 'in', which may be associated with proclisis or enclisis (see (i) below):

 (i) Tinham   pressa em {se   afastarem   /afastarem-se}
     had-3.PL hurry in themselves move.away-INF-3PL move.away-INF-
                                                      3PL-themselves
     dali.   (EP)
     from.there
     'They were in a hurry to get away from there.'

b. Não ficámos   nada   contentes com {*o reprovar /reprová-**lo**}.
      *not stayed-1.PL nothing content   with **him** fail-INF fail-INF-him*
      'We were not at all happy in letting him down.'
   c. Não sabemos   se {***lhe** dizer   /dizer-**lhe**} a verdade hoje
      not know-1.PL if him   tell-INF tell-INF-him the truth today
      ou amanhã.
      or tomorrow
      'We don't know if we should tell him the truth today or tomorrow.'

(c) particles that may be specified as complementizers or prepositions, triggering proclisis or enclisis according to this specification: for instance, the particles *de* 'of' (see (5.195)), *para* 'to' (see (5.198a)), *sem* 'without' (see (5.198b)), *em* 'in', and *por* 'by' when introducing uninflected infinitivals:

(5.198) EP:
   a. Vim   para   {**te**   ajudar   /ajudar-**te**}.
      came-1.SG to   you.SG help-INF help-INF-you.SG
      'I came to help you(SG).'
   b. O   João   saiu   sem   {**se**   despedir
      the João left   without himself say.good-bye-INF
      /despedir-**se**}
      say.good-bye-INF-himself
      'João left without saying good-bye.'
   c. Ela estava interessada em   {**o** impressionar /impressioná-**lo**}.
      she was   interested   in him impress-INF impress-INF-him
      'She wanted to make a good impression on him.'
   d. Eles   acabaram   por {**lhe** pagar   /pagar-**lhe**} mais dinheiro
      they   finished   by   him pay-INF pay-INF-him more money
      do que deviam}.
      than   owed
      'They ended up paying him more money than they owed.'

Although descriptive, the characterization above is not devoid of empirical consequences, as the proclisis and enclisis possibilities may independently correlate with different phenomena related to the structural complexity of the infinitival. Take the contrast in (5.199) below involving the secondary predicate *doente* 'sick', for example. If the infinitival has enclisis, as in (5.199a), *doente* may be interpreted as referring to the object of the embedded verb or to the subject of the matrix clause. On the other hand, if the infinitival has proclisis, as in (5.199b), the matrix subject reading becomes strongly disfavored (if at all available). If infinitival clauses with proclisis are structurally more complex than their counterparts with enclisis due to the additional layer of structure introduced by the prepositional complementizer, the contrast in (5.199) can be accounted for if this additional layer of structure disrupts interclausal interpretative processes.

(5.199) EP:
    a. Eu não gostava de vê-**lo** doente.
       I not liked of see-INF-him sick
       'I didn't want to see him while he was sick.': OK
       'I didn't want to see him while I was sick.': OK
    b. Eu não gostava <u>de</u> o ver doente.
       I not liked of him see-INF sick
       'I didn't want to see him while he was sick.': OK
       'I didn't want to see him while I was sick.': ???

Similar considerations apply to the intriguing contrasts in (5.200) and (5.201) below. If the infinitival has enclisis, the interpretive possibilities for the null subject of the infinitival are more restrictive. In (5.200a), the null subject must find its antecedent in a designated position in the matrix clause (i.e. the matrix object position) and in (5.201a) it must establish a self-referring interpretation parallel to the one established in the matrix clause. On the other hand, if the infinitival has proclisis, the interpretation of the null subject is less dependent on specific properties of the matrix clause; hence, in (5.200b) the null subject may also be interpreted as João and Maria together and in (5.201b) a non-self-referring reading is also available. Again, this contrast may be explained if the infinitival with proclisis has a prepositional complementizer and the extra layer of structure it adds to the infinitival clause disrupts the relevant interclausal interpretive relations.

(5.200) EP:
    a. Essa música, o João convidou a Maria para Ø dançá-**la**
       this music the João invited the Maria to dance-INF-it
       na peça.
       in-the play
       Ø = Maria: OK 'João invited Maria to dance this music in the play.'
       Ø = João and Maria: *'João invited Maria for the two of them to dance this music in the play.'
    b. Essa música, o João convidou a Maria para Ø **a** dançar
       this music the João invited the Maria to it dance-INF
       na peça.
       in-the play
       Ø = Maria: OK 'João invited Maria to dance this music in the play.'
       Ø = João and Maria: **OK** 'João invited Maria for the two of them to dance this music in the play.'

(5.201) EP:
    a. Fiquei   aliviada por livrar-**me**   dele e a Maria
       stayed-1.SG relieved for rid-INF-myself of-he and the Maria
       também ficou.
       also   stayed
       'I was relieved to get rid of him and Maria was relieved to get rid of him, as well.': OK
       'I was relieved to get rid of him and Maria too was relieved that I got rid of him.': *
    b. Fiquei   aliviada <u>por</u> **me**   livrar dele e a Maria
       stayed-1.SG relieved for myself rid-INF of-he and the Maria
       também ficou.
       also   stayed
       'I was relieved to get rid of him and Maria was relieved to get rid of him, as well.': OK
       'I was relieved to get rid of him and Maria too was relieved that I got rid of him.': **OK**

So far, in all the cases that we have seen, enclisis arises when there are no proclisis triggers. However, two tenses do not allow enclisis in (standard) EP, namely, the indicative future and the indicative conditional, as illustrated in (5.202).

(5.202) EP:
    a. *Eu escreverei-**te**   no mês que vem.
       I write-INDIC.FUT-1.SG-you.SG in-the month that comes
       'I'll write you(SG) next month.'
    b. *Eles comprariam-**no**   amanhã se tivessem dinheiro.
       they buy-INDIC.COND-3.PL-it tomorrow if had   money
       'They would buy it tomorrow if they had the money.'

In this case, EP resorts to what is traditionally referred to as *mesoclisis*, that is, the clitic appears in the "middle" of the verb, as shown in (5.203).

(5.203) EP:
    a. Eu escrever-**te**-ei   no mês que vem.
       I write-INDIC.FUT-you.SG-1.SG in-the month that comes
       'I'll write you(SG) next month.'
    b. Eles comprá-**lo**-iam   amanhã se tivessem dinheiro.
       they buy-INDIC.COND-it-3.PL tomorrow if had   money
       'They would buy it tomorrow if they had the money.'

Diachronically, these two tenses evolved from Latin verbal periphrases involving an infinitival verb plus the verb *habere* 'have' in the present or imperfective past, as sketched in (5.204) below. Interestingly, there are also verbal periphrases with the verb *haver* in EP (and BP), whose meaning is close to the indicative future and indicative conditional, as illustrated in (5.205).

(5.204) a. scribere habeo   > escrever hei   > escreverei
             write   have-1.SG   write-INDIC.FUT-1.SG
        b. scribere habebam > escrever havia > escreveria
             write   had-1.SG   write-INDIC.COND-1.SG

(5.205) EP:
        a. Eu hei   de vencer.
           I   have-1.SG of win-INF
           'I shall win.'
        b. Eu havia   de vencer.
           I   had-1.SG of win-INF
           'I should win.'

These facts suggest that, in sentences such as those in (5.203), we actually have enclisis of *te* and *o* to the main verb, with the ending that follows being an affixal auxiliary.[102] Or more broadly, mesoclisis is but a morphological variant of enclisis, which explains why mesoclisis is not possible in the presence of a proclisis trigger, as illustrated in (5.206) below with negation. The fact that BP does not have mesoclisis is also accounted for, as BP generally excludes enclisis (see Section 5.6.2).[103]

(5.206) Eu não {o pagarei   /*pagá-**lo**-ei}.   (EP)
         I   not it pay-INDIC.FUT-1.SG pay-INDIC.FUT-it-1.SG
         'I won't pay for it.'

Let us now consider clitic placement in verbal periphrases in EP, starting with periphrases with a participial main verb. Absolute participles cannot host clitics, as illustrated in (5.207) below. Accordingly, a participial verb in a periphrasis cannot host a clitic, regardless of whether it is active (see (5.208a)) or passive (see (5.208b)). In this situation, the clitic associated with the participial main verb must "climb" and its placement will then be duly computed with respect to the auxiliary verb, that is, enclisis to the auxiliary verb obtains if there are no proclisis triggers, as shown in (5.209).

(5.207) *Enviados-**lhe**   os documentos, o processo foi
        send-PPLE-MASC-PL-him the documents   the process   was
        arquivado.   (EP)
        filed
        'Once the documents were sent to him, the lawsuit was ended.'

---

[102] For discussion see e.g. Duarte and Matos 2000.
[103] In some EP dialects mesoclisis has been replaced by enclisis.

(5.208) EP:
    a. *O médico tinha observado-**a** na semana passada.
       the doctor had observed-her in-the week passed
       'The doctor had examined her last week.'
    b. *Os documentos foram enviados-**lhe**.
       the documents were send-PPLE-MASC-PL-him
       'The documents were sent to him.'

(5.209) EP:
    a. O médico {***a** tinha /tinha-**a**} observado na semana passada.
       the doctor her had had-her examined in-the week passed
       'The doctor had examined her last week.'
    b. O médico <u>não</u> {**a** tinha /*tinha-**a**} observado na semana passada.
       the doctor not her had had-her examined in-the week passed
       'The doctor had not examined her last week.'
    c. Os documentos {*__lhe__ foram /foram-**lhe**} enviados.
       the documents him were were-him send-PPLE-MASC-PL
       'The documents were sent to him.'
    d. Os documentos <u>não</u> {**lhe** foram /*foram-**lhe**} enviados.
       the documents not him were were-him send-PPLE-MASC-PL
       'The documents were not sent to him.'

Verbal periphrases involving gerunds also typically behave in a way parallel to the paradigm in (5.209), as illustrated in (5.211), despite the fact that gerunds can host a clitic when not in a periphrasis, as shown in (5.210).[104]

---

[104] Enclisis to the gerund in a periphrasis, as illustrated in (i), is dialectally/idiolectally allowed, though infrequent (see e.g. Martins 2013b, 2021a for discussion).

(i)   %EP:
    a. E hoje, esses rapazes é a mesma coisa: a baleia já está quase para morrer, fraca, mas parada em cima do mar, a gente dá a lança para os rapazes irem **experimentando-a**.
       and today these youngsters is the same thing the whale already is almost for die weak but stopped in above of-the sea we give the spear for the youngsters go-INF-3PL trying-it
       'And today, it's the same thing with these youngsters: when the whale is weak and almost dying, but floating at the surface of the sea, we give them the spear for them to poke it.'
       (CORDIAL-SIN, PIC16)
    b. Quando vinha das terras, a gente tirava-o e ia **puxando-o**.
       when came of-the lands we took-it and went pulling-it
       'When we returned from working in the fields, we took it and dragged it.'
       (CORDIAL-SIN, CLH20)

(5.210) Vendo-**os** felizes, fico feliz. (EP)
seeing-them happy stay-1SG happy
'I'm happy when I see them happy.'

(5.211) EP:
a. %Ela ia distanciando-**se** da família.
   she went distancing-herself from-the family
b. Ela {***se** ia /ia-**se**} distanciando da família.
   she herself went went-herself distancing from-the family
   'She was distancing herself from her family.'
c. <u>Só</u> ela {**se** ia /*ia-**se**} distanciando da família.
   only she herself went went-herself distancing from-the family
   'She was the only person distancing herself from her family.'

Finally, let us look at the pattern displayed by infinitives. As we have seen above, infinitives can independently host clitics (see (5.192b) and (5.193b), for instance). When part of a periphrasis, the infinitival may host the clitic (see (5.212a)) or allow it to climb, in which case the clitic is computed with respect to the auxiliary and default enclisis placement is enforced in the absence of proclisis triggers (see (5.212b) vs. (5.212c)).

(5.212) EP:
a. O João vai despedir-**se** dos amigos amanhã.
   the João goes say.good-bye-himself of-the friends tomorrow.
b. O João {***se** vai / vai-**se**} despedir dos amigos amanhã.
   the João himself goes goes-himself say.good-bye of-the friends tomorrow.
   'João will say good-bye to his friends tomorrow.'
c. <u>Até</u> o João {**se** vai /*vai-**se**} despedir dos amigos amanhã.
   even the João himself goes goes-himself say.good-bye of-the friends tomorrow.
   'Even João will say good-bye to his friends tomorrow.'

A class of verbs referred to as *restructuring* verbs may optionally form a kind of verbal periphrasis with an infinitival verb[105] and, in this case, we will find the same pattern as that which we saw with temporal auxiliaries in (5.212), as illustrated in (5.213) with the modal *poder* 'can' and in (5.214) with the volitive verb *querer* 'want'.

---

[105] For discussion see e.g. Gonçalves 1999 and Martins 2000a.

(5.213) EP:
 a. Posso   sempre   ajudar-**te**.
    can-1.SG   always   help-INF-you.SG
 b. Posso-**te**   sempre   ajudar.
    can-1.SG-you.SG always   help-INF
    'I'm always willing to help you(SG).'

(5.214) EP:
 a. Não   quero   ver-**te**.
    not   want-1.SG   see-INF-you.SG
 b. <u>Não</u> **te**   quero   ver.
    not   you.SG   want-1.SG   see-INF
    'I don't want to see you(SG).'

If a verbal periphrasis contains more than one auxiliary or restructuring verb, clitic placement may be computed with respect to each member of the periphrasis, as illustrated in (5.215).[106]

(5.215) EP:
 Não   posso   entrar?
 not   can-1.SG   enter
 a. Devo   poder   ir   dar-**lhe**   um abraço, pelo   menos.
    might-1.SG   can-INF   go-INF   give-INF-him   a   hug   for-the less
 b. Devo   poder   ir-**lhe**   dar   um abraço, pelo   menos.
    might-1.SG   can-INF   go-INF-him   give-INF a   hug   for-the less
 c. Devo   poder-**lhe**   ir   dar   um abraço, pelo   menos.
    might-1.SG   can-INF-him   go-INF   give-INF a   hug   for-the less
 d. Devo-**lhe**   poder   ir   dar   um abraço, pelo   menos.
    might-1.SG-lhe   can-INF   go-INF   give-INF a   hug   for-the less
    'Can't I come in? I could at least give him a hug.'

5.6.2 Clitic Placement in Brazilian Portuguese

Three factors greatly interfere with a proper description of clitic placement in BP. The first is that the inventory of clitics in the grammar of BP (in the sense specified in Chapter 1) is much more reduced than that of EP, being essentially restricted to *me* (ACC/DAT.1.SG), *te* (ACC/DAT.2.SG), reflexive *se* (ACC/DAT.2/3.SG/PL), and indefinite *se*. The clitic *vos* 'you-PL. ACC/DAT' has died out, the clitics *lhe* 'him/her.DAT' and *lhes* 'they.DAT' have become dialectally restricted (and in some dialects replaced the accusative clitics), and the clitics *nos* (ACC/DAT.1.PL) and the third person accusative clitics *o(s)* (MASC(-PL)) and *a(s)* (FEM(-PL)) have become associated

---

[106] For discussion see e.g. Gonçalves 1999 and Martins 2013b.

with formal style, written language, and schooling (see Section 2.4 and references therein).

The second factor is that there is a sharp contrast between spoken and written language with respect to clitic placement. Whereas spoken BP is essentially proclitic, written BP resorts to both proclisis and enclisis. The fact that enclisis is acquired through schooling lends it sociolinguistic prestige (in written language). Interestingly, though, the distribution of proclisis and enclisis in written BP does not correspond to the EP system and displays substantial variation among writers.[107]

The third factor is the more interesting one.[108] First, indefinite *se* in BP has a specific pattern of placement that sets it aside from the other clitics that are regularly employed (*me*, *te*, and reflexive *se*). Second, when the clitics *lhe(s)* and *nos* are used in BP in the relevant dialects and registers, they do not differ from the clitics *me*, *te*, and reflexive *se* with respect to clitic placement, but when the clitics *o(s)* and *a(s)* are used (in written language), their pattern of placement corresponds to neither that of other clitics in BP nor that of EP. We will therefore analyze indefinite *se* and *o(s)/a(s)* separately.

Following the methodology outlined in Chapter 1, we will put aside clitic placement in written BP and will not discuss the placement of *nos* and *lhe(s)*. We will however make an exception with respect to third person accusative clitics, as their different pattern of placement (be it in spoken or written language) provides an additional support for the claim that they are not part of the grammar of BP (as defined in Chapter 1).

Let us then start with the general pattern of clitic placement in BP. As illustrated in (5.216) below with simple nonperiphrastic verbs, proclisis is the norm, irrespective of verbal inflectional morphology or clausal type.[109] The clauses may be affirmative (see (5.216a)), negative (see (5.216b)), embedded (see (5.216c)), nonembedded (see (5.216a)), finite (see (5.216a)), or nonfinite (see (5.216d)); the clitic may be in a clause-initial position (see (5.216e)); and if it is the subject of an embedded clause, the clitic surfaces left-attached to the selecting verb (see (5.216f)).

---

[107] For discussion see e.g. Pagotto 1993, Abaurre and Galves 1996, Galves 2001, Carneiro 2005, Kato 2005, 2017, and Carneiro and Galves 2010.
[108] For discussion see e.g. Abaurre and Galves 1996, Nunes 2015a, 2019a, and Martins and Nunes 2016.
[109] For discussion see e.g. Pagotto 1993, Abaurre and Galves 1996, Galves 2001, Galves, Ribeiro, and Torres Morais 2005, and Luís and Kaiser 2016.

(5.216) BP:
a. A Maria {**me** viu /*viu-**me**} no cinema.
   the Maria me saw saw-me in-the cinema
   'Maria saw me at the movies.'
b. A Maria não {**me** viu /*viu-**me**} no cinema.
   the Maria not me saw saw-me in-the cinema
   'Maria didn't see me at the movies.'
c. A Maria parece que {**me** viu /*viu-**me**} no cinema.
   the Maria seems that me saw saw-me in-the cinema
   'It seems that Maria saw me at the movies.'
d. Você {**me** ligando /*ligando-**me**}, eu lido com o problema.
   you.SG me call-GER call-GER-me I deal with the problem
   'When you(SG) call me, I'll handle the problem.'
e. {**Me** telefone /*Telefone-**me**} amanhã.
   me call call-me tomorrow
   'Call me tomorrow.'
f. A Maria {**me** viu /*viu-**me**} saindo.
   the Maria me saw saw-me leaving.
   'Maria saw me leaving.'

As for clitic placement in clauses with verbal periphrases, we find general proclisis to the main verb, as illustrated in (5.217) below. The only exception involves passive participles, which host clitics neither in proclisis nor in enclisis positions, as shown in (5.218a).[110] In this case, the clitic climbs and procliticizes to the auxiliary, as shown in (5.218b).

(5.217) BP:
a. Ele está {**se** preparando /*preparando-**se**} para a corrida.
   he is himself prepare-GER prepare-GER-himself for the race
   'He is preparing himself for the race.'
b. Ele tinha {**me** dado /*dado-**me**} uma chance.
   he had me give-PPLE give-PPLE-me a chance
   'He had given me a chance.'
c. Eu vou {**te** dar /*dar-**te**} um conselho.
   I go you.SG give give-you.SG an advice
   'I'm going to give you(SG) a piece of advice.'

(5.218) BP:
a. Foi {*****me** dito / /*dito-**me**} que o João estava aqui.
   was me said said-me that the João was here
b. {**Me** foi /*foi-**me**} dito que o João estava aqui.
   me was was-me said that the João was here
   'I was told that João was here.'

---

[110] For discussion see e.g. Figueiredo Silva 1990.

It should be stressed that although the clitics in (5.217) sit between the auxiliary and the main verb, they are syntactically and phonologically attached to the main verb and not the auxiliary. This becomes evident when we have additional material between the two verbs, as shown in (5.219).

(5.219) BP:
    a. Ele {*está-se sempre preparando /está sempre se
        he   is-himself always preparing   is   always himself
        preparando} para uma nova   corrida.
        preparing   for a   new   race
        'He is always preparing himself for another race.'
    b. Ele {*tinha-me novamente dado /tinha novamente me dado}
        he   had-me   again   given had   again   me given
        uma chance.
        a   chance
        'He had given me another chance.'
    c. Eu {*vou-te   novamente dar /vou novamente te   dar} um conselho.
        I   go-you.SG again   give go   again   you give an advice
        'I'm going to give you(SG) another piece of advice.'

Finally, as mentioned above, passive participles are the only case in which the clitics are not positioned with respect to the main verb (see (5.218)). In particular, BP has no clitic climbing with verbs that in EP behave like restructuring verbs, as illustrated in (5.220).[111,112]

(5.220) BP:
    a. Você   não {*me pode despedir /pode [me despedir]}.
        you.SG not   me   can   fire   can   me fire
        'You(SG) can't fire me.'
    b. Quem {*te   quer   contratar} /quer [te   contratar]}?
        who   you.SG wants hire   wants you.SG hire
        'Who wants to hire you(SG)?'

Given the overall proclitic nature of BP, the pattern of clitic placement displayed by indefinite *se* in BP, as illustrated in (5.221) below, is really puzzling.[113] It cannot be clause-initial (see (5.221a)); it is sensitive to proclisis triggers such as negation (see (5.221b)); and it obligatorily undergoes climbing (see (5.221c) vs. (5.221d)).

---

[111] For clarity, we will add square brackets in (5.220), (5.225)–(5.227), (5.229)–(5.232), and (5.234) to indicate right attachment of the clitic when there is no material intervening between the verbs.
[112] For discussion see e.g. Cyrino 2008.
[113] For discussion see e.g. Abaurre and Galves 1996 and Martins and Nunes 2016.

5.6 Clitic Placement

(5.221) BP:
    a. {Contratou-**se** /***se** contratou} um novo professor.
        hired-SE_{IND} SE_{IND} hired   a new teacher
        'A new teacher was hired.'
    b. Não {**se** contratou /***contratou-se**} um novo professor.
        not SE_{IND} hired   hired-SE_{IND} a new teacher
        'No new teachers were hired.'
    c. *Deve, sem sombra de dúvida, **se** contratar um novo professor.
        should without shade of doubt SE_{IND} hire a new teacher
    d. Deve-**se**, sem sombra de dúvida, contratar um novo professor.
        should-SE_{IND} without shade of doubt hire a new teacher
        'No doubt a new teacher should be hired.'

It is not clear why indefinite *se* should have this peculiar behavior in BP, though. Interestingly, indefinite *se* in BP also differs from its counterpart in EP in respect of the co-occurrence restriction with the reflexive clitic *se* illustrated in (5.222a) below.[114] As discussed in Section 2.4.3, in EP this restriction is more syntactic in nature as it rules out structures with verbs with the reflexive *se* that take indefinite *se* as their subject. Take (5.222b), for instance. Although indefinite *se* and reflexive *se* surface far away from each other, the sentence is ruled out because indefinite *se* is the understood subject of all the verbs, including the verb with reflexive *se*. In contrast, in BP the co-occurrence restriction involving *se* takes into account just phonological adjacency, as the contrasts in (5.223) illustrate.[115]

(5.222) EP:
    a. *Levanta-**se**-**se** cedo neste país.
        gets.up-SE_{REFL}-SE_{IND} early in-this country
        'People get up early in this country.'
    b. *Tentou-**se** conseguir evitar sentar-**se** na última fila.
        tried-SE_{IND} manage avoid sit-SE_{REFL} in-the last row
        'One tried to manage to avoid sitting in the last row.'

(5.223) BP:
    a. *Pode-**se**   **se**   sentar em qualquer lugar.
        can.3SG-SE_{IND} SE_{REFL} sit   in any   place
        'One can sit anywhere.'
    a'. Pode-**se**, salvo engano, **se** sentar em qualquer lugar.
        can-SE_{IND} saving mistake SE_{REFL} sit in any   place
        'I think one can sit anywhere.'

---

[114] See Martins and Nunes 2016, 2017b for discussion.
[115] An amelioration effect is noted with respect to (5.223a) and (5.223b) in BP if a pause is inserted between the two clitics.

b. *Deve-**se**   se   levantar cedo.
    should-SE_{IND} SE_{REFL} raise late
    'One should get up early.'
b'. Não **se**   deve   se   levantar tarde.
    not SE_{IND} should SE_{REFL} raise late
    'One shouldn't get up late .'

Let us now consider the syntactic placement of the third person accusative clitics (3PACs) *o(s)* and *a(s)*, by comparing it with the placement of the clitics *me* and *te* in (5.224)–(5.227) below. The two sets of clitics share the same pattern of placement only when the verb is finite and not part of a periphrasis and the clitic is not in a clause-initial position (see (5.224a,a′) and (5.224b,b′)). In cases involving verbal periphrases, *me* and *te* stick to the pattern of proclisis to the main verb, whereas 3PACs display proclisis to the auxiliary if the main verb is a participle (see (5.225b′)) or a gerund (see (5.226b′)) and enclisis to the main verb if it is infinitival (see (5.227a′)). The cases with proclisis of 3PACs to the auxiliary in (5.225b′) and (5.226b′) are nevertheless restricted to written language.

(5.224) BP:
  a. *Eu vi-**te**   ontem   na   universidade.
      I   saw-you.SG yesterday in-the university
      'I saw you(SG) yesterday at the university.'
  a'. *Eu vi-**a**   ontem   na   universidade.
      I   saw-her   yesterday in-the university
      'I saw her yesterday at the university.'
  b. Eu **te**   vi   ontem   na   universidade.
      I   you.SG saw   yesterday in-the university
      'I saw you(SG) yesterday at the university.'
  b'. Eu **a**   vi   ontem   na   universidade.
      I   her   saw   yesterday in-the university
      'I saw her yesterday at the university.'
  c. **Te**   vi   ontem   na   universidade.
      you.SG saw   yesterday in-the university
      'I saw you(SG) yesterday at the university.'
  c'. ***A**   vi   ontem   na   universidade.
      her   saw   yesterday in-the university
      'I saw her yesterday at the university.'

(5.225) BP:
  a. O   João tinha [**me** visto].
      the João had   me   seen
      'João had seen me.'
  a'. *O João tinha [**os** visto].
      the João had   them seen
      'João had seen them.'

b. *O João **me** tinha visto.
   the João me had seen
   'João had seen me.'
b'. O João **os** tinha visto.
   the João them had seen
   'João had seen them.'

(5.226) BP:
a. O João está [**te** vendo].
   the João is you.SG seeing
   'João is watching you(SG).'
a'. *O João está [**o** vendo].
    the João is him seeing
    'João is seeing him.'
b. *O João **te** está vendo.
   the João you.SG is seeing
   'João is seeing you(SG).'
b'. O João **o** está vendo.
    the João him is seeing
    'João is seeing him.'

(5.227) BP:
a. *O João vai contratar-**te**.
   the João goes hire-you.SG
   'João is going to hire you(SG).'
a'. O João vai contratá-**las**.
    the João goes hire-them.FEM
    'João is going to hire them(FEM).'
b. O João vai [**te** contratar].
   the João goes you.SG hire
   'João is going to hire you(SG).'
b'. *O João vai [**as** contratar].
    the João goes them.FEM hire
    'João is going to hire them(FEM).'
c. *O João **te** vai contratar.
   the João you.SG goes hire
   'João is going to hire you(SG).'
c'. *O João **as** vai contratar.
    the João them.FEM goes hire
    'João is going to hire them(FEM).'

The complex pattern seen above suggests that 3PACs behave like (object) agreement markers, as they seek potentially agreeing hosts and compete with subject agreement morphology for a morphological slot in the verbal template.[116] More specifically, the positioning of 3PACs may be taken to follow from the interaction of four conditions: (a) the host of a 3PAC can have agreement morphology; (b) subject agreement takes precedence over 3PACs to occupy the suffixal agreement slot; (c) climbing can be only employed as a strategy of last resort; and (4) 3PACs cannot surface clause-initially. Let us see how these conditions interact by reconsidering the data in (5.224)–(5.227).

In (5.224a′), (5.224b′) and (5.224c′), the finite verb counts as a proper host because it can bear agreement. However, subject agreement takes precedence over the 3PAC *a* to occupy the suffixal agreement slot even if it is a Ø-morpheme. This excludes (5.224a′) and *a* must procliticize to the finite verb, as in (5.224b′) and (5.224c′). However, 3PACs, like indefinite *se* in BP (see (5.221a)), cannot appear in clause-initial position, though; hence, only (5.224b′) is well formed. In (5.225), in turn, the main verb is not an appropriate host for the 3PAC *os*, as active participles cannot inflect for agreement in BP (see (5.225a′)). The clitic then climbs as a strategy of last resort and is computed with respect to the finite auxiliary, which is an appropriate host for agreement morphology. However, since subject agreement takes precedence for surfacing as a suffix of the verb, *os* procliticizes to the auxiliary (see (5.225b′)). The same considerations apply to (5.226), for gerunds cannot host agreement morphology in BP either. Finally, in (5.227) the main verb is an infinitival, and both EP and BP have inflected infinitivals, as discussed in Section 3.3.2.2.2. So, from a morphological point of view, the infinitive in (5.227a′) counts as a proper host. Furthermore, with verbal periphrases with the main verb in the infinitive, subject agreement (if existent) is encoded on the highest auxiliary only, as illustrated in (5.228) below. In other words, the morphological slot that is available for agreement in the infinitival of (5.227) is vacant in (5.228). The 3PAC *as* then occupies this suffixal position, surfacing in an enclitic rather than a proclitic position (see (5.227a′) vs. (5.227b′)). Furthermore, once *as* is licensed in (5.227a′), climbing as a rescuing strategy is not activated and the sentence in (5.227c′) (with climbing and proclisis to the auxiliary) is ruled out.

(5.228) a. Nós vamos cumprimentar(*mos) o João.
we go-1.PL greet-INF(-1.PL) the João
'We are going to greet João.'
b. Os meninos vão cumprimentar(*em) o João.
the boys go-3.PL greet-INF(-3.PL) the João
'The boys are going to greet João.'

---

[116] See Nunes 2015a, 2019a for discussion.

This general pattern is replicated if the 3PAC is the subject of the embedded clause (see (5.216f)), as shown in (5.229). As the clitic must be positioned with respect to the subordinating clause in this configuration, the 3PAC *a* procliticizes to the causative verb if the verb is finite (see (5.229a′)) or to the auxiliary if the causative verb is an active participle or a gerund (see (5.229b″) and (5.229c″)), and encliticizes to the causative verb if it is an infinitival (see (5.229d″)). As with (5.225b′) and (5.226b′), attachment of 3PACs to the highest verb in (5.229a′), (5.229b″), and (5.229c″) is also restricted to written language.

(5.229) BP:
    a.   O   João **me** fez   rir.
         the João me made laugh
         'João made me laugh.'
    a′. O   João **a**   fez   rir.
         the João her made laugh
         'João made her laugh.'
    b.   O   João tinha [**me** feito] rir.
         the João had me made laugh
         'João had made me laugh.'
    b′. *O João tinha [**a** feito] rir.
         the João had her made laugh
    b″. O João **a** tinha feito rir.
         the João her had made laugh
         'João had made her laugh.'
    c.   O   João estava [**me** fazendo] rir.
         the João was me making laugh
         'João was making me laugh.'
    c′. *O João estava [**a** fazendo] rir.
         the João was her making laugh
    c″. O João **a** estava fazendo rir.
         the João her was making laugh
         'João was making her laugh.'
    d.   O   João vai   [**me** fazer] rir.
         the João goes me make laugh
         'João is going to make me laugh.'
    d′. *O João vai [**a** fazer] rir.
         the João goes her make laugh
    d.″ O João vai fazê-**la** rir.
         the João goes make-her laugh
    d.‴ *O João **a** vai fazer rir.
         the João her goes make laugh
         'João is going to make her laugh.'

When a 3PAC is forced to climb, the result will depend on the morphological properties of the auxiliary. In the cases discussed thus far, the auxiliary has always been finite. Let us then examine cases when the auxiliary is nonfinite, by considering the contrast between (5.230) and (5.231).

(5.230) BP:
   a. Ter   [**me** visto] na   reunião surpreendeu o   João.
      have-INF me seen   in-the meeting surprised   the João.
      'It surprised João to see me at the meeting.'
   b. *Ter   [**a** visto] na   reunião surpreendeu o   João.
      have-INF her seen   in-the meeting surprised   the João.
   b'. Tê-**la**   visto na   reunião surpreendeu o   João.
      have-INF-her seen   in-the meeting surprised   the João.
      'It surprised João to see her at the meeting.'

(5.231) BP:
   a. Tendo [**me** encontrado] na   reunião, o   João foi   direto
      having me meet.PPLE in-the meeting the João went straight
      ao   assunto.
      to-the subject
      'Having met me at the meeting, João went straight to business.'
   b. *Tendo [**a** encontrado] na   reunião, o   João foi   direto
      having her meet.PPLE in-the meeting the João went straight
      ao   assunto.
      to-the subject
   b'. *Tendo-**a** encontrado na   reunião, o   João foi   direto
      having-her meet.PPLE in-the meeting the João went straight
      ao   assunto.
      to-the subject
   b". ***A** tendo   encontrado na   reunião, o   João foi   direto
      her having meet.PPLE in-the meeting the João went straight
      ao   assunto.
      to-the subject
      'Having met her at the meeting, João went straight to business.'

(5.230b) and (5.231b) are ruled out because the active participle cannot host agreement morphology. The 3PACs are then allowed to climb. In (5.230b'), the auxiliary is an infinitival and thus a proper host; furthermore, the infinitive in this configuration may be uninflected for subject agreement. The 3PAC then encliticizes and yields a well-formed sentence. By contrast, there is no acceptable output if the auxiliary is a gerund, as shown in (5.231b',b"), for gerunds are not proper hosts of morphological agreement in BP. (5.231b") sounds even worse than (5.231b') as it also violates the ban on 3PACs in clause-initial position.

Let us consider two interesting consequences of this characterization of 3PACs as agreement markers in BP.[117] Because 3PACs and the *bona fide* clitics *me*, *te*, and reflexive *se* have different placement requirements, it is possible to find both types of clitics attached to the same verb, as illustrated

---

[117] See Nunes 2011, 2015a, 2019a for additional discussion.

in (5.232), where the clitics *me* and *te* occupy their usual position of proclisis to the main verb and the 3PACs occupy the morphological slot reserved for agreement morphology.

(5.232) BP:
    a. Você pode [**me** enviá-**lo**] por e-mail.
       you.SG may me send-it by e-mail
       'You(SG) may send it to me by e-mail.'
    b. Eu não poderia [**te** recomendá-**la**], porque ela ainda é nova no trabalho.
       I not could you.SG recommend-her because she still is new in-the work
       'I couldn't recommend her to you(SG) because she's still new to the job.'

In EP, by contrast, the possibility of more than one clitic independently attached to a single verb is completely impossible. In such potential cases, either EP resorts to fused clitics (see Section 2.4.3), as illustrated in (5.233), or each clitic surfaces on a different host, as shown in (5.234). Neither possibility is available in BP.

(5.233) EP:
    a. O João enviou-**lha**.   ({lhe/lhes} + a)
       *the João sent-**pron.DAT.3**$_{[CL]}$-**pron.ACC.3.FEM.SG**$_{[CL]}$*
       'João sent it to {him/her/them}.'
    b. A Maria recomendou-**no-las**.   (nos + as)
       *the Maria recommended-**pron.DAT.1.PL**$_{[CL]}$-**pron.ACC.3.FEM-PL**$_{[CL]}$*
       'João recommended them to us.'

(5.234) EP:
    a. Vou-**lhe** já devolvê-**lo**.
       go.1.PL-him/her already return-it
       'I'm going to return it to {him/her} right away.'
    b. [Posso-**te**] confirmá-**lo** sem hesitação.
       can-1.SG-you confirm-it without hesitation
       'I can confirm it without hesitation.'

The second interesting consequence of treating 3PACs as agreement markers has to do with their placement in structures involving inflected infinitivals and the subjunctive future. The data in (5.235) below, for instance, show the expected pattern with respect to infinitives. We find enclisis of the 3PAC *o* when the infinitive is uninflected, thus having the morphological slot for agreement available (see (5.235a)), but proclisis if the infinitive is inflected (see (5.235b)), for the suffixal morphological slot is already taken by subject agreement. Interestingly, when the inflected infinitival is to be associated with a Ø-morpheme for subject agreement (see Section 3.4.2), proclisis and enclisis become acceptable, as shown in (5.236).

(5.235) BP:
    a. Não era permitido {*o criticar /criticá-**lo**} em público.
        not was permitted him criticize-INF criticize-INF in public
        'It was not allowed to criticize him in public.'
    b. Não era adequado nós {**o** recomendarmos
        not was adequate we him recommend-INF-1.PL
        /***recomendarmo-lo**} para o cargo.
        recommend-INF-1.PL-him for the position
        'It was not appropriate for us to recommend him for the position.'

(5.236) BP:
    a. Não era adequado {eu/você/a gente/ele}
        not was adequate I/you.SG/we/he
        o recomendar para o cargo.
        him recommend-**INF-3.SG** for the position
    b. Não era adequado {eu/você/a gente/ele}
        not was adequate I/you.SG/we/he
        recomendá-lo para o cargo.
        recommend-**INF**-him for the position
        'It was not appropriate for {me/you(SG)/us/him} to recommend him for the position.'

The inflected infinitive in (5.236a) does not differ phonetically from the uninflected form. Given the overall weakening of verbal agreement in BP, as discussed in Section 3.3.2.2, the well-formedness of (5.236b) in sharp contrast to the enclisis option in (5.235b) suggests that the grammar has already made it possible for uninflected infinitivals to replace inflected infinitivals with phonetically null agreement inflection.

Another case parallel to (5.236) can be found in clauses with subjunctive future tense, as illustrated in (5.237).

(5.237) BP:
    a. Se você **o** encontrar, me avise.
        if you.SG him meet-**SUBJ.FUT.3.SG** me warn
    b. Se você encontrá-**lo**, me avise.
        if you.SG meet-**INF**-him me warn
        'If you(SG) find him, let me know.'

As shown in Table 5.1 below, the subjunctive future can be morphologically distinguished from the inflected infinitival only in the case of irregular verbs. The double possibility for clitic placement in (5.237) can then be accounted for if uninflected infinitivals may be used in place of homophonous

Table 5.1 *Conjugations of the inflected infinitive and subjunctive future in BP for a regular and an irregular verb*

Nominative pronoun	Regular verb: *falar* 'speak'		Irregular verb: *deter* 'detain'	
	Inflected infinitive	Subjunctive future	Inflected infinitive	Subjunctive future
eu 'I' *você* 'you(SG)' *ele* 'he', *ela* 'she' *a gente* 'we'	*falar*	*falar*	*deter*	*detiver*
nós 'we'	*falarmos*	*falarmos*	*determos*	*detivermos*
vocês 'you(PL)' *eles* 'they(MASC)', *elas* 'they(FEM)'	*falarem*	*falarem*	*deterem*	*detiverem*

subjunctive future forms with no overt markings of subject agreement. In other words, in (5.237a) the verb is in its subjunctive form and its subject agreement morphology, although phonetically null, prevents the 3PAC from surfacing enclitically. (5.237b), in turn, resorts to the uninflected infinitival form and enclisis is enforced, as the suffixal morphological slot for agreement is available.

As the glosses of the verbs in (5.237) indicate, we have different morphological specifications for the verbs, rather than a double option for clitic placement. This becomes clearer when we consider irregular verbs. As exemplified in (5.238), the syncretism involving the inflected infinitive and the subjunctive future is also being extended to irregular verbs in BP, and the subjunctive future forms *vir* and *detiver* are losing ground to the uninflected forms *ver* 'see' and *deter* 'detain'. Remarkably, the position of 3PACs is sensitive to whether the verb surfaces with the irregular or the regularized conjugation, as shown in (5.239).

(5.238) BP:
    a. %Se você **vir** o João, me
        *if you.SG see.***SUBJ.FUT.3.SG*** *the João me*
        avise.   [*irregular conjugation*]
        warn
    a'. Se você **ver** o João, me avise. [*regularized conjugation*]
        *if you.SG see.***INF*** *the João me warn*
        'If you(SG) see João, tell me.'
    b. Se a polícia **deter** esse senador, isso
        *if the police detain.***SUBJ.FUT.3.SG*** *this senator this*
        vai ser uma grande novidade. [*irregular conjugation*]
        goes be a big novelty

b'. Se   a   polícia   **deter**   esse senador, isso vai ser
    if   the   police   detain-**INF** this senator   this goes be
    uma grande novidade.   [*regularized conjugation*]
    a   big   novelty
    'If the police arrest this senator, it will be big news.'

(5.239)   BP:
    a. *Se   você   vi-**lo**,   me
        if   you.SG   see.***SUBJ.FUT.3.SG***-him   me
        avise.   [*irregular conjugation*]
        warn
    a'. %Se   você   **o**   vir,   me
        if   you.SG   him   see.***SUBJ.FUT.3.SG***   me
        avise.   [*irregular conjugation*]
        warn
    b.   Se   você   **o**   ver,   me
        if   you.SG   him   see.***SUBJ.FUT.3.SG***   me
        avise.   [*regularized conjugation*]
        warn
    b'. Se você   **vê-lo**,   me avise.   [*infinitive*]
        if you.SG see.**INF**-him me warn
        'If you(SG) see him, let me know.'

(5.240)   BP:
    a. *Quando a   polícia detivé-**los**,   isso
        when   the police detain.***SUBJ.FUT.3.SG***-them this
        vai   ser   uma   grande   novidade.   [*irregular conjugation*]
        goes   be   a   big   novelty
    a'. Quando a   polícia **os**   detiver,   isso
        when   the police   them   detain.***SUBJ.FUT.3.SG*** this
        vai   ser   uma   grande   novidade.   [*irregular conjugation*]
        goes   be   a   big   novelty
    b.   Quando a   polícia **os**   deter,   isso
        when   the police   them   detain.***SUBJ.FUT.3.SG*** this
        vai   ser   uma   grande novidade.   [*regularized conjugation*]
        goes   be   a   big   novelty
    b'. Quando a   polícia detê-**los**,   isso
        when   the police   detain.**INF**-them this
        vai   ser   uma   grande   novidade.   [*infinitive*]
        goes   be   a   big   novelty
        'When the police arrest them, it will be big news.'

(5.239a,a') and (5.240a,a') involve unambiguous cases of subjunctive future. Enclisis is therefore blocked by the null morpheme of subject agreement and proclisis is enforced. In (5.239b,b') and (5.240b,b'), the verb is ambiguous between a regularized subjunctive future form and an uninflected infinitival form. So, we have proclisis in the first case and enclisis in the second.

Unsurprisingly, the clitics *me* and *te* are not sensitive to such fine morphological distinctions and proclisis is uniformly enforced, as shown in (5.241).

(5.241) a. %Se eu **te** vir,
if I you.SG see-SUBJ.FUT.3.SG
eu dou um sinal. [*irregular conjugation*]
I give a signal
a'. Se eu **te** ver,
if I you.SG see-SUBJ.FUT.3.SG
eu dou um sinal. [*regularized conjugation*]
I give a signal
'If I see you(SG), I'll give a signal.'
b. Se a polícia **me** detiver,
if the police me detain-SUBJ.FUT.3.SG
ligue pro meu advogado. [*irregular conjugation*]
call to-the my lawyer
b'. Se a polícia **me** deter,
if the police me detain-SUBJ.FUT.3.SG
ligue pro meu advogado. [*regularized conjugation*]
call to-the my lawyer
'If the police arrest me, call my lawyer.'

5.7 Summary

In the preceding sections we have seen that EP and BP significantly differ with respect to how they employ word order to encode context-sensitive information and to satisfy morphological restrictions in the case of clitics. By and large, BP always has fewer possibilities of word order variation than EP and, even when they converge on the same orders, they may be subject to different restrictions. For instance, both EP and BP generally allow VS order to encode thetic judgments if the verb is intransitive (unergative and unaccusative), but not if it is transitive (see Section 5.2.1.1). However, when the allowed VS orders are examined in more detail in each variety, we find that VS is much more lexically restricted in BP than in EP and that this order is subject to definiteness restrictions in BP and evidentiality conditions in EP.

VS order actually turns out to mark a watershed between the two varieties. We have seen, for instance, that the fronting of focus in declarative sentences and *wh*-phrases in interrogative sentences is generally accompanied in EP by subject–verb inversion, whereas BP tends to stick to the unmarked SVO order, encoding the relevant focus information through stress assignment (see Sections 5.2.2 and 5.3). VS also arises in different types of exclamatives in EP, being quite restricted in BP (see Section 5.4). In fact, in essentially every domain (finite or nonfinite; see Section 5.5) we examined, BP exhibits a more rigid word order.[118] This becomes crystal-clear when we discuss clitic placement. Whereas EP exhibits a complex interaction of factors that yields both enclisis and proclisis outputs, BP rigidly converges on proclisis to the main verb, with the exception of indefinite *se* and third person accusative clitics. Even so, the latter exception is arguably not part of the grammar of BP as defined in Chapter 1, which makes BP even more rigid with respect to clitic placement.

In Chapter 2 we saw that the reduction of the inventory of pronouns in BP has led to a good amount of case syncretism, drastically reducing case distinctions in its pronominal system. In Chapter 3, we also saw that, although EP and BP on the surface look basically the same with respect to their verbal agreement inflection, at a morphological level the agreement system of BP is greatly underspecified. It also happens that when languages lose case distinctions and have their agreement system weakened, they lean towards a more rigid word order. Thus, the fact that EP and BP so distinctively diverge with respect to word order possibilities appears to be a reflex of these other changes that BP has undergone.

---

[118] The distinction between affirmative and negative clauses also has a greater impact on word order in EP than on that in BP. For instance, affirmative and negative clauses have a different pattern of clitic placement in EP, but not in BP (see Section 5.6) and focus fronting of negative words makes the otherwise obligatory VS order optional in EP, but does not interfere with the SV order in BP (see Section 5.2.2.2).

6

Null Objects and Null Possessors

6.1 Introduction

In Chapter 4 we discussed the differences between European Portuguese (EP) and Brazilian Portuguese (BP) with respect to null subjects. In this chapter we return to the interesting issue of syntactic structures that are not phonetically realized, examining how the two varieties pattern with respect to null objects in the verbal domain and null possessors in the nominal domain.

Consider the data in (6.1) below, for instance, which show that the verb *comprar* 'buy' selects a direct object and the verb *gostar* 'like' an oblique complement headed by the preposition *de* 'of'. Given an appropriate context, these complements may also be left unexpressed, as respectively shown in (6.2a) and (6.2b).

(6.1)   a. Eu comprei o vaso.
           I bought the vase
           'I bought the vase.'
      b. Eu gostei do livro.
           I liked of-the book
           'I liked the book.'

(6.2)   a. Olha [que vaso bonito]$_i$! Vou comprar Ø$_i$ para a Maria.
           look what vase beautiful go-1.SG buy   for the Maria
           'What a beautiful vase! I'm going to buy it for Maria.'
      b. Eu li [o livro]$_i$, mas não gostei Ø$_i$.
           I read the book but not liked
           'I read the book, but didn't like it.'

The data in (6.3) and (6.4), in turn, respectively show that the relevant "possessive" relation between *pai* 'father' and *o João* may be realized by a possessive pronoun (in EP; see Section 2.4.3), an oblique pronoun preceded by the preposition *de*, or left unexpressed.

(6.3) a. [O João]ᵢ telefonou para o **seu**ᵢ pai.   (EP)
the João called to the his father
b. [O João]ᵢ telefonou para o pai **dele**ᵢ.
the João called to the father of-him
'Joãoᵢ called hisᵢ father.'

(6.4) [O João] telefonou para o pai Øᵢ.
the João called to the father
'Joãoᵢ called hisᵢ father.'

Remarkably, although EP and BP allow for null direct objects, null oblique objects, and null possessors in sentences like (6.2a), (6.2b), and (6.4), they display substantial differences with respect to the licensing or the interpretation of each of these empty expressions, as we shall see. It is also worth pointing out that EP and BP also allow ellipsis of verbal constituents; this may give rise to ambiguous cases where a given sentence may be analyzed as involving a null object or involving ellipsis of a verbal constituent containing an object. In order to avoid an undesirable confusion between the two types of lack of phonetic realization, we will start our discussion with a brief description of ellipsis of verbal constituents.

The chapter is organized as follows. In Section 6.2 we discuss some properties of constructions with ellipsis of verbal constituents in EP and BP that allow us to distinguish them from null object constructions, which are the topics of Section 6.3 (null direct objects) and 6.4 (null oblique objects). Section 6.5 discusses null possessors. Finally, Section 6.6 summarizes the differences between EP and BP in respect of null objects and null possessors.

6.2 Ellipsis of Verbal Projections

Ellipsis of syntactic constituents is a very interesting phenomenon, as natural languages may differ with respect to the types of constituents that can be elided and the conditions that license it. In this section we will focus on some properties of ellipsis of verbal constituents in Portuguese, which will be helpful for the characterization of null objects to be presented in Sections 6.3 and 6.4.[1]

Let us start with *VP ellipsis*, a relatively infrequent crosslinguistic pattern that is available in both EP and BP. VP ellipsis involves lack of phonetic

---

[1] For discussion see e.g. Raposo 1986, Matos 1992, 2013a, Martins 1994b, 2006b, 2016b, Cyrino and Matos 2002, 2005, 2016, Kato 2003, Kato and Raposo 2007, and Costa, Martins, and Pratas 2012.

realization of the main verb, its complements and (optionally) its adjuncts, when the verbal constituent containing these elements is the complement of an auxiliary verb, as illustrated in (6.5a) and (6.5b) below. The material without phonetic realization is interpretively recovered based on some discourse-salient parallel material available in the same sentence or in previous discourse – commonly referred to as the *antecedent* of the elided material.[2] In the sentences in (6.5), for instance, the second clause is understood as involving the whole verb phrase of the first clause in (6.5a) and the verb and the direct object of the previous utterance in (6.5b), as represented by the crossed-out material in (6.5a′) and (6.5b′), respectively.

(6.5)   a. A Maria já tinha conversado com o Pedro
the Maria already had-3.SG talked with the Pedro
ontem, mas o João ainda não tinha.
yesterday but the João still not had-3.SG
'Maria had already talked to Pedro yesterday, but João hadn't.'
a′. ... mas o João ainda não tinha [conversado com o Pedro ontem]
b. A: – A Maria vai comprar a passagem amanhã.
the Maria go-3.SG buy the ticket tomorrow
'Maria will buy the ticket tomorrow.'
B: – E o João vai no domingo.
and the João go-3.SG in-the Sunday
'And João will on Sunday.'
b′. E o João vai [comprar a passagem] no domingo.

Let us now consider the data in (6.6) and (6.7) below. The answer by B in (6.6) and the second conjunct of (6.7) cannot be simply analyzed as a potential combination of a null direct object with a null oblique object, for their interpretation is that Maria put the books on the bookshelf in alphabetical order. In other words, the unexpressed constituent in (6.6B) and (6.7) must also include the manner adverbial in addition to the complements of the verb.

(6.6)   A: – A Maria colocou os livros na estante
the Maria put PAST.3.SG the books in-the bookshelf
em ordem alfabética?
in order alphabetical
'Did Maria put the books on the bookshelf in alphabetical order?'
B: – Colocou.
put.PAST.3.SG
'Yes, she did.'

---

[2] See e.g. Matos 1992, 2013a for a characterization of these contexts and discussion.

334   6 Null Objects and Null Possessors

(6.7)   O   João   não   colocou   os   livros   na   estante
        the João   not   put PAST.3.SGt   the   books   in-the   bookshelf
        em   ordem   alfabética,   mas   a   Maria   colocou.
        in   order   alphabetical   but   the   Maria   put PAST.3.SG
        'João did not put the books on the bookshelf in alphabetical order, but
        Maria did.'

Given the similarities between (6.5), on the one hand, and (6.6) and (6.7), on the other, one would expect the latter to also involve ellipsis of a verbal constituent. A unified analysis of (6.5)–(6.7) can be achieved if one takes into account the way verbs are associated with their tense and agreement inflections. As the first clauses of (6.5a) and (6.5b) show, the finite tense and agreement inflections are realized not on the main verb, but on the auxiliary verb. Suppose that the inflection (Infl) in fact always sits in a position external to the verb phrase (VP) even when auxiliaries are not present, as illustrated in (6.8a) below. If there is no auxiliary to support the inflection, the main verb then moves to the left of Infl, as sketched in (6.8b).[3] Finally, if VP ellipsis applies to (6.8b), as shown in (6.8c), the output will have the main verb phonetically realized, but not its complements and adjuncts. This is exactly what we find in (6.6B) and the second conjunct of (6.7). The verb *colocar* 'put' moves to the left of Infl and the whole verb phrase is elided, as sketched in (6.9). Crosslinguistically, this pattern of ellipsis, generally referred to as *verb-stranding VP ellipsis* (VSVPE), is more infrequent than the VP ellipsis illustrated in (6.5). In EP and BP, VSVPE typically occurs in answers to *yes/no* questions (see Section 7.5.1), as illustrated in (6.6B), but can also occur in declarative sentences, as shown in (6.7).[4]

(6.8)   a. [Infl [VP V ...]]
        b. [V-Infl [VP __ ...]]
        c. [V-Infl [VP ...]]

---

[3] For the original proposals on verb movement to Infl, see Emonds 1976 and Pollock 1989. For discussion on verb movement in Portuguese, see e.g. Ambar 1992a, Figueiredo Silva 1996, Costa 1998, Galves 2001, and Tescari Neto 2012.

[4] For discussion see e.g. Raposo 1986, Matos 1992, Martins 1994b, 2006b, 2007, 2016b, Cyrino and Matos 2002, 2005, 2016, and Kato 2016. In (6.9), the thematic vowel of *colocar* ({-a-}) is realized as [o] when preceding the indicative perfective past tense morpheme {-u}. For purposes of presentation, we set aside the possibility that the verb and its inflection may further move leftwards, with ellipsis targeting a constituent larger than VP. For arguments for such an approach and discussion, see Martins 1994b, 2006b, 2007, 2016b, Costa, Martins, and Pratas 2012, and Kato 2016.

(6.9)   a. [-u [VP coloca- os livros na estante em ordem alfabética]]
         b. [coloca-u [VP __ os livros na estante em ordem alfabética]]
         c. [coloca-u [VP __ ~~os livros na estante em ordem alfabética~~]]

The fact that VP ellipsis strands an auxiliary verb, as seen in (6.5a) with the perfective auxiliary *ter* 'have' or in (6.5b) with the future auxiliary *ir* 'go', makes it clear that these are not cases of null object constructions like (6.2a) and (6.2b), for the auxiliary *ter* cannot take *com o Pedro* 'with Pedro' as an oblique object in (6.5a), neither can *ir* take *a passagem* 'the ticket' as a direct object in (6.5b). Sentences like (6.10a) below, on the other hand, whose verb phrase involves just a verb and a direct object, are indeed potentially ambiguous between a null direct object construction, as shown in the simplified representation in (6.10b), and a VSVPE construction, as represented in (6.10c) (see footnote 4 above).[5]

(6.10)   a. A Maria já comprou o livro, mas o João ainda não comprou.
           the Maria already bought the book but the João still not bought
           'Maria has already bought the book, but João hasn't.'
          b. ... mas o João ainda não comprou Ø
          c. ... mas o João ainda não [compra-u [VP __ ~~o livro~~]]

One test that helps disambiguate the two constructions is an identity requirement that applies to ellipsis.[6] In particular, the stranded verb of VSVPE must be identical in lexical content to its antecedent, as illustrated in (6.11) below. Although the verbs *pôr* 'put' and *colocar* 'put' are synonymous and select the same types of complements, the one cannot license VSVPE involving the other.

(6.11)   *A Maria **pôs** os documentos em ordem, mas o João não **colocou**.
           the Maria put the documents in order but the João not placed
           'Maria put the documents in order, but João didn't.'

The sentence in (6.10a) may thus be a case of VSVPE (see (6.10c)), but not that in (6.12a) below, for the verbs in (6.12a) correspond to different lexical items; hence, (6.12a) is to be analyzed as involving a null object, as represented in (6.12a'). Similarly, (6.12b) is acceptable despite having distinct

---

[5] See e.g. Raposo 1986, Matos 1992, Martins 1994b, Kato 2003, 2016, Kato and Raposo 2007, and Cyrino and Matos 2016 for discussion.

[6] For discussion see e.g. Raposo 1986, Duarte 1987, Matos 1992, 2013a, Cyrino and Matos 2002, 2005, Zocca 2003, Nunes and Zocca 2009, and Costa and Duarte 2013.

verbs, because it is not an instance of VSVPE either. Notice that only one of the complements of *colocar* is missing in (6.12b); hence, it is also to be analyzed as involving a null object, as represented in (6.12b′).

(6.12) a. O João **encontrou** o livro, mas não **comprou**.
  the João found the book but not bought
  'João found the book, but didn't buy it.'
  a′. …mas não comprou Ø.
  b. A Maria **pôs** os documentos em ordem, mas
  the Maria put the documents in order but
  não **colocou** no local adequado.
  not placed in-the place adequate
  Maria put the documents in order, but didn't put them in the proper place.'
  b′. …mas não colocou Ø no local adequado.

We leave a discussion of additional properties of VSVPE to the next section, as we proceed to laying out the properties of null objects in EP and BP.

6.3 Null Direct Objects

In this section we discuss differences between EP and BP with respect to null definite direct objects like that exemplified in (6.2a).[7] Before we move to the discussion proper, we still need to put aside two other different cases of empty object positions that have different properties and should not be conflated with the type of null direct object that is the major focus of this section. The first involves indefinite generic null objects, as illustrated in (6.13).[8]

(6.13) a. Esse argumento leva Ø a uma conclusão bem interessante.
  this argument takes to a conclusion well interesting
  'This argument leads to a rather interesting conclusion.'
  b. Muitos dentifrícios protegem Ø contra bactérias.
  many dentifrices protect against bacteria-PL
  'Many toothpastes protect against bacteria.'

---

[7] For discussion see e.g. Moreira da Silva 1983, Tarallo 1983, Duarte 1986, 1989, Raposo 1986, 1998a, Duarte 1987, Galves 1989, Farrell 1990, Corrêa 1991, Kato 1993b, 1994, 2003, Nunes 1993, Bianchi and Figueiredo Silva 1994, Cyrino 1993, 1997, 2016, 2019, 2020, Ferreira 2000, Kato and Raposo 2001, 2005, 2007, Costa and Duarte 2003, 2013, Creus and Menuzzi 2004, Marafoni 2010, Cyrino and Lopes 2016, Cyrino and Matos 2016, and Panitz 2018.

[8] See e.g. Costa and Duarte 2013 and Cyrino and Matos 2016 for discussion.

The verbs *levar* 'take' in (6.13a) and *proteger* 'protect' in (6.13b) may take an overt direct object. However, if the direct object is left unexpressed, as in (6.13), it receives an indefinite generic reading similar to 'one'. The interpretation of this type of null object is fixed and the class of verbs that allows it is lexically restricted.

The other case we will leave aside involves deictic null inanimate objects that are generally found with imperatives.[9] The null object of the sentences in (6.14) below, for example, may be interpreted as a null demonstrative akin to 'this', referring to some salient object deictically identifiable. (6.14a) may, for instance, be an instruction written on an envelope stating that the envelope itself should be sent with the payment and (6.14b) may be written on a box containing fragile material as a warning that the box itself should be handled carefully. Interestingly, languages that do not allow null objects such as those in (6.2), whose interpretation is linked to an overt expression in the sentence or in the previous discourse, may allow null object constructions analogous to (6.13) and (6.14). This is the case with English, for example.

(6.14)   a. Envie Ø com o pagamento.
           send   with the payment
           'Send with payment.'
         b. Carregue Ø com cuidado.
           carry   with care
           'Handle with care.'

Once we set aside seemingly related constructions such as (6.13) and (6.14), there are four major factors that are relevant for the licensing and interpretation of null definite direct objects (henceforth, simply *null objects*) such as those in (6.2) in EP and BP: [person] and [human] specifications, the position of the antecedent, and syntactic islands. Let us consider each of these in turn.

Null objects in EP and BP display sensitivity to the feature [person]. Consider the sentence in (6.15b) below, for instance, as a potential answer to each of the questions in (6.15a) in a context where people are discussing who is taking whom to the party. (6.15b) can mean only that Maria will take him or João, but cannot mean that she will take you or me. In other words, EP and BP do not allow null objects to be interpreted as first or second person pronouns.

(6.15)   [*Context*: People are discussing who is taking whom to the party.]
         a. A: –   E   {eu/você/ele/o João}?
                and   I/you.SG/he/the João
                'What about {me/you(SG)/him/João}?'

---

[9] See e.g. Kato 1994 and R. Lopes 2003 for discussion.

b. B: – A   Maria   leva   Ø.   (EP/BP)
        the Maria   takes
        'Maria will take {*you(SG)/*me/him/João}.'
b'. B: – A   Maria leva   {-te/-me/-o}.   (EP)
        the Maria takes -you/-me/-him
b''. B: – A   Maria {{te/me} leva   / leva ele}. (BP)
        the Maria you.SG/me takes / takes him
        'Maria will take {you(SG)/me/him}.'

This is another property that sets null object constructions apart from ellipsis constructions. As the VP ellipsis construction in (6.16a) and the VSVPE construction in (6.16b) show, elliptical structures can be interpreted as having first and second person pronouns.

(6.16) a. A Maria não tinha me visto, mas o Pedro tinha.
            the Maria not had   me seen   but the Pedro had
            'Maria had not seen me, but Pedro had.'
      b. A: – A   Maria não me viu.
              the Maria not me saw.3.SG
              'Maria didn't see me.'
         B: – Viu,   sim.
              saw.3.SG yes
              'Yes, she did.'

The null object of (6.15b) can also be interpreted as [-hum] given the appropriate context, as illustrated in (6.17a–b) below. In contexts such as (6.17), the null object is actually preferred over the corresponding overt alternative in both EP (see (6.17b′)) and BP (see (6.17b″)). In fact, the interpretation of null objects as [-hum] is much less restricted than its [+hum] counterpart, as there seems to be no structural configuration where a null object can be interpreted as [+hum], but not as [-hum]. Even in configurations where [+hum] interpretation is allowed, as in (6.15b), speakers tend to find parallel configurations with a [-hum] interpretation, like that in (6.17b), more natural. Speakers also display more variation in acceptability judgments with respect to [+hum] third person null objects in sentences like (6.15b), generally preferring an overt pronoun, instead – a clitic in EP, as seen in (6.15b′), and a clitic or a weak pronoun in BP, as seen in (6.15b″) (see Section 2.4.3).[10]

---

[10] For discussion see e.g. Omena 1978, Tarallo 1983, Duarte 1986, 1989, Corrêa 1991, Kato, Cyrino, and Corrêa 2009, Marafoni 2010, Rinke, Flores, and Barbosa 2018, and Rinke 2021.

(6.17) [*Context*: People are discussing who is bringing what to the picnic.]
    a. A: – E   o   bolo?
           and the cake
          'What about the cake?'
    b. B: – A   Maria leva   Ø.   (EP/BP)
           the Maria takes
    b′. B: – ?A Maria leva-o.   (EP)
           the Maria takes-it
    b.″ B: – ?A   Maria leva   **ele**. (BP)
           the Maria takes it
          'Maria will bring it.'

This contrast between [+hum] and [-hum] specifications also appears in the context of strong syntactic islands. Relative clauses, sentential subjects, and adverbial clauses are generally referred to as strong syntactic islands, for they do not allow syntactic movement from within them, as illustrated in (6.18) below. Recall that EP and BP allow focused constituents to remain *in situ* or move to a designated sentence-initial position (see Section 5.2.2.1). The contrasts in (6.18) show that movement of the focus across a strong island yields unacceptable sentences.

(6.18)   a. A Maria entrevistou um escritor [island que escreveu **só um livro**].
          the Maria interviewed a writer   that wrote   only one book

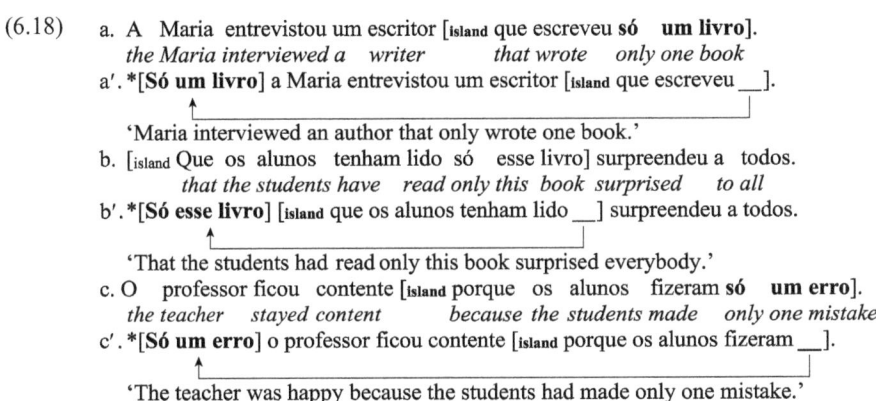

      a′. *[**Só um livro**] a Maria entrevistou um escritor [island que escreveu __].
          'Maria interviewed an author that only wrote one book.'
      b. [island Que os alunos tenham lido só esse livro] surpreendeu a todos.
            that the students have read only this book surprised to all
      b′. *[**Só esse livro**] [island que os alunos tenham lido __] surpreendeu a todos.
          'That the students had read only this book surprised everybody.'
      c. O professor ficou contente [island porque os alunos fizeram **só um erro**].
           the teacher stayed content   because the students made   only one mistake
      c′. *[**Só um erro**] o professor ficou contente [island porque os alunos fizeram __].
          'The teacher was happy because the students had made only one mistake.'

Interestingly, [-hum] null objects within strong islands like those in (6.19) below are judged to be plainly acceptable by BP speakers, but are generally rejected or only marginally accepted by (some) EP speakers.[11] EP speakers

---

[11] It is possible that the EP speakers that marginally allow constructions with null objects within strong islands are actually assigning a more complex structure to these constructions, involving movement of some verbal projection other than VP, followed by its deletion (see Kato 2003, Costa and Duarte 2003, and Kato and Raposo 2007 for specific proposals and discussion). For presentation purposes, we will disregard this variation within EP and focus on the major contrasts between EP and BP.

strongly prefer the clitic versions in (6.20) instead, whereas BP speakers interchangeably allow the null object constructions in (6.19) and their counterparts with a weak pronoun in (6.20).

(6.19) [*Context*: People are talking about a given car.]
    a. O   rapaz   [_{island} que comprou Ø] é meu vizinho. (EP: ?*; BP: OK)
       the young.man   that bought   is my neighbor
       'The young man who bought it is my neighbor.'
    b. [_{island} Que o   João   tenha conseguido consertar Ø sozinho]
             that the   João   has   managed   fix   alone
       foi   uma surpresa.   (EP: *; BP: OK)
       was a   surprise
       'That João managed to fix it by himself was a surprise.'
    c. O   João ficou admirado [_{island} porque a   Maria queria
       the   João stayed   surprised   because the Maria wanted
       vender Ø].   (EP: ?* BP: OK)
       sell
       'João was surprised that Maria wanted to sell it.'

(6.20) a. O   rapaz   [_{island} que **o** comprou] é meu vizinho.   (EP)
       the young.man   that it bought   is my neighbor
    a′. O   rapaz   [_{island} que comprou **ele**] é meu vizinho. (BP)
        the young.man   that bought   it is my neighbor
        'The young man who bought it is my neighbor.'
    b. [_{island} Que o   João   tenha conseguido consertá-**lo** sozinho]
             that the   João   has   managed   fix-it   alone
       foi   uma surpresa.   (EP)
       was a   surprise
    b′. [_{island} Que o   João   tenha conseguido consertar **ele** sozinho]
             that the   João   has   managed   fix   it alone
       foi   uma surpresa.   (BP)
       was a   surprise
       'That João managed to fix it by himself was a surprise.'
    c. O   João ficou admirado [_{island} porque a   Maria queria
       the   João stayed   surprised   because the Maria wanted
       vendê-**lo**].   (EP)
       sell-it
    c′. O   João ficou admirado [_{island} porque a   Maria queria
        the   João stayed   surprised   because the Maria wanted
       vender **ele**].   (BP)
       sell   it
       'João was surprised that Maria wanted to sell it.'

By contrast, sentences analogous to (6.19) but referring to a [+hum] antecedent in the discourse are judged as unacceptable in both EP and BP, as illustrated in (6.21) below. As expected (see Section 2.4.3), in such configurations EP resorts to a clitic instead of the null object and BP a weak pronoun, as shown in (6.22).

(6.21) [*Context*: People are talking about Pedro.]
    a. *O gerente [island que contratou Ø] foi promovido. (EP/BP)
        the manager   that hired   was promoted
       'The manager who hired him was promoted.'
    b. *[island Que a Maria tenha despedido Ø] foi uma
              that the Maria has fired   was a
       surpresa. (EP/BP)
       surprise
       'That Maria had fired him was a surprise.'
    c. *A Maria ficou contente [island porque o chefe
        the Maria stayed content   because the boss
       promoveu Ø]. (EP/BP)
       promoted
       'Maria was happy because the boss promoted him.'

(6.22) a. O gerente [island que o contratou] foi promovido. (EP)
        the manager   that him hired   was promoted
    a'. O gerente [island que contratou **ele**] foi promovido. (BP)
        the manager   that hired   him was promoted
       'The manager who hired him was promoted.'
    b. [island Que a Maria o tenha despedido foi uma surpresa. (BP)
            that the Maria him has fired   was a   surprise
    b'. [island Que a Maria tenha despedido **ele**] foi uma surpresa. (BP)
            that the Maria has fired   him was a   surprise
       'That Maria had fired him was a surprise.'
    c. A Maria ficou contente [island porque o chefe **o**
        the Maria stayed content   because the boss him
       promoveu]. (EP)
       promoted
    c'. A Maria ficou contente [island porque o chefe promoveu
        the Maria stayed content   because the boss promoted
       ele]. (BP)
       him
       'Maria was happy because the boss promoted him.'

Again, this interaction between [+hum] and [-hum] specifications and strong islands distinguishes null object constructions from ellipsis constructions. The VP ellipsis and VSVPE constructions in (6.23a) and (6.23b) below, for instance, both allow the elliptical material to include a [+hum] object (notice that (6.23b) also involves a strong island).[12]

---

[12] See e.g. Kato 2003 and Kato and Raposo 2007 for discussion.

342   6 Null Objects and Null Possessors

(6.23)   a. A Joana vai trazer **o noivo**, mas a Maria não vai.
            the Joana goes bring the fiancé but the Maria not goes
            'Joana is going to bring her fiancé, but Maria isn't.'
         b. O gerente elogiou **o João**, mas eu conversei com
            the manager praised the João but I talked with
            uma pessoa [island que disse que o presidente não elogiou].
            a person   that said that the president not praised
            'The manager praised João, but I talked with someone who said that
            the chairman didn't.'

So far, we have discussed cases where the antecedent of the null object is not in its sentence, but in the previous discourse. When the antecedent is within the same sentence as the null object, an intricate interaction between the specification [±hum] and the position of the antecedent appears.[13] Two syntactic positions are particularly relevant: the subject position and the sentence-initial topic position. If the intrasentential antecedent is [-hum] and no strong island intervenes between the null object and its antecedent, the null object is generally accepted in EP and BP, as illustrated in (6.24a–c) below. If an island intervenes, the pattern seen earlier with an antecedent in the previous discourse reappears: a null object is allowed in BP, but not in EP, as illustrated in (6.24d–e).

(6.24)   a. O dono d[o **apartamento**]$_i$ mudou de opinião
            the owner of-the apartment   changed of opinion
            e decidiu não vender Ø$_i$.   (EP/BP)
            and decided not sell
            'The owner of the apartment changed his mind and decided
            not to sell it.'
         b. O João trouxe [os **documentos**]$_i$ e deixou
            the João brought the documents   and left
            Ø$_i$ em cima da mesa.   (EP/BP)
            in top of-the table
            'João brought the documents and left them on the table.'
         c. [**Este livro**]$_i$, todos os meus amigos leram Ø$_i$. (EP/BP)
            this book   all   the my friends   read
            'All my friends read this book.'
         d. [**Este prato**]$_i$, a pessoa [island que recomendou Ø$_i$] sabe
            this dish   a person   that recommended   knows
            bem o que é uma boa comida japonesa.   (EP: ?*; BP: OK)
            well what is a   good food   Japanese
            'The person who recommended this dish really knows what good
            Japanese food is.'

---

[13] For discussion see e.g. Bianchi and Figueiredo Silva 1994 and Ferreira 2000.

e. O   Pedro foi   procurar [o   artigo]ᵢ [island
    the   Pedro went   search   the   article
    porque o   orientador tinha citado Øᵢ].   (EP: *; BP: OK)
    because the advisor   had   cited
    'Pedro searched for the article because his advisor had cited it.'

However, the two varieties split if the [-hum] antecedent sits in a subject position, as shown in (6.25) below. In this case, the null object is not allowed in EP, which must then resort to the clitic version; by contrast, BP allows both the null object and the weak pronoun versions, with a preference for the empty category.

(6.25) a. [Esse   prato]ᵢ exige   que o cozinheiro acabe de
           this   dish   demands that the cook   finishes of
           preparar Øᵢ   na   mesa.   (EP: ?*; BP: OK)
           prepare   in-the   table
     a'.   [Esse prato]ᵢ exige   que o   cozinheiro acabe de prepará-loᵢ
           this dish   demands that the cook   finishes of prepare-it
           na   mesa.   (EP)
           in-the table
     a''. [Esse   prato]ᵢ exige   que o   cozinheiro acabe   de
           this   dish   demands that the cook   finishes of
           preparar eleᵢ   na   mesa.   (BP)
           prepare   it   in-the   table
           'This dish requires that the cook finishes preparing it at the table.'
       b. [Esse   brinquedo]ᵢ permite que as crianças montem Øᵢ
           this   toy   permits that the children assemble
           sem   ajuda.   (EP: *; BP: OK)
           without   help
     b'.   [Esse brinquedo]ᵢ permite que as crianças oᵢ montem sem
           this toy   permits that the children it assemble without
           ajuda.   (EP)
           help
     b''. [Esse brinquedo]ᵢ permite que as crianças montem eleᵢ sem
           this toy   permits that the children assemble it without
           ajuda.   (BP)
           help
           'This toy allows children to assemble it without help.'
       c. [Esse livro]ᵢ desapontou as   pessoas [island que tentaram ler
           this book   disappointed the   people   that tried   read
           Øᵢ].   (EP: *; BP: OK)
     c'.   [Esse livro]ᵢ desapontou as   pessoas [island que tentaram
           this book   disappointed the   people   that tried
           lê-loᵢ].   (EP)
           read-it

c″. [**Esse livro**]$_i$ desapontou as pessoas [$_{island}$ que tentaram ler
    this book disappointed the people that tried read
    ele$_i$]. (BP)
    it
    'This book disappointed the people who tried to read it.'

If the intrasentential antecedent is [+hum], the sentence is generally unacceptable in both EP and BP, as shown in (6.26) below. As seen earlier, EP employs a clitic instead of the null object and BP a weak pronoun.

(6.26) a. *A mãe d[o **João**]$_i$ disse que a Maria vai visitar
    the mother of-the João said that the Maria goes visit
    Ø$_i$. (EP/BP)
  a′. A mãe d[o **João**]$_i$ disse que a Maria vai
    the mother of-the João said that the Maria goes
    visitá-**lo**$_i$. (EP)
    visit-him
  a″. A mãe d[o **João**]$_i$ disse que a Maria vai visitar
    the mother of-the João said that the Maria goes visit
    ele$_i$. (BP)
    him
    'João's mother said that Maria was going to visit him.'
  b. *O João recomendou [esses alunos]$_i$, mas ninguém contratou
    the João recommended these students but nobody hired
    Ø$_i$. (EP/BP)
  b′. O João recomendou [esses alunos]$_i$, mas ninguém **os**$_i$
    the João recommended these students but nobody them
    contratou. (EP)
    hired
  b″. O João recomendou [esses alunos]$_i$, mas ninguém contratou
    the João recommended these students but nobody hired
    eles$_i$. (BP)
    them
    'João recommended these students, but no one hired them.'
  c. *[**Esse juiz**]$_i$ não gosta que os advogados contradigam
    this judge not likes that the lawyers contradict
    Ø$_i$. (EP/BP)
  c′. [**Esse juiz**]$_i$ não gosta que os advogados **o**$_i$
    this judge not likes that the lawyers him
    contradigam. (EP)
    contradict
  c″. [**Esse juiz**]$_i$ não gosta que os advogados contradigam
    this judge not likes that the lawyers contradict
    ele$_i$. (BP)
    him
    'This judge does not like lawyers contradicting him.'

d. *[**Essa atriz**]ᵢ desapontou as pessoas [ᵢₛₗₐₙd que tentaram
   this actress disappointed the people that tried
   cumprimentar Øᵢ]. (EP/BP)
   greet

d'. [**Essa atriz**]ᵢ desapontou as pessoas [ᵢₛₗₐₙd que tentaram
   this actress disappointed the people that tried
   cumprimentá-**la**ᵢ]. (EP)
   greet-her

d". [**Essa atriz**]ᵢ desapontou as pessoas [ᵢₛₗₐₙd que tentaram
   this actress disappointed the people that tried
   cumprimentar **ela**ᵢ]. (BP)
   greet her
   'This actress disappointed the people who tried to greet her.'

e. *A chefe promoveu [**o secretário**]ᵢ [ᵢₛₗₐₙd porque todos
   the boss promoted the secretary because all
   elogiaram Øᵢ]. (EP/BP)
   praised

e'. A chefe promoveu [o secretário]ᵢ [ᵢₛₗₐₙd porque todos
   the boss promoted the secretary because all
   oᵢ elogiaram]. (EP)
   him praised

e". A chefe promoveu [o secretário]ᵢ [ᵢₛₗₐₙd porque todos
   the boss promoted the secretary because all
   elogiaram **ele**ᵢ]. (BP)
   praised him
   'The boss promoted the secretary because everyone praised him.'

However, if the [+hum] antecedent appears in the sentence-initial topic position, the presence of island configurations containing the null object becomes relevant again. If no strong island is present, the sentence is acceptable in EP and BP, along with the corresponding clitic and weak pronoun versions, as shown in (6.27) below. On the other hand, if the null object occurs within a strong island, it is accepted only in BP, as illustrated in (6.28).

(6.27) a. [**O Obama**]ᵢ, o João disse que todos queriam
   the Obama the João said that all wanted
   cumprimentar Øᵢ. (EP/BP)
   greet

a'. [**O Obama**]ᵢ, o João disse que todos queriam
   the Obama the João said that all wanted
   cumprimentá-**lo**ᵢ. (EP)
   greet-him

a". [**O Obama**]ᵢ, o João disse que todos queriam cumprimentar
   the Obama the João said that all wanted greet
   eleᵢ. (BP)
   him
   'Obama, João said that everyone wanted to greet him.'

b. [O **Bolsonaro**]$_i$, a Maria disse que todos fingiam não
   the Bolsonaro the Maria said that all pretended not
   ver Ø$_i$. (EP/BP)
   see

b′. [O **Bolsonaro**]$_i$, a Maria disse que todos fingiam não
    the Bolsonaro the Maria said that all pretended not
    vê-**lo**$_i$. (EP)
    see-him

b″. [O **Bolsonaro**]$_i$, a Maria disse que todos fingiam não ver
    the Bolsonaro the Maria said that all pretended not see
    ele$_i$. (BP)
    him

'Bolsonaro, Maria said that everyone pretended not to see him.'

(6.28) a. [Esse **cantor**]$_i$, eu não conheço uma única
       this singer I not know a unique
       pessoa [$_{island}$ que tenha elogiado Ø$_i$]. (EP: ?*; BP: OK)
       person that has praised

a′. [Esse **cantor**]$_i$, eu não conheço uma única
    this singer I not know a unique
    pessoa [$_{island}$ que **o**$_i$ tenha elogiado]. (EP)
    person that him has praised

a″. [Esse **cantor**]$_i$, eu não conheço uma única pessoa
    this singer I not know a unique person
    [$_{island}$ que tenha elogiado **ele**$_i$]. (BP)
    that has praised him

'This singer, I don't know of a single person who has praised him.'

b. [Esse **ditador**]$_i$, os jornalistas [$_{island}$ que criticaram
   this dictator the journalists that criticized
   Ø$_i$] acabaram na prisão. (EP: *; BP: OK)
   finished in-the prison

b′. [Esse **ditador**]$_i$, os jornalistas [$_{island}$ que **o**$_i$
    this dictator the journalists that him
    criticaram] acabaram na prisão. (EP)
    criticized finished in-the prison

b″. [Esse **ditador**]$_i$, os jornalistas [$_{island}$ que
    this dictator the journalists that
    criticaram **ele**$_i$] acabaram na prisão. (BP)
    criticized him finished in-the prison

'This dictator, the journalists that criticized him ended up in prison.'

Putting aside differences between EP and BP regarding their specific preferences in respect of a null object and a clitic or a weak pronoun, Table 6.1 below summarizes the observations made thus far.

The first thing to notice in Table 6.1 is that islands have a bigger impact on EP than on BP. In EP a null object inside a strong island yields unacceptable results,

Table 6.1 Licensing of null objects in European Portuguese and Brazilian Portuguese

			[+hum]		[-hum]	
			EP	BP	EP	BP
No island	antecedent in discourse cf. (6.15b)/(6.17b)		OK	OK	OK	OK
	antecedent in the same sentence	in topic position cf. (6.27a)/(6.24c)	OK	OK	OK	OK
		in subject position cf. (6.26c)/(6.25b)	*	*	*	OK
		in other positions cf. (6.26a)/(6.24b)	*	*	OK	OK
Null object inside strong island	antecedent in discourse cf. (6.21a)/(6.19b)		*	*	*	OK
	antecedent in the same sentence	in topic position cf. (6.28b)/(6.24d)	*	OK	?*	OK
		in subject position cf. (6.26d)/(6.25c)	*	*	*	OK
		in other positions cf. (6.26e)/(6.24e)	*	*	*	OK

whereas in BP strong islands are relevant only when computed in tandem with the specification [+hum] and the position of the antecedent. Consider the sentences in (6.29) and (6.30) below, for instance.

(6.29) a. [Este carro]$_i$, a Maria disse que o João
 this car the Maria said that the João
 lavou Ø$_i$ ontem. (EP/BP)
 washed yesterday
 'This car, Maria said that João washed it yesterday.'
 b. A: – E [este carro]$_i$?
 and this car
 'What about this car?'
 B: – A Maria disse que o João lavou Ø$_i$
 the Maria said that the João washed
 ontem. (EP/BP)
 yesterday
 'Maria said that João washed it yesterday.'

(6.30) a. [Este carro]$_i$, o mecânico [$_{island}$ que ia
 this car the mechanic that went
 consertar Ø$_i$] ficou doente. (EP: *; BP: OK)
 fix stayed sick
 'The mechanic who was going to fix this car got sick.'
 b. A: – E [este carro]$_i$?
 and this car
 'What about this car?'
 B: – O mecânico [$_{island}$ que ia consertar Ø$_i$]
 the mechanic that went fix
 ficou doente. (EP: ?*; BP: OK)
 stayed sick
 'The mechanic who was going to fix it got sick.'

Given that the antecedent of a null object is interpreted as a topic and that strong islands block syntactic movement, the contrast between (6.29) and (6.30) in EP indicates that null object constructions in EP are derived via movement, regardless of whether or not the topic is overtly realized in the sentence.[14] In other words, sentences such as (6.29a) and (6.29b) in EP are derived along the simplified lines of (6.31a), where the embedded direct object is syntactically dislocated to a designated sentence-initial topic position (see Section 5.2.1.2). Suppose EP allows third person object topics to be

---

[14] See Raposo 1986 for the original proposal and Duarte 1987 for further elaboration and discussion.

"dropped."[15] Thus, if the topicalized object is phonetically realized, as in (6.31a), the structure surfaces as (6.29a); if the topic is dropped, as represented in (6.31b), the structure surfaces as (6.29b), with a null object being identified in the previous discourse.

(6.31)   a. [Este carro]$_i$, a Maria disse que o João lavou __ ontem   (cf. (6.29a))

b. [Este carro]$_i$, a Maria disse que o João lavou __ ontem   (cf. (6.29b))

What about BP? Given that sentences such as (6.30), which involve a strong island, are perfectly acceptable in BP, we are led to conclude that at least sentences like those in (6.30) cannot be derived via syntactic movement. Furthermore, given that one of the salient properties of BP is that it has lost its third person accusative clitics (see Sections 2.4.3 and 5.6.2), a possibility that arises is that BP came to have a null pronominal object (*pro*).[16] From this perspective, sentences such as (6.30) are to be represented as in (6.32), where the null pronoun, like pronouns in general, may be anaphorically anchored in the sentence or in the discourse.

(6.32)   BP:
a. [Este carro]$_i$, o mecânico [$_{island}$ que ia consertar ***pro**$_i$*] ficou doente.   (cf. (6.30a))
b. O mecânico [$_{island}$ que ia consertar ***pro***] ficou doente.   (cf. (6.30b))

The question now is whether sentences with no islands such as (6.29) are also to be derived in terms of *pro* in BP or whether BP also has available the movement strategy sketched in (6.31). At first sight, it does not seem possible to provide an answer, for the two possibilities should yield the same result. Interestingly, however, an answer can be reached if we take some phonological properties of BP into account. Let us consider (6.33a) below in BP, for instance, where the capital letters in bold annotate primary stress. The verb *comeu* 'ate.3.SG' has its primary stress on its last syllable and the noun *bolo* 'cake', on its first syllable. When two stressed syllables within the same phonological phrase are adjacent, as is the case in (6.33a), BP may allow the first stress to be shifted to the

---

[15] Recall that null objects in neither EP nor BP can be first or second person (see (6.15)). Hence, under a derivation where the null object is derived by movement and topic drop, it must be the case that, for independent reasons, topic drop cannot apply to first and second person object pronouns (see also footnote 19 below).
[16] For different proposals and discussion, see e.g. Galves 1989, Farrel 1990, Kato 1994, and Ferreira 2000.

previous syllable.[17] The configuration of stress clash in (6.33a), therefore, may be resolved via stress shift, yielding (6.33b).

(6.33) BP:
    a. A   Maria [coMEU BOlo]→
       the   Maria ate   cake
       'Maria ate some cake.'
    b. A Maria [COmeu BOlo]

Relevant to our current discussion is the situation where an empty syntactic position intervenes between two stressed syllables. Take the sentences in (6.34a) and (6.35a) below in BP, for example. We have seen earlier that, in both EP and BP, a focalized expression in a sentence-initial position reaches this position via movement, as it cannot cross a syntactic island (see (6.18)). So, it must be the case that, in the focalization construction in (6.34a), the embedded object has been moved to the sentence-initial position, as shown in the simplified representation in (6.34b). In turn, the null object in the topic construction in (6.35a) is separated from its antecedent by an island, which indicates that we have a null pronoun occupying this position in BP, as represented in (6.35b). Surprisingly, although we have a phonologically empty position intervening between the two stressed syllables in both (6.34b) and (6.35b), the gap produced by movement does not block stress shift, as shown in (6.34c), but *pro* does, as shown in (6.35c).[18]

(6.34)   a. [Só esse casaco]$_i$ o   João disse que ele vesTIU Ø$_i$ HOje
          only this coat   the João said that he dressed   today
          'It's only this coat that João said he put on today.'
    b. [Só esse casaco]$_i$ o João disse que ele vesTIU __ HOje →
    c. [Só esse casaco]$_i$ o João disse que ele VEStiu __ HOje

(6.35) BP:
    a. [Esse   casaco]$_i$,   a   Maria   ficou   elegante
       this   coat   the   Maria   stayed   elegant
      [$_{island}$ depois   que   ela   vesTIU   Ø$_i$ HOje.]
          after   that   she   dressed   today
      'This coat, Maria looked elegant in it after she put it on today.'
    b. [Esse casaco]$_i$, a Maria ficou elegante [$_{island}$ depois que ela vesTIU *pro*$_i$ HOje]→
    c. *[Esse casaco]$_i$, a Maria ficou elegante [$_{island}$ depois que ela VEStiu *pro*$_i$ HOje]

---

[17] For discussion on stress shift in BP, see e.g. Abousalh 1997, Guimarães 1998, Sândalo and Truckenbrodt 2002, and R. S. Santos 2002, 2003.
[18] See R. S. Santos 2002, 2003 for the original observation and Nunes and Santos 2009 for further discussion.

Returning to the relevant structure of the topic construction without islands in (6.29) in BP, we can see in (6.36a) and (6.37a) below that stress retraction is possible in this configuration. Therefore, the general conclusion is that, in the absence of islands, null objects in BP may be derived via movement, as sketched in (6.36b) and (6.37b).

(6.36)   a. [Este carro]$_i$, a Maria disse que o João laVOU Ø$_i$ ONtem →
           [Este carro]$_i$, a Maria disse que o João LAvou Ø$_i$ ONtem
       b. [Este carro]$_i$, a Maria disse que o João lavou __ ontem   (cf. (6.29a))

(6.37)   a. A Maria disse que o João laVOU Ø ONtem →
           A Maria disse que o João LAvou Ø ONtem
       b. [Este carro]$_i$, a Maria disse que o João lavou __ ontem   (cf. (6.29b))

Let us finally consider the relevance of the position of the antecedent and the [±hum] specification depicted in Table 6.1, bearing in mind that the specification [+hum] applies only to third person expressions, as EP and BP do not allow first and second person null objects (see footnote 15 above). In BP, a [-hum] null object is generally permitted regardless of the presence of islands or the position of the antecedent (see the last column of Table 6.1); by contrast, a [+hum] null object is allowed only when there are no strong islands and the antecedent is to be found in the previous discourse or when the antecedent sits in a designated topic position. This set of facts can be accounted for if *pro* in BP is underspecified in not having the feature [hum]. As far as interpretation is concerned, not being specified for the feature [hum] is quite compatible with being negatively specified for this feature ([-hum]), which would explain why a null object in BP is always able to take a [-hum] element for its antecedent, regardless of whether it is to be found in the sentence (see (6.24)) or in the discourse (see (6.17b)/(6.19)). The [+hum] possibility with an antecedent in the discourse in the absence of syntactic islands can be obtained via movement and topic drop. The answer by B in (6.38a) below, for instance, is to be analyzed along the lines sketched in (6.38b), with movement of the direct object to sentence-initial topic position, followed by its deletion. Recall that, in both EP and BP, sentences such as (6.38B) sound less natural than analogous sentences with a [-hum] interpretation for the null object (see (6.15) vs. (6.17)). From the current perspective, this may be taken to indicate that topic drop of objects sounds more natural with [-hum] expressions.

352   6 Null Objects and Null Possessors

(6.38) a. A: – E   o   Bolsonaro?
and the Bolsonaro
'What about Bolsonaro?'
B: – O   João disse que ninguém elogiou.
the João said that nobody praised
'João said that no one praised him.'
b.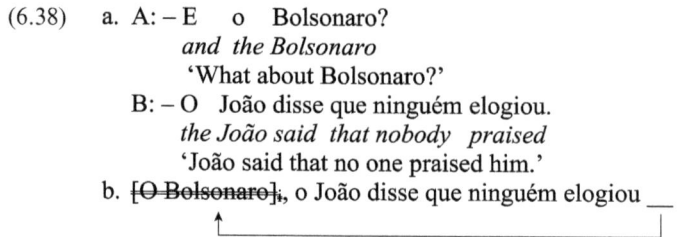

Lastly, the allowed [+hum] interpretation of a null object in BP when the [+hum] antecedent sits in the designated topic position seems to be enforced by the topic rather than the pronoun. In a sentence such as (6.39a) below, for instance, the pronoun in object position may take *o João* as its antecedent or some other compatible expression in the previous discourse; by contrast, in (6.39b) the pronoun can take only *o João* as its antecedent. The contrast in (6.39) stems from the fact that *o João* sits in a subject position in (6.39a), but in a topic position in (6.39b). This entails that in (6.39b) the material following *o João* must be about him, restricting the interpretive possibilities for the pronoun. Notice that we find the same situation in (6.28b), repeated below in (6.40), where the null pronoun can refer back only to *esse ditador* 'this dictator' in the topic position. Recall that we are assuming that object/accusative *pro* in BP does not have the feature [hum]; thus, there is no incompatibility in the specifications of *esse ditador* and *pro* in (6.40). An anaphoric relation between accusative *pro* and a [+hum] antecedent such as that illustrated in (6.40) is nevertheless established only when forced by independent interpretive requirements triggered by the antecedent.[19]

(6.39) BP:
a. [O João]$_i$ disse que todo mundo adora ele$_{i/k}$.
the João   said that all   world   adores him
'João$_i$ said that everyone loves him$_{i/k}$.'
b. [O João]$_i$, a Maria disse que todo mundo adora ele$_{i/*k}$.
the João   the Maria said that all   world   adores him
'Maria said that everyone loves João.'

---

[19] Notice that the null object pronoun in BP is not specified for the feature [hum], but is specified as third person. Hence, a null object inside an island in BP cannot be identified as first or second person, even in the presence of a first or second person pronoun in the topic position, as illustrated in (i) below. In other words, (i) is unacceptable for the same reason as (6.39b) or (6.40) when the pronoun has index *k*, namely, a topic is introduced and is not talked about in the comment. Thanks to Ezekiel Panitz for having brought this issue to our attention.

(i)   *{Eu/você},   o   professor   [$_{island}$ que entrevistou *pro* parecia de mau
I/you.SG   the teacher   that interviewed   seemed of bad
humor].   (BP)
humor
'The teacher who interviewed {me/you(SG)} seemed to be in a bad mood.'

(6.40)   BP:

   [**Esse ditador**]$_i$, os   jornalistas [$_{island}$ que   criticaram **pro**$_{i/*k}$]
   this   dictator   the journalists   that criticized
   acabaram   na   prisão.
   finished   in-the prison
   'This dictator, the journalists that criticized him ended up in prison.'

Let us now return to EP. We have seen that null objects in EP are derived only by movement to the sentence-initial topic position. Thus, the relevance of the [±hum] specification will be noted only in constructions with no islands. As seen in (6.26c) and (6.25b), repeated here in (6.41), a null object in EP cannot take a subject for its antecedent, regardless of whether it is [+hum] or [-hum]. On the other hand, if the antecedent occupies other positions, an asymmetry arises, with only [-hum] antecedents being allowed, as seen in (6.26b) and (6.24b), repeated below in (6.42).

(6.41)   EP:
   a. *[**Esse juiz**]$_i$ não gosta que   os   advogados contradigam Ø$_i$.
      this   judge not   likes that   the   lawyers   contradict
      'This judge does not like lawyers contradicting him.'
   b. *[**Esse brinquedo**]$_i$ permite que as crianças montem Ø$_i$ sem   ajuda.
      this   toy   permits that the children assemble   without help
      'This toy allows children to assemble it without help.'

(6.42)   EP:
   a. *O João recomendou [**esses alunos**]$_i$, mas ninguém contratou Ø$_i$.
      the João recommended these students but nobody   hired
      'João recommended these students, but no one hired them.'
   b. O João trouxe [**os documentos**]$_i$ e   deixou Ø$_i$ em cima da   mesa.
      the João brought the documents   and left   in top of-the table
      'João brought the documents and left them on the table.'

As null object constructions in EP are generated via movement, the unacceptability of the sentences in (6.41) is not unexpected. A general property of syntactic movement is that it is subject to a "strong crossover" restriction, which rules out movement of a nominal constituent across a coreferring subject, as illustrated in (6.43) below. Finally, the contrast between [+hum] and [-hum] specifications seen in (6.42) is also found in (6.44), where the topic moves to the sentence-initial position, crossing a coreferential element that is not in subject position (an instance of "weak crossover"). The sentence is allowed if the crossed coreferential element is [-hum] (see (6.44b)), but not if it is [+hum] (see (6.44a)). If null object constructions in EP involve movement of the object to a topic position, followed by its deletion, as seen above, it is no surprise that the type of restrictions independently found in topic constructions like (6.44) is replicated in null object constructions like (6.42).²⁰

(6.43)   EP:
a. *[Que professor]ᵢ disse eleᵢ que os alunos elogiaram?
    which teacher   said he that the students praised
    '*[Which teacher]ᵢ did heᵢ say that the students praised?'
b. *[Que professor]ᵢ disse eleᵢ que os alunos elogiaram __?

(6.44)   EP:
a. *[Este ator]ᵢ, as pessoas que oᵢ criticam não conhecem.
    this   actor   the people   that him criticize not know
    'The people who criticize this actor don't know him.'
b. [Este livro]ᵢ, as pessoas que oᵢ criticaram não leram.
    this   book   the people   that it criticized not read
    'The people who criticized this book didn't read it.'

6.4 Null Oblique Objects

Let us now examine constructions like (6.2b), repeated here in (6.45).

(6.45)   Eu li   [o livro]ᵢ, mas não gostei Øᵢ.
         I read the book   but not liked
         'I read the book, but didn't like it.'

First of all, notice that the two clauses in (6.45) have different verbs. So, the null complement of the verb *gostar* 'like' in (6.45) is not to be derived based on VSVPE (see Section 6.2). It also differs from the type of null object discussed in Section 6.3 in that it corresponds to an oblique complement, for the verb *gostar* selects for the preposition *de* 'of', as shown in (6.46). We will accordingly refer to these null complements as *null oblique objects*.²¹

(6.46)   a. *Eu gostei o   livro.
             I liked the book
         b. Eu gostei do   livro.
             I liked of-the book
             'I liked the book.'

Null oblique objects clearly differ from null direct objects in productivity. Null direct objects are by and large oblivious to the lexical properties of the

---

[20] For discussion, see Duarte 1987 and Ferreira 2000.
[21] For discussion see e.g. Duarte 1996, 2003a, 2013b, Nunes 2008b, Kato and Nunes 2009, 2014, Kato 2010, 2012, and Nunes and Kato forthcoming.

6.4 Null Oblique Objects   355

verbs they are associated with. Null oblique objects, by contrast, are highly sensitive to the (sometimes idiosyncratic) lexical properties of the verbs that admit them. Thus, although EP and BP both allow null oblique objects, they do not converge on the same set of verbs that license them and we also find individual variation among speakers with respect to the acceptability of the verbs that admit them. (6.47) below gives examples with the null oblique object taking an antecedent in the same sentence and (6.48) in the previous discourse (the verbs within the parentheses are followed by the preposition they select when not taking a null complement):

(6.47) a. (*discordar de*, lit.: *disagree of*)
   A   Maria disse   que   eu   concordei com [o
   the Maria said   that   I   agreed   with the
   João]$_i$, mas na   verdade eu **discordei Ø$_i$**.   (EP: OK; BP: OK)
   João   but in-the truth   I disagreed
   'Maria said I agreed with João, but I actually disagreed with him.'

   b. (*confiar em*, lit.: *trust in*)
   Eu   não desconfio d[este   candidato]$_i$, mas
   I   not mistrust   of-this candidate   but
   também não posso   dizer eu **confio   Ø$_i$**   (EP: OK; BP: OK)
   also   not can-1.SG say   I trust-1.SG
   'I don't mistrust this candidate, but I can't say that I trust him either.'

   c. (*precisar de*, lit.: *need of*)
   Eu   não guardei [os   livros]$_i$ [island
   I   not shelved the   books
   porque a   Maria ainda podia **precisar Ø$_i$**]. (EP: OK; BP: OK)
   because the Maria still could need
   'I didn't put the books away because Maria could still need them.'

(6.48) a. (*assistir a*, lit.: *watch to*)[22]
   A: – Gostei   muito d[a   primeira conferência do   congresso]$_i$.
         liked-1.SG much of-the first   lecture   of-the conference
   'I really liked the first lecture of the conference.'
   B: – Infelizmente, não pude   **assistir Ø$_i$** porque
         unfortunately not could-1.SG watch   because
         não consegui   chegar   a   tempo. (EP: OK; BP: OK)
         not managed-1.SG arrive   to   time
   'Unfortunately, I couldn't attend it because I didn't arrive in time.'

---

[22] The verb *assistir* 'watch' in BP no longer obligatorily selects for the preposition *a* 'to', as illustrated in (i). The presence of *a* preceding the complement of *assistir* in BP is associated with written language and formal style.

  (i) Eu vou assistir esta conferência hoje. (EP: *; BP: OK)
       I go watch   this lecture   today
       'I'm going to attend this lecture today.'

b. (*gostar de*, lit.: *like of*)
   A: – A Maria disse que adora [esse tipo de filme]ᵢ.
       the Maria said that adores this type of movie
       'Maria said that she loves this kind of movie.'
   B: – [island Que ela **goste** Øᵢ] não me
                that she likes-*SUBJ* not me
       surpreende. (EP: OK; BP: OK)
       surprises
       'That she likes it doesn't surprise me.'
c. (*concordar com*, lit.: *agree with*)
   A: – E [a nova proposta de lei]ᵢ?
       and the new proposal of law
       'What about the new law proposal?'
   B: – Não falei com ninguém [island que tenha
       not spoke-*1.SG* with nobody that has.*SUBJ*
       concordado Øᵢ]. (EP: OK; BP: OK)
       agreed
       'I haven't spoken with anybody that agrees with it.'

(6.47c), (6.48b) and (6.48c) show that null oblique objects can appear within strong islands. This indicates that null oblique objects cannot be generated via movement (see Section 6.3). In other words, null oblique objects in EP and BP are probably null pronouns (*pro*) lexically licensed.[23]

In both EP and BP, relative clauses constitute the most favorable environment for the occurrence of null oblique objects. If the relativized constituent is the object of a preposition, there are in principle three different ways to form a relative clause, as illustrated in (6.49).[24]

(6.49) a. Despediram [uma professora]ᵢ [**de quem**ᵢ eu gostava
            fired-*3PL*   a   teacher   of whom   I liked
            muito]. (EP: OK; BP: %)
            much
        a'. Despediram [uma professora]ᵢ [**que** eu gostava muito
            fired-*3PL*   a   teacher   that   I liked   much
            delaᵢ]. (EP: %; BP: OK)
            of-her

---

[23] See e.g. Kato and Nunes 2009, 2014 and Nunes and Kato forthcoming for discussion.
[24] For discussion see e.g. Tarallo 1983, Brito 1991a, Móia 1992, Peres and Móia 1995, Kato 1993a, Alexandre 2000, Kenedy 2003, 2007, Lessa de Oliveira 2008, Kato and Nunes 2009, 2014, Cardoso 2010, 2016, Veloso 2013, Medeiros Júnior 2014, and Nunes and Kato forthcoming.

a″. Despediram [uma professora]$_i$ [**que** eu gostava
    fired-3PL   a   teacher   that I liked
    muito   Ø$_i$].   (EP: %; BP: OK)
    much
    'A teacher that I liked a lot was fired.'

b. [O   mecânico]$_i$ [**com**   **quem**   eu
   the   mechanic   with   whom   I
   conversei ontem]   era excelente.   (EP: OK; BP: %)
   talked   yesterday   was excellent

b′. [O   mecânico]$_i$ [**que** eu   conversei **com**
    the   mechanic   that I   talked   with
    ele$_i$ ontem]   era excelente.   (EP: %; BP: OK)
    him yesterday   was excellent

b″. [O   mecânico]$_i$ [**que** eu   conversei
    the   mechanic   that I   talked
    Ø$_i$ ontem]   era excelente.   (EP: *; BP: OK)
    yesterday   was excellent
    'The mechanic that I talked to yesterday was excellent.'

In (6.49a) and (6.49b), the preposition and the relative pronoun are fronted together to a position adjacent to the element that anchors the interpretation of the relative pronoun; in (6.49a′) and (6.49b′), the relative clause begins with the invariable complementizer *que* 'that' and the object position contains the preposition and a "resumptive" pronoun, whose interpretation is anaphorically anchored on the expression that precedes the relative clause; finally, in the "chopping" type in (6.49a″) and (6.49b″), the relative clause also starts with *que* but has a null oblique object, instead. Each of these possibilities has a different sociolinguistic status. (6.49a) and (6.49b) represent the standard form in both EP and BP. In BP this type is generally associated with written language and formal style. The acceptability of the two nonstandard possibilities is subject to several factors, including the question of whether or not the verb inside the relative clause belongs to the class that licenses null oblique objects in the relevant variety. When this is the case, the alternative with a null oblique object in both EP and BP is generally preferred over (or has more sociolinguistic prestige than) the alternative with an overt resumptive pronoun.

Differences between EP and BP with respect to the strategy with a null oblique pronoun may follow from their differences regarding the set of verbs allowing null oblique objects. The verb *conversar* 'talk', for instance, more easily allows for a null oblique object in BP than EP, as shown in (6.50); hence, chopping relatives with *conversar* are acceptable in BP but not in EP (see (6.49b″)).

(6.50) Este professor, eu conversei ontem.   (EP: *; BP: OK)
this teacher I talked yesterday
'I talked to this teacher yesterday.'

BP seems to have a larger number of verbs that allow null oblique objects than EP. This becomes very clear when we consider oblique expressions headed by the preposition *em* 'in'. The first thing to observe is that both EP and BP allow chopping relatives associated with time and place expressions when they are headed by *em*, as illustrated in (6.51a′) and (6.51b′) below. Interestingly, directional verbs in BP have undergone a wholesale diachronic change replacing the preposition *a* 'to' by *em* as the head of their complements, as illustrated in (6.52).[25] This in turn has paved the way for directional verbs to be included in the set of verbs that allow null oblique objects in BP, as shown in (6.53).

(6.51) a. Nós estávamos num momento [em que todos passavam por
we were in-a moment in which all passed by
dificuldades].   (EP: OK; BP: OK)
difficulties

a′. Nós estávamos num momento [que todos passavam por
we were in-a moment that all passed by
dificuldades].   (EP: %; BP: OK)
difficulties
'We were going through a time when everyone was experiencing problems.'

b. Eles estavam à procura de uma escola [em
they were to.the search of a school in
que os alunos não se sentissem como numa
which the students not themselves felt-SUBJ as in-a
prisão].   (EP: OK; BP: OK)
prison

b′. Eles estavam à procura de uma escola [que os
they were to.the search of a school that the
alunos não se sentissem como numa
students not themselves felt-SUBJ as in-a
prisão].   (EP: %; BP: OK)
prison
'They were looking for a school where the students did not feel like they were in a prison.'

(6.52) a. O João foi ao mercado.   (EP)
the João went to-the market
a′. O João foi no mercado.   (BP)
the João went in-the market
'João went to the market.'

---

[25] See e.g. Wiedemer 2013 for description and discussion.

b. A Maria já chegou **a** casa. (EP)
   the Maria already arrived to house
b'. A Maria já chegou **em** casa. (BP)
   the Maria already arrived in house
   'Maria has already arrived home.'
c. O Pedro veio **à** festa. (EP)
   the Pedro came to-the party
c'. O Pedro veio **na** festa. (BP)
   the Pedro came in-the party
   'Pedro came to the party.'
d. A Maria levou o filho **ao** cinema hoje. (EP)
   the Maria took the son to-the cinema today
d'. A Maria levou o filho **no** cinema hoje. (BP)
   the Maria took the son in-the cinema today
   'Maria took her son to the movies today.'

(6.53) a. A farmácia [que o João foi Ø] estava fechada. (EP: *; BP: OK)
   the drugstore that the João went was closed
   'The drugstore João went to was closed.'
b. A cidade [que a Maria chegou Ø] era bem
   the city that the Maria arrived was well
   hospitaleira. (EP: *; BP: OK)
   welcoming
   'The city where Maria arrived was very welcoming.'
c. A festa [que o Pedro veio Ø] ficou famosa. (EP: *; BP: OK)
   the party that the Pedro came stayed famous
   'The party Pedro went to became famous.'
d. O cinema [que a Maria levou o filho Ø] fica
   the cinema that the Maria took the son stays
   perto daqui. (EP: *; BP: OK)
   near of-here
   'The movie theater Maria took her son to is nearby.'

6.5 Null Possessors

As seen in Sections 2.3.4.3, 2.3.4.5, and 2.4, possession may be encoded in EP and BP in different ways, as illustrated in (6.54a) below with a possessive (genitive) pronoun, in (6.54b) with the dummy preposition *de* 'of', and in (6.54c) with a dative clitic.[26]

---

[26] For discussion see e.g. Oliveira e Silva 1984, Perini 1985, Miguel 1992, 1996, 2004, Cerqueira 1993, 1996, Menuzzi 1996, 1999, Müller 1996, Negrão and Müller 1996, Floripi 2003, Rodrigues 2004, 2010, 2020, Avelar 2004, 2006, 2009b, Barros 2006, A. Castro 2006, Estrela 2006, Floripi and Nunes 2009, Lobo 2013a, and Nunes 2018.

360   6 Null Objects and Null Possessors

(6.54) a. O João telefonou para o **meu** pai.
the João called to the my father
'João called my father.'
b. A Maria telefonou para o pai **dele**.
the Maria called to the father of-him
'Maria called his father.'
c. Ninguém **me** segurou a mão.
nobody me.DAT held the hand
'Nobody held my hand.'

In addition to employing overt expressions to encode possession, EP and BP also have different types of constructions where a possessor is not phonetically realized. In the main, these null possessors can be divided into three groups depending on their specific interpretation and licensing: deictic null possessors, lexically conditioned null possessors, and syntactically conditioned null possessors. Before we examine the third group, which is the focus of this section, let us briefly discuss the first two.

(6.55) below illustrates cases of deictic null possessors. In these sentences, the null possessor is interpreted as 'my' or 'our' and the "possessee" is a kinship noun that indicates a "top member" of the family tree like *pai* 'father', *mãe* 'mother', *vô* 'grandpa', *vó* 'grandma', *tio* 'uncle' or *tia* 'aunt'. As the kinship nouns associated with deictic null possessors receive a hypocoristic interpretation, these constructions are pragmatically circumscribed to utterances where the speaker and the addressee are relatives or very close friends. This type of construction is dialectically or idiolectally restricted in both EP and BP and individual speakers may differ with respect to the nouns that license this reading and how "close" the speaker and the addressee must be in order for the sentences to be licensed pragmatically. The coreference between the null possessor and the subject in (6.55a) under this reading is just a coincidence. The relevant interpretation is maintained with a different subject, as shown in (6.55b), which also allows an interpretation referring to *Maria*'s mother, or even if there is no potential antecedent in the sentence, as in (6.55c).

(6.55) a. %Ontem eu conversei com o pai.
yesterday I talked with the father
'Yesterday I talked to Dad.'
b. %Ontem a Maria visitou a mãe.
yesterday the Maria visited the mother
'Yesterday Maria visited Mom.'
c. %O vô ainda não chegou.
the grandpa still not arrived
'Grandpa has not arrived yet.'

(6.56) below shows another construction with a deictic null possessor that is available in both EP and BP. It involves nouns referring to pets or things which the speaker is somehow emotionally connected to. The null possessor is interpreted as 'my'.

(6.56) O   gato (está) doente, o   carro (está) avariado, a   casa
        the   cat   is   sick   the   car   is   damaged   the house
        (está) em   obras, como   posso estar contente?
        is   in   works, how   can-1SG be   content
        'My cat is sick, my car is damaged, and my house is being repaired ... How can I be happy?

Null possessors may also be lexically licensed by the verbs that select for their noun phrases, as illustrated in (6.57)–(6.59) below.[27] These sentences involve inalienable possession referring to body parts, and the null possessor is interpreted as coreferential with the subject of the clause. The verbs that allow these constructions are lexically restricted, encompassing three sub-classes: transitive verbs whose subject is the agent of the action described by the verb (see (6.57)), transitive verbs whose subject has some control over the action but the action is executed by a different agent (see (6.58)), and unaccusative verbs whose subjects have no control over the event being described and are just affected by it (see (6.59)).

(6.57) a. As crianças lavaram as mãos.
           the children washed the hands
           'The children washed their hands.'
        b. O João enxugou o rosto.
           the João dried the face
           'João dried his face.'

(6.58) a. O Pedro cortou o cabelo.
           the Pedro cut the hair
           'Pedro had his hair cut.'
        b. O Fernando arrancou o dente do siso.
           the Fernando extracted the tooth of-the wisdom
           'Fernando had his wisdom tooth pulled out.'

(6.59) a. O João queimou a mão.
           the João burned the hand
           'João burned his hand.'
        b. A Maria magoou o pé.   (EP)
           the Maria hurt the foot

---

[27] For discussion see e.g. Cançado 2010, Cançado and Negrão 2010, Cançado and Gonçalves 2016, and Rodrigues 2020.

b'. A Maria machucou o pé. (BP)
   the Maria hurt   the foot
   'Maria hurt her foot.'

A null possessor may also be externally licensed if the selecting verb itself encodes possession. In EP, these cases are construed with *ter* 'have' and in BP with *estar com* 'be with', as illustrated in (6.60).[28]

(6.60) a. Temos   o   carro avariado.   (EP)
          have-1.PL the car damaged
       a'. Nós estamos com o   carro avariado. (BP)
          we are   with the car   damaged
          'Our car is damaged.'
       b. O João tem o tio   doente.   (EP)
          the João has the uncle sick
       b'. O João está com o tio   doente. (BP)
          the João is   with the uncle sick
          'João's uncle is sick.'

In this section we will put aside cases of null possessors that have a fixed interpretation (see (6.55) and (6.56)) or are lexically conditioned (see (6.57)–(6.60)), and focus on the interpretation of anaphoric null possessors that are syntactically licensed (from now on simply *null possessors*).[29] Although EP and BP both allow null possessors of this type, they may assign different interpretations to these phonetically null expressions, depending on the syntactic configurations containing them. In a sentence such as (6.61) below, for instance, the null possessor could potentially be interpreted as Maria, yielding a pragmatically odd incestuous reading where Maria is marrying her own father, or João, yielding a pragmatically more neutral reading where João is talking about Maria's marriage with his father. In EP, both readings are available, whereas in BP only the incestuous reading is possible.

(6.61) O João disse que a Maria vai casar com o pai.
       the João said that the Maria goes marry with the father
       'João said that Maria$_i$ is going to marry her$_i$ own father.' (EP: OK; BP: OK)
       'João$_k$ said that Maria is going to marry his$_k$ father.'   (EP: OK; BP: *)

Four major factors regulate the licensing and interpretation of these null possessors in EP and BP: person specifications, the presence of syntactic islands, the position of the antecedent, and the definiteness specification of

---

[28] For discussion see e.g. Avelar 2004, 2009b.
[29] See e.g. Floripi 2003, Rodrigues 2004, 2010, Floripi and Nunes 2009, and Nunes 2018 for discussion.

the "possessee." Let us start our discussion by examining the interaction between person and definiteness specifications. Consider the data in (6.62) and (6.63) below under the reading in which the null possessor within the object takes the subject as its antecedent, as indicated by the translations (the sentences in (6.62a-b) are also grammatical in EP but not in BP under a reading in which the null possessor takes a discourse referent for its antecedent). (6.62) and (6.63) show that a first and second person null possessor can take the subject as its antecedent only when it is inside an indefinite noun phrase, whereas third person null possessors are licensed in both definite and indefinite noun phrases.

(6.62) a. *Ontem   eu encontrei o   amigo   na   biblioteca. (EP/BP)
            yesterday I   met   the friend at-the   library
            'Yesterday I met my friend at the library.'
        b. *Você   não ia   contratar o   primo?   (EP/BP)
            you.SG not went   hire   the cousin
            'Weren't you(SG) going to hire your(SG) cousin?'
        c. O   João contratou o   primo.   (EP/BP)
           the João hired   the cousin
           'João hired his cousin.'

(6.63) a. Ontem   eu encontrei um amigo   na   biblioteca. (EP/BP)
            yesterday I   met   a   friend at-the   library
            'Yesterday I met a friend of mine at the library.'
        b. Você   não ia   contratar um primo?   (EP/BP)
           you.SG not went   hire   a   cousin
           'Weren't you(SG) going to hire a cousin of yours(SG)?'
        c. O   João contratou um primo.   (EP/BP)
           the João hired   a   cousin
           'João hired a cousin of his.'

Interestingly, the contrast above mirrors the contrast we find with respect to the linear order of possessors within the noun phrase. As shown in (6.64) and (6.65) below, an indefinite noun phrase allows postnominal possessors regardless of their person specifications, but definite noun phrases allow only third person postnominal possessors (of the oblique variety).[30]

---

[30] As seen in Section 2.4.3, *seu* in (6.64) and (6.65) may also mean 'his/her' in EP, but not in BP. We put this difference aside, as it is not relevant to the current discussion. Some EP dialects allow prenominal genitive pronouns within indefinite noun phrases, as illustrated in (i) below. For discussion see e.g. Miguel 2002, 2004 and A. Castro 2006.

(i)   uma {minha/tua/sua/nossa} tia   (%EP)
      a   my/your/his/our   aunt
      'an aunt of {mine/yours/his/ours}'

(6.64) a. um primo {meu /seu /dele}
　　　 a　 cousin {my /your /of-him}
　　 b. um {%meu /%seu /*dele} primo
　　　 a　 my　 /your /of-him　 cousin
　　　 'a cousin of {mine/yours/his}'

(6.65) a. o　 primo {*meu /*seu /dele}
　　　 the cousin　 my　 /your /of-him
　　 b. o　 {meu /seu /*dele} primo
　　　 the　 my　 /your /of-him　 cousin
　　　 '{my/your/his} cousin'

The data in (6.62)–(6.65) show that a null possessor is licensed only if its overt counterpart can appear in postnominal position. (6.62) and (6.63) can thus receive a simple account if null possessors are to be licensed in the postnominal position, as sketched in (6.66) below. The question we now have to address regards the syntactic nature of the empty category in (6.66).

(6.66) [N Ø$_{possessor}$]

Consider the data in (6.67) below, for instance.

(6.67) a. [A　médica　d[o　 Pedro]$_k$]$_i$ ligou　para [o　irmão　 Ø]].
　　　　 the　doctor　of-the　Pedro　 called　to　 the　brother
　　　　 Ø$_i$ ('Pedro's doctor called her brother.') → EP: OK; BP: OK
　　　　 Ø$_k$ ('Pedro's doctor called his brother.') → EP: OK; BP: *
　　 b. [O suspeito]$_k$ disse que [o detetive]$_i$ interrogou [os amigos Ø].
　　　　 the suspect　 said that the detective　 interrogated the friends
　　　　 Ø$_i$ ('The suspect said that [the detective]$_i$
　　　　 questioned his$_i$ friends.')　　　　　　　　　　 → EP: OK; BP: OK
　　　　 Ø$_k$ ('[The suspect]$_i$ said that the detective
　　　　 questioned his$_k$ friends.')　　　　　　　　　　 → EP: OK; BP: *

In both (6.67a) and (6.67b), the noun phrase containing the null possessor is definite; hence, the null possessor must be interpreted as a third person pronoun (see (6.62) and (6.65)). As indicated by the indices, there are two potential antecedents for the null possessor in each sentence, but in an out-of-the-blue context, there is a pragmatic bias favoring *o Pedro* in (6.67a) and *o suspeito* 'the suspect' in (6.67b) as an actual antecedent. EP patterns as expected: although the two readings are indeed available, the preferred interpretation in an out-of-the-blue context is that Pedro's doctor called Pedro's brother in (6.67a) and that the detective questioned the suspect's friends in (6.67b). BP, on the other hand, seems to ignore the pragmatic biases: the interpretation obtained is that Pedro's doctor called her own brother in (6.67a) and that the detective questioned his own friends in (6.67b) (in a way similar to what we saw in (6.61)).

The contrast between EP and BP regarding (6.67) suggests that null possessors have a different syntactic status in each variety. The restrictive interpretation of null possessors in BP resembles the interpretation of its third person null subjects (see Chapter 4) in that they look for an antecedent in the closest subject position. In the case of third person null subjects in BP, this restrictive interpretation was analyzed in terms of movement: the relevant null subjects correspond to gaps when the subjects move to the next higher subject position (see Section 4.3.1.2). Let us then tentatively suppose that null possessors in BP are derived in a similar manner. The sentences in (6.67), for example, are to be derived in BP as sketched in (6.68).

(6.68) a. [A médica do Pedro] ligou para [o irmão __]
        b. O suspeito disse que [o detetive] interrogou [os amigos __]

In EP, on the other hand, the sentences in (6.67) may be taken to involve a null pronominal, as represented in (6.69).

(6.69) EP:
        a. [A médica d[o Pedro]$_k$]$_i$ ligou para [o irmão *pro*$_{k/i}$]
        b. [O suspeito]$_k$ disse que [o detetive]$_i$ interrogou [os amigos *pro*$_{k/i}$]

The different representations in (6.68) and (6.69) account for why the interpretation of null possessors is sensitive to pragmatic biases in EP, but not in BP. In BP, the interpretation of the null postnominal position in (6.68) is syntactically determined; in EP, on the other hand, the interpretation does not substantially differ from the interpretation of overt pronouns. In (6.70) below, for instance, the pronoun *ele* 'him' may take either the matrix or the embedded subject as its antecedent, but pragmatic information regarding suspects and detectives tends to prime the reading under which *ele* is interpreted as the suspect, in an out-of-the blue context.

(6.70) EP/BP:
        [O suspeito]$_k$ disse que [o detetive]$_i$ interrogou [os amigos dele$_{k/i}$].
        the suspect said that the detective interrogated the friends of-***him***
        '[The suspect]$_k$ said that [the detective]$_i$ questioned his$_{k/i}$ friends.'

The representations in (6.68) and (6.69) also lead to different predictions regarding syntactic islands. Given that movement operations are sensitive to syntactic islands but pronominal interpretation is not, the expectation is that the presence of a strong island intervening between a null possessor and its antecedent should change the interpretive possibilities of null possessors in BP, but not in EP. The data in (6.71) show that this prediction is fulfilled.

(6.71)   EP/BP:

a. [A Maria]$_i$ ligou para [o João]$_k$ [$_{island}$ quando [o pai Ø$_{i/k}$]
    the Maria   called to   the João   when   the father
    foi demitido].
    was fired
    'Maria called João when her/his father was fired.'

b. [A Maria]$_i$ disse que [o João]$_k$ atendeu o pedido [$_{island}$ que
    the Maria   said that   the João   granted the request   that
    [o irmão Ø$_{i/k}$] fez].
    the brother   made
    'Maria said that João had granted the request that her/his brother made.'

The null possessor is separated from its antecedent by an adverbial clause in (6.71a) and a relative clause in (6.71b), both constituting strong syntactic islands for movement. Interestingly, EP and BP now pattern alike in displaying a pronominal behavior, as represented in (6.72) below, with the null possessor being able to take either João or Maria as its antecedent.

(6.72)   EP/BP:

a. [A Maria]$_i$ ligou para [o João]$_k$ [$_{island}$ quando [o pai *pro*$_{i/k}$] foi demitido].
b. [A Maria]$_i$ disse que [o João]$_k$ atendeu o pedido [$_{island}$ que [o irmão *pro*$_{i/k}$] fez].

The uniform behavior displayed by null possessors in EP indicates that nouns in EP simply license a null pronoun in the postnominal position. The contrast between (6.67) and (6.71) in BP (see (6.68) vs. (6.72)), in turn, shows that pronominal null possessors in BP are employed only as a "last resort," when movement from the postnominal position is not possible.[31] This is further confirmed by constructions with null possessors taking a discourse antecedent. Consider the data in (6.73) in a context where the detective's girlfriend is not the suspect.

(6.73)   A: – E   o   suspeito?
              and   the   suspect
              'What about the suspect?'

a. B: – [A namorada   Ø]   já   foi   interrogada.
         the girlfriend   already was   interrogated
         'The suspect's girlfriend has already been
         questioned.'   (EP: OK; BP: OK)

b. B': – O   detetive   prendeu   [a   namorada   Ø].
         the detective   arrested   the girlfriend
         'The detective arrested the suspect's
         girlfriend.'   (EP: OK; BP: *)
         'The detective arrested his own girlfriend.'   (EP: OK; BP: OK)

---

[31] See Nunes 2018 for discussion.

Given this context, the most natural interpretation for the responses prompted by A's question is that they refer to the suspect's girlfriend. This is indeed the reading we have in (6.73a) for both EP and BP. As for (6.73b), the null possessor could also take *o detetive* 'the detective' as its antecedent, yielding a nonsensical reading in this context (the detective arrested his own girlfriend). Although available in EP, this reading is overshadowed by the pragmatically sound reading where the null possessor takes the suspect as its antecedent. In BP, on the other hand, only the pragmatically disparate reading is available for (6.73b). These differences can be accounted for if the null possessor has a different grammatical status in each variety. In EP, the null possessor displays a uniform pronominal behavior, as represented in (6.74) below. In BP, on the other hand, a null pronoun is resorted to, only if movement is prevented; in order words, if available, movement is more economical than pronominalization, so to speak. Observe that movement from the postnominal position is a possibility available in (6.73b), but not in (6.73a). Hence, only in (6.73a) is the pronominal last resort option activated, yielding an appropriate answer; in (6.73b) movement is implemented – because it is possible – as illustrated in (6.75), yielding a disparate answer. The pragmatically appropriate alternative for (6.73b) in BP must involve an overt pronoun, as shown in (6.76) (which is also permitted in EP, though it is not the preferred option).

(6.74)   EP:
         A: –   E [o suspeito]$_i$?
    a.   B: – [A namorada *pro*$_i$] já foi interrogada pelo detetive.
    b.   B': – O detetive prendeu [a namorada *pro*$_i$].

(6.75)   A: – E [o suspeito]$_i$?
    a. B: – [A namorada *pro*$_i$] já foi interrogada pelo detetive.
    b. B': – [O detetive] prendeu [a namorada __].

(6.76)   A: – E   o   suspeito?
             and   *the*   *suspect*
             'What about the suspect?'
        B: – O   detetive   prendeu   [a   namorada   **dele**].
             the   *detective*   *arrested*   *the*   *girlfriend*   *of-him*
             EP/BP: 'The detective arrested the suspect's girlfriend.'

6.6 Summary

Although EP and BP both admit null direct objects, null possessors, and null oblique objects they systematically differ with respect to each of these null expressions. As far as null direct objects are concerned, these arise as the result of syntactic movement in EP, but may result from movement or be a null pronominal in BP (see Section 6.3). This implies that BP displays a more widespread distribution of null direct objects than EP. As for null possessors, we find the opposite pattern, with EP licensing more interpretations than BP, as EP makes use of null pronominals, whereas BP resorts to a null pronominal only when the relevant null possessor is within a syntactic island and movement from the possessor position is precluded (see Section 6.5). Finally, null oblique objects correspond to null pronominals in both EP and BP, but they are licensed by a larger set of verbs in BP than EP (see Section 6.4). These contrasts clearly show that inaudible expressions may have different sources and, consequently, affect the grammar of each variety in a distinctive way.

7

Affirmation, Negation, and *yes/no* Questions and Answers

7.1 Introduction

In this chapter, we discuss affirmation, negation, *yes/no* (polar) questions, and answers in European Portuguese (EP) and Brazilian Portuguese (BP). We will pay special attention to the way in which each variety grammatically encodes these locutions in non-neutral contexts. The chapter is organized as follows. In Section 7.2, we discuss how emphatic affirmation is grammatically encoded. In Section 7.3, we discuss the syntactic and interpretive properties associated with different types of negation. In Section 7.4, we discuss biased polar questions. In Section 7.5 we discuss different types of answers to polar questions. Finally, Section 7.6 briefly summarizes the similarities and differences between EP and BP with respect to the domains discussed.

7.2 Emphatic Affirmation

In both EP and BP, there is no special marking to encode neutral affirmative declarative sentences. A neutral affirmative declarative displays the unmarked SVO word order and a falling intonational contour (↓), as illustrated in (7.1).

(7.1) A Maria pôs os livros na estante.↓
the Maria put the books in-the bookshelf
'Maria put the books on the bookshelf.'

In this section, we discuss emphatic affirmation – a non-neutral type of affirmation that encodes positive disagreement with respect to some previous negative statement. Consider (7.2) below, for instance. Given speaker A's negative statement in the preceding context, the sentences in (7.2a–b) convey the meaning that speaker B denies what A says, stressing that the relevant event (João's purchase of the car) did indeed occur.

(7.2) [*Context*:
    A: – O João não comprou o carro.
          the João not bought the car
    'João did not buy the car.']
   a. B: – O João comprou o carro, **sim**. (EP: OK; BP: OK)
          the João bought the car yes
   b. B: – O João **comprou** o carro, **comprou**. (EP: OK; BP: *)
          the João bought the car bought
    'João did buy the car.'

There are two general patterns of emphatic affirmation: one employs affirmative particles like *sim* 'yes' in sentence-final position, as in (7.2a), and the other (available only in EP) employs verb reduplication, also in sentence-final position, as in (7.2b). A common property shared by the two patterns is that emphatic affirmation is restricted to the matrix domain. Given the contexts in (7.3) and (7.4) below, for example, the affirmative particle can be used to indicate that Maria is indeed aware that João was hired in (7.3a), but cannot be used in (7.4a) to indicate that João was indeed hired. Accordingly, the matrix verb can be reduplicated (see (7.3b)), but not the embedded verb (see (7.4b)).[1]

---

[1] When emphatic affirmation reverses the polarity of an assertion with both matrix and embedded negation, the affirmative particle *sim* 'yes' more naturally follows the matrix verb, as illustrated in (ia) below. In (ia) there is a pause following *sim*, which suggests that the clausal complement is extraposed to the right of the affirmative particle. Interestingly, such extraposition is blocked with verb reduplication, as shown in (ib) in contrast with (ic).

(i) [*Context*:
    A: – A Maria não sabe que o João não foi contratado.
          the Maria not knows that the João not was hired
    'Maria doesn't know that João was not hired.']
   a. B: – A Maria sabe, **sim**, que o João
        the Maria knows yes that the João
        não foi contratado.
        not was hired (EP: OK; BP: OK)
   b. B: – *A Maria **sabe**, **sabe**, que o João
        the Maria knows knows that the João
        não foi contratado.
        not was hired (EP: *; BP: *)
   c. B: – A Maria **sabe** que o João não
        the Maria knows that the João not
        foi contratado, **sabe**.
        was hired knows (EP: OK; BP: *)
    'Maria does know that João was not hired.'

(7.3) [*Context*:
A: – A Maria não sabe que o João foi contratado.
the Maria not knows that the João was hired
'Maria doesn't know that João was hired.']
a. B: – A Maria sabe que o João foi contratado, **sim**. (EP: OK; BP: OK)
the Maria knows that the João was hired yes
b. B: – A Maria **sabe** que o João foi contratado, **sabe**. (EP: OK; BP: *)
the Maria knows that the João was hired knows
'Maria does know that João was hired.'

(7.4) [*Context*:
A: – A Maria sabe que o João não foi contratado.
the Maria knows that the João not was hired
'Maria knows that João was not hired.']
a. B: – #A Maria sabe que o João foi contratado, **sim**.
the Maria knows that the João was hired yes
b. B: – *A Maria sabe que o João **foi** contratado, **foi**.
the Maria knows that the João was hired was
'Maria know that João was indeed hired.'

Below we examine each of the patterns illustrated in (7.2) in more detail.

7.2.1 *Emphatic Affirmation with* sim, pois, *and* já

Whereas emphatic affirmation with particles in BP is restricted to the affirmative particle *sim* 'yes', EP may also employ the confirmative (CONFIRM) particle *pois*, as shown in (7.5).[2]

(7.5) [*Context*:
A: – A Maria não terminou o trabalho.
the Maria not finished the job
'Maria didn't finish the job.']
a. B: – A Maria terminou o trabalho, **sim**. (EP: OK; BP: OK)
the Maria finished the work yes

---

[2] For discussion see e.g. Martins 2006b, 2013a, 2016a.

b. B: – A   Maria   terminou   o
       the   Maria   finished   the
       trabalho, **pois**.   (EP: OK; BP: *)
       work   CONFIRM
       'Maria did finish the work.'

Although *pois* and *sim* can be used to mark emphatic affirmation in constructions such as (7.5) in EP, *pois* behaves unlike *sim* in being unable to function as a neutral positive answer to a *yes/no* question, as illustrated in (7.6).

(7.6)   EP:
         [*Context*:
         A: – O   João   comprou   um   carro?
              the João   bought   a   car
              'Did João buy a car?']
         a.   B: – **Sim**.
                   yes
         b.   B: – ***Pois**.
                   CONFIRM
                   'Yes, he did.'

Pois in EP can nonetheless express agreement with both an affirmative and a negative declarative, as illustrated in (7.7) and (7.8) below. In other words, *pois* in EP is not an answering particle, but a particle that expresses confirmation of a previous statement, as indicated by its gloss. In BP, on the other hand, *pois* is used as a confirmative particle only in the frozen expression *pois é* (lit. *CONFIRM is*), which is employed in both positive and negative contexts, as shown in (7.7c) and (7.8c) (see Section 7.5.3 for discussion).

(7.7)   [*Context*:
         A: – O   João   comprou   um   carro.
              the João   bought   a   car
              'João bought a car.']
         a.   B: – **Pois**   comprou.   (EP: OK; BP: *)
                   CONFIRM   bought
         b.   B: – **Pois**   foi.   (EP: OK; BP: *)
                   CONFIRM   was
         c.   B: – **Pois**   é.   (EP: %; BP: OK)
                   CONFIRM   is
                   'He surely did.'

(7.8)   [*Context*:
         A: – O   João   não   comprou   um   carro.
              the João   not   bought   a   car
              'João didn't buy a car.']

a. B: – **Pois**   não.   (EP: OK; BP: *)
           CONFIRM   no
b. B: – **Pois**   foi.   (EP: OK; BP: *)
           CONFIRM   was
c. B: – **Pois**   é.   (EP: %; BP: OK)
           CONFIRM   is
    'He surely didn't.'

This difference between EP and BP regarding *pois* is also reflected in their tag questions (see Section 7.4.2). Tag questions with a negative statement preceding the tag provide a felicitous context for emphatic affirmation in that they anticipate a negative answer. The question tag itself is a copy of the main verb in BP, but the expression *pois não* (lit. *CONFIRM not*) in EP, as illustrated in (7.9).³

(7.9)   [*Context*:
        A: – O   João não **comprou** um carro, **comprou**?   (BP)
             the João not bought   a   car   bought
        A′: – O   João não comprou um carro, **pois**   não?   (EP)
              the João not bought   a   car   CONFIRM   no
        'João didn't buy a car, did he?']
    a. B: – Comprou, sim.   (EP: OK; BP: OK)
              bought   yes
    b. B: – Comprou, pois.   (EP: OK; BP: *)
              bought   CONFIRM
        'Yes, he did, indeed.'

---

³ In BP *pois não* is a frozen expression with two different meanings, depending on its intonation. When associated with rising intonation, as in (ia) below, it may be used as a polite way for the speaker to say that it is the interlocutor's turn to say what s/he needs. With this intonation, it may be a polite way to greet a customer, for instance. When associated with falling intonation, it provides a polite formal positive response to a request for assistance, as illustrated in (ib), for instance.

(i)   BP:
    a. Pois   não?↑
        CONFIRM   no
        'Can I help you?'
    b. [*Context*:
        A: – Você   pode   me dar   uma   ajudinha?
             you.SG   can   me give   a   help-DIM
        'Can you(SG) give me a hand?']
        B: – Pois   não.↓
             CONFIRM   no
        'Sure.'

374   7 Affirmation, Negation, Questions, and Answers

EP can also express emphatic affirmation with reduplication of the adverb *já* 'already' in sentence-final position, as illustrated in (7.10).

(7.10) [*Context*:
  A: – O   João   ainda   não   saiu.
        the João   still   not   left
        'João hasn't left yet.']
  B: – O   João   **já**   saiu, **já**.   (EP: OK; BP: *)
        the João   already left   already
        'Of course, João has already left.'

Já is the only adverb that can be reduplicated in EP as a means to express emphatic affirmation. The adverb *sempre* 'always', for instance, which behaves like *já* in being able to function as answer to *yes/no* questions, as we will see in Section 7.5.2, cannot be duplicated, as shown in (7.11a) below. Notice that (7.11) does have a context compatible with emphatic affirmation (and duplication), as the structure in (7.11b) shows.

(7.11)   EP:
  [*Context*:
  A: – O   João   nem   sempre   apoiou   a   Maria.
        the João   not   always   supported the Maria
        'João hasn't always supported Maria.']
  a. B: – *O João **sempre** apoiou   a   Maria, **sempre**.
             the João   always   supported the Maria   always
  b. B: – O João sempre apoiou   a   Maria, **sim**.
             the João   always   supported the Maria   yes
        'Of course João has always supported Maria.'

Finally, it is worth observing that although preverbal *já* is compatible with *sim* and *pois* (see (7.12a) and (7.12b)) and can be reduplicated (see (7.12c)), its reduplication is blocked in the presence of these particles (see (7.12d) and (7.12e)) and so is the reduplication of the verb in the presence of *já* (see (7.12f)).

(7.12)   EP:
  [*Context*:
  A: – O   João   ainda   não   saiu,   pois   não?
        the João   yet   not   left   CONFIRM no
        'João hasn't left yet, has he?']
  a. B: – (Já)   saiu, **sim**.
             already left   yes
  b. B: – (Já)   saiu, **pois**.
             already left   CONFIRM
  c. B: – **Já**   saiu, **já**.
             already left   already

d. B: – *Já saiu, já sim.↑ [with rising intonation; see Section 7.2.2 below]
   already left already yes
e. B: – *Já saiu, já pois.↑ [with rising intonation; see Section 7.2.2 below]
   already left already CONFIRM
f. B: – *Já **saiu, saiu.**
   already left left
   'Yes, he has, indeed.'

The ungrammaticality of (7.12d) and (7.12e) indicate that *sim*, *pois* and the reduplicated adverb compete for sentence-final position. In turn, the contrast between (7.12c) and (7.12f) suggests that in the competition between *já* and the verb, the adverb counts as the optimal target for reduplication (perhaps for being structurally higher).

7.2.2 *Emphatic Affirmation with Verb Reduplication in European Portuguese*

Let us now examine emphatic affirmation with verb reduplication, which, as we mentioned above, is possible in EP, but not in BP.[4] The first thing we have to ensure is that these constructions do involve morphosyntactic reduplication within a sentence and not just two discourse fragments, with the second of them involving repetition of the previous verb. Let us then compare the cases of emphatic affirmation with verb reduplication in (7.13a) and (7.14a) with the cases of repetition in (7.13b) and (7.14b), for instance.

(7.13) EP:
[*Context*:
A: – O João não chegou tarde.
the João not arrived late
'João didn't arrive late.']
a. *Emphatic affirmation*:
B: – O João **chegou** tarde, **chegou**.↑
the João arrived late, arrived
'João did arrive late.'
b. *Fragment repetition*:
B: – Ele na verdade chegou tarde.↓ Chegou tarde, como
he in-the truth arrive late arrived late as
é o seu costume.↓
is the his custom
'He in fact arrived late. He arrived late, as usual.'

---
[4] For discussion see e.g. Martins 2007, 2016a.

(7.14) EP:
[*Context*:
A: – O João não saiu, pois   não?
    the João not left   CONFIRM no
    'João didn't leave, did he?']
a. *Emphatic affirmation*:
   B: – **Saiu,   saiu.**↑
        left   left
        'Yes, he did, indeed.'
b. *Fragment repetition*:
   B: – Saiu,↓ saiu,↓ saiu.↓ Quantas vezes vais   repetir essa
        left   left   left   how.many times go-2.SG   repeat   this
        pergunta?
        question
        'Yes, he did. How many times are you(SG) going to repeat this question?'

In the repetition of discourse fragments there is generally a pause separating the fragments, with each fragment being assigned a falling intonation contour (see (7.13b) and (7.14b)); it may also reiterate, as with the verb shown in (7.14b). By contrast, emphatic affirmation with reduplication involves only a single copy of the verb, is assigned a rising intonational contour, and there is no prosodic break preceding the reduplicated verb. The use of a comma in the written transcription of (7.13a) and (7.14a), for instance, is just an orthographic convention and does not correspond to a pause.[5]

Verb reduplication under emphatic affirmation may also be phonologically distinguished from repetition. In EP, the dental voiceless fricative phoneme /s/ may be phonetically realized as [ʃ], [ʒ], or [z] when it occurs in coda positions. The voiceless palatal fricative [ʃ] occurs word-internally or between words when preceding a voiceless consonant or in word-final position before a pause (e.g. *três cestas* [treʃseʃteʃ] 'three baskets'); the voiced palatal fricative [ʒ] emerges before a voiced consonant, both word-internally and between words if they are not separated by a prosodic break (e.g. *osgas grandes* [ɔʒgeʒgrẽdiʃ], lit.: geckos big, 'big geckos'); and the voiced dental realization [z] shows up when the fricative coda is followed by a word-initial vowel, with no intervening pause (e.g. *três amigos* [trezemiguʃ] 'three friends'). Bearing this in mind, let us examine the data in (7.15).

(7.15) EP:
[*Context*:
A: – Eu não ando a fazer nada   de mal.
    I not walk to do nothing of wrong
    'I'm not doing anything wrong.']

---

[5] It is also worth observing that, although verb reduplication is not available in BP, sentences with fragment repetition analogous to those in (7.13b) and (7.14b) are perfectly acceptable in this variety.

a. *Emphatic affirmation*:
   B: – *Anda[ʃ]   anda[ʃ].↑
         walk-2.SG walk-2.SG
   B': – Anda[z]   anda[ʃ].↑
         walk-2.SG walk-2.SG
         'Of course you(SG) are.'
b. *Fragment repetition*:
   B: – Anda[ʃ].↓ Anda[ʃ], sim.↓
         walk-2.SG walk-2.SG
         'You(SG) are. Of course you(SG) are.'

The last phoneme of the first verb can be realized as the palatal allophone [ʃ] in (7.15b), but not in (7.15a). Notice that the rising intonational contour in (7.15a) enforces the verb reduplication reading. This contrast between (7.15a) and (7.15b) with respect to the realization of [ʃ] can be accounted for if a pause can be introduced before the repeated verb in (7.15b), but not before the reduplicated verb in (7.15a). If there is no pause between the verbs of (7.15a), the rule for the realization of [z] is triggered and the sentence surfaces as in the utterance by speaker B'.

It is also worth noting that, although sentences with fragment repetition may be pragmatically felicitous in contexts that license emphatic affirmation, as seen in (7.13b) and (7.14b), fragment repetition itself does not encode positive disagreement. As shown in (7.16) below, repetition may also express positive agreement, in sharp contrast with emphatic affirmation with verb reduplication:[6]

(7.16) EP:
        [*Context*:
           A: – Felizmente, correu tudo bem.
                fortunately ran   all   well
                'Fortunately, everything went well.']

---

[6] It is worth emphasizing that the answer in (7.16a) in EP is pragmatically inadequate with the rising intonation that signals positive disagreement (see Section 7.5.1). If it is assigned a flat intonation (→), as represented in (i), it receives an ironic interpretation indicating that things in fact did not go well (see footnote 21 below for a similar case).

(i)   [*Context*:
         A: – Felizmente, correu   tudo   bem.
              fortunately ran   everything well
              'Fortunately, everything went well.']
         B: – Correu,   correu.→   (EP)
              ran   ran
              'Of course, it didn't.'

378   7 Affirmation, Negation, Questions, and Answers

    a. *Emphatic affirmation*:
       B: – #**Correu, correu.**↑
           ran   ran
       'It certainly did.'
    b. *Fragment repetition*:
       B: – Correu.↓ (Pois)   correu.↓
           ran   CONFIRM ran
       'It did. It really did.'

Similarly, given that verb reduplication grammatically encodes emphatic affirmation, it is incompatible with negation, as shown in (7.17a) below. By contrast, verb repetition is not subject to this restriction, as shown in (7.17b). Likewise, verb reduplication is incompatible with evidential adverbial expressions such as *realmente* 'really', *certamente* 'certainly', *efetivamente* 'effectively', *obviamente* 'obviously', or *de facto* 'in fact', presumably because they convey the same meaning as the reduplication; by contrast, reiterative repetition does not display this incompatibility, as illustrated in (7.18).

(7.17)   EP:

    [*Context*:

    A: – O João ganhou a   lotaria.
           the João won   the lottery
       'João won the lottery.']

    a. *Emphatic verb reduplication*:
       B: – *O João não **ganhou** a   lotaria, **ganhou.**↑
           the João not won   the lottery won
       B': – *O João **não** **ganhou** a   lotaria, **não** **ganhou.**↑
            the João not won   the lottery not   won
       'João did NOT win the lottery.'

    b. *Fragment repetition*:
       B: – O João não ganhou a   lotaria.↓
           the João not won   the lottery.
           Não   ganhou   (infelizmente).↓
           not   won   regrettably
       'João didn't win the lottery. Regrettably, he didn't.'

(7.18)   EP:

    [*Context*:

    A: – O João não gosta de ler.
           the João not   likes   of read
       'João doesn't like to read.']

    a. *Emphatic affirmation*:
       B: – *O João realmente **gosta** de ler, **gosta.**↑
           the João really   likes   of read likes
       'João does like to read.'

7.2 Emphatic Affirmation 379

    b. *Fragment repetition*:
       B: – O   João realmente gosta de ler.↓ Gosta, mas finge
            the   João really   likes of read likes but pretends
            que não gosta.↓
            that not likes
       'João really likes to read. He does, but pretends he doesn't.'

Finally, as the reader can check in previous examples, verb reduplication just targets the finite matrix verb, whereas there is no such constraint on repetition. In (7.19) and (7.20) below, for example, only the auxiliary verb may be reduplicated, whereas the whole verb cluster can be repeated.

(7.19)   EP:
        [*Context*:
        A: – Eu não fui avisada.
            I not was warned
            'I wasn't warned.']
    a. *Emphatic affirmation*:
       B: – Tu   **foste** avisada, **foste**.↑
            you   were warned were
       B′: – *Tu   **foste avisada, foste   avisada**.↑
            you.SG were warned were   warned
       'Of course you(SG) were warned.'
    b. *Fragment repetition*:
       B: – Tu   foste avisada.↓ Foste avisada.↓ Não finjas
            you.SG were warned   were warned   not pretend-2.SG
            que não.
            that not
       'You(SG) were warned. I'm sure you(SG) were warned. Don't pretend you(SG) were not.'

(7.20)   EP:
        [*Context*:
        A: – O   João não vai vir.
            the João not goes come
            'João is not coming.']
    a. *Emphatic affirmation*:
       B: – O   João **vai** vir, **vai**.↑
            the João goes come goes
       B′: – *O   João **vai vir, vai vir**.↑
            the João goes come goes come
       'Of course João is coming.'
    b. *Fragment repetition*:
       B: – Tem calma. O   João vai vir.↓ Vai vir.↓
            have calm   the João goes come goes come
       'Calm down. João will come. He certainly will.'

380   7 Affirmation, Negation, Questions, and Answers

Now that the distinction between verb reduplication and repetition has been clarified, it is worth mentioning that verb reduplication can occur with any type of verbal predicate, as illustrated below with a transitive verb in (7.21a), a ditransitive verb in (7.21b), an unergative verb in (7.21c), an unaccusative verb in (7.21d), a copula in (7.21e), and the existential verb *haver* in (7.21f).

(7.21)   EP:

    a. Ele **recusou** a proposta, **recusou**.
       he refused the offer refused
       'He did refuse the offer.'

    b. Eu **dei** ontem esse livro ao João, **dei**.
       I gave yesterday this book to-the João gave
       'I did give João this book yesterday.'

    c. Tu **sorriste, sorriste**.
       you.SG smiled, smiled
       'You(SG) did smile.'

    d. O mau tempo **chegou** cá, **chegou**.
       the bad weather arrived here arrived
       'The bad weather did arrive here.'

    e. Dormir oito horas **é** saudável, **é**.
       sleep eight hours is healthy is
       'Of course to sleep eight hours is healthy.'

    f. **Há** demasiadas pessoas nesta sala, **há**.
       have too-many persons in-this room have
       'Of course there are too many people in this room.'

Verb reduplication is not generally unconstrained, though. Compound verbs like *fotocopiar* 'photocopy' (lit. *photo-copy*), *radiografar* 'x-ray' (lit. *radio-write*), *manuscrever* 'handwrite' (lit. *hand-write*), *maniatar* 'strap' (lit. *hand-tie*), *bendizer* 'bless' (lit. *well-say*), *maldizer* 'curse' (lit. *badly-say*), or *maltratar* 'mistreat' (lit. *badly-treat*) and verbs taking stressed prefixes such as *contra* (e.g. *contra-atacar* 'counter-attack'), *super* (e.g. *super-enfatizar* 'super-emphasize'), *pré* (e.g. *pré-inscrever* 'pre-register') or *pós* (e.g. *pós-graduar* 'post-graduate') render verb reduplication marginal, as illustrated in (7.22) and (7.23).

(7.22)   EP:

    a. [*Context*:
       A: – Ele não copiou o livro sem a tua autorização,
            he not copied the book without the your permission
          pois não?
          CONFIRM no
       'He didn't copy the book without your permission, did he?']
       B: – **Copiou, copiou**.
          copied, copied
       'Yes, he DID.'

b. [*Context*:
      A: – Ele   não   fotocopiou   o   livro sem   a   tua autorização,
           he   not   photocopied the book without the your permission,
           pois   não?
           CONFIRM   no
           'He didn't photocopy the book without your permission, did he?']
      B: – ??**Fotocopiou, fotocopiou.**
           photocopied   photocopied
      B′: – Fotocopiou, sim.
           photocopied   yes
           'Yes, he DID.'

(7.23) EP:
   a. [*Context*:
      A: – Ele   não   atacou   o   candidato,
           he   not   attacked   the candidate
           pois   não?
           CONFIRM   no
           'He didn't attack the candidate, did he?']
      B: – **Atacou,   atacou.**
           attacked   attacked
           'Yes, he DID.'
   b. [*Context*:
      A: – O   candidato   não   contra-atacou,   pois   não?
           the candidate   not   counter-attacked   CONFIRM   no
           'The candidate didn't counter-attack, did he?']
      B: – ??**Contra-atacou, contra-atacou.**
           counter-attacked counter-attacked
      B′: – Contra-atacou, sim.
           counter-attacked yes
           'Yes, he DID.'

(7.22a) and (7.23a) show that in their underived forms, the verbs *copiar* 'copy' and *atacar* 'attack' can undergo reduplication without any problems. In turn, the utterances by B′ in (7.22b) and (7.23b) show that the compound forms *fotocopiar* 'photocopy' and *contra-atacar* 'counter-attack' can independently appear in an emphatic affirmation construction. Given the acceptability of these examples, the marginality of the utterances by B in (7.22b) and (7.23b) may be taken to indicate that verb reduplication may be sensitive to morphological complexity.

One could think that the marginality of reduplication with *fotocopiar* and *contra-atacar* might simply be a matter of phonological length, with longer words being unable to undergo reduplication. The perfect acceptability of

(7.24), whose reduplicated verb has more syllables than the reduplicated verbs in (7.22b) and (7.23b), shows that phonological length is not what is at stake.

(7.24) EP:
 [*Context*:
 A: – As plantas não descontaminaram a água.
   the plants not decontaminated the water
  'The plants did not decontaminate the water.']
 B: – **Descontaminaram, descontaminaram**.
   decontaminated *decontaminated*
  'Of course they did.'

 The fact that the reduplicated verb in (7.24) also has a prefix (*des-*) shows that affixation *per se* is not the relevant trouble-maker in (7.23b) either. The common property between the two groups of verbs that resist reduplication is actually related to their stress pattern. In both groups, the addition of an adverb-like constituent in the case of the compound verbs like that in (7.22) or a stressed prefix in cases like (7.23) gives rise to a complex prosodic word, i.e. a word with two word stress domains; this seems to be what disrupts reduplication. Notice that the prefixes that yield marginal results in verb reduplication can be coordinated or appear in isolation, as illustrated in (7.25).

(7.25) EP:
 a. Houve um acordo entre os contra e os
   had an agreement between the counter- and the
  anti-terroristas.
  anti-terrorists
  'There was an agreement between the counter- and the anti-terrorists.'
 b. A: – Eles são contra-terroristas ou anti-terroristas?
    they are counter-terrorists or anti-terrorists
  'Are they counter-terrorists or anti-terrorist?'
  B: – Contra.
    counter
  'They are counter-terrorists.'

 Another effect of morphological complexity on verb reduplication in EP is illustrated by verbal forms in the indicative future or the indicative conditional. In (7.22a) and (7.23a), we saw that the verbs *copiar* and *atacar* independently allow verb reduplication. Interestingly, if these verbs are in the indicative future or the indicative conditional, their reduplication yields a marginal result, as shown in (7.26).

7.2 Emphatic Affirmation

(7.26)   EP:
    a. [*Context*:
       A: – Ele não atacará o candidato, pois
           *he not attack-**INDIC.FUT**-3.SG the candidate CONFIRM*
       não?
       no
       'He will not attack the candidate, will he?']
      B: – ??**Atacará**, **atacará**.
          attack-INDIC.FUT-3.SG attack-INDIC.FUT-3.SG
       'Yes, he WILL.'
    b. [*Context*:
       A: – Ele não copiaria o
           *he not copy-**INDIC.COND**-3.SG the*
       livro sem a tua autorização,
       book without the your authorization
       pois não?
       CONFIRM no
       'He wouldn't copy the book without your permission, would he?']
      B: – ??**Copiaria**, **copiaria**.
          copy-INDIC.COND-3.SG copy-INDIC.COND-3.SG
       'He surely would.'

As discussed in Section 5.6.1, the indicative future and the indicative conditional diachronically evolved from Latin verbal periphrases involving an infinitival verb plus the verb *habere* 'have' in the present or imperfective past, as sketched in (7.27) below. Interestingly, these two tenses in EP are the only ones that allow mesoclisis, as illustrated in (7.28) (see Section 5.6.1; (7.27) and (7.28) reproduce (5.203) and (5.204)).

(7.27)   a. scribere habeo   > escrever hei   > escreverei
        write have-1.SG   *write-INDIC.FUT-1.SG*
    b. scribere habebam > escrever havia > escreveria
        write had-1.SG   *write-INDIC.COND-1.SG*

(7.28)   EP:
    a. Eu escrever-**te**-ei no mês que vem.
       I write-INDIC.FUT-you.SG-1.SG in-the month that comes
      'I'll write you(SG) next month.'
    b. Eles comprá-**lo**-iam amanhã se tivessem dinheiro.
       they buy-INDIC.COND-it-3.PL tomorrow if had money
      'They would buy it tomorrow if they had the money.'

The exceptional pattern of clitic placement with these tenses in EP suggests that we may in fact have enclisis to the main verb, with the ending following the clitic being a reduced auxiliary (see Section 5.6.1).⁷ That being so, it is no surprise that the morphological complexity of the verbal forms in (7.26) hinders reduplication.⁸ We should also expect a cumulative hindering effect if reduplication targets compound verbs or verbs with stressed prefixes, in the indicative future or the indicative conditional form. This is indeed what happens, as shown in (7.29), whose reduplications are completely unacceptable, strongly contrasting with the corresponding emphatic affirmation with *sim*.

(7.29) EP:
    a. [*Context*:
        A: – O   candidato   não contra-atacará,
             the   *candidate* *not* *counter-attack-**INDIC.FUT**-3.SG*
             pois   não?
             CONFIRM *no*
             'The candidate won't counter-attack, will he?']
        B: – ***Contra-atacará, contra-atacará.** *counter-attack-INDIC.FUT-3.SG*
                                                                         counter-attack-INDIC.FUT-3.SG
        B': – Contra-atacará,   sim.
             counter-attack-INDIC.FUT-3.SG   *yes*
             'Yes, he WILL.'
    b. [*Context*:
        A: – Ele   não   fotocopiaria   o
             he   *not*   *photocopy-**INDIC.COND**-3.SG* *the*
             livro   sem   a   tua   autorização, pois   não?
             book *without* *the your authorization* *CONFIRM* *no*
             'He wouldn't photocopy the book without your permission, would he?']
        B: – ***Fotocopiaria, fotocopiaria.**   *photocopy-INDIC.COND.FUT-3.SG*
                                                            photocopy-INDIC.COND.FUT-3.SG
        B': – Fotocopiaria,   sim.
             photocopy-INDIC.COND-3.SG *yes*
             'Yes, he WOULD.'

Let us discuss one final case of morphological complexity affecting verb reduplication. Although answering a *yes/no* question with a bare verb is more natural in EP (see Section 7.5.1), a verb+clitic sequence is also a possible grammatical answer, as shown in (7.30a) below. The clitic can also occur in emphatic affirmation with *sim*, as shown in (7.30b). However, if the verb is

---

⁷ See e.g. Duarte and Matos 2000 for discussion.
⁸ Vigário (2003) in fact shows that verbal units that host a mesoclitic pronoun function as complex prosodic words (with two word stress domains) like compound verbs and verbs with stressed prefixes.

reduplicated, the presence of the clitic yields an unacceptable result, as illustrated in (7.31).

(7.30) EP:
  a. [*Context*:
    A: – Devolveste-me   o   livro   que   te   emprestei?
        returned-2.SG-me   the   book   that you.SG   lent-1.SG
        'Did you(SG) return me the book I lent you(SG)?']
    B: – Devolvi.
        returned-1.SG
    B′: – Devolvi-**to**.
        returned-1.SG-you$_{[CL]}$.it$_{[CL]}$
        'Yes, I did.'
  b. [*Context*:
    A: – Não   me   devolveste   o   livro   que
        not   me   returned-2.SG   the   book   that
        eu   te   emprestei,   pois   não?
        I   you.SG   lent-1.SG   CONFIRM   no
        'You(SG) haven't returned me the book I lent you, have you(SG)?']
    B: – Devolvi(-**to**),   sim.
        returned-1.SG-you.SG$_{[CL]}$.it$_{[CL]}$ yes
        'Yes, I DID.'

(7.31) EP:
  a. [*Context*:
    A: – Não lhe trouxeste   o   livro   que   ele   te   pediu.
        not him brought-2.SG   the book that he   you.SG   asked
        'You(SG) didn't take him the book that he asked you(SG) for.']
    B: – Eu **trouxe**-lhe   o   livro   que ele me pediu, **trouxe**.
        I   brought-him   the book that he me asked, brought
    B′: – *Eu **trouxe-lhe**   o   livro   que ele me pediu, **trouxe-lhe**.
        I   brought-him   the book that he me asked, brought-him
        'Yes, I did take him the book.'
  b. [*Context*:
    A: – Não   me   devolveste   o   livro   que   eu   te
        not   me   returned-2.SG   the   book   that   I   you.SG
        emprestei,   pois   não?
        lent-1.SG   CONFIRM   no
        'You(SG) haven't returned me the book I lent you(SG), have you(SG)?']
    B: – **Devolvi,**   **devolvi**.
        returned-1.SG   returned-1.SG
    B′: – *Devolvi-to,   devolvi-to.
        returned-1.SG-you$_{[CL]}$.it$_{[CL]}$ returned-1.SG-you$_{[CL]}$.it$_{[CL]}$
        'Yes, I surely did.'

Given the discussion above, the unacceptability of the reduplication sentences in (7.31) can be accounted for, if the sequence verb+clitic counts as morphologically too complex for reduplication.

7.3 Syntactic Patterns of Negation

As seen in Section 7.2, there is no overt marker for affirmation in neutral sentences; affirmation is grammatically encoded only when emphatic. We will see below that negation, on the other hand, always requires overt expression and that different types of expression may correspond to different types of negation. To put it differently, affirmation is the default value for the polarity of a clause and negation is its marked value. In this section, we discuss different types of negation and how they are grammatically encoded.[9] We examine clausal negation in Section 7.3.1, emphatic negation in Section 7.3.2, metalinguistic negation in Section 7.3.3, and expletive negation in Section 7.3.4.

7.3.1   Clausal Negation and Negative Concord

In both EP and BP, clausal negation is obligatorily expressed preverbally, as illustrated by the predicative negation marker *não* 'not' in (7.32a), the negative coordination conjunction *nem* 'nor' in (7.32b–c), and the negative focusing word *nem* 'not even' in (7.32d).[10]

---

[9] Unless it is relevant for the discussion of clausal polarity, we will set aside cases of "constituent negation," where negation has scope not over the entire clause, but over one of its constituents or a discourse fragment, as illustrated in (i). For discussion see e.g. Vitral 1999 and Cavalcante 2012.

(i) a. A **não**-aprovação do projeto deixou todos furiosos.
    the non-approval of-the project left all furious
    'The non-approval of the project made everyone furious.'
   b. **Não** poucos alunos reclamaram.
    not few students complained
    'Not a few students complained.'
   c. Ele **não**.
    he not
    'Not him!' [campaign slogan against Bolsonaro in Brazilian presidential elections in 2018]

[10] For discussion see e.g. Mioto 1992, Peres 1995, 1997, 2013, Abreu 1998, Biberauer and Cyrino 2009, and Teixeira de Sousa 2012, 2015.

(7.32) a. O João **não** saiu.
 the João not left
 'João didn't go out.'
 b. O João {não/**nem**} saiu, **nem** dormiu.
 the João not/neither left neither slept
 'João neither went out nor slept.'
 c. **Nem** o João **nem** a Maria saíram.
 nor the João nor the Maria left
 'Neither João nor Maria went out.'
 d. **Nem** o João dormiu.
 not.even the João sleep
 'Not even João slept.'

As seen in (7.32), the clausal negation marker *não* has a tighter positional requirement than *nem* in that it must immediately precede the verb. In fact, only pronominal clitics are allowed to disrupt the adjacency between the clausal negation marker *não* and the verb, as shown by the contrast between *não* and *nem* in (7.33), within a similar context.[11]

(7.33) a. Ele não **me** viu.
 he not me_{[CL]} saw
 'He didn't see me.'
 b. *Ele não **lá** mora.
 he not there lives
 'He doesn't live there.'
 c. Ele nem **me** viu.
 he not.even me_{[CL]} saw
 'He didn't even see me.'
 d. Ele nem **lá** mora.
 he not.even there lives
 'He doesn't even live there.'

The clausal negative marker *não* 'not' is homophonous with the clause-external negative word *não* 'no'. While the former is strictly dependent on the verbal form it precedes (see (7.32a) and (7.33a–b)), the latter has a wider distributional pattern, as illustrated in (7.34) below. Besides occurring in sentence-initial position in answers to *yes/no* questions, where it surfaces in tandem with the clausal negation marker *não* 'not' (see (7.34a) below), clause-external *não* 'no' can appear in isolation (see (7.34b)), in clause-final position after the complementizer *que* 'that' (see (7.34c)), between two occurrences of *que* in "recomplementation" structures (see (7.34d)), and in clause-final positions where it expresses emphatic negation (see (7.34e)).

---

[11] See e.g. Costa and Martins 2010 for discussion.

(7.34) [*Context*:
　　　　A: – Ele vem?
　　　　　　　he comes
　　　　　　　'Is he coming?']
　　a. B: – **Não**, não vem.
　　　　　　　no not comes
　　b. B: – **Não**.
　　　　　　　no
　　　　　　　'No, he isn't.'
　　c. B: – Ele disse que **não**.
　　　　　　　he said that no
　　　　　　　'He said he wasn't.'
　　d. B: – Ele disse que **não**, que não vem.
　　　　　　　he said that no that not comes
　　　　　　　'He said that he was not coming.'
　　e. [*Context*:
　　　　A: – Ele vem, não vem?
　　　　　　　he comes not comes
　　　　　　　'He is coming, isn't he?']
　　　　B: – Não vem **não**.
　　　　　　　not comes no
　　　　　　　'No, he is not.'

In a number of BP and EP dialectal varieties, the two types of *não* can be phonetically distinguished in that the clausal negative marker *não* 'not' may undergo phonological weakening (with the diphthong being reduced to a single vowel that can be further denasalized), but the clause-external *não* 'no' cannot, as illustrated in (7.35).[12]

(7.35)　a. %EP: Eu {**não/nã/na**} quero, {**não/*nã/*na**}.
　　　　　　　　　 I not　　　　　 want　 no
　　　　b. %BP: Eu {**não/num/nu**} quero, {**não/*num/*nu**}.
　　　　　　　　　 I not　　　　　　 want　 no
　　　　　　　　'I do not want it.'

Another difference between the two types of *não* regards their positive counterparts. In BP, the positive marker *sim* 'yes' in (7.36a–b) below is generally restricted to formal registers (hence the annotation "%"), as will be discussed in Section 7.5.1. But putting this aside for the moment, clause-external *não* 'no' displays the same syntactic distribution as *sim*, as can be seen in (7.36). By contrast, the clausal negative marker *não* 'not' has no overt positive morphosyntactic counterpart, as mentioned above.

---

[12] For discussion see e.g. Vasconcelos 1901, E. Martins 1997, Ramos 2002, and Cavalcante 2004.

(7.36) [*Context*:
A: – Ele vem?
    he comes
    'Is he coming?']
a. B: – **Sim**, vem.   (EP: OK; BP: %)
       yes comes
b. B: – **Sim**.   (EP: OK; BP: %)
       yes
       'Yes, he is.'
c. B: – Ele disse que **sim**.
       he said that yes
       'He said he was.'
d. B: – Ele disse que **sim**, que vem.
       he said that yes that comes
       'He said that he was coming.'
e. [*Context*:
   A: – Ele não vem.
       he not comes
       'He's not coming.']
   B: – Vem, **sim**.
        comes yes
        'Yes, he is.'

The requirement that clausal negation be marked preverbally can be satisfied if negative polarity items (NPIs) like the indefinites *nenhum* 'no', *nada* 'nothing', *ninguém* 'nobody', or the adverb *nunca* 'never' precede the verb, as illustrated in (7.37) below; in this case, the clausal negation marker *não* 'not' is blocked.[13] If the NPIs follow the verb, as shown in (7.38), clausal negation must again be overtly expressed.[14]

---

[13] In (7.37), the NPIs occupy canonical positions reserved for the subject and preverbal adverbs. EP also allows the NPI *nada* 'nothing' to appear preverbally when it is an object, as illustrated in (ia). The NPIs *ninguém* 'nobody' and *nenhum* 'no' do not have this possibility, as shown in (ib) and (ic). The contrast between (ia), on the one hand, and (ib) and (ic), on the other, also exists in BP, although (ia) has a formal or literary ring to it.

(i) a. Ele **nada** fez para me ajudar.
       he nothing did to me help
       'He didn't do anything to help me.'
    b. *Ele **ninguém** contratou para me ajudar.
        he nobody   hired   to me help
        'He didn't hire anybody to help me.'
    c. ??Ele **nenhuma** palavra disse para me consolar.
         he no   word   said to me console
         'He didn't say a word to console me.'

[14] On the nature of negative polarity items in Portuguese and their interplay with negation, see e.g. Martins 2000b. In Portuguese, in contrast to most Romance languages, NPIs are not allowed in *positive non-assertive* contexts (e.g. questions, conditionals, complements of prohibition predicates, and *antes que* 'before' clauses), as shown in (i):

(7.37) a. **Ninguém** telefonou.
nobody called
a′. *Ninguém **não** telefonou.
nobody not called
'Nobody called.'
b. **Nenhum** deles foi demitido.
none of-them was fired
b′. *Nenhum deles **não** foi demitido.
none of-them not was fired
'None of them was fired.'
c. **Nada** aconteceu.
nothing happened
c′. *Nada **não** aconteceu.
nothing not happened
'Nothing happened.'
d. Eles **nunca** telefonam.
they never call
d′. *Eles nunca **não** telefonam.
they never not call
'They never call.'

(7.38) a. **Não** telefonou ninguém.
not called nobody
a′. *Telefonou **ninguém**.
called nobody
'Nobody called.'

(i) a. O João queria saber se viria {**alguém**
 the João wanted know if come-INDIC.COND somebody
 /***ninguém**}.
 nobody
 'João wanted to know if anyone would come.'
 b. Se você quiser comer {**alguma coisa** /*nada},
 if you.SG want.SUBJ.FUT eat some thing nothing
 é só dizer.
 is only say
 'If you(SG) want anything to eat, just let me know.'
 c. O comandante proibiu que {**alguém** /***ninguém**}
 the commander prohibited that somebody nobody
 saísse do quartel.
 leave-SUBJ.FUT from-the barracks
 'The commander prohibited anybody from leaving the barracks.'
 d. O Pedro saiu antes que {**alguém** /***ninguém**}
 the Pedro left before that somebody nobody
 pudesse fazer {**um** /***nenhum**} gesto.
 could do a no move
 'Pedro left before anyone could make a move.'

b. **Não** foi   demitido nenhum deles.
    not   was   fired   no   of-them
b'. *Foi   demitido **nenhum** deles.
    was   fired   no   of-them
    'None of them was fired.'
c. **Não**   aconteceu nada.
    not   happened   nothing
c'. *Aconteceu **nada**.
    happened   nothing
    'Nothing happened.'
d. Eles **não** telefonam nunca.
    they not   call   never
d'. *Eles telefonam **nunca**.
    they   call   never
    'They never call.'

The sharp asymmetry between preverbal and postverbal NPIs regarding their interaction with negation seen in (7.37) and (7.38) also shows that the cooccurrence of the clausal negation marker *não* 'not' and a postverbal NPI within the same clause does not give rise to a double negation reading, with each negative element making an independent semantic contribution. The grammatical sentences of (7.38) unambiguously express standard negation, showing that we have an instance of "negative concord," where the postverbal NPI simply agrees with the predicative negation marker and does not make a semantic contribution of its own.

Negative concord also emerges when two or more NPIs are stacked within the same clause, as shown in (7.39) below. If the relevant negative elements are in different clauses, a double negation reading arises, as illustrated in (7.40) with one negation cancelling the other.

(7.39) a. O   João **nunca** fala   com   **ninguém** durante as reuniões.
          the João never   speaks   with nobody   during   the meetings
          'João never speaks to anybody during the meetings.'
       b. Aqui, **nunca** **ninguém** vê **nada**.
          here   never   nobody   sees nothing
          'Here, nobody ever sees anything.'

(7.40) a. **Não** passa   um dia em que   eu **não** pense   nele.
          not   passes a   day in that I   not   think   of-him
          'There isn't a single day I don't think of him.'
          [= 'I always think of him.']
       b. Ele **nunca** lhe   acontece **não** saber   o que dizer.   (EP)
          he   never   him.DAT   happens   not   know-INF   what   say-INF

b'. **Nunca**   acontece   de   ele   **não**   saber   o que dizer. (BP)
   never   happens   of   he   not   know-INF what   say-INF
   'It never happens to him to not know what to say.'
   [= 'He always knows what to say.']

An apparent exception to the obligatoriness of negative concord within a single clause involves the negative preposition *sem* 'without' in sentences like (7.41), in which one negation cancels the other.

(7.41) a. Ela   **não**   sai   **sem**   chapéu.
          she   not   leaves   without   hat
          'She doesn't go out without wearing a hat.'
          [= 'She always wears a hat when going out.']
       b. Ela   **nunca** sai   **sem**   chapéu.
          she   never   leaves   without   hat
          'She never goes out without wearing a hat.'
          [= 'She always wears a hat when going out.']
       c. Aqui **ninguém** sai   **sem**   chapéu.
          here nobody   leaves   without   hat
          'Here, nobody goes out without wearing a hat.'
          [= 'Here, everybody wears a hat when going out.']

The negative specification of *sem* can be detected in sentences like those in (7.42) below, for instance, which show that *sem* can license a negative polarity expression. However, the sentences in (7.42) also show that *sem* is unable to negate the whole clause; after all, in (7.42a) João did arrive and in (7.42b) Maria did travel. In other words, *sem* is a case of constituent negation (see footnote 9 above) and constituent negation is unable to undergo negative concord. Hence, the exceptionality of (7.41) is only apparent.

(7.42) a. O   João chegou   **sem**   **nada**   nos   bolsos.
          the João arrived without   nothing   in-the   pockets
          'João arrived with nothing in his pockets.'
       b. A   Maria viajou   **sem**   **um tostão furado**.
          the Maria travelled without   a   cent   holed
          'Maria travelled without a red cent on her.'

That constituent negation cannot participate in negative concord is illustrated by the interesting paradigm in (7.43) below. The postverbal position of *não* in (7.43a) indicates that this is a case not of clausal negation, but of constituent negation. That being so, the contrast between (7.43b) and (7.43c) follows straightforwardly. In (7.43b), postverbal *não* targets the constituent headed by *sem*, cancelling the negative import of the latter, which can no longer license the NPI *um tostão furado* 'a red cent'. In (7.43c), on the other hand, the negative specification of *sem* is not canceled and it is independently able to license the NPI, regardless of whether the matrix clause is negated or not.

(7.43)   a. O Pedro saiu **não sem** antes dizer adeus.
           the Pedro left not without before say-INF goodbye
           'Pedro left but not before saying goodbye.'
       b. *O Pedro vai viajar **não sem** ter **um tostão furado**.
           the Pedro goes travel-INF not without have-INF a cent holed
           'Pedro is going to travel but not without a red cent.'
       c. O Pedro (**não**) vai viajar **sem** ter **um tostão furado**.
           the Pedro not goes travel-INF without have-INF a cent holed
           'Pedro is (not) going to travel without a red cent.'

A restricted set of predicates (not necessarily the same ones in EP and BP) allows negative concord across clause boundaries, as shown in (7.44) below.[15] Infinitivals are generally more porous to interclausal negative concord than finite clauses, as illustrated by the contrasts in (7.45).

(7.44)   a. Eu **não** quero que ele compre **nada**.
           I not want that he buy-SUBJ nothing
           'I don't want him to buy anything.'
       b. Eu **não** acredito que ele tenha mexido **um dedo**
           I not believe that he has-SUBJ moved a finger
           para me ajudar.
           to me help
           'I don't believe him to have lifted a finger to help me.'
       c. **Não** senti que esse tratamento tivesse efeito colateral
           not felt-1.SG that this treatment had-SUBJ effect collateral
           nenhum.
           none
           'I didn't feel that this medical treatment had any side-effects.'
       d. Ela **não** pediu que eu trouxesse **nada**.
           she not asked that I brought-SUBJ nothing
           'She didn't ask me to bring anything.'

(7.45)   a. Eu **não** vi o João falar com **ninguém**.
           I not saw the João speak-**INF** with nobody
           'I didn't see João speak with anybody.'
       a'. *Eu **não** percebi que o João dançou com **ninguém**.
           I not realized that the João danced with nobody
           'I didn't notice that João danced with no one.'
       b. Ele **não** mexeu um dedo para ajudar **ninguém**.
           he not moved a finger to help-**INF** nobody
           'He didn't lift a finger to help anybody.'

---

[15] For discussion see e.g. Mioto 1992 and Peres 1995, 1997, 2013.

b'. *Ele **não** mexeu um dedo para que socorressem
he not moved a finger to that help-SUBJ.IMPERF-3.PL
ninguém.
nobody
'He didn't lift a finger so that they could help someone.'

7.3.2 Emphatic Negation

Emphatic negation describes the type of negation that contradicts/ denies a previous positive assertion, usually presented as a statement or as a tag question that anticipates a positive answer, as respectively illustrated in (7.46a) and (7.46b).[16]

(7.46) a. [Context:
A: – Vocês saíram sem pagar.
you-PL left without pay-INF
'You(PL) left without paying.']
B: – A gente não saiu sem pagar **não**.   (EP/BP)
we not left without pay no
'We did not leave without paying!'
b. [Context:
A: – Ele gosta de bacalhau, não gosta?
he likes of cod not likes
'He likes cod, doesn't he?']
B: – Não gosta **não**.   (EP/BP)
not likes no
'No, he does not.'

Emphatic negation with sentence-final *não* 'no' behaves in a way parallel to emphatic affirmation with sentence-final *sim* 'yes' (see Section 7.2.1): while sentence-final *sim* amplifies an affirmative declarative, sentence-final *não* amplifies a negative declarative, functioning as a reinforcing tag with respect to the truth-conditional content of the declarative sentence it is attached to. Thus, two negation items surface in emphatic negation constructions like those in (7.46), namely, the clause-internal predicative negation marker *não* 'not' and the clause-external negative marker *não* 'no'.

Although EP and BP may both express emphatic negation with sentence-final *não* 'no', as in (7.46), the distribution of clause-internal in tandem with clause-external *não* is wider in BP. In particular, in BP but not in EP, the

---

[16] For discussion see e.g. Mioto 1992, Biberauer and Cyrino 2009, Cavalcante 2012, Teixeira Sousa 2012, and Martins 2013a, 2016a.

clause-external *não* can be associated with negation in an embedded complement clause, as shown in (7.47), with a negative imperative, as illustrated in (7.48),[17] and can be used to tilt a *yes/no* question towards a positive answer, as shown by the confirmation question in (7.49) and the polite invitation in (7.50). However, the two varieties converge in ruling out clause-external *não* in *wh*-questions, as illustrated in (7.51).

(7.47) A Maria disse que ele **não** compromou aquela casa
the Maria said that he not bought that house
não. (EP: *; BP: OK)
no
'Maria said that he did not buy that house.'

(7.48) **Não** convide o João **não**. (EP: *; BP: OK)
not invite the João no
'Do not invite João.'

(7.49) Você **não** terminou o relatório **não**? (EP: *; BP: OK)
you.SG not finished the report no
'Didn't you(SG) finish the report?'

(7.50) Você **não** quer tomar um cafezinho **não**? (EP: *; BP: OK)
you.SG not want take a coffee-DIM no
'Wouldn't you(SG) like to have some coffee?'

(7.51) a. *O que é que o João **não** comprou **não**? (EP: *; BP: *)
what is that the João not bought no
'What did João not buy?'
b. *Quem é que o João **não** cumprimentou **não**?
whom is that the João not greeted no
'Who did João not greet?'

EP and BP can also make use of the negative indefinite *nada* 'nothing' to express emphatic negation, although with differences with respect to the position where it is licensed and the obligatoriness of clause-internal negation.[18] In EP, the emphatic negation marker *nada* must immediately follow the verb and clause-internal negation is obligatory, as illustrated in (7.52) below. By contrast, in BP *nada* occurs in sentence-final position and clause-internal negation is optional, as shown in (7.53). Notice that an emphatic negation construction such as (7.54) is acceptable in both varieties because there is no material other than *nada* following the verb; hence, (7.54)

---

[17] (7.48) may in fact be acceptable in EP (and in BP, as well) with a flat intonation, in which case it is interpreted as a kind of threat: If you do not invite João, something bad may happen to you.
[18] See e.g. Pinto 2010 and Cavalcante 2012 for discussion.

can satisfy the postverbal adjacency requirement of EP, as well as the sentence-final requirement of BP. In fact, emphatic negation with *nada* in BP sounds more natural when the predicate involves only the verb, as in (7.54), thus corresponding to the negative counterpart of short answers with emphatic affirmation (see Section 7.2.1).[19]

(7.52)   EP:
         [*Context*:
         A: – Vi   o   teu   namorado   a   beijar a   Maria.
             saw-1.SG   the   your.SG   boyfriend   to   kiss   the Maria
             'I saw your(SG) boyfriend kissing Maria.']
         B: – **Não** viste   **nada**   o   meu   namorado a   beijar
             not   saw-2.SG   nothing   the   my   boyfriend to kiss
             a   Maria.
             the   Maria
             'You(SG) did NOT see my boyfriend kissing Maria.'

(7.53)   BP:
         [*Context*:
         A: – O   mecânico   disse que   consertou o   carro.
             the   mechanic   said   that   fixed   the car
             'The mechanic said that he fixed the car.']
         B: – **(Não)** consertou (o   carro) **nada**.
             not   fixed   the   car   nothing
             'He definitely did not fix the car.'

(7.54)   [*Context*:
         A: – Ontem   o   João   chegou   na   hora   certa.
             yesterday the   João   arrived   in-the   hour   right
             'Yesterday João arrived at the right time.']
         B: – Não   chegou   nada.   (EP/BP)
             not   arrive   nada
             'He did NOT.'

---

[19] *Nada* as a non-argumental negative word can also be found in imperative-like structures such as that in (i) or in the negative exclamatives in (ii).

(i)   Meninos, **nada**   de comerem   os bombons   todos.
      boys   nothing   of eat-INF-3.PL   the chocolates all
      'Children, don't you(PL) dare eat all the chocolates.'
(ii) [*Context*:
      A: – Ele   telefonou para te   dar   os   parabéns?
          he   called   to   you   give the congratulations
          'Did he call to congratulate you(SG)?']
      B: – **Nada**   disso!   (EP)
          nothing   of-that
      B': – Que   **nada**!   (BP)
          what   nothing
          'Not at all!'

7.3 Syntactic Patterns of Negation

Some dialects of BP (in particular, Northeastern dialects) allow sentence-final *não* without clause-internal negation in several types of constructions, as illustrated in (7.55a) below with an answer to a *yes/no* question and (7.55b) with a negative imperative. These dialects also use this frame to express emphatic negation, as illustrated in (7.56).[20]

(7.55) %BP:
    a. [*Context*:
        A: – Você   fez   o   trabalho?
            you.SG did the work
            'Did you(SG) do the work?']
        B: – Fiz   **não**.
            did.1.SG no
            'No, I didn't.'
    b. Convide ele **não**.
       invite   he   no
       'Don't invite him.'

(7.56) %BP:
    a. [*Context*:
        A: – Cê   demorou   pra   chegar.
            you.SG   took.long   to   arrive
            'It took you(SG) a long time to get here.']
        B: – Demorei   **não**.
            took.long-1.SG   no
            'No, it didn't.'
    b. [*Context*:
        A: – O   João vai   viajar amanhã.
            the   João goes travel tomorrow
            'João is going to travel tomorrow.']
        B: – Vai **não**.
            goes no
            'No, he isn't.'

Interestingly, it is not the case that these BP dialects have substituted constructions like (7.56) for the emphatic negation construction with clause-internal negation. The two structures occur side by side, although the version without clause-internal negation is more restricted in that it is banned from embedded clauses. A sentence such as (7.57) below, for instance, can be interpreted as denying the saying, but not denying the buying (cf. (7.47)). Besides, the version without a clause-internal negative marker is able to license an NPI like *nada* 'nothing', for instance, but not a minimizer like *um*

---

[20] See e.g. Biberauer and Cyrino 2009, Cavalcante 2007, 2010, Fonseca 2011, and Teixeira Sousa 2012 for discussion.

tostão furado 'a red cent', as illustrated in (7.58). This indicates that sentences such as (7.56) in these dialects cannot be analyzed simply as not having clause-internal negation, for otherwise (7.58a) would be excluded because the post-verbal NPI *nada* would not be licensed; conversely, they cannot be analyzed as simply involving phonological deletion of the clause-internal negative maker *não* 'not', for otherwise the minimizer in (7.58b) should be licensed. In other words, these constructions seem to involve a null clause-internal negative marker with a featural specification distinct from predicative *não*, for it can enter a negative concord relation, as in (7.58a), but cannot license a minimizer, as shown in (7.58b). It is also worth noting that the postulation of such null negation marker is compatible with the generalization that predicative/propositional negation is necessarily preverbal.[21]

(7.57) %BP:

    A   Maria disse que ele comprou aquela casa **não**.
    the Maria said that he bought that house no
    'Maria did not say that he bought that house.'
    *'Maria said that he did not buy that house.'

(7.58) %BP:

  a. [*Context*:
      A: – Você comprou alguma coisa?
           you.SG bought some thing
           'Did you(SG) buy anything?]
      B: – Comprei nada **não**.
           bought nothing no
           'No, I didn't buy anything.'

---

[21] Thus far, we have restricted our attention to the more general case of emphatic negation involving the denial of a previous positive assertion. However, it should be pointed out that emphatic negation may also contradict a previous negative statement, in which case it requires some special marking. In the EP sentence in (ia) below, for instance, the double negation reading is enforced by the complementizer-like element *que* 'that', whereas in (ib) the double negation reading requires a special flat intonation (⇢) in both EP and BP. The fact that the affirmative sentence in (ic) in EP displays the same kind of intonation as that which characterizes (ib) (see also footnote 6 above) suggests that this intonational contour is perhaps a prosodic indicator/clue for irony.

(i)   [*Context*:
    A: – A Maria não gosta de viajar.
        the Maria not likes of travel
        'Maria doesn't like traveling.']
    a. B: – Não que não gosta.   (EP)
           no that not likes
    b. B: – Não gosta não.⇢   (EP/BP)
           not likes no
    c. B: – Gosta pouco gosta.⇢   (EP)
           likes little likes
           'Of course she does like it.'

b. [*Context*:
   A: – O   João   é   rico!
           the   João   is   rich
           'João is rich!']
   B: – *O quê? Ele tem um tostão furado **não**.
           what   he has a   cent   holed   no
           'What?! He doesn't have a red cent!'

7.3.3 Metalinguistic Negation

Metalinguistic negation describes the type of negation that signals objection to a previous utterance, not necessarily with respect to its truth but with respect to its appropriateness and the types of inference it may invite.[22] Consider the exchange in (7.59) below, for instance. From a logical point of view, if João got all the answers wrong, it is necessarily true that he got some answers wrong. The negative marker in (7.59) does not make B's utterance contradictory or nonsensical, though. B is not actually denying that João got some answers wrong, but questioning the appropriateness of A's utterance in a context where João got all answers wrong, for it invites the inference that at least some of the answers were right. We thus have here an instance of metalinguistic negation.

(7.59)   [*Context*:
   A: – O   João   errou   algumas questões na   prova.
           the   João   erred   some   questions in-the   exam
           'João got some answers wrong in the exam.']
   B: – Ele **não** errou   algumas questões. Ele errou todas.
           he   not   erred   some   questions he   erred   all
           'He didn't get some answers wrong. He got all of them wrong.'

In addition to the all-purpose negative marker *não* 'not' seen in (7.59), EP and BP employ two other general patterns to encode metalinguistic negation. The first involves *wh*-like pronouns, as illustrated in (7.60) for EP.[23]

(7.60)   EP:
   [*Context*:
   A: – Eles humilharam-no.
          they   humiliated-him
          'They humiliated him.']

---

[22] For discussion on metalinguistic negation in Portuguese, see e.g. Martins 2010, 2012, 2014, 2020a, 2021b, Pinto 2010, 2020, Cavalcante 2012, Pereira 2010, 2013, and Marcelino 2018.
[23] See e.g. Martins 2020a, 2021b for discussion.

a.   B: – **Qual** humilharam-no!
            which   humiliated-him
a′.   B: – *Humilharam-no **qual**!
           humiliated-him   which
b.   B: – Humilharam-no **o quê**!
           humiliated-him   the what
b′.   B: – ***O quê** humilharam-no!
           the what   humiliated-him
c.   B: – **Qual (quê)**!
           which (what)
d.   B: – **Qual** humilharam-no {**qual quê** /**o quê**}!
           which   humiliated-him   which what /the what
           'Like hell they did.'

EP uses the *wh*-determiners/pronouns *qual* 'which', *o quê* 'what', and *quê* 'what' with a very interesting distribution. *Qual* can appear in isolation (see (7.60c)) or in sentence-initial position (see (7.60a) vs. (7.60a′)). By contrast, *o quê* must appear in sentence-final position (see (7.60b) vs. (7.60b′)). Finally, *quê* can occur only in combination with *qual*, either in isolation (see (7.60c)) or in sentence-final position, doubling a sentence-initial *qual* (see (7.60d)). The latter possibility is also available for *o quê* (see (7.60d)). Interestingly, the preverbal *wh*-element in (7.60a) and (7.60d), as opposed to standard *wh*-determiners and *wh*-pronouns (see Section 5.6.1), does not trigger proclisis.

As for BP, it resorts to *que* 'what' and *o que* 'what', as illustrated in (7.61) below.[24] These *wh*-elements also occupy different peripheral positions, with *que* occurring sentence-initially (see (7.61a) vs. (7.61a′)) and *o que* sentence-finally (see (7.61b) vs. (7.61b′)), which also allows them to be combined (see (7.61c)). In this regard, *que* in (7.61a) and (7.61c) contrasts with interrogative *que* 'what', which cannot appear clause-initially in BP unless it is preceded by a preposition or is followed by the homophonous complementizer-like *que* (see Section 5.3.2).[25,26]

---

[24] For discussion see e.g. Rocha 2021.

[25] In Section 5.3.2, it was suggested that this behavior of interrogative *que* in BP could be accounted for if it were a weak pronoun. Interestingly, *que* in (7.61a) has its vowel lengthened (annotated by a colon), which may perhaps be viewed as a way of circumventing the relevant clause-initial restriction.

[26] Some dialects of BP also allow the expression *que mané* as another clause-initial marker of metalinguistic negation, as illustrated in (i), which may be optionally doubled by *que nada* (lit. *what nothing*). For discussion see e.g. Rocha 2021.

(i)   %BP:

     a. [*Context*:
        A: – Ele   não   vai   poder   jogar   videogame   hoje.
            he   not   goes   can   play   videogame   today
       'He won't be able to play videogames today.']

(7.61) BP:
[Context:
A: – O João não vai comer sobremesa.
the João not goes eat dessert
'João is not going to have dessert.']
a. B: – **Que:** não vai!
what not goes
a'. B: – *Não vai **que:**!
not goes what
b. B: – Não vai **o quê**!
not goes what
b'. B: – ***O que** não vai!
what not goes
c. B: – **Que:** não vai comer sobremesa **o quê**!
that not goes eat dessert what
'Of course he is.'

The second general pattern that grammatically encodes metalinguistic negation involves three specific lexical items that originated from deictic adverbials, namely, *lá* (lit. *there*), *cá* (lit. *here*), and *agora* (lit. *now*), as illustrated in (7.62) for EP and (7.63) for BP.

(7.62) EP:
[Context:
A: – Tu estavas um pouco preocupado.
you.SG were a little worried
'You(SG) were a little worried.']
a. B: – Eu estava {**lá/cá/agora**} um pouco preocupado.
I was there/here/now a little worried.
Estava morto de preocupação.
was dead of worry
'I wasn't a little worried, my friend; I was worried sick.'

B: – **Que mané** não vai poder jogar videogame hoje
NEG not goes can play videogame today
(**que nada**)!
what nothing
'How come he won't be able to play videogames today?! Of course he will!'
b. [Context:
A: – Você disse que ia trazer sobremesa.
you.SG said that went bring dessert
'You(SG) said you(SG) were going to bring dessert.']
B: – **Que mané** sobremesa (**que nada**)! Eu disse que
NEG dessert what nothing I said that
ia trazer cerveja, como sempre.
went bring beer, as always
'What dessert?! I said I was going to bring beer, as usual.'

402   7 Affirmation, Negation, Questions, and Answers

    b. B: – *Eu {lá/cá/agora} estava um pouco preocupado.
            I   there/here/now   was   a   little   worried.
            Estava morto de preocupação.
            was   dead   of worry
    c. B: – Eu   estava um pouco preocupado {*lá/*cá/agora}.
            I   was   a   little   worried.   there/here/now
            Estava morto de preocupação.
            was   dead   of worry
    d. B: – *Eu   estava {lá/cá}   um pouco   preocupado
            I   was   there/here a   little   worried.
            agora. Estava morto de preocupação.
            now   was   dead   of   worry
            'I wasn't a little worried. I was worried sick.'

(7.63) BP:
       [Context:
       A: – Eu trouxe   esses exercícios pra você   me ajudar.
            I   brought these   exercises   for you.SG me help
       'I brought these exercises for you(SG) to help me with them.']
    a. B: – E eu {lá/agora} entendo   de matemática?!
            and I there/now   understand of mathematics
    b. B: – E eu entendo   {lá/agora} de matemática?!
            and I understand there/now of mathematics
    c. B: – E eu entendo   de matemática {*lá/agora}?!
            and I understand of mathematics there/now
    d. B: – E eu **lá**   entendo   de matemática **agora**?!
            and I there understand of mathematics now
    e. B: – E eu entendo lá de matemática **agora**?!
            and I understand there of mathematics now
       'Am I supposed to know math?!'

The contrast between (7.62) and (7.63), on the one hand, and (7.64) below, on the other, shows that metalinguistic negation is a matrix clause phenomenon.

(7.64) a. EP:
       [Context:
       A: – A   Maria   disse   que   tu   estavas um   pouco
            the Maria   said   that you.SG   were   a   little
            preocupado.
            worried
       'Maria said that you(SG) were a little worried.']
       B: – *A   Maria   disse [que eu   estava   **agora** um   pouco
            the Maria   said   that I   was   now   a   little
            preocupado]. Estava morto   de preocupação.
            worried.   was   dead   of worry
       'Maria said that I wasn't a little worried. I was sick with worry.'

b. BP:
   [*Context*:
   A: – Eu   trouxe   esses   exercícios   pra   você   me   ajudar.
           I   brought   these   exercises   for   you.SG   me   help
           'I brought these exercises for you(SG) to help me with them.']
   B: – *E   eu   lamento   [que   eu   **lá**   entendo   de   matemática]?!
           and I   regret   that   I   there   understand   of   mathematics
           'I'm sorry but I don't know math!'

Let us examine *lá*, *cá*, and *agora* as markers of metalinguistic negation in more detail, as this usage has passed unnoticed in Portuguese grammars due to its colloquial nature. The first thing to point out is that *cá* is used as a metalinguistic negation marker only in EP (see (7.62)). *Lá* and *agora* are used in both varieties, although in BP they are basically restricted to contexts involving rhetorical questions as replies, as seen in (7.63). The second point worth noting is that EP and BP differ with respect to the position of these specialized metalinguistic negation markers. In EP, *lá* and *cá* always occur immediately following the verb, whereas *agora* may follow the verb or appear sentence-finally, as seen in (7.62).[27]

In BP, on the other hand, these markers may either immediately precede or immediately follow the verb, as shown in (7.63a) and (7.63b), but only *agora* can appear sentence-finally (see (7.63c)). In BP, but not in EP, one may also have one marker in the verb-adjacent position and the other one occupying the sentence-final position, as illustrated by the contrast between (7.62d) in EP and (7.63d) and (7.63e) in BP.

Lá in BP also displays exceptional behavior when idiomatically associated with *sei* 'know.1.SG'. Consider the data in (7.65) and (7.66) below, for example. (7.65a) and (7.66b) exhibit the expected pattern for *lá* (see (7.63)), with a rising intonation characteristic of a rhetorical question and *lá* preceding or following the verb.[28] Interestingly, the subject cannot be dropped in (7.65a), as shown in

---

[27] Some Northwestern dialects of EP also allow *agora* in sentence-initial position, as illustrated in (i) below. See Pereira 2010, 2013 for discussion. Although *agora* is usually pronounced in EP as [ɐ'gɔrɐ], with the unstressed vowel reduction that is chracteristic of EP, the sentence-initial *agora* in sentences like (i) is pronounced as [a'gɔrɐ]. Thus the metalinguistic negation marker *agora* behaves like BP *que*: (see (7.61) above) in undergoing phonological strengthening in sentence-initial position.

(i)   [*Context*:
       A: – Tu   estavas   um   pouco   preocupado.
               you.SG   were   a   little   worried
               'You(SG) were a little worried?']
       B: – **Agora**   estava.   (%EP)
               now   was
               'Nonsense.'

[28] Another possible pattern in the same context as (7.65) and (7.66) is shown (i), which appears to combine (7.65a) with the typical BP clefting with *que* (see Section 5.2.2.3).

404   7 Affirmation, Negation, Questions, and Answers

(7.65c). The unexpected pattern with postverbal *lá* is presented in (7.66): it has a falling intonation, its subject has been dropped, and, although interpreted as a negative answer (stating that B does not know the answer to A's question), it does not necessarily receive a metalinguistic negation reading (questioning the appropriateness of A's question). (7.67) shows that the exceptionality of (7.66) is restricted to the first person singular form of the verb *saber* 'know' in the indicative present, for the analogous construction with the indicative imperfective past form in (7.66d) is completely unacceptable.

(7.65)   BP:
   [*Context*:
   A: – Eles   vão   casar?
        they   go   marry
        'Are they going to get married?']
   a. B: – Eu   **lá**   sei   (se eles vão casar)?!
            I   there   know.1.SG   if   they go marry
   b. B: – Eu sei   **lá**   (se eles vão casar)?!
            I know.1.SG   there   if   they go marry
   c. B: – *Lá   sei   (se   eles   vão   casar)?!
            there   know.1.SG   if   they   go   marry
        'I don't know (if they are going to get married)! [What made you think I would?]'

(7.66)   BP:
   [*Context*:
   A: – Eles   vão   casar?
        they   go   marry
        'Are they going to get married?']
   B: – Sei   **lá**   (se   eles   vão   casar)?!
        know.1.SG   there   if   they   go   marry
        'I don't know (if they are going to get married).'

(7.67)   BP:
   [*Context*:
   A: – Por que você   não   me   contou   que   eles
        why   you.SG   not   me   told   that   they
        iam   casar?
        went   marry
        'Why didn't you(SG) tell me that they were going to get married?']

(i)   B: – Eu   **lá**   que   sei   (se   eles   vão   casar?   (BP)
            I   there   that   know.1.SG   if   they   go   marry
        'I don't know (if they are going to get married)! [What made you think I would?]'

a. B: – E   eu   **lá**   sabia   (que
           and   I   there   know-INDIC.IMPERF.1.SG   that
           eles   iam   casar)?!
           they   went marry
b. B: – E   eu   sabia   **lá**   *(que
           and   I   know-INDIC.IMPERF.1.SG   there   that
           eles   iam   casar)?!
           they   went marry
c. B: – *E   **lá** sabia   (que   eles
           and   there   know-INDIC.IMPERF.1.SG   that   they
           iam   casar)?!
           went marry
d. B: – *Sabia   **lá**   (que   eles   iam
           know-INDIC.IMPERF.1.SG   there   that   they   went
           casar)?!
           marry
           'I didn't know (that they were going to get married)!
           [What made you think I would?]'

In EP, the metalinguistic negation markers *lá* and *cá* also differ from *agora* in several respects. *Agora* has stricter requirements than *lá* and *cá* with respect to discourse licensing as it must object to an actual utterance, while *lá* and *cá* can contradict an implied presupposition. So, *agora* can be licensed in (7.62a) or (7.68) below, but not in (7.69). Thus, if *agora* takes the position of *cá* in (7.68), as shown in (7.70), the second sentence becomes ungrammatical.

(7.68)   EP:
         [*Context*:
         A: – Vem   para   o   nosso   grupo   de filosofia.
              come   to   the   our   group   of philosophy
              'Join us in our philosophy group.']
         B: – (Vou   **agora**). Eu sei   **cá**   alguma   coisa   de filosofia.
              go.1.SG   now   I know   here   some   thing   of philosophy
              'Nonsense. What do I know about philosophy?'

(7.69)   EP:
         [*Context*:
         A: – O   João   estará   em   casa?
              the   João   be-INDIC.FUT   in   house
              'Could João be at home?']
         a.   B: – Sei   **lá**.
                    know.1.SG   there
         b.   B: – *Sei   **agora**.
                    know.1.SG   now
              'I don't know. (Why am I supposed to know?)'

406   7 Affirmation, Negation, Questions, and Answers

(7.70)   EP:
         [*Context*:
         A: – Vem   para   o   nosso   grupo   de   filosofia.
             come   to   the   our   group   of   philosophy
             'Join us in our philosophy group.']
         B: – (Vou   **agora**). *Eu sei   **agora**   alguma   coisa   de   filosofia.
             go.1.SG now   I   know now   some   thing   of   philosophy
             'Nonsense. What do I know about philosophy?'

Another difference is that *agora* can occur in isolation or preceding a nominal responsive fragment, but *lá* and *cá* cannot, as illustrated in (7.71) and (7.72).

(7.71)   EP:
         [*Context*:
         A: – Ele   pagou   o   jantar?
             he   paid   the dinner
             'Did he pay for the dinner?']
     a. B: – **Agora**.
                now
     b. B: – {*Lá/*cá}.
               there/here
               'Like hell he did.'

(7.72)   EP:
         [*Context*:
         A: – O   João   vai   comprar   mas   é   a   bicicleta.
             the   João   goes   buy   but   is   the bicycle
             'It is the bike that João is going to buy.']
     a. B: – **Agora**   a   bicicleta.
                now   the   bicycle
     b. B: – {*Lá/*cá}   a   bicicleta.
               there/here   the   bicycle
               'The bike my eye.'

Agora is also compatible with VP ellipsis and VSVPE (see Section 6.2), as opposed to *lá* and *cá*, as illustrated in (7.73) and (7.74).[29]

(7.73)   EP:
         [*Context*:
         A: – O   João   tem   lido   todos   os   livros.
             the   João   has   read   all   the   books
             'João has been reading all the books.']

---

[29] The fact that *lá* and *cá* cannot occur in isolation or with nominal fragments and block VP ellipsis suggests that they form a morphological unit with the verb they attach to, affecting the identity computations that apply to ellipsis (see Section 6.2).

a. B: – Tem **agora**.
   　　has　now
b. B: – *Tem **lá**.
   　　has　there
c. B: – O João tem **lá** lido todos os livros.
   　　the João has there read all the books
   'Like hell he has.'

(7.74) EP:
[*Context*:
A: – A Maria ofereceu um cão à filha.
　　the Maria offered a dog to-the daughter
'Maria gave her daughter a dog.']
a. B: – Ofereceu **agora**.
   　　offered now
b. B: – *Ofereceu **cá**.
   　　offered here
c. B: – A Maria ofereceu **cá** um cão à filha.
   　　the Maria offered here a dog to-the daughter
   'Like hell she did.'

Lá and *cá* are completely incompatible with *não*, as shown in (7.75) below, whereas *agora* can co-occur with *não* in contexts such as that in (7.76). However, in these contexts *agora* objects to a previous negative utterance and induces a double negation interpretation (hence the contrast between (7.75b) and (7.76) regarding *agora*). In other words, none of these metalinguistic negation markers can be licensed through negative concord.[30]

---

[30] It should be pointed out that, in both EP and BP, postverbal *lá* can also be used as a degree-expressing negative polarity item, in which case it is licensed only in negative clauses and is interpreted as a paucal degree word, as illustrated in (i) and (ii) below. In EP, but not in BP, the degree-expressing NPI *lá* usually precedes the degree adverb *muito* 'very' (thus, (iib) is also acceptable in EP; in (iia) EP could resort to *cá*, with a similar interpretation).

(i) EP:
a. Ele não gosta **lá** muito de trabalhar.
   he not likes there much of work
   'He doesn't particularly like to work.'
b. Ele não fala inglês **lá** muito bem.
   he not speaks English there very well
   'He doesn't speak English particularly well.'

(ii) BP:
a. Eu não sou **lá** de fazer essas coisas, mas eu vou tentar.
   I not am there of do those things but I go try
   'That isn't quite my type of thing to do, but I'll try.'

(7.75) EP:
[Context:
A: – Tens   de pedir-lhe desculpa.
        have-2.SG of ask-him apology
        'You(SG) must apologize to him.']
a.   B: – Peço-lhe   {**lá/cá/agora**} desculpa.
              ask-1.SG-him there/here/now apology
b.   B: – ***Não** lhe peço   {**lá/cá/agora**} desculpa (**não**).
              not him ask-1.SG there/here/now apology no
        'I will apologize to him my eye.'

(7.76) EP:
[Context:
A: – Eu não vou pedir-lhe desculpa.
      I not go ask-him apology
      'I will not apologize to him.']
     B: – **Não** vais   **agora** pedir-lhe desculpa.
           not go-2.SG now ask-him apology
      'You(SG) will not apologize to him my eye.'

EP and BP also have a class of idiomatic expressions and swear words that may behave as markers of metalinguistic negation when they occur in sentence-final position or are clefted in sentence-initial position. We take *uma ova* 'a fish roe' to be representative of this class, as exemplified in (7.77) below. *Lá*, *cá*, and *agora* cannot co-occur with *uma ova*, as shown in (7.78) and (7.79).[31]

(7.77) [Context:
A: – O João vai   tomar conta de tudo.
        the João goes take care of everything
        'João is going to take care of everything.']
a.   B: – Vai tomar conta de tudo   **uma   ova**.   (EP/BP)
              goes take care of everything a   fish.roe
b.   B: – **Uma ova**   é   que vai tomar conta de tudo. (EP)
              a fish.roe is that goes take care of everything
b'. B: – **Uma ova**   que ele vai tomar conta de tudo. (BP)
              a fish.roe that he goes take care of everything
        'Like hell he will.'

---

b.   Ele não é **lá** de trabalhar muito.
       he not is there of work   much
       'He doesn't particularly/especially like to work.'

[31] (7.79c) and (7.79d) may be acceptable in BP if *agora* is interpreted as 'now' and not as a marker of metalinguistic negation.

(7.78) EP:
[*Context*:
A: – Tens   de pedir-lhe   desculpa.
     have-2.SG of ask-him   apology
     'You(SG) must apologize to him.']
a. B: – Peço-lhe   {**lá/cá/agora**}   desculpa.
       ask-1.SG-him there/here/now apology
b. B: – Peço-lhe   desculpa **uma** **ova**.
       ask-1.SG-him apology   a   fish.roe
c. B: – *Peço-lhe   {**lá/cá/agora**}   desculpa   **uma** **ova**.
       ask-1.SG-him there/here/now apology a   fish.roe
d. B: – ***Uma** **ova**   é   que   lhe   peço   {**lá/cá/agora**}
       a   fish.roe is   that him ask-1.SG there/here/now
       desculpa.
       apology
       'Like hell I will.'

(7.79) BP:
[*Context*:
A: – O João disse que ele paga as contas em dia.
     the João said that he pays the bills in day
     'João said that he pays his bills on time.']
a. B: – E ele {**lá/agora**} paga as contas em dia?!
       and he there/now pays the bills in day
b. B: – Ele paga as contas em dia **uma** **ova**!
       he pays the bills in day a fish.roe
c. B: – *E ele {**lá/agora**} paga as contas em dia **uma** **ova**!
       and he there/now pays the bills in day a fish.roe
d. B: – ***Uma** **ova** que ele {**lá/agora**} paga as contas em dia!
       a fish.roe that he there/now pays the bills in day
       'Like hell he pays his bills on time!'

By contrast, *lá* and *cá* can form a cluster with *agora*. In BP, the order within the cluster is fixed with *lá* preceding *agora*, as shown in (7.80), but in EP, *lá* and *cá* can cluster with *agora* in either order, as shown in (7.81). Interestingly, as opposed to what we saw in (7.71b), the clusters formed with *lá* or *cá* and *agora* can appear in isolation, as shown in (7.82).

(7.80) BP:
[*Context*:
A: – Eu trouxe   esses exercícios pra   você   me   ajudar.
     I brought these exercises for   you.SG me   help
     'I brought these exercises for you(SG) to help me with.']
a. B: – E eu **lá**   **agora** entendo   de   matemática?!
       and *there*   now   understand of   mathematics
b. B: – *E eu **agora** **lá**   entendo   de   matemática?!
       and *there*   now   understand of   mathematics
       'Am I supposed to know math?!'

(7.81)   EP:
[*Context*:
A: – Ele viveu sempre em Paris.
he lived always in Paris
'He has always lived in Paris.']
a. B: – Ele viveu **agora** {**lá/cá**} sempre em Paris.
he lived now there/here always in Paris
b. B: – Ele viveu {**lá/cá**} **agora** sempre em Paris.
he lived there/here now always in Paris
'Like hell he has always lived in Paris.'

(7.82)   EP:
[*Context*:
A: – Ele pagou o jantar?
he paid the dinner
'Did he pay for the dinner?']
a. B: – **Agora lá**.
now there
b. B: – **Agora cá**.
now here
'Like hell he did.'

Given that metalinguistic negation involves the denial of the assertability of a previous utterance, unambiguous metalinguistic negation markers are not felicitous when uttered in out-of-the-blue situations, to initiate a conversation; hence the contrast between the all-purpose negative marker *não* in (7.83a) and *lá*, *cá*, and *agora* in (7.83b), for example.

(7.83)   EP:
a. A: – Ah, **não** trouxe a carteira. Pagas-me o café?
oh not brought.1.SG the wallet pay-2.SG-me the coffee
b. A: – *Ah, trouxe {**lá/cá/agora**} a carteira. Pagas-me
oh brought.1.SG there/here/now the wallet pay-2.SG-me
o café?
the coffee
'Oh, I didn't bring my wallet. Will you(SG) pay for my coffee?'

That the metalinguistic negation markers *lá*, *cá*, and *agora* are not (logical) propositional negation operators is also confirmed by contrasts such as that in (7.84) below. Corrective *mas* 'but' is licensed only when preceded by (logical) propositional negation; hence, it may by licensed by *não* in (7.84a), but not by *lá/cá/agora* in (7.84b).

(7.84)   EP:
a. Ele **não** tem três filhos, mas quatro.
he not has three sons but four

b. *Ele tem {**lá/cá/agora**} três filhos, mas quatro.
   he has there/here/now three sons but four
   'He doesn't have three children, but four.'

Since *lá*, *cá*, and *agora* cannot establish negative concord relations, they cannot license NPIs either, as shown by their contrast with *não* in (7.85) and (7.86).

(7.85)   EP:
   a. [*Context*:
      A: – Tu   é   que   conheces   uma   pessoa
          you.SG is   that   know-2.SG a   person
          que   sabe   arranjar   isto.
          that   knows   fix   this
          'You(SG) do know someone that can fix this.']
      B: – Eu   **não**   conheço   **ninguém**   que   saiba
          I   not   know   nobody   that   know-SUBJ
          arranjar   isso.
          fix   that
      B′: – Eu   conheço   {**lá/cá**}   {alguém/***ninguém**}   que   saiba
          I   know   there/here   someone/nobody   that   know-SUBJ
          arranjar   isso.
          fix   this
          'I do not know anyone who can fix that.'
   b. [*Context*:
      A: – Eu   sei   que   tu   gostas
          I   know   that   you.SG   like
          de   marisco.
          of   seafood
          'I know you(SG) like seafood.']
      B: – Eu   **não**   gosto   de   marisco   **de   todo**.
          I   not   like   of   seafood   of   all
      B′: – *Eu   gosto   **agora**   de   marisco   **de   todo**.
          I   like   now   of   seafood   of   all
          'I don't like seafood at all.'

(7.86)   BP:
   a. [*Context*:
      A: – Vem   para   o   nosso   grupo   de   filosofia.
          come   to   the   our   group   of   philosophy
          'Join us in our philosophy group.']
      B: – Eu   **não**   sei   **nada**   de   filosofia.
          I   not   know   nothing   of   philosophy
      B′: – E   eu   **agora**   sei   {alguma coisa/***nada**}   de   filosofia?!
          and I   now   know   something/nothing   of   philosophy
          'I know nothing about philosophy.'

b. [*Context*:
   A: – Hoje você vai sair comigo.
        today you.SG go leave with.me
       'Today we are going out together.']
   B: – Eu **não** saio com você **nem** **morta**.
        I not leave with you.SG not.even dead
   B′: – *Eu **lá** saio com você **nem** **morta**?!
        I there leave with you.SG not.even dead
       'No way I will go out with you(SG).'

Finally, it is worth mentioning that *lá*, *cá*, and *agora* are actually compatible with *positive* polarity items (PPIs). In (7.87) and (7.88) below, for example, we see that they are compatible with the PPIs *e peras* (lit. *and pears*) in EP, *e tanto* (lit. *and so much*) in BP, and *do diabo* (lit. *of the devil*) in both, contrasting with negative elements such as *ninguém* 'nobody'.

(7.87)   EP:
   a. [*Context*:
     A: – Ele é um nadador e peras.
        he is a swimmer and pears
      'He is a great swimmer.']
     B: – ***Ninguém** é um nadador **e** **peras**.
        nobody is a swimmer and pears
      'Nobody is a great swimmer.'
     B′: – Ele é **cá** um nadador **e** **peras**.
        he is here a swimmer and pears
      'He is a great swimmer my eye.'
   b. [*Context*:
     A: – Tiveste uma sorte do diabo.
        had-2.SG a luck of-the devil
      'You(SG) were so lucky!']
     B: – ***Ninguém** teve uma sorte **do** **diabo**.
        nobody had a luck of-the devil
      'Nobody was that lucky.'
     B′: – Tive **lá** uma sorte do diabo.
        had.1.SG there a luck of-the devil
      'I was so lucky my eye!'

(7.88)   BP:
   a. [*Context*:
     A: – Ele é um nadador e tanto.
        he is a swimmer and so.much
      'He is a great swimmer.']
     B: – ***Ninguém** é um nadador **e** **tanto**.
        nobody is a swimmer and so.much
      'Nobody is a great swimmer.'

B': – Ele **lá** é um nadador e **tanto**?!
  he there is a swimmer and so.much
  'He is not a great swimmer.'

b. [*Context*:
  A: – Você teve uma sorte do diabo.
    you.SG had a luck of-the devil
    'So lucky you(SG) were!']
  B: – *****Ninguém** teve uma sorte **do diabo**.
    nobody had a luck of-the devil
    'Nobody was that lucky.'
  B': – E eu **agora** tive uma sorte do
    and I now had.1.SG a luck of-the
    diabo?! Eu joguei foi muito bem!
    devil I played was very well
    'I was lucky my eye! I actually played very well!'

7.3.4 Expletive Negation

Expletive negation describes cases where a negative marker does not negate or deny something, but instead adds emphasis to a positive non-assertive sentence.[32] EP and BP restrict expletive negation to exclamative sentences, as exemplified in (7.89) and (7.90).

(7.89) a. O que o João **(não)** faz pela família!
  what the João not does by-the family
  'João does so much for his family!'
  b. O que o meu pai **(não)** diria
    what the my father not say-COND-3.SG
    se soubesse!
    if know-SUBJ.IMPERF-3.SG
    'What my father would say if he knew about that!'
  c. Quantos acidentes **(não)** poderiam ser evitados!
    how.many accidents not could be avoided
    'So many accidents could be avoided!'
  d. Quantos livros ela **(não)** leu!
    how.many books she not read
    'She read so many books!'

(7.90) a. **Não** é que ele sabia a resposta!
    not is that he knew the answer
    'He knew the answer! (Can you believe it?)'

---

[32] See e.g. Matos 2003 for discussion.

b. **Não** é que ela comeu tudo!
   not is that she ate everything
   'She has eaten everything! (Can you believe it?)'

Although BP and EP pattern alike in licensing expletive negation in *wh*-exclamatives like those in (7.89) and in exclamatives with the expression *não é que* (lit. *not is that*) like those in (7.90), expletive negation is actually more restricted in BP than EP, as seen in Section 5.4. In particular, EP allows expletive negation with quantifying non-*wh* exclamatives, but BP does not, as shown in (7.91).[33,34]

(7.91)   a. Muito ele (**não**) lê!   (EP: OK; BP: *)
            much he not reads
            'How much he reads!'
         b. Os livros que ele (**não**) lê!   (EP: OK; BP: *)
            the books that he not reads
            'He reads so many books!'
         c. As coisas que ele (**não**) me disse! (EP: OK; BP: *)
            the things that he not me told
            'What things he has told me!'

Not being a true instance of negation, expletive negation is unable to license NPIs, as shown in (7.92) below, and is incompatible with the emphatic negation marker *nada* (see Section 7.3.2), as shown in (7.93).[35] In fact, expletive negation is compatible with positive polarity items, as illustrated in (7.94) with the PPI *do diabo* (lit. *of the devil*).

---

[33] The sentences in (7.91a–c) may be acceptable in BP under different interpretations, though. For instance, (7.91a) is acceptable under a contrastive focus reading for the fronted adverb (see Section 5.2.2.2) and (7.91b) and (7.91c) may be interpreted as simple exclamatives expressing surprise regarding the books that he read or did not read and the things that he said or did not say.

[34] The EP idiomatic expression in (i) combines expletive negation with the emphatic marker *lá* 'there' (see Section 7.3.3) in a non-quantifying exclamative.

   (i)   **Não** querem lá ver o idiota!   (EP)
         not want-3.PL there see the idiot
         '{You are/he is} such an idiot!'

[35] Recall that expletive negation is compatible with VS even in BP, as shown in (i) (see Section 5.4). Thus, in both EP and BP, the ungrammaticality of (7.92a) is due to the lack of a licenser for the postverbal NPI (see Section 7.3.1).

   (i)   O que não **faz um pai** pelos filhos!
         what not does a father by-the sons
         'A parent does so much for her/his children!'

7.3 Syntactic Patterns of Negation   415

(7.92) a. *O que **não** faz **nenhum** pai   pelos filhos!
             what   not does no   father by-the sons
             'A parent does so much for her/his children!'
        b. ***Não** é **que** ela   criticou   **ninguém**!
             not   is that she   criticized   nobody
             'She didn't criticize anyone! (Can you believe it?)'

(7.93) [*Context*:
        A: – Você   nunca vai   lá.
            you.SG never go   there
            'You(SG) never go there.']
        a. B: – Eu?! Quantas vezes eu **não** fui   lá!   (EP/BP)
                  I   how.many times I   not   went   there
        b. B: – Eu?! *Quantas vezes **não** fui **nada** lá!   (EP)
                  I   how.many times not   went nothing there
        b'. B: – Eu?! *Quantas vezes eu **não** fui   lá **nada**!   (BP)
                  I   how.many times I   not   went   there nothing
             'Me? I went there all the time.'

(7.94) Quantos imbecis **não** têm   uma sorte **do**   diabo!
        how.many idiots not   have a   luck of-the devil
        'So many idiots are the luckiest guys!'

Let us finally consider the contrasts in (7.95) and (7.96) below. A reduced coordinated structure may be licensed by the adverbial *também* 'also' if the relevant coordinating structure is positive or by the complex *também não* 'also not' if the coordinating structure is negative. As illustrated in (7.95) and (7.96), *também* is compatible with a coordinating structure containing expletive negation, but *também não* is not. This further confirms that clauses with expletive negation do not count as negative clauses.

(7.95) a. O que **não** diria   o   seu   pai   se
            what   not   say-COND-3.SG   the your   father   if
            soubesse   e   o   meu **também**!
            know-SUBJ.IMPERF-3.SG and the my   also
        b. *O que **não**   diria   o   seu   pai   se
            what   not   say-COND-3.SG   the your   father   if
            soubesse   e   o   meu **também não**!
            know-SUBJ.IMPERF-3.SG and the my   also   not
            'What your father would say if he knew! And mine too!'

(7.96) a. **Não** é **que** o Pedro sabia tudo   e   a   Maria **também**!
            not   is that the Pedro knew everything and the Maria also
        b. ***Não** é **que** o Pedro sabia tudo   e   a   Maria **também não**!
            not   is that the Pedro knew everything and the Maria also   not
            'Pedro knew everything and Maria did, too! (Can you believe it!)'

7.4 Biased Polar Questions

We have seen in Section 5.3.1 that in EP and BP, neutral *yes*/*no* (polar) questions and neutral affirmative declarative sentences display the same unmarked SVO word order, differing only in terms of their intonational contour (typically, a falling contour (↓) in declaratives and a rising contour (↑) in polar questions), as illustrated in (7.97).

(7.97)   a. A   Maria   pôs   os   livros   na   estante.↓
             the   Maria   put   the   books   in-the   bookshelf
             'Maria put the books on the bookshelf.'
       b. A   Maria   pôs   os   livros   na   estante?↑
             the   Maria   put   the   books   in-the   bookshelf
             'Did Maria put the books on the bookshelf?'

A positive polar question such as (7.97b) is also neutral with respect to the positive or negative answer it requests, for it does not signal that the relevant context may favor one answer over the other. However, if negation is added to the picture, the question becomes biased towards one or the other answer, as we shall see below.[36] In the subsections that follow we examine two types of biased polar interrogatives, namely, negative polar questions and tag questions.

7.4.1 Negative Polar Questions

Negative polar questions are always biased towards either the negative or the positive answer and denote in one way or another the questioner's point of view.[37] The bias may be reflected in the prosodic properties and/or the lexical choices of the question, as illustrated in (7.98) and (7.99) below. It may also simply be inferred from the discourse context, including assumptions about the speaker's intentions and beliefs. Confirmation questions, for example, favor a positive bias in contexts where there is evidence for (or a strong belief in favor of) a certain state of affairs and a negative bias in contexts where there is evidence against it. So, the same question may be intended for a positive or a negative answer, as illustrated in (7.100).

---

[36] For discussion see e.g. Dimitrova 2020.
[37] EP and BP do not substantially differ with respect to this type of question. Thus, the identification of some examples in this section as EP or BP is not meant to indicate that the relevant description applies to only one variety, but is merely the reflex of irrelevant specific lexical choices or grammatical structures present in one variety but not the other.

7.4 Biased Polar Questions 417

(7.98) a. Ele não comeu **já** a salada? (EP) [*positive bias*]
  he not ate already the salad
  'Hasn't he eaten the salad already?'
  b. Ele **ainda** não comeu a salada? [*negative bias*]
  he yet not ate the salad
  'Hasn't he eaten the salad yet?'

(7.99) a. Não existe **um** restaurante tailandês aqui perto? [*positive bias*]
  not exists a restaurant Thai here close
  'Isn't there a/some Thai restaurant around here?'
  b. Não existe **nenhum** restaurante tailandês aqui perto? [*negative bias*]
  not exists none restaurant Thai here close
  'Aren't there any Thai restaurants around here?'

(7.100) a. Você não vem amanhã? [*positive or negative bias*]
  you.SG not come-2.SG tomorrow
  'Aren't you(SG) coming tomorrow?'
  b. A Maria não gostou do bacalhau? [*positive or negative bias*]
  the Maria not liked-3SG of-the cod
  'Didn't Maria like the cod?'

Questions expressing an indirect reproach also allow both sides of the polar bias, as exemplified in (7.101) and (7.102) below. In (7.101c) *já* 'already' tips the balance towards a positive bias, whereas in (7.102b) and (7.102c) *ainda* 'still', *nothing* 'nada' and *nem* 'not even' tip the balance towards a negative bias.

(7.101) a. Eu não te pedi pra você ficar calado? (BP) [*positive bias*]
  I not you.DAT ask for you.SG be silent
  'Didn't I ask you(SG) to be quiet?'
  b. Não sabias que era o teu dia de
  not knew-2.SG that was the your.SG day of
  fazer o jantar? (EP) [*positive bias*]
  do the dinner
  'Didn't you(SG) know it was your(SG) turn to make dinner?'
  c. Não tens **já** o que querias? (EP) [*positive bias*]
  not have-2.SG already what wanted-2SG
  'Haven't you(SG) already got what you(SG) wanted?'

(7.102) a. Não tens vergonha? (EP) [*negative bias*]
  not have-2.SG shame
  'Aren't you(SG) ashamed?' ['You ought to be ashamed of yourself.']
  b. Você **ainda** não está satisfeito? **Nada** te
  you.SG still not are satisfied nothing you
  satisfaz? (BP) [*negative bias*]
  satisfies
  'Aren't you(SG) satisfied yet? Does nothing satisfy you(SG)?'
  c. Não queres **nem** um café? (EP) [*negative bias*]
  not want-2.SG not.even a coffee
  'Won't you(SG) even have a coffee?'

418   7 Affirmation, Negation, Questions, and Answers

Negative polar questions may also express a polite request (see (7.103a,b)) or offer (see (7.103c)), in which case they have a positive bias (even if, or despite the fact that, the speaker does not have evidence for a positive answer).

(7.103)   a. Cê   não pode me dar   uma ajudinha
             you.SG   not can   me give a   help-DIM
             com   isso?   (BP) [positive bias]
             with   this
             'Couldn't you(SG) give me a hand with this?'
          b. Não me compras   o   jornal   quando
             not me buy-2.SG the   newspaper when
             fores   à   rua?   (EP) [positive bias]
             go.SUB.FUT-2.SG   to-the   street
             'Couldn't you(SG) buy me the newspaper when
             you(SG) go out?'
          c. Não queres   um cafezinho?   (EP) [positive bias]
             not want-2.SG   a   coffee-DIM
             'Wouldn't you(SG) care for a little coffee?'

Negative polar questions expressing evaluative comments, as exemplified in (7.104) below, or challenging an earlier assertion by the interlocutor, as illustrated in (7.105), unambiguously carry a positive bias and may be compatible with a PPI like *dos diabos*, lit. *of the devils* (see (7.104c) and (7.105c)).

(7.104)   a. Não está crescido o   meu filho?   [positive bias]
             not is   grown-up the my son
             'Hasn't my son grown up?'
          b. Não está horrível esta sopa?   [positive bias]
             not is   horrible this soup
             'Isn't this soup horrible?'
          c. Não está um frio dos   diabos?   [positive bias]
             not is   a cold of-the devils
             'Isn't it freezing today?'

(7.105)   a. [Context:
              A: – Estou com   fome.
                  am   with   hunger
                  'I'm hungry.']
              B: – Não há   comida no   frigorífico? (EP) [positive bias]
                   not have.3.SG food   in-the   refrigerator
                   'Isn't there food in the fridge?']
          b. [Context:
              A: – Ele é   tão sem   sal.   (BP)
                   he   is   so   without   salt
                   'He is so uninteresting.']
              B: – Ele não   escreveu um   bestseller?   [positive bias]
                   he not   wrote   a   bestseller
                   'Hasn't he written a bestseller?'

c. [*Context*:
   A: – Todos   gostam   dele.
        all   like   of-him
        'Everybody likes him.']
   B: – (Mas)   ele   não   é   um
         but   he   not   is a
         sacana   dos   diabos?   [*positive bias*]
         scoundrel of-the devils
         'But isn't he an utter scoundrel?'

The fact that negative polar questions are always biased towards an answer has interesting pragmatic implications. In particular, they may be interpreted as some sort of declarative, thus not requiring a genuine answer, which is already provided by the bias. Take the conversation exchange in (7.106) below, for example. Using a negative polar question, B tells A that she would prefer to have lunch outside. A does not, strictly speaking, answer the question, but by means of another negative polar question, he lets B know that he does not think her suggestion is a good idea. Finally, B does not answer A's negative polar question either, but expresses agreement with respect to the hidden affirmation induced by the biased question.

(7.106) A: – Vou   pôr   a   mesa   para o   almoço.
              go.1.SG put   the table   for   the lunch
              'I'll set the table for lunch.'
         B: – Não vamos   comer lá   fora?
              not go-1.PL eat   there out
              'Aren't we eating outside?'
         A: – Não está frio?
              not is   cold
              'Isn't it cold?'
         B: – Tá bom, então! Eu corto o   pão.
              is good then   I   cut   the bread
              'OK, then. I'll slice the bread.'

Similarly, the addressee may also simply take the biased answer implied by a negative polar question for granted and add a coordination structure, as if it were truly preceded by a declarative. This is exemplified by interactions of the type illustrated in (7.107) and (7.108).

(7.107) A: – O   João não   terminou já   o   curso?
              the João not   finished already the course
              'Hasn't João graduated already?'
         B: – Mas ainda não arranjou trabalho.
              but yet   not found   job
              '[He has graduated,] but he hasn't found a job yet.'

(7.108) A: – Não está alto o meu filho?
           not is   tall the my son
           'Didn't my son get tall?'
         B: – E bonito também.
           and beautiful also
           '[He got tall] and also handsome.'

7.4.2 Tag Questions

A tag question is a particular type of polar question made up of a *declarative anchor* (affirmative or negative) and an *interrogative coda* (the *tag*), which inverts the polarity of the anchor.[38] In (7.109a) below, for example, the anchor is positive and the coda is negative; in (7.109b) the anchor is negative and the coda is positive.

(7.109) a. A Maria **terminou** o trabalho, **não terminou**?
            the Maria finished the work not finished
            'Maria finished the work, didn't she?'
         b. A Maria **não terminou** o trabalho, **terminou**? (BP)
            the Maria not finished the work finished
            'Maria didn't finish the work, did she?'

Tag questions are always strongly biased: if the declarative anchor is positive, a positive answer is anticipated; if the declarative anchor is negative, the speaker expects a negative answer. Below we show the different types of tags EP and BP resort to, depending on the polarity of the anchor.

When the anchor is positive, the tag may involve some specialized expressions, as illustrated in (7.110).

(7.110) Vocês pediram bacalhau, a. **não é verdade?** (EP/BP)
         you-PL asked   cod   not is truth
                                  b. **não é assim?** (EP/*BP)
                                     not is so
                                  c. **não é?** (EP/BP)
                                     not is
                                  d. **é?** (EP/*BP)
                                     is
         'You(PL) have ordered cod, am I right?'

In addition to its fixed form in the third person singular indicative present form, the verb *ser* in (7.110c) may also agree with the tense of the anchor if the verb is in the indicative perfective or imperfective past form, as respectively illustrated in (7.111a,b).

---

[38] See e.g. Hagemeijer and Santos 2004 for discussion.

(7.111) a. Vocês   pediram   bacalhau, **não**
         you-PL   ask-***INDIC.PERF***-3.PL cod   not
         foi?   (EP/BP)
         be-***INDIC.PERF***-3.SG
         'You(PL) have ordered cod, am I right?'
    b. Vocês, nesse   restaurante, costumavam
       you-PL in-this   restaurant   used.to-***INDIC.IMPERF***-3.PL
       pedir   bacalhau, **não era?**   (EP/BP)
       ask   cod   not be-***INDIC.IMPERF***-3.SG
       'You(PL) used to order cod in this restaurant, am I right?'

Interestingly, though, the most common type of tag for a positive anchor is the one involving the negative marker *não* 'not' and a copy of the finite verb of the anchor, as illustrated in (7.112).

(7.112) a. Eu **fiz**   um   bom   negócio, **não fiz?**
         I made.1.SG   a   good   business not made.1.SG
         'I made a good deal, didn't I?'
    b. A   Maria **fala**   bem   inglês, **não fala?**
       the Maria speaks   well   English not speaks
       'Maria speaks English well, doesn't she?'
    c. **Vamos** precisar contratar mais   um estagiário, **não vamos**?
       go-1.PL need   hire   more   one trainee   not go-1.PL
       'We'll need to hire another trainee, won't we?'
    d. As   crianças **brincaram**   bastante, **não brincaram**?
       the children played-3.PL   much   not played-3.PL
       'The children played a lot, didn't they?

If the positive anchor contains expressions that carry a negative implicature (e.g. the adverb *só* 'only' or a cleft structure), the tag cannot repeat the verb, as shown in (7.113), and one of the fixed tags must be employed, instead, as illustrated in (7.114).

(7.113) a. *Só   a   Maria **chegou**   hoje de   Paris, **não chegou**?
         only the Maria arrived.3.SG   today of   Paris, not arrived.3.SG
         'Only Maria arrived today from Paris, isn't that so?'
    b. *Ontem   **é que** a   Maria **regressou**   de Paris, **não regressou**?
       yesterday is that   the Maria returned.3.SG   of Paris, not returned.3.SG
       'It was yesterday that Maria returned from Paris, wasn't it?'

(7.114) a. **Só**   a   Maria **chegou**   hoje de Paris,   **não é verdade**?
         only   the   Maria arrived.3.SG today of Paris,   not is truth
         'Only Maria arrived today from Paris, isn't that so?'
    b. Ontem   **é que** a   Maria **regressou**   de Paris, **não**
       yesterday   is that the Maria returned.3.SG   of Paris, not
       foi?
       be-***INDIC.PERF***-3.SG
       'It was yesterday that Maria returned from Paris, wasn't it?'

As in the case of emphatic affirmation (see Section 7.2.1), if the positive anchor involves the adverb *já* 'already' in EP, the adverb itself can be copied into the tag, but not if it is accompanied by the verb, as shown in (7.115).[39]

(7.115)   EP:
  a. A   Maria   já   regressou   de Paris, **não regressou**?
     the   Maria   already returned.3.SG   of Paris   not returned.3.SG
  b. A   Maria   já   regressou   de Paris, **não já**?
     the   Maria   already returned.3.SG   of Paris   not already
  c. *A   Maria   já   regressou   de Paris, **não já**
     the   Maria   already returned.3.SG   of Paris   not already
     regressou?
     returned.3.SG
  'Maria has already returned from Paris, hasn't she?'

Let us now examine tag questions with a negative anchor. This type of polar question is compatible with the fixed tags seen in (7.110), as shown below in (7.116). It is also compatible with the tense-agreeing tag with *ser* 'be' seen in (7.111), as shown in (7.117).

(7.116)   Vocês   **não** pediram bacalhau, a. **não é verdade?** (EP/BP)
          you-PL   not   asked   cod   not is   truth
                                               b. **não é assim?**   (EP/*BP)
                                                  not is   so
                                               c. **não é?**   (EP/BP)
                                                  not is
                                               d. **é?**   (EP/*BP)
                                                  is
  'You(PL) haven't ordered cod, am I right?'

(7.117)   a. Vocês   não   pediram   bacalhau, **não**
             you-PL   not   ask-**INDIC.PERF**-3.PL   cod   not
             foi?   (EP/BP)
             be-**INDIC.PERF**-3.SG
  'You(PL) have ordered cod, am I right?'
          b. Eles   nunca   se   decidiam,   **não**
             they-PL   never   themselves   decide-**INDIC.IMPERF**-3.PL   not
             era?   (EP/BP)
             be-**INDIC.IMPERF**-3.SG
  'They would never make a decision, am I right?'

Interestingly, EP and BP display a sharp contrast in their most common form of tag questions with a negative anchor, as shown in (7.118) below (see Section 7.2.1). BP simply copies the finite verb into the tag – a possibility that is not available in EP. In turn, EP makes use of the confirmation particle *pois*

---
[39] For discussion see e.g. Martins 2006b.

in tandem with the negative marker *não* – a possibility that is not available in BP.⁴⁰

(7.118) a. Eu **não** **fiz** um bom negócio, **pois** **não**? (EP)
 I not made.1.SG a good business CONFIRM no
 a'. Eu **não** **fiz** um bom negócio, **fiz**? (BP)
 I not made.1.SG a good business made.1.SG
 'I didn't make a good deal, did I?'
 b. A Maria **não** **fala** bem inglês, **pois** **não**? (EP)
 the Maria não speaks well English CONFIRM no
 b'. A Maria **não** **fala** bem inglês, **fala**? (BP)
 the Maria não speaks well English speaks
 'Maria doesn't speak English well, does she?'
 c. **Não vamos** precisar contratar mais estagiários, **pois**
 not go-1.PL need hire more trainees CONFIRM
 não? (EP)
 no
 c'. **Não vamos** precisar contratar mais estagiários,
 not go-1.PL need hire more trainees
 vamos? (BP)
 go-1.PL
 'We won't need to hire more trainees, will we?'
 d. As crianças **não** **brincaram** muito, **pois** **não**? (EP)
 the children not played-3.PL much CONFIRM no
 d'. As crianças **não** **brincaram** muito, **brincaram**? (BP)
 the children not played-3.PL much played-3.PL
 'The children did not play much, did they?'

7.5 Minimal Answers to *yes/no* Questions

An appropriate answer to a *yes/no* (polar) question can be viewed as encompassing two pieces of information: (i) an assertion as to whether or not the state of affairs referred to in the question holds, which is expressed by the opposition *positive/negative*; and (ii) whether such an assertion agrees or disagrees with the way in which the question was framed with respect to its

---

⁴⁰ In Northern EP dialects, the confirmative particle *pois* may also occur in tandem with a copied verb in tags associated with a positive anchor, as illustrated in (i).

(i) a. O João **não** **comeu** a sopa, **pois** **não**? (EP)
 the João not ate the soup, CONFIRM no
 'John hasn't eaten the soup, has he?'
 b. O João **comeu** a sopa, **pois** **comeu**? (%EP)
 the João ate the soup, CONFIRM ate
 'John has eaten the soup, hasn't he?'

polarity, which is expressed by the opposition *agreement/disagreement*. The distinction between these two pieces of information is not obvious in the case of unmarked (positive) polar questions, but becomes clearer in the case of negative polar questions (see Section 7.4). Consider the contrast between (7.119a) and (7.119b) in EP, for instance, in a context where B's response is meant to inform that João sold the car (a positive answer).

(7.119) EP:
    a. A: – O   João vendeu o   carro?
            the João sold   the car
            'Did João sell the car?'
       B: – Sim.
            yes
            'Yes.'
    b. A: – O   João não vendeu o   carro, pois   não?
            the João not sold   the car CONFIRM no
            'João didn't sell the car, did he?'
       B: – *Sim.
            yes
            'Yes, he did.'

A positive answer agrees with the polarity of the unmarked (affirmative) question in (7.119a), but not with the polarity of the marked (negative) question in (7.119b). The fact that *sim* 'yes' can be an appropriate answer in (7.119a), but not in (7.119b), shows that an adequate account of answers to polar questions must take into consideration the agreement/disagreement opposition in addition to the usual positive/negative opposition.

Below we examine in detail how EP and BP grammatically encode positive and negative responses in contexts where they are in agreement or disagreement with the polarity of the relevant questions.[41] We will focus on minimal answers, that is, answers that count as appropriate responses even though they do not repeat all the lexical items in the question.[42] In Section 7.5.1 we discuss minimal answers involving bare verbs and/or the responsive particles *sim* 'yes' and *não* 'no'; in Section 7.5.2, minimal answers with certain adverbs and quantifiers; and in Section 7.5.3 minimal answers with the verb *ser* 'be'.

---

[41] Pragmatic and prosodic factors may also distinguish positive agreement from positive disagreement and negative disagreement from negative agreement, but in this chapter we will be concerned only with lexical and syntactic ways of encoding polarity distinctions.
[42] For discussion see e.g. Kato and Tarallo 1992, Martins 1994b, 2006b, 2016a, Oliveira 1996, A. L. Santos 2002, 2003, 2009, Sell 2003, Kato 2016, and Teixeira de Sousa 2020.

7.5.1 Minimal Answers with Bare Verbs and Responsive Particles

Let us consider some of the possible minimal answers to the questions by A and A' in (7.120).

(7.120) A: – Ele vai sair hoje?
he go.3.SG go.out today
'Is he going out today?'
A': – Ele vai sair hoje, não vai?
he go.3.SG go.out today not go.3.SG
'He's going out today, isn't he?'

a. B: – Vai. [*positive agreement*] (EP/BP)
go.3.SG
b. B: – Sim. [*positive agreement*] (EP/%BP)
yes
c. B: – *Pois. [*positive agreement*] (*EP/*BP)
CONFIRM
'Yes.'
d. B: – Sim, vai. [*positive agreement*] (EP/%BP)
yes go.3.SG
e. B: – Não. [*negative disagreement*] (EP/BP)
no
'No.'
f. B: – Não, não vai. [*negative disagreement*] (EP/BP)
no not go.3.SG
'No, he isn't.'

Given that the question by A in (7.120) is framed as an unmarked (positive) question and the tag question by A' in (7.120) is biased towards a positive answer (see Section 7.4.2), answers with a positive assertion count as positive agreement and answers with a negative assertion counts as negative disagreement. In both EP and BP, bare verb answers like that in (7.120a) constitute the unmarked pattern of minimal positive answers to such questions and the short *não* answer in (7.120e) represents the unmarked option for minimal negative responses. As mentioned in Section 7.2.1, *pois* is not a responsive particle in EP and in BP: it is either part of the frozen expression *pois não* (see footnote 3 above) or part of the confirmative expression *pois é* (see Section 7.5.3); hence the ungrammaticality of (7.120c) in both varieties. Finally, answers with *sim* 'yes' both in their short version as in (7.120b) and in their extended version in (7.120d) can also be used as regular positive answers in EP, but not in BP. By and large, short and extended *sim* answers in BP are restricted to formal registers, generally in somewhat ritualized contexts that involve lists of questions and answers. Thus, they sound more natural in quiz-show competitions, as in (7.121a) below, and legal interrogatories, as in (7.121b–c), for instance. In these types of contexts, it is not uncommon that the question is hidden under a statement to be evaluated, as in (7.121a), or that the question itself explicitly involves the choice between *sim* and *não*, as illustrated in (7.121c).

(7.121) BP:

   a. A: – Martin Luther King Jr. ganhou o Nobel da Paz.
             Martin Luther King Jr. won the Nobel of-the peace
          'Martin Luther King Jr. won the Nobel Peace Prize.'
     B: – Sim.
          yes
          'Yes.'

   b. A: – O senhor conhece a testemunha?
             the mister knows the witness
          'Do you[formal] know the witness?'
     B: – Sim, conheço.
          yes know-1.SG
          'Yes, I do.'

   c. A: – O suspeito falou com a vítima no dia do
             the suspect spoke with the victim in-the day of-the
             crime? Sim ou não?
             crime yes or no
          'Did the suspect speak to the victim on the day of the crime? Yes or no?'
     B: – Sim.
          yes
          'Yes.'

As discussed in detail in Section 7.4.2, the biased tag question by A′ in (7.120) can also be answered by a minimal answer with emphatic negation, as illustrated in (7.122), in which case it encodes negative disagreement.

(7.122) A: – Ele vai sair hoje, não vai?
           he go.3.SG go.out today not go.3.SG
        'He's going out today, isn't he?'
      B: – Não vai, não.   [*negative disagreement*] (EP/BP)
           not go.3.SG no
         'No, he isn't.'

Let us now examine minimal answers to the negative polar question by A in (7.123) below. As discussed in Section 7.4.1, negative polar questions may be interpreted as biased towards a positive or negative answer. Thus, the question by A in (7.123) should be considered under these two different scenarios. When it is biased towards a positive answer, we find the same patterns of answers as those already seen in (7.120a–f), with the affirmative answers encoding positive agreement and the negative answers, negative disagreement. Let us then consider answers to A's question in (7.123) when it is biased towards a negative answer so that we can examine them together with answers to the tag questions by A' and A″ in (7.123), which are negatively biased.

(7.123) A: – Ele não vai   sair   hoje?   [*under negative bias*]
              he   not go.3.SG go.out   today
              'Is he not going out today?'
         A': – Ele não vai   sair   hoje, pois   não?   (EP)
              he   not go.3.SG go.out   today CONFIRM   no
         A″: – Ele não vai   sair   hoje, vai?   (BP)
              he   not go.3.SG go.out   today go.3.SG
              'He's not going out today, is he?'
    a.   B: – Vai.   [*positive disagreement*]   (EP/BP)
                go.3.SG
    b.   B: – *Sim.   [*positive disagreement*]   (*EP/*BP)
                yes
    c.   B: – Sim, vai.   [*positive disagreement*]   (?EP/%BP)
                yes go.3.SG
    d.   B: – Vai,   sim.   [*positive disagreement*]   (EP/BP)
                go.3.SG yes
    e.   B: – Vai,   pois.   [*positive disagreement*]   (EP/*BP)
                go.3.SG CONFIRM
    f.   B: – Vai,   vai.   [*positive disagreement*]   (EP/*BP)
                go.3.SG go.3.SG
                'Yes, he is.'
    g.   B: – Não.   [*negative agreement*]   (EP/BP)
                no
                'No.'
    h.   B: – Não, não vai.   [*negative agreement*]   (EP/BP)
                no   not go.3.SG
    i.   B: – Sim, não vai.   [*negative agreement*]   (EP/*BP)
                yes not go.3.SG
                'Yes, he's not.'

As in (7.120), bare verb answers like that in (7.123a) constitute the unmarked pattern of minimal positive answers in both EP and BP, whereas the short response with *não* 'no' in (7.123g) represents the unmarked option for minimal negative answers. Under a negative bias interpretation for A's question in (7.123), a positive response to the questions by A and A'/A″ in (7.123) counts as a disagreement answer and a negative response counts as an agreement answer. The answers in (7.123d–f), with *sim*, *pois*, and the reduplicated verb in sentence-final position, are therefore interpreted as cases of emphatic affirmation, as discussed in detail in Section 7.2.

The comparison between (7.120) and (7.123) reveals an interesting pattern associated with *sim*. In the relevant registers and contexts, *sim* in BP cannot encode positive disagreement by itself (see (7.123b)), unless it is extended by a positive assertion (see (7.123c)). EP also disallows the short answer with *sim* in this scenario (see (7.123b)), contrasting with what we saw in (7.120b). In the face of an answer such as (7.123b) in this context in EP, the interlocutor could ask *Sim o quê?* (lit. *yes what*), indicating that (7.123b) does not actually provide a proper answer to a negative polar question in EP. Even when extended as in (7.123c), the *sim* answer does not sound as a truly adequate positive disagreement response. Interestingly, *sim* may actually constitute an adequate negative agreement response if associated with a negative extension as in (7.123i), which is not at all possible in BP. The data in (7.120) and (7.123) thus indicate that *sim* is a positive word in the relevant registers of BP, but an agreeing word in EP. To put it differently, a short answer with *sim* encodes agreement in EP (see (7.120b)) and is at odds with contexts of positive disagreement (cf. (7.123b) vs. (7.123d)). When *sim* appears clause-initially in EP, it agrees with the preceding utterance in the discourse, be it positive (see (7.120b,c)) or negative (see (7.123i)); when it appears clause-finally as in (7.123d), it agrees with the positive assertion of its sentence, giving rise to an emphatic interpretation.

This agreement behavior of *sim* in EP is confirmed by the fact that a short answer with *sim* is permitted in EP if the relevant negative interrogative is not an actual negative question, but a polite request, invitation or comment, as illustrated in (7.124).

(7.124) EP:
 a. A: – Não me podes emprestar uma caneta, por favor?
    not me can-2.SG lend a pen by favor
   'Could you(SG) lend me a pen, please?'
  B: – Sim (claro).
    yes clear
   'Yes, of course.'
 b. A: – Não queres um cafezinho?
    not want-2.SG a coffee-DIM
   'Would you(SG) like some coffee?'
  B: – Sim (obrigado).
    yes obliged
   'Yes, thank you.'
 c. A: – Não está crescido o meu filho?
    not is grown.up the my   son
   'Isn't my son so grown up?'
  B: – Sim.   [with a smile]
    yes
   'Yes, he is.'

Thus far, we have examined grammatical cases of bare verbal answers encoding positive agreement (see (7.120a)) or positive disagreement (see (7.123a)). A bare verbal answer does not count as an appropriate response to an unmarked (positive) interrogative, though, if the question carries negative implicatures. Take the sentences in (7.125) below, for instance. (7.125a) conveys the implication that he did not win the race; (7.125b) that he did not eat up what he was supposed to eat; (7.125c) that he does nothing other than sleep; (7.125d) that people other than him did not confess everything; and (7.125e) that he would not be in jail if he had not confessed everything. In all these cases, the *sim* answer is chosen over the bare verb answer. This suggests that bare verb answers carry positive specifications, thus being unable to recover the content of questions containing negative implicatures: this would be a case of negative agreement. On the other hand, *sim* answers are not that strict, as we saw with respect to (7.123i).[43,44]

(7.125) a. A: –   Ele   quase   venceu a   corrida?
                  he   almost   won   the race
                  'Did he almost win the race?'

---

[43] If the adverb that introduces negative implicatures appears postverbally, a bare verb answer becomes available, as illustrated in (i) with *quase* 'almost' and *só* 'only'.

(i)   a. A: –   Ele   comeu   **quase**   o   bolo   todo?
                he   ate   almost   the cake   all
                'Did he almost eat the whole cake?'
         B: –   Comeu.
                ate
         B': – Sim.   (EP/%BP)
                yes
                'Yes, he did.'
      b. A: –   Ele   comeu   **só**   as   batatas?
                he   ate   only   the   potatoes
                'Did he only eat the potatoes?'
         B: –   Comeu.
                ate
         B': – Sim.   (EP/%BP)
                yes
                'Yes, he did.'

[44] Another environment that blocks bare verbal answers in favor of *sim* answers involves questions with clausal coordination (see (i) below):

(i)   A: –   Eles   compraram   os   ingredientes   e   fizeram   o   bolo?
              they   bought-3.PL the ingredients   and   made-3.PL   the cake
              'Did they buy the ingredients and make the cake?'
      B: –   *Compraram.
              bought-3.PL
      B': –   *Fizeram.
              made-3.PL
      B'': – Sim.   (EP/%BP)
              yes
              'Yes, they did.'

B: – *Venceu.
   won
B′: – Sim.   (EP/%BP)
   yes
   'Yes, he almost did.'

b. A: – Ele   mal   tocou   na   comida?
       he   hardly   touched   in-the   food
       'Did he hardly eat?'
   B: – *Tocou.
       touched
   B′: – Sim.   (EP/%BP)
       yes
       'Yes, he hardly did.'

c. A: – Ele   só   dorme?!
       he   only   sleeps
       'Does he only sleep?!'
   B: – *Dorme.
       sleeps
   B′: – Sim.   (EP/%BP)
       yes
       'Yes, that's the only thing he does.'

d. A: – Foi   ele   que   confessou   tudo?
       was   he   that   confessed   everything
       'Was it him who confessed everything?'
   B: – *Confessou.
       confessed
   B′: – Sim.   (EP/%BP)
       yes
       'Yes, it was him.'

e. A: – Ele   está   na   prisão   porque   contou   tudo?
       he   is   in-the   jail   because   told   everything
       'Is he in jail because he confessed everything'/'Is it because he confessed everything that he is in jail?'
   B: – *Está.
       is
   B′: – Sim.   (EP/%BP)
       yes
       'Yes, that's why he is in jail.'

Actually, *sim* answers in EP may felicitously incorporate (weak) epistemic modal values, in contrast to bare verb answers. The data in (7.126) below, for instance, show that a *sim* answer may express a "weak commitment" agreement with what the speaker takes to be the interlocutor's expectation. Once this general agreement is set, it can be nuanced by a continuation that weakens it. Such a strategy is not available when a bare verb answer is chosen to express positive agreement.

(7.126) EP:
  a. A: – Gostas   de   comida   picante?
        like-2.SG of   food   spicy
        'Do you(SG) like spicy food?'
     B: – Sim,   talvez   goste.
          yes   maybe   like-SUBJ.1.SG
     B′: #Gosto,   talvez   goste.
          like-1.SG   maybe   like-SUBJ.1.SG
          'Well ... maybe.'
  b. A: – E   se   saíssemos   hoje   à   noite?
        and   if   leave-SUBJ.IMPERF.1.PL today   at-the night
        'What about going out tonight?'
     B: – Sim,   vamos   pensar   nisso.
          yes   go-1.PL   think   in-this
     B′: – #Saímos,   vamos   pensar   nisso.
          leave.INDIC.PRES-1.PL   go.INDIC.PRES-1.PL think   in-this
          'Why not, let's think about it.'
  c. A: – Ele   seguramente   vai   apoiar   a   proposta?
        he   undoubtedly   go.3.SG support the proposal
        'Will he undoubtedly support the proposal?'
     B: – Sim,   pode   ser   que   apoie.
          yes   may   be   that   support-SUBJ.PRES.3.SG
     B′: – #Vai.   Pode   ser   que   apoie.
          go.3.SG   may   be   that   support-SUBJ.PRES.3.SG
          'Well ... he may support it.'

The data in (7.127) below further show that short *sim* answers in EP must in fact recover the whole antecedent. A short positive answer to a polar question with a modal verb like *poder* 'can' may involve either the modal, the main verb, or *sim*, as shown by the answer by B in (7.127). As expected, the continuation in the answer by B′ in (7.127a) sounds inappropriate (in fact, contradictory) in the case of the main verb, but is acceptable with the modal. Interestingly, the short answer with *sim* also admits the same continuation, which shows that *sim* is at least compatible with the modal reading. (7.127b) in turn shows that the recovery of the whole content of the question, including the modal, is actually obligatory, which leads to the same contradiction induced by a short answer with the modal.

(7.127) EP:
  a. A: – Podes   emprestar-me   uma   caneta?
         can-2.SG   lend.me   a   pen
         'Can you(SG) lend me a pen?'
      B: – {Posso   /Empresto   /Sim}.
           can-1.SG   /lend-1.SG   /yes
           'Yes, I can.'
      B′: – {Posso   /#Empresto   /Sim},   mas   não   empresto.
            can-1.SG /lend-1.SG   /yes   but   not   lend-1.SG
            'I can but I won't.'

b. A: – Podes   emprestar-me dinheiro?
       can-2.SG lend.me   money
       'Can you(SG) lend me some money?'
   B: – {#Posso /Empresto /#Sim}, embora não possa.
       can-1.SG/ lend-1.SG /yes   though not can-SUBJ.PRES
       'I can't, but I will.'

The general pattern of short answers to polar questions in EP and BP with bare verbs and the responsive particles *sim* and *não* is summarized in Table 7.1 below.

Before we leave this section, let us consider a couple of additional details with respect to some of the answers summarized in Table 7.1. The first observation has to do with the scope of short answers with *sim* and *não*, on the one hand, and short answers with bare verbs, on the other. In both EP and BP, *sim* and *não* cannot by themselves provide a proper answer to an embedded question. (7.128a) and (7.128b) below, for instance, can be interpreted only as answers to the matrix clause.

(7.128) A: – Você sabe se o João (não) vem?
         you.SG know if   the João not   come.3.SG
         'Do you(SG) know if João is coming?'
  a. B: – Sim.   (EP/%BP)
         yes
         'Yes, I do.'/*'Yes, he is.'
  b. B: – Não.
         no
         'No, I don't.'/*'No, he isn't.'

By contrast, verbal responses can constitute appropriate answers to embedded questions. Interestingly, there are in fact more possibilities for appropriate answers where embedded questions are concerned. First, a sentence-final *sim* or *não* is no longer interpreted as contrastive (as a case of disagreement); thus, (7.129c) and (7.130b) below also count as adequate answers to the relevant embedded questions, in addition to the expected positive answers in (7.129a) and (7.129b) and the negative answer in (7.130a). Moreover, a negative answer to a positive embedded question may take the format in (7.129d), with just the negation preceding the verb, which does not sound natural in the case of a matrix interrogative, as shown in (7.131).

Table 7.1 *Short answers with bare verbs and responsive particles in European Portuguese and Brazilian Portuguese*

Interpretation	Short answers	EP	BP
Positive agreement	*Verb.* cf. (7.120a)	✓	✓
	Sim. cf. (7.120b)	✓	%
	Sim, *verb.* cf. (7.120d)	✓	%
Negative disagreement	Não. cf. (7.120e)	✓	✓
	Não, não *verb.* cf. (7.120f)	✓	✓
	Não *verb*, não. cf. (7.122)	✓	✓
Positive disagreement	*Verb.* cf. (7.123a)	✓	✓
	Sim, *verb.* cf. (7.123c)	?	%
	Verb, sim. cf. (7.123d)	✓	✓
	Verb, pois. cf. (7.123e)	✓	*
	Verb, verb. cf. (7.123f)	✓	*
Negative agreement	Não. cf. (7.123g)	✓	✓
	Não, não *verb.* cf. (7.123h)	✓	✓
	Sim, não *verb.* cf. (7.123i)	✓	*

(7.129) A: – Você sabe se o João vem?
         you.SG know if the João come.3.SG
         'Do you(SG) know if João is coming?'
    a.   B: – Vem.
              come.3.SG
    b.   B: – Sim, vem.
              yes come.3.SG
    c.   B: – **Vem,   sim.**
              come.3.SG yes
              'Yes, he is.'
    d.   B: – Não vem.
              not come.3.SG
    e.   B: – Não, não vem.
              not not come.3.SG
              'No, he isn't.'

(7.130) A: – Você sabe se o João não vem?
         you.SG know if the João not come.3.SG
         'Do you(SG) know if João is coming?'
    a.   B: – Não, não vem.
              not not come.3.SG
    b.   B: – **Não vem,   não.**
              not come.3.SG no
              'No, he isn't.'

(7.131) A: – O João vem?
              the João come.3.SG
              'Is João coming?'
    a.   B: – ??Não vem.
              not come.3.SG
    b.   B: – Não, não vem.
              not not come.3.SG
              'No, he isn't.'

Verbal answers repeating an embedded verb are restricted to indirect questions, though. As shown in (7.132), the embedded verb of a factive complement clause or an adjunct clause, for instance, is not an adequate source for a verbal answer.[45]

---

[45] An exception to this generalization involves questions with raising verbs (see Section 3.4.3) in the matrix clause. As shown in (i), in this case the embedded verb may be the source for a bare verb answer.

(i)   A: – Ele acabou   por ler   o   livro? (EP)
            he   finished-3.SG by read the   book
      A': – Ele acabou   lendo   o   livro?   (BP)
            he   finished-3.SG reading the book
            'Did he end up reading the book?'
      B: – *Acabou.
             finished-3.SG
      B': – Leu
             read-IND.PAST.3.SG
             'Yes, he did.'

(7.132) a. A: – A Maria sabe que o João contou tudo?
 the Maria knows that the João told everything
 'Does Maria know that João confessed everything?'
 B: – Sabe.
 knows
 'Yes, she does.'
 B': *Contou.
 told
 'Yes, he did.'
 b. A: – O João estava na prisão quando contou tudo?
 the João was in-the jail when told everything
 'Was João in jail when he confessed everything?'
 B: – Estava.
 was
 'Yes, he was.'
 B': *Contou.
 told
 'Yes, he did.'

By and large, verbal answers repeat the tense of the finite verb occurring in the question, with the relevant adjustment in person if the verb in the question has first or second person inflection. This is just the general case, though. We have already seen in (7.127) that a (finite) verbal answer may be based on an infinitival verb associated with the modal *poder* 'can'. A similar pattern also occurs with perfective tenses with the auxiliary *ter* 'have' (prefective past and perfective present in EP and only prefective past in BP). As illustrated in (7.133) below, a verbal answer in this case may be based on the auxiliary or on the participial main verb.

(7.133) a. A: – Ele tinha feito isso de propósito?
 he had.3.SG done this of purpose
 'Had he done this on purpose?'
 B: – Tinha.
 had.3.SG
 'Yes, he had.'
 B': – **Fez**.
 did.3.SG
 'Yes, he did.'
 b. A: – Ele tem tomado os comprimidos?
 he has taken the pills
 'Has he been taking his pills?'
 B: – Tem.
 has
 B': – **Toma**. (EP)
 takes
 'Yes, he has.'

Another interesting pattern is observed in EP with the indicative future tense morphology. If the indicative future tense morphology of the verb in the question is semantically interpreted as future, the answer sounds more natural with the present tense rather than the future tense form, as illustrated in (7.134) below. If the future tense morphology in the question encodes a modal value (doubt/uncertainty/probability) instead, answers with future tense morphology or bare *sim* are blocked and the present tense is used, as shown in (7.135) and (7.136). Similarly, if the indicative conditional morphology in the question encodes modality, as illustrated in (7.137), answers with indicative conditional morphology or bare *sim* are ruled out and a bare answer with past tense morphology is employed instead.[46]

(7.134)   EP:

       A: – **Farás**   isso por mim?
           do-*INDIC.FUT-2.SG* this by me
           'Will you(SG) do that for me?'

   a.   B: – ?Farei.
           do-*INDIC.FUT-1.SG*

   b.   B: – **Faço**.
           do-*INDIC.PRES.1.SG*

(7.135)   EP:

       [*Context*: A and B are knocking at their friends' door.]

       A: – Eles (não) **estarão**   em casa?
           they not   be-*INDIC.FUT-3.PL*   in home
           'Could it be that they are not at home?'

   a.   B: – *Estarão.
           be-*INDIC.FUT-3.PL*

   b.   B: – *Sim.
           yes
           'Yes, they are.'

   c.   B: – **Estão**.   (Acabei   de ouvir passos
           be-*INDIC.PRES.3.PL* finished-*1.SG* of hear steps
           lá   dentro.)
           there   inside
           'Yes, they are. (I have just heard footsteps inside).'

(7.136)   EP:

       A: – Ela **terá**   30 anos?
           she have-*INDIC.FUT.3.SG* 30 years
           'Is she maybe 30 years old?'

---

[46] For some EP speakers, *sim* answers in (7.135)–(7.137) are allowed if they have a particular intonation, with heavy stress on the word *sim*.

a. B: – *Terá.
       have-INDIC.FUT.3.SG
b. B: – *Sim.
       yes
       'Yes, she is.'
c. B: – **Tem.**   (Ela   na   verdade   tem 31.)
       *have-**INDIC.PRES**.3.SG   she   in-the   truth   has 31*
       'Yes, she is. (She is actually 31).'
d. B: – **Deve**   **ter**.
       *may-**INDIC.PRES**.3.SG   have-INF*
       'She might well be.'

(7.137) EP:
A: – Estou   tão   nervosa.   O   João   **teria**
    *be-PRES.1.SG   so   nervous   the   João   have-**INDIC.COND**.3.SG*
    passado   no   exame?!
    passed   in-the   exam
    'I'm so nervous. Will João have passed the exam?'
a. B: – *Teria.
       have-INDIC.COND.3.SG
b. B: – *Sim.
       yes
       'Yes, he has.'
c. B: – **Passou.**   (Era ele ao   telefone.)
       *pass-**INDIC.PAST**.3.SG   was   he   to-the   telephone*
       'Yes, he has. (It was him on the phone.)'

Lastly, let us briefly discuss answers to fragment polar questions, that is, nonverbal elliptical structures that may function as well-formed polar questions in the appropriate discourse context. Putting aside the formality associated with *sim* answers in BP, we may find three different patterns. If the fragment can be interpreted as the argument of the implicit verb recovered by the context, both bare verb answers and *sim* answers are available, as illustrated in (7.138) below. If the fragment is interpreted as a topicalized argument in the sense that it is singled out as a discourse-salient member of the set denoted by the argument of the verb, a bare verb answer is allowed but not a *sim* answer, as shown in (7.139). Finally, if the question is not an argument of the verb, but some modifier, *sim* answers are allowed but not bare verb answers, as shown in (7.140). In this case, answers with just a preposition may also be allowed, as shown in (7.140b–d).

(7.138) a. A: – {Café?/Vinho?}
  coffee/wine
  '{Coffee?/Wine?}'
  B: – Quero   (, por   favor).
  want-1.SG by   favor
  B': – Sim   (, por   favor).   (EP/%BP)
  yes   by   favor
  'Yes, please.'

b. [*Context*: A and B are going out for the day but have not quite decided where to go. When they get into the car, A asks B:]
  A: – Para   a   praia?
  to   the   beach
  'To the beach?'
  B: – Vamos.
  go-1.PL
  B': – Sim.   (EP/%BP)
  yes
  'Yes, let's go.'

(7.139) a. [*Context*: B is showing A what he bought at the supermarket for their dinner party.]
  A: – E   as   bebidas?
  and   the   drinks
  'What about the drinks?'
  B: – Comprei.
  bought-1.SG
  B':   *Sim.
  yes
  'I bought them.'

b. [*Context*: A and B are going to watch a movie at B's place. B is suggesting different options.]
  A: – E   filmes   espanhóis?
  and   movies   Spanish
  'What about Spanish movies?'
  B: – Tenho.
  have-1.SG
  B': – *Sim.
  yes
  'I have [some].'

(7.140) a. [*Context*: A is offering wine to B.]
  A: – Tinto?
  red
  'Red [wine]?'
  B: – *Quero   (,por   favor).
  want-1.SG   by   favor
  B': – Sim   (,por   favor).   (EP/%BP)
  yes   by   favor
  'Yes, please.'

b. [*Context:* A is offering coffee to B.]
   A: – **Com**   leite?
          with   milk
          'Milk?'
   B: –   *Quero   (, por favor).
          want-1.SG by   favor
   B′: – Sim   (, por favor).   (EP/%BP)
          yes   by   favor
   B″:–   **Com**   (, por favor).   (?EP/BP)
          with   by   favor
   B‴:–   **Sim, com**   (, por favor).   (EP/%BP)
          yes   with   by   favor
          'Yes, please.'
   B⁗:–   **Sem**   (, por favor).   (EP/BP)
          without by   favor
          'No milk, please.'
c. [*Context*: A is offering tea to B.]
   A: –   **Sem**   açúcar?
          without   sugar
          'No sugar?'
   B: –   *Quero   (, por favor).
          want-1.SG by   favor
   B′: – Sim   (, por favor).   (EP/%BP)
          yes   by   favor
   B″: – **Sem**   (, por favor).   (?EP/BP)
          without by   favor
   B‴: – **Sim,   sem**   (, por favor).   (EP/%BP)
          yes   without by   favor
          '[No sugar], please.'
   B⁗: – **Com**   (, por favor).   (EP/BP)
          with   by   favor
          'With sugar, please.'
d. [*Context*: A is offering coffee to B.]
   A: – **Com**   ou **sem**   açúcar?
          with   or   without sugar
          'With sugar or without?'
   B: –   **Com**.   (EP/BP)
          with
          'With sugar.'
   B′: – **Sem**.   (EP/BP)
          without
          'Without.'

7.5.2 *Minimal Answers with Adverbs and Quantifiers*

Adverbial expressions may also constitute minimal answers to polar questions in EP and BP.[47] The first general pattern, which is quite common across languages, involves answers with evidential or epistemic adverbials not present in the relevant question, as illustrated in (7.141) below. EP and BP also allow this type of answer with the degree adverb *quase* 'almost' and the temporal adverbs *sempre* 'always' and *nunca* 'never', as shown in (7.142). (7.143) further shows that this pattern of adverbial answers is lexically conditioned and does not include adverbs like *também* 'also' or *só* 'only', for instance, even in contexts where they would be pragmatically appropriate.

(7.141) A: – O João vai conseguir terminar o trabalho a tempo?
  the João goes manage finish the work to time
  'Is João going to get the work done in time?'
  B: – {Claro /Evidentemente /Sem dúvida /Talvez}.
  clear /evidently /without doubt /maybe
  '{Of course/Sure/No doubt/Maybe.}'

(7.142) a. A: – O Pedro terminou o trabalho?
  the Pedro finished the work
  'Did Pedro finish the work?'
  B: – Quase.
  almost
  'Nearly.'

  b. A: – A Maria visita os pais no fim de semana?
  the Maria visits the parents in-the end of week
  'Does Maria visit her parents on weekends?'
  B: – Sempre.
  always
  'Always.'

  c. A: – O João já tinha feito esse comentário antes?
  the João already had made this comment before
  'Had João already made this comment?'
  B: – Nunca.
  never
  'No, never.'

(7.143) a. A: – O Pedro pediu cerveja. E você, quer cerveja?
  the Pedro asked beer and you.SG want beer
  'Pedro ordered beer. What about you(SG)? Do you(SG) want beer?'
  B: – *Também.
  also
  'I do too.'

---

[47] For discussion see e.g. Santos 2002, 2003, 2009, Kato 2016, and Martins 2016a.

b. A: –   Ele   toma   vinho?
          he   drinks   wine
          'Does he drink wine?'
   B: –   *Só.
          only
          'He only drinks wine.'

In this section we will focus on another type of minimal adverbial answer in EP and BP, which repeats an adverb present in the question. This pattern involves the adverbs *também* 'also', *sempre* 'always', *nunca* 'never', *só* 'only', *quase* 'almost', *talvez* 'maybe', *já* 'already', and *ainda* 'still'. Let us then examine the properties of each of these responsive adverbs, starting with *também*, *sempre*, and *nunca*, illustrated in (7.144)–(7.146).[48]

(7.144) a. A: –   Ele   **também**   vai   viajar?
                 he   also   goes travel
                 'Is he going to travel too?'
        B: –   Também.   [*positive agreement*]
               also
               'Yes, he is.'
        B′: – *Também não.   [*negative disagreement*]
               also   not
               'No, he is not.'
     b. A: –   Ele   **também**   não vai viajar?
                 he   also   not goes travel
                 'Is he not going to travel either?'
        B: –   Também   não.   [*negative agreement*]
               also   not
               'No, he isn't either.'
        B′: – *Também.   [*positive disagreement*]
               also
               'Yes, he is.'

---

[48] Typically, minimal adverbial responses can also be extended along the lines of bare verb answers discussed in Section 7.5.1, as illustrated in (i).

(i)   A: – O   João   **já**   fechou   a   loja?
            the   João   already   closed   the store
            'Has João already closed?'
      B: – Já.
            already
      B′: – Sim,   já.   (EP/%BP)
            yes   already
      B″: – Sim,   já   fechou.   (EP/%BP)
            yes   already closed
            'Yes, he has.'

(7.145) a. A: – Ele   **sempre**   usou chapéu?
              he   always   used hat
              'Has he always worn a hat?'
       B: – Sempre.   [*positive agreement*]
              always
              'Yes, always.'
       B′: – Nem   sempre.   [*negative disagreement*]
              not   always
              'Not always.'
    b. A: – Ele   nem **sempre** usava   chapéu, pois   não? (EP)
              he   not   always   use-IMPERF hat   CONFIRM   no
       A′: – Ele   nem **sempre** usava   chapéu, usava?   (BP)
              he   not   always   use-IMPERF hat
              'Didn't he always wear a hat?'
       B: – Nem   sempre.   [*negative agreement*]
              not   always
              "Not always.'
       B′: – *Sempre.   [*positive disagreement*]
              always
              'Always.'

(7.146) A: – Ele   **nunca** viaja   de avião?
                he   never   travels of airplane
                'Does he never travel by plane?'
         B: – Nunca.   [*negative agreement*]
                never
                'No, never.'

As seen in (7.144) and (7.145), *também* 'also' and *sempre* 'always' encode positive agreement when alone (see (7.144a) and (7.145a)). When accompanied by a negative expression, *sempre* can express both negative agreement (see (7.145b)) and negative disagreement (see (7.145a)), whereas *também* is restricted to negative agreement (see (7.144b)). The adverb *nunca* 'never', in turn, is inherently negative; hence, it will give rise only to a negative agreement response (see (7.146)).

The adverbs *talvez* 'maybe' and *só* 'only' differ from the previous adverbs in that they are compatible with either positive or negative agreement when unaccompanied by other expressions, as shown in (7.147) and (7.148) below.[49] However, they pattern like the previous adverbs in not supporting a positive

---

[49] Interrogative sentences that include the modal adverb *talvez* 'maybe' display subjunctive mood, which cannot surface in a bare verb answer. A bare verb answer with indicative mood is possible, as shown in (id) below, but contrasts with the adverbial and *sim* answers in (ia) and (ib) in being unable to recover the modality expressed by the question (cf. (7.126) and (7.127)). Thus, the bare verb answer allows a continuation like (id) but not like (ic).

disagreement interpretation. In negative contexts like (7.147b) and (7.148b), a response with bare *talvez* or *só* can be interpreted only as negative agreement.[50]

(7.147) a. A: – Ele **talvez** venha?
           he   maybe   come-SUBJ.3SG
           'Might it be that he will come?'
        B: – Talvez.   [*positive agreement*]
             maybe
             'Maybe.'
        B′: – Talvez não.   [*negative disagreement*]
             maybe not
             'Maybe not.'

(i)   A: – O João talvez saia   do   hospital hoje?
             the João maybe leave-SUBJ.3.SG of-the hospital today
             'Might João be leaving the hospital today?'
    a. B: – Talvez. Mas também pode não sair.
             maybe but also may not leave
    b. B: – Sim. Mas também pode não sair.   (EP/%BP)
             yes but also may not leave
             'Yes, he might. But maybe he won't.'
    c. B: – **Sai**.   #Mas também pode não sair.
             leave-**IND**.3.SG but   also   may not leave
             'Yes, he will. #But maybe he won't.'
    d. B: – **Sai**.   Acabaram de ligar do   hospital.
             leave-**IND**.3.SG finished-3.PL of call of-the hospital
             'Yes, he will. They have just called from the hospital.'

[50] Answers to questions with adverbs like *talvez* and *só* may express positive disagreement if associated with metalinguistic negation expressions (see Section 7.3.3), as illustrated in (i).

(i) a. [*Context*:
        A: – Ele   talvez não venha?
             he   maybe not come-SUBJ.3SG
             'Might it be that he won't come?']
        B: – Uma ova   que ele talvez não venha!   (BP)
             a   fish.roe that he   maybe   not come-SUBJ.3SG
        B′: – **Que:** talvez não venha   **o quê**!   (BP)
             that may   not come-SUBJ.3SG what
             'Like hell he won't come!'
     b. [*Context*:
        A: – Só   ele disse a   verdade?
             only he   said   the truth
             'Was he the only one to tell the truth?']
        B: – **Agora** só   ele!   (EP)
             now   only he
        B′: – Só   ele disse a verdade   **o quê**?   (EP)
             only he   said the truth   what
             'Only he told the truth my eye!'

b. A: – Ele   **talvez**   não venha?
            he   maybe   not come-SUBJ.3SG
            'Might it be that he won't come?'
      B: – Talvez.   [*negative agreement*]/*[*positive
            maybe   disagreement*]
      B': – Talvez não.   [*negative agreement*]
            maybe not
            'Maybe not.'

(7.148) a. A: – **Só** ele   disse a   verdade?
               only   he   said the   truth
               'Was he the only one to tell the truth?'
         B: – Só.   [*positive agreement*]
               only
               'Yes, he was.'
         B': – Não só.   [*negative disagreement*]
               not only
               'No, he wasn't.'
      b. A: – **Só** ele   não disse a   verdade?
               only he   not said the   truth
               'Was he the only one not to tell the truth?'
         B: – Só.   [*negative agreement*]/
               only   *[*positive disagreement*]
               'Right(, he was the only one not to tell the truth).'
         B': – Não só.   [*negative disagreement*
               not only   (double negation)]
               'Wrong(, he wasn't the only one not to tell the truth).'

The adverb *quase* 'almost' patterns like *talvez* and *só* in being compatible with both positive and negative agreement, as shown by the answers by B in (7.149a) and (7.149b). Differently, though, its association with negation is not compatible with negative disagreement (see the answer by B' in (7.149a) and yields a marginal result in EP and a completely unacceptable result in BP as a way to encode negative agreement (see the answer by B' in (7.149b)).

(7.149) a. A: – Ela   **quase** ganhou a   corrida?
               she   almost   won   the race
               'Did she almost win the race?'
         B: – Quase.   [*positive agreement*]
               Almost
               'Yes, almost.'

> B': – *Quase não. [negative disagreement]
> almost not
> 'No, she didn't.'
> b. A: – Ela **quase** não ganhou a corrida?
> she almost not won the race
> 'Did she almost not win the race?'
> B: – Quase. [negative agreement]
> almost
> 'Yes, almost.'
> B': – Quase não. (?EP/*BP) [negative agreement]
> almost not
> 'No, she didn't.'

Let us finally consider *já* 'already' and *ainda* 'still', which do not necessarily trigger repetition and may instead stand for each other, as illustrated in (7.150) and (7.151).[51]

> (7.150) a. A: – Ela **já** terminou o livro?
> she already finished the book
> 'Has she already finished the book?'

---

[51] As opposed to adverbs like *sempre* 'always' or *só* 'only', which may license a responsive adverbial answer regardless of whether they are preverbal or postverbal, as shown in (i) below, the licensing of an adverbial response by postverbal *já* is accepted by only some speakers, as illustrated in (ii). See Santos 2002 for discussion.

> (i) a. A: – {Ele **sempre** gostou dela? /Ele gostou **sempre** dela?}
> he always liked of-her /he liked always of-her
> 'Has he always liked her?'}
> B: – Sempre.
> always
> 'Yes, always.'
> b. A: – {Ele só disse mentiras? /Ele disse só mentiras?
> he only said lies /he said only lies
> 'Did he only tell lies?'
> B: – Só.
> only
> 'Yes, he did.'
> (ii) a. A: – Ele nessa idade **já** tinha problemas?
> he in-this age already had problems
> 'Did he already have problems at this age?'
> B: – Já.
> already
> 'Yes, he did.'
> b. A: – Ele nessa idade tinha **já** problemas?
> he in-this age had already problems
> 'Did he already have problems at this age?'
> B: – %Já.
> already
> 'Yes, he did.'

	B: –	**Já**.		[*positive agreement*]
		already		
		'Yes, she has.'		
	B′: –	**Ainda** não.		[*negative disagreement*]
		still not		
		'Not yet.'		
b. A: –		Ela **já** não quer mais correr a maratona?		
		she already not wants more run the marathon		
		'Doesn't she want to run the marathon anymore?'		
	B: –	***Já**.		[*positive disagreement*]/
		already		[*negative agreement*]
		'Yes, she does.'		
	B′: –	**Já** não.	(EP/*BP)	[*negative agreement*]
		already not		
		'No, she doesn't.'		

(7.151) a. A: –   Ela **ainda** trabalha naquele escritório?
                  she still works in-that office
                  'Does she still work in that office?'
        B: –   **Ainda**.   [*positive agreement*]
                  still
                  'Yes, she does.'
        B′: –   **Já** não.   (EP/*BP)   [*negative disagreement*]
                  already not
                  'Not anymore.'
     b. A: –   Você **ainda** não viu esse filme?
                  you.SG still not saw this movie
                  'Haven't you(SG) watched this movie yet?'
        B: –   **Ainda** não.   [*negative agreement*]
                  still not
                  'Not yet.'
        B′: –   **Já**.   (EP/*BP)   [*positive disagreement*]
                  already
                  'Yes, I have.'
        B″: –   **Já**, sim.   (EP/BP)   [*positive disagreement*]
                  already yes
                  'Yes, I have.'

Já 'already' is the only responsive adverb that can by itself encode positive disagreement, although only when the question involves *ainda não* (lit. *still not*) and only in EP, as can be seen by the contrast between answers by B in (7.151b) and by B′ in (7.151b). Also interesting is the fact that *já* can combine with *não* in EP to encode both negative agreement (see the answer by B''' in (7.150b)) and negative disagreement (see the answer by B'' in (7.151a)), neither of which is allowed in BP. This exceptional behavior is certainly related to the fact that *já* is also exceptional in EP in being the only adverb that can express positive disagreement through a reduplication pattern similar to that of the verb, as illustrated in (7.152a) below (see Section 7.2.1), and form a tag question, as illustrated in (7.152b) (see Section 7.4.2).

(7.152) EP:
    a. [*Context*:
       A: – O   João ainda não saiu.
             the João still   not   left
            'João hasn't left yet.']
       B: – O   João **já**   saiu, **já**.
             the João already left already
             'Of course, João has already left.'
    b. **Já**   viste   este   filme, não   **já**?
       already saw-2.SG this   movie not   already
       'You(SG) have already seen this movie, haven't you(SG)?'

Finally, it is worth noting that the quantifiers *tudo* 'everything' and *nada* 'nothing' can also function as minimal answers to polar questions, as illustrated in (7.153) and (7.154) below.[52] In isolation, *tudo* encodes positive agreement (see the answer by B in (7.153a)) and *nada*, negative agreement (see the answer by B in (7.154a)), which allows them to be associated with *sim* and *não*, as respectively illustrated by the answers by B' in (7.153a) and (7.154a). A diminutive morpheme may also be added to each of these quantifiers, as shown in (7.153b) and (7.154b), giving rise to an emphatic reading.

(7.153) A: – A   Maria   fez   **tudo**   sozinha?
              the Maria   did   everything alone
         'Did Maria do everything all by herself?'
    a. B: – Tudo.   [*positive agreement*]
            everything
      B': – Sim,   tudo.   (EP/%BP) [*positive agreement*]
            yes   everything
    b. B: – Tud**inho**.   [*positive agreement*]
            everything-***DIM***
         'Yes, she did.'

---

[52] See e.g. Kato 2016 for discussion.

448   7 Affirmation, Negation, Questions, and Answers

    c. B: – Nem   tudo.   [*negative disagreement*]
               not   everything
              'No, she didn't.'

(7.154) A: – O   João não comprou **nada**?
               the João not bought   nothing
            'Didn't João buy anything?'
    a. B: – Nada.   [*negative agreement*]
           nothing
        B': – Não,   nada.   [*negative agreement*]
           no   nothing
    b. B'': – Nad**inha**.   (EP) [*negative agreement*]
           nothing-*DIM*
        B''': – Nad**ica**   de nada. (BP) [*negative agreement*]
           nothing-*DIM* of nothing
           'No, nothing.'
    c. B: – Comprou (, sim).   [*positive disagreement*]
           bought   yes
           'Yes, he did.'

Nada can also convey an emphatic negative disagreement response in negative exclamatives, as illustrated in (7.155) below (see footnote 19 above). In this case, however, *nada* need not be a repetition.

(7.155) A: – O   João chegou antes da   hora desta vez?
               the   João arrived before of-the hour of-this time
            'Did João arrive early this time?'
        B: – Nada   disso!   (EP)
           nothing of-this
        B': – Que   nada!   (BP)
           what   nothing
           'Not at all.'

7.5.3 Minimal Answers with the Copula *ser* 'be'

EP and BP may also (marginally) allow minimal answers with the third person singular form of the copula *ser* 'be' either uniformly in the present tense or agreeing with the tense of the question, as illustrated in (7.156).[53]

---

[53] For discussion, see A. L. Santos 2003, 2009, Kato 2016, and Martins 2016a.

(7.156) A: – Os organizadores perderam o voo?
                the organizers   missed   the flight
        'Did the organizers miss their flight?'
    a. B: – Foi.   (%EP/*BP) [*positive agreement*]
            be.PAST.3.SG
    b. B: – %É.   (%EP/%BP) [*positive agreement*]
            be.PRES.3.SG
    c. B: – Pois   é.   (*EP/BP)   [*positive agreement*]
            CONFIRM be.PRES.3.SG
            'Yes, they did.'

Ser answers are not universally accepted by EP speakers, who may judge such answers within a range from very unnatural (when *ser* agrees with the tense of the question, as in (7.156a)) to ungrammatical (when the invariable form *é* 'is' is employed, as in (7.156b) above). The same EP speakers who dislike *ser* answers allow their counterparts as confirmations of a previous declarative sentence (especially the forms agreeing in tense), which may be optionally accompanied by the confirmative particle *pois*, as illustrated in (7.157).

(7.157) A: – Eles   já   encontraram as chaves.
              they   already   found   the keys
        'They already found the keys.'
        B: – (Pois)   foi.   (EP/*BP)
             CONFIRM be.PAST.3.SG
             'They did, indeed.'

In BP, the use of the invariant copula as a minimal response may be subject to individual variation (see (7.156b)) and *pois é* is employed as a confirmative expression (see (7.156c)). So the answer in (7.156c) sounds more adequate in a context in which A already has evidence of or suspicions about the organizers missing their flight. Accordingly, *pois é* cannot be employed as an answer to a genuine request for information, as shown in (7.158a) (see also (7.162d), (7.163d) and (7.164c) below), but it is an appropriate comment to a previous declarative sentence, as illustrated in (7.158b) (see Section 7.2.1).

(7.158) BP:
    a. A: – Você   lembrou   de trazer os documentos?
             you.SG   remembered   of bring the documents
            'Did you(SG) remember to bring the documents?'
        B: – *Pois   é.
             CONFIRM be-PRES.3.SG
             'Yes, I did.'

b. A: – A   inflação   voltou.
       the inflation returned
       'Inflation is back.'
   B: – Pois   é.
       CONFIRM be-PRES.3.SG
       'It is, indeed.'

Ser answers and BP *pois é* answers unequivocally express agreement with the question, be it positive agreement as in (7.156) or negative agreement, as in (7.159) below. However, they cannot be expanded in association with *sim* or *não*, as shown in (7.160) and (7.161).

(7.159) A: – Ele   não   veio?
             he   not   came
             'Did he not come?'
     a. B: – Foi.   (%EP/*BP) [*negative agreement*]
           be.PAST.3.SG
     b. B: – %É.   (%EP/%BP) [*negative agreement*]
           be.PRES.3.SG
     c. B: – Pois   é.   (*EP/BP)   [*negative agreement*]
           CONFIRM be.PRES.3.SG
           'No, he didn't.'

(7.160) A: – O   João   já   voltou   de   férias?
             the João   already returned of   vacations
             'Has João already come back from his vacations?'
     a. B: – Foi.   (%EP/*BP) [*positive agreement*]
           be.PAST.3.SG
     a′. B: – *Sim, foi.   (*EP/*BP) [*positive agreement*]
           yes be.PAST.3.SG
     b. B: – %É.   (%EP/%BP) [*positive agreement*]
           be.PRES.3.SG
     b′. B: – *Sim, é.   (*EP/*BP) [*positive agreement*]
           yes be.PRES.3.SG
     c. B: – Pois   é.   (*EP/BP)   [*positive agreement*]
           CONFIRM be.PRES.3.SG
     c′. B: – *Sim, pois   é.   (*EP/*BP) [*positive agreement*]
           yes   CONFIRM be.PRES.3.SG
           'Yes, he has.'

(7.161) A: – O   João   não   gostou   do   filme?
             the João   not   liked   of-the movie
             'Didn't João like the movie?'
     a. B: – Foi.   (%EP/*BP) [*negative agreement*]
           be.PAST.3.SG

a'. B: – *Não, não foi.   (*EP/*BP) [*negative agreement*]
         no   not be.PAST.3.SG
b. B: – %É.   (%EP/%BP) [*negative agreement*]
         be.PRES.3.SG
b'. B: – *Não, não é.   (*EP/*BP) [*negative agreement*]
         no   not be.PRES.3.SG
c. B: – Pois   é.   (*EP/BP) [*negative agreement*]
         CONFIRM   be.PRES.3.SG
         'Yes, he did.'
c'. B: – *Não, pois   não é. (*EP/*BP) [*positive agreement*]
         no   CONFIRM not be.PRES.3.SG
         'No, he didn't.'

S*er* answers and *pois é* answers differ from bare verbal answers in being unable to be interpreted as a response to an embedded question, as shown in (7.162).

(7.162) A: – Vocês   sabem se o   João telefonou?
             you.PL know   if the João called
             'Do you(PL) happen to know if João has called?'
   a. B: – Telefonou.
           called
   b. B: – *Foi.
           be.PAST.3.SG
   c. B: – *É.
           be.PRES.3.SG
   d. B: – *Pois   é.
           CONFIRM   be.PRES.3.SG
           'Yes, he has.'

Due to their agreement nature, *ser* answers and *pois é* answers are also unable to express a proper response to questions that are to be interpreted as polite ways to make a request or offer something, for instance, as illustrated in (7.163) and (7.164).

(7.163) A: – O   senhor pode assinar nesta   linha?
             the mister can   sign   in-this   line
             'Could you(SG) sign on this line, sir?'
   a. B: – Posso.
           can-1.SG
   b. B: – Assino.
           sign-1.SG
   c. B: – *É.
           be.PRES.3.SG
   d. B: – *Pois   é.
           CONFIRM   be.PRES.3.SG
           'Sure.'

(7.164) A: – Vai   um cafezinho?
go.3.SG a   coffee-DIM
'Would like some coffee?'
a. B: – Vai.
go-3.SG
b. B: – *É.
be.PRES.3.SG
c. B: – *Pois   é.
CONFIRM be.PRES.3.SG
'Sure.'

In BP, *ser* answers seems to have filled the gap left by the obsolescence of *sim* answers in its system (see Section 7.5.1). Thus, the most natural context for a *ser* answer in BP involves environments where a bare verb answer is not available (see Section 7.5.2), as in the case of questions with a clefted constituent, questions with negative implicatures, or questions with coordinated verbs, for instance, as illustrated in (7.165).[54]

(7.165) BP:
a. A: – Esse filme que você queria ver?
this movie that you wanted see
'Is it this movie that you(SG) wanted to watch?'
B: – *Queria.
wanted
B′: – É.
be.PRES.3.SG
'Yes, it is.'
b. A: – O João só escreveu um parágrafo?
the João only wrote one paragraph
'Did João only write one paragraph?'
B: – *Escreveu.
wrote
B′: – É.
be.PRES.3.SG
'Yes, he did.'
c. A: – A Maria terminou as aulas e viajou?
the Maria finished the classes and traveled
'Did Maria finish her classes and travel?'
B: – *Terminou.
finished

---

[54] As opposed to the cases of (7.156b), (7.159b), (7.160b), and (7.161b), the answers by B′ in (7.165b) and by B″ in (7.165c) are more uniformly judged as acceptable by EP speakers (along with the tense-agreeing alternative *foi* lit. *was*). Unsurprisingly, (7.165b) and (7.165c) involve contexts where a bare verb answer is not allowed in EP (see Section 7.5.1).

B′: – *Viajou.
    traveled
B″: – É.
    be.PRES.3.SG
    'Yes, she did.'

7.6 Summary

In this chapter we have examined how polarity is encoded in EP and BP. We have seen that a salient property that singles out EP and BP crosslinguistically is the fact that they may use bare verbs and some adverbs as minimal responses to polar questions, as shown in (7.166) and (7.167).

(7.166) A: – O João vendeu o carro?
         the João sold the car
         'Did João sell the car?'
      B: – Vendeu.   (EP/BP)
         sold
         'Yes, he did.'

(7.167) A: – A Maria já saiu?
         the Maria already left
         'Has Maria already left?'
      B: – Já.   (EP/BP)
         already
         'Yes, she has.'

We have also seen that EP and BP diverge considerably with respect to specific polarity configurations. EP has a much wider spectrum of possibilities to encode affirmation, as illustrated in (7.168), whereas negation is much less restricted in BP, as shown in (7.169).

(7.168) [*Context*:
      A: – O João ainda não saiu.
         the João still not left
         'João hasn't left yet.']
   a. B: – Saiu, sim.   (EP: OK; BP: OK)
          left yes
   b. B: – Saiu, pois.   (EP: OK; BP: *)
          left CONFIRM
   c. B: – Saiu, saiu.   (EP: OK; BP: *)
          left left
   d. B: – Já saiu, já.   (EP: OK; BP: *)
          already left already
          'Of course, João has already left.'

454   7 Affirmation, Negation, Questions, and Answers

(7.169) a. Ele   não   comprou   aquela casa   não.   (EP: OK; BP: OK)
           he   not   bought   that   house   no
        'He definitely did not buy that house.'
     b. A   Maria   disse   que   ele   **não**
        the Maria   said   that he   not
        comprou aquela casa   **não**.   (EP: *; BP: OK)
        bought that   house no
        'Maria said that he did not buy that house.'
     c. **Não** convide   o   João   **não**.   (EP: *; BP: OK)
        not   invite   the João   no
        'Do not invite João.'
     d. Você   **não**   terminou o   relatório **não**?   (EP: *; BP: OK)
        you.SG not   finished the report   no
        'Didn't you(SG) finish the report?'
     e. Você   **não**   quer   tomar um   cafezinho
        you.SG not   want   take a   coffee-DIM
        não?   (EP: *; BP: OK)
        no
        'Wouldn't you(SG) like to have some coffee?'

The interaction between these general tendencies results in interesting and intricate patterns, as we have seen in detail in the preceding sections.

8

Conclusion

In the preceding chapters we have discussed major syntactic similarities and differences between European Portuguese (EP) and Brazilian Portuguese (BP). Starting with their pronominal systems in Chapter 2, we observe that, at first sight, EP and BP share basically the same pronominal system, which differs only with regard to the fact that some pronouns are more commonly used in one variety than the other. However, when we examine the case distinctions of the two pronominal systems, a very different picture arises. Tables 8.1 and 8.2 below (adapted from Tables 2.8 and 2.9) show that, while in EP case syncretism involving the default nominative form is restricted to some pronouns (depicted by the darker shaded areas), in BP case syncretism is the norm, rather than the exception.

It is well known that, when a language loses case distinctions, its word order tends to become more rigid. Given the pervasiveness of case syncretism in BP and its associated loss of case distinctions, we are led to expect BP to display a much more rigid word order than EP. As discussed in detail in Chapter 5, this expectation is indeed fulfilled. Although SVO is the basic word order in both varieties, EP commonly resorts to VS order in several syntactic configurations, whereas BP sticks to the basic word order in the same configurations, generally restricting VS order to configurations encoding thetic judgments and, even in this case, VS is lexically conditioned (see Sections 5.2.1.1, 5.3, 5.4, and 5.5). EP and BP also clearly differ with respect to clitic placement (see Section 5.6). EP exhibits a complex interaction of factors that yields both enclisis and proclisis outputs, whereas BP by and large converges on proclisis to the main verb.

The different pronominal systems depicted in Tables 8.1 and 8.2 also closely interact with nominal and verbal agreement. We saw in Chapter 3 that BP generally favors agreementless forms whenever possible. In the case of noun phrases, in particular, BP allows for number to be morphologically recorded just on the determiner, which opens the way for the emergence of bare singulars with countable nouns in the language. This general preference for underspecified forms in BP is not restricted to the surface realization of agreement, but affects the underlying specification of its pronouns. As

Table 8.1 *Syncretism of personal pronouns with the default form in European Portuguese*

	[+REFL]		[-REFL]		[+REFL]	[-REFL]	prepositional	synthetic
	ACC	DAT	ACC	DAT	OBL	NOM	GEN	GEN
1.SG	me[CL]				mim / comigo	eu		meu[MASC.SG] / meus[MASC-PL] / minha[FEM.SG] / minhas[FEM-PL]
2.SG[+close]	te[CL]				ti / contigo	tu		teu[MASC.SG] / teus[MASC-PL] / tua[FEM.SG] / tuas[FEM-PL]
2.SG[-close]			o[MASC.CL] / a[FEM.CL]	lhe[CL]	si / consigo	*você*		seu[MASC.SG] / seus[MASC-PL] / sua[FEM.SG] / suas[FEM-PL]
3.SG	se[CL]					ele[MASC] / ela[FEM]		
3-PL			os[MASC.CL] / as[FEM.CL]	lhes[CL]		eles[MASC] / elas[FEM]		
2-PL			vos[CL]		convosco	*vocês*		vosso[MASC.SG] / vossos[MASC-PL] / vossa[FEM.SG] / vossas[FEM-PL]
1.PL			nos[CL]		connosco	*a gente* / nós		nosso[MASC.SG] / nossos[MASC-PL] / nossa[FEM.SG] / nossas[FEM-PL]

The first column displays the traditional description of the nominative pronouns in boldface (see Section 3.4.2 for revisions and refinements).

Table 8.2 *Syncretism of personal pronouns with the default form in Brazilian Portuguese*

	[+REFL]	[-REFL]		[+REFL]	[-REFL]	[-REFL]	prepositional	synthetic
	ACC	DAT	ACC	DAT	OBL	NOM	GEN	GEN
1.SG	*me*[CL]	*me*[CL]	*me*[CL]	*mim / comigo*	*mim / comigo*	*eu*		*meu*[MASC.SG] *meus*[MASC-PL] *minha*[FEM.SG] *minhas*[FEM-PL]
2.SG	*se*[CL]		*te*[CL]	*te*[CL]	*você*	*você*		*seu*[MASC.SG] *seus*[MASC-PL] *sua*[FEM.SG] *suas*[FEM-PL]
			cê[W]			*cê*[W]		
2-PL	*se*[CL]		*cês*[W]		*vocês*	*vocês*		
						cês[W]		
3.SG/3-PL	*se*[CL]					*ele*[MASC.SG] *ela*[FEM.SG] *eles*[MASC-PL] *elas*[FEM-PL]		
1.PL	*se*[CL]				*a gente / nós*	*a gente / nós*		*nosso*[MASC.SG] *nossos*[MASC-PL] *nossa*[FEM.SG] *nossas*[FEM-PL]

The first column displays the traditional description of the nominative pronouns in boldface (see Section 3.4.2 for revisions and refinements).

458   8 Conclusion

shown in Table 3.12, repeated in Table 8.3, although EP and BP trigger the same surface form for verbal agreement, the underlying specifications of their nominative pronouns and the verbal inflection associated with them are very different.

The analysis underlying Table 8.3 allows us to account for the fact that the number of verbal agreement distinctions in EP and BP does not suffice to account for their differences in several domains and, in particular, where null subjects are concerned. We have seen in Chapter 4 that the same surface verbal agreement inflection may or may not morphologically license a null subject depending on its underlying featural information. More specifically, we have argued that the morphological licensing of null subjects is governed by the Prominent Feature Valuation Condition, restated in (8.1).

(8.1)   *Prominent Feature Valuation Condition*
A given verbal inflection Infl can morphologically license the ellipsis of a definite pronominal subject in Portuguese only if the most prominent feature of Infl is valued, where feature prominence has the following scale: *person > number > gender > case*.

According to (8.1), the licensing of a given null subject – interpreted here as pronominal ellipsis – depends on whether the most prominent feature of the verbal agreement inflection associated with the pronoun that is the target of ellipsis is valued or not. Given that different tense–aspect inflections may have different features, the prediction is that a given null subject may give rise to different degrees of acceptability, depending on the composition and valuation of the features of the specific tense–aspect inflection it is associated with. We saw in Chapter 4 that the feature specifications in Table 8.3, coupled with the Prominent Feature Valuation Condition in (8.1), indeed provide a straightforward account of the complex pattern of null subject licensing depicted in Tables 4.22 and 4.23, repeated as Tables 8.4 and 8.5 below.

The loss of third person accusative clitics and third person possessors in BP seen in Table 8.2 has also had an impact on the distribution and interpretation of null objects and null possessors in this variety (see Chapter 6). Interestingly, it is not simply the case that BP is more restricted than EP with respect to empty categories. We find a larger distribution and wider range of interpretations for null subjects and null possessors in EP (see Chapters 4 and 6), but a larger distribution and wider range of interpretations for null objects in BP, as illustrated in Table 6.1, adapted here as Table 8.6 below.

In the same vein, EP and BP treat polarity differently, as EP has a much wider spectrum of possibilities to encode affirmation, whereas negation is much less restricted in BP, as discussed in Chapter 7.

Table 8.3 *Pronominal specifications for person and number and verbal agreement in Portuguese*

Nominative pronouns	Morphological specification for person and number				Surface forms: *dançar* 'dance' (indicative present)
	EP		BP		
	Pronoun specification	Agreement inflection	Pronoun specification	Agreement inflection	
tu 'you(SG)'	[P:N:2:SG]	[P:N:2:SG]			*danças*
eu 'I'	[P:N:1:SG]	[P:N:1:SG]	[P:N:SG]	[P:N:SG]	*danço*
nós 'we'	[P:N:1:PL]	[P:N:1:PL]	[P:N:1]	[P:N:1]	*dançamos*
você 'you(SG)'	[P:2:N:SG]	[P:2:N:SG]	[P-N]	[P:u-N:u]	*dança*
ele 'he/it(MASC)' *ela* 'she/it(FEM)'	[P:3:N:SG]	[P:3:N:SG]			
a gente 'we'	[P.N]	[P:u-N:u]	[P.N]		
vocês 'you(PL)'	[P:2-N:PL]	[P:2-N:PL]	[P-N:PL]	[P:u-N:PL]	*dançam*
eles 'they(MASC)' *elas* 'they(FEM)'	[P:3-N:PL]	[P:3-N:PL]			

Table 8.4 Morphological licensing of definite null subjects in European Portuguese

		Finite clauses		Inflected infinitivals	Participials	Agreementless case-marking gerunds
		Fuller paradigm	Impoverished paradigm			
Null counterpart of	eu 'I'	✓	✓	✓	✓	✓
	tu 'you(SG)'	✓	✓	✓	✓	✓
	você 'you(SG)'	✓	✓	✓	✓	✓
	ele 'he' / ela 'she'	✓	✓	✓	✓	✓
	nós 'we'	✓	✓	✓	✓	✓
	vocês 'you(PL)'	✓	✓	✓	✓	✓
	eles 'they(MASC)' / elas 'they(FEM)'	✓	✓	✓	✓	✓
	a gente 'we'	*	*	*	*	✓

Table 8.5 *Morphological licensing of definite null subjects in Brazilian Portuguese*

		Finite clauses		Inflected infinitivals	Participials	Agreementless case-marking gerunds
		Fuller paradigm	Impoverished paradigm			
Null counterpart of	*nós* 'we'	✓	✓	✓	*	✓
	vocês 'you(PL)'	??	??	??	*	✓
	eles 'they(MASC)' *elas* 'they(FEM)'	??	??	??	✓	✓
	eu 'I'	??	*	*	*	✓
	você 'you(SG)'	*	*	*	*	✓
	ele 'he' *ela* 'she'	*	*	*	✓	✓
	a gente 'we'	*	*	*	*	✓

Table 8.6 Licensing of null objects in European Portuguese and Brazilian Portuguese

			[+hum]		[-hum]	
			EP	BP	EP	BP
No island	antecedent in discourse		OK	OK	OK	OK
	antecedent in the same sentence	in topic position	OK	OK	OK	OK
		in subject position	*	*	*	OK
		in other positions	*	*	OK	OK
Null object inside strong island	antecedent in discourse		*	*	*	OK
	antecedent in the same sentence	in topic position	*	OK	?*	OK
		in subject position	*	*	*	OK
		in other positions	*	*	*	OK

8 Conclusion

In sum, the differences between EP and BP discussed in the preceding chapters are shown to stem from their different underlying specifications even when they have the same surface form.

Ø esperamos que Ø tenha-Ø-Ø gostado do livro! (EP)
[P.N:1.PL] hope-1.PL that [P:2-N:SG] have-P:2-N:SG liked of-the book
Ø esperamos que você tenha-Ø-Ø gostado do livro! (BP)
[P.N:1] hope-1 that [P-N] have-P:u-N:u liked of-the book
'We hope you(SG) enjoyed this book!'

References

Abaurre, Maria Bernadete and Charlotte Galves. 1996. Os clíticos no português brasileiro: Elementos para uma abordagem sintático-fonológica. In *Gramática do português falado: Estudos descritivos*, ed. by Ataliba de Castilho and Margarida Basílio, 273–319. Campinas: Editora da UNICAMP.

Abney, Steven. 1987. The noun phrase in its sentential aspect. Doctoral dissertation, Massachusetts Institute of Technology.

Abreu, Sabrina. 1998. A negação sentencial: Da Teoria de Princípios e Parâmetros para o Programa Minimalista – Uma investigação através do português brasileiro. Doctoral dissertation, Pontifícia Universidade Católica do Rio Grande do Sul.

Absousalh, Elaine. 1997. Resolução de choques de acento no português brasileiro: Elementos para uma reflexão sobre a interface fonologia–sintaxe. Master's thesis, Universidade Estadual de Campinas.

Alexandre, Nélia. 2000. A estratégia resumptiva em relativas restritivas do português europeu. Master's thesis, Universidade de Lisboa.

Alexandre, Nélia. 2006. Estruturas em movimento: Alguns tópicos sobre as construções-Q e de clivagem. *Letras de Hoje* 41: 99–119.

Alexiadou, Artemis and Janayna Carvalho. 2017. The role of location in (partial) pro-drop languages. In *Order and structure in syntax II: Subjecthood and argument structure*, ed. by Michelle Sheehan and Laura Bailey, 41–67. Berlin: Language Science Press.

Ambar, Manuela. 1992a. *Para uma sintaxe da inversão sujeito–verbo em português*. Lisbon: Edições Colibri.

Ambar, Manuela. 1992b. Temps et structure de la phrase en portugais. In *Structure de la phrase et théorie du liage*, ed. by Hans-Georg Obenauer and Anne Zribi-Hertz, 29–49. Paris: Presses Universitaires de Vincennes.

Ambar, Manuela. 1994. "Aux-to-COMP" and lexical restrictions on verb movement. In *Paths toward Universal Grammar: Studies in honor of Richard Kayne*, ed. by Guglielmo Cinque, Jan Koster, Jean-Yves Pollock, Luigi Rizzi, and Raffaella Zanuttini, 1–23. Washington, D.C.: Georgetown University Press.

Ambar, Manuela. 1998. Inflected infinitives revisited: Genericity and single event. *Canadian Journal of Linguistics/Revue Canadienne de Linguistique* 43: 5–36.

Ambar, Manuela. 1999. Aspects of the syntax of focus in Portuguese. In *The grammar of focus*, ed. by George Rebuschi and Laurice Tull, 23–53. Amsterdam/Philadelphia: John Benjamins.

Ambar, Manuela. 2000. Infinitives *vs.* participles. In *Portuguese syntax: New comparative studies*, ed. by João Costa, 14–30. Oxford/New York: Oxford University Press.
Ambar, Manuela. 2002. *Wh*-questions and *wh*-exclamatives unifying mirror effects. In *Romance languages and linguistic theory 2000 – Selected papers from "Going Romance" 2000*, ed. by Claire Beyssade, Reineke Bok-Bennema, Frank Drijkoningen, and Paola Monachesi, 15–40. Amsterdam/Philadelphia: John Benjamins.
Ambar, Manuela. 2003. Wh-asymmetries. In *Asymmetries in grammar*, ed. by Anna Maria Di Sciullo, vol. 1, 209–249. Amsterdam/Philadelphia: John Benjamins.
Ambar, Manuela. 2005. Clefts and tense asymmetries. In *UG and external systems*, ed. by Anna Maria Di Sciullo, 95–127. Amsterdam/Philadelphia: John Benjamins.
Ambar, Manuela 2013. Yes-no questions, subjects, adverbs and left periphery – New evidence from Portuguese. In *Language use and linguistic structure: Proceedings of the Olomouc Linguistics Colloquium 2013*, ed. by Joseph Emonds and Markéta Janebová, 15–32. Olomouc: Palacký University.
Ambar, Manuela. 2016. On finiteness and the left periphery. In *Mood, aspect, modality revisited: New answers to old questions*, ed. by Joanna Blaszczak, Anastasia Giannakidou, Dorota Klimek-Jankowska, and Krzysztof Migdalski, 125–176. Chicago: University of Chicago Press.
Ambar, Manuela and Ángel Jiménez-Fernández. 2017. Overtly/non-overtly inflected infinitives in Romance. In *The Blackwell companion to syntax*, ed. by Martin Everaert and Henk van Riemsdijk, 1996–2037. Oxford: Wiley-Blackwell.
Ambar, Manuela, Mary A. Kato, Carlos Mioto, and Rita Veloso. 2003. Padrões de interrogativas-Q no português europeu e no português brasileiro: Uma análise inter- e intralinguística. *Boletim da ABRALIN* 25: 400–404.
Ambar, Manuela, Esmeralda Negrão, Rita Veloso, and Luís Graça. 2007. Tense domains in BP and EP – *v*P, CP and phases. In *Romance languages and linguistic theory – Selected papers from "Going Romance" Amsterdam 2007*, ed. by Enoch Aboh, Elisabeth van der Linden, Joseph Quer, and Petra Sleeman, 1–24. Amsterdam/Philadelphia: John Benjamins.
Ambar, Manuela and Rita Veloso. 2001. On the nature of *wh*-phrases, word order and *wh*-in-situ: Evidence from Portuguese, French, Hungarian and Tetum. In *Romance languages and linguistic theory 1999 – Selected papers from "Going Romance" 1999*, ed. by Yves D'hulst, Johan Rooryck, and Jan Schroten, 1–38. Amsterdam/Philadelphia: John Benjamins.
Andrade, Aroldo de and Charlotte Galves. 2014. A unified analysis for subject topics in Brazilian Portuguese. *Journal of Portuguese Linguistics* 13: 117–147.
Armelin, Paula. 2015. A relação entre gênero e morfologia avaliativa nos nominais do português brasileiro: Uma abordagem sintática da formação de palavras. Doctoral dissertation, Universidade de São Paulo.
Augusto, Marina, José Ferrari Neto, and Letícia Corrêa. 2006. Explorando o DP: A presença da categoria NumP. *Revista de Estudos da Linguagem* 14: 245–275.
Avelar, Juanito. 2004. Dinâmicas morfossintáticas com *ter*, *ser* e *estar* em português brasileiro. Master's thesis, Universidade Estadual de Campinas.
Avelar, Juanito. 2006. Adjuntos adnominais preposicionados no português brasileiro. Doctoral dissertation, Universidade Estadual de Campinas.

Avelar, Juanito. 2009a. Inversão locativa e sintaxe de concordância no português brasileiro. *Matraga* 16: 232–252.
Avelar, Juanito. 2009b. *Ter, ser e estar: Dinâmicas morfossintáticas no português brasileiro*. Campinas: Editora RG.
Avelar, Juanito and Dinah Callou. 2007. Sobre a emergência do verbo possessivo em contextos existenciais no português brasileiro. In *Descrição, aquisição e história do português brasileiro*, ed. by Ataliba de Castilho, Maria Aparecida Torres Morais, Ruth Lopes, and Sonia Cyrino, 375–402. Campinas: Pontes/FAPESP.
Avelar, Juanito and Sonia Cyrino. 2008. Locativos preposicionados em posição de sujeito: Uma possível contribuição das línguas Bantu à sintaxe do português brasileiro. *Revista de Estudos Linguísticos da Universidade do Porto* 3: 49–65.
Avelar, Juanito and Charlotte Galves. 2011. Tópico e concordância em português brasileiro e português europeu. In *Textos seleccionados do XXVI Encontro da Associação Portuguesa de Linguística*, ed. by Armanda Costa, Isabel Falé, and Pilar Barbosa, 49–65. Lisbon: Associação Portuguesa de Linguística.
Bacelar do Nascimento, Maria Fernanda. 1989. A gente, um pronome de 4ª pessoa? In *Actas do congresso sobre a investigação e ensino do português – 18/22 Maio 1997*, 480–490. Lisbon: ICALP.
Bacelar do Nascimento, Maria Fernanda. 2020. Formas de tratamento. In *Gramática do português*, ed. by Eduardo Paiva Raposo, Maria Fernanda Bacelar do Nascimento, Maria Antónia Mota, Luísa Segura, and Amália Mendes, vol. 2, 2701–2732. Lisbon: Fundação Calouste Gulbenkian.
Barbosa, Pilar. 1995. Null subjects. Doctoral dissertation, Massachusetts Institute of Technology.
Barbosa, Pilar. 1996. A new look at the null subject parameter. In *Proceedings of ConSole IV*, ed. by João Costa, Rob Goedemans, and Ruben van de Vijver. Leiden: HIL.
Barbosa, Pilar. 1997. Subject positions in the null subject languages. *Seminários de Linguística* 1: 39–63.
Barbosa, Pilar. 2000. Clitics: A window to the null subject property. In *Portuguese syntax: New comparative studies*, ed. by João Costa, 31–93. Oxford/New York: Oxford University Press.
Barbosa, Pilar. 2001. On inversion in *wh*-questions in Romance. In *Subject inversion in Romance and the theory of Universal Grammar*, ed. by Aafke Hulk and Jean-Yves Pollock, 20–59. Oxford/New York: Oxford University Press.
Barbosa, Pilar. 2002. A propriedade do sujeito nulo e o princípio da projecção alargado. In *Saberes no tempo: Homenagem a Maria Henriqueta Costa Campos*, ed. by Maria Helena Mira Mateus and Clara Correia, 51–71. Lisbon: Colibri.
Barbosa, Pilar. 2006. Ainda a questão dos sujeitos pré-verbais em português europeu: Uma resposta a Costa (2001). *D.E.L.T.A.* 22: 345–402.
Barbosa, Pilar. 2009. Two kinds of subject pro. *Studia Linguistica* 63: 2–58.
Barbosa, Pilar. 2013. As construções pseudoclivadas: Perguntas e respostas. In *XXVIII Encontro Nacional da Associação Portuguesa de Linguística – Textos selecionados*, ed. by Maria de Fátima da Silva, Isabel Falé, and Sandra Pereira, 131–148. Braga: Associação Portuguesa de Linguística.
Barbosa, Pilar. 2019. *pro* as a minimal NP: Toward a unified approach to pro-drop. *Linguistic Inquiry* 50: 487–526.

Barbosa, Pilar and Fátima Cochofel. 2005. O infinitivo preposicionado em PE. In *Actas do XX Encontro Nacional da Associação Portuguesa de Linguística*, ed. by Inês Duarte and Isabel Leiria, 387–400. Lisbon: Associação Portuguesa de Linguística.

Barbosa, Pilar, Maria Eugênia Duarte, and Mary A. Kato. 2001. A distribuição do sujeito nulo no português europeu e no português brasileiro. In *Actas do XVI Encontro Nacional da Associação Portuguesa de Linguística*, ed. by Clara Correia and Anabela Gonçalves, 539–550. Lisbon: Associação Portuguesa de Linguística.

Barbosa, Pilar, Maria Eugênia Duarte, and Mary A. Kato. 2005. Null subjects in European and Brazilian Portuguese. *Journal of Portuguese Linguistics* 4: 11–52.

Barbosa, Pilar, Cristina Flores, and Cátia Pereira. 2018. On subject realization in infinitival complements of causative and perceptual verbs in European Portuguese. Evidence from monolingual and bilingual speakers. In *Language acquisition and contact in the Iberian Peninsula*, ed. by Alejandro Cuza and Pedro Guijarro-Fuentes, 125–158. Berlin/Boston: de Gruyter.

Barbosa, Pilar and Eduardo Paiva Raposo. 2013. Subordinação argumental infinitiva. In *Gramática do português*, ed. by Eduardo Paiva Raposo, Maria Fernanda Bacelar do Nascimento, Maria Antónia Mota, Luísa Segura, and Amália Mendes, vol. 2, 1901–1977. Lisbon: Fundação Calouste Gulbenkian.

Barbosa, Pilar, Pedro Santos, and Rita Veloso. 2020. Tipos de frase e força ilocutória. In *Gramática do português*, ed. by Eduardo Paiva Raposo, Maria Fernanda Bacelar do Nascimento, Maria Antónia Mota, Luísa Segura, Amália Mendes, and Amália Andrade, vol. 3, 2517–2586. Lisbon: Fundação Calouste Gulbenkian.

Barros, Evângela. 2006. Construções de posse com clítico no PB: Percurso diacrônico. Doctoral dissertation, Universidade Federal de Minas Gerais.

Bassani, Indaiá and Marcus Lunguinho. 2011. Revisitando a flexão verbal do português à luz da Morfologia Distribuída: Um estudo do presente, pretérito perfeito e pretérito imperfeito do indicativo. *ReVEL* 5, special issue: 199–227.

Bastos, Ana Claudia. 2001. Fazer, eu faço! Topicalização de constituintes verbais em português brasileiro. Master's thesis, Universidade Estadual de Campinas.

Bastos-Gee, Ana Claudia. 2009. Topicalization of verbal projections in Brazilian Portuguese. In *Minimalist essays on Brazilian Portuguese syntax*, ed. by Jairo Nunes, 161–190. Amsterdam/Philadelphia: John Benjamins.

Bastos-Gee, Ana Claudia. 2011. Information structure within the traditional nominal phrase: The case of Brazilian Portuguese. Doctoral Dissertation, University of Connecticut.

Baxter, Alan. 2009. A concordância de número. In *O português afro-brasileiro*, ed. by Dante Lucchesi, Alan Baxter, and Ilza Ribeiro, 269–293. Salvador: EDUFBA.

Berlinck, Rosane. 1996a. La position du sujet en portugais: Étude diachronique des variétés brésilienne et européenne. Doctoral dissertation, Katholieke Universiteit Leuven.

Berlinck, Rosane. 1996b. The Portuguese dative. In *The dative: Descriptive studies*, ed. by William van Belle and Willy van Langendonck, 119–151. Amsterdam/Philadelphia: John Benjamins.

Berlinck, Rosane. 2000. Brazilian Portuguese VS order: A diachronic analysis. In *Brazilian Portuguese and the null subject parameter*, ed. by Mary A. Kato and

Esmeralda Negrão, 175–194. Madrid and Frankfurt am Main: Iberoamericana/Vervuert.
Berlinck, Rosane and Izete Coelho. 2018. A ordem do sujeito em construções declarativas na história do português brasileiro. In *Mudança sintática do português brasileiro: Perspectiva gerativista*, ed. by Sonia Cyrino and Maria Aparecida Torres Morais, 308–381. São Paulo: Contexto.
Betoni, Simone. 2013. O expletivo *ele* em domínios dependentes em português europeu. Master's thesis, Universidade de Lisboa.
Bianchi, Valentina and Maria Cristina Figueiredo Silva. 1994. On some properties of agreement-object in Italian and Brazilian Portuguese. In *Issues and theory in Romance linguistics – Selected papers from the LSRL XXIII*, ed. by Michael Mazzola, 181–197. Washington, DC: Georgetown University Press.
Biberauer, Theresa and Sonia Cyrino. 2009. Negative developments in Afrikaans and Brazilian Portuguese. Paper delivered at the 19th Colloquium on Generative Grammar. University of the Basque Country, 2009.
Boeckx, Cedric, Norbert Hornstein, and Jairo Nunes. 2010. *Control as movement*. Cambridge: Cambridge University Press.
Bolrinha, Márcia. 2017. Clivada de *ser* e estrutura enfática com *mas ser*: Uma mesma estrutura ou estruturas diferentes? Master's thesis, Universidade Nova de Lisboa.
Bonet, Eulàlia. 1991. Morphology after syntax: Pronominal clitics in Romance. Doctoral dissertation, Massachusetts Institute of Technology.
Brito, Ana Maria. 1991a. *A sintaxe das orações relativas em português*. Oporto: INIC.
Brito, Ana Maria. 1991b. Ligação, co-referência e o princípio evitar pronome. In *Homenagem a Óscar Lopes*, ed. by Ana Maria Brito, 101–121. Lisbon: Associação Portuguesa de Linguística.
Brito, Ana Maria. 2007. European Portuguese possessives and the structure of DP. *Cuadernos de Lingüística* 14: 27–50.
Britto, Helena. 1994. Reduzidas gerundivas: Teoria do Caso e inversão verbo–sujeito Master's thesis, Universidade Estadual de Campinas.
Britto, Helena. 1998. Deslocamento à esquerda, resumptivo-sujeito, ordem SV e a codificação sintáctica de juízos categórico e tético no português do Brasil. Doctoral dissertation, Universidade Estadual de Campinas.
Britto, Helena. 2000. Syntactic codification of categorial and thetic judgments in Brazilian Portuguese. In *Brazilian Portuguese and the null subject parameter*, ed. by Mary A. Kato and Esmeralda Negrão, 195–222. Madrid and Frankfurt am Main: Iberoamericana/Vervuert.
Brocardo, Maria Teresa and Célia Lopes. 2016. Main morphosyntactic changes and grammaticalization processes. In *Handbook of Portuguese linguistics*, ed. by Leo Wetzels, João Costa, and Sergio Menuzzi, 471–486. Malden: Wiley Blackwell.
Buthers, Christina and Fábio Duarte. 2012. Português brasileiro: Uma língua de sujeito nulo ou de sujeito obrigatório? *Diacrítica* 26: 65–89.
Calindro, Ana. 2015. Introduzindo argumentos: Uma proposta para as sentenças ditransitivas do português brasileiro. Doctoral dissertation, Universidade de São Paulo.

Calindro, Ana. 2020. Ditransitive constructions: What sets Brazilian Portuguese apart from other Romance languages? In *Dative constructions in Romance and beyond*, ed. by Anna Pineda and Jaume Mateu, 75–95. Berlin: Language Science Press.
Camacho, José. 2013. *Null subjects*. Cambridge: Cambridge University Press.
Camacho, José. 2016. The null subject parameter revisited: The evolution from null subject Spanish and Portuguese to Dominican Spanish and Brazilian Portuguese. In *The morphosyntax of Portuguese and Spanish in Latin America*, ed. by Mary A. Kato and Francisco Ordóñez, 27–48. Oxford: Oxford University Press.
Câmara Jr., Joaquim Mattoso. 1970. *Estrutura da língua portuguesa*. Petrópolis: Vozes.
Cançado, Márcia. 1995. Verbos psicológicos: A relevância dos papéis temáticos vistos sob a ótica de uma semântica representacional. Doctoral dissertation, Universidade Estadual de Campinas.
Cançado, Márcia. 1997. Verbos psicológicos no português brasileiro e a análise inacusativa de Belletti & Rizzi: Indícios para uma proposta semântica. *D.E.L.T.A.* 13: 119–139.
Cançado, Márcia. 2006. O quantificador *tudo* no PB. *Revista Letras* 70: 157–182.
Cançado, Márcia. 2010. Verbal alternations in Brazilian Portuguese. *Studies in Hispanic and Lusophonic Linguistics* 3: 77–111.
Cançado, Márcia, Luísa Godoy, and Luana Amaral. 2013. *Catálogo de verbos do português brasileiro: Classificação verbal segundo a decomposição de predicados*, vol. 1: *Verbos de mudança*. Belo Horizonte: Editora da UFMG.
Cançado, Márcia and Anabela Gonçalves. 2016. Lexical semantics: Verb classes and alternations. In *Handbook of Portuguese linguistics*, ed. by Leo Wetzels, João Costa, and Sergio Menuzzi, 374–391. Malden: Wiley Blackwell.
Cançado, Márcia and Esmeralda Negrão. 2010. Two possessor raising constructions in Brazilian Portuguese. Paper presented at VIII Workshop on Formal Linguistics, Universidade de São Paulo, 8/6–7/2010.
Cardinaletti, Anna and Michal Starke. 1999. The typology of structural deficiency: On the three grammatical classes. In *Clitics in the languages of Europe*, ed. by Henk van Riemsdijk, 145–234. Berlin: De Gruyter Mouton.
Cardoso, Adriana. 2010. Variation and change in the syntax of relative clauses. Doctoral dissertation, Universidade de Lisboa.
Cardoso, Adriana. 2016. *Portuguese relative clauses in synchrony and diachrony*. Oxford: Oxford University Press.
Cardoso, Adriana and Nélia Alexandre. 2013. Relativas clivadas em variedades não *standard* do PE. In *XXVIII Encontro Nacional da Associação Portuguesa de Linguística – Textos selecionados*, ed. by Maria de Fátima da Silva, Isabel Falé, and Sandra Pereira, 205–227. Braga: Associação Portuguesa de Linguística.
Cardoso, Adriana, Ernestina Carrilho, and Sandra Pereira. 2011. On verbal agreement variation in European Portuguese: Syntactic conditions for the 3SG/3PL alternation. *Diacrítica* 25: 135–158.
Cardoso, Daisy. 2006. O imperativo gramatical no português do Brasil. *Revista de Estudos da Linguagem* 14: 317–340.
Carneiro, Zenaide. 2005. Cartas da Bahia: Um estudo linguístico-filológico. Doctoral dissertation, Universidade Estadual de Campinas.
Carneiro, Zenaide and Charlotte Galves. 2010. Variação e gramática: Colocação de clíticos na história do português brasileiro. *Revista de Estudos da Linguagem* 18: 7–38.

Carrilho, Ernestina. 2003. Construções de expletivo visível em português europeu (não-padrão). In *Gramática e léxico em sincronia e diacronia – Um contributo da linguística portuguesa*, ed. by Alexandre Veiga, 29–38. Santiago de Compostela: Universidade de Santiago de Compostela.

Carrilho, Ernestina. 2005. Expletive *ele* in European Portuguese dialects. Doctoral dissertation, Universidade de Lisboa.

Carrilho, Ernestina. 2008. Beyond doubling: Overt expletives in European Portuguese dialects. In *Syntax and semantics*, vol. 36: *Microvariation in syntactic doubling*, ed. by Sjef Barbiers, Olaf Koeneman, Marika Lekakou, and Margreet van der Ham, 301–323. Bingly: Emerald.

Carrilho, Ernestina. 2009. Sobre o expletivo *ele* em português europeu. *Estudos de Linguística Galega* 1: 7–26.

Carrilho, Ernestina and Sandra Pereira. 2009. On the areal distribution of non-standard syntactic constructions in European Portuguese. Paper presented at the Congress of Dialectology and Geolinguistics, University of Maribor, 11/14–18/2009.

Carvalho, Danniel. 2018. O traço de gênero na morfossintaxe do português. *D.E.L.T.A.* 34: 635–660.

Carvalho, Janayna. 2016. A morfossintaxe do português brasileiro e sua estrutura argumental: Uma investigação sobre anticausativas, médias, impessoais e a alternância agentiva. Doctoral dissertation, Universidade de São Paulo.

Carvalho, Janayna. 2018. Diferentes tipos de sujeito nulo no português brasileiro. *ReVEL* 16: 78–107.

Carvalho, Janayna. 2019. Teasing apart 3rd person null subjects in Brazilian Portuguese. In *Romance languages and linguistic theory 2016. Selected papers from "Going Romance" 30 Frankfurt*, ed. by Ingo Feldhausen, Martin Elsig, Imme Kuchenbrandt, and Mareike Neuhaus, 237–254. Amsterdam/Philadelphia: John Benjamins.

Casteleiro, João Malaca. 1979. Sintaxe e semântica das construções enfáticas com "é que". *Boletim de Filologia* 25: 97–166.

Castro, Ana. 2006. On possessives in Portuguese. Doctoral dissertation, Universidade Nova de Lisboa/Université Paris 8.

Castro, Ivo. 2006. *Introdução à história do português*. Lisbon: Edições Colibri.

Cavalcante, Rerisson. 2004. Construções negativas no português falado em Salvador. *Hyperion* 7.

Cavalcante, Rerisson. 2007. A negação pós-verbal no português brasileiro: Análise descritiva e teórica dos dialetos rurais de afro-descendentes. Master's thesis, Universidade Federal da Bahia.

Cavalcante, Rerisson. 2009. Complementos dativos sem preposição no dialeto mineiro. *ReVEL* 7: 1–19.

Cavalcante, Rerisson. 2012. Negação anafórica no português brasileiro: Negação sentencial, negação enfática e negação de constituinte. Doctoral dissertation, Universidade de São Paulo.

Cavalcante, Sílvia. 2006. O uso de *se* com infinitivo na história do português: Do português clássico ao português europeu e brasileiro modernos. Doctoral dissertation, Universidade Estadual de Campinas.

Cerqueira, Vicente. 1993. A forma genitiva *dele* e a categoria de concordância (AGR) no português brasileiro. In *Português brasileiro: Uma viagem*

diacrônica, ed. by Ian Roberts and Mary A. Kato, 129–161. Campinas: Editora da UNICAMP.
Cerqueira, Vicente. 1996. A sintaxe do possessivo no português brasileiro. Doctoral Dissertation, Universidade Estadual de Campinas.
Chao, Wynn. 1983. The interpretation of null Subjects: Brazilian Portuguese. *Cahiers Linguistiques d'Ottawa* 11: 69–74.
Chomsky, Noam. 1973. Conditions on transformations. In *A Festschrift for Morris Halle*, ed. by Stephen R. Anderson and Paul Kiparsky, 232–286. New York: Holt, Rinehart, and Winston.
Chomsky, Noam. 1981. *Lectures on government and binding*. Dordrecht: Foris.
Chomsky, Noam. 1986. *Knowledge of language: Its nature, origin and use*. New York: Praeger.
Chomsky, Noam. 2000. Minimalist inquiries: The framework. In *Step by step: Essays on minimalist syntax in honor of Howard Lasnik*, ed. by Roger Martin, David Michaels, and Juan Uriagereka, 89–155. Cambridge, Mass.: MIT Press.
Chomsky, Noam. 2001. Derivation by phase. In *Ken Hale: A life in language*, ed. by Michael Kenstowicz, 1–52. Cambridge, Mass.: MIT Press.
Chomsky, Noam and Howard Lasnik. 1993. The theory of principles and parameters. In *Syntax: An international handbook of contemporary research*, ed. by Joachim Jacobs, Arnim von Stechow, Wolfgang Sternefeld, and Theo Vennemann, 506–569. Berlin/New York: Walter de Gruyter.
Cinque, Guglielmo. 1988. On *si* constructions and the theory of arb. *Linguistic Inquiry* 19: 521–582.
Cintra, Luís Lindley. 1971. Nova proposta de classificação dos dialectos galego-portugueses. *Boletim de Filologia* 22: 81–116.
Cintra, Luís Lindley. 1972. *Sobre "formas de tratamento" na língua portuguesa*. Lisbon: Livros Horizonte.
Ciríaco, Larissa and Márcia Cançado. 2006. Inacusatividade e inergatividade no PB. *Cadernos de Estudos Linguísticos* 46: 207–225.
Coelho, Claudia, Jairo Nunes, and Leticia Santos. 2018. On the movement analysis of null subjects in Brazilian Portuguese: Experimental results from extraction of embedded subjects. *Isogloss* 4: 85–112.
Coelho, Izete. 2000. A ordem VDP em construções monoargumentais: Uma restrição sintático-semântica. Doctoral dissertation, Universidade Federal de Santa Catarina.
Coelho, Izete and Marco Antonio Martins. 2012. Padrões de inversão do sujeito na escrita brasileira do século 19: Evidências empíricas para a hipótese de competição de gramáticas. *Alfa* 56: 11–28.
Colaço, Madalena. 2005. Configurações de coordenação aditiva: Tipologia, concordância e extracção. Doctoral dissertation, Universidade de Lisboa.
Colaço, Madalena. 2016. Especificidades das estruturas de coordenação: Padrões de concordância. In *Manual de linguística portuguesa*, ed. by Ana Maria Martins and Ernestina Carrilho, 481–522. Berlin/Boston: De Gruyter.
Corrêa, Vilma. 1991. O objeto direto nulo no português do Brasil. Master's thesis, Universidade Estadual de Campinas.
Costa, Doris. 2000. Os verbos psicológicos e a queda da preposição *a* no português do Brasil. Master's thesis, Universidade Federal de Santa Catarina.

Costa, Igor, Marina Augusto, and Erica Rodrigues. 2014. Verbos meteorológicos flexionados no plural e a hipótese da inacusatividade biargumental: Explorando a sintaxe do português brasileiro. *Veredas* 18: 257–280.
Costa, João. 1998. *Word order variation: A constraint-based approach*. The Hague: Holland Academic Graphics.
Costa, João. 2001. Postverbal subjects and agreement in unaccusative contexts in European Portuguese. *The Linguistic Review* 18: 1–17.
Costa, João. 2003. Null vs overt Spec,TP in European Portuguese. In *Romance languages and linguistic theory 2001*, ed. by Josep Quer, Jan Schroten, Mauro Scorretti, Petra Sleeman, and Els Verheugd-Daatzelaar, 31–47. Amsterdam/Philadelphia: John Benjamins.
Costa, João. 2004. *Subject positions and interfaces: The case of European Portuguese*. Berlin/New York: Mouton de Gruyter.
Costa, João and Inês Duarte. 2001. Minimizando a estrutura: Uma análise unificada das construções de clivagem em português. In *Actas do XVI Encontro Nacional da Associação Portuguesa de Linguística*, ed. by Clara Correia and Anabela Gonçalves, 627–638. Lisbon: APL/Colibri.
Costa, João and Inês Duarte. 2003. Objectos nulos em debate. In *Razões e emoção: Miscelânea de estudos em homenagem a Maria Helena Mira Mateus*, ed. by Ivo Castro and Inês Duarte, 249–260. Lisbon: INCM.
Costa, João and Inês Duarte. 2013. Objeto nulo. In *Gramática do português*, ed. by Eduardo Paiva Raposo, Maria Fernanda Bacelar do Nascimento, Maria Antónia Mota, Luísa Segura, and Amália Mendes, vol. 2, 2339–2348. Lisbon: Fundação Calouste Gulbenkian.
Costa, João and Maria Cristina Figueiredo Silva. 2006a. Nominal and verbal agreement in Portuguese: An argument for Distributed Morphology. In *Studies on agreement*, ed. by João Costa and Maria Cristina Figueiredo Silva, 25–46. Amsterdam/Philadelphia: John Benjamins.
Costa, João and Maria Cristina Figueiredo Silva. 2006b. On the (in)dependence relations between syntax and pragmatics. In *The architecture of focus*, ed. by Valéria Molnar and Susanne Winkler, 83–104. Berlin: Mouton de Gruyter.
Costa, João and Maria Lobo. 2009. Estruturas clivadas: Evidência dos dados do português europeu não-standard. *Anais do Congresso Internacional da ABRALIN – João Pessoa 2009*: 3800–3806.
Costa, João and Ana Maria Martins. 2003. Clitic placement across grammar components. Paper presented at "Going Romance" 2003, Nijmegen University, 11/20–22/2003.
Costa, João and Ana Maria Martins. 2010. Middle scrambling with deictic locatives in European Portuguese. In *Romance Languages and Linguistic Theory* 2, ed. by Reineke Bok-Bennema, Brigitte Kampers-Manhe, and Bart Hollebrandse, 59–76. Amsterdam/Philadelphia: John Benjamins.
Costa, João and Ana Maria Martins. 2011. On focus movement in European Portuguese. *Probus* 23: 217–245.
Costa, João, Ana Maria Martins, and Fernanda Pratas. 2012. VP ellipsis: New evidence from Capeverdean. In *Romance languages and linguistic theory 2010 – Selected papers from "Going Romance" Leiden 2010*, ed. by Irene Franco, Sara Lusini and Andrés Saab, 155–176. Amsterdam/Philadelphia: John Benjamins.

Costa, João, Denilda Moura, and Sandra Pereira. 2001. Concordância com *a gente*: Um problema para a teoria de verificação de traços. In *Actas do XVI Encontro Nacional da Associação Portuguesa de Linguística*, ed. by Clara Correia and Anabela Gonçalves, 639–655. Lisbon: Associação Portuguesa de Linguística.

Costa, João and Sandra Pereira. 2005. Phases and autonomous features: A case of mixed agreement. In *Working Papers in Linguistics 49 – Perspectives on phases*, ed. by Martha McGinnis and Norvin Richards, 115–124. Cambridge, Mass.: MIT Press.

Costa, João and Sandra Pereira. 2012. *A gente*: revisitando o estatuto pronominal e a concordância. In *Por amor à linguística: Miscelânea de estudos linguísticos dedicados à Maria Denilda Moura*, ed. by Adeilson Sedrins, Ataliba de Castilho, Marcelo Sibaldo, and Rafael de Lima, 101–122. Alagoas: Editora da UFAL.

Costa, João and Sandra Pereira. 2013. *A gente*: Pronominal status and agreement revisited. *Linguistic Review* 30:161–184.

Creus, Susana and Sérgio Menuzzi. 2004. Sobre o papel do gênero na alternância entre objetos nulos e pronomes plenos em português brasileiro. *Revista da ABRALIN* 3: 149–176.

Cyrino, Sonia. 1993. Observações sobre a mudança diacrônica no português do Brasil: Objeto nulo e clíticos. In *Português brasileiro: Uma viagem diacrônica*, ed. by Ian Roberts and Mary A. Kato, 163–184. Campinas: Editora da UNICAMP.

Cyrino, Sonia. 1997. *O objeto nulo no português do Brasil: Um estudo sintático-diacrônico*. Londrina: Editora UEL.

Cyrino, Sonia. 2008. The loss of clitic climbing in Brazilian Portuguese revisited. Paper presented at the 10th Diachronic Generative Syntax Conference – DiGS X, Cornell University, 9/7–9/2008.

Cyrino, Sonia. 2016. The null object in Romania Nova. In *The morphosyntax of Portuguese and Spanish in Latin America*, ed. by Mary A. Kato and Francisco Ordóñez, 177–203. Oxford: Oxford University Press.

Cyrino, Sonia. 2019. O objeto nulo do português brasileiro: Sincronia e diacronia. In *Português brasileiro: Uma segunda viagem diacrônica*, ed. by Charlotte Galves, Mary A. Kato, and Ian Roberts, 173–200. Campinas: Editora da UNICAMP.

Cyrino, Sonia. 2020. Objetos nulos em português brasileiro. *Cuadernos de la ALFAL* 12: 387–410.

Cyrino, Sonia, Maria Eugênia Duarte, and Mary A. Kato. 2000. Visible subjects and invisible clitics in Brazilian Portuguese. In *Brazilian Portuguese and the null subject parameter*, ed. by Mary A. Kato and Esmeralda Negrão, 55–74. Madrid and Frankfurt am Main: Iberoamericana/Vervuert.

Cyrino, Sonia and M. Teresa Espinal. 2015. Bare nominals in Brazilian Portuguese: More on the DP/NP analysis. *Natural Language and Linguistic Theory* 33: 471–521.

Cyrino, Sonia and Ruth Lopes. 2016. Null objects are ellipsis in Brazilian Portuguese. *The Linguistic Review* 33: 483–502.

Cyrino, Sonia and Gabriela Matos. 2002. VP ellipsis in European and Brazilian Portuguese: A comparative analysis. *Journal of Portuguese Linguistics* 1: 177–214.

Cyrino, Sonia and Gabriela Matos. 2005. Local licensers and recovering in VP ellipsis. *Journal of Portuguese Linguistics* 4: 79–112.

Cyrino, Sonia and Gabriela Matos. 2016. Null objects and VP ellipsis in European and Brazilian Portuguese. In *Handbook of Portuguese linguistics*, ed. by Leo Wetzels, João Costa, and Sergio Menuzzi, 294–316. Malden: Wiley Blackwell.

d'Albuquerque, Alair. 1984. A perda dos clíticos num dialeto mineiro. *Tempo Brasileiro* 78/79.

Dias Martins, Maria José. 1954. Etnografia, linguagem e folclore de uma pequena região da Beira Baixa (Póvoa de Atalaia, Alcongosta, Tinalhas e Sobral do Campo). "Licenciatura" thesis, Universidade de Lisboa.

Dimitrova, Margarita. 2020. On the syntax of yes-no questions in Bulgarian and Portuguese. Doctoral dissertation, Universidade de Lisboa.

Dobrovie-Sorin, Carmen. 2010. Number neutral amounts and pluralities in Brazilian Portuguese. *Journal of Portuguese Linguistics* 9: 53–74.

Dobrovie-Sorin, Carmen and Roberta Pires de Oliveira. 2008. Reference to kinds in Brazilian Portuguese: Definite singulars *vs.* bare singulars. In *Proceedings of SuB12*, ed. by Atle Grønn, 107–121. Oslo: ILOS.

Duarte, Inês. 1987. A construção de topicalização na gramática do português. Doctoral dissertation, Universidade de Lisboa.

Duarte, Inês. 1996. A topicalização em português europeu: Uma análise comparativa. In *Actas do Congresso Internacional sobre o Português (Lisboa 1994)*, ed. by Inês Duarte and Isabel Leiria, 327–360. Lisbon: APL/Colibri.

Duarte, Inês. 1997. Ordem de palavras: Sintaxe e estrutura discursiva. In *Sentido que a vida faz: Estudos para Óscar Lopes*, ed. by Ana Maria Brito, Fátima Oliveira, Isabel de Lima, and Rosa Martelo, 581–592. Oporto: Campo das Letras.

Duarte, Inês. 2003a. Frases com tópicos marcados. In *Gramática da língua portuguesa*, ed. by Maria Helena Mira Mateus, Ana Maria Brito, Inês Duarte, Isabel Faria, Sónia Frota, Gabriela Matos, Fátima Oliveira, Marina Vigário, and Alina Villalva, 489–506. Lisbon: Caminho.

Duarte, Inês. 2003b. Padrões de colocação dos pronomes clíticos. In *Gramática da língua portuguesa*, ed. by Maria Helena Mira Mateus, Ana Maria Brito, Inês Duarte, Isabel Faria, Sónia Frota, Gabriela Matos, Fátima Oliveira, Marina Vigário, and Alina Villalva, 847–867. Lisbon: Caminho.

Duarte, Inês. 2013a. Construções ativas, passivas, incoativas e médias. In *Gramática do português*, ed. by Eduardo Paiva Raposo, Maria Fernanda Bacelar do Nascimento, Maria Antónia Mota, Luísa Segura, and Amália Mendes, vol. 1, 427–458. Lisbon: Fundação Calouste Gulbenkian.

Duarte, Inês. 2013b. Construções de topicalização. In *Gramática do português*, ed. by Eduardo Paiva Raposo, Maria Fernanda Bacelar do Nascimento, Maria Antónia Mota, Luísa Segura, and Amália Mendes, vol. 1, 401–426. Lisbon: Fundação Calouste Gulbenkian.

Duarte, Inês, Anabela Gonçalves, and Matilde Miguel. 2005. Propriedades de C em frases completivas. In *Actas do XX Encontro Nacional da Associação Portuguesa de Linguística*, ed. by Inês Duarte and Isabel Leiria, 549–562. Lisbon: Associação Portuguesa de Linguística.

Duarte, Inês and Gabriela Matos. 2000. Romance clitics and the minimalist program. In *Portuguese syntax: New comparative studies*, ed. by João Costa, 116–142. Oxford/New York: Oxford University Press.

Duarte, Inês, Ana Lúcia Santos, and Anabela Gonçalves. 2016. O Infinitivo flexionado na gramática do adulto e na aquisição de L1. In *Manual de linguística portuguesa*, ed. by Ana Maria Martins and Ernestina Carrilho, 451–480. Berlin/Boston: De Gruyter.
Duarte, Maria Eugênia. 1986. Variação e sintaxe: Clítico acusativo, pronome lexical e categoria vazia no português do Brasil. Master's thesis, Pontifícia Universidade Católica de São Paulo.
Duarte, Maria Eugênia. 1989. Clítico acusativo, pronome lexical e categoria vazia no português do Brasil. In *Fotografias sociolinguísticas*, ed. by Fernando Tarallo, 19–34. Campinas: Pontes/Editora da UNICAMP.
Duarte, Maria Eugênia. 1992. A perda da ordem V(erbo) S(ujeito) em interrogativas qu- no português do Brasil. *D.E.L.T.A.* 8: 37–52.
Duarte, Maria Eugênia. 1993. Do pronome nulo ao pronome pleno: A trajetória do sujeito no português do Brasil. In *Português brasileiro: Uma viagem diacrônica*, ed. by Ian Roberts and Mary A. Kato, 107–128. Campinas: Editora da UNICAMP.
Duarte, Maria Eugênia. 1995. A perda do princípio "Evite Pronome" no português brasileiro. Doctoral dissertation, Universidade Estadual de Campinas.
Duarte, Maria Eugênia. 1998. Left-dislocated subjects and parametric change in Brazilian Portuguese. In *Proceedings of the 16th International Congress of Linguists*, ed. by Bernard Caron, 219. CD-Rom. Amsterdam: Elsevier.
Duarte, Maria Eugênia. 2000. The loss of the Avoid Pronoun principle in Brazilian Portuguese. In *Brazilian Portuguese and the null subject parameter*, ed. by Mary A. Kato and Esmeralda Negrão, 17–36. Madrid and Frankfurt am Main: Iberoamericana/Vervuert.
Duarte, Maria Eugênia. 2004. On the embedding of a syntactic change. In *Language variation in Europe: Papers from the second international conference on language variation in Europe*, ICLaVE 2, ed. by Britt-Louise Gunnarsson, Lena Bergström, Gerd Ekrund, Staffan Fridell, 145–155. Uppsala: Universitetstryckeriet.
Duarte, Maria Eugênia. 2007. Sobre outros frutos de um projeto herético: O sujeito expletivo e as construções de alçamento. In *Descrição, aquisição e história do português brasileiro*, ed. by Ataliba de Castilho, Maria Aparecida Torres Morais, Ruth Lopes, and Sonia Cyrino, 35–48. Campinas: Pontes/FAPESP.
Duarte, Maria Eugênia and Mary A. Kato. 2002. A diachronic analysis of Brazilian Portuguese *wh*-questions. *Santa Barbara Portuguese Studies* 6: 326–339.
Duarte, Maria Eugênia and Mary A. Kato. 2008. Mudança paramétrica e orientação para o discurso. Paper presented at XXIV Encontro Nacional da Associação Portuguesa de Linguística, Universidade do Minho, 9/20–22/2008.
Duguine, Maia. 2013. Null arguments and linguistic variation: A minimalist analysis of pro-drop. Doctoral dissertation, University of the Basque Country/University of Nantes.
Eliseu, André. 1984. Verbos ergativos do português: Descrição e análise. "Trabalho de síntese para provas de aptidão pedagógica e capacidade científica," MS, Universidade de Lisboa.
Emonds, Joseph E. 1976. *A transformational approach to English syntax: Root, structure-preserving, and local transformations*. New York: Academic Press.

Estrela, Antónia. 2006. A Teoria da Ligação: Dados do português europeu. Master's thesis, Universidade Nova de Lisboa.
Faraco, Carlos. 1982. The imperative sentence in Portuguese: A semantic and historical discussion. Doctoral dissertation, University of Salford.
Faraco, Carlos. 1986. Considerações sobre a sentença imperativa no português do Brasil. *D.E.L.T.A.* 2: 1–15.
Faraco, Carlos. 1996. O tratamento *você* em português: Uma abordagem histórica. *Fragmenta* 13: 51–82.
Farrell, Patrick. 1990. Null objects in Brazilian Portuguese. *Natural Language and Linguistic Theory* 8: 325–346.
Ferreira, Marcelo. 2000. Argumentos nulos em português brasileiro. Master's thesis, Universidade Estadual de Campinas.
Ferreira, Marcelo. 2009. Null subjects and finite control in Brazilian Portuguese. In *Minimalist essays on Brazilian Portuguese syntax*, ed. by Jairo Nunes, 17–49. Amsterdam/Philadelphia: John Benjamins.
Ferreira, Marcelo. 2010. The morpho-semantics of number in Brazilian Portuguese bare singulars. *Journal of Portuguese Linguistics* 9: 95–116.
Fiéis, Alexandra and Maria Lobo. 2010. Aspectos da sintaxe das orações gerundivas no português medieval e no português europeu contemporâneo. In *XXV Encontro Nacional da Associação Portuguesa de Linguística – Textos Seleccionados*, ed. by Ana Maria Brito, Fátima Silva, João Veloso, and Alexandra Fiéis, 419–434. Lisbon: Associação Portuguesa de Linguística.
Figueiredo Silva, Maria Cristina. 1990. Les clitiques en portugais du Brésil: Notes pur une étude. MS, Université de Genève.
Figueiredo Silva, Maria Cristina. 1996. *A posição do sujeito no português brasileiro: Frases finitas e infinitivas*. Campinas: Editora da UNICAMP.
Figueiredo Silva, Maria Cristina. 2007. A perda do marcador dativo e algumas de suas consequências. In *Descrição, aquisição e história do português brasileiro*, ed. by Ataliba de Castilho, Maria Aparecida Torres Morais, Ruth Lopes, and Sonia Cyrino, 85–110. Campinas: Pontes/FAPESP.
Figueiredo Silva, Maria Cristina and Elaine Grolla. 2016. Some syntactic and pragmatic aspects of WH-in-situ in Brazilian Portuguese. In *The morphosyntax of Portuguese and Spanish in Latin America*, ed. by Mary A. Kato and Francisco Ordóñez, 259–285. Oxford: Oxford University Press.
Floripi, Simone. 2003. Argumentos nulos dentro de DPs em português brasileiro. Master's thesis, Universidade Estadual de Campinas.
Floripi, Simone and Jairo Nunes. 2009. Movement and resumption in null possessor constructions in Brazilian Portuguese. In *Minimalist essays on Brazilian Portuguese syntax*, ed. by Jairo Nunes, 51–68. Amsterdam/Philadelphia: John Benjamins.
Fonseca, Hely. 2011. Marcador negativo final no português brasileiro. *Cadernos de Estudos Linguísticos* 46: 5–20.
Franchi, Carlos, Esmeralda Negrão, and Evani Viotti. 1998. Sobre a gramática das orações impessoais com *ter/haver*. *D.E.L.T.A.* 14: 105–131.
Frota, Sónia and João António de Moraes. 2016. Intonation in European and Brazilian Portuguese. In *Handbook of Portuguese linguistics*, ed. by Leo Wetzels, João Costa and Sérgio Menuzzi, 141–166. Malden: Wiley Blackwell.

Galves, Charlotte. 1986a. A interpretação "reflexiva" do pronome no português brasileiro. *D.E.L.T.A.* 2: 249–264.
Galves, Charlotte. 1986b. *Aluga-(se) casas: Um problema de sintaxe portuguesa na teoria de regência e vinculação*. Campinas: Preedição 2.
Galves, Charlotte. 1987. A sintaxe do português brasileiro. *Ensaios de Linguística* 13: 31–50.
Galves, Charlotte. 1989. O objeto nulo no português brasileiro: Percurso de uma pesquisa. *Cadernos de Estudos Lingüísticos* 17: 65–90.
Galves, Charlotte. 1993. O enfraquecimento da concordância no português brasileiro. In *Português brasileiro: Uma viagem diacrônica*, ed. by Ian Roberts and Mary A. Kato, 387–408. Campinas: Editora da UNICAMP.
Galves, Charlotte. 1997. La syntaxe pronominale du portugais brésilien et la typologie des pronoms. In *Les pronoms*, ed. by Anne Zribi-Hertz, 11–34. Paris: Presses Universitaires de Vincennes.
Galves, Charlotte. 1998. Tópicos, sujeitos, pronomes e concordância no português brasileiro. *Cadernos de Estudos Lingüísticos* 34: 7–21.
Galves, Charlotte. 2001. *Ensaios sobre as gramáticas do português*. Campinas: Editora da UNICAMP.
Galves, Charlotte, Ilza Ribeiro, and Maria Aparecida Torres Morais. 2005. Syntax and morphology in the placement of clitics in European and Brazilian Portuguese. *Journal of Portuguese Linguistics* 4: 143–177.
Gonçalves, Anabela. 1999. Predicados verbais complexos em contextos de infinitivo não preposicionado em português europeu. Doctoral dissertation, Universidade de Lisboa.
Gonçalves, Anabela, Ernestina Carrilho, and Sandra Pereira. 2016. Predicados complexos numa perspetiva comparativa. In *Manual de linguística portuguesa*, ed. by Ana Maria Martins and Ernestina Carrilho, 523–557. Berlin/Boston: De Gruyter.
Gonçalves, Anabela and Inês Duarte. 2001. Construções causativas em português europeu e em português brasileiro. In *Actas do XVI Encontro Nacional da Associação Portuguesa de Linguística*, ed. by Clara Correia and Anabela Gonçalves, 657–671. Lisbon: Associação Portuguesa de Linguística.
Gonçalves, Anabela and Matilde Miguel. 2019. Porque é que os relógios não quebram os ponteiros em português europeu? In *Estudos linguísticos e filológicos oferecidos a Ivo Castro*, ed. by Ernestina Carrilho, Ana Maria Martins, Sandra Pereira, and João Paulo Silvestre, 713–738. Lisbon: Centro de Linguística da Universidade de Lisboa.
Gonçalves, Anabela, Ana Lúcia Santos, and Inês Duarte. 2014. (Pseudo-)inflected infinitives and control as Agree. In *Romance languages and linguistic theory 2012*, ed. by Karen Lahousse and Stefania Marzo, 161–180. Amsterdam/Philadelphia: John Benjamins.
Gonçalves, Fernanda. 2004. Riqueza morfológica e aquisição da sintaxe em português europeu e brasileiro. Doctoral dissertation, Universidade de Évora.
Gonçalves, Perpétua. 2012. Lusofonia em Moçambique com ou sem glotofagia? Paper presented at the II Congresso Internacional de Linguística Histórica. Universidade de São Paulo, 2/7–10/2012.
González Rodríguez, Raquel. 2008. Exclamative wh-phrases as positive polarity items. *Catalan Working Papers in Linguistics* 7: 91–116.

Guesser, Simone. 2011. La sintassi delle frasi *cleft* in portoghese brasiliano. Doctoral dissertation, Università di Siena.
Guilherme, Ana Rita and Víctor Lara Bermejo. 2015. Quão cortês é *você*? O pronome de tratamento *você* em Português Europeu. *Labor Histórico* 1: 167–180.
Guimarães, Maximiliano. 1998. Repensando a interface fonologia–sintaxe a partir do Axioma de Correspondência Linear. Master's thesis, Universidade Estadual de Campinas.
Guy, Gregory. 1981. Linguistic variation in Brazilian Portuguese: Aspects of the phonology, syntax, and language history. Dissertation, University of Pennsylvania.
Haegeman, Liliane. 1990. Non-overt subjects in diary contexts. In *Grammar in Progress, GLOW essays for Henk van Riemsdijk*, ed. by Joan Mascaro and Marina Nespor, 167–174. Dordrecht: Foris.
Haegeman, Liliane. 2013. The syntax of registers: Diary subject omission and the privilege of the root. *Lingua* 130: 88–110.
Hagemeijer, Tjerk. 2016. O português em contacto em África. In *Manual de linguística portuguesa*, ed. by Ana Maria Martins and Ernestina Carrilho, 43–67. Berlin/Boston: De Gruyter.
Hagemeijer, Tjerk and Ana Lúcia Santos. 2004. Elementos polares na periferia direita. In *Actas do XIX Encontro Nacional da Associação Portuguesa de Linguística*, ed. by Clara Correia and Anabela Gonçalves, 465–476. Lisbon: Associação Portuguesa de Linguística.
Halle, Morris and Alec Marantz. 1993. Distributed morphology and the pieces of inflection. In *The view from building 20*, ed. by Kenneth Hale and S. Jay Keyser, 111–176. Cambridge, Mass.: MIT Press.
Holmberg, Anders, Aarti Nayudu, and Michelle Sheehan. 2009. Three partial null-subject languages: A comparison of Brazilian Portuguese, Finnish and Marathi. *Studia Linguistica* 63: 59–97.
Hornstein, Norbert. 1999. Movement and control. *Linguistic Inquiry* 30: 69–96.
Hornstein, Norbert, Ana Maria Martins, and Jairo Nunes. 2006. Infinitival complements of perception and causative verbs: A case study on agreement and intervention effects in English and European Portuguese. *University of Maryland Working Papers in Linguistics* 14: 81–110.
Hornstein, Norbert, Ana Maria Martins, and Jairo Nunes. 2008. Perception and causative structures in English and European Portuguese: ɸ-feature agreement and the distribution of bare and prepositional infinitivals. *Syntax* 11: 198–222.
Houaiss, Antônio and Mauro de Salles Villar. 2001. *Dicionário Houaiss da língua portuguesa*. Rio de Janeiro: Objetiva.
Huang, C.-T. James. 1984. On the distribution and reference of empty pronouns. *Linguistic Inquiry* 15: 531–574.
Kato, Mary A. 1989. Tópico e sujeito: Duas categorias em sintaxe? *Cadernos de Estudos Lingüísticos* 17: 109–132.
Kato, Mary A. 1992. Variação sintática e estilo. *Cadernos de Estudos Lingüísticos* 20: 127–138.
Kato, Mary A. 1993a. Recontando a história das relativas. In *Português brasileiro: Uma viagem diacrônica*, ed. by Ian Roberts and Mary A. Kato, 223–261. Campinas: Editora da UNICAMP.

Kato, Mary A. 1993b. The distribution of pronouns and null elements in object position in Brazilian Portuguese. In *Linguistic Perspectives on Romance languages: Selected Papers from the XXI Linguistic Symposium of Romance Languages*, ed. by William Ashby, Marianne Mithun, and Giorgio Perissinotto, 225–235. Amsterdam/Philadelphia: John Benjamins.
Kato, Mary A. 1994. A theory of null objects and the development of a Brazilian child grammar. In *How tolerant is Universal Grammar*, ed. by Rosemarie Tracy and Elsa Lattey, 125–153. Tübingen: Niemeyer.
Kato, Mary A. 1999. Strong pronouns, weak pronominals and the null subject parameter. *Probus* 11: 1–37.
Kato, Mary A. 2000. The partial pro-drop nature and the restricted VS order in Brazilian Portuguese. In *Brazilian Portuguese and the null subject parameter*, ed. by Mary A. Kato and Esmeralda Negrão, 223–258. Madrid and Frankfurt am Main: Iberoamericana/Vervuert.
Kato, Mary A. 2002a. Pronomes fortes e fracos na sintaxe do português brasileiro. *Revista Portuguesa de Filologia* 24: 101–122.
Kato, Mary A. 2002b. The reanalysis of unaccusative constructions as existentials in Brazilian Portuguese. *Revista do GEL*, special issue: 157–186.
Kato, Mary A. 2003. Null objects, null resumptives and VP-ellipsis in European and Brazilian Portuguese. In *Romance languages and linguistic theory 2001*, ed. by Josep Quer, Jan Schroten, Mauro Scorretti, Petra Sleeman, and Els Verheugd-Daatzelaar, 131–154. Amsterdam/Philadelphia: John Benjamins.
Kato, Mary A. 2005. Gramática do letrado: Questões para a teoria gramatical. In *Ciências da linguagem: 30 anos de investigação e ensino*, ed. by Maria Aldina Marques, 131–145. Braga: Universidade do Minho/CEHUM.
Kato, Mary A. 2006. Comentários a respeito do artigo: "Gramática, competição e padrões de variação: casos com *ter/haver* e *de/em* no português brasileiro," de Juanito Avelar. *Revista de Estudos da Linguagem* 14: 145–149.
Kato, Mary A. 2007. Free and dependent small clauses in Brazilian Portuguese. *D.E.L.T.A.* 23: 85–111.
Kato, Mary A. 2009. Mudança de ordem e gramaticalização na evolução das estruturas de foco no português brasileiro. *Revista do GEL* 38: 375–385.
Kato, Mary A. 2010. Optional prepositions in Brazilian Portuguese. In *Romance linguistics 2008: Interactions in Romance*, ed. by Karlos Arregi, Zsuzsanna Fagyal, Silvina Montrul, and Annie Tremblay, 171–184. Amsterdam/Philadelphia: John Benjamins.
Kato, Mary A. 2012. Caso inerente, Caso "default" e ausência de preposições. In *Por amor à linguística: Miscelânea de estudos linguísticos dedicados à Maria Denilda Moura*, ed. by Adeilson Sedrins, Ataliba de Castilho, Marcelo Sibaldo, and Rafael de Lima, 86–99. Alagoas: Editora da UFAL.
Kato, Mary A. 2013. Deriving "wh-in-situ" through movement in Brazilian Portuguese. In *Information structure and agreement*, ed. by Victoria Camacho-Taboada, Ángel Jiménez-Fernández, Javier Martín-González, and Mariano Reyes-Tejedor, 175–191. Amsterdam/Philadelphia: John Benjamins.
Kato, Mary A. 2014. Focus and *wh*-questions in Brazilian Portuguese. In *Linguistic variation: Confronting fact and theory*, ed. by Nathalie Dion, Andrés Lapierre, and Rena Torres Cacoullos, 111–130. London: Routledge.

Kato, Mary A. 2016. Affirmative polar replies in Brazilian Portuguese. In *Romance linguistics 2013 – Selected papers from the 43rd Linguistic Symposium on Romance Languages (LSRL)*, ed. by Christina Tortora, Marcel den Dikken, and Ignacio Montoya, 195–212. Amsterdam/Philadelphia: John Benjamins.

Kato, Mary A. 2017. A variação no domínio dos clíticos no português brasileiro. *Revista da ALFAL* 33: 133–149.

Kato, Mary A. 2018. Morphological doublets in Brazilian Portuguese *wh*-constructions. In *Romance languages and linguistic theory 14: Selected papers from the 46th Linguistic Symposium on Romance Languages (LSRL)*, ed. by Lori Repetti and Francisco Ordóñez, 135–152. Amsterdam/Philadelphia: John Benjamins.

Kato, Mary A. 2019. As interrogativas-Q e as estruturas de foco na diacronia e na sincronia do PB. In *Português brasileiro: Uma segunda viagem diacrônica*, ed. by Charlotte Galves, Mary A. Kato, and Ian Roberts, 313–336. Campinas: Editora da UNICAMP.

Kato, Mary A. 2020a. *Wh*-questions in Brazilian Portuguese and Quebec French. In *Brazilian Portuguese, syntax and semantics, 20 years of Núcleo de Estudos Gramaticais*, ed. by Roberta Pires de Oliveira and Sandra Quarezemin, 135–150. Amsterdam/Philadelphia: John Benjamins.

Kato, Mary A. 2020b. Uma narrativa sincrônica das interrogativas-Q em português brasileiro. *Cuadernos de la ALFAL* 12: 126–144.

Kato, Mary A., Sonia Cyrino, and Vilma Corrêa. 2009. Brazilian Portuguese and the recovery of lost clitics through schooling. In *Minimalist inquiries into child and adult language acquisition: Case studies across Portuguese*, ed. by Acrisio Pires and Jason Rothman, 245–272. Berlin/New York: De Gruyter Mouton.

Kato, Mary A. and Maria Eugênia Duarte. 2018. A codificação dos juízos tético e categórico no português brasileiro. In *O apelo das árvores: Estudos em homenagem a Miriam Lemle*, ed. by Alessandro Medeiros and Andrew Nevins, 15–44. Campinas: Pontes.

Kato, Mary A. and Maria Eugenia Duarte. 2021. Parametric variation: The case of Brazilian Portuguese null subjects. In *Syntactic architecture and its consequences III: Inside syntax*, ed. by András Bárány, Theresa Biberauer, Jamie Douglas, and Sten Vikner, 357–398. Berlin: Language Science Press.

Kato, Mary A. and Ana Maria Martins. 2016. The main varieties of Portuguese: An overview on word order. In *Handbook of Portuguese linguistics*, ed. by Leo Wetzels, João Costa, and Sergio Menuzzi, 15–40. Malden: Wiley Blackwell.

Kato, Mary A. and Carlos Mioto. 2005. A multi-evidence study of European and Brazilian Portuguese *wh*-questions. In *Linguistic evidence: Empirical, theoretical, and computational perspectives*, ed. by Stephan Kepser and Marga Reis, 307–328. Berlin/New York: Mouton de Gruyter.

Kato, Mary A. and Carlos Mioto. 2011. Pseudo-clivadas e os efeitos de conectividade. In *Estudos formais das línguas naturais*, ed. by Rozana Naves and Heloisa Salles, 51–66. Brasília: Cânone.

Kato, Mary A. and Carlos Mioto. 2015. Sobre a estrutura das sentenças pseudo-clivadas e semi-clivadas. *Cadernos de Estudos Linguísticos* 57: 23–40.

Kato, Mary A. and Carlos Mioto. 2016. Pseudo-clefts and semi-clefts: An analysis based on Portuguese. In *The morphosyntax of Portuguese and Spanish in Latin America*, ed. by Mary A. Kato and Francisco Ordóñez, 286–331. Oxford: Oxford University Press.
Kato, Mary A. and Esmeralda Negrão (eds.). 2000. *Brazilian Portuguese and the null subject parameter*. Madrid and Frankfurt am Main: Iberoamericana/Vervuert.
Kato, Mary A. and Jairo Nunes. 2009. A uniform raising analysis for standard and nonstandard relative clauses. In *Minimalist essays on Brazilian Portuguese syntax*, ed. by Jairo Nunes, 93–120. Amsterdam/Philadelphia: John Benjamins.
Kato, Mary A. and Jairo Nunes. 2014. Uma análise unificada dos três tipos de relativas restritivas do português brasileiro. *Sociodialeto* 4: 575–590.
Kato, Mary A. and Francisco Ordóñez. 2019. Topic subjects in Brazilian Portuguese and clitic left dislocation in Dominican Spanish. *Syntax* 22: 229–247.
Kato, Mary A. and Eduardo Paiva Raposo. 1996. European and Brazilian Portuguese word order: Questions, focus and topic Constructions. In *Aspects of Romance linguistics*, ed. by Claudia Parodi, Carlos Quicoli, Mario Saltarelli, and Maria Luisa Zubizarreta, 267–277. Washington, D.C.: Georgetown University Press.
Kato, Mary A. and Eduardo Paiva Raposo. 2001. O objeto nulo definido no português europeu e no português brasileiro: Convergências e divergências. In *Actas do XVI Encontro Nacional da Associação Portuguesa de Linguística*, ed. by Clara Correia and Anabela Gonçalves, 673–685. Lisbon: Associação Portuguesa de Linguística.
Kato, Mary A. and Eduardo Paiva Raposo. 2005. Obje(c)tos e artigos nulos : Similaridades e diferenças entre o português europeu e o português brasileiro. In *Reflexões sobre a sintaxe do português*, ed. by Denilda Moura, 73–96. Maceió: Edufal.
Kato, Mary A. and Eduardo Paiva Raposo. 2007. Topicalization in European and Brazilian Portuguese. In *Romance Linguistics 2006: Selected papers from the 36th Linguistic Symposium on Romance languages (LSRL)*, ed. by José Camacho, Nydia Flores-Ferrán, Liliana Sánchez, Viviane Déprez, and María José Cabrera, 199–212. Amsterdam/Philadelphia: John Benjamins.
Kato, Mary A. and Ilza Ribeiro. 2006. A evolução das estruturas clivadas no português: Período V2. In *Para a história do português brasileiro*, ed. by Tânia Lobo, Ilza Ribeiro, Zenaide Carneiro, Norma Almeida, 165–182. Salvador: EDUFBA.
Kato, Mary A. and Ilza Ribeiro. 2009. Cleft sentences from Old Portuguese to Modern Brazilian Portuguese. In *Focus and background in Romance languages*, ed. by Andreas Dufter and Daniel Jacob, 123–154. Amsterdam/Philadelphia: John Benjamins.
Kato, Mary A. and Fernando Tarallo. 1992. *Sim*: Respondendo afirmativamente em português. In *Lingüística aplicada: Da aplicação da lingüística a uma lingüística transdisciplinar*, ed. by Mara Paschoal and Maria Antonieta Celani, 259–278. São Paulo: EDUC.
Kato, Mary A. and Fernando Tarallo. 2003. The loss of VS syntax in Brazilian Portuguese. In *Dialogue between schools: Sociolinguistics, conversational analysis and generative theory in Brazil*, ed. by Brigitt Schliebe-Lange, Ingedore Koch, and Konstanze Jungbluth, 101–129. Münster: Nodus Publikationen, Klaus D. Dutz.

Kenedy, Eduardo. 2003. Aspectos estruturais da relativização em português – Uma análise baseada no modelo de *raising*. Master's thesis, Universidade Federal do Rio de Janeiro.

Kenedy, Eduardo. 2007. A antinaturalidade de pied-piping em orações relativas. Doctoral dissertation, Universidade Federal do Rio de Janeiro.

Kiparsky, Paul. 1973. "Elsewhere" in phonology. In *A Festschrift for Morris Halle*, ed. by Stephen R. Anderson and Paul Kiparsky, 93–106. New York: Holt, Rinehart, and Winston.

Kuroda, Shige-Yuki. 1972. The categorical and the thetic judgments. *Foundations of Language* 9: 153–185.

Lacerda, Renato. 2020. Middle-field syntax and information structure in Brazilian Portuguese. Doctoral dissertation, University of Connecticut.

Lacerda, Renato. 2011. Todos os quantificadores têm cada um as suas particularidades. In *Anais do VII Congresso Internacional da ABRALIN*, 3701–3712.

Lacerda, Renato. 2016. Rebel without a Case: Quantifier floating in Brazilian Portuguese and Spanish. In *The morphosyntax of Portuguese and Spanish in Latin America*, ed. by Mary A. Kato and Francisco Ordóñez, 78–106. Oxford: Oxford University Press.

Lara Bermejo, Víctor. 2015. Los tratamientos de 2PL en Andalucía occidental y Portugal: Estudio geo- y socio-lingüístico de un proceso de gramaticalización. Doctoral dissertation, Universidad Autónoma de Madrid.

Lara Bermejo, Víctor. 2017. La generalización de *vocês* en el portugués europeo continental y su patrón de difusión geográfica. *Hispanic Research Journal* 18: 93–117.

Lara Bermejo, Víctor and Ana Rita Guilherme. 2018. The politeness of *você* in European Portuguese. *Studies in Hispanic and Lusophone Linguistics* 11: 337–366.

Lasnik, Howard and Mamoru Saito. 1984. On the nature of proper government. *Linguistic Inquiry* 15: 235–289.

Lemle, Miriam and Anthony J. Naro. 1977. Competências básicas do português. Final research report, MOBRAL-MEC/Fundação Ford, Rio de Janeiro.

Lessa de Oliveira, Adriana. 2003. Aquisição do constituinte-Q em dois dialetos do português brasileiro. Master's Thesis, Universidade Estadual de Campinas.

Lessa de Oliveira, Adriana. 2008. As sentenças relativas em português brasileiro: Aspectos sintáticos e fatos de aquisição. Doctoral dissertation, Universidade Estadual de Campinas.

Lightfoot, David. 1991. *How to set parameters: Arguments from language change*. Cambridge, Mass.: MIT Press.

Lobato, Lucia. 2006. Sobre a questão da influência ameríndia na formação do português do Brasil. In *Língua, gramática e discurso*, ed. by Denize Silva, 54–86. Goiânia: Cânone.

Lobo, Maria. 1995. Para uma redefinição do parâmetro do sujeito nulo. Master's thesis, Universidade de Lisboa.

Lobo, Maria. 2001. On gerund clauses of Portuguese dialects. In *El verbo: Entre el léxico y la gramática*, ed. by Alexandre Veiga, Víctor Longa, and JoDee Anderson, 107–118. Lugo: Trim Tram.

Lobo, Maria. 2003. Aspectos da sintaxe das orações subordinadas adverbiais do português. Doctoral dissertation, Universidade Nova de Lisboa.

Lobo, Maria. 2006. Assimetrias em construções de clivagem em português: Movimento *vs.* geração na base. In *Textos seleccionados do XXI Encontro Nacional da Associação Portuguesa de Linguística*, ed. by Fátima Oliveira and Joaquim Barbosa, 457–474. Lisbon: Associação Portuguesa de Linguística.
Lobo, Maria. 2013a. Dependências referenciais. In *Gramática do português*, ed. by Eduardo Paiva Raposo, Maria Fernanda Bacelar do Nascimento, Maria Antónia Mota, Luísa Segura, and Amália Mendes, vol. 2, 2177–2230. Lisbon: Fundação Calouste Gulbenkian.
Lobo, Maria. 2013b. Sujeito nulo: Sintaxe e interpretação. In *Gramática do português*, ed. by Eduardo Paiva Raposo, Maria Fernanda Bacelar do Nascimento, Maria Antónia Mota, Luísa Segura, and Amália Mendes, vol. 2, 2309–2335. Lisbon: Fundação Calouste Gulbenkian.
Lobo, Maria. 2016a. O gerúndio flexionado no português dialetal. In *Manual de linguística portuguesa*, ed. by Ana Maria Martins and Ernestina Carrilho, 481–501. Berlin/Boston: De Gruyter.
Lobo, Maria. 2016b. Sujeitos nulos: Gramática do adulto, aquisição de L1 e variação dialetal. In *Manual de linguística portuguesa*, ed. by Ana Maria Martins and Ernestina Carrilho, 558–580. Berlin/Boston: De Gruyter.
Lobo, Maria and Ana Maria Martins. 2017. Subjects. In *Manual of Romance morphosyntax and syntax*, ed. by Andreas Dufter and Elisabeth Stark, 27–88. Berlin/Boston: De Gruyter.
Lopes, Célia. 1998. *Nós* e *a gente* no português falado culto do Brasil. *D.E.L.T.A.* 14: 405–422.
Lopes, Célia. 2003. *A inserção de* a gente *no quadro pronominal do português*. Frankfurt: Iberoamericana/Vervuert.
Lopes, Célia. 2008. Retratos da variação entre *você* e *tu* no português do Brasil: Sincronia e diacronia. In *Português brasileiro II – Contato lingüístico, heterogeneidade e história*, ed. by Cláudia Roncarati and Jussara Abraçado, 55–71. Niterói: EDUFF.
Lopes, Célia and Maria Eugênia Duarte. 2007. Notícias sobre o tratamento em cartas escritas no Brasil dos séculos XVIII e XIX. In *Para a história do português brasileiro*, vol. 5: *Estudos sobre mudança lingüística e história social*, ed. by Jânia Ramos and Mônica Alkmim, 329–357. Belo Horizonte: Editora FALE/UFMG.
Lopes, Célia and Márcia Rumeu. 2007. O quadro de pronomes pessoais do português: As mudanças na especificação dos traços intrínsecos. In *Descrição, aquisição e história do português brasileiro*, ed. by Ataliba de Castilho, Maria Aparecida Torres Morais, Ruth Lopes, and Sonia Cyrino, 419–435. Campinas: Pontes/FAPESP.
Lopes, Ruth. 2003. The production of subject and object in Brazilian Portuguese by a young child. *Probus* 15: 123–146.
Lopes, Ruth. 2005. Bare nouns and DP number agreement in the acquisition of Brazilian Portuguese. In *Selected proceedings of the 9th Hispanic Linguistics Symposium*, ed. by Nuria Sagarra and Almeida Jacqueline Toribio, 252–262. Somerville: Cascadilla Press.
Lopes-Rossi, Maria Aparecida. 1993. Estudo diacrônico sobre as interrogativas no português do Brasil. In *Português brasileiro: Uma viagem diacrônica*, ed.

by Ian Roberts and Mary A. Kato, 241–266. Campinas: Editora da UNICAMP.

Lucchesi, Dante. 2009. A concordância de gênero. In *O português afro-brasileiro*, ed. by Dante Lucchesi, Alan Baxter, and Ilza Ribeiro, 295–318. Salvador: EDUFBA.

Luís, Ana R. and Georg. A. Kaiser. 2016. Clitic pronouns: Phonology, morphology, and syntax. In *Handbook of Portuguese linguistics*, ed. by Leo Wetzels, João Costa, and Sergio Menuzzi, 210–233. Malden: Wiley Blackwell.

Lunguinho, Marcus. 2006. Partição de constituintes no português brasileiro: características sintáticas. In *Língua, gramática e discurso*, ed. by Denize Silva, 133–147. Goiânia: Cânone.

Lunguinho, Marcus and Paulo Medeiros Jr. 2009. Inventou um novo tipo de sujeito: Características sintáticas e semânticas de uma estratégia de indeterminação do sujeito no português brasileiro. *Interdisciplinar: Revista de Estudos em Língua e Literatura* 9: 7–21.

Machado-Rocha, Ricardo. 2016. O redobro de clítico no português brasileiro dialetal. Doctoral dissertation, Universidade Federal de Minas Gerais.

Machado-Rocha, Ricardo and Jânia Ramos. 2016. Clitic doubling and pure agreement person features. *Revista de Estudos da Linguagem* 24: 378–416.

Magalhães, Telma. 2003. Aprendendo o sujeito nulo na escola. *Letras de Hoje* 38: 189–202.

Magalhães, Telma. 2004. Valorando traços de concordância dentro do DP. *D.E.L.T.A.* 20: 149–170.

Magalhães, Telma. 2006. O sistema pronominal sujeito e objeto na aquisição do português europeu e do português brasileiro. Doctoral dissertation, Universidade Estadual de Campinas.

Magalhães, Telma. 2007. A aquisição de pronomes sujeitos no PB e no PE. *Letras de Hoje* 42: 97–112.

Magalhães, Telma and Ana Lúcia Santos. 2006. As respostas verbais e a freqüência de sujeito nulo na aquisição do português brasileiro e português europeu. *Letras de Hoje* 41: 179–193.

Magro, Catarina. 2005. Introdutores de orações infinitivas: O que diz a sintaxe dos clíticos. In *Actas do XX Encontro Nacional da Associação Portuguesa de Linguística*, ed. by Inês Duarte and Isabel Leiria, 649–664. Lisbon: Associação Portuguesa de Linguística.

Magro, Catarina. 2007. Clíticos: Variações sobre o tema. Doctoral dissertation, Universidade de Lisboa.

Marafoni, Renata. 2010. A distribuição do objeto nulo no português europeu e no português brasileiro. Doctoral dissertation, Universidade Federal do Rio de Janeiro.

Marcelino, Nara. 2018. Sentenças de negação com *é ruim* e *nem a pau* em português brasileiro. Doctoral dissertation, Universidade Federal do Rio Grande do Norte.

Martins, Ana Maria. 1994a. Clíticos na história do português. Doctoral dissertation, Universidade de Lisboa.

Martins, Ana Maria. 1994b. Enclisis, VP deletion, and the nature of Σ. *Probus* 6: 173–206.

Martins, Ana Maria. 1997. "Alguns," "poucos," "muitos," "todos" e a relação sintaxe-semântica. In *Sentido que a vida faz: Estudos para Óscar Lopes*, ed. by

Ana Maria Brito, Fátima Oliveira, Isabel de Lima, and Rosa Martelo, 679–692. Oporto: Campo das Letras.
Martins, Ana Maria. 2000a. A minimalist approach to clitic climbing. In *Portuguese syntax: New comparative studies*, ed. by João Costa, 169–190. Oxford/New York: Oxford University Press.
Martins, Ana Maria. 2000b. Polarity items in Romance: Underspecification and lexical change. In *Diachronic syntax: Models and mechanisms*, ed. by Susan Pintzuk, George Tsoulas, and Anthony Warner, 191–219. Oxford: Oxford University Press.
Martins, Ana Maria. 2001. On the origin of the Portuguese inflected infinitive: A new perspective on an enduring debate. In *Historical Linguistics 1999: Selected Papers from the 14th International Conference on Historical Linguistics, Vancouver, 9– 13 August 1999*, ed. by Laurel Brinton, 207–222. Amsterdam/Philadelphia: John Benjamins.
Martins, Ana Maria. 2003. Construções com *se*: Mudança e variação no português europeu. In *Razões e emoção: Miscelânea de estudos em homenagem a Maria Helena Mira Mateus*, ed. by Ivo Castro and Inês Duarte, 19–41. Lisbon: INCM.
Martins, Ana Maria. 2006a. Aspects of infinitival constructions in the history of Portuguese. In *Historical Romance linguistics: Retrospective and perspectives*, ed. by Deborah Arteaga and Randall Gess, 327–355. Amsterdam/Philadelphia: John Benjamins.
Martins, Ana Maria. 2006b. Emphatic affirmation and polarity: Contrasting European Portuguese with Brazilian Portuguese, Spanish, Catalan and Galician. In *Romance languages and linguistic theory 2004*, ed. by Jenny Doetjes and Paz González, 197–223. Amsterdam/Philadelphia: John Benjamins.
Martins, Ana Maria. 2007. Double realization of verbal copies in European Portuguese emphatic affirmation. In *The copy theory of movement*, ed. by Norbert Corver and Jairo Nunes, 77–118. Amsterdam/Philadelphia: John Benjamins.
Martins, Ana Maria. 2009. Subject doubling in European Portuguese dialects: The role of impersonal *se*. In *Romance languages and linguistic theory – Selected papers from "Going Romance" Amsterdam 2007*, ed. by Enoch Aboh, Elisabeth van der Linden, Joseph Quer, and Petra Sleeman, 179–200. Amsterdam/Philadelphia: John Benjamins.
Martins, Ana Maria. 2010. Negação metalinguística (*lá*, *cá* e *agora*). In *Actas do XXV Encontro da Associação Portuguesa de Linguística*, ed. by Ana Maria Brito, 567–587. Lisbon: Associação Portuguesa de Linguística.
Martins, Ana Maria. 2011. Clíticos na história do português à luz do teatro vicentino. *Estudos de Lingüística Galega* 3: 55–83.
Martins, Ana Maria. 2012. Deictic locatives, emphasis and metalinguistic negation. In *Parameter theory and linguistic change*, ed. by Charlotte Galves, Sonia Cyrino, Ruth Lopes, Filomena Sândalo, and Juanito Avelar, 213–236. Oxford: Oxford University Press.
Martins, Ana Maria. 2013a. Emphatic polarity in European Portuguese and beyond. *Lingua* 128: 95–123.
Martins, Ana Maria. 2013b. Posição dos pronomes pessoais clíticos. In *Gramática do português*, ed. by Eduardo Paiva Raposo, Maria Fernanda Bacelar do

Nascimento, Maria Antónia Mota, Luísa Segura, and Amália Mendes, vol. 2, 2231–2302. Lisbon: Fundação Calouste Gulbenkian.

Martins, Ana Maria. 2013c. The interplay between VSO and coordination in two types of non-degree exclamatives. *Catalan Journal of Linguistics* 12: 1–27.

Martins, Ana Maria. 2014. How much syntax is there in metalinguistic negation?. *Natural Language and Linguistic Theory* 32: 635–672.

Martins, Ana Maria. 2016a. O sistema responsivo: Padrões de resposta a interrogativas polares e a asserções. In *Manual de linguística portuguesa*, ed. by Ana Maria Martins and Ernestina Carrilho, 501–609. Berlin/Boston: De Gruyter.

Martins, Ana Maria. 2016b. VP and TP Ellipsis: Sentential polarity and information structure. In *Manual of grammatical interfaces in Romance*, ed. by Susann Fischer and Christoph Gabriel, 457–485. Berlin/Boston, De Gruyter.

Martins, Ana Maria. 2020a. Metalinguistic negation. In *The Oxford handbook of negation*, ed. by Viviane Déprez and M. Teresa Espinal, 349–368. Oxford: Oxford University Press.

Martins, Ana Maria. 2020b. Some notes on postverbal subjects in declarative (and other non *wh*-) sentences. *Diadorim* 22: 98–119.

Martins, Ana Maria. 2021a. Microvariação na sintaxe dos clíticos: Os dialetos portugueses dos Açores e Madeira. *Estudos de Lingüística Galega* 13: 67–105.

Martins, Ana Maria. 2021b. Syntactic aspects of metalinguistic negation. *Revue Roumaine de Linguistique* 66 (2–3): 175–197.

Martins, Ana Maria and João Costa. 2016. Ordem dos constituintes frásicos: sujeitos invertidos, objetos antepostos. In *Manual de linguística portuguesa*, ed. by Ana Maria Martins and Ernestina Carrilho, 371–400. Berlin/Boston: De Gruyter.

Martins, Ana Maria and Maria Lobo. 2020. Estratégias de marcação de foco: Ordem dos constituintes frásicos e estruturas clivadas. In *Gramática do português*, ed. by Eduardo Paiva Raposo, Maria Fernanda Bacelar do Nascimento, Maria Antónia Mota, Luísa Segura, Amália Mendes, and Amália Andrade, vol. 3, 2617–2664. Lisbon: Fundação Calouste Gulbenkian.

Martins, Ana Maria and Jairo Nunes. 2005. Raising issues in Brazilian and European Portuguese. *Journal of Portuguese Linguistics* 4: 53–77.

Martins, Ana Maria and Jairo Nunes. 2009. Syntactic change as *chain reaction*: The emergence of hyper-raising in Brazilian Portuguese. In *Historical syntax and linguistic theory*, ed. by Paola Crisma and Giuseppe Longobardi, 144–157. Oxford: Oxford University Press.

Martins, Ana Maria and Jairo Nunes. 2010. Apparent hyper-raising in Brazilian Portuguese: Agreement with topics across a finite CP. In *The complementiser phase: Subjects and operators*, ed. by Phoevos Panagiotidis, 142–163. Oxford: Oxford University Press.

Martins, Ana Maria and Jairo Nunes. 2016. Passives and *se* constructions. In *Handbook of Portuguese linguistics*, ed. by Leo Wetzels, João Costa, and Sergio Menuzzi, 318–337. Malden: Wiley Blackwell.

Martins, Ana Maria and Jairo Nunes. 2017a. Deletion of reflexive clitics with the verb *custar* in European Portuguese: An MTC Account. *Journal of Portuguese Linguistics* 16: 1–25.

Martins, Ana Maria and Jairo Nunes. 2017b. Identity avoidance with reflexive clitics in European Portuguese and minimalist approaches to control. *Linguistic Inquiry* 37: 627–649.

Martins, Ana Maria and Jairo Nunes. 2017c. Subespecificação de traços-ϕ em infinitivos flexionados e variação dialetal/idioletal em português. Paper presented at Romania Nova IX/ALFAL XVIII, Universidade Nacional de Colombia, 7/25–26/2017.

Martins, Ana and Jairo Nunes. 2021. Brazilian and European Portuguese and Holmberg's 2005 typology of null subject languages. In *Romance languages and linguistic theory 2018: Selected papers from "Going Romance" 32, Utrecht*, ed. by Sergio Baauw, Frank Drijkoningen, and Luisa Meroni, 171–190. Amsterdam/Philadelphia: John Benjamins.

Martins, Eneida. 1997. Sentential negation in Spoken Brazilian Portuguese. Master's thesis, Georgetown University, Washington.

Mateus, Maria Helena Mira, Ana Maria Brito, Inês Duarte, Isabel Faria, Sónia Frota, Gabriela Matos, Fátima Oliveira, Marina Vigário, and Alina Villalva. 2003. *Gramática da língua portuguesa*. Lisbon: Caminho.

Matos, Gabriela. 1985. Clítico verbal demonstrativo. Master's thesis, Universidade de Lisboa.

Matos, Gabriela. 1992. Construções de elipse de predicado em português: SV nulo e despojamento. Doctoral dissertation, Universidade de Lisboa.

Matos, Gabriela. 2003. Aspectos sintácticos da negação. In *Gramática da língua portuguesa*, ed. by Maria Helena Mira Mateus, Ana Maria Brito, Inês Duarte, Isabel Faria, Sónia Frota, Gabriela Matos, Fátima Oliveira, Marina Vigário, and Alina Villalva, 770–793. Lisbon: Caminho.

Matos, Gabriela. 2013a. Elipse. In *Gramática do português*, ed. by Eduardo Paiva Raposo, Maria Fernanda Bacelar do Nascimento, Maria Antónia Mota, Luísa Segura, and Amália Mendes, vol. 2, 2349–2386. Lisbon: Fundação Calouste Gulbenkian.

Matos, Gabriela. 2013b. Quotative inversion in Peninsular Portuguese and Spanish, and in English. *Catalan Journal of Linguistics* 12: 111–130.

Mattos e Silva, Rosa Virgínia. 1993. *O português arcaico – Morfologia e sintaxe*. São Paulo: Contexto.

Mattos e Silva, Rosa Virgínia. 2008. *O português arcaico – Uma aproximação*. Lisbon: Imprensa Nacional – Casa da Moeda.

Maurer Jr., Theodoro. 1968. *O infinitivo flexionado português: Estudo histórico-descritivo*. São Paulo: Companhia Editora Nacional.

Medeiros Júnior, Paulo. 2014. Relativas livres do PB: Sintaxe, semântica e diacronia. Doctoral dissertation, Universidade Estadual de Campinas.

Meireles, Letícia and Márcia Cançado. 2020. A alternância parte-todo com verbos transitivos no PB: Um caso de fatoração de argumento. *D.E.L.T.A.* 36: 1–28.

Menon, Odete. 1984. O imperativo no português do Brasil. Master's thesis, Universidade Católica do Paraná, Curitiba.

Menon, Odete. 1996. *A gente*: um processo de gramaticalização. *Estudos Lingüisticos* 25: 622–628.

Menon, Odete and Loremi Loregian-Penkal. 2002. Variação no indivíduo e na comunidade: *tu/você* no sul do Brasil. In *Variação e mudança no português falado no Sul*, ed. by Paulino Vandresen, 147–188. Pelotas: Educat.

Mensching, Guido. 2000. *Infinitive constructions with specified subjects: A syntactic analysis of the Romance languages*. Oxford: Oxford University Press.
Menuzzi, Sérgio. 1994. Adjectival positions inside DP. In *Linguistics in the Netherlands 1994*, ed. by Reineke Bok-Bennema and Crit Cremers, 127–138. Amsterdam/Philadelphia: John Benjamins.
Menuzzi, Sergio. 1996. 3rd person possessives in Brazilian Portuguese: On the syntax–discourse relation. In *Proceedings of the Discourse Anaphora and Anaphora Resolution Colloquium*, ed. by Simon Botley, 191–210. Lancaster: Lancaster University.
Menuzzi, Sergio. 1999. *Binding theory and pronominal anaphora in Brazilian Portuguese*. The Hague: Holland Academic Graphics.
Menuzzi, Sergio. 2000. First person plural anaphora in Brazilian Portuguese: Chains and constraint interaction in binding. In *Portuguese syntax: New comparative studies*, ed. by João Costa, 191–240. Oxford/New York: Oxford University Press.
Menuzzi, Sergio. 2004. Pronomes como determinantes: Algumas propriedades do elemento interrogativo QUE em português brasileiro. *Leitura* 33: 65–86.
Menuzzi, Sergio. 2012. Algumas observações sobre foco, contraste e exaustividade. *Revista Letras* 86: 95–121.
Menuzzi, Sérgio, Maria Cristina Figueiredo Silva, and Jenny Doetjes. 2015. Subject bare singulars in Brazilian Portuguese and information structure. *Journal of Portuguese Linguistics* 14: 7–44.
Menuzzi, Sergio and Maria Lobo. 2016. Binding and pronominal forms in Portuguese. In *Handbook of Portuguese linguistics*, ed. by Leo Wetzels, João Costa, and Sergio Menuzzi, 338–355. Malden: Wiley Blackwell.
Miguel, Matilde. 1992. O possessivo e a estrutura predicativa do sintagma nominal. Master's thesis, Universidade de Lisboa.
Miguel, Matilde. 1996. A preposição *a* e os complementos genitivos. In *Quatro estudos em sintaxe do português*, ed. by Anabela Gonçalves, Madalena Colaço, Matilde Miguel, and Telmo Móia, 101–147. Lisbon: Colibri.
Miguel, Matilde. 2004. O sintagma nominal: Posições de sujeito. Doctoral dissertation, Universidade de Lisboa.
Miguel, Matilde, Anabela Gonçalves, and Inês Duarte. 2010. Possessive and personal datives in Portuguese. Paper presented at IV Workshop Romania Nova. Campos do Jordão, 24–26/11/2010.
Mioto, Carlos. 1992. Negação sentencial em português brasileiro e a teoria da gramática. Doctoral dissertation, Universidade Estadual de Campinas.
Mioto, Carlos. 1994. As interrogativas WH no português brasileiro e o critério-WH. *Letras de Hoje* 96: 19–33.
Mioto, Carlos. 2011. Interrogativas WH no português europeu e no português brasileiro. In *Percursos em teoria da gramática*, ed. by Roberta Pires de Oliveira and Carlos Mioto, 43–72. Florianópolis: Editora da UFSC.
Mioto, Carlos. 2012. Reduced pseudoclefts in Caribbean Spanish and in Brazilian Portuguese. *In Enjoy Linguistics! Papers offered to Luigi Rizzi on the occasion of his 60th birthday*, ed. by Valentina Bianchi and Cristiano Chesi, 287–302. Siena: CISCL Press.
Mioto, Carlos and Maria Cristina Figueiredo Silva. 1995. Wh que = wh é que?. *D.E.L.T.A.* 11: 301–311.

Mioto, Carlos and Maria Lobo. 2016. *Wh*-movement: Interrogatives, relatives and clefts. In *Handbook of Portuguese linguistics*, ed. by Leo Wetzels, João Costa, and Sergio Menuzzi, 275–293. Malden: Wiley Blackwell.

Mioto, Carlos and Esmeralda Negrão. 2007. As sentenças clivadas não contêm uma relativa. In *Descrição, aquisição e história do português brasileiro*, ed. by Ataliba de Castilho, Maria Aparecida Torres Morais, Ruth Lopes, and Sonia Cyrino, 159–183. Campinas: Pontes/FAPESP.

Modesto, Marcello. 2000. On the identification of null arguments. Doctoral dissertation, University of Southern California.

Modesto, Marcello. 2001. *As construções clivadas no português do Brasil: Relações entre interpretação focal, movimento sintático e prosódia*. São Paulo: Humanitas.

Modesto, Marcello. 2011. Infinitivos flexionados em português brasileiro e sua relevância para a teoria do controle. In *Estudos da Linguagem – Casamento entre temas e perspectivas*, ed. by Dermeval da Hora and Esmeralda Negrão, 63–87. João Pessoa: UFPB/Ideia.

Modesto, Marcello. 2016. Inflected infinitives and restructuring in Brazilian Portuguese. In *The morphosyntax of Portuguese and Spanish in Latin America*, ed. by Mary A. Kato and Francisco Ordóñez, 157–176. Oxford: Oxford University Press.

Móia, Telmo. 1992. A sintaxe das orações relativas sem antecedente expresso do português. Master's thesis, Universidade de Lisboa.

Moreira da Silva, Samuel. 1983. Études sur la symétrie et l'asymétrie sujet/objet dans le portugais du Brésil. Doctoral dissertation, Université de Paris VIII.

Mota, Maria Antónia. 1997. Les traits nombre et personne/nombre en portugais – l'oral dans ses variétés. In *Analyse linguistique et approches de l'oral – Recueil d'études offert à Claire Blanche-Benveniste* (Orbis, Supplementa 10), ed. by Mireille Bilger, Karel van den Eynde, and Françoise Gadet, 339–345. Louvain/Paris: Peeters.

Mota, Maria Antónia. 2016. Morfologia nas interfaces. In *Manual de linguística portuguesa*, ed. by Ana Maria Martins and Ernestina Carrilho, 156–177. Berlin/Boston: De Gruyter.

Mota, Maria Antónia. 2020a.Introdução à morfologia. In *Gramática do português*, ed. by Eduardo Paiva Raposo, Maria Fernanda Bacelar do Nascimento, Maria Antónia Mota, Luísa Segura, Amália Mendes, and Amália Andrade, vol. 3, 2783–2831. Lisbon: Fundação Calouste Gulbenkian.

Mota, Maria Antónia. 2020b. Morfologia do nome e do adjetivo. In *Gramática do português*, ed. by Eduardo Paiva Raposo, Maria Fernanda Bacelar do Nascimento, Maria Antónia Mota, Luísa Segura, Amália Mendes, and Amália Andrade, vol. 3, 2835–2930. Lisbon: Fundação Calouste Gulbenkian.

Müller, Ana. 1996. A gramática das formas possessivas no português do Brasil. Doctoral dissertation, Universidade Estadual de Campinas.

Müller, Ana. 2002. Nomes nus e o parâmetro nominal no português brasileiro. *Revista Letras* 58: 331–344.

Müller, Ana and Fátima Oliveira. 2004. Bare nominals and number in Brazilian and European Portuguese. *Journal of Portuguese Linguistics* 3: 9–36.

Munhoz, Ana. 2011. A estrutura argumental das construções de tópico-sujeito: O caso dos sujeitos locativos. Master's thesis, Universidade de Brasília.

Munhoz, Ana and Rozana Naves. 2012. Construções de tópico-sujeito: Uma proposta em termos de estrutura argumental e de transferência de traços de C. *Signum* 15: 245–265.

Munn, Alan and Cristina Schmitt. 2005. Number and indefinites. *Lingua* 115: 821–855.

Mutali, Henrique. 2019. A colocação dos pronomes clíticos no português angolano escrito. Master's thesis, Universidade de Lisboa.

Naro, Anthony. 1976. The genesis of the reflexive impersonal construction in Portuguese: A study in syntactic change as a surface phenomenon. *Language* 52: 779–810.

Naro, Anthony and Marta Scherre. 2007. *Origens do português brasileiro*. São Paulo: Parábola.

Naro, Anthony and Sebastião Votre. 1986. Discurso e ordem vocabular. In *Anais do IV Encontro de Variação Lingüística e Bilingüismo na Região Sul*, 2–24. Porto Alegre: Universidade Federal do Rio Grande do Sul.

Naro, Anthony and Sebastião Votre. 1999. Discourse motivations for linguistic regularities: Verb/subject order in spoken Brazilian Portuguese. *Probus* 11: 76–100.

Nascimento, Milton do. 1984. Sur la posposition du sujet dans le portugais du Brésil. Doctoral dissertation, Université de Paris VIII.

Negrão, Esmeralda. 1986. Anaphora in Brazilian Portuguese complement structures. Doctoral dissertation, University of Wisconsin.

Negrão, Esmeralda. 1997. Asymmetries in the distribution of overt and empty categories in Brazilian Portuguese. In *Clitics, pronouns and movement*, ed. by James Black and Virginia Motapayane, 217–235. Amsterdam/Philadelphia: John Benjamins.

Negrão, Esmeralda. 1999. O português brasileiro: Uma língua voltada para o discurso. "Tese de livre-docência," Universidade de São Paulo.

Negrão, Esmeralda and Ana Müller. 1996. As mudanças no sistema pronominal do português brasileiro: Substituição ou especialização de formas. *D.E.L.T.A.* 12: 125–152.

Negrão, Esmeralda and Evani Viotti. 2008. Estratégias de impessoalização no português brasileiro. In *África no Brasil: A formação da língua portuguesa*, ed. by José Luiz Fiorin and Margarida Petter, 179–203. São Paulo: Contexto.

Negrão, Esmeralda and Evani Viotti. 2015. Elementos para a investigação semântica do clítico *se* em português brasileiro. *Cadernos de Estudos Linguísticos* 57: 41–59.

Neves, Maria Helena Moura. 2000. *Gramática de usos do português*. São Paulo: Editora da Unesp.

Nunes, José Joaquim. 1919. *Compêndio de gramática histórica portuguesa – Fonética e morfologia*. Lisbon: Clássica Editora.

Nunes, Jairo. 1990. O famigerado *se*: Uma análise sincrônica e diacrônica das construções com *se* apassivador e indeterminador. Master's thesis, Universidade Estadual de Campinas.

Nunes, Jairo. 1991. *Se* apassivador e *se* indeterminador: O percurso diacrônico no português brasileiro. *Cadernos de Estudos Lingüísticos* 20: 33–57.

Nunes, Jairo. 1993. Direção de cliticização, objeto nulo e pronome tônico na posição de objeto em português brasileiro. In *Português brasileiro: Uma viagem*

diacrônica, ed. by Ian Roberts and Mary A. Kato, 207–222. Campinas: Editora da UNICAMP.
Nunes, Jairo. 1995. Ainda o famigerado *se*. *D.E.L.T.A.* 11: 201–240.
Nunes, Jairo. 2001. Sideward movement. *Linguistic Inquiry* 31: 303–344.
Nunes, Jairo. 2004. *Linearization of chains and sideward movement*. Cambridge, Mass.: MIT Press.
Nunes, Jairo. 2007. Triangulismos e a sintaxe do português brasileiro. In *Descrição, aquisição e história do português brasileiro*, ed. by Ataliba de Castilho, Maria Aparecida Torres Morais, Ruth Lopes, and Sonia Cyrino, 25–34. Campinas: Pontes/FAPESP.
Nunes, Jairo. 2008a. Inherent Case as a licensing condition for A-movement: The case of hyper-raising constructions in Brazilian Portuguese. *Journal of Portuguese Linguistics* 7: 83–108.
Nunes, Jairo. 2008b. Preposition insertion in the mapping from Spell-Out to PF. *Linguistics in Potsdam* 28: 133–156.
Nunes, Jairo. 2009. Dummy prepositions and the licensing of null subjects in Brazilian Portuguese. In *Romance languages and linguistic theory: Selected papers from "Going Romance" Amsterdam 2007*, ed. by Enoch Aboh, Elisabeth van der Linden, Josep Quer, and Petra Sleeman, 243–265. Amsterdam/Philadelphia: John Benjamins.
Nunes, Jairo. 2010a. A note on *wh*-islands and finite control in Brazilian Portuguese. *Estudos da Língua(gem)* 8: 79–103.
Nunes, Jairo. 2010b. Relativizing minimality for A-movement: φ- and θ-relations. *Probus* 22: 1–25.
Nunes, Jairo. 2011. On the diachronic reanalysis of null subjects and null objects in Brazilian Portuguese. In *The development of grammar: Language acquisition and diachronic change – In honor of Jürgen M. Meisel*, ed. by Esther Rinke and Tanja Kupish, 331–354. Amsterdam/Philadelphia: John Benjamins.
Nunes, Jairo. 2013. *Edge features* legitimando movimento-A. *ReVEL* 7, special issue: 35–50.
Nunes, Jairo. 2014. Adjunct control and edge features. In *Minimalism and beyond: Radicalizing the interfaces*, ed. by Peter Kosta, Steven Franks, Teodora Radeva-Bork, and Lilia Schürcks, 79–108. Amsterdam/Philadelphia: John Benjamins.
Nunes, Jairo. 2015a. De clítico a concordância: O caso dos acusativos de terceira pessoa em português brasileiro. *Cadernos de Estudos Linguísticos* 57: 61–84.
Nunes, Jairo. 2015b. Subespecificação de traços-φ e hiperalçamento em português brasileiro. In *Diálogos com Ribeiro: Sobre gramática e história da língua portuguesa*, ed. by Cristina Figueiredo and Edivalda Araújo, 121–148. Salvador: Edufba.
Nunes, Jairo. 2016. Subject and topic hyper-raising in Brazilian Portuguese: A case study on reference sets for economy computations. In *The morphosyntax of Portuguese and Spanish in Latin America*, ed. by Mary A. Kato and Francisco Ordóñez, 107–134. Oxford: Oxford University Press.
Nunes, Jairo. 2017. Circumventing φ-minimality: On some unorthodox cases of A-movement in Brazilian Portuguese. In *Romance languages and linguistic theory 12: Selected papers from the 45th Linguistic Symposium on Romance languages*, ed. by Ruth Lopes, Juanito Avelar, and Sonia Cyrino, 159–183. Amsterdam/Philadelphia: John Benjamins.

Nunes, Jairo. 2018. Movimento-*wh* e controle de adjunto em português. In *O apelo das árvores: Estudos em homenagem a Miriam Lemle*, ed. by Alessandro Medeiros and Andrew Nevins, 45–77. Campinas: Pontes.
Nunes, Jairo. 2019a. Clíticos acusativos de terceira pessoa em PB como concordância de objeto. In *Português brasileiro: Uma segunda viagem diacrônica*, ed. by Charlotte Galves, Mary A.Kato, and Ian Roberts, 151–172. Campinas: Editora da UNICAMP.
Nunes, Jairo. 2019b. Remarks on finite control and hyper-raising in Brazilian Portuguese. *Journal of Portuguese Linguistics* 18: 1–50.
Nunes, Jairo. 2020a. Especificação morfológica de pronomes nominativos, concordância verbal e sujeitos nulos em português brasileiro. *Fórum Linguístico* 17, special issue: 4658–4672.
Nunes, Jairo. 2020b. Hiperalçamento em português brasileiro. *Cuadernos de la ALFAL* 14: 199–227.
Nunes, Jairo. 2021a. Edge features and multiple *wh*-questions. *Cadernos de Linguística* 2: 1–29.
Nunes, Jairo. 2021b. On the locus and licensing of edge features. *Glossa* 6: 1–35.
Nunes, Jairo and Mary A. Kato. Forthcoming. Approaching "topic-subjects" in Brazilian Portuguese from below. To appear in *Formal approaches to languages of South America*, ed. by Cilene Rodrigues and Andrés Saab. New York: Springer.
Nunes, Jairo and Eduardo Paiva Raposo. 1997. Are non-trivial chains needed for feature checking? Evidence from Portuguese infinitives. Paper delivered at "Going Romance" 1997, University of Groningen, 12/13/1997.
Nunes, Jairo and Eduardo Paiva Raposo. 1998. Portuguese inflected infinitivals and the configurations for feature checking. Paper delivered at GLOW 21 (Generative Linguistics in the Old World), Universiteit van Tilburg, 4/15–18/1998.
Nunes, Jairo and Raquel S. Santos. 2009. Stress shift as a diagnostics for identifying empty categories in Brazilian Portuguese. In *Minimalist essays on Brazilian Portuguese syntax*, ed. by Jairo Nunes, 121–136. Amsterdam/Philadelphia: John Benjamins.
Nunes, Jairo and Cristina Ximenes. 2009. Prepositional contractions and morphological sideward movement in Brazilian Portuguese. In *Minimalist essays on Brazilian Portuguese syntax*, ed. by Jairo Nunes, 191–214. Amsterdam/Philadelphia: John Benjamins.
Nunes, Jairo and Cynthia Zocca. 2009. Lack of morphological identity and ellipsis resolution in Brazilian Portuguese. In *Minimalist essays on Brazilian Portuguese syntax*, ed. by Jairo Nunes, 215–236. Amsterdam/Philadelphia: John Benjamins.
Oliveira e Silva, Giselle. 1984. Variação no sistema possessivo de terceira pessoa. *Tempo Brasileiro* 78/79: 54–72.
Oliveira, Ireniza. 2009. They are really tough, but also middle: Diferentes estruturas para sentenças com predicado *tough*. Doctoral dissertation, Universidade Estadual de Campinas.
Oliveira, Marilza de. 1996. Respostas assertivas e sua variação nas línguas românicas: O seu papel na aquisição. Doctoral dissertation, Universidade Estadual de Campinas.

Omena, Nelise. 1978. Pronome pessoal de terceira pessoa: Suas formas variantes em função acusativa. Master's thesis, Pontifícia Universidade Católica do Rio de Janeiro.
Omena, Nelise and Maria Luísa Braga. 1996. A gente está se gramaticalizando? In *Variação e discurso*, ed. by Alzira Macedo, Cláudia Roncaratti, and Maria Cecília Mollica, 75–84. Rio de Janeiro: Tempo Brasileiro.
Othero, Gabriel. 2013. Revisitando o status do pronome *cê* no português brasileiro. *Revista de Estudos da Linguagem* 21: 135–156.
Pagotto, Emilio. 1993. Clíticos, mudança e seleção natural. In *Português brasileiro: Uma viagem diacrônica*, ed. by Ian Roberts and Mary A. Kato, 185–206. Campinas: Editora da UNICAMP.
Panitz, Ezekiel. 2018. Argument ellipsis and strong islands. Doctoral dissertation, University College London.
Paredes Silva, Vera. 1998. Variação e funcionalidade no uso de pronomes de 2ª pessoa do singular no português carioca. *Revista de Estudos da Linguagem* 7: 121–138.
Paredes Silva, Vera. 2003. O retorno do pronome *tu* à fala carioca. In *Português brasileiro: Contato lingüístico, heterogeneidade e história*, ed. by Cláudia Roncarati and Jussara Abraçado, 160–169. Rio de Janeiro: Sete Letras.
Pereira, Bruna. 2016. Feature interpretability and the positions of 2nd person possessives in dialectal Brazilian Portuguese. *Filologia e Linguística Portuguesa* 18: 199–229.
Pereira, Sandra. 2003. Gramática comparada de *a gente*: Variação no português europeu. Master's thesis, Universidade de Lisboa.
Pereira, Sílvia. 2010. O marcador de negação metalinguística *agora* nos dialectos do português europeu. Master's thesis, Universidade de Lisboa.
Pereira, Sílvia. 2013. "Àgora" no dialecto minhoto. *Estudos de Lingüística Galega* 5: 105–126.
Peres, João Andrade. 1995. Concordância negativa através de fronteiras frásicas. In *Actas do X Encontro Nacional da Associação Portuguesa de Linguística (Évora 1994)*, 435–451. Lisbon: Associação Portuguesa de Linguística.
Peres, João Andrade. 1997. Extending the notion of negative concord. In *Negation and polarity: Syntax and semantics*, ed. by Danielle Forget, Paul Hirschbühler, France Martineau, and Maria-Luisa Rivero, 289–310. Amsterdam/Philadelphia: John Benjamins.
Peres, João Andrade. 2013. Aspetos gerais da negação. In *Gramática do português*, ed. by Eduardo Paiva Raposo, Maria Fernanda Bacelar do Nascimento, Maria Antónia Mota, Luísa Segura, and Amália Mendes, vol. 1, 461–498. Lisbon: Fundação Calouste Gulbenkian.
Peres, João Andrade and Telmo Móia. 1995. *Áreas críticas da língua portuguesa*. Lisbon: Caminho.
Perini, Mário. 1974. A grammar of Portuguese infinitives. Doctoral dissertation, University of Texas.
Perini, Mário. 1985. O surgimento do sistema possessivo do português coloquial: Uma abordagem funcional. *D.E.L.T.A.* 1: 1–16.
Perlmutter, David. 1971. *Deep and surface constraints in syntax*. New York: Holt, Rinehart & Winston.
Petersen, Carol. 2008. A tripartição pronominal e o estatuto das formas *cê, ocê* e *você*. *D.E.L.T.A.* 24: 283–308.

Petersen, Maria Carolina. 2011. O licenciamento do sujeito nulo em orações subjuntivas no português brasileiro: Contribuições para a teoria de controle por movimento. Master's thesis, Universidade de São Paulo.

Pilati, Eloisa. 2006. Aspectos sintáticos e semânticos das orações com ordem verbo–sujeito no português do Brasil. Doctoral dissertation, Universidade de Brasília.

Pinto, Clara. 2010. Negação metalinguística e estruturas com *nada* no português europeu. Master's thesis, Universidade de Lisboa.

Pinto, Clara. 2020. Polarity, expression of degree and negation: The vernacular form caraças. *Estudos de Lingüística Galega* 12: 115–139.

Pires, Acrisio. 2006. *The minimalist syntax of defective domains*. Amsterdam/Philadelphia: John Benjamins.

Pires, Acrisio and Heather Taylor. 2007. The syntax of wh-in-situ and common ground. In *Proceedings from the 43rd Annual Meeting of the Chicago Linguistic Society*, ed. by Malcolm Elliott, James Kirby, Osamu Sawada, Eleni Staraki, and Suwon Yoon, 201–215. Chicago: Chicago Linguistic Society.

Pires de Oliveira, Roberta and Susan Rothstein. 2011. Bare singular noun phrases are mass in Brazilian Portuguese. *Lingua* 121: 2153–2175.

Pollock, Jean-Yves. 1989. Verb movement, UG and the structure of IP. *Linguistic Inquiry* 20: 365–424.

Pontes, Eunice. 1987. *O tópico no português do Brasil*. Campinas: Pontes.

Quicoli, Antonio Carlos. 1982. *The structure of complementation*. Ghent: E. Story-Scientia.

Ramos, Jânia. 1996. O uso das formas *você, ocê* e *cê* no dialeto mineiro. In *Diversidade lingüística no Brasil*, ed. by Dermeval da Hora, 43–60. João Pessoa: Idéia.

Ramos, Jânia. 2002. A alternância entre "não" e "num" no dialeto mineiro: Um caso de mudança linguística. In *Dialeto mineiro e outras falas: Estudos de variação e mudança linguística*, ed. by Jânia Ramos and Maria Antonieta Cohen, 155–167. Belo Horizonte: FALE/UFMG.

Raposo, Eduardo Paiva. 1985. Some asymmetries in the binding theory in Romance. *The Linguistic Review* 5: 75–110.

Raposo, Eduardo Paiva. 1986. On the null object construction in European Portuguese. In *Studies in Romance Linguistics*, ed. by Osvaldo Jaeggli and Carmen Silva-Corvalán, 373–390. Dordrecht: Foris.

Raposo, Eduardo Paiva. 1987a. Case theory and Infl-to-Comp: The inflected infinitive. *Linguistic Inquiry* 18: 85–109.

Raposo, Eduardo Paiva. 1987b. Romance infinitival clauses and Case Theory. In *Studies in Romance languages*, ed. by Carol Neidle and Rafael Núñez-Cedeño, 237–249. Dordrecht: Foris.

Raposo, Eduardo Paiva. 1989. Prepositional infinitival constructions in European Portuguese. In *The null subject parameter*, ed. by Osvaldo Jaeggli and Kenneth Safir, 277–305. Dordrecht: Kluwer.

Raposo, Eduardo Paiva. 1994. Affective operators and clausal structure in European Portuguese and European Spanish. Paper presented at the 24th Linguistic Symposium on Romance languages, University of California at Los Angeles, 10–13/3/1994.

Raposo, Eduardo Paiva. 1995. Próclise, ênclise e posição do verbo em português europeu. In *O amor das letras e das gentes – In honor of Maria de Lourdes Belchior Pontes*, ed. by João Camilo dos Santos and Frederick Williams, 455–481. Santa Barbara: University of California at Santa Barbara.

Raposo, Eduardo Paiva. 1998a. Definite/zero alternations in Portuguese: Towards a unification of topic constructions. In *Romance linguistics: Theoretical perspectives*, ed. by Armin Schwegler, Bernard Tranel and Myriam Uribe-Etxebarria, 197–212. Amsterdam/Philadelphia: John Benjamins.

Raposo, Eduardo Paiva. 1998b. Some observations on the pronominal system of Portuguese. *Catalan Woking Papers in Linguistics* 6: 59–93.

Raposo, Eduardo Paiva. 2000. Clitic positions and verb movement. In *Portuguese syntax: New comparative studies*, ed. by João Costa, 266–297. Oxford/New York: Oxford University Press.

Raposo, Eduardo Paiva. 2013. Pronomes. In *Gramática do português*, ed. by Eduardo Paiva Raposo, Maria Fernanda Bacelar do Nascimento, Maria Antónia Mota, Luísa Segura, and Amália Mendes, vol. 1, 881–918. Lisbon: Fundação Calouste Gulbenkian.

Raposo, Eduardo Paiva and Juan Uriagereka. 1995. Two types of small clauses. In *Small clauses*, ed. by Anna Cardinaletti and Maria Teresa Guasti, 179–206. New York: Academic Press.

Raposo, Eduardo Paiva and Juan Uriagereka. 1996. Indefinite SE. *Natural Language and Linguistic Theory* 14: 749–810.

Resenes, Mariana. 2014. A sintaxe das construções semiclivadas e pseudoclivadas do português brasileiro. Doctoral dissertation, Universidade de São Paulo.

Ribeiro, Ilza. 1993. A formação dos tempos compostos: A evolução históricas das formas *ter, haver* e *ser*. In *Português brasileiro: Uma viagem diacrônica*, ed. by Ian Roberts and Mary A. Kato, 343–386. Campinas: Editora da UNICAMP.

Ribeiro, Ilza. 1995a. A sintaxe da ordem no português arcaico: O efeito V2. Doctoral dissertation, Universidade Estadual de Campinas.

Ribeiro, Ilza. 1995b. Evidence for a verb-second phase in Old Portuguese. In *Clause structure and language change*, ed. by Adrian Battye and Ian Roberts, 110–139. Oxford: Oxford University Press.

Ribeiro, Maria Raquel. 2002. As ocorrências da forma de gerúndio na variedade padrão e numa variedade dialectal do português europeu. Master's thesis, Universidade Nova de Lisboa.

Rinke, Esther. 2021. Does animacy matter for the realization of null objects in European Portuguese? Evidence from monolingual and bilingual language acquisition and use. Paper presented at the International Meeting on Null Objects from a Crosslinguistic and Developmental Perspective, Universidade do Minho, 29–30/1/2021.

Rinke, Esther, Cristina Flores, and Pilar Barbosa. 2018. Null objects in the spontaneous speech of monolingual and bilingual speakers of European Portuguese. *Probus* 30: 93–120.

Rio-Torto, Graça. 2020. Derivação. In *Gramática do português*, ed. by Eduardo Paiva Raposo, Maria Fernanda Bacelar do Nascimento, Maria Antónia Mota, Luísa Segura, Amália Mendes, and Amália Andrade, vol. 3, 3029–3149. Lisbon: Fundação Calouste Gulbenkian.

Roberts, Ian. 2010. A deletion analysis of null subjects. In *Parametric variation: Null subjects in minimalist theory*, ed. by Theresa Biberauer, Anders Holmberg, Ian Roberts, and Michelle Sheehan, 58–87. Cambridge: Cambridge University Press.
Rocha, Paula da. 2021. "Que adiar a formatura o quê; já tô entregando o TCC": Um estudo sobre as construções [que mané X], [que X o quê] e [que X que nada] do português brasileiro. "Trabalho de conclusão de curso," Universidade Federal do Rio de Janeiro.
Rodrigues, Cilene. 2002. Morphology and null subjects in Brazilian Portuguese. In *Syntactic effects of morphological change*, ed. by David Lightfoot, 160–178. Oxford: Oxford University Press.
Rodrigues, Cilene. 2004. Impoverished morphology and A-movement out of Case domains. Doctoral dissertation, University of Maryland.
Rodrigues, Cilene. 2010. Possessor raising through thematic positions. In *The movement theory of control*, ed. by Norbert Hornstein and Maria Polinsky, 119–146, Amsterdam/Philadelphia: John Benjamins.
Rodrigues, Cilene. 2020. Estruturas com alçamento de possuidor e a restrição de entidade afetada: Evidência para controle como movimento. *Cuadernos de la ALFAL* 14.2: 228–250.
Rodrigues, Erica. 2006. O processamento da concordância de número entre sujeito e verbo na produção de sentenças. Doctoral dissertation, Pontifícia Universidade Católica do Rio de Janeiro.
Rodygina, Olga. 2009. Colocação dos pronomes átonos nas orações infinitivas no português europeu. Master's thesis, Universidade do Minho.
Rooryck, Johan and João Costa. 2000. Pseudo-raising. In *Configurations of sentential complementation: Perspectives from Romance languages*, by Johan Rooryck, 54–72. London/New York: Routledge.
Ross, John R. 1967. Constraints on variables in syntax. Doctoral dissertation, Massachusetts Institute of Technology.
Ross, John R. 1982. Pronoun deleting processes in German. Paper presented at the Annual Meeting of the Linguistic Society of America, San Diego.
Saab, Andrés. 2016. On the notion of partial (non-) *pro*-drop in Romance. In *The morphosyntax of Portuguese and Spanish in Latin America*, ed. by Mary A. Kato and Francisco Ordóñez, 49–77. Oxford: Oxford University Press.
Salles, Heloisa. 1997. Prepositions and the syntax of complementation. Doctoral dissertation, University of Wales.
Sândalo, Maria Filomena and Hubert Truckenbrodt. 2002. Some notes on phonological phrasing in Brazilian Portuguese. *MIT Working Papers in Linguistics* 42: 285–310.
Santos, Ana Lúcia. 1999. O particípio absoluto em português e em outras línguas românicas. Master's thesis, Universidade de Lisboa.
Santos, Ana Lúcia. 2002. Answers to yes/no questions and clitic placement: the question of adverbs. In *Actas do XVII Encontro Nacional da Associação Portuguesa de Linguística*, ed. by Anabela Gonçalves and Clara Correia, 445–455. Lisbon: Associação Portuguesa de Linguística.
Santos, Ana Lúcia. 2003. The acquisition of answers to yes/no questions in Portuguese: Syntactic, discourse and pragmatic factors. *Journal of Portuguese Linguistics* 2: 61–91.

Santos, Ana Lúcia. 2009. *Minimal answers: Ellipsis, syntax and discourse in the acquisition of European Portuguese*. Amsterdam/Philadelphia: John Benjamins.
Santos, Leticia. 2018. Estruturas finitas de repetição verbal em português brasileiro. Master's thesis, Universidade de São Paulo.
Santos, Raquel S. 2002. Categorias sintáticas vazias e retração de acento em português Brasileiro. *D.E.L.T.A.* 18: 67–86.
Santos, Raquel S. 2003. Traces, pro and stress retraction in Brazilian Portuguese. *Journal of Portuguese Linguistics* 2: 101–113.
Saraiva, Maria Elizabeth. 1996. O SN nu objeto em português: Um caso de incorporação semântica e sintática. Doctoral dissertation, Universidade Federal de Minas Gerais.
Saraiva, Maria Elizabeth. 1997. *"Buscar menino no colégio": A questão do objeto incorporado em português*. Campinas: Pontes.
Scher, Ana Paula. 1996. As construções com dois complementos no inglês e no português do Brasil: Um estudo sintático comparativo. Master's thesis, Universidade Estadual de Campinas.
Scherre, Maria Marta. 1988. Reanálise da concordância nominal em português. Doctoral dissertation, Universidade Federal do Rio de Janeiro.
Scherre, Maria Marta. 1994. Aspectos da concordância de número no português do Brasil. *Revista Internacional de Língua Portuguesa* 12: 37–49.
Scherre, Maria Marta. 2004. Norma e uso: O imperativo no português brasileiro. In *O português do Brasil: Perspectivas da pesquisa atual*, ed. by Wolf Dietrich and Volker Noll, 231–260. Madrid: Iberoamericana.
Scherre, Maria Marta. 2007. Aspectos sincrônicos e diacrônicos do imperativo gramatical no português brasileiro. *Alfa* 51: 189–222.
Scherre, Maria Marta, Daisy Cardoso, Marcus Lunguinho, and Heloisa Salles. 2007. Reflexões sobre o imperativo em português. *D.E.L.T.A.* 23, special issue: 193–241.
Scherre, Maria Marta and Maria Eugênia Duarte. 2016. Main current processes of morphosyntactic variation. In *Handbook of Portuguese linguistics*, ed. by Leo Wetzels, João Costa, and Sergio Menuzzi, 526–544. Malden: Wiley Blackwell.
Scherre, Maria Marta and Anthony Naro. 1998a. Restrições sintáticas e semânticas no controle da concordância verbal em português. *Fórum Lingüístico* 1: 54–71.
Scherre, Maria Marta and Anthony Naro. 1998b. Sobre a concordância de número no português falado do Brasil. In *Atti del XXI Congresso Internazionale di Linguistica e Filologia Romanza*, ed. by Giovanni Ruffino, 509–523. Tübingen: Niemeyer.
Schmitt, Cristina and Alan Munn. 1999. Against the nominal mapping parameter: Bare nouns in Brazilian Portuguese. In *Proceedings of NELS 29*, ed. by Pius Tamanji, Masako Hirotani, and Nancy Hall, 339–353. Amherst: University of Massachusetts.
Schmitt, Cristina and Alan Munn. 2002. The syntax and semantics of bare arguments in Brazilian Portuguese. *Linguistic Variation Yearbook* 2: 185–216.
Segura, Luísa. 2013. Variedades dialetais do português europeu. In *Gramática do português*, ed. by Eduardo Paiva Raposo, Maria Fernanda Bacelar do Nascimento, Maria Antónia Mota, Luísa Segura, and Amália Mendes, vol. 1, 85–142. Lisbon: Fundação Calouste Gulbenkian.

Sell, Fabíola. 2003. As interrogativas do português brasileiro: Perguntas e respostas. Doctoral dissertation, Universidade Federal de Santa Catarina.

Selph, Blake. 2021. *Vós, vocês* and the null subject in European Portuguese. Master's thesis, Universidade de Lisboa.

Sheehan, Michelle. 2016. Subjects, null subjects and expletives. In *Manual of grammatical interfaces in Romance*, ed. by Susann Fischer and Christoph Gabriel, 329–362. Berlin/Boston: DeGruyter.

Silva, Gláucia. 2013. *Word order in Brazilian Portuguese*. Berlin/Boston: De Gruyter Mouton.

Silva-Villar, Luis. 1998. Subject positions and the roles of CP. In *Romance linguistics – Theoretical perspectives*, ed. by Armin Schwegler, Bernard Tranel, and Myriam Uribe-Etxebarria, 247–270. Amsterdam/Philadelphia: John Benjamins.

Simioni, Leonor. 2010. The relationship among subject positions, focus, and agreement in passive constructions in Brazilian Portuguese. *Estudos da Língua(gem)* 8: 173–187.

Simioni, Leonor. 2011. Concordância em construções passivas como argumentos pré- e pós verbais e incorporação de nomes nus no PB. Doctoral dissertation, Universidade de São Paulo.

Simões, Luciene. 1997. Sujeito nulo na aquisição do português brasileiro: Um estudo de caso. Doctoral dissertation, Pontifícia Universidade Católica do Rio Grande do Sul.

Simões, Luciene. 1999. Sujeito nulo na aquisição do português do Brasil. *Cadernos de Estudos da Linguagem* 36: 105–130.

Sória, Maíra. 2013. *Nós, a gente* e o sujeito nulo de primeira pessoa do plural. Master's thesis, Universidade de Lisboa.

Tarallo, Fernando. 1983. Relativization strategies in Brazilian Portuguese. Doctoral dissertation, University of Pennsylvania.

Tarallo, Fernando and Mary A. Kato. 1989. *Harmonia trans-sistêmica: Variação intra- e inter-linguística*. Campinas: Preedição.

Taylor, Michael. 2009. On the pronominal status of Brazilian Portuguese *a gente*. *New York University Working Papers in Linguistics* 2: 1–36.

Teixeira de Sousa, Lílian. 2012. Sintaxe e interpretação de negativas sentenciais no português brasileiro. Doctoral dissertation, Universidade Estadual de Campinas.

Teixeira de Sousa, Lílian. 2015. Three types of negation in Brazilian Portuguese. *Lingua* 159: 27–46.

Teixeira de Sousa, Lílian. 2020. O sistema responsivo do português brasileiro. *Diadorim* 22: 497–515.

Tescari Neto, Aquiles. 2012. On verb movement in Brazilian Portuguese: A cartographic study. Doctoral dissertation, Università Ca' Foscari di Venezia.

Torres Morais, Maria Aparecida. 1993. Aspectos diacrônicos do movimento do verbo, estrutura da frase e caso nominativo no português do Brasil. In *Português brasileiro: Uma viagem diacrônica*, ed. by Ian Roberts and Mary A. Kato, 263–306. Campinas: Editora da UNICAMP.

Torres Morais, Maria Aparecida. 2007. Os dativos. "Tese de livre docência," Universidade de São Paulo.

Torres Morais, Maria Aparecida and Rosane Berlinck. 2007. "Eu disse pra ele" ou "Disse-lhe a ele": A expressão do dativo nas variedades brasileira e europeia do português. In *Descrição, aquisição e história do português brasileiro*, ed. by Ataliba de Castilho, Maria Aparecida Torres Morais, Ruth Lopes, and Sonia Cyrino, 61–83. Campinas: Pontes/FAPESP.

Torres Morais, Maria Aparecida and Heloisa Salles. 2010. Parametric change in the grammatical encoding of indirect objects in Brazilian Portuguese. *Probus* 22: 181–209.

Torres Morais, Maria Aparecida and Heloisa Salles. 2016. The external possessor construction in European Portuguese and Brazilian Portuguese. In *The morphosyntax of Portuguese and Spanish in Latin America*, ed. by Mary A. Kato and Francisco Ordóñez, 204–235. Oxford: Oxford University Press.

Uriagereka, Juan. 1995a. An F position in Western Romance. In *Discourse configurational languages*, ed. by Katalin Kiss, 153–175. Oxford: Oxford University Press.

Uriagereka, Juan. 1995b. Aspects of the syntax of clitic placement in Western Romance. *Linguistic Inquiry* 26: 79–123.

Uriagereka, Juan. 2004. A peripheral pleonastic in Western Iberian. Talk presented at *EXPLetive subjects in Romance and Germanic languages*. University of Konstanz, 11–13/11/2004.

Vasconcelos, José Leite de. 1901. *Esquisse d'une dialectologie portugaise*. Paris: Aillaud & Cie.

Veloso, Rita. 2013. Subordinação relativa. In *Gramática do português*, ed. by Eduardo Paiva Raposo, Maria Fernanda Bacelar do Nascimento, Maria Antónia Mota, Luísa Segura, and Amália Mendes, vol. 2, 2061–2136. Lisbon: Fundação Calouste Gulbenkian.

Vercauteren, Aleksandra. 2010. Como é que é com o *é que*? Análise de estruturas com *é que* em variedades não standard do português europeu. Master's thesis, Universidade Nova de Lisboa.

Vercauteren, Aleksandra. 2015. A conspiracy theory for clefts: The syntax and interpretation of cleft constructions. Doctoral dissertation, Universidade Nova de Lisboa/University of Ghent.

Vergnaud, Jean-Roger. 2008. Letter to Noam Chomsky and Howard Lasnik on "Filters and Control," April 17, 1977. In *Foundational issues in linguistic theory: Essays in honor of Jean-Roger Vergnaud*, ed. by Robert Freidin, Carlos Otero, and Maria Luisa Zubizarreta, 3–16. Cambridge, Mass.: MIT Press.

Vianna, Juliana. 2006. A concordância de *nós* e *a gente* em estruturas predicativas na fala e na escrita carioca. Master's thesis, Universidade Federal do Rio de Janeiro.

Vicente, Helena. 2006. O quantificador flutuante "todos" no português brasileiro e no inglês: Uma abordagem gerativa. Doctoral dissertation, Universidade de Brasília.

Vigário, Marina. 2003. *The prosodic word in European Portuguese*. Berlin: Mouton de Gruyter.

Villalva, Alina. 2000. *Estruturas morfológicas – Unidades e hierarquias nas palavras do português*. Lisbon: Fundação Calouste Gulbenkian/FCT.

Villalva, Alina. 2003. Estrutura morfológica básica. In *Gramática da língua portuguesa*, ed. by Maria Helena Mira Mateus, Ana Maria Brito, Inês Duarte, Isabel Faria, Sónia Frota, Gabriela Matos, Fátima Oliveira, Marina Vigário, and Alina Villalva, 917–938. Lisbon: Caminho.

Villalva, Alina. 2020. Composição. In *Gramática do português*, ed. by Eduardo Paiva Raposo, Maria Fernanda Bacelar do Nascimento, Maria Antónia Mota, Luísa Segura, Amália Mendes, and Amália Andrade, vol. 3, 3151–3210. Lisbon: Fundação Calouste Gulbenkian.

Viotti, Evani. 1998. Uma história para *ter* e *haver*. *Cadernos de Estudos Lingüísticos* 34: 41–50.

Viotti, Evani. 1999. A sintaxe das sentenças existenciais no português do Brasil. Doctoral dissertation, Universidade de São Paulo.

Viotti, Evani. 2005. O Caso *default* no português do Brasil: Revisitando o Caso dos inacusativos. *Revista Estudos da Linguagem* 13: 53–71.

Viotti, Evani. 2007. Ordem VS no português brasileiro: Questionando a existência de expletivos nulos. In *Descrição, aquisição e história do português brasileiro*, ed. by Ataliba de Castilho, Maria Aparecida Torres Morais, Ruth Lopes, and Sonia Cyrino, 131–158. Campinas: Pontes/FAPESP.

Vitral, Lorenzo. 1996. A forma CÊ e a noção de gramaticalização. *Revista Estudos da Linguagem* 4: 115–124.

Vitral, Lorenzo. 1999. A negação: Teoria da checagem e mudança lingüística. *D.E.L.T.A.* 15: 57–84.

Wall, Albert. 2017. *Bare nominals in Brazilian Portuguese – An integral approach*. Amsterdam/Philadelphia: John Benjamins.

Weingart, Anja. 2020. Anaphoric dependencies in Spanish and European Portuguese: A minimalist analysis. Doctoral Dissertation, Georg-August-Universität Göttingen.

Wheeler, Dana. 1982. Portuguese pseudo-clefts: Evidence for free relatives. In *Papers from the eighteenth regional meeting of the Chicago Linguistic Society*, ed. by Kevin Tuite, Robinson Scheider, and Robert Chametzky, 507–520. Chicago: University of Chicago.

Whitaker-Franchi, Regina. 1989. As construções ergativas: Um estudo semântico e sintático. Master's thesis, Universidade Estadual de Campinas.

Wiedemer, Marcos. 2013. Variação e gramaticalização no uso de preposições em contextos de verbo de movimento no português brasileiro. Doctoral dissertation, Universidade Estadual Paulista.

Williams, Edwins. 1938. *From Latin to Portuguese – Historical phonology and morphology of the Portuguese language*. Philadelphia: University of Philadelphia Press.

Ximenes, Cristina. 2002. Contração de preposição em estruturas coordenadas. Master's thesis, Universidade Estadual de Campinas.

Ximenes, Cristina and Jairo Nunes. 2004. Contraction and duplication of prepositions in coordinated structures in Brazilian Portuguese. In *WCFFL 23: Proceedings of the 23rd West Coast Conference on Formal Linguistics*, ed. by Vinneta Chand, Ann Kelleher, Angelo Rodriguez, and Benjamin Schmeiser, 815–828. Somerville: Cascadilla Press.

Zilles, Ana. 2005. The development of a new pronoun: The linguistic and social embedding of *a gente* in Brazilian Portuguese. *Language Variation and Change* 17: 19–53.

Zocca, Cynthia. 2003. O que não está lá? Um estudo sobre morfologia flexional em elipses. Master's thesis, Universidade Estadual de Campinas.

Corpora

CORDIAL-SIN. *Corpus Dialectal para o Estudo da Sintaxe / Syntax-Oriented Corpus of Portuguese Dialects*, coordinated by Ana Maria Martins. CC licensed: CORDIAL-SIN by Centro de Linguística da Universidade de Lisboa:

http://clul.ulisboa.pt/recurso/cordial-sin-syntax-oriented-corpus-portuguese-dialects.

Also available (with sound) at:

http://corpora.ugr.es/synapse/index.php?action=home

CRPC. Corpus de Referência do Português Contemporâneo, do Centro de Linguística da Universidade de Lisboa:

https://clul.ulisboa.pt/projeto/crpc-corpus-de-referencia-do-portugues-contemporaneo.

Searchable with CPQweb (http://alfclul.clul.ul.pt/CPQweb) and TEITOK (http://teitok.clul.ul.pt/teitok/crpcoral/).

Index

[±close], 12, 37
[±hum], 9, 43, 225
[±REFL], 21–25, 28, 36, 48

absolutive constructions, 73
acquisition of Portuguese, 1, 148
address forms, 12, 35, 36
affirmation, 369–386, 453, 458
   affirmation particles, 370, 371–375
   and reduplication, 370, 374, 375–386, 447
   emphatic affirmation, 369–386, 422, 427
   positive agreement, 377
   positive disagreement, 377
   positive polarity item (PPI), 412, 414, 418
agreement, syntactic, 57, 455
   -mo(s), 76, 79, 82, 98, 99, 106, 121, 127, 141
   Agree, 92, 100
   and morphophonological adjustments, 65, 69
   and semantic agreement, 99, 110, 114, 205, 208
   and vowel lowering, 59, 61, 66, 69
   and word order, 127–134
   attribute, 88, 100
   default, 74, 79, 82, 84, 87, 90, 95, 96, 99, 100, 102, 104, 111, 114, 122, 130, 134, 137, 141, 169, 170, 171, 211, 263
   defective, 120, 123, 127, 141
   gender, 16, 58, 60, 62, 73, 137
   in finite clauses, 81, 92, 116, 120, 121, 127
   in inflected gerunds, 92
   in inflected infinitivals, 81–85
   in participials, 73–75, 92, 137
   in *se* constructions, 139
   mismatch, 88, 89, 95, 96, 100, 101, 107, 111, 141
   nonagreement, 62, 66, 107
   number, 16, 60–63, 64, 73, 74, 75, 86, 100
   partial agreement, 62, 66, 455
   person, 11, 22, 75, 86, 100
   traditional analysis, 87–90, 101, 141, 143, 150, 231
   value, 88
   with coordinated subjects, 110, 132–134
   with impersonal predicates, 136
   with nominal and adjectival predicates, 70–73, 96, 97, 100
   with partitive expressions, 72
   with postverbal subjects, 74, 129, 130, 132, 133, 134, 138, 220
   with unaccusative verbs, 130
   within nominal domains, 57, 58, 71
allomorphy, 16, 44
answers, minimal, 152, 423–452
   negative agreement, 424, 427, 428, 429, 442, 443, 444, 447, 450
   negative disagreement, 424, 425, 426, 444, 447, 448
   positive agreement, 424, 425, 426, 428, 429, 430, 442, 447, 449, 450
   positive disagreement, 424, 427, 428, 429, 443, 446
   to embedded questions, 432, 451
   with bare adverbs, 440–447, 453
   with bare prepositions, 437
   with bare quantifiers, 447
   with bare verbs, 425–439, 442, 452, 453
   with responsive particles, 425–439, 442, 450
   with *ser*, 448–452; *see also* tense agreement: in minimal answers with *ser*
argument, 129
   external, 129, 216
   internal, 129, 130, 134, 135, 136, 138, 139, 217

bare plurals, 70
bare singulars, 66–70, 72; *see also* agreement, syntactic: nonagreement

Index

case, 13, 53, 131, 143, 144, 207, 213, 330, 455
   accusative, 16, 92, 93, 139, 239
   Case Filter, 144
   dative, 17–19, 230, 239, 243
   default, 14, 131, 134
   ECM (Exceptional Case Marking), 16, 19, 36, 84, 85, 92, 93
   genitive, 20, 22, 50
   inherent, 135
   nominative, 15, 22, 75, 87, 88, 92, 93, 100, 116, 117, 120, 123, 124, 131, 134, 137, 138, 139, 176, 198, 213
   oblique, 19–20, 144
categorical judgments. *See* judgments (categorical and thetic)
clefting, 260–265, 282–286, 408, 452; *see also* tense agreement: in clefts; word order: in clefted *wh*-questions; word order: in clefts
clitics, 7, 23, 341, 343, 344, 383, 384; *see also* word order: clitic placement
   lhe(s), 37, 49, 315
   me, 315
   nos, 315
   se, indefinite, 7, 46, 51–52, 98, 136, 137, 139, 216, 315, 316, 319
   se, passive, 138, 139
   se, reflexive, 315
   te, 6, 8, 37, 315
   vos, 315
   3PAC (third person accusative clitic), 2, 44, 47, 299, 315, 316, 320–329, 458
   as agreement markers, 321, 324, 325
   doubling, 9, 10, 29, 98, 137, 242, 257
   fusion, 46, 325
compounds, 70
control, 81, 82, 130, 207, 208
coordination, 6, 110, 145, 256, 287, 415, 419, 429, 452
correspondence rules, 95, 99, 114
   and agreement with *tu*, 108
   in BP, 108, 121, 122, 162, 171, 179
   in EP, 95, 102, 155, 171, 178
   in hyper-raising, 123
   indicative perfective past, 102, 108, 155
   indicative present, 95, 102, 108, 155

default. *See under* agreement, syntactic; case
determiners, 64, 67, 69
   null, 67, 69, 72

ellipsis, 152, 162, 169, 179, 183, 187, 190, 208, 215, 332, 334; *see also* null subjects; Prominent Feature Valuation Condition
   identity requirement, 335
   verb stranding VP ellipsis (VSVPE), 334, 335, 336, 338, 341
   VP ellipsis, 333, 335, 338, 341, 406
Empty Category Principle (ECP), 281
enclisis. *See* word order: clitic placement
EPP (Extended Projection Principle), 147, 219
exclamatives, 286–293, 396, 413, 414
   concessive, 287
   coordinate nondegree, 287
   negative, 448
   qualifying, 292, 293
   quantifying, 288, 289, 291, 293, 414
expletives
   null, 130, 131, 134, 147, 215, 220, 221, 223
   overt, 43, 130, 147, 219, 222, 229

features. *See* morphological features; semantic features
focalization, 6, 245, 339, 350
   and clitic placement, 257, 258, 301, 302
   and extraposition, 259
   and prosodic prominence, 246, 252, 253
   contrastive focus, 9, 252, 260, 291, 292, 301, 414
   focus particles, 6, 248, 255, 258, 259, 303
   information focus, 260
   with *mas*, 264

gapping, 133
gender, 13, 89, 92, 109, 200, 202, 205, 208
gerunds, 208–215, 308
   agreementless case-marking, 208, 212–215, 295
   inflected, 14, 85–87, 99, 114, 208, 210–212, 297
   obligatorily controlled, 208
   uninflected, 211
grammar, 2–3, 44, 48, 53, 118, 152, 316
grammaticalization, 25, 89, 90, 102, 249

hyper-raising, 115, 116–127, 141, 176, 177, 194, 195, 198

imperative mood, 14, 75, 80, 145, 163
impoverishment, 104, 170, 171, 172, 175, 176, 177, 187, 189, 190, 191, 194, 195, 200, 211

indicative mood, 14, 75, 287, 306, 442
  conditional, 169, 268, 311, 312, 382, 383, 384, 436
  future, 104, 149, 157, 268, 311, 312, 382, 383, 384, 436
  imperfective past, 77, 102, 104, 169, 172, 177, 194, 195, 239, 420
  perfective past, 77, 104, 127, 149, 157, 404, 420, 435
  perfective present, 435
  periphrastic future, 104, 149
  present, 75, 76, 80, 81, 82, 87, 104, 127, 149, 157, 194, 249, 260, 404, 420
infinitives, 92, 309
  inflected, 81, 82, 84, 86, 92, 116, 119, 120, 121, 127, 187–200, 298, 308, 326
  uninflected, 19, 81, 84, 85, 86, 92, 116, 189, 194, 207, 208, 309, 326, 329
interrogatives, 153, 154, 155, 265–286
  biased polar questions, 268, 423
  clefted *wh*-questions, 282–286
  echo questions, 270
  embedded questions, 308, 432
  fragment questions, 437
  multiple *wh*-questions, 279–282, 285
  negative polar questions, 419, 426, 428
  rhetorical questions, 164
  tag markers, 420, 421, 422, 423
  tag questions, 241, 267, 373, 394, 423, 426, 427; *see also* tense agreement: in tag questions
  wh-questions, 246, 259, 266
  yes/no questions, 152, 164, 266, 267–269, 416
islands, 165, 166, 167, 169, 184, 186, 272, 339, 341, 346, 348, 349, 351, 353, 356, 362, 365, 366

judgments (categorical and thetic), 232–241, 455

mesoclisis. *See* word order: clitic placement
movement
  to the left periphery, 8, 153, 155, 165, 253, 257, 259, 269, 272, 278, 280, 288, 291, 339
  to the subject position, 116–127, 135, 136, 141, 176, 183, 186, 187, 198, 207, 218, 223
  traces of movement, 183, 350

negation, 386–415, 453, 458
  and clitic placement, 305

  and *wh*-questions, 395
  clausal negation, 393
  constituent negation, 301, 386, 392
  double negation, 391, 398
  emphatic negation, 399, 426
  expletive negation, 289, 290, 291, 292, 413–415
  external negation, 387, 394, 397
  metalinguistic negation, 399–412, 443
  minimizers, 397
  negative concord, 391, 392, 393, 407
  negative markers, 386, 394, 395, 396, 397, 399, 400, 401, 403, 406, 408, 413, 414, 421
  negative polarity items (NPIs), 301, 389, 391, 392, 397, 407, 414
morphological features. *See* gender; impoverishment; number; person; Prominent Feature Valuation Condition; pronouns: feature composition; pronouns: underspecification. *See also under* agreement, syntactic: default, defective, gender, in finite clauses, in inflected gerunds, in inflected infinitivals, in participials, mismatch, number, partial agreement, person, traditional analysis.

null direct objects, 153, 331, 336–354, 458
  and [±hum], 338–345, 348, 351, 352
  and islands, 339, 342, 345, 348, 351
  and null topics, 349
  and person, 338, 349, 352
  and stress retraction, 351
  and strong crossover, 354
  and the position of the antecedent, 342, 343, 345, 348, 351, 352
  and verb stranding VP ellipsis (VSVPE), 333, 335, 336, 338, 341
  and VP ellipsis, 335, 338, 341
  and weak crossover, 354
  as *pro*, 349, 350, 351, 352, 368
  as traces of movement, 349, 351, 354
  deictic inanimate, 337
  indefinite generic, 337
null objects. *See* null direct objects; null oblique objects
null oblique objects, 331, 354–358
  and chopping relatives, 358
  and directional verbs, 358
  and islands, 356
  and syntactic movement, 356

as *pro*, 356
lexical conditioning, 355
null possessors, 331, 359–367, 458
   and (in)definiteness, 364
   and islands, 365
   and person, 364
   as *pro*, 365, 366, 367
   as traces of movement, 365
   deictic, 360
   lexically conditioned, 360, 361, 362
   syntactically conditioned, 360
null subjects, 12, 35, 240, 458; *see also*
   Prominent Feature Valuation Condition; pronouns
   and fuller agreement, 149, 190
   and illocutionary force, 163, 164, 168
   and impoverished agreement, 169–177, 187–195
   and subject–verb inversion, 154
   and topic drop, 153, 155, 159, 160, 168, 177, 178, 179, 180, 183, 216, 273
   as *pro*, 81, 82, 145, 147, 153, 154, 159, 160, 181, 182, 185, 187, 194, 205, 207, 208, 224, 225, 272, 273, 349, 368
   as PRO, 81, 82, 145, 147, 153, 154, 159, 160, 181, 182, 185, 187, 194, 205, 207, 208, 224, 225, 272, 273, 349, 368
   as traces of movement, 165, 169, 183, 186, 365
   Avoid Pronoun Principle, 145, 166, 185, 224, 226
   definite, 146, 147–215, 216, 218, 223, 226
   expletive, 147, 220, 229
   first and second persons, 149–177, 186, 187–195, 207, 225
   frequency, 148, 225
   in adjunct clauses, 207
   in agreementless case-marking gerunds, 215
   in diary contexts, 159
   in embedded clauses, 159, 160, 163, 165, 166, 167, 179, 181, 183, 191
   in finite clauses, 149–187, 196
   in imperatives, 163
   in inflected gerunds, 210–212
   in inflected infinitivals, 187–200
   in islands, 165, 166, 167, 169, 184, 186
   in participials, 200–208
   in transparent domains, 165, 166, 167, 169, 184, 186
   in uninflected gerunds, 164
   in uninflected infinitivals, 310
   in *wh*-questions, 154, 155, 163, 177, 272

   indefinite, third person plural, 146, 216
   indefinite, third person singular, 139, 216–218, 229
   non-*pro*-drop, 145, 159, 219
   pro-drop, 145, 154, 158, 177, 178, 180, 181, 182, 183, 185, 219, 220, 222, 224, 226
   third person, 149, 177–187, 196–198, 201–202, 225
number, 12, 92, 94, 95, 96, 109, 120, 162, 169, 170, 176, 179, 186, 187, 190, 191, 195, 196, 200, 202, 205, 210, 211

participials, 92, 200–208, 297, 298
passives, 74, 92
person, 5, 90, 92, 94, 100, 109, 120, 157, 162, 163, 169, 176, 187, 190, 191, 196, 200, 210, 212, 337
Principles and Parameters Theory, 2, 3, 21, 145, 147, 281
proclisis. *See* word order: clitic placement
Prominent Feature Valuation Condition, 157, 162, 169, 171, 172, 175, 176, 187, 189, 191, 200, 205, 211, 213, 226, 273, 458
pronouns, 145, 455
   a gente, 25–32, 49, 79, 82, 87, 89, 93, 95–100, 101, 102, 104, 108, 110, 115, 122, 123, 126, 149, 155, 157, 160, 162, 163, 164, 165, 169, 175, 187, 191, 200, 204, 205, 207, 208, 211, 215, 226, 272
   cê(s), 6–8, 40, 106, 109, 111, 122, 150, 152, 225, 279
   consigo, 36, 49
   ela(s)/ele(s), 3, 8–10, 45, 91, 93, 98, 106, 107, 109, 111, 122, 123, 126, 165, 187, 225
   eu, 25, 82, 91, 102, 105, 106, 108, 110, 119, 121, 122, 125, 126, 130, 143, 149, 157, 160, 162, 166, 167, 169, 170, 171, 172, 175, 176, 187, 189, 190, 191, 200, 211
   nós, 25–32, 79, 82, 91, 98, 105, 106, 108, 111, 115, 117, 122, 124, 125, 126, 149, 157, 158, 160, 162, 166, 169, 187, 189, 195, 206
   ocê(s), 39
   que, interrogative, 61, 64, 276, 277, 279, 400
   seu(s)/sua(s), 50, 458
   si, 36, 49
   tu, 36, 37, 78, 80, 82, 85, 87, 91, 104, 105, 107, 114, 149, 152, 157, 189
   você(s), 6, 10, 12, 35, 36, 37, 76, 89, 93, 95, 97, 101, 102, 106, 109, 111, 122, 123, 126, 149, 155, 160, 162, 163, 164, 165, 169, 175, 176, 187, 191, 273

pronouns (cont.)
  vós, 3, 37, 38, 76, 80, 94, 97, 102
  feature composition, 87–115, 178, 215, 226, 455
  first person, 5, 11, 25–32, 149
  gender, 58
  interrogative, 266
  null. *See* null direct objects: as *pro*; null oblique objects: as *pro*; null possessors: as *pro*; null subjects: as *pro*; null subjects: as PRO
  number, 111
  person, 11, 53, 111
  pro. *See* null direct objects: as *pro*; null oblique objects: as *pro*; null subjects: as *pro*
  PRO. *See* null subjects: as PRO
  relative, 59, 60, 62
  second person, 5, 11, 38, 40, 45, 149
  strong, 6–11, 23, 43, 145, 225, 241
  third person, 5, 11, 40–51, 149
  underspecification, 105–115, 120, 141, 178, 179, 351, 455
  weak, 6–11, 23, 43, 145, 225, 241, 242, 257, 279, 340, 343, 344, 400
proper names, 12

questions. *See* interrogatives

registers, 18, 32, 38, 44, 48, 77, 106, 125, 139, 158, 162, 249, 299, 316, 357, 388, 389, 425, 428

schooling, 2, 32, 44, 48, 136, 139, 148, 299, 316
semantic features, 11, 13, 87, 88, 89, 95, 96, 97, 99, 101, 108, 110, 111
sociolinguistic stigmatization, 3, 29, 69, 71, 79
spoken language, 2, 136, 285, 316
stigmatization. *See* sociolinguistic stigmatization
subjunctive mood, 14, 75, 169, 181, 286, 287, 306, 442
  future, 77, 325, 326, 327, 328
  imperfective past, 77, 169
  present, 80, 81, 102, 169, 172, 175
suppletion, 13, 59

tense agreement
  in clefts, 261–265
  in minimal answers with *ser*, 448–452
  in tag questions, 420

thetic judgments. *See* judgments (categorical and thetic)
topicalization, 6, 126, 153, 245, 348
  and clitic placement, 244, 257, 258, 302
  and doubling, 257
  and extraposition, 259
  marked topics, 242–245
  null topics, 153, 154, 159, 160
  topic drop. *See* null topics *in this entry*

verb reduplication, 369–386; *see also* affirmation: emphatic affirmation
  and repetition, 379
  morphological restrictions, 386
  phonological properties, 377
  pragmatic restrictions, 378
verbs
  auxiliary, 238, 295, 435
  causative, 15, 120
  compound, 380
  copula, 16, 233, 260, 262, 274, 448; *see also* answers, minimal: with *ser*; clefting; tense agreement: in minimal answers with *ser*
  directional, 358
  ditransitive, 17, 237, 251
  existential, 16, 135, 219
  factive, 295
  impersonal, 18, 135, 219
  irregular, 326, 327
  passive, 216, 219
  perception, 15, 92, 120
  psychological, 18
  raising, 116, 136, 163, 434
  transitive, 15, 73, 235, 237, 238, 239, 247, 253, 255, 256, 289, 292, 361
  unaccusative, 73, 128, 129, 130, 133, 134, 216, 219, 220, 232, 234, 235, 248, 253, 255, 269, 274, 275, 276, 277, 283, 289, 292, 295, 361
  unergative, 128, 129, 132, 216, 232, 234, 235, 238, 239, 248, 253, 255, 269, 274, 275, 276, 289
  weather, 219
VSVPE. *See under* ellipsis

word order, 455
  SV(O), 230, 232–242, 246, 247, 248, 249, 250, 251, 253, 275, 276, 280, 283, 288, 292, 294, 295, 297
  V(X)S, 247, 248, 249, 250, 277, 283
  VOS, 250, 294

VS, 232–242, 244, 251, 253, 255, 256, 259, 263, 268, 273, 275, 276, 278, 280, 283, 287, 289, 292, 294, 295, 297, 329, 455
VS(O), 232, 250
VSX, 248, 249, 283, 286, 287
and (in)definiteness, 234, 235, 329
and categorical and thetic judgements, 232–241, 329
and contrastive focus, 237, 259
and evidentiality, 235, 237, 329
and expletive negation, 289, 291
and focalization, 257, 329
and information focus, 236, 246–252
and subject doubling, 240, 241
and topicalization, 242–245
between topics and foci, 259
clitic climbing, 315, 317, 318, 320, 323
clitic placement in BP, 315–329, 330, 455
clitic placement in EP, 300–314, 330, 455
in agreementless case-marking gerunds, 295
in clefted *wh*-questions, 282–286
in clefts, 260–265, 278
in declaratives, 230, 265
in embedded questions, 271, 276
in exclamatives, 286–293
in inflected gerunds, 297
in inflected infinitives, 295
in interrogatives, 265–286, 330
in multiple *wh*-questions, 282
in negative sentences, 236, 300, 330, 387, 389, 391, 403
in participials, 297
in single *wh*-questions, 269–279
in *yes/no* questions, 267–269, 416
quotative inversion, 251
subject–verb inversion, 153, 232, 240, 330
unmarked, 230, 246, 252, 253, 416
written language, 2, 32, 38, 44, 48, 139, 158, 162, 299, 316, 320, 323, 357

For EU product safety concerns, contact us at Calle de José Abascal, 56–1°,
28003 Madrid, Spain or eugpsr@cambridge.org.